Debian® GNU®/ Linux® 3.1 Bible

Debian® GNU®/ Linux® 3.1 Bible

Benjamin Mako Hill
David B. Harris
Jaldhar Vyas

WILEY

Wiley Publishing, Inc.

Debian® GNU®/Linux® 3.1 Bible

Published by
Wiley Publishing, Inc.
10475 Crosspoint Boulevard
Indianapolis, IN 46256
www.wiley.com

ISBN-10: 0-7645-7644-5

ISBN-13: 978-0-7645-7644-7

Manufactured in the United States of America

10 9 8 7 6 5 4 3 2 1

1O/SV/QX/QV/IN

For general information on our other products and services or to obtain technical support, please contact our Customer Care Department within the U.S. at (800) 762-2974, outside the U.S. at (317) 572-3993 or fax (317) 572-4002.

Wiley also publishes its books in a variety of electronic formats. Some content that appears in print may not be available in electronic books.

Library of Congress Cataloging-in-Publication Data

Hill, Benjamin Mako, 1980-
    Debian GNU/Linux 3.1 Bible / Benjamin Mako Hill, David B. Harris.
        p. cm.
    Includes index.
    ISBN 0-7645-7644-5 (paper/cd-rom)
    1. Linux. 2. Operating systems (Computers) I. Harris, David B., 1980– II. Title.
    QA76.76.O63H57135 2005
    005.4'32–dc22

                        2004027963

About the Authors

Benjamin Mako Hill is an intellectual property researcher and activist and a professional Free/Open Source Software (FOSS) advocate, developer, and consultant. He is an active participant in the Debian Project in both technical and nontechnical roles, and is a founder of Debian-Nonprofit and several other Free Software projects. He is the author of the *Free Software Project Management HOWTO* and many published works on Free and Open Source Software in addition to academic and nonacademic work in both technical and nontechnical fields. He is currently working full time for Canonical Ltd. on Ubuntu, a Debian-based distribution.

David B. Harris is a professional systems administrator who works with Debian systems daily. He is an active and recognized member of the Debian community, where he maintains a number of Debian components. David also serves as the point of first contact for numerous Debian users and developers, and is known for providing excellent personalized technical support. Aside from Debian, he manages all the technical aspects of the Open and Free Technology Community, a group formed early in 2000 to provide services to Open Source projects.

Jaldhar Vyas is a 34-year-old Hindu priest and consultant specializing in Perl and Linux who lives in Jersey City, New Jersey, with his wife Jyoti, daughter Shailaja, and son Nilagriva. Jaldhar has been a Debian developer for eight years and a Linux user for 10. His current major area of interest is Debian-IN, subproject to improve Debian's support of Indian-language speakers.

Credits

Acquisitions Editor
Debra Williams Cauley

Development Editor
Sara Shlaer

Production Editor
William A. Barton

Technical Editors
Micah Anderson, Elizabeth Barclay,
Andrew Suessmuth

Copy Editor
Publication Services

Editorial Manager
Mary Beth Wakefield

**Vice President & Executive Group
Publisher**
Richard Swadley

Vice President and Publisher
Joseph B. Wikert

Project Coordinator
Erin Smith

Graphics and Production Specialists
Carrie A. Foster
Denny Hager
Joyce Haughey
Jennifer Heleine
Amanda Spagnuolo

Quality Control Technicians
David Faust
John Greenough
Brian H. Walls

Permissions Editor
Laura Moss

Media Development Specialist
Kit Malone

Proofreading and Indexing
TECHBOOKS Production Services

Preface

Debian's reputation often precedes it. Over more than a decade, Debian has earned its share of both admirers and critics. In any case, Debian is becoming increasingly difficult to ignore.

It seems that a Linux User Group is somehow incomplete without at least one token Debian fanatic preaching the virtues of apt-get and the distinction between Open Source and Free Software (both areas are covered in this book if you're unfamiliar with either concept). As a semiprofessional Debian fanatic, I have certainly assumed that role in groups I've participated in. Debian has cultivated an enduring Linux subculture that has grown steadily but surely — often faster than any other Linux distribution.

Love it or hate it, people who know Debian will tell you that it is a different kind of GNU/Linux distribution. Debian is unique among other Free Software distributions for a number of reasons. Debian is the only major distribution, with the possible exception of Gentoo, that is fully institutionally independent and primarily volunteer-based. Debian is the largest Linux distribution in terms of the number of volunteers and in terms of the number of packages included. It is arguably the largest Free Software project ever. Debian has a reputation for a powerful non-RedHat–based package manager, a strict adherence to Free Software principles, and a guiding philosophy of software freedom, open processes, and committment to users and a community. It is these strengths that have made Debian such an attractive base for those making derived GNU/Linux distributions. On the other hand, Debian also has a less favorable reputation for its slow and unpredictable release cycle and difficult installer.

Debian is a *distribution* of computer software. The software contained in Debian is, for the most part, the same software that is included in every other major Linux distribution, such as Red Hat or Mandrake. As such, there is overlap between this book and any other Linux book. The differences can be subtle, but they can also be aggravating — especially over time and especially to new users. Debian deserves its own book to cater to its eccentricities. This book focuses on describing how to do Debian things and how to do non-Debian things *the Debian way*.

If you are serious about using Debian — or even just seriously considering it — it's worth learning a little bit about the project and the product.

Who Should Read This Book

This book is written to appeal to a variety of users with varying degrees of experience. In most cases, it is designed to complement and augment the documentation included in Debian and the documentation for individual programs included in Debian packages. As a result, anyone with a Debian installation can benefit from this book, not just those that want a paper copy to refer to.

For those with no experience on Debian, Linux of any sort, or even a UNIX or UNIX-like operating system, this book begins slowly and introduces fundamental concepts. For beginners ("newbies"), it will be wise to start at the beginning of the book and work your way through it until you are confident enough to start jumping around.

Readers who have some familiarity with Linux or a UNIX-like operating system will be able to take a more random-access approach to the book. Several chapters are very useful in documenting the Debian-specific parts of a Debian system. Others go into a good deal of depth on subjects that, while not wholly Debian specific, still make an effort to address highly Debian-specific differences.

This book was not written for the seasoned Debian power user. That said, the authors of this book have taught me, a long-time Debian developer and a Debian user for nearly a decade, a great deal in the process and something new in nearly every chapter. I suspect everyone can learn something from this book.

How This Book Is Organized

The *Debian GNU/Linux 3.1 Bible* is organized into five parts.

Part I: The Fundamentals

The first part of the book introduces Debian. Chapter 1 introduces *Debian the project*. The remaining chapters deal with *Debian the distribution* and *Debian the Linux operating system*. It is good reading for anyone new to Linux or UNIX and contains useful information for those that are new specifically to Debian or who would like to fill a few gaps in their knowledge. The section introduces the basics of administering a Debian system and includes the process of making backups — knowledge that will apply to every Debian system.

Part II: The Linux Desktop

This part goes into detail on using Debian as a desktop operating system. Chapter 7 walks the user through graphics and sound setup. Chapter 8 introduces KDE and GNOME, the two major desktop environments. Chapters 9–12 walk the user through a sampling of the desktop applications and programs available in Debian and high-light some classic programs and hidden gems within Debian. These chapters cover publishing, using multimedia, and playing games in Debian.

Part III: The Internet Server

Part III opens with an important chapter on the dangers of having your Debian machine connected to the Internet, and it discusses measures to secure your machine against threats. Other chapters walk you through setting up and maintaining e-mail, Web, file, and domain servers. Part III closes with a more general chapter on remote access.

Part IV: The Intranet Server

Part IV focuses on the network services that are of particular use on an internal network or intranet. It covers a number of topics, including file serving, intranet e-mail, printing, and database serving.

Part V: The Developer

Part V goes into the specifics of development on Debian. Chapter 25 provides a description of the Debian community, and Chapter 26 offers coverage of Debian packages that will help you gain more power over your Debian system. Chapter 27 explains how to find and use Debian archives. This section offers a good overview for users wishing to take control of their Debian system and is a good introduction to readers interested in joining the Debian project or just giving back.

Appendixes

This book contains two appendixes. Appendix A describes the contents of the companion CD-ROMs. Appendix B reproduces the Debian Constitution.

About the Companion CD-ROMs

This book contains two CDs. The first CD is the first CD of a Debian installation. This includes the Debian installer and the most popular Debian packages. Debian is a very large project, and a full Debian distribution will not fit on a single CD — or even a single DVD! This CD contains all of the software you'll need to get a minimal Debian system up and running, though. If you want to install a full desktop system, you'll need to either supplement the CD by downloading additional software with an Internet connection, or you'll need to get additional CDs. You can buy these from many vendors, which are listed at `www.debian.org/CD/vendors/`. You are more than welcome to use the included CD to get a minimal installation and then upgrade.

The second CD is a *Live CD* distribution based on Debian. When run, this CD will put you in a full Debian environment, very much like the one you'll be using once you have installed Debain, but it will not copy anything to your hard drive and will not overwrite your data. It's a great way to preview Debian before you are ready to commit to a real installation, and it's also a great way to turn any computer into a Debian workstation in seconds!

To use either of these CDs, place the CD in the drive and then reboot your computer. Your computer should automatically load up the CD instead of booting your default operating system, and you should be able to follow directions, or follow along in the rest of this book, from there.

The source code for the Debian install DVD included with this book is available via mail. To order the Debian Linux 3.1 source code, go to www.wiley.com/go/debianlinuxsource to download a coupon with further details.

Conventions Used in This Book

The book uses a variety of conventions to help you scan through it and quickly find information of interest. Commands and code text, for example, are presented in a monospaced font:

```
Code looks like this.
```

Here are some of the other conventions you will see in the book:

This icon presents a quick aside to the general topic.

This icon presents brief shortcuts and hints to make you more effective in using Debian.

This icon reminds you to take special care when executing a procedure to avoid damaging your system or losing your data.

This icon shows you where to find additional information on the topic under discussion.

Acknowledgments

A year and a half ago, my academic research focused on issues of collaborative authorship. Had I worked on this book two years earlier, my thesis would have been dealt a fine case in point. The collaborative nature of writing that went into this book surpassed my wildest claims on the pervasiveness and extent of collaborative writing in modern publishing. I cannot take individual credit for this book but am proud to stand in the group of talented hackers, writers, and editors that made it possible.

Due to the inherent unpredictability of life, primary responsibility for this book has changed hands in the process of the book's production: I was brought in at a late point to write several chapters and to take control of the book as a whole. Meanwhile, Debra Williams Cauley worked hard to make sure that every other piece of the book was being written by a competent author. The team she was able to put together worked hard to produce the high-quality text. I want to thank and acknowledge each author for his essential contributions: David B. Harris, Micah Anderson, John Goerzen, Jim Keogh, Jaldhar Vyas, and Kurt Wall. Their experience, advice, and knowledge helped make this book the deep resource that it is.

Even my insular responsibilities could not have been carried out without the help of others. In particular, Sara Shlaer worked closely with me to raise questions in places I might miss them and was patient with me as I caught up to speed. She helped me plan out work on the book and walked me through the plan to completion. I would have been completely lost without her help, and I thank her for her patience.

Benjamin Mako Hill

Contents at a Glance

Contents

• •

Part II: The Linux Desktop   163

Chapter 7: Configuring Graphics and Sound 165

Chapter 8: The KDE and GNOME Desktop Environments 177

Chapter 9: Internet Applications 207

The Fundamentals

The Debian Project

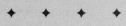

We've come a long way. In 1992, Linus Torvalds made
the decision to release his new operating system kernel, *Linux*, to the public under a copyright license that gave
users the right to modify and distribute software based on
the Linux kernel in any manner they chose. The GNU Project
(www.gnu.org) had been releasing pieces of a complete UNIX-
like operating system under the "GNU General Public License"
for quite some time. With the release of Linux, however, users
now had a complete system — the kernel and its hardware
drivers, along with administration utilities, word processors,
and myriad other games, tools, and applications from the GNU
Project and the wider community.

It wasn't long until companies and members of the community
collected this software and presented it to users as an integrated operating system. Thus in August of 1993 was the
Debian software distribution born. It was one of the first such
distributions, and it's one of the longest lived. Created by Ian
Murdock (and named after a combination of his name and the
name of his wife, Debra), the original announcement reads in
part:

> Distributions are essential to the future of Linux.
> Essentially, they eliminate the need for the user to
> locate, download, compile, install, and integrate a fairly
> large number of essential tools to assemble a working
> Linux system. Instead, the burden of system construc-
> tion is placed on the distribution creator, whose work
> can be shared with thousands of other users. Almost all
> users of Linux will get their first taste of it through a dis-
> tribution, and most users will continue to use a distribu-
> tion for the sake of convenience even after they are
> familiar with the operating system. Thus, distributions
> play a very important role indeed.

Murdock couldn't have been more correct, and today almost all Linux users (even most of those who put together a Linux system from scratch) use a Linux software distribution.

This chapter walks you through the components of a software distribution. It introduces the concepts of distributions, packages, architectures, releases, and specific pieces of software including an operating system kernel. It then introduces Debian and the way that it is structured within this system.

The Components of a Software Distribution

Over 900 Debian package maintainers worldwide currently contribute to the Debian software distribution, integrating over 13,000 pieces of software into a cohesive whole. The task is truly daunting when you consider that the latest release of Debian (code named *Sarge*) includes 13 installation CDs for Intel-compatible computers alone. Note, however, that only the first of these 13 CDs is required for a typical installation; the most popular software is contained on the first CD, the least popular on the thirteenth.

Packages

Any Linux distribution (such as Debian, Red Hat, or SUSE) is composed of pieces of software bundled into discrete components referred to as *packages* for distribution and management. Debian was the first major distribution to fully embrace this concept. Without packages, people install the raw version in what is called *tarballs* in such a way that installed programs are largely unaccounted for, or are accounted for in an inconsistent way.

In Debian, everything comes in a package. The work of most Debian developers is packaging documentation and software of all sorts. These packages give users a consistent way to install, monitor, reconfigure, and remove applications. With packages, and a package management system, you are able to do the following things:

✦ You can find out information about your software, such as who made it or what software is included when you unpack it.

✦ You can know whether any other software is needed to make the software in the package work and whether there is anything already installed on your system that could prevent this software from working.

✦ After you've installed software, you can easily uninstall it.

✦ Setup can be done automatically. Cleanup upon uninstallation can be done as well.

✦ When you install a new version or upgrade, your changes should be preserved.

A distinctive feature of Debian as opposed to other Linux distributions is that software packages are called *debs* after their .deb file extension. A deb contains some software, *metadata* that describes it, and scripts that are run at install and uninstall time. The metadata contains information such as the name of the program, a description of the program, who packaged it, and so forth. It also includes information on dependencies — which other packages are needed for this package to function, which packages conflict, and which packages are related. The deb records which files it contains in a central database, so uninstalling it completely is a snap. It can also mark some files as configuration files, so on upgrade, you are warned about upgrades that include a newer configuration and given the opportunity to accept the new file or keep your old one.

Another package format that is popular in the Linux world is *rpm*, originally created by Red Hat, Inc. for its own Linux distribution but since adopted by others. rpms offer benefits similar to debs, but the two are incompatible. The only point at which a Debian user is likely to feel the lack of rpm support, however, is for certain commercial software that is available only in rpm format. You can use the `alien` package to convert rpms into debs for those cases.

There are a number of reasons why packages became so successful. I address some of the most common reasons for this in the section of this chapter entitled "Reasons for Choosing Debian."

The kernel

Basically, a software distribution consists of an operating system and *kernel*, the tools that support it and the applications that run atop it. A kernel typically provides the following:

✦ **Device drivers:** Each device driver is a bit of software that allows you to use one particular piece of your computer hardware. For instance, if you wish to use a keyboard and a mouse, there will be device drivers for them. Likewise, if you use graphics, you'll be using Linux's drivers for your graphics card. The Linux kernel contains device drivers for almost all common hardware in use today, with more drivers being regularly added.

✦ **Filesystems:** A filesystem is a full-blown database for files, and it is used for common data storage and retrieval tasks. Part of Linux's rise to prominence has been the ability to read from and write to a plethora of filesystems used in other operating systems. NTFS, ext3, and VFAT are examples of common filesystems.

✦ **The network stack:** A network stack allows all the applications running on the system to use a network quickly and easily. The network stack can be considered as a layer on top of the network card's device driver. It provides common networking facilities such as error correction and quality control.

✦ **A programming interface:** The programming interface is the way that most programs speak to the kernel. Libraries and applications build upon the kernel's programming interface to gain access to common functionality managed by the kernel. Most of the kernel interfaces on a modern GNU/Linux system are common system libraries, which are called by applications.

Though these items may seem rather mundane, their value cannot be understated. Instead of an application needing to write its own database software to store your data, it can use the kernel's filesystem. Instead of a game needing to drive the video card directly (and, thus, having to know about each and every video card out there), it can simply call upon the kernel to do that work.

In Debian's case, the only officially supported kernel is Linux. There are several projects underway to support other kernels as well, such as FreeBSD, NetBSD, and the GNU HURD kernel. When these projects are complete, they will allow you to use the same tools and applications you're already familiar with in a Debian or "Linux" system without using Linux.

Other components

Though the kernel's name (in our case, Linux) is certainly the most recognizable part of a software distribution, it's just that—one part. The kernel is important, but it's tiny compared to the rest of the distribution. A carefully crafted Linux kernel can be entirely contained on a single floppy disk, while the entirety of Debian consumes 13 CDs (and that's just for Intel-compatible hardware). In addition to the kernel, a distribution (such as Debian) also provides one or more of the following:

✦ A set of higher-level libraries to ease the task of developing applications. Applications rarely speak to the kernel directly; instead they call upon common system libraries. The GNU C library is a famous example of an essential library on any Debian system.

✦ Utilities to work with the system at a basic level, such as a command shell and the utilities available through it. The Bourne Shell and BASH are two shells that are packaged in Debian and are common on most GNU/Linux systems.

✦ Services or *daemons* that allow the computer to provide functionality to other computers over a network. On a modern Linux system, daemons also perform many tasks of interest only to applications running on your own computer. This allows for an environment that is *network-transparent*—an environment where software is just as easy to run across a network connection as it is to run on the computer itself. The Apache Web server, or an FTP or DNS system like BIND, are each examples of daemons packaged in Debian.

✦ Software that provides a consistent graphical user interface. GNOME and KDE are two large sets of packages in Debian that fill this role.

✦ Applications that are used directly by the user, such as a Web browser or e-mail client. Mozilla is an example of a popular Web browser packaged for Debian. Evolution is a good example of an e-mail client application that is packaged and installed on most Debian systems.

Architectures

The Linux kernel was originally designed for Intel processor–based PCs and therefore so was Debian. Soon Linux was ported to other platforms, and naturally, Debian followed suit. Although the PC is still by far the most popular architecture, Debian can now be used on anything from small handhelds based upon the ARM processor to IBM z-series mainframes based on the S/390 architecture. Another direction in which Debian has spread is beyond Linux itself to other kernels. GNU's own kernel project, known as the HURD (`www.gnu.org/software/hurd/`), which lived mostly in the shadow of Linux, got a much-needed boost by being integrated into a Debian distribution (though it is still not quite ready for wide use). There are also ports underway to the FreeBSD and NetBSD kernels. You can even run a Debian derivative on Apple's Mac OS X thanks to the Fink project (`http://fink.sourceforge.net/`), which has ported `apt-get`, `dpkg`, and many other Debian packages to the Macintosh so users can get access to free, high-quality Open Source applications in an easy-to-use format.

Some users wonder why all this effort is put into porting to sometimes rather obscure or obsolete architectures when that effort could be put into improving the PC version of Debian. Even if all you ever use are standard Intel processor–based beige boxes, you benefit from porting. The process of making software work in environments other than the ones they were designed for reveals hidden assumptions and hard-to-find bugs that would otherwise have gone unnoticed. Currently, the Debian project officially supports these architectures:

✦ **i386** — Intel's 80386 and its descendants and clones. Except for the kernel and a few packages where such optimization would actually make a difference, Debian doesn't optimize for Pentiums, AMD Athlons, and the like. Should a user wish to do so himself, he can recompile, but there isn't enough benefit to do this on a global basis.

✦ **m68k** — Motorola 68000 chips as used in Sun3, early Apple Macintosh, Atari, and Amiga machines.

✦ **sparc/sparc64** — Sun's 32- and 64-bit SPARC processors.

✦ **alpha** — Compaq's (formerly Digital's) Alpha processors.

✦ **powerpc** — IBM and Motorola PowerPC processors used in IBM servers and newer Apple Macintoshes.

✦ **arm** — ARM processors used in many PDAs and embedded devices.

✦ **mips/mipsel** — MIPS processors with different byte orders. These were used on machines from SGI and DEC.

✦ **hppa** — Hewlett-Packard's PA-RISC processors.

✦ **ia64** — Intel's Itanium processors.

✦ **s390** — IBM's S/390 mainframes.

✦ **sh** — Hitachi Super/H processors as used in the Sega Dreamcast.

✦ **amd64** — AMD's Opteron processors.

✦ **all** — software that is architecture neutral such as documentation or scripts. This is referred to as being of architecture all.

Distributions and Releases

A Debian *distribution* consists of a number of packages designed to work with one another and built for the same architecture. At any given time there are three distributions:

✦ **unstable** — New packages go here. This distribution is referred to as *unstable*, not necessarily because the packages are broken, but because they are in flux. While a package is in the unstable distribution, it may undergo many revisions, alterations in dependencies, and other changes. Think of unstable as the assembly plant for new Debian releases.

✦ **testing** — If a package has managed to remain bug-free for a certain amount of time, it is promoted to the *testing* distribution. When all the packages have entered the testing distribution, a short freeze period is declared, the testing distribution is fully tested (hence the name) for any integration problems, and the distribution is considered stable.

✦ **stable** — This is the released Debian distribution, the one recommended for the general public and available on CDs. A stable release has a version number and a code name.

Note   It was Debian Project leader Bruce Perens who started the tradition of giving Debian releases code names. Because Bruce was working for the Pixar animation studio at the time, the names are based on characters from the Pixar film *Toy Story*. The current stable distribution is called *sarge*. The proposed code name for the current testing distribution is *etch*. The unstable distribution also has a code name — *sid*. Some people will tell you *sid* is an acronym for *Still In Development*, but actually it is named after the naughty boy in *Toy Story* who liked to break his toys.

On the FTP archive, each distribution consists of three sections, only one of which is technically part of Debian:

✦ **main:** This is the Debian distribution proper. It consists solely of packages that meet the Debian Free Software Guidelines.

✦ **nonfree:** This section is for packages containing software that does not meet the Debian Free Software Guidelines but is otherwise legal to distribute. As explained in Section 5 of the Social Contract (see Chapter 25), it is made available solely as a concession to the fact that some software a user might need has no good free replacement. It is not considered part of the official Debian distribution.

✦ **contrib:** This section is for packages of software that are free but require a nonfree component to be useful. Examples include a game that requires you to purchase levels for it to be played or a Java program that requires Sun's proprietary Java virtual machine. It also is not considered part of the official Debian distribution.

Which Distribution Should You Use?

At some point, you will need to choose which distribution you are going to use, so it's good to get an overview here. (If you are new to Debian and find this confusing, you might want to refer back to it later.)

After a stable release has been issued, a new testing distribution is started, and the "freeze" on changes is lifted, allowing packages to enter testing again. A stable release is never updated with new packages except at release time because new packages could potentially introduce bad interactions, meaning everything would have to be tested all over again. Even in the event of a security problem being discovered after a release, the fix is back-ported to the version in the stable release rather than adding a new version.

Together with Debian's long release cycles, this policy means the software in the stable distribution is often several versions behind the current state of development. Debian is often criticized for this perceived obsolescence. What the critics misunderstand is that the whole point of a stable distribution is to be boring! If, for instance, you are using Debian to run an experiment on the space shuttle (as has been done), you don't want surprises. You want something that is tried and true and rock solid. If you want the fun and insanity of the bleeding edge, you should pick the unstable or testing version instead. Packages often enter unstable the same day as they are released upstream. In return, you sometimes have to deal with breakage, but you would be surprised how well most unstable packages hold up for noncritical uses. Many Debian users run the unstable version; by doing so, they help improve stability for everyone by finding and reporting bugs.

If the unstable version is a bit too raw and chaotic for you, the testing distribution should be the one you run. It receives newer packages, but at a slower rate than the unstable. The downside is that it may receive packages you need, such as security fixes, at a slower rate too. One last distribution option I should mention is to use the stable version with backports of packages from the unstable. There is an organized effort to provide such backports at www.backports.org/. Although this project is not officially part of Debian, it is run by Debian developers, and the packages taken from the unstable and recompiled for the stable distribution are just as high quality as official packages.

What Does Debian Do?

Debian is a *general-purpose* distribution, meaning that it includes software packages for every conceivable use. That isn't to say that Debian wrote all this software. Quite the opposite, in fact—Debian is the system integrator. There are numerous bits and pieces of Debian-specific software, but a huge majority (over 99 percent) is standard Free Software/Open Source software that can also be found in other GNU/Linux distributions. Debian's role is to serve in the place of a traditional proprietary vendor, and to put all this software into a form that's easy for the user to install, use, and maintain. Not only does this benefit the user by providing a clear and consistent operating environment, but it also allows developers to focus on creating applications without needing to worry about every little detail of the user's installation.

The table of contents for this book should provide you with an idea of what sort of common purposes a Debian installation is used for, but here's a quick rundown:

✦ **Desktop Workstation:** The power of traditional UNIX workstations, the administrative ease of a modern Linux distribution, and the breadth of software available—all these combine to allow Debian to serve as a first-class desktop operating system. Whether you're publishing a book, browsing the Web, modeling in 3-D, reading your e-mail, playing games, managing your digital photo album, or enjoying multimedia files, you'll find mature and easy-to-use applications available to meet your needs.

Cross-Reference   This book was written using OpenOffice.org, an excellent desktop productivity suite covered in Chapter 10. It's fully capable of interoperating with Microsoft Word—the software my editors use.

✦ **Internet Servers:** Probably the most common use of Linux is to act as an Internet server performing any number of roles, including but not limited to that of Web server, FTP server, e-mail server, VPN server, or DNS server. Debian's ease of administration makes it one of the most popular choices for skilled administrators. Professional administrators don't enjoy a system that's hard to maintain any more than a desktop user just looking to browse the Web, and Debian's consistent packaging standards allow for minimal fuss and bother.

✦ **Intranet Servers:** Providing a wide range of services, intranet servers (servers that are run on an internal network, providing services you don't want to offer to the general public) are the workhorses of modern companies. What's more, the wide availability of free Linux distributions has resulted in more and more homes having intranet servers as well. Often they perform the relatively simple task of allowing multiple desktops to share a single Internet connection, but I've been pleased to witness a trend of users providing more advanced services to their families and housemates such as media sharing and playback, schedule sharing, e-mail, printing, backups, and databases.

✦ **A Development Platform:** Debian's massive software archive (unequalled anywhere) makes for a compelling development platform for both experienced developers and those just getting their feet wet. Since developer tools and libraries are easily accessible, and since systems administration is really quite simple, a developer can feel comfortable having the best tools available quickly and easily, while not needing to spend too much time on "system administrator" problems.

Though some Debian Developers and users say this tongue-in-cheek, Debian tries to be a "universal operating system." We're well on our way to accomplishing this goal. Not only can Debian fulfill many roles (far more than are covered here), but it's also built from the ground up in a manner that allows others to create their own "mini" Debians. Though there are more widely used Linux distributions and operating systems in existence, there's scarcely a single task that can't be accomplished with a Debian system today.

For each of the architectures Debian supports, it includes the following:

✦ An installer, such as a CD-ROM, allowing the user to perform an initial installation of the Debian distribution.

✦ A full archive of software already compiled for that architecture. (Most software must be processed or *compiled* for a given architecture before it can be used on that architecture — a time-consuming and difficult task.)

✦ Documentation in the form of an installation manual that covers most if not all of the common questions specific to that architecture.

Linux and Its Pedigree

At the heart of Debian is the Linux kernel described above. All of the software that's available in Debian runs atop Linux. As such, it makes sense to spend some time discussing Linux, its roots, and how that affects the software you see in Debian.

As mentioned previously, Linux was originally created by (and is still primarily maintained by) Linus Torvalds. It's technically modeled after traditional UNIX systems, but it does not contain any of their copyrighted material. The Linux kernel was developed in an environment of open exchange that allowed for rapid development and maturation.

Contrast this to UNIX, which was controlled primarily by commercial interests. Each vendor had a vested interest in ensuring that its variation of UNIX was the most popular. A result of this interest was the exploitation of the vendors' customers: If a traditional UNIX vendor could make its own variant different enough from the others to discourage easy migration, they could charge exorbitant fees for maintenance, hardware, and new software releases. Nontechnical pushes to

become distinctive and different made administration and programming more difficult and resulted in steeper learning curves. It didn't help that traditional UNIX
vendors saw their software primarily as a means of selling (expensive) hardware.
Perhaps they weren't as motivated as they could have been to improve the software.

The end result of this marketplace fractioning was the rise of other operating systems, notably those from Microsoft. During the UNIX days, Microsoft was the new
kid on the block. While its software was comparatively immature and lacking in features, it was usable on common hardware available from multiple vendors.
Companies large and small flocked to the lower cost of these platforms, while at the
same time shedding the bonds their proprietary UNIX vendors held them with.

The self-destructive practices of these traditional UNIX vendors also gave rise to
another contender — Linux. Not only can you use it on the most mundane commod-
ity hardware, but you can also use it on the hardware that those traditional UNIX
vendors designed, built, and sold.

Given that, Linux can be seen in some ways as the evolution of the UNIX philosophy. UNIX was, for a very long time, acknowledged as the superior operating system in technical terms. The steady decline of UNIX in importance is mainly due to
the actions of the vendors, and not due to the basic technology itself.

Since Linux takes after traditional UNIX in its technical aspects, there are some
basic features that are common to any Linux distribution, including Debian:

   ✦ Linux systems are heavily abstracted or layered. There are clear interface lay-
     ers — for instance, between the standard C library and applications. This
     allows for layers to be replaced wholesale with minimal disruption if some-
     thing better is developed, or if a particular layer needs even a minor upgrade.

   ✦ The environment is also segmented horizontally: One subsystem is kept care-
     fully segregated from its peers. For instance, two applications may use the
     same libraries, but they're kept separate. This again allows for flexibility,
     while at the same time minimizing the impact of any bugs and making the sys-
     tem more stable and secure.

   ✦ Linux is a true multi-user, multitasking operating system, and it has been since
     its birth. Unlike other operating systems that had such functionality added to
     them later, or whose focus is elsewhere, Linux allows multiple people to
     simultaneously use the same machine in a safe, secure, and high-performance
     manner. Likewise, users aren't limited to running a single desktop environ-
     ment or a single application. Resources will be shared amongst applications,
     and the only limit to the number you're able to run is the capacity of your
     computer.

   ✦ Access to hardware is done through the kernel (or in some rare cases, a sys-
     tem library or daemon). As such, applications are almost entirely device inde-
     pendent. You can replace your digital camera and use the same application to

manage your digital photography. Instead of requiring each hardware vendor to design, develop, test, and distribute such applications, efforts can be concentrated into a small number of applications that meet every user's needs.

✦ Linux has several industrial-strength filesystems available for use. Thanks to the layering of a Linux system, your choice of filesystem can be tailored to your needs. For instance, if you need high performance, you might be willing to sacrifice some storage space efficiency to get it. Perhaps you really would rather have a very solid filesystem that is very resistant to data loss, and you're willing to accept a small tradeoff in terms of performance. Maybe you need a filesystem that's okay at everything, even though it may not stand out as the best at anything. No single filesystem can be the best at everything, but with a well-constructed system like Linux, you're able to choose the particular tradeoffs you'd like to make. Your applications will continue to function regardless of the filesystem you choose.

The Debian Project and Debian Community

Thus far we've discussed the Debian software distribution. The term *Debian* is also used to refer to the community that builds and maintains the associated software distribution.

 The Debian community is discussed in more depth in Chapter 25.

The wider Free Software/Open Source community

Software isn't like a piece of furniture. A piece of furniture takes time to design, energy and raw materials to build (not to mention the factory), and time and energy to transport it to the customer. Software, on the other hand, only needs time to be written once. Thanks to the Internet, copying and distribution costs are negligible.

Software is also quite complex. The Linux kernel (a small but important part of a full operating environment) has more than 5 million functional lines of source code. There are many people in the world who don't feel comfortable trusting such complex things implicitly. Similarly, there aren't many people who would feel comfortable flying in a plane whose workings were entirely sealed to everybody but the manufacturer. (The airline mechanics should be able to check to see if the wiring is well-insulated.)

These properties of software — its complexity and the need for accountability, its one-time cost of writing, and its lack of cost to duplicate and distribute — gave rise to the Free Software/Open Source movement. In this movement, companies and individual volunteers work together to create software to meet their needs.

Instead of paying large and recurring license fees to traditional software vendors, these individuals and companies choose instead to put some of that money toward the development of part of the system while pocketing the balance or spending it elsewhere. In turn, other companies and individuals put some of their own money and time into improving other parts of the system. The net result is a huge community of individuals and companies working together to build a computer operating environment for less than it would cost them to license a proprietary solution.

With the mainstream popularity that Linux has been gaining over the past few years, a number of companies have opted to pay licensing fees to a commercial Linux distributor (such as Red Hat, Inc.), which in turn employs developers working to improve the software while offering support and corporate accountability.

Not only have these models of collective contribution proven to lower costs for the user as well as generally create higher-quality software, but each and every participant (whether a random user, an individual developer, or a company of any size) has full access to every portion of the system. If they wish to ensure the security of the system and integrity of their data, they can do so by auditing the source code themselves. If a portion of the system needs to be altered slightly to meet their specific needs, they can do so. Additionally, if there's a problem with the software, it's impossible to hide and is always fixable. Last but certainly not least, all this access to information allows users to maintain the software themselves should the need arise — instead of relying on a vendor that may decide the software the user needs to perform critical business functions is no longer profitable enough (or perhaps has just gone out of business, as so many software companies have). Users of Free Software/Open Source software aren't contractually — or otherwise — bound to upgrade their software and pay the associated licensing and maintenance fees; if the user doesn't wish to disrupt his business by upgrading his infrastructure, he can instead opt to pay any number of companies to help maintain the older software, or can develop that capability in-house.

The Debian Project's goals and people

The Debian Project itself follows the Free Software/Open Source model very closely. It even has a Social Contract (www.debian.org/social_contract), which is a constitution of sorts that all Debian Developers must adhere to in their Debian work. I encourage you to read the contract if you're interested in the details, but here's a rough overview:

Cross-Reference   The entire Social Contract can be read in Chapter 25.

✦ Debian users have the right to view and modify any part of the system as they see fit, to meet their own specific needs.

✦ Debian will participate in the wider Free Software/Open Source community by making any of its own source code available under licenses acceptable to that community.

✦ Debian will not attempt to hide mistakes or bugs from its users, understanding that this information must be available for timely and high-quality system administration, and that it's harmful to the community to attempt to keep this information secret.

✦ Our priorities are our users and the Free Software/Open Source community. Their needs will be foremost in our mind when we make any decisions. We do not object to companies or other users using Debian as a base for a commercial Linux distribution, nor do we object to commercial software designed to work with our distribution.

✦ We understand that not all software licenses meet our standards for transparency, ease of distribution, and the ability for the user to make arbitrary modifications. Thus, while no such software is part of Debian, we will support its use.

These are the rules that we apply to the Debian distribution and to the act of maintaining it. Debian Developers have, in fact, agreed to a lot more than the conditions listed here. There are hundreds of pages of documentation describing specific conventions used, specific technologies exercised, and how everything fits together.

Black and white text though, dry and impersonal, simply doesn't express the variety and richness in the Debian community. At its core, Debian is all about putting together software that we can use on a day-to-day basis. Individual developers come from many backgrounds. Many are volunteers who prefer to use Debian on their personal machines and servers. A fair number are representative of companies who use Debian to conduct their business. These people, whether volunteers or paid, come from dozens of countries in all parts of the world. What's common, however, is that they're all interested in using and producing a Linux distribution that meets their needs. There are also differences of opinion on a regular basis. They make for lively debates and an excellent distribution.

Official *Debian Developers* are the only people allowed to add or update packages in the Debian archive. *New Maintainers* (aspiring Debian Developers) are put through a rigorous screening process that usually takes several months. During this process, their skills in reading and understanding software licenses are checked, they must agree to uphold Debian's principles, they're asked to provide example packages for evaluation, and they're asked to answer myriad questions concerning their ability to maintain a package — everything from responding to bug reports to responding to security alerts to tracking new versions of software.

Cross-Reference   See Chapter 25 for an in-depth look at the steps a New Maintainer must follow to become an official Debian Developer.

Though applicants aren't able to directly upload packages to the Debian archive as they're proceeding through the New Maintainer process, there are many Debian Developers who enjoy auditing the New Maintainers' packages and commenting on them. It's a form of mentoring. The Debian Developer can then — once satisfied with the package's quality — upload it to Debian on the New Maintainer's behalf. Many important packages in Debian are maintained by New Maintainers being mentored and sponsored by official Debian Developers.

Though individual developers are ultimately responsible for the state of the packages they maintain, sometimes a package is simply too large and complex for one person to handle. In these cases, *group maintainership* has become a popular solution. This form of package maintenance has gained prominence in recent years within Debian, to more evenly spread the burden of package maintenance across numerous maintainers. In this model, each individual in the group is treated as the package's maintainer; any actions they take with respect to the package are taken with full authority.

Custom Debian distributions

In addition to the general Debian roles described previously, there are numerous Debian subprojects to develop customized distributions underway (www.debian.org/devel/#projects and http://wiki.debian.net/index.cgi?CustomDebian). Since Debian is a general-purpose distribution, it offers people a platform from which to target specific audiences. There are a number of sub-projects within Debian to do exactly that. The intent is to provide installation media, preselected package lists, and custom configuration and documentation that have been designed specifically for the target audience to further ease their Debian use. Instead of creating a distribution from scratch, these groups instead make small changes to the installer, package lists, and default configurations to allow their users to more easily install and use Debian in their particular environment. Examples of custom distributions are Debian-JR for children, Debian-Med for doctors and hospitals, Debian-Edu for use in schools, and Debian-NP, which is targeted at nonprofit organizations.

There are also commercial derivatives of Debian. Two major distributions are UserLinux, spearheaded by Bruce Perens, and Ubuntu. UserLinux tries to do its work entirely within Debian. It adds certifications and a support infrastructure distributed among many consultants who want to support Debian but who find it difficult to do this directly, given Debian's institutionally independent nature. More information on UserLinux can be found at www.userlinux.org.

Ubuntu, the employer of one of the authors of this book, is pursuing a monolithic support model organizationally, although others are welcome and encouraged to compete. Ubuntu is focusing much more on development and is working on a branched version of Debian and contributing its changes back as they are made. Ubuntu offers a version of Debian with an easier and less verbose installer, a tightly integrated GNOME installation, and a schedule that releases a version with new software every six months. Information on Ubuntu is available at www.ubuntulinux.org.

Both projects are young and remain largely unproven. They are joined by a number of other commercial Debian derivatives that include Linspire and others. I am singling out these two because they are dedicated to keeping the difference between their work and Debian proper. As a result, almost everything in this book will apply not only to Debian but also to UserLinux and Ubuntu and, to a differing extent, to other Debian derivatives.

Reasons for Choosing Debian

I've already mentioned some of the reasons why Debian is popular and why it's used where it's used. As you read through more of this book, you'll find more reasons as well. However, there's no better place in this book for a good, technical (or at least semitechnical) list of reasons why you might be interested in learning about Debian and using it on your computers, so here it is.

The breadth of software

One of Debian's selling points has long been the breadth of software officially available. Unlike many commercial Linux distributions, Debian offers a full archive of the available Free Software/Open Source software. Almost everything that runs on Linux is available in Debian for easy installation and use, as opposed to the smaller, approved subset available through other distributions.

This may not sound like a particularly compelling argument at first; after all, those commercial distributions do have good taste, and they choose very good software. However, Debian acknowledges that not every user can use the same software to solve the same problem or fill the same role. Instead of requiring users to manually maintain that particular bit of software on their own without any support from the vendor, Debian provides it right from the start. What's more, even if the user is a skilled administrator, many software installations can quickly become a drain on the administrator's time, which could be much better spent tending to the more immediate needs of her users.

Completely aside from the amount of software available within Debian itself, we also go to great lengths to make sure that it's easy for you to use regardless of which hardware platform you have. Instead of selling an old and unused Sun server that cost $10,000 at the time of purchase for a paltry $1,000 on eBay, you can turn that quite capable server into a Debian machine for a variety of purposes. Perhaps it's a Hewlett-Packard HP-UX server that isn't being used. Perhaps it's an IBM AIX server. Chances are that if you can buy it or build it, Debian can run on it.

This portability—the capability for Debian to run on so many different architectures—also allows for an unrivaled amount of standardization. No longer do you need to learn a half-dozen different software systems (or, worse yet, hire a half-dozen very expensive and often underworked specialists); you can simply use Debian and apply it wherever needed.

Debian currently contains over 13,000 software packages that are officially supported on 10 different hardware platforms (with unofficial support on another 5).

For a complete list of architectures supported by Debian, visit `www.debian.org/ports/`.

The ease of administration

Debian was one of the first Linux distributions to fully embrace now-commonplace packaging practices, and even today Debian's support for this means of administering systems is unequalled. While every distribution of note uses packages these days, Debian has been doing it for longer and has used this time to refine the concept to a fine art.

Part of this refinement has been in the tools available to the system administrator or user for managing these packages. Much of a system administrator's time is spent installing, configuring, upgrading, and removing software. With tools such as `apt-get` and `aptitude` to install, upgrade, and remove packages, and the standardized debconf configuration framework, software maintenance and configuration have never been easier.

Software management with `apt-get` and `aptitude` is discussed in Chapter 4, "Software Management," as is Debian's configuration framework, `debconf`.

A phenomenon I've seen in other Linux distributions has been that of extremely large default installations. Without specifically telling the distribution's installer anything, you're left with massive numbers of packages on your hard drive that you'll never use. Many of them will be running unnecessary processes in the background. This, I believe, is often due to the relatively poor nature of the package maintenance system of most distributions. When system administrators find it difficult to locate and install software, their tendency is to install a great deal of software during the installation to save themselves the hassle later.

Contrast this to Debian, where a package can be installed in seconds, simply by knowing the package's name. The side effect of this property is that Debian doesn't install large amounts of software unless you actually tell it to. There's simply no need because it's always painless to install more software.

When a package is installed in Debian, package management software will automatically install any software upon which your package depends and will automatically upgrade to the newest version of the package if the software is already installed.

Limiting the software contained on your computer does more than simply save disk space (which, while a concern for high-performance servers, is not terribly important); it also allows for easier maintenance. Installations and upgrades are less time-consuming and error prone. Security updates are less frequent because you have less software installed that might be insecure and require a patch. The system is smaller and easier to understand, aiding in troubleshooting, education, and documentation.

Since Debian packages are so easy to install and maintain, and because there are so many of them, Debian has also been forced to come up with a standard package-configuration framework (hinted at earlier). This framework is called *debconf*, short for "Debian configuration." The highly segmented nature of Debian packages allows each maintainer to provide tailored configuration scripts for packages where such configuration makes sense. To reconfigure such a package, it's only a matter of knowing the package's name and running the command `dpkg-reconfigure packagename`. A centralized, monolithic configuration application would have been totally unusable for a Debian user and would be unstable and breakable. Instead, Debian has offered a streamlined, purpose-built configuration system that allows the user to selectively configure small portions of the system at a time, on an as-needed basis, or to be prompted with questions only at a certain priority while accepting the same default for others.

This heavy focus on packages has resulted in a very rich package-development environment. It's not difficult for a system administrator to create his or her own software packages (perhaps for an in-house application, or just a package containing configuration information) and distribute them using standard Debian tools.

Your independence

The Debian distribution was built from the ground up by system administrators and users. The people who build the distribution are those who most benefit from being able to easily maintain their own computer systems. Unlike a commercial vendor, which may have a vested interest in support contracts, Debian has a vested interest in the exact opposite. Debian is maintained by volunteers and individuals working for companies, and both these groups of maintainers have other things to do with their time than nursing day-to-day problems with a terrible software distribution; they'd rather make the distribution good in the first place.

This attitude, combined with the licensing requirements for software included in Debian, means that your computers do not rely on the existence of a second or third party to function properly. Not only is the system built for easy self-maintenance, but also all the software officially available via Debian (that is, everything included on the CDs and in the main archives) has full source code available and licensed in such a way that you're free to modify and redistribute the applications should the need ever arise.

Summary

The Debian Project is formed by nearly a thousand developers who, over the course of the last decade, have built a distribution of 13,000 pieces of software—*packages* in the Debian world—that run on top of the Linux kernel. Packages are convenient ways of wrapping up software, and a *distribution* is a collection of such packages. These packages within Debian will run on many architectures. In addition to a distribution, Debian is a project that produces and maintains a distribution that, for a number of technical, economic, and philosophical reasons, provides a compelling alternative to other Free Software/Open Source and proprietary operating systems.

✦   ✦   ✦

Installing Debian

Debian has long been criticized for its installer. While features like `apt-get` and the massive size of its repository have drawn many users and much praise to the Debian Project, the difficult installer — the first thing a typical new user sees — has proven a prohibitively difficult hurdle for many users. Many Debian Developers joked that the advanced package-management tools and large archive in Debian were so good at allowing for seamless upgrades over long periods of time that Debian Developers never had to reinstall and as a result put less emphasis into the installer.

The installer familiar to anyone who has installed Debian in the past is a system called *boot floppies*. It was used for the woody release and most of Debian's earlier releases. "Boot floppies" is something of a misnomer because most people who used that installer probably ran it off a CD-ROM, not from floppies. The system did little or no hardware detection and asked a lot of questions that proved either too intimidating or too technical for many users. For this and for other technical reasons, a new Debian Installer project was created.

During planning for woody (Debian 3.0), the release managers chose to stick with boot floppies for one more release. Sarge (Debian 3.1), the most recent Debian release, is the first release of Debian to be built off this brand-new installer, which has been in the works for more than half a decade.

At first glance, the new installer, with its blue backgrounds and dialog boxes, appears graphically similar to boot floppies, but these similarities are purely superficial. The project is a rewrite from the ground up, and you can feel this when you start using it.

The new installer sports advanced hardware detection and automatic partitioning. Like the old system, it will install on a wide number of different architectures. Debian Installer (abbreviated "d-i" or "di") will look and act the same on everything from your old Motorola 6800 series Macintosh to your IBM S/390 mainframe. In the simplest configurations, the new installer can install Debian onto a bare system in less than a dozen clicks. In terms of speed of portability, the new Debian Installer is unmatched in the Linux world.

However, since Debian Installer is relatively late in coming, a number of people and organizations have already created their own tools for installing Debian. While this chapter describes only the official process using the Debian Installer, there are others that may be worth reviewing. Most notable (and currently maintained) among these is Progeny's project, which has modified Red Hat, Inc.'s Anaconda installer so that, in addition to being able to install Red Hat, it can also install a Debian sarge system. A long list of Debian installers and derivatives is online at `www.linuxmafia.com/faq/Debian/installers.html`. At least one project, Ubuntu, is installing its operating system using a modified version of Debian's "d-i" installer. Ubuntu's Web site is `www.ubuntulinux.org`.

While you may have more luck with other installers for Debian, I focus on the Debian Installer because it's the default installer and the one supported by the Debian Project. In this chapter, I cover the details of working with the new Debian Installer.

A Quick Walk-Through of the Debian Installer

The first step in installing Debian is booting from the CD image. On many computers, this simply means placing the CD-ROM accompanying this book into the drive and rebooting your computer. If your computer is not configured to boot from a CD, you will have to enter your computer's BIOS on boot-up (typically done by pressing the Delete key) and change the boot configuration or sequence so that your computer attempts to boot from the CD-ROM *before* it tries to boot from the hard disk. The specifics of this change will vary depending on the particular BIOS on your computer. These instructions are outside the scope of this book, but you can get help either online or in the manual that came with your computer or motherboard.

1. When you boot off the CD, you are prompted with a screen similar to the one in Figure 2-1.

   In most situations, you can press Enter to continue. If, after you've pressed Enter, your system doesn't boot, becomes unreadable, or never reaches the language choice prompt detailed in the next step, you can use this prompt to pass in low-level options. You can see these options by pressing **F1** at this prompt. After pressing Enter, the installation system will initialize and boot.

Figure 2-1: The initial boot screen appears when you put the CD in your drive and reboot.

2. Next, choose your language by following the prompt shown in Figure 2-2.

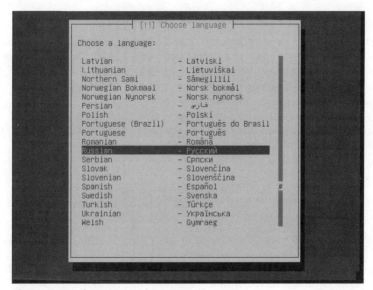

Figure 2-2: Choose your language.

Simply choose the language corresponding to the language you speak and would like to install Debian in and press Enter.

Note
You will not be forced to use your computer in a single language based on what you answer here.

3. The next two screens ask for your country and your keyboard layout. Answer appropriately. Your country and keyboard layout do not necessarily need to correspond to the language that the installer is in.

Note
You will be able to change your language at any point later and can even have several different languages supported on a single machine if you have multiple users that like to use the computer in different languages.

4. After you respond to these prompts, the installer will load installer components from the CD and start automatic hardware detection to find network devices. If a network device cannot automatically be detected, the installer prompts you with a list of choices of network cards and also enables you to choose one not listed on the list and to install a driver stored on a floppy drive or from another external source instead.

Note
You'll find that a network interface is extremely useful during a Debian installation. Debian includes thousands of pieces of software, and only the most popular will fit on the first CD — the only one that is included with this book. Chances are good that unless you're installing a bare-bones system, you'll benefit from being able to download some extra packages. Luckily, all of these packages are located on Internet-accessible servers, so once your network is up, you'll be good to go.

If you don't have network access and need packages not provided on the installation CD, you can order them from the many resellers listed at www.debian.org/CD/vendors/. With vendors all around the world, Debian will be able to connect you with someone nearby to get either the top few Debian CDs or the complete set.

5. After your network interface is up and you are online, the system will configure the network either by DHCP (automatic IP assignment) or by asking you to provide the necessary information. Many networks support automatic or DHCP networking, but if yours does not, you will either need to get the appropriate information — including an IP address, DNS address, netmask, gateway, and nameserver — from your local network administrator, or copy it from your current operating system if you are replacing it.

6. With the network online, the installer asks you for your new system's hostname. Many people, myself included, will attest to the fact that this is the most entertaining part of the install. Thinking up a naming scheme for all your computers can be fun. Comparing these naming schemes is a common conversation among groups of geeks.

7. The next step that the installer leads you through is the partitioning of your disks in such a way that you can install Debian. Basically, you need to designate a space on your hard drive where the Debian install can store all of its files. Drawing the boundaries on the disks to designate this space is called *partitioning*. The system loads a piece of software, the partitioner, and then presents you with a menu like the one in Figure 2-3.

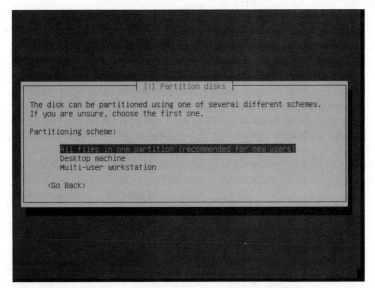

Figure 2-3: Choose a partitioning scheme for your disk.

Caution

Partitioning will break your hard disk into separate chunks. If there is data on the drive that you need to access, partitioning, or repartitioning, can make accessing that data difficult or impossible when things go wrong. If you are installing onto a drive with essential data, it's a good idea to back up your data before you proceed with the partitioning process.

In this step, the installer asks what partitioning scheme you prefer. For the majority of users, the default answer, "All files in one partition," is the best choice.

8. With the default option selected, the system runs an auto-partitioning program to create the appropriate drive partitions, and then goes to work doing the partitioning itself. Before it begins the actual partitioning, the system prompts you for confirmation with a screen like the one in Figure 2-4.

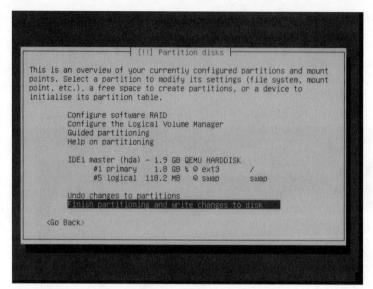

Figure 2-4: Confirm the installer's choices for partitioning.

9. Scan the choices to make sure they look sane. If so, you can confirm the partition by pressing Enter. The installer will ask you to verify this decision because this type of installation will destroy any data that was on the disk before. Confirm it once you are sure you have taken appropriate precautions. At this point, the installer will partition the drives and then create filesystems as presented in the previous screen. The default behavior is to create what is called an *EXT3* filesystem.

Note   While EXT3 is the default filesystem, there are several other popular types, including ReiserFS and XFS. Each of these filesystems has unique performance benefits and weaknesses. Choosing a different filesystem will not have any effect on the computer as you use it or trade files with other people. It's merely the internal database format that your computer uses to keep track of information for itself.

The system now starts installing the base Debian system onto your hard drive in your newly created partition. This may take quite a while and will vary heavily depending on the speed of your CD-ROM drive and your computer. After installing the packages, the installer configures these essential packages for you according to defaults and the answers you gave in the earlier part of the install.

After finishing the configuration, the system begins wrapping up the first stage of the install. It prompts you to install a *boot loader*—the program that loads up your operating system (or systems if you have more than one). The default boot loader in Debian is called the *GRand Unified Bootloader* (GRUB).

It can allow you to boot Debian, Windows, and other operating systems on your computer from a menu. Assuming you started with a clean system, as in the example in this chapter, Debian is the only OS on your computer. The installer will notice this, as indicated in Figure 2-5, and will prompt you to set GRUB accordingly. Select Yes at this prompt.

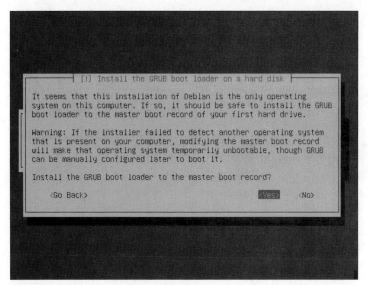

Figure 2-5: Confirm GRUB installation.

10. Upon confirming this and installing a boot loader, you've reached the end of the first stage of installation. You now have a Debian system on your hard drive! Before you start celebrating, though, you should realize that the installation is not finished. You'll need to reboot your system and finalize the installation by configuring the base system and then selecting what additional nonbase software that you want to install. The installer will prompt you about this reboot with a message like the one in Figure 2-6. Select Continue to reboot.

With that click, you will leave the Debian Installer. When your machine reboots, you will no longer be using the installer but will be using the similar-appearing base configuration program. Remember to remove the CD before rebooting or you will go right back into the installer again.

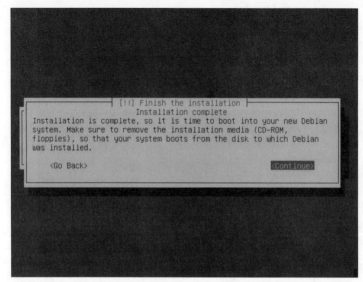

Figure 2-6: Reboot your system and finish installation.

11. Upon reboot, if all has gone well, you will be greeted by the GRUB boot loader menu, which is similar to the screen in Figure 2-7. Press Enter to select the default mode (nonrecovery mode) to boot your system.

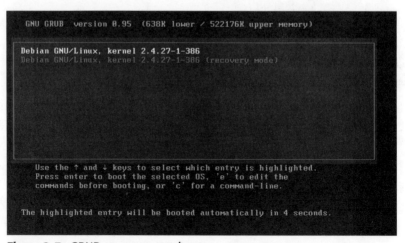

Figure 2-7: GRUB menu upon reboot.

Configuring Your System

After your system boots, you will be greeted by a screen that welcomes you to your Debian system and gives you an overview of what's coming in the rest of the setup procedure. Basically you'll be asked to:

✦ Set up a time zone

✦ Select a root password

✦ Create a system user

✦ Install additional software

The first three steps should be self-explanatory. If you are uncertain about the terminology of root and system users, remember that you'll use your system as a normal user but will keep a *superuser* identity — always named root — for doing privileged system administration tasks where you could break things. The password for this privileged superuser is, conveniently enough, called the *root password*. Normal system users are all other nonprivileged users, including the identity you will use to access the machine and that you will be prompted to created now. Many people choose a first name, nickname, or initials as their username, but it can be anything you like as long as it doesn't have a space. Follow the prompts to complete this portion of the installation.

Caution   It's important that you remember your root password. It may be wise to write it down and keep it somewhere safe and out of the way where others will not find it. It's not impossible to recover from a lost root password, but it is a lot of work and is not a lot of fun, either.

Installing Software

After entering your user password, you will come to a section on apt configuration. apt is the Debian package manager, and it's very powerful. (apt is discussed in depth later in this book, particularly in Chapter 4.)

1. At this point, you need to choose the methods by which apt accesses the Debian archive. Because you're installing off of the CD, you can choose "cdrom."

2. Because you only have one CD, which does not hold all the available Debian distribution software, you'll want to add a network resource (that is, as long as you have network access). Either FTP or HTTP is an equally appropriate choice at this point.

3. Upon selecting your network resource, you will be prompted to select a mirror: first by narrowing down the list by country and then by selecting an actual mirror. After you have done this, you can progress through the installer.

   With your mirror in hand, `apt` will update its list of possible packages by downloading lists of available packages off of the CD (or CDs if have you have more than one) and by downloading similar lists from any mirrors that you have selected.

4. The installer will then ask you to select the software you want to install from a list like the one in Figure 2-8.

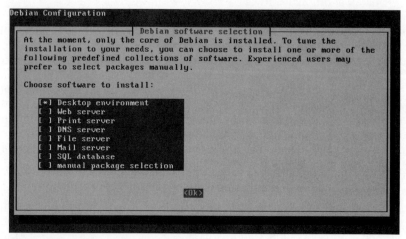

Figure 2-8: Select software to install.

You can select whatever you are comfortable with and whatever you want. You do not need to select anything at this point unless you need it. If you are installing a particular type of server, such as a Web server or mail server, it is a good idea to select these from the list. If you are planning on using this installation as a desktop machine, you should select Desktop Environment here. Desktop Environment will install both the GNOME and KDE desktop packages. (GNOME and KDE are covered in detail in Chapter 8.)

At the bottom of the list in Figure 2-8 you should see an option for Manual Package Selection. Manual package selection can be powerful, but it may be a little too complicated for most beginners. It presents users with a list of all of the available packages and allows them to select what they wish. Keep in mind, though, that the sheer number of packages can be overwhelming.

Once you have selected and confirmed the groups of packages, or individual packages, that you wish to install, `apt` will kick into gear. You will see a lot of scrolling text as `apt` downloads packages that are not available on the CD or the local filesystem and configures and installs them.

Based on the software you select, you will be asked additional questions to aid in the configuration of these packages. The questions will vary depending on the software you have chosen to install. The more software you install, the more questions you will likely be asked. Most of these are relatively straightforward, but some can be tricky, especially for novices.

Many of these questions are addressed in descriptions of installing the individual pieces of software later in this book. There are two alternatives I suggest for those wary of answering questions on their own:

✦ Do not select any groups of software at the "select software" stage (step 4 in the previous list). This will leave you with the bare minimum system. As you progress through this book, though, you can install pieces of software as you go. Debian includes a very advanced package dependency management system that makes installing software, even complex software with many dependencies, an absolute breeze.

✦ Select the software you want and proceed now. Try your best to answer questions and when you get stumped, refer to later sections in this book that are relevant to the questions and the piece of software that is asking the question. For example, GNOME installation questions are covered in "The GNOME Desktop Environment" section in Chapter 8.

Note   As you proceed through this book and as you use Debian, you will undoubtedly install more software. As you will quickly learn, Debian makes installing software so painless many people do it dozens of times a day!

That's it for now. You should have everything you need to install a bare-bones Debian system. Congratulations!

Summary

This chapter introduced you to the process and the history of Debian installation. Because hands-on experience is the best way to learn anything, it walked you through an installation of Debian. After the installer itself, the walk-through continued with a discussion of the initial system configuration stage through the selection and installation of packages.

✦   ✦   ✦

Using the Shell and Filesystem

In today's GNU/Linux world, a user can be fully satisfied using the rich set of graphical applications, utilities, and games available in Debian and other distributions. However, this book isn't just for a user interested solely in browsing the Web or word processing; it's also for users who want to know (and administrators who *need* to know) what's going on behind the scenes. Crucial to understanding the workings of a GNU/Linux system like Debian is a basic familiarity with the system's file storage database or *filesystem*. The easiest way to learn about this filesystem is to use another important layer of a GNU/Linux system — the command shell.

Linux has several different filesystem types available. Some specialize in performance, others integrity. Since each filesystem presents a standardized interface to the user and applications, this book will discuss the ext3 filesystem — the Linux standard. It's very mature and capable, has broad compatibility and acceptance, and is well rounded, though it is not particularly notable for any one feature. In the default Debian installation, ext3 is the filesystem that you will be using. In day-to-day usage, the filesystem type will be invisible to the user.

Shells, on the other hand, are not only meant to be a user interface to working with the filesystem, but also as a general-purpose interface to any number of subsystems and applications. Accomplished administrators spend a great deal of their time in a shell, and they'll usually pick a shell that best suits their workflow and style. For simplicity's sake, this chapter will examine the bash shell. bash is a full-featured, mature, and portable shell. It's the default shell in Debian (mainly due to its widespread availability on multiple platforms).

The following sections provide grounding in shell usage and filesystem examination and manipulation. The concepts and basic commands introduced here are required for administering even the most basic Debian system.

Filesystem Structure

Before you dive into using the shell to examine your filesystem, it's prudent to discuss some of the structure common to today's GNU/Linux systems. Since the filesystem plays such a central role in administration, software management, and day-to-day use, its layout is well defined and largely standardized. Equally important is an understanding of the various types of files that live in the filesystem and the properties associated with them.

Namespaces and trees

These days, with hard drives commonly holding 80GB of data or more, it's more crucial than ever to organize information so that it's easy to access. This is done, of course, by naming the different bits of information. It may seem obvious, but this concept wasn't applied broadly to computers until the 1970s. Before the 1970s, information was mostly stored and retrieved using numeric, non-human-readable addresses. Applying names to individual pieces of information created a *namespace* — a virtual area where no two pieces of information can have the same name.

Flat namespaces versus trees

Given the large amount of data stored on computers, another important aspect is categorization or subdivision. A *flat* namespace is one in which there are no categories or subdivisions; it's essentially unorganized. Though the individual files can be accessed by their names, you'll have trouble finding a file if you don't know its name.

A *hierarchical* namespace, or *tree*, allows you or an application to find and work with data by referring to its category. Categories in a GNU/Linux system are, of course, *directories* and are often represented graphically as folders. There is a single root directory that contains files and other directories. Those directories, in turn, can contain other files and directories, and so on.

When referring to a file, you refer to both the file itself and the directory that contains it. For example, /usr/share/doc/base-files/README.FHS is a full address or *pathname*. /usr/share/doc/base-files/ is the directory that contains the file or its *path*, and README.FHS is the filename.

> **Note**
>
> You'll note in the example above that the path separator on a GNU/Linux system is the slash (/), as opposed to the backslash (\), which you may be more familiar with from the Windows world. If you've been using a backslash for a long time, you'll quickly get used to the difference; the slash isn't as far a reach on most keyboard layouts as the backslash.

The GNU/Linux filesystem tree

Since finding data should be easy, standard structures for filesystem trees have been adopted. These standards specify what sort of data belongs in which directory, and why.

The Filesystem Hierarchy Standard

The Filesystem Hierarchy Standard (or *FHS*) is the standard filesystem layout for GNU/Linux systems. Debian has adopted it, as have a number of other distributions. Those systems that haven't officially adopted it still appear to be very similar. The FHS wasn't a committee standard; it simply documented the common practices of most GNU/Linux distributions. Debian's current policy adheres to the FHS version 2.1 dated April 12, 2000. The most recent version is 2.3, but the changes between versions haven't been major.

 You can view the current (and past) versions of the Filesystem Hierarchy Standard, in full, at www.pathname.com/fhs/.

Notable directories

Table 3-1 describes the contents for some of the more important directories on the system.

Table 3-1
Notable Directories

Directory	Contents
/	The root directory is the root or head of the tree.
/bin/	Basic command-line utilities intended to be used by all users.
/sbin/	Basic command-line utilities intended to be used primarily by the system administrator.
/lib/	Shared libraries required by the utilities in /bin/ and /sbin/.
/etc/	System-wide configuration files. Files in this portion of the namespace either set system-wide defaults for applications, or contain configuration information about the system itself (such as any network cards, the local time zone, and so on).
/boot/	The kernel and other files vital to booting the computer are contained here.
/dev/	This directory contains the *device nodes* on a system. These are files that represent the various hardware devices on your system.

Continued

Table 3-1 *(continued)*	
Directory	**Contents**
/mnt/	Since all filesystems, even those of removable media such as CD-ROMs and DVDs, as well as other computers, are grafted onto the same namespace, an area set aside for such temporary *mount points* is required. /mnt/ is where temporarily mounted filesystems are represented.
/usr/	This directory is a major part of the namespace, and includes /usr/bin/, /usr/sbin/, /usr/lib/, /usr/share/, and other directories. In the interests of keeping the root filesystem small, most nonessential software on the system is kept here in /usr/. /usr/ is also shareable between machines of the same architecture; you can mount this filesystem over the network onto your own /usr/ (instead of putting it in /mnt/), for instance, allowing local disk space to be saved by having a single server provide all this data.
/var/	/var/, short for *variable*, is where most system-wide volatile data is stored. Database applications, e-mail storage, backups, and more are stored in /var/.
/home/	By default, every user on a GNU/Linux system has his own directory in /home/, allowing him to manage his own portion of the namespace. This also aids in system administration because most of a user's data isn't stored in multiple application-specific directories, but is rather stored in the user's home directory. Home directories, by default, are /home/*username*/.
/root/	This is the root user's (the system administrator's) home directory. It's not in /home/ because /home/ may be on a separate filesystem — one that might be inaccessible if there's a problem with the computer. Since root's home directory is kept separate, her files and user-specific configuration data are available even if /home/ is not.

Cross-Reference   You may be interested in jumping ahead to the "Navigation and Pathnames" section of this chapter. The information about relative and absolute paths may be of particular usefulness at this point.

Filesystem object types, permissions, and ownership

In UNIX-like systems, one of the predominant themes is "treat everything like a file." This allows for consistent manipulation and access control methods, predictable behavior, and a somewhat less steep learning curve for new users. As such, there are actually several types of filesystem objects that appear as files even though they represent more abstract or more physical objects. For example, hardware devices can be represented as a file in the form of a device node. Of course, a directory isn't really a regular file either. Table 3-2 describes the various filesystem object types. The first column lists the letter associated with each object; these letters are used as shorthand in the output of many utilities, so they're worth noting here.

Table 3-2
Filesystem Object Types

Letter	Full Name	Description
d	Directory	Directories can contain any object, including other directories. Equally, every filesystem object must be in a directory.
-	Regular file	Regular files store data. The data stored within the file is irrelevant at this level; anything can be in there. Files are a generic storage mechanism.
l	Symbolic link	A symbolic link is a special file that points to another file.
b	Block device	A block device node is a special file that an application can use to access any block devices (such as hard drives, USB memory sticks, and so on). There is one block device node on the filesystem for every block device available in your computer. An application wanting to manipulate such a device, such as a partition manager, typically does so via a block device node instead of accessing the hardware directly or manually.
c	Character device	A character device node special file is similar to a block device node, except in the ways that it can be accessed. Whereas a block device can have separate portions of the underlying device addressed, a character device can deal only with continuous streams of data, either being read from the device or written to the device. A sound card is a good example of a character device; a stream of audio is either sent to the device (which then goes to the speakers), or read from the device (from a microphone, for instance, to be stored on the filesystem).
s	Domain socket	A domain socket special file, otherwise known as a UNIX domain socket, is the filesystem representation of an interapplication communication method. An application may create a socket file and listen to commands written to it—for instance, an mp3 player might create a socket so that an infrared remote control application can send commands to it.
p	Named pipe	Pipes are similar to domain sockets. Their behavior more closely matches shell pipes (discussed later in this chapter).

Users, groups, and ownership

Since GNU/Linux is a multi-user system, it's important that users be able to access only what they're supposed to be able to access. To accomplish this, a simple model for identification and access control was developed. Each user of the system receives a personal identity, or *username*. In addition to the username, a user may be a member of one or more *groups*. This allows for access to be controlled on a per-user or per-group basis. For instance, if you have a project with a number of employees who need to access the same files, you can put them all in a group and make the files group-owned by that group. When a new person joins the project, you can add them to that group and they're all set. The alternative is specifying each and every user who gets access to the files in question; when a new person joined the project, they would need to be added to each and every file's access control list. Obviously, using groups is a lot easier, especially when a particular group needs access to thousands of files or has hundreds of members.

Each filesystem object has a single user who *owns* the object. That person is the only user (aside from the system administrator using the root account) who is allowed to modify the object's *permissions*, which control access to the object. Additionally, each object may also be accessible to a group of users. The differentiation between a single user-owner and a group-owner is important because it allows users to keep their private files private, while allowing other files they create to be read from or written to by other members of a group. The user who owns an object can change the object's group-owner, but only to groups the user is a member of. For instance, if Joe is a member of group writers and there's another group named editors that Joe isn't a part of, Joe can't assign editors as the group-owner of an object he owns. Note that groups can't be members of other groups.

Basic permissions

The standard form of access control for a filesystem object is the *permissions* of the object. Separate permissions can be set for the user-owner, group-owner, and *other* users (and people who are neither the owner nor a member of the object's group). For each category of owner, group, and other users, three separate permissions can be set: read access, write access, and execute access.

Permissions are textually represented by nine characters, as shown in Figure 3-1, where r indicates read access, w indicates write access, and x indicates executable access. The first three characters define the owner's permissions, the next three characters define the group permissions, and the final three define the permissions for other users.

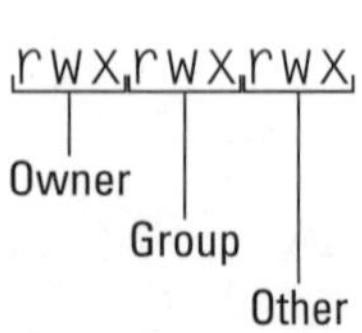

Figure 3-1: Filesystem permissions.

The meanings of the different permission bits (read, write, and execute) depend on context, but they are always either *on* or *off* (or *set* and *unset*). When the owner of an object is allowed to write to the file, the second character is a w. When the owner has opted to disable write access, perhaps to avoid accidentally changing the file, a hyphen or dash (-) is displayed instead, indicating that the write bit is unset. Though these permissions exist for all filesystem objects, they may take on different meanings when applied to different types of objects. When applied to a directory, they mean one thing, and when applied to a file they may have an altogether different meaning. Table 3-3 provides summaries of how these permissions affect the ability of the owner, group, and other users to operate upon the filesystem object.

Table 3-3
Basic Permissions

Object Type	Permission	Description
File	Read	If this permission bit is set, the file can be read from.
	Write	If this permission bit is set, the file's contents can be changed, deleted, or added to. Note, however, that the ability to entirely remove or rename a file from the filesystem is dependent upon the permissions of the directory that contains it (see below).
	Execute	On UNIX-like systems, including GNU/Linux, an application can't be run unless its code is marked as executable in the filesystem. This allows the user and administrator to control whether other applications can easily execute given files (for instance, e-mail attachments won't be marked executable by default).
Directory	Read	If the read bit is present on a directory, the user can list its contents. If this bit is unset, then the user must know the full name of any files or directories she wishes to access.
	Write	The write bit on a directory controls the deletion of files and the creation of new files. Renaming files is also included here.
	Execute	The execute bit allows the user to list files within the directory. With the read bit set but the execute bit unset, a user can list the contents of the directory but cannot read any of the files contained therein, nor list the contents of any subdirectories.

When you attempt to access a filesystem object, the first permissions that are checked are the owner-user permissions. If you are the file's owner, those permissions are the ones that control your access to the object. If you aren't the file's owner but you are a member file's group-owner, the group permissions control your access. If you are neither the file's owner nor in the group of the file's group-owner, the third set of permissions (for everybody else, or other users) applies.

This system may seem quite complex and confusing at first, but it is very powerful and flexible, and the alternatives are even more complex. This user/group/other, read/write/execute scheme allows for every common access control scenario to be expressed. A simpler system would not allow for the expression of restrictions common to daily life in a multi-user system.

Extended permissions

Linux also provides the *setuid*, *setgid*, and *sticky* permissions. These are a superset of the basic permissions described above. Textually, when the setuid and setgid permissions are set, they appear as an s instead of x. For example, rwxrws--- means that the owner's read, write, and execute bits are set, in addition to the group read, write, execute, and setgid bits.

The setuid and setgid permissions, when applied to files, are relevant only when the file is executable. When you run an executable that has its setuid bit set, instead of the executable being run as yourself, it's run as the file's owner. For instance, your administrator may allow you to run some particular commands as root by setting the executable's owner to root, as well as setting the setuid permission bit. Setgid is similar in that the executable, when run, runs as if you're a member of that file's group-owner.

Setuid has no relevance when applied to a directory. When a directory has its setgid bit set, any files created in that directory are created with the same group-owner the directory has.

Directories also have their own special extended permission, the sticky bit. When this bit is set, only the owner of the files in that directory may move those files. This is in contrast to normal directories without the sticky bit set; in that instance, anybody who has write access to the directory — in other words, anybody who can create files — can also remove any files. When a directory has its sticky bit set, the last character in the nine-character textual representation of its permissions will be t; for instance, rwxrwxrwt.

Table 3-4 summarizes these extended permissions.

Table 3-4
Extended Permissions

Object Type	Permission	Description
File	setuid (- - s - - - - - -)	When executed, the program will run as if the user who owns the file was running it.
	setgid (- - - - - s - - -)	When executed, the program will run as if it was a member of the file's group.
	sticky (- - - - - - - - t)	No effect.
Directory	setuid (- - s - - - - - -)	No effect.
	setgid (- - - - - s - - -)	When a new file is created in the directory, the new file will have the same group-owner as the directory.
	sticky (- - - - - - - - t)	Files can be deleted only by their owner.

Cross-Reference   See the section of this chapter titled "Filesystem Manipulation" for details on how to change the permissions and ownership of filesystem objects.

Getting Started with Your Shell

Now that you've got the theory out of the way, you're going to actually do some work and examine the filesystem hands-on using the shell and the utilities available therein. In this section, I introduce the shell and how to run commands, and then move on to some specific commands used for examining and manipulating the filesystem.

If you aren't already logged in, log in now. Do so using your regular user account, however, not the root account. As you'll see in Chapter 5, spending as much time as possible in your regular user account will protect against inadvertent data loss and corruption, and you should have no need for root privileges in this chapter.

After logging in, you'll see a prompt similar to the one in Figure 3-2. This is the default bash command prompt. The word before the @ is your username, and the word after the @ is the computer name or *hostname*. The colon is a separator, and the dollar sign ends the line. When you're logged in as root, your prompt will be different—for example, the dollar sign will be replaced by a pound sign (#). The text between the colon and the dollar sign indicates your location in the filesystem; after you've logged in, this will show your *home directory*, whose location is typically represented as a tilde (~) for brevity.

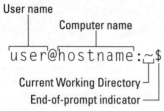

Figure 3-2: Default bash prompt.

Running commands

Your shell is primarily a text, line-based environment. You issue commands by typing them; when you press Enter, the command is run by the shell, and any output appears on-screen. Most commands also accept *options* and *arguments*, which allow you to fine-tune their behavior or provide a specific bit of data for them to work with, respectively. Keep in mind that (nearly) everything you type into a UNIX-like system is case-sensitive, including commands, their options, and their arguments. That is to say that a is not the same as A, and that pwd is not the same as PwD. So it's important to type commands exactly as they're presented, otherwise the results may be different from what you expected — sometimes in an unpleasant way.

Let's use a simple example, pwd, which means "print the working directory."

```
user@hostname:~$ pwd
/home/user
user@hostname:~$
```

Every application running on the system has its own *current working directory*, in this case, /home/user. When you provide a filename (as opposed to a full pathname that starts with a forward slash), the file is assumed to be in the working directory. For instance, the touch command below creates a new, empty file. Since we're providing only a filename as opposed to a full pathname, the file is created in /home/user/.

```
user@hostname:~$ touch testfile
user@hostname:~$
```

This example demonstrates two shell concepts. The first is passing an argument to a command. In this case, the argument testfile is passed to the command touch as the name of the file to be created. The second concept is illustrated by the lack of any output from the command. It's common for command-line utilities and applications to simply finish their work without saying anything, given the understanding that unless something bad happens, there's not much point in being chatty. You see only the prompt for the next command, as Debian waits patiently for you to tell it what to do.

Look at another command, ls, which means "list files." You just created a new file, so take a look at it in detail. (The output from this command is explained in detail in the "Listing files and directories" section later in this chapter.)

```
user@hostname:~$ ls -l testfile
-rw-r--r--    1 user      user         0 2004-04-11 13:48 testfile
user@hostname:~$
```

I passed ls both an option and an argument. I passed the -l option to tell ls to use its *long* mode—to provide many details in the listing. With the -l option issued, ls shows the permissions of the file followed by information about the owner and group of the file and the date and time it was created in addition to the name of the file. Options are generally preceded by at least one dash. In many situations, single letter options are preceded by a single dash, and full word options are preceded by two dashes. The argument I passed was, again, testfile, telling ls to list only that file (the default of ls is to list every file in the current working directory). I cover the use of ls in more detail later in this chapter.

Using tab-completion

Tab-completion is the closest thing a Linux system can offer to reading a user's mind. Auto-completion in other operating systems, where a partially typed URL or file causes a list of possible files to be displayed for easy selection, is similar conceptually to tab-completion. Basically, when you wish to supply a filename to a command, simply type out a few characters from the file and press your Tab key. The rest of the filename will be inserted into the command line. For instance, type the following but don't press Enter:

```
user@hostname:~$ ls -l test
```

Now press Tab, and your newly tab-completed filename should result in a command line that looks like the one below.

```
user@hostname:~$ ls -l testfile
```

In the example above, if you had had multiple files that started with the specified string (test), you would have received a beep upon hitting the Tab key. That's an audible cue to let you know that more characters are required for a unique match. If you'd like to see a list of possible completions, you could hit Tab again to see a list of possible matches. After this point you could continue typing characters either to finish the filename yourself, or to include enough characters so that tab-completion can find a unique match.

Tab-completion is pretty easy to get used to, but be warned: After you've used it for a while, it's nearly impossible to do without.

Reading documentation in the shell: manpages

Before moving further into specific shell commands, it's worth examining a common form of documentation for shell commands — manual pages or *manpages*. Manpages are the primary source of on-demand documentation in the Linux and UNIX world. Manpages typically aren't intended to be tutorials or guides; they're provided as reference material. As such, they may seem quite terse, and if you intend to learn a tool from scratch by reading its manpage, you may have to read it a few times to grasp the meaning of everything. That said, the reference nature of manpages makes them excellent for quickly looking up a tool's option that you've forgotten, double-checking the format a tool takes its arguments in, and the like.

Manpages typically start with a summary of the command, as well as a synopsis of its usage. While manpages are usually used to document commands or programs, they are also sometimes available for C functions or Perl modules. These sections are usually followed by a section detailing each individual option and argument the tool accepts. The end of the manpage often contains references to other manpages of interest, which are related in some way to the tool you're reading about.

To read a manpage, simply type man *command*:

```
user@hostname:~$ man ls
```

Tip

In Debian, it's considered a bug if a shell command doesn't have a manpage. As such, virtually every command you can run has a manpage named after the command. So you can typically type man *command* to get that command's manpage.

This will format ls' manpage and display it in less, the standard manpage viewer. less is actually a generic *pager*, which is used to display text that doesn't fit on a single screen. It supports the kind of scrolling and navigation you would expect. Pressing the H key after less has started will display less' own help file, but Table 3-5 summarizes the useful keys.

	Table 3-5	
	less Keyboard Commands	
Key	*Alternatives*	*Description*
Down arrow	j	Scroll down one line.
Up arrow	k	Scroll up one line.
Page down	Space, f	Scroll down one screen.
Page up	b	Scroll up one screen.
/	None	Start a search. After pressing /, you're prompted at the bottom of the screen for a search term. Keep them simple because some characters, like [,] and many others, are treated specially.

Key	Alternatives	Description
n	None	Repeat the previous search.
N	None	Repeat the previous search, but in the reverse direction. This key, N, and the other repeat-search key, n, allow you to quickly jump through a manpage looking for terms.
q	None	Quit less.

Note If you're curious about less' name, here's a bit of history: Before less was developed, a small utility called more was the standard pager. more was quite feature-less and unpleasant to use. Thus, less was released. After all, less is more. An even more advanced pager, most, has also been created. most is also packaged in Debian.

Finding manpages

Finding manpages should generally be pretty easy. In Debian, all commands available in the shell have manpages. Simply using man *command* should do in most cases, although commands aren't the only thing documented in manpages. However, sometimes you will not know the exact name of the command you're looking for, or what ancillary documentation is available for it. Thus you should know about the apropos tool. apropos is a tool designed to search the short descriptions of all the manpages on your system to find relevant programs using a keyword. The following example shows a search for programs that involve the term "bash."

```
user@hostname:~$ apropos bash
bash (1)              - GNU Bourne-Again SHell
bash-builtins (7)     - bash built-in commands, see bash(1)
bashbug (1)           - report a bug in bash
builtins (7)          - bash built-in commands, see bash(1)
rbash (1)             - restricted bash, see bash(1)
user@hostname:~$
```

As you can see, there are numerous available manpages relating to bash. You might be curious about the numbers beside each manpage title. Those refer to the manpage's section. Manpages are categorized into broad sections, which allow more than one manpage of the same name to exist on the system. This can be useful because sometimes a file format manpage will have the same name as a command manpage (for instance, if the command operates on a file of a particular format). If you wish to refer to a manpage in a specific section, simply use a second argument to man, man *sectionnumber manpage*. For example,

```
user@hostname:~$ man 7 bash-builtins
```

Continued

Continued

You don't always need to specify the section because `man` will use the first manpage it finds, and it's often the one you want. `man` searches the categories in a particular order, which is intended to reduce the number of times you need to specify a section. The following table describes the various manpage sections.

Section Number	Section Contents
1	Executable programs or shell commands
2	System calls (programming functions provided by the kernel)
3	Library calls (programming functions provided by system libraries)
4	Special files (usually found in `/dev/`)
5	File formats and conventions (for example, the manpage "passwd" for `/etc/passwd`)
6	Games
7	Miscellaneous and overview manpages, which provided either an overview of other manpages, or nonfile conventions and formats
8	System administration commands (usually only for `root`)
9	Kernel routines (this section is nonstandard and very rarely used)

Navigation and Pathnames

When you wish to refer to a file or directory, you have two options: use its absolute pathname or its relative pathname. An *absolute pathname* gives enough information to get to a file from anywhere on a system. All absolute paths begin with / and give the full path of directories leading from / to the location of the file or directory being described. The *relative pathname* of a file depends on the current working directory. Changing the current working directory is equivalent to navigating the filesystem.

The current working directory

Each program or application has a working directory. When you log in, your current working directory is automatically set to your home directory because this is where most of your personal data will be stored. Changing your working directory with the `cd` command (for "change directory") is like changing the default for every application that accesses files and directories when you use them from that shell, such as `ls`. For example, without any arguments, `ls` displays the contents of the current working directory. By changing your current working directory, you change the directory `ls` displays.

The current working directory plays a surprisingly large role in day-to-day shell usage because without it every single file would need to be referred to by its full pathname. For instance, instead of using `ls testfile` like you did in the previous examples, you would need to supply the full pathname, `/home/user/testfile`. That would be a lot of typing if you had to do it constantly. The following code is a simple example of the `cd` command and how it affects the current working directory and `ls`.

```
user@hostname:~$ pwd
/home/user
user@hostname:~$ cd /usr
user@hostname:/usr$ ls
X11R6  bin  doc  games  include  info  lib  local  sbin  share  src
user@hostname:/usr$ cd /usr/games
user@hostname:/usr/games$ ls
banner
user@hostname:/usr/games$ cd
user@hostname:~$ pwd
/home/user
user@hostname:~$
```

In this example, you start in the user's home directory. The command `pwd` returns the name of the current working directory with a full path. In this case, it tells you that you are in the directory `/home/user`. The next command issued is the `cd` command, which changes to the directory specified—in this case, `/usr`. `ls` is run to list the files in that directory. One of the files in the `/usr/` directory is the `games` subdirectory. Use the `cd` command again with a full path to change into the `/usr/games` directory and then issue `ls` again to see the contents of `/usr/games`. In this case, the directory contains only a single file, called `banner`.

Note that the final `cd` command issued did not include any arguments. Again, the importance of the home directory is demonstrated; without any arguments, `cd` returns to your home directory.

Relative pathnames

The current working directory provides a sort of default setting for any filesystem references. If you reference an object and that reference doesn't begin with a forward slash, your current working directory is prepended to the reference. By not including a starting forward slash and instead relying on the current working directory to fill in the missing information, you're making a reference *relative* to the current working directory, or a relative path. Here's an example:

```
user@hostname:~$ pwd
/home/user
user@hostname:~$ ls testfile
testfile
user@hostname:~$ ls /home/user/testfile
/home/user/testfile
user@hostname:~$
```

These two filesystem references, `testfile` and `/home/user/testfile`, refer to the same file, but the first took far less effort to type. Filesystem trees can become quite deep in a GNU/Linux system, which is a result of the increasing amount of data stored on computers. Relative directories can be used for any form of filesystem object and in any place where a filesystem object is expected as an argument. For instance, the `cd` command below refers to a directory — `/home/user/` — in relative terms.

```
user@hostname:~$ cd /home
user@hostname:~$ pwd
/home
user@hostname:/home$ cd user
user@hostname:~$ pwd
/home/user
user@hostname:~$
```

Virtual directories

Each directory has a set of virtual directories named `.` and `..`, known respectively as the *dot directory* and the *double-dot directory*. These are virtual directories; they exist in every single directory on the system and are part of a directory's basic structure. The dot directory always refers to the directory that the dot is contained in. For instance, `/usr/.` refers to the `/usr/` directory. This allows you to use `.` in the shell in place of the current working directory on a command line without needing to type out the full current working directory. The double-dot directory refers to the directory immediately above the one containing it. For instance, `/home/user/..` refers to `/home/`. This allows you to more easily access "nearby" files. Take a look at the following fictitious example:

```
user@hostname:~$ cd /really/long/fake/directory/
user@hostname:/really/long/fake/directory$ ls /really/long/fake
directory  a-file
user@hostname:/really/long/fake/directory $ ls ../a-file
a-file
user@hostname:/really/long/fake/directory $ ls /really/long/fake/a-file
a-file
user@hostname:/really/long/fake/directory $ cd
user@hostname:~$
```

Though the example is fake, it's quite obvious that using the double-dot directory can save keystrokes when working in deep directory structures, which tend to be common on a GNU/Linux system. In the example above, you may have noted that `../a-file` was a relative pathname; it didn't start with a forward slash. That's quite correct, and there's not much point in using the dot directory or double-dot directory when using absolute pathnames. `/home/user/../` would simply turn into `/home/`.

Examining the Filesystem

Now that you've got the basics out of the way, let's return to an earlier example to do a detailed exploration of the simple tools available to examine the filesystem, including `ls`, and `stat`.

Listing files and directories

`ls` is a real workhorse. It is, for all intents and purposes, your eyes into the filesystem. As you've already seen, without any options or arguments, `ls` simply lists the files in the current working directory in a plain manner.

```
user@hostname:~$ ls
testfile
user@hostname:~$
```

This output is plain, however, and doesn't really tell us much about the file(s) in question. It's a good default in that it allows large numbers of files to be listed on a single screen, and it doesn't load down the user with information. However, as I demonstrated earlier, you can add the `-l` option to get more verbose output:

```
user@hostname:~$ ls -l
-rw-r--r--   1 user     user            0 2004-04-11 13:48 testfile
user@hostname:~$
```

In this output, the first column displays the object type and permissions. (The first character is `-` in this example, meaning this particular object is a regular file.) The second column (1, in the example) indicates how many references to this file exist on the filesystem. The third and fourth columns list the user and the group that own the file. The fifth column (currently 0) indicates the file's size in bytes; remember that we used `touch` to create this file, so it's empty. The sixth column (2004-04-11) tells us the date the file was last modified, while the seventh column (13:48) tells us the time of that day the file was last modified. The last column is simply the filename.

Cross-Reference See the "Basic permissions" section earlier in this chapter for a more detailed explanation of what the first field of `ls  -l` output means.

It's worth noting that your default home directory has more than just one file in it by default. The others are not being listed by `ls`. The convention on UNIX-like systems is to not display files whose names start with a period by default; `ls` follows this convention. To tell `ls` to list all files, even those that begin with a dot, supply the `-a` option.

```
user@hostname:~$ ls -a
.  ..  .bash_history  .bash_profile  .bashrc
user@hostname:~$
```

Note that most multiple options can be provided to a command and even grouped together. You could specify `-l -a` or `-la` to list all files *and* use long mode, and `ls` would behave identically. Another possibility is the `--color` option, which *colorizes* `ls`' output. In colorized mode, `ls` will provide output in color with directories listed as dark blue, symbolic links as cyan, executable files as green, and other files as different colors. Notice that `--color` is a *long option*, and so is preceded by two dashes instead of one. Long options are also referred to as named options; they're easier to read. There tend to be many long options with no short option equivalent; there are only 26 letters in the alphabet (52 in a case-sensitive system like GNU/Linux) and ten numerals, and many commands have more options than a single-character-only system would allow for.

Take a look at the following example:

```
user@hostname:~$ ls -la --color
total 12
drwxr-xr-x    2 user     user           75 2004-04-11 13:48 .
drwxrwsr-x    8 root     staff          86 2004-04-09 03:23 ..
-rw-------    1 user     user          425 2004-04-09 12:54 .bash_history
-rw-r--r--    1 user     user          570 2004-04-09 03:23 .bash_profile
-rw-r--r--    1 user     user         1256 2004-04-09 03:23 .bashrc
-rw-r--r--    1 user     user            0 2004-04-11 13:48 testfile
user@hostnmame:~$
```

This gives you more information to work with. Note the filenames in the rightmost column. First in the list are two virtual "files," `.` and `..`, which appear in blue in the actual code, indicating that they are really virtual directories, the ones that are present in every directory. Following these are four regular files. The three *dotfiles*—the term for files that start with a period—are for bash. `.bash_history` keeps a record of all the commands you've typed. (It's pruned automatically so as not to get too large.) `.bash_profile` and `.bashrc` are shell initialization files and are used to configure the shell environment (more on that later). Try using the `--color` option on your screen to see the results in living color.

If you want to view a directory and its properties directly, pass `ls` the `-d` option:

```
user@hostname:~$ ls -ld /home/
drwxrwsr-x    8 root     staff          86 2004-04-09 03:23 /home/
user@hostname:~$
```

Excruciating detail with stat

Though ls's long mode provides all sorts of useful information, it doesn't provide all the information about a given filesystem object. There's quite a bit more, and you can imagine that being able to display it succinctly in a single line would be a pretty tough job. As such, there's another tool that can be used to more closely examine the properties of a file—stat. Look at the following example:

```
user@hostname:~$ stat testfile
  File: `testfile'
  Size: 0              Blocks: 0          IO Block: 4096    regular empty
file
Device: fe07h/65031d    Inode: 3237752    Links: 1
Access: (0644/-rw-r--r--) Uid: ( 1005/    user)  Gid: ( 1005/    user)
Access: 2004-04-11 13:48:27.000000000 -0400
Modify: 2004-04-11 13:48:27.000000000 -0400
Change: 2004-04-11 13:48:27.000000000 -0400
user@hostname:~$
```

Far more information is revealed with stat than with ls. The first line is the filename, and the second line indicates—among other things—the file's size and type. The third line describes where exactly the file exists, on which device it exists—hard drive or what have you—and where on that device it exists, as well as how many links to the file exist. The fourth line displays in both numeric and human-readable forms the file's permissions, its owner, and its group. The fifth, sixth, and seventh lines respectively display the time the file was last accessed, the time the file was last modified, and the time the file was created—sort of. The last line actually indicates when the filesystem record for that object was last changed to accommodate either a shrinking or a growing of the file. Creation counts as the file growing, and in the example's case the last line indicates when the file was created.

Shell Quoting and Escaping

You should recall from the earlier discussion of commands that spaces separate commands, arguments, and options. Because space takes on this extra meaning, it is called a *metacharacter*. This means it's interpreted specially by the shell; in this case, the shell interprets a space to mean the end of one argument and the beginning of another. A space is just one example of a metacharacter, however. There are many others. Because filenames can contain spaces and other special characters, there needs to be some way to tell the shell not to interpret a particular space as a separator—to instead treat it as a *literal* space. Two methods for handling this problem are *quoting* and *escaping*.

Quoting

Quoting is the simplest means of telling the shell to treat a particular set of characters literally. Your shell will recognize two forms of quotes: double-quotes and single-quotes. In the following example, I use `touch` to create a new file as I did earlier, but I use quotes to create a file with spaces in the name. I then use `ls` to list the files in the directory and verify that I have created the file with `touch`. Look at an example file with spaces in it:

```
user@hostname:~$ touch "test file with spaces in it"
user@hostname:~$ ls -l testfile "test file with spaces in it"
-rw-r--r--   1 user     user           0 2004-04-11 13:48 testfile
-rw-r--r--   1 user     user           0 2004-04-12 11:41 test file with
spaces in it
user@hostname:~$
```

Here you see the test file you originally created at the beginning of the chapter, as well as the new file that has spaces in the name. Without putting quotes around `test file with spaces in it`, you would instead get the following results:

```
user@hostname:~$ ls -l testfile test file with spaces in it
-rw-r--r--   1 user     user           0 2004-04-11 13:48 testfile
ls: test: No such file or directory
ls: file: No such file or directory
ls: with: No such file or directory
ls: spaces: No such file or directory
ls: in: No such file or directory
ls: it: No such file or directory
user@hostname:~$
```

As you can see, `ls` is trying to display a file for every word in the command and, since these files do not exist, is giving an error message.

Cross-Reference For information on the difference between single and double quotation marks, refer to the section "Intermediate Shell Usage" later in this chapter.

Escaping

As an alternative to quoting a string, you can escape a character. *Escaping* involves specifying to a program that a character should be taken literally. This usually means prefixing the character you want to have interpreted literally with a special character. As this description implies, escaping is a character-by-character behavior. As in many other places on the Debian system, the escape character in the `bash` shell is the backslash (\). To make the shell interpret a space (or other metacharacter) as the character itself, you must precede the character with a backslash. An example should make this concept clear:

```
user@hostname:~$ ls -l test\ file\ with\ spaces\ in\ it
-rw-r--r--   1 user     user           0 2004-04-12 11:41 test file with
spaces in it
user@hostname:~$
```

In this example, I escaped the spaces instead of quoting the entire string of characters. Each space must be escaped separately. Escaping is particularly useful when you want to include a literal quote because quotes are metacharacters, too; after all, they're treated specially by the shell.

```
user@hostname:~$ touch test\'\"
user@hostname:~$ ls -l test\'\"
-rw-r--r--   1 user     user           0 2004-04-12 11:52 test'"
user@hostname:~$
user@hostname:~$ touch test\'\"
>
```

The > in the last code line tells you that bash is still waiting for the end of the command. In this case, it's waiting for the closing quotation marks to signify that you are done.

A backslash is also a metacharacter! If you need to use a backslash as a regular character, you can either escape it (with a second backslash) or include it in single-quotes:

```
user@hostname:~$ touch test\\
user@hostname:~$ ls -l 'test\'
-rw-r--r--   1 user     user           0 2004-04-12 12:16 test\
user@hostname:~$
```

Note how the backslash didn't escape the closing single-quote. This is a property specific to single-quotes; even backslashes are passed to the command literally.

Cross-Reference Figuring out the most appropriate times to use different types of quotes or whether to use escapes is difficult to describe succinctly because it often depends on context. The rest of this chapter covers a range of shell usage, and where using quotes is required, the reasons for doing so are explained.

Shell Wildcards and Globbing

In addition to spaces, *wildcards* or *globs* are also interpreted by the shell instead of being passed on to commands. You may already be familiar with wildcards or *globbing* from other platforms or previous experience with GNU/Linux. If you aren't, though, globbing is a technique that allows you to refer to a large number of files or directories without needing to type each one manually.

Asterisks and question marks

The simplest bash globbing characters are * and ?. * will match any character any number of times, while ? will expand to any character exactly once. For example, foo* will match any word of any length that starts with foo, while foo? will match only words that start with foo and are followed by zero or one extra characters.

First, make a file called nottest with touch nottest.

```
user@hostname:~$ ls -l *
-rw-r--r--    1 user      user           0 2004-04-11 13:48 nottest
-rw-r--r--    1 user      user           0 2004-04-12 11:41 test file with
spaces
-rw-r--r--    1 user      user           0 2004-04-12 11:52 test'"
-rw-r--r--    1 user      user           0 2004-04-12 12:16 test\
-rw-r--r--    1 user      user           0 2004-04-11 13:48 testfile
user@hostname:~$
```

That wasn't a particularly impressive example, since ls will display those files even without any options or arguments. However, you can combine wildcard characters and regular characters. If you want to see only the files that start with test, you can use ls test* and you'll see the following example:

```
user@hostname:~$ ls -l *
-rw-r--r--    1 user      user           0 2004-04-12 11:41 test file with
spaces
-rw-r--r--    1 user      user           0 2004-04-12 11:52 test'"
-rw-r--r--    1 user      user           0 2004-04-12 12:16 test\
-rw-r--r--    1 user      user           0 2004-04-11 13:48 testfile
user@hostname:~$
```

Notice that the file nottest, which does not begin with test, was not returned.

If you want to see all files with five-character filenames that *start* with test, you can use test?:

```
user@hostname:~$ ls -l test?
-rw-r--r--    1 user      user           0 2004-04-12 12:16 test\
user@hostname:~$
```

Or, perhaps you'd like to see all filenames that have the string file in them:

```
user@hostname:~$ ls -l *file*
-rw-r--r--    1 user      user           0 2004-04-12 11:41 test file with
spaces
-rw-r--r--    1 user      user           0 2004-04-11 13:48 testfile
user@hostname:~$
```

You can combine wildcard characters as well. Here's a more complex example. Perhaps you'd like to see all files that start with `test` and have a minimum of six characters (but can have more):

```
user@hostname:~$ ls -l test??*
-rw-r--r--    1 user     user             0 2004-04-12 11:41 test file with
spaces
-rw-r--r--    1 user     user             0 2004-04-12 11:52 test'"
-rw-r--r--    1 user     user             0 2004-04-11 13:48 testfile
user@hostname:~$
```

\ and ? are metacharacters, and as such they need to be quoted or escaped if they're to be taken literally. In the following example, to create a filename that includes the wildcard characters, you must escape the name:

```
user@hostname:~$ touch 'test??*'
user@hostname:~$ ls -l test??*
-rw-r--r--    1 user     user             0 2004-04-12 11:41 test file with
spaces
-rw-r--r--    1 user     user             0 2004-04-12 11:52 test'"
-rw-r--r--    1 user     user             0 2004-04-12 13:20 test??*
-rw-r--r--    1 user     user             0 2004-04-11 13:48 testfile
user@hostname:~$ ls -l 'test??*'
-rw-r--r--    1 user     user             0 2004-04-12 13:20 test??*
user@hostname:~$
```

As you might be able to imagine, you could just as easily use escaping as quoting by typing `touch test\?\?\*`, and you would create the same file with the same name. As you can see, if you wish to refer to the file named `test??*` directly, the filename needs to be quoted or otherwise escaped.

Sequences

Another useful type of glob is the *sequence* glob. This is indicated by enclosing the string within curly brackets ({ }). Represented as {*string1*,*string2*,*stringN*}, sequence globs let you include as many terms as you'd like. A sequence is similar to a question mark in that it will match only a simple expression, but unlike a question mark, the expression you are matching can include as many or as few characters as you'd like, and which characters in particular. Take a look at an example:

```
user@hostname:~$ touch test1
user@hostname:~$ touch test2
user@hostname:~$ touch testFOO
user@hostname:~$ touch testBAR
user@hostname:~$ ls -l test{1,2,FOO,BAR}
-rw-r--r--    1 user     user             0 2004-04-12 13:37 test1
-rw-r--r--    1 user     user             0 2004-04-12 13:37 test2
-rw-r--r--    1 user     user             0 2004-04-12 13:37 testBAR
-rw-r--r--    1 user     user             0 2004-04-12 13:37 testFOO
user@hostname:~$
```

You can even embed other globs in the sequence, as the following example demonstrates:

```
user@hostname:~$ ls -l test{?,FOO,BAR}
-rw-r--r--    1 user       user              0 2004-04-12 13:37 test1
-rw-r--r--    1 user       user              0 2004-04-12 13:37 test2
-rw-r--r--    1 user       user              0 2004-04-12 13:37 testBAR
-rw-r--r--    1 user       user              0 2004-04-12 13:37 testFOO
-rw-r--r--    1 user       user              0 2004-04-12 12:16 test\
user@hostname:~$
```

In this example, test{?,FOO,BAR}, I matched any file that began with test and had exactly one additional character (any character), or began with test and ended with FOO, or began with test and ended with BAR. Of course, that you can use globs inside of a sequence means that if you want to refer to a file with a globbing character in its name, you have to escape it, as in the following example:

```
user@hostname:~$ ls -l test{file,\?\?\*}
-rw-r--r--    1 user       user              0 2004-04-11 13:48 testfile
-rw-r--r--    1 user       user              0 2004-04-12 13:20 test??*
user@hostname:~$
```

You can't use single- or double-quotes to enclose the entire expression or term because by doing so, you tell the shell not to interpret any wildcards — including the sequence. For instance, "test{file,??*}" would literally have looked for a file named test{file,??*}. You can, however, use quotes within the sequence:

```
user@hostname:~$ ls -l test{file,'??*'}
-rw-r--r--    1 user       user              0 2004-04-11 13:48 testfile
-rw-r--r--    1 user       user              0 2004-04-12 13:20 test??*
user@hostname:~$
```

Like every other metacharacter, { and } need to be quoted or escaped if you want to use them literally as an option or an argument.

Character ranges and lists

Character ranges are another form of glob. The term *range* is a bit of a misnomer, however, because the same globbing character can be used to match a list of characters. The glob characters for a range are the square brackets [and]. [denotes the start of the range, and] closes it. If the range contains a list of characters, these will be interpreted as a list. If there is a - character in the middle of a set of letters or numbers, the shell automatically expands the characters in the brackets to include all of the intervening numbers or letters. Table 3-6 gives some examples.

	Table 3-6	
	Character Range and List Globs	
Glob	*Description*	*Examples*
[a-z]	Match any character from a through z.	test[d-f]ile would match testdile, testeile, and testfile.
[ahij]	Match characters a, h, i, and j.	test[ahij]file would match testafile, testhfile, testifile, and testjfile.
[-a-z]	Match character - and any character from a through z	test[-a-z]file would match test-file, testafile, testbfile, and so on through testzfile.

Like every other metacharacter, both [and] must be escaped or quoted to be used literally.

Filesystem Manipulation

Be careful when modifying or deleting files in your Linux filesystem. Under the hood, the filesystem is very advanced, including such features as automatic journaling of changes to prevent data loss, special allocation patterns to almost entirely prevent fragmentation, and space-saving techniques such as tail-packing, which puts several files into a single disk sector. Unfortunately, these features are not without their price; it's generally not possible to undelete a file or revert a change on any standard Linux filesystem. There was a time when you could manually go through the raw data on a drive to find the information you were interested in, but in these days of 100GB hard drives and file sizes to match, recovering data manually isn't a fun prospect.

Creating directories

Creating directories is simple with the mkdir command. You can supply multiple directories, and the command will create them in turn. Here's a simple example; you'll be using this directory shortly:

```
user@hostname:~$ mkdir testdir
user@hostname:~$ ls -ld testdir
drwxr-xr-x    2 user     user           6 2004-04-11 23:58 testdir
user@hostname:~$
```

Removing files and directories

Removing files is done with the `rm` command. In its simplest form, you simply pass it a filename to delete; for instance:

```
user@hostname:~$ ls -l testfile
-rw-r--r--    1 user     user              0 2004-04-11 13:48 testfile
user@hostname:~$ rm testfile
user@hostname:~$ ls -l testfile
ls: testfile: No such file or directory
user@hostname:~$
```

There are a number of options that `rm` accepts, which are summarized in Table 3-7.

<table>
<tr><td colspan="2" align="center">Table 3-7
rm Options</td></tr>
<tr><td>Option</td><td>Description</td></tr>
<tr><td>-r</td><td>Recursive delete; if any directories are specified on the command-line, all the files contained therein are deleted, and then the directory is deleted. This is true for any directories contained within the given directory, as well. The act of going directory through directory is called recursing.</td></tr>
<tr><td>-f</td><td>Force delete; under some circumstances (for instance, when you don't have write access on a given file), rm will ask you to confirm the delete. This option overrides this behavior, and all files will be deleted without interaction. Combined with -r, this option allows for quick deletion of large trees.</td></tr>
<tr><td>-i</td><td>Interactive; normally rm doesn't prompt to remove a file unless there's something special about it (for instance, when you don't have write access for the file). With this option, rm will prompt for each and every removal.</td></tr>
<tr><td>--</td><td>End of option arguments; any arguments supplied to rm that start with a dash are assumed to be options, and if you specify an option rm doesn't recognize, it will produce an error and abort. However, sometimes you have a file with a dash as the first character in its name; when this is the case, you must supply the -- option to rm; for example, you would supply run <code>rm -- -filename-with-starting-dash</code>.</td></tr>
</table>

Moving and renaming files

Moving a file in Linux is identical to renaming it; all you're doing is changing the place in the filesystem where the data appears. In other words, the data stays right where it is; only the pathname it's accessible by is changed. The command to move and rename files is the same: `mv`.

mv accepts many options; see the mv manpage for more information. The options aren't commonly used, so I don't cover them here. More important is the format mv accepts its arguments in; first you supply one or more *sources* and then exactly one *destination*. If you supply more than one source file (or directory), the destination *must* be a directory. If you supply only a single source file, the destination can either be an existing file (to overwrite), a new file (thus renaming/moving the file), or a directory. (The file will then keep its basename, but will be in a new directory.)

Here are some examples that demonstrate using the mv command:

```
user@hostname:~$ touch movetest
user@hostname:~$ ls -l movetest
-rw-r--r--    1 user     user             0 2004-04-11 23:59 movetest
user@hostname:~$ mv movetest testmove
user@hostname:~$ ls -l movetest testmove
ls: movetest: No such file or directory
-rw-r--r--    1 user     user             0 2004-04-11 23:58 testmove
user@hostname:~$ mv testfile movetest testdir
user@hostname:~$ ls -l testdir/
total 0
-rw-r--r--    1 user     user             0 2004-04-11 13:48 testfile
-rw-r--r--    1 user     user             0 2004-04-11 23:59 testmove
user@hostname:~$ mv testdir/testfile ./
user@hostname:~$ ls -l testfile
-rw-r--r--    1 user     user             0 2004-04-11 13:48 testfile
user@hostname:~$ rm -rf testdir
user@hostname:~$
```

Changing ownership and permissions

Changing ownership and permissions is just as complex as the underlying access control mechanisms used; in other words, it's not too simple, but it's not too complex, and it's very powerful. If you haven't done so already, read the sections of this chapter titled "Basic permissions" and "Extended permissions"; you'll need them here.

As discussed in those sections, there are single-letter representations for the various permissions. Briefly, those are r, w, x, s, and t. Though they weren't covered earlier, there are also single-letter representations for the users the three sets of permissions apply to: for the user-owner it's u, for the group-owner it's g, and for other users it's o. There's also a special character, a, which refers to everybody: user-owner, group-owner, and others.

These letters combine to allow for easy specification of permissions on the command-line. In this representation, roughly speaking, each letter is followed by a sign (either -, =, or +), followed by a permission or set of permissions. Thus u-x means "remove execute permissions from the user-owner," o=rw means "make the permissions for other users equal to read and write permissions," and g+w means "add write permissions for the group-owner." These strings are used with the chmod command to change the permissions of files and directories. chmod stands for "change mode." (Mode is UNIX and GNU/Linux jargon for the permissions that a file has.) Look at the following example, and note carefully each call to chmod and the changing ls output:

```
user@hostname:~$ touch chmodtest
user@hostname:~$ ls -l chmodtest
-rw-r--r--    1 user     user         0 2004-04-12 00:12 chmodtest
user@hostname:~$ chmod a-rwx chmodtest
user@hostname:~$ ls -l chmodtest
----------    1 user     user         0 2004-04-12 00:12 chmodtest
user@hostname:~$ chmod u+rw chmodtest
user@hostname:~$ ls -l chmodtest
-rw-------    1 user     user         0 2004-04-12 00:12 chmodtest
user@hostname:~$ chmod u-w chmodtest
user@hostname:~$ ls -l chmodtest
-r--------    1 user     user         0 2004-04-12 00:12 chmodtest
user@hostname:~$ chmod a+r chmodtest
user@hostname:~$ ls -l chmodtest
-r--r--r--    1 user     user         0 2004-04-12 00:12 chmodtest
user@hostname:~$ chmod u+xs chmodtest
user@hostname:~$ ls -l chmodtest
-r-sr--r--    1 user     user         0 2004-04-12 00:12 chmodtest
user@hostname:~$ chmod g=w chmodtest
user@hostname:~$ ls -l chmodtest
-r-s-w-r--    1 user     user         0 2004-04-12 00:12 chmodtest
user@hostname:~$ rm -f chmodtest
user@hostname:~$
```

You can supply more than a single file or directory to chmod. If you supply the -r option and one or more directories, chmod will recurse through the directories given and change all the permissions of files and directories underneath it to your specification. You can also provide different user-owner, group-owner, and others permissions on the command-line in a combined form by separating them with commas. For instance, chmod u=rwx,g=rx,o=rx filename would change filename's permissions to read/write/execute for the user-owner, read/execute for the group-owner, and read/execute for everybody else.

 Caution   Be careful using chmod recursively because directories need to be executable in order to change into them. If you recursively remove execute privileges, your directories will become unusable until you add the execute privilege back to them.

Changing ownership is a far easier task. You can use the chown and chgrp commands to change ownership and permissions, but note again that if you wish to change group-ownership, you must be a member of the target group, and if you want to change user-ownership of a file, you need to be root. To change user-ownership, run chown newuser filename; to change group-ownership, run chgrp newgroup filename. chown and chgrp both accept the -r option, as chown, described earlier.

Editing files

Many Linux users are probably familiar with the text editors vi or vim, which have historical importance on UNIX and UNIX-like operating systems. Because many tasks in GNU/Linux involve editing files — including configuration files — a text editor is an essential tool. The default text-mode editor for Debian GNU/Linux is nano. You can practice editing a test file by running the command nano -w nanotest.

Note   You should supply the -w option because without it, nano will wrap lines. This is acceptable for English text, but is not acceptable for scripts or configuration files, which programs can be much pickier about. Remember to supply the -w option when you are writing documents that programs will be using, and leave it off when you are writing documents for human beings to read. (See the next section for directions on how to create shortcuts for commands so that you don't need to keep typing the full command-line.)

Having run nano -w nanotest, you should be presented with a rather plain, empty display. Type some random characters; they're inserted into the file automatically. Navigating through a file in nano should be fairly intuitive; the Page Up, Page Down, and arrow keys function normally. At the bottom of the screen is a helper bar, which documents the most frequently used commands. The notation may be new to you, however — a single caret (^) followed by a single letter. The caret indicates that the Control key should be held down while you press the letter. The exit key binding (Ctrl+X) will ask you whether you'd like to save your file before you exit. Press Ctrl+C at that prompt to abort your exit and return to editing. The editing system is pretty obvious; just look at the bottom of the screen if you're ever lost.

Caution   If you're a vi user (vi is a traditional UNIX editor, also the only formally standardized screen-based editor), take care using Debian's default vi — the nvi package. I have found this package somewhat buggy, and I would strongly encourage the use of vim instead. If you haven't used it before, you may appreciate some of its nicer features, like syntax highlighting. vim also includes a built-in help browser, simply use the :help command when you've started it.

Intermediate Shell Usage

bash and other shells actually implement a full programming language called, simply, *shell*. There are all sorts of features in this language, and most of the basic features are covered here.

Note   If you are new to a UNIX or GNU/Linux shell, you might want to stop here and use the shell for some period to become more at home with it before continuing with this section. You'll be ready for the more advanced shell usage described in this section very soon.

Variables and variable substitution

The basic idea behind shell substitution is to take part of your command line and turn it into something else. For example, if you find yourself referring often to /home/user/personal-data/finances/2004/march/purchases.txt, you might find it easier to set a variable for part or all of that pathname to make it easier to refer to later. The shell takes this variable reference and substitutes in the contents of the variable — in this case, the really long pathname. Shell variables, also called *environment variables*, are also used by other applications, as you'll see later.

```
user@hostname:~$ MyVariable="foo bar"
user@hostname:~$
```

Though it may not be apparent, you've just assigned the text foo bar to the variable MyVariable. Shell quoting applies to anything on the command-line, by the way, not just filenames, as in the previous example. The generic form of assigning a value to a variable is *variablename=value*. There can't be spaces between the variable name and the equal sign, nor between the equal sign and the value. For instance, consider this example:

```
user@hostname:~$ MyVariable = "foo bar"
bash: MyVariable: command not found
user@hostname:~$
```

With the inappropriate spaces in place, bash thinks you're trying to run a command named MyVariable with the arguments = and foo bar. After setting a variable, you can refer to it using the $ metacharacter, which, when prefixing an expression, tells the shell to interpret the following phrase as a variable name:

```
user@hostname:~$ echo $MyVariable
foo bar
user@hostname:~$
```

Note   The echo command simply prints its arguments to the screen. For instance, if I had run echo hi, a message would have been printed saying hi.

Resetting an environment variable is done by setting the variable to something else. You will not receive an error if you set a variable twice — often called "stomping" a variable. If you set a variable to 1 and then set it again to 2, you will silently overwrite the value of 1 and replace it with 2. You can see a complete list of your current shell variables (as well as other virtual things like aliases, which are discussed in the "Aliases" section later in this chapter) by issuing the set command without passing it any options or arguments.

Quoting variables and building variables

If the value you are setting a variable to includes a space, you need to quote it when you use it to make sure that the command understands the spaces as well. Take a look at the following example:

```
user@hostname:~$ touch 'test file'
user@hostname:~$ MyVariable='test file'
user@hostname:~$ ls -l $MyVariable
ls: test: No such file or directory
ls: file: No such file or directory
user@hostname:~$ ls -l "$MyVariable"
-rw-r--r--    1 user      user           0 2004-04-12 16:18 test file
user@hostname:~$
```

To build upon a variable, for instance to add the word `test` to `MyVariable` from the earlier example, you can use the variable's current contents in setting the new value, as here:

```
user@hostname:~$ echo "$MyVariable"
test file
user@hostname:~$ MyVariable="test $MyVariable"
user@hostname:~$ echo "$MyVariable"
test test file
user@hostname:~$
```

If for some reason (and it's actually quite common in day-to-day shell usage) you need to append a string to an already-existing variable without adding a space, you need to use a special form of variable reference, `${VariableName}`. Take the following shell session, for example:

```
user@hostname:~$ echo "$MyVariable"
test test file
user@hostname:~$ MyVariable="${MyVariable}string"
user@hostname:~$ echo "$MyVariable"
test test filestring
user@hostname~$
```

Without using the curly braces notation, the shell would have interpreted `$MyVariablestring` as a full variable name, as opposed to a variable reference and then a separate string.

Because $ is a metacharacter, to include a literal $ in any argument you're supplying on the command-line, you need to quote it using single-quotes or escape it. Variable references (as well as command substitution, covered later) are expanded in a string if the string is double-quoted. See the following example for examples of quoting variables:

```
user@hostname:~$ echo $NonExistentVariable

user@hostname:~$ echo \$NonExistentVariable
$NonExistentVariable
user@hostname:~$ echo '$NonExistentVariable'
$NonExistentVariable
user@hostname:~$
```

Variable persistence and inheritance

When you run a command from your shell, the new command runs as a new process, and its environment is *inherited*. By inherited, I mean that it receives a copy of all the various environment variables that have been set. If that process (perhaps it's a new shell, perhaps an application — what have you) changes any environment variables, the new variables aren't applied to the parent process (the shell you ran the command from). Thus, inheritance is a one-way street; any time you change or set an environment variable, the change will be applied to new commands run only from *that process*.

This is relevant because some variables control some common behaviors in applications. For instance, the PATH environment variable is a colon-separated list of directories. When you or an application attempts to run a command, each directory in that list is checked for the command; if it can't be found in any directory, you get a familiar command not found message.

Variables in bash are closely related to environment variables, but they're not exactly the same. The difference between a regular variable and an environment variable is that an environment variable is passed to new processes. To make a given variable available to a process, you need to export it. Take the following shell session as an example:

```
user@hostname:~$ TestVariable=test
user@hostname:~$ echo $TestVariable
test
user@hostname:~$ bash
user@hostname:~$ echo $TestVariable

user@hostname:~$ exit
user@hostname:~$
```

As you can see, TestVariable wasn't in the new shell process you started. You must export it with the export shell command. Exporting a variable will make the variable available to all child processes; there is no need to target an export:

```
user@hostname:~$ TestVariable=test
user@hostname:~$ export TestVariable
user@hostname:~$ bash
user@hostname:~$ echo $TestVariable
test
user@hostname:~$ exit
user@hostname:~$
```

You can modify an exported variable normally; the new value will be passed onto any new processes. You don't need to reexport it.

Variables also aren't saved automatically; if you want them to be persistent, you need to set them in your shell start-up files (see the "Personalizing Your Shell" section of this chapter). Setting them in your shell start-up file will also cause them to become global in that any time you log in, via whatever means (perhaps you'll install a graphical login manager), your variables will be set the way you want them to be.

Aliases

Aliases allow you to create shortcuts for commonly used command-lines. For instance, I have an alias named ll that, when run, runs ls -lh --color. Setting an alias is simple, as you can observe in the following session:

```
user@hostname:~$ ll
bash: ll: command not found
user@hostname:~$ alias ll='ls -lh -color'
user@hostname:~$ ll testfile
-rw-r--r--    1 user     user            0 2004-04-11 13:48 testfile
user@hostname:~$
```

As you can see, you can supply arguments and options to your alias. Anything supplied to the alias will be appended to the command-line you set with the alias command. Note that, like variables, aliases aren't persistent. If you wish to have aliases created whenever your shell is started, see the "Personalizing Your Shell" section of this chapter.

Command substitution

In addition to inserting variables into the command-line, you can also insert the output of other commands. For instance, take the following command:

```
    user@hostname:~$ echo 'test file'
    test file
    user@hostname:~$
```

You can take the output from the command and use it as an argument in another command, like so:

```
user@hostname:~$ ls "$(echo 'test file')"
-rw-r--r--    1 user     user          0 2004-04-12 16:18 test file
user@hostname:~$
```

As you can see, the format for the command substitution is $(command). Everything within the parentheses is treated as if it was a new command-line, so you can use variables and quotes and aliases and further command substitution as you normally would. Backticks (`) can serve as a shortcut to using $(), but they're primarily kept around for compatibility and are considered more difficult to read in scripts, as you can see in the following session:

```
user@hostname:~$ ls "`echo 'test file'`"
-rw-r--r--    1 user     user          0 2004-04-12 16:18 test file
user@hostname:~$
```

Note that I double-quoted the command substitutions; the output from the command I'm running (echo 'test file') contains spaces, and thus to make sure ls sees the two separate words as a single argument, I need to quote them. Using single-quotes isn't acceptable because single-quotes tell the shell to ignore *all* special characters and treat them as normal characters. In the examples here, both $(*command*) and `*command*` need to be interpreted specially, and thus I can't single-quote them. From the example, it should be evident that using backticks makes for harder reading.

Command substitution can be quite useful. The seq command, for instance, outputs a simple list of numbers. If given a single numerical argument, it will count from 1 to the numerical value of the argument. For example,

```
user@hostname:~$ seq 3
1
2
3
user@hostname:~$
```

Combine this with command substitution, and you can perform a number of operations at once, quickly and easily:

```
user@hostname:~$ touch $(seq 3)
user@hostname:~$ ls -l $(seq 3)
-rw-r--r--    1 user      user               0 2004-04-16 14:06 1
-rw-r--r--    1 user      user               0 2004-04-16 14:06 2
-rw-r--r--    1 user      user               0 2002-04-16 14:06 3
user@hostname:~$
```

I didn't quote the command substitution in this example because I wanted each line of output to be interpreted as a separate argument. (I created and listed three different files, instead of creating one single file whose name would span three separate lines.)

Redirection

Similar to command substitution discussed above, where the output from a utility was inserted directly into the command-line, output from a command can be redirected into files.

Output redirection

The special characters for output redirection are > and >>, and their use is simple: *command* > *file* and *command* >> *file*. Using > will cause *file* to be overwritten, while using >> will cause the output of *command* to be appended to *file*. To do this, use the cat command. cat is a simple utility that takes the content from one place, usually a file, and prints it out (to the terminal by default):

```
user@hostname:~$ seq 3 > testoutput
user@hostname:~$ cat testoutput
1
```

```
2
3
user@hostname:~$ echo hello >> testoutput
user@hostname:~$ cat testoutput
1
2
3
hello
user@hostname:~$ ls -l $(seq 3) > testoutput
user@hostname:~$ cat testoutput
-rw-r--r--   1 user     user              0 2004-04-16 14:06 1
-rw-r--r--   1 user     user              0 2004-04-16 14:06 2
-rw-r--r--   1 user     user              0 2002-04-16 14:06 3
user@hostname:~$
```

This can be used to save and transfer the output from a file to somewhere else, as well as for a number of other purposes. Perhaps a command takes, as an argument, a filename. The file will be interpreted as a list of files, one per line, upon which it will perform some operation. You can use `ls -1 > filelist` (`-1` tells `ls` to output only one filename per line) to populate the file `filelist`, which you can then pass to the hypothetical command that wants the type of argument described previously.

Error redirection

Whenever you run a command, there are actually two streams of output available. The standard output stream, or `STDOUT`, is used for regular messages and output. The second stream, the standard error stream or `STDERR`, is used explicitly for error and warning messages. Redirecting errors is done using the same special characters as redirecting normal output, except that they're prefixed with 2, for the second stream; `2>` and `2>>`. See the following example:

```
user@hostname:~$ ls nonexistent-file
ls: nonexistent-file: No such file or directory
user@hostname:~$ ls nonexistent-file 2> erroroutput
user@hostname:~$ cat erroroutput
ls: nonexistent-file: No such file or directory
user@hostname:~$
```

The two standard output streams, `STDOUT` and `STDERR`, are entirely separate by default. This allows you to keep logs of the different types of messages; for instance, you could run `ls file-which-exists nonexistent-file > output.log 2> error.log`. You would have two files then, `output.log` and `error.log`, with the segregated output streams. There are times, however, when you wish to merge both streams; you can do so by appending `2>&1` to the end of the command-line. This isn't just a simple shortcut; you can't safely redirect two entirely separate streams to a single file, thus you need to merge them into a single stream first. The next demonstration sends all the output from `ls` to `combined.log`:

```
user@hostname:~$ ls testfile nonexistent-file > combined.log 2>&1
user@hostname:~$
```

This form of output redirection is used most often when you wish to have a command run entirely silently. It's also often used for debugging, to send all the output (both normal and error) from a command to another person for analysis.

Pipes

Pipes are another form of output redirection. Unlike file redirection, pipes redirect the output to another command. Many standard UNIX utilities accept input in this manner. The `grep` command, for instance, provides for very advanced regular expression searching (see `man 7 regex`) and accepts input via a pipe. To use a pipe, append the command whose output you'd like piped with a pipe character (`|`, obtained by holding down Shift and pressing the backslash key on most U.S.-style keyboard layouts), followed by the command you'd like to accept the output. For instance, see the following example:

```
user@hostname:~$ ls -l /usr | grep info
lrwxrwxrwx    1 root       root              10 Apr 18 18:39 info -> share/info
user@hostname:~$
```

Like any other special character, the pipe character (`|`) must be quoted or escaped if you wish to use it literally (as opposed to using it to pipe output).

Personalizing Your Shell

There are many ways to personalize your shell, but the most common forms of personalization are shortcuts or *aliases* for frequently used command-lines, as well as altering variables that control the shell's behavior. Personalization for the `bash` shell is controlled through two dotfiles in your home directory, `.bash_profile` and `.bashrc`.

These two files are your shell initialization files. They're read during `bash` start-up and serve to populate your shell with environment variables and aliases and to run any commands you'd like run at start-up. Both files are *sourced* by the `bash` shell, meaning they're run in-place. Any commands run, whether they are setting variables or aliases, are run in the context of your current shell.

`bash` can be run in two modes — normal mode and login mode. In login mode, `.bash_profile` is read first. If your shell isn't a login shell, it's not read at all. Though `bash` can be made to act as if it's a login shell at any time by passing it the `--login` option, most applications that launch a shell won't do so automatically. As such, the only settings you should have in this file are environment variable settings, which will be inherited by all processes run by the shell. `.bashrc`, on the other hand, is read only when the shell is a nonlogin interactive shell.

This behavior is difficult to explain and even more difficult to work with. Suffice it to say that if you want your shell to be consistent, you'll source your `.bashrc` from your `.bash_profile` unconditionally and just stick with modifying the first file.

To cause your ~/.bash_profile to source your ~/.bashrc unconditionally, open your ~/.bash_profile in your favorite editor; use nano if you don't have a favorite. You should have three lines identical to the following:

```
#if [ -f ~/.bashrc ]; then
#    . ~/.bashrc
#fi
```

These lines are ignored by the shell at the moment because they start with the # character, which indicates that the lines are comments and aren't to be executed. Uncomment those lines by removing the # characters, and then save the file and exit. Next time you log in, your shell will read both files. The first and last lines of that three-line snippet just check for the existence of ~/.bashrc before the shell sources it. If the file wasn't there, and the script didn't check for its existence before it sources it, the shell would produce an error. Reading the file is done using the . command; this is the *source* command, which informs the shell to read the file directly and execute it.

Setting aliases was covered in the "Aliases" section of this chapter, so it is not rehashed here. Just include alias commands in ~/.bashrc as you would on the command-line, and the next time the shell starts, the aliases will be available. (Of course, if you want to apply it to your current shell instance, run . ~/.bashrc to source it.)

Environment variables have also been discussed, but largely in a theoretical way. I mentioned earlier that there are some standard variables that control the behavior of many applications; most notable is the PATH variable. (Other variables will be referenced in a given program's documentation, and I'll leave them to explain their uses; you likely won't need to use them unless you need to consult their documentation, anyhow.)

However, PATH makes a good working example because it's common for an administrator to alter it as one of the first personalizations they perform. This is common because the default user's PATH environment variable doesn't include the /usr/local/sbin/, /usr/sbin/, and /sbin/ directories. These commands are used mainly by system administrators, but they don't always need to be run with root privileges. For instance, in your current regular-user shell, run echo $PATH. The output should be similar to my own, shown here:

```
user@hostname:~$ echo $PATH
/usr/local/bin:/usr/bin:/bin:/usr/bin/X11:/usr/games
user@hostname:~$
```

As you can see, no sbin/ directories are included. You may want to prepend those sbin/ directories to the default PATH because the first directories listed are the first directories checked for commands. Open up your ~/.bashrc in your favorite editor, and near the top of the file (just after the first block of comments), add the following line:

```
PATH="/usr/local/sbin:/sbin:/usr/sbin:$PATH"
```

Save the file, and then log out and log back in. If you're running `bash` in a terminal, you can just close the terminal and start a new one. When you're logged in, run `echo $PATH` again, and you should see output similar to the example output here:

```
user@hostname:~$ echo $PATH
/usr/local/sbin:/sbin:/usr/sbin:/usr/local/bin:/usr/bin:/bin:/usr/bin/X11:
/usr/games
user@hostname:~$
```

Summary

The first part of this chapter was devoted entirely to basic command and filesystem manipulation, which you'll need to use if you want to administer any Debian GNU/Linux system, even if it's your own desktop. The most important aspect, by far, is filesystem coverage. It's important because many applications assume a basic understanding of the filesystem they run on. A Linux filesystem isn't totally different from the filesystems available under other platforms, but as Linux users say, "It's similar enough to look the same, but different enough to give you a headache."

The second part of this chapter should have given you a decent overview of some of the intermediate uses your shell can be put to, namely as the basis for a scripting language. If you're interested in learning more about the shell, I strongly recommend you visit the Advanced Bash-Scripting Guide at `www.tldp.org/LDP/abs/html/`, which provides an excellent hands-on approach to flow control and other advanced concepts. That guide assumes a fairly basic knowledge of shell, however, and I hope you can say that you gained it here.

✦   ✦   ✦

Software Management

The basic unit of software in Debian—and, indeed, in almost every major operating system today—is the *package*. A lot of effort goes into making a package that's easy to install and works on the first try. Each package needs to declare its relationship to other packages; perhaps it needs a library written by another author, or a separate program to round out functionality. Packages also need to monitor and work with their configuration files to ease upgrades and preserve changes.

A large part of administering a system—whether by a home user or a paid administrator taking care of thousands of machines—is maintaining the software installed on the computers. This chapter provides some basic background on packaging systems in general, as well as hands-on examples for maintaining software on a Debian system.

The Anatomy of a Software Package

This section reviews the properties common to almost all packaging systems, as well as some traits unique to Debian packages.

Common package properties

Everything about a packaging system, whether source or binary, is designed around standardization and ease of use. With the source code available, each user is perfectly capable of configuring and compiling (*building*, which is not to be confused with writing) his own software, but the end result is a very unique machine that can be difficult to administer.

Source packages versus binary packages

A *source package* is a package that is made up completely of source code. Source code is useful for programmers but must be built or compiled before it can actually be run. Building packages can take long periods of time even on fast machines, and it takes even longer on older and slower machines. *Binary packages* are already compiled and are distributed in a ready-to-use manner. A perennial debate in the GNU/Linux world is whether to distribute source packages or binary packages to end-users. The difference is simple: If *source* packages are distributed, the user builds and installs the software on his machine; if *binary* packages are distributed, only the installation part is necessary. In each case, the package system will configure the source, compile it, install it, and throughout the process run any scripts that are required.

Compiling a package doesn't necessarily need to be complex. There are several source-based packaging systems in use, and they all make the job of configuring the source package, compiling it, and installing it relatively pain-free. In fact, this is a basic precept of any packaging system: Do as much of the work as possible for the user.

In the case of source packages, there are typically numerous default source-configuration values that users can, should they choose to, override. This allows for a degree of build-time customization that can vary from package to package. However, most of these systems allow for one notable customization — the ability to specify compiler settings. Customizing compiler settings allows a greater degree of control over the compilation process, which can include performance-related optimization.

Caution   There have been many studies conducted on the effect of changing default compiler settings, and in almost every common case it proved that the resulting software was slower and more crash prone than software compiled with conservative settings — the settings that Debian package maintainers choose by default. If you wish to investigate changing compiler settings and rebuilding packages, avail yourself of the compiler documentation and take some time to research studies that have been done in the field.

Though source-based packaging systems exist and are used by some, binary-based packaging systems are far more prevalent. In these systems, the package maintainer configures the source and compiles the software, and then packages the result into a simple file, which is distributed to the end-user. Compared to compiling a source package, installing a binary package is very fast. A large source package can take hours to compile on high-end hardware, whereas a binary package created from that source code can be installed in seconds. Binary packages also result in a far more consistent end-user installation because each end-user installs the same binary package. Last but certainly not least, a binary package maintainer will typically be very familiar with the package she is producing and will have in-depth knowledge of the ideal compiler and source settings to use.

Binary packages are not without their drawbacks, however. Notably, they tend to require more ancillary software to be installed because disabling the use of this software must be done with the source code. In the interests of making the package applicable to the widest audience, most of the knobs that control the use of external software are turned all the way up.

Debian is a binary-based distribution. It was decided long ago that the tradeoffs for using a binary packaging format far outweighed the added flexibility gained by requiring users to compile each and every bit of software on their system. Debian does distribute source packages, though: Each binary package in Debian that the user installs has an associated source package from which the binary package is built. So while Debian's primary means of providing software for installation is via binary packages, users who really need to change compile-time settings can do so without *too* much trouble.

Dependencies

Whether dealing with source packages or binary packages, another common theme is *dependencies*, or more generally, *package relationships*. Over the years, more and more common tasks have been moved into shared libraries — code that each developer can use instead of writing their own each time. Every time this happens, a dependency is created.

Package relationships in their most common form allow a package to declare a dependency on another package. A calculator might declare a dependency on a library containing common math functions. Graphical applications would declare a dependency on a common graphical user interface toolkit library. Though *dependencies*, as they're called, are the most widely understood and implemented package relationships, they're not the only kind. In advanced packaging systems like Debian's, packages can also declare a number of other relationships (see the list of possible relationships in the "Package relationships" section of this chapter).

Installation scripts

Aside from containing the software itself, as well as declaring any dependencies or other package relationships, packages typically include *installation scripts*. These are small programs that act on the user's machine in a fairly intelligent manner. These scripts might migrate configuration files to new locations or upgrade configuration files to new versions. They might print a warning telling the user to be careful with a particularly dangerous piece of software. Because these are programs in their own right — typically small, but not necessarily — they're the active portion of a given package.

Debian's packages

As I hinted in the previous subsection, Debian's package management system is quite advanced. It's been evolving for a decade and has been continually refined, though that's not to say it's the be-all and end-all of package management. However, most users find the most compelling aspect of Debian to be its package management system. This subsection discusses its particular properties in detail.

Package relationships

The quality of a package in Debian has a lot to do with how well it declares its relationships to other packages, and there certainly can be a lot of relationships to declare. The full list of package relationships available for a Debian package to declare includes *Depends*, *Pre-Depends*, *Recommends*, *Suggests*, *Conflicts*, *Provides*, and *Replaces*. Table 4-1 describes how each of these fields is used.

Table 4-1
Package Relationships

Relationship Field	Description and Usage
Depends	If package A requires package B for use by the user, or if package B is required for package A to be configured, package A must declare that it Depends on package B.
Pre-Depends	If package A's installation procedure requires package B, package A must declare that it Pre-Depends upon package B.
Recommends	When package A's functionality is enhanced with an additional package, B, then package A must declare that it Recommends the installation of package B.
Suggests	The Suggests relationship is a weaker form of the Recommends relationship. It's usually used to indicate that some related software can be used alongside the package declaring the relationship.
Conflicts	When package A absolutely can *not* exist on the user's machine at the same time as package B, package A must declare that it Conflicts with package B.
Provides	When package A provides identical functionality to package B, it may declare that it Provides package B. Therefore, when a package Depends on package B, its dependency may be satisfied by package A or B.
Replaces	Occasionally, as when a package maintainer is reorganizing a set of closely related packages, package A will contain the same files as another package, B. When this is the case, package A declares that it Replaces package B, and any files from package A will overwrite files in package B. Without this relationship being declared, if two packages claim the same file, the package management system will produce an error and abort the operation.

Maintaining package relationships is a large part of a Debian maintainer's job
because these relatively simple concepts make software management easy and
painless for the user. However, choosing which relationships to declare with which
packages is something of an art.

Maintainer scripts

Debian packages have *maintainer scripts*, which are scripts the package maintainer
writes to help ease the installation, removal, or upgrade of his packages by the user.
There isn't a single installation script. Rather, there are five scripts that the maintainer can use, although not every package uses every script: the *pre-installation*
script, the *post-installation* script, the *pre-removal* script, the *post-removal* script,
and the debconf script. These scripts are all run automatically during different portions of package management operations.

The names should be self-explanatory, except for perhaps the debconf script.
During the installation of your Debian system, you were asked a number of questions. These were done using Debian's configuration framework, the self-titled
debconf. debconf scripts primarily serve to collect information from the user to
provide a sensible default configuration for a package. However, debconf scripts
are also occasionally used to print messages and warnings to the user.

Each of the maintainer scripts is provided with a great deal of information about
the user's system before they're run, including whether the package is being
upgraded, what version of the package was last installed, any errors that might
have occurred, and so on.

Configuration files

In addition to the regular files that make up the software, the declarations of package relationships, and the maintainer scripts that ease installation and upgrades, a
major component of a Debian package is its configuration files. Unlike regular files,
which overwrite old versions or preexisting versions without any prompting on the
part of the user, configuration files are treated specially. A large part of Debian's
appeal to system administrators is the care taken to preserve any changes made to
a configuration file.

Preserving changes made to a configuration file isn't easy. There are many different
configuration file formats, and sometimes a single configuration file will have multiple formats — depending on which version of the package you have installed. As
such, there are two standard methods of dealing with configuration files in a Debian
package: dpkg's *conffile* handling and a debconf-based handler called *ucf* (which
stands for "update configuration file").

Cross-Reference   Dealing with configuration files is presented in detail in the "Installing Packages"
section of this chapter.

Package repositories

Package repositories are large archives of packages that are stored, usually on the Internet, for users to pull from when they want to install or upgrade software on their system. Though obviously not a part of a package, *repositories* are nevertheless very important to the implementation of package management systems. Though some package management systems require users to operate directly on package files themselves, advanced systems keep databases describing the packages contained in a repository and can pull from them automatically. Not only does this allow the user to retrieve information with only the package name to work with, but it also avoids the tedious step of first finding a package file and then downloading it.

Debian's package repository contains approximately 15,000 binary packages for each architecture it supports. The database that describes the packages in this repository is copied to the user's machine on a regular basis by the user (in a process described later in this chapter). With the database stored locally, package searches and information retrieval are fast and convenient. The form that a Debian repository takes varies — for instance, installation CDs are partial repositories. However, most users prefer using Debian's Internet servers, which allow the user to download only those packages they're interested in (as opposed to either downloading all 13 CDs' worth of packages or purchasing and carrying around a small library of CDs).

Configuring which Debian repositories to use is as simple as editing `/etc/apt/sources.list` (type `man sources.list` for more information on how to do this) or removing `/etc/apt/sources.list` and then running `apt-setup`.

Package Management Tools

Getting into the meat of package management, this section simply provides an overview of the various package management tools in Debian. In addition to graphical front ends and package management systems, there are three main tools that can be used for different purposes at different times:

✦ **The `apt` family** — Probably the most famous part of Debian, `apt-get` is a command-line tool to install and remove packages. `apt-get` is part of the `apt` family of tools, where `apt` stands for "advanced package tool." `apt-get`'s simplicity is unmatched — to install a package, you issue a command such as `apt-get install` *packagename*. Though it doesn't provide pretty buttons and lots of colorful icons, `apt-get` is easy to learn and simple to use. Its command-line nature also allows it to be used remotely over very low-bandwidth or unreliable connections.

apt-get, however, is just one part of the apt family. apt-cache, for example, is the apt family's command-line search and display tool. apt-cache shares the same advantages as apt-get, namely simplicity and ease of use. apt-setup, which was mentioned above, is yet another in the family of apt tools.

✦ aptitude — aptitude is a fullscreen console-based package management front end browser. It's based on the apt libraries, meaning that the functionality provided by the apt family of command-line tools is available within aptitude. aptitude's strengths lie in its presentation of the data. With so many components in the distribution, it can be a bit difficult to find exactly what you want. Even examining your current system can be a chore. With aptitude, you can "drill down" through the various levels of the system, quickly collecting whatever data you need.

A special feature specific to aptitude — and the reason why I recommend its use — is its ability to track packages that were installed automatically. As an example, say you install package foo. During foo's installation, the library bar was installed automatically to satisfy foo's dependencies. When you remove package foo, library bar will be removed as well, so long as no other package still depends on it.

Tip

aptitude can actually be used on the command-line as well, by providing the same arguments you would give apt-get and apt-cache. So not only does aptitude provide a fullscreen package browser that can often aid in your searching and system examination, but it can also be used with the same simplicity as apt-get and apt-cache — with the added benefit of the tracking of automatically installed packages.

✦ dpkg — At the bottom of the pile is dpkg, Debian's basic package management tool. Whenever apt-get or aptitude install, remove, or otherwise operate on a package, they're calling dpkg to do the heavy lifting. dpkg provides a lower-level interface to the packaging system, allowing you to override particular behaviors. These low-level package operation interfaces should be used only when you know exactly what you need to do, however, because making a mistake with dpkg might require some painful hand-editing of package databases, which requires expert knowledge.

Finding and Examining Packages

One of the harder parts of dealing with a Debian system is finding the package you want from among the many available. Though finding packages can be difficult, it isn't the only sort of information-gathering you'll need to use routinely. You'll also need to list packages, list packaging details, determine which files belong to which packages, and even occasionally view information about packages available in a different Debian tree than the one you use. This section covers these sorts of tasks.

Listing installed packages

Listing installed packages is a pretty easy task, and you can use either dpkg or aptitude to do it.

Using dpkg to list packages

dpkg has a listing mode that doesn't affect the packaging system databases, so it's safe to use on a regular basis. It can be the most convenient way to quickly see whether a package is installed, as you can see with the following shell session:

```
user@hostname:~$ dpkg -l dpkg
Desired=Unknown/Install/Remove/Purge/Hold
| Status=Not/Installed/Config-files/Unpacked/Failed-config/Half-installed
|/ Err=(none)/Hold/Reinst-required/X=both(Status,Err:uppercase=bad)
||/ Name           Version        Description
+++-==============-==============-============================================
ii  dpkg           1.9.21         Package maintenance system for Debian
user@hostname:~$
```

dpkg's -l option turns on listing mode, and you can supply it with a list of arguments or none at all. If you provide no arguments, dpkg will list all the packages that have records in the database. If you provide it with a list of arguments, dpkg will interpret it as a list of package names. In our example, we asked dpkg to list its own information. dpkg also supports the use of wildcards, as discussed in Chapter 3, to allow you to easily list a set of related packages, as in this example:

```
user@hostname:~$ dpkg -l "base*"
Desired=Unknown/Install/Remove/Purge/Hold
| Status=Not/Installed/Config-files/Unpacked/Failed-config/Half-installed
|/ Err?=(none)/Hold/Reinst-required/X=both(Status,Err: uppercase=bad)
||/ Name           Version        Description
+++-==============-==============-============================================
un  base           <none>         (no description available)
ii  base-config    1.33.18        Debian base configuration package
ii  base-files     3.0.2          Debian base system miscellaneous files
ii  base-passwd    3.4.1          Debian Base System Password/Group Files
user@hostname:~$
```

Note the double-quotes surrounding base*. Without the quotes, your shell will interpret the wildcards itself, which might produce unexpected results. The last three fields in the output, Name, Version, and Description, should be self-explanatory. The first field, however, could use a closer examination.

Those two letters in the first field indicate the state the package should be in, and the state the package is actually in. Even though Debian goes to great lengths to ensure easy package management, bugs do occasionally creep in and interrupt a package installation or removal halfway through. Likewise, if your computer were to lose power during a package maintenance session, the database would be left in an inconsistent state. There's actually a third space there for another letter, which is the error indicator. See Table 4-2 for the meanings of the three status letters.

Table 4-2
Status Indicators

Letter	Description
First Character – Desired Status	
u	Unknown: For package names that dpkg has never had to install or remove, this character is displayed.
i	Install: The package is supposed to be installed.
r	Remove: The package is supposed to be removed.
p	Purge: The package is supposed to be purged (removed, and with all configuration files deleted as well).
h	Hold: Any packages that the administrator has put on hold won't be automatically upgraded or removed.
Second Character – Actual Status	
n	Not Installed: The package is not installed.
i	Installed: The package is installed.
c	Config-files: The package's configuration files remain.
u	Unpacked: The package has been unpacked, and its files have overwritten old ones, but the package's post-installation script has not been run.
f	Failed-config: The package's post-installation script ran, but it failed for some reason.
h	Half-installed: The package's installation was interrupted.
Third Character – Error Status	
	A single space in this position means there are no errors with the package.
H	Held: A package can also be put on hold by the packaging system; for instance, if its dependencies are broken (this often happens when the administrator forces a package's installation, ignoring the package's dependencies).
R	Reinst-required: If a package is in a particularly poor state, its reinstallation may be required, and this letter indicates that.
X	Both problems: When a package is both put on hold by the system *and* needs to be reinstalled, X is the character displayed.

dpkg can also display which files are part of a given package and search for which package owns a particular file. These actions are done using the -L and -S options, respectively. The following example illustrates the use of these options:

```
user@hostname:~$ dpkg -L base-passwd
/.
/usr
/usr/sbin
/usr/sbin/update-passwd
/usr/share
/usr/share/doc
/usr/share/doc/base-passwd
/usr/share/doc/base-passwd/README
/usr/share/doc/base-passwd/copyright
/usr/share/doc/base-passwd/changelog.gz
/usr/share/man
/usr/share/man/man8
/usr/share/man/man8/update-passwd.8.gz
/usr/share/base-passwd
/usr/share/base-passwd/group.master
/usr/share/base-passwd/passwd.master
user@hostname:~$ dpkg -S /usr/share/base-passwd
base-passwd: /usr/share/base-passwd
user@hostname:~$
```

Cross-Reference   dpkg -S and dpkg -L function only for packages that you have installed. See the subsection "Searching using the Debian package Web site" for information on how to look at packages in this manner when you don't have them installed.

Using aptitude to list packages

As mentioned previously, one of aptitude's great strengths is its ability to flexibly display information about your package database. The following instructions walk you step-by-step through an example description of using aptitude:

1. Open aptitude with this command:

   user@hostname:~$ aptitude

   Your screen should look similar to the one shown in Figure 4-1.

   As you can see, aptitude's main display is nicely organized.

2. By default, the bottom half of the screen is used to display the long descriptions of packages. Toggle that off by pressing Shift+D, giving you more real estate to work with in the top half.

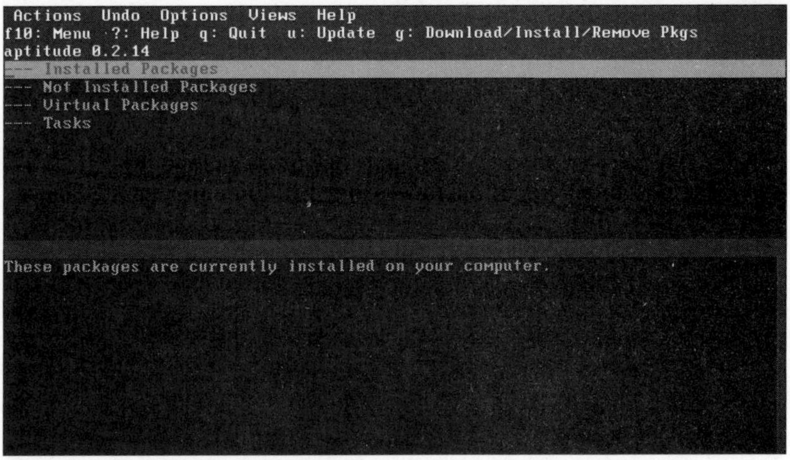

Figure 4-1: aptitude's main display.

3. Aside from the categories shown in Figure 4-1, at times others will appear, such as New Packages and Upgradeable Packages. We're primarily interested now in the packages that are currently installed, so use the up and down arrow keys to highlight that category, and press the Enter key. The category will expand into a number of subcategories. Each package in Debian is assigned a particular category, and this listing shows how the results are often displayed.

4. Now highlight Editors and press Enter. The next (lower) category level is displayed; this is the license level, and it allows you to restrict your listing to a particular style of license. Packages in the main archive on this level are totally free for use, modification, and redistribution. Though you likely don't see any on your screen, packages in the contrib and non-free archives have other licensing or use restrictions that may require a careful license examination on your part.

5. Press Enter to expand the main category. You should now see three packages: ed, nano, and nvi. These are the only text editors installed on the system by default. Examine an example line:

```
i    ed                          0.20-20    0.20-20
```

The first few characters in the line are equivalent to dpkg's listing mode, as is the second field (the package name). The third field indicates the currently installed version of the package, and the fourth field indicates the most recent available version of the package. (If an upgrade is available, for instance, the new version of the package is displayed here.)

6. Highlight the package's line, and the bottom line of the screen will display the package's short description. You can press Shift+D to turn the extended description area back on and view the package's long description.

Don't quit `aptitude` yet because we'll examine the `ed` package in more detail later in this chapter.

Showing package details

Of course, performing a package operation—whether install, remove, purge, or what have you—may require that you understand what the package is and how it works within the system as a whole. You can use `aptitude` or `apt-cache` to see the package details.

Using aptitude to show package details

Examining the package system in detail is where `aptitude` can really shine. Any place where a package name is displayed by `aptitude`, you can press Enter to view that package's details. Using the example from the previous section, highlight `ed` and press Enter. You're now presented with a new screen detailing all sorts of information about the package. Wherever you can highlight a line that starts with three dashes, you can press Enter to expand the tree and get more information. Go ahead and expand the `Packages which depend on ed` tree. Use the down-arrow key to scroll down, and you can see all the packages that use `ed` in some way or another, as well as their status (again, status is indicated in the first field). At the bottom of this detailed package display, you can see all versions of the package that are available; sometimes the package has an upgrade available. You can press Enter on any of those to view that version's particular details.

Press the Q key to leave the package detail screen and return to the main screen. If you decided to explore a bit and view other packages' details, just keep pressing Q until you're back at the main screen. Then press Q one last time to quit, and confirm that you wish to quit.

Using apt-cache to show package details

Though I really love `aptitude`, it isn't suitable for every purpose. For instance, the fullscreen nature of the detail view can make it more difficult to use. It's also darned near impossible to use `aptitude`'s fullscreen display in a script to automatically retrieve information. A good alternative utility is `apt-cache`. Take a look at how `apt-cache` displays the `ed` package's details, using the `apt-cache show` command followed by the package name:

```
user@hostname:~$ apt-cache show ed
Package: ed
Priority: important
Section: editors
Installed-Size: 144
Maintainer: James Troup <james@nocrew.org>
Architecture: i386
Version: 0.2-20
```

```
Depends: libc6 (>= 2.3.1-1)
Filename: pool/main/e/ed/ed_0.2-20_i386.deb
Size: 44718
MD5sum: 0c466ce6a160c62fa558fbbb46a4ea45
Description: The classic unix line editor
 ed is a line-oriented text editor.  It is used to
 create, display, modify and otherwise manipulate text
 files.
 .
 red is a restricted ed: it can only edit files in the
 current directory and cannot execute shell commands.

user@hostname:~$
```

The information `apt-cache` displays is much the same as what `aptitude` presented, but it allows for easier scripting.

Searching with apt-cache

Finding packages to install can be a tough job, but there are a few good options. Though `aptitude` is by far the most flexible, allowing for all sorts of search queries and narrowing-down of the results, `apt-cache` is definitely the easiest to use, especially for short queries. For searching, try `apt-cache`'s `search` option, as shown in the following example. The format is `apt-cache search` *one or more search terms*. This command will search the package names, short description, and package long descriptions and return a list of package names and short one-line descriptions for packages that contain the search term or terms. If you get too many results, try adding words to the search to narrow it down:

```
user@hostname:~$ apt-cache search debian goodies
debian-goodies - Small toolbox-style utilities for Debian systems
emacs-goodies-el - Miscellaneous add-ons for Emacs
python - An interactive high-level object-oriented language (default
version)
user@hostname:~$
```

When you find a package that looks interesting, you can use `apt-cache show` (as explained in the previous subsection) to display the details about a listed package, including its long description.

Searching with aptitude

`aptitude` has great browsing facilities and really flexible searching facilities. However, the cool stuff is a bit complex, so I'll discuss the simplest search method in `aptitude`. Go ahead and run it so that you're at the main screen. Type in a single forward slash followed by a single term, and then press Enter. Pressing the forward slash key tells aptitude that you will be typing in a term to search for. This term will be searched for in all packages' names. aptitude will show your search's first hit. To repeat the search again and find subsequent hits, press the N key until you find what you're looking for. Here's that same process broken down into steps:

1. At the prompt, type **aptitude** to start the program:

   ```
   user@hostname:~$ aptitude
   ```

   The main aptitude window should now be displayed.

2. Once you are in aptitude, type a single forward slash (/) to bring up the search prompt. Now type the term you want to search for. Press Enter to start the search.

3. aptitude will jump to the first package it can find that matches or includes the word you have searched for. If this is not the package you are looking for, press N to go to the next match. Keep repeating until you find a satisfactory package.

Tip   For more information regarding aptitude's searching and filtering capabilities, see /usr/share/doc/aptitude/README.

Searching using the Debian package Web site

All the tools described above work on the package lists stored locally on your computer. This means that they describe only packages that are available on your particular architecture for the Debian tree you're using (stable, testing, or sid). This is a lot of packages, but it will never be all of them. If you are using Debian stable, there may be new software that is uploaded only into testing or even sid. Occasionally you'd like to see what's available anywhere in Debian. http://packages.debian.org/ is the Debian package Web site, and it's a great resource for these sorts of situations. The most useful sections of the site are the "Search package directories" and "Search the contents of packages" windows located toward the bottom of the page. Using these tools, you can enter a search term and search the complete list of packages in the Debian archive through the archive's Web interface.

"Search package directories" functions like apt-cache search. "Search the contents of packages" functions like dpkg -S and dpkg -L, but you don't need to have the package installed on your machine to get results. Additionally, after clicking on a package's name in the results page, you can see other information like the package's copyright license and its change log because this information is all provided at the bottom of the page.

Caution   You can—but shouldn't—download package files from packages.debian.org and install them manually with dpkg. This will not always work, though, and it can possibly break your system. apt-get and aptitude do a lot of consistency-checking behind the scenes. Use packages.debian.org to find the name of the package you want, and then install it with either apt-get or aptitude.

Installing Packages

Now that you know how to find packages, you likely want to install some. I'll use several example packages, one for each tool available. First, if you aren't logged in as `root` (and you shouldn't be), do so now. You can either switch to a different console with `Ctrl+Alt+F`*n*, where *n* is a number from 1 (the first console) through 6 (`Ctrl+Alt+F7` is reserved for X Windows). Alternatively, you can use the `su` command, as in the following:

```
user@hostname:~$ su
Password:
hostname:~#
```

`su` means "super user," and it allows you to switch to the `root` account from a regular user account. The password you type is the `root` password, which you initially configured during the installation. Note the prompt change; the terminator is now a pound sign (#) instead of a dollar sign, indicating that you're logged in as `root`. Since you know you're logged in as `root` from the pound sign, the prompt doesn't include the username at the beginning.

Installing packages using apt-get

The simplest is usually the best way to start, so let's start with `apt-get`. While I recommend `aptitude` for regular use (due mainly to its ability to track automatically installed packages), you can't beat `apt-get` as a learning tool. First and foremost, before you install any new packages or upgrade old packages with `apt-get`, you need to run `apt-get update`, as shown in the following code example. This downloads the latest list of packages from Debian servers, and it ensures that you get the latest versions of packages available for the Debian tree you have installed:

```
hostname:~# apt-get update
Hit http://ftp.us.debian.org stable/main Packages
Hit http://ftp.us.debian.org stable/main Release
Hit http://ftp.us.debian.org stable/main Sources
Hit http://ftp.us.debian.org stable/main Release
Get:1 http://security.debian.org stable/updates/main Packages
[183kB]
Hit http://non-us.debian.org stable/non-US/main Packages
Hit http://non-us.debian.org stable/non-US/main Release
Hit http://non-us.debian.org stable/non-US/main Sources
Hit http://non-us.debian.org stable/non-US/main Release
Get:2 http://security.debian.org stable/updates/main Release
[110B]
Fetched 183kB in 2s (85.7kB/s)
Reading Package Lists... Done
Building Dependency Tree... Done
user@hostname:~$
```

The output you get won't be identical to the output here, but it should be close. If you get any errors, chances are your /etc/apt/sources.list is broken. If this is the case, go ahead and remove that file with rm /etc/apt/sources.list, and run apt-setup to generate a new one.

Having updated the package list, go ahead and install vim. vim is an editor, a Vi clone, but it has far more features:

```
hostname:~# apt-get install vim
Reading Package Lists... Done
Building Dependency Tree... Done
The following extra packages will be installed:
  libgpmg1
The following NEW packages will be installed:
  libgpmg1 vim
0 packages upgraded, 2 newly installed, 0 to remove and 0  not upgraded.
Need to get 0B/3796kB of archives. After unpacking 12.3MB will be used.
Do you want to continue? [Y/n] y
Get:1 http://ftp.us.debian.org stable/main libgpmg1 1.19.6-12 [45.2kB]
Get:2 http://ftp.us.debian.org stable/main vim 6.1.018-1 [3751kB]
Selecting previously deselected package libgpmg1.
(Reading database ... 6633 files and directories currently installed.)
Unpacking libgpmg1 (from .../libgpmg1_1.19.6-12_i386.deb) ...
Selecting previously deselected package vim.
Unpacking vim (from .../vim_6.1.018-1_i386.deb) ...
Setting up libgpmg1 (1.19.6-12) ...

Setting up vim (6.1.018-1) ...

hostname:~#
```

Here you see Debian's dependency-resolution at play. vim depends on libgpmg1, so that package was marked for installation automatically. apt-get wanted to be sure that the extra installation was acceptable, so it asked for confirmation. Then it went ahead and downloaded and installed the packages. Pretty simple, and that's it.

To reinstall a package, use apt-get --reinstall install *packagename*.

Installing packages using aptitude

Before using aptitude, you should run aptitude update, which has a similar purpose and effect as running apt-get update. Alternatively, you can press the U key when in aptitude's normal interactive fullscreen mode.

aptitude can be used in the same way as apt-get, right on the command-line. In this example, you'll install mutt, a common console-based e-mail client. First, look at mutt's package relationships more closely, using the apt-cache show command:

```
hostname:~# apt-cache show mutt | grep -E '^(Depends|Recommends)'
Depends: libc6 (>= 2.3.2.ds1-4), libidn11, libncursesw5
(>= 5.3.20030510-1), libsasl2 (>= 2.1.15), exim | mail-transport-agent
Recommends: locales, mime-support
hostname:~#
```

As you can see, `mutt` recommends both the `locales` and `mime-support` packages. `locales` is installed as part of the basic installation, but `mime-support` is not. Whereas `apt-get installs` installs only Depends packages, by default `aptitude` will also install recommended packages in the field "Recommends," as shown in the following code sample:

```
hostname:~# aptitude install mutt
Reading Package Lists... Done
Building Dependency Tree
Reading extended state information... Done
The following NEW packages will be automatically installed:
  libidn11 libncursesw5 libsasl2 libsasl2-modules mime-support
The following NEW packages will be installed:
  libidn11 libncursesw5 libsasl2 libsasl2-modules mime-support mutt
0 packages upgraded, 6 newly installed, 0 to remove and 62 not upgraded.
Need to get 2185kB of archives. After unpacking 5788kB will be used.
Do you want to continue? [Y/n/?] y
Writing extended state information... Done
Get:1 http://http.us.debian.org sid/main libsasl2 2.1.18-2 [255kB]
Get:2 http://http.us.debian.org sid/main libidn11 0.4.1-1 [90.2kB]
Get:3 http://http.us.debian.org sid/main libncursesw5 5.4-3 [287kB]
Get:4 http://http.us.debian.org sid/main mime-support 3.26-1 [28.6kB]
Get:5 http://http.us.debian.org sid/main mutt 1.5.5.1-20040112+1 [1375kB]
Get:6 http://http.us.debian.org sid/main libsasl2-modules 2.1.18-2 [150kB]
Fetched 2185kB in 9s (230kB/s)
Selecting previously deselected package libsasl2.
(Reading database ... 17338 files and directories currently installed.)
Unpacking libsasl2 (from .../libsasl2_2.1.18-2_i386.deb) ...
Selecting previously deselected package libidn11.
Unpacking libidn11 (from .../libidn11_0.4.1-1_i386.deb) ...
Selecting previously deselected package libncursesw5.
Unpacking libncursesw5 (from .../libncursesw5_5.4-3_i386.deb) ...
Selecting previously deselected package mime-support.
Unpacking mime-support (from .../mime-support_3.26-1_all.deb) ...
Selecting previously deselected package mutt.
Unpacking mutt (from .../mutt_1.5.5.1-20040112+1_i386.deb) ...
Selecting previously deselected package libsasl2-modules.
Unpacking libsasl2-modules (from .../libsasl2-modules_2.1.18-2_i386.deb)
...
Setting up libsasl2 (2.1.18-2) ...

Setting up libidn11 (0.4.1-1) ...

Setting up libncursesw5 (5.4-3) ...
```

```
Setting up mime-support (3.26-1) ...

Setting up mutt (1.5.5.1-20040112+1) ...

Setting up libsasl2-modules (2.1.18-2) ...
Reading Package Lists... Done
Building Dependency Tree
Reading extended state information... Done
hostname:~#
```

Now mutt is installed. aptitude installed everything mutt really absolutely required for functioning (the Depends), and an additional package that mutt's maintainer feels adds a good deal of value (the Recommends). The other recommended package, locales, and the package on which mutt depended, libc6, were already installed. As a result, neither of them was installed. Both of these packages were already installed because they are in the core Debian distribution and are always included in new installs. The output from the command should look very much like of apt-get's output. Not only do apt-get and apttiude share a lot of code, but they also both end up calling dpkg to do the messy work of installation. apt-get and aptitude are responsible for selecting and downloading the packages to install (to satisfy the various package relationships), while dpkg does the heavy lifting.

Now go ahead and run aptitude without any arguments on the command-line to open up a fullscreen session. Press / to begin a search, type elinks, and press Enter. You should now have the elinks package highlighted. To mark the package for installation, type +. The color of the line will change to green, and in the far left column an i will appear; both of these are intended to indicate that the package will be installed when you initiate operations.

Speaking of initiating operations, here's a quick note about aptitude in fullscreen mode: You first tell it what you want to do, and then you press the G key, for "go." aptitude displays a staging screen, showing you what operations it will perform. Look over the list of changes and then press G at this staging screen to confirm its actions. The screen changes, and you can see that aptitude is going to install two extra packages — liblua50 and liblualib50 — to satisfy elinks' dependencies. Press G a third and final time to begin the installation process.

When the downloads have completed, you'll be asked to confirm for the last time that you want to continue, at which point aptitude will call upon dpkg to perform the package installations.

To reinstall a package with aptitude, use either aptitude reinstall *packagename* or browse to the package in the fullscreen interface and press L to mark the package for reinstallation. It will be reinstalled when you next initiate packaging operations.

Removing and Purging Packages

In Debian, great pains are taken to ensure that configuration data is kept intact. When a package is simply removed, its configuration files and data are left in place in case you ever want to reinstall the package. To tell the packaging system to remove the configuration files too (so that the next time you install the package you get the default configuration), you need to purge the package.

Removing and purging packages using apt-get

Once again, apt-get is a quite simple way to solve this problem. Simply run apt-get remove *packagename*, and it will remove the package. Remove vim, as seen in the following session:

```
hostname:~# apt-get remove vim
Reading Package Lists... Done
Building Dependency Tree... Done
The following packages will be REMOVED:
  vim
0 packages upgraded, 0 newly installed, 1 to remove and 0  not upgraded.
Need to get 0B of archives. After unpacking 12.2MB will be freed.
Do you want to continue? [Y/n] y
(Reading database ... 7567 files and directories currently installed.)
Removing vim ...
dpkg - warning: while removing vim, directory `/etc/vim' not empty so not
removed.
hostname:~#
```

apt-get will always ask you before it removes a package. You'll note that dpkg issued a warning saying that it wasn't able to remove a directory — /etc/vim/ — because it wasn't empty. That's not surprising, since you just removed the package instead of purging it — thus vim's configuration files remain. To purge a package, pass apt-get the --purge option:

```
hostname:~# ls /etc/vim/
vimrc
hostname:~# apt-get --purge remove vim
Reading Package Lists... Done
Building Dependency Tree... Done
The following packages will be REMOVED:
  vim*
0 upgraded, 0 newly installed, 1 to remove and 61 not upgraded.
Need to get 0B of archives.
After unpacking 1700kB disk space will be freed.
Do you want to continue? [Y/n] y
(Reading database ... 17629 files and directories currently installed.)
Removing vim ...
```

```
Purging configuration files for vim ...
hostname:~# ls /etc/vim/
ls: /etc/vim/: No such file or directory
hostname:~#
```

apt-get again asked us for permission to perform this operation; it indicated it was purging the package by appending an asterisk to the package's name. The final ls command verifies that that directory is in fact now gone. Now that vim is purged, if you reinstall it, its default configuration file will be installed freshly again.

Note, however, that apt-get didn't remove libgpmg1, which was installed alongside vim to satisfy a dependency. If packages are installed as dependencies of another package, apt-get will not look to see whether they are still needed when you uninstall the original package and will simply leave them there. Now take a look at how aptitude deals with that scenario.

Removing and purging packages using aptitude

Let's get rid of mutt first, which we installed earlier via aptitude:

```
hostname:~# aptitude remove mutt
Reading Package Lists... Done
Building Dependency Tree
Reading extended state information... Done
The following packages are unused and will be REMOVED:
  libidn11 libncursesw5 libsasl2 libsasl2-modules mime-support
The following packages will be REMOVED:
  mutt
0 packages upgraded, 0 newly installed, 6 to remove and 61 not upgraded.
Need to get 0B of archives. After unpacking 5788kB will be freed.
Do you want to continue? [Y/n/?] y
Writing extended state information... Done
(Reading database ... 17519 files and directories currently installed.)
Removing mutt ...
Removing libidn11 ...
Removing libncursesw5 ...
Removing libsasl2-modules ...
Removing libsasl2 ...
Removing mime-support ...
Reading Package Lists... Done
Building Dependency Tree
Reading extended state information... Done
hostname:~#
```

Note   You can purge a package on the command-line with aptitude by running the command aptitude purge *packagename*. Note the difference between this and apt-get, which accepts purge as a double-dash option to remove.

As you can see, the packages that were installed alongside mutt were also removed when you asked for mutt's removal. This is because you installed it with aptitude, removed it with aptitude, and mutt was the only installed package that declared dependencies on these packages. If another package had required, say, mime-support, the mime-support package would have been left intact. Unfortunately, aptitude can only know whether other packages need a given package. You may have, after installing a package automatically to satisfy a dependency, started using the package directly, so be careful and read aptitude's output before telling it to go ahead with the operation. If you want to keep some of those automatically installed packages, one way to do it is to use aptitude's fullscreen interactive interface.

So, as usual, fire up aptitude. Press / to start a search, type elinks, and press Enter. elinks should be highlighted. To mark a highlighted package for removal, press the minus/dash key (-). To purge it, type in an underscore (_). For this example, you want to purge elinks, so type an underscore. You'll note that the line once again changes color, this time to purple. Press the G key to go to the summary screen, and you'll see that both liblua50 and liblualib50 are also going to be uninstalled. Suppose you'd like to keep liblua50 around. Highlight that package and press +, the same key you would use to mark a package for installation. The color of the line changes back to normal, and now liblua50 won't be removed. If you want to mark packages as automatically or manually installed, highlight the packages and press M or m, respectively. Press the minus key to mark liblua50 for removal again, and then press G to start the operation. When you're done, quit aptitude.

Configuring and Configuration Files

There are two forms of configuration on a Debian system: *application-specific* configuration and *debconf-based* configuration. Application-specific configuration typically means that the configuration for programs is stored in configuration files. Changing or customizing this type of configuration usually means editing a configuration file by hand and changing or adding variables and values. Debian attempts to make package installation painless, and most package maintainers avoid using interactive debconf prompts during a package install, but sometimes it's unavoidable. If a package can't provide a sensible default configuration file, it will instead ask some debconf questions. The advantage of debconf is that the user can decide what sorts of questions he'd like to see, and how to see them.

Configuring packages using debconf

debconf is the standard Debian configuration system. Many packages use debconf to provide a single interface to configuration that eliminates the need to have users edit files by instead providing sane defaults and a way to prompt users with questions. debconf questions are generally asked as part of the package's installation, but you can also invoke them later on to reconfigure the package. This is done by running `dpkg-reconfigure` *packagename*:

```
hostname:~# dpkg-reconfigure debconf
```

Reconfiguring `debconf` allows you to set a variety of parameters used to display and process questions asked via packaged `debconf` scripts. The first question `debconf`'s own configuration script asks is "What interface should be used for configuring packages?" You can safely leave it at the default. After you've selected which interface you'd like to use, press Enter. You're then asked what priority of questions you'd like to see. Low-priority questions aren't displayed by default; they're usually only of interest to obsessive-compulsive knob-twiddlers like myself.

Note   I selected medium-priority questions, and you should as well. Unlike changing the `debconf` interface, changing which questions are asked will result in subtly different configuration files, which may break the instructions given in this book. When you're done with this book, or when you're familiar with the system as a whole, feel free to reconfigure `debconf` and choose whichever priority level you'd like.

Configuration file handling

Configuration files are always handled specially in Debian because they're far more important than most other software files. Configuration files are meant to be edited by the administrator, and as such may have hours of work put into them. Given that, and because your installation can break badly if a package blindly overwrites your carefully crafted configuration file, extra prompts are displayed whenever something damaging might happen.

Prompts are displayed whenever:

1. A new package is being installed for the first time, and there is a preexisting configuration file — perhaps copied from an older installation.

2. A package is being upgraded, but the administrator has manually changed a configuration file so that it's no longer the same one that was contained in the package.

Prompts are *not* displayed when:

1. The administrator has removed a configuration file; if you want to get a configuration file back from a package, you need to purge and reinstall it.

2. A new version of a configuration file exists in the new version of the package, and the administrator hasn't changed the current version.

Let's take a working example, and reinstall vim. If you haven't purged it already, do so now with aptitude purge vim. This will remove all its configuration files and tell the packaging system that when the package is installed later, it should restore the packaged configuration files. With vim no longer installed on the system in any way, create a fake /etc/vim/vimrc and see what happens when you reinstall it:

```
hostname:~# mkdir /etc/vim
hostname:~# echo Testing > /etc/vim/vimrc
hostname:~# cat /etc/vim/vimrc
Testing
hostname:~# aptitude install vim
Reading Package Lists... Done
Building Dependency Tree
Reading extended state information... Done
The following NEW packages will be installed:
  vim
0 packages upgraded, 1 newly installed, 0 to remove and 61 not upgraded.
Need to get 774kB of archives. After unpacking 1704kB will be used.
Writing extended state information... Done
Get:1 http://http.us.debian.org sid/main vim 1:6.2-426+1 [774kB]
Fetched 774kB in 11s (69.6kB/s)
Selecting previously deselected package vim.
(Reading database ... 17306 files and directories currently installed.)
Unpacking vim (from .../vim_1%3a6.2-426+1_i386.deb) ...
Setting up vim (6.2-426+1) ...

Configuration file `/etc/vim/vimrc'
 ==> File on system created by you or by a script.
 ==> File also in package provided by package maintainer.
   What would you like to do about it ?  Your options are:
    Y or I  : install the package maintainer's version
    N or O  : keep your currently-installed version
      D     : show the differences between the versions
      Z     : background this process to examine the situation
 The default action is to keep your current version.
*** vimrc (Y/I/N/O/D/Z) [default=N] ?
```

As you can see, it's a somewhat ugly-looking prompt. It's simple and gets the job done, however. It tells us that there's a configuration file of the same name in the same directory in the package we're installing, and that tells us which configuration file it is talking about.

Your choices at this prompt are simple: Press the Y key and press Enter to have the packaged configuration file overwrite your own. Press the N key if you know that the file you have is good. You can press D to see the differences between the current file and the new file; you'll be returned to the prompt after you've finished reading the differences. Lastly, if you choose the Z option, you're dropped into a shell where you can manually poke about and perhaps merge the two configuration files by hand in a text editor. When you exit the shell, you're returned to the prompt.

Configuration File Handling with ucf

The information on configuration file handling in this section refers to regular configuration files, the kind that are included in the package normally and aren't generated at install time. In that simple case, dpkg itself is displaying the prompt and handling the configuration file. However, pretty much any package that uses debconf scripts also creates a default configuration file on the fly during the package's installation. As such, the handling is slightly different. ucf emulates the standard dpkg prompt in many ways, with the exception that it uses debconf for its user interface. The options will be the same, and the reasons are the same, although the display will look different.

Since the configuration file you created is fake, press Y and press Enter to use the packaged version. The installation will complete normally after that.

Upgrading Packages

As mentioned in the introduction of this book, sarge users won't be getting updates very often; it's a stable release and will only occasionally get a security update. However, when sarge does get an update, it's more than likely a very important fix. As such, it's important to go through the upgrade process at least once daily to check for upgrades. sid users will likely go through this upgrading process daily anyway, since sid receives updates on a continual basis.

 If you use sid, see http://people.debian.org/~dbharris/tracking-sid/ for some helpful tips on upgrading that are specific to sid. Whether you use sid or sarge, visit http://people.debian.org/~dbharris/check-updates/ for details on getting your Debian system to automatically check for updates and e-mail you when any are available.

Upgrading using apt-get

As usual, before attempting to install or upgrade a package, run apt-get update to download the latest package lists from the Debian servers. After having done so, upgrading is as simple as running apt-get upgrade. apt-get upgrade won't, by default, allow any packages to be removed. If there's a case where a package needs to be removed, some packages will be *held back*. This is often the case where a package has been renamed; the procedure in that case is for apt-get to remove the old package and install the new one. This is typically a trouble-free process, performed automatically, but it's always safer to act conservatively. If you see a package being held back, you can instead use apt-get dist-upgrade, which will then allow apt-get to satisfy package relationships by removing packages. Carefully examine the output, however, to make sure that nothing you care about is being removed — or at least that nothing you care about is being removed without being replaced.

If there are a number of upgrades available but you want to upgrade only one or more specific packages, you can instead use `apt-get install` and supply it with a package or list of packages on the command-line. This will upgrade only those packages that you've specified, as well as any other upgrades that absolutely must take place to install the newer versions of the packages you've specified.

Upgrading using aptitude

In terms of upgrading, `aptitude` is used in the exact same way on the command-line as `apt-get`. However, as usual, `aptitude` has a fullscreen interface available as well. In the case of upgrades, this is particularly useful because it allows you to fine-tune which packages get upgraded quickly and easily. By default, `aptitude` will mark every package that has a newer available version than the one you've got installed, so simply running `aptitude` and then pressing the G key to go to the operation summary screen will show you what packages will be upgraded, added, or removed. If you wish to put a package on hold to prevent it from being upgraded, press the = (equal sign) key. This package will be displayed as being held back every time you go to the operation summary screen, and you can decide to upgrade it later; just highlight the package and press the + (plus sign) key.

Integrity-Checking Packages

To test the validity of your system, you may want to verify that the files on your machine match those that were contained in the original package. Almost every package in Debian includes cryptographic signatures for all the files it contains. Using the `debsums` tool, you can compare the files on your system against these cryptographic signatures.

Once you have `debsums` installed, run `debsums` to see whether any of the files on your system have been modified from the packaged version. Since you just did an installation, it's very unlikely. Typically, a file will have changed if you tried to install, from source, some of the same software you already had installed. Ignore any output that warns that some packages don't contain `md5sums`. It's just a warning, not an error.

Caution   The other reason for wanting to check your files' consistency is if you believe your machine's security has been compromised. There is no absolute way to ensure that your system hasn't been subverted. At best you can confirm that it *has* been broken into. Since the cryptographic signatures contained in Debian packages are stored on your hard drive after the package has been installed, an attacker could just as easily modify those signatures to match any modifications they might have made to the system files. In the event of a security breach, the *only* option is reinstalling from scratch and copying only nonexecutable files from the old installation. There are many reasons to do this, but I'll leave that to the next chapter, "Basic System Administration." Suffice it to say that if you care about such things, you'll keep your system up to date with respect to any security updates available and closely read all the chapters in this book relating to security.

Package Repositories and /etc/apt/sources.list

Although Debian's package repositories are very large and complete, they don't quite contain everything. The two primary reasons for using unofficial package repositories are to get patent-encumbered software, or to retrieve newer versions of packages than are available in sarge, without using the sid development tree.

Though specifics differ from repository to repository, the general idea is the same: add one or more lines to /etc/apt/sources.list. Since /etc/apt/sources.list is the file apt-get update and aptitude update read to determine which package lists to download, it's worth discussing the makeup of that file.

Each line describes a single repository and is made up of three parts: the binary/source keyword, the repository's URL, and the components within that repository. Standard lines look like the following:

```
deb http://http.us.debian.org/debian stable main
deb-src http://http.us.debian.org/debian stable main
```

The first word in the line is the binary/source indicator. deb means the repository contains binary packages you can install, and deb-src is for source packages. Most archives have both binary and source, so lines are often added in pairs. The second part of the line is simply the URL to the repository. Everything after the URL reflects the components of the repository. Though the components you want to add are repository specific, there needs to be *some* text there. The examples here refer to a standard Debian package repository for the stable distribution — sarge, in this case — and the main portion of that repository.

Note   Whenever you change anything in /etc/apt/sources.list, **run** aptitude update **or** apt-get update.

apt Pinning

The ability to add multiple sources to /etc/apt/sources.list makes it possible to seamlessly integrate unofficial repositories of Debian packages. These repositories may contain packages not found in Debian or newer or enhanced versions of official packages.

What happens if the same package exists in two or more repositories? (As far as the packaging system is concerned, it is the same package if it has the same name, regardless of the contents.) By default, apt will use the package with the higher version number. If two packages have the same version number, apt will select the one that best fits your current release (that is, sarge), which in most cases will be the official Debian package. If the packages have the same version number and belong to the same release, apt will pick the first one it comes across in its database, or in other words, essentially pick one at random.

Sometimes the default is not good enough. apt's "pinning" feature lets you change it. Here are a few scenarios where you might want to change the way apt prioritizes upgrades.

Using selected packages from another release

Sometimes you need a newer version of a package on your stable system, but you don't want to move entirely to testing or unstable. Debian also has an experimental distribution for packages whose state is too raw even for unstable. You will want to be very careful about installing and upgrading such packages, too careful to trust the computer to do the right thing. apt pinning will help in both these and other situations.

/etc/apt/sources.list

Start by adding the apt sources for each release to /etc/apt/sources.list. A file that includes stable, testing, unstable, and experimental will look something like this:

```
# Debian sarge (stable)
deb http://security.debian.org sarge/updates main contrib non-free
deb http://http.us.debian.org/debian/ sarge main contrib non-free
# Debian etch (testing)
deb http://http.us.debian.org/debian/ etch main contrib non-free
# Debian sid (unstable)
deb http://http.us.debian.org/debian/ sid main contrib non-free
# Debian experimental
deb http://http.us.debian.org/debian/ experimental main contrib non-free
```

After adding these lines, run

```
# apt-get update
```

so apt can add all the packages in these sources to its database. You can now install packages from any of these distributions. But which will apt-get pick?

apt-cache policy

The command

```
$ apt-cache policy <packagename>
```

will tell you what it is going to do. For instance, as I write this, I get the following report for the KDE word processor kword on a system running sarge with the same sources.list as above:

```
$ apt-cache policy kword
kword:
  Installed: 1:1.3.2-1.sarge.1
```

```
Candidate: 1:1.3.4-1
Version Table:
    1:1.3.4-1 0
        500 http://http.us.debian.org sid/main Packages
        500 http://http.us.debian.org etch/main Packages
*** 1:1.3.2-1.sarge.1 0
        100 /var/lib/dpkg/status
    1:1.3.2-1.sarge.1 0
        500 http://http.us.debian.org sarge/main Packages
```

(The version numbers may be different by the time you read this, but the same principles apply.) What the output is telling you is that I currently have version 1:1.3.2-1 of kword installed. (/var/lib/dpkg/status, which is dpkg's database, is treated as the source of the package.) apt has assigned this version a score of 100. Sarge currently has the same version, which has a score of 500, as does 1:1.3.4-1 in etch/sid. kword doesn't exist in experimental. As both the versions in sarge and etch/sid have the same score, the tie is broken by the higher version. The number after the version is the priority of the package, which is set only if you pin by version—see the "Installing (or keeping) a specific version" section)—so it is 0 here.

/etc/apt/preferences

Were I to do an upgrade of kword now, the version from testing/unstable would be the candidate for installation. Because kword 1:1.3.4-1 depends on other packages from testing/unstable, installing it could inadvertently result in a large part of my system being upgraded to unstable. So be very careful in using pinning with common library packages such as libc6, which large numbers of packages depend on. This can be prevented by creating a file called /etc/apt/preferences with contents like this:

```
Explanation: Sarge
Package: *
Pin: release a=stable
Pin-Priority: 999

Explanation: Etch
Package: *
Pin: release a=testing
Pin-Priority: 90

Explanation: Sid
Package: *
Pin: release a=unstable
Pin-Priority: 80

Package: *
Pin: release a=experimental
Pin-Priority: 10
```

Each stanza of this file consists of several fields, each on their own line. (Within a stanza, fields don't need to be in any particular order, however.) The first field, `Explanation`, can be used for comments, a short description of what you are trying to do with the pin. `Package` describes which packages are affected by this pin. The special value * means all packages, or you can give one or more package names here. The next field contains the criterion you want to use to pick packages to pin. In this case, the keyword `release` in the first half of the line means you want to sort packages based on the information in the `release` file that should accompany each package repository. (For more information on the subject, see Chapter 27.) The second half of the line specifies which field of the release file is to be used; a means archive. Unfortunately, `apt` doesn't support release code names, so you have to use the archive name (stable, testing, unstable) instead of sarge, etch, and sid. You can also use c for component (such as `main`, `contrib`, or `nonfree`), v for release version (such as 3.0 for Debian's woody release,) o for origin, or l for label. Other keywords you can use in the first half are `origin`, which is confusingly not the same as the `origin` field in the `release` file, but the Internet address of the package repository (such as `ftp.debian.org`), and `version`, which also is unconnected to the similarly named field in the `release` file and instead refers to a package version. This will be explained in greater detail further on. The last field is the score you want `apt` to give to this pin. By default, an installed package gets a score of 100, and any other sources get 500, unless a default release has been specified in `apt`'s configuration, in which case packages belonging to that release are assigned 990.

In the example preferences file, packages belonging to the stable release get the highest priority. Testing, unstable, and experimental are both less than 100, so assuming you have a package installed, you will not be prompted to upgrade it even if a newer version is available than what is in stable. If you run `apt-cache policy` again, you can see the difference pinning makes:

```
$ apt-cache policy kword
kword:
  Installed: 1:1.3.2-1.sarge.1
  Candidate: 1:1.3.2-1.sarge.1
  Version Table:
     1:1.3.4-1 0
         80 http://http.us.debian.org sid/main Packages
         90 http://http.us.debian.org etch/main Packages
 *** 1:1.3.2-1.sarge.1 0
        100 /var/lib/dpkg/status
     1:1.3.2-1.sarge.1 0
        999 http://http.us.debian.org sarge/main Packages
```

Installing from multiple distributions

With pinning set up as shown previously, you are protected from accidental upgrades to a different release. But what if you want to install a different version of kword? You can temporarily override your pinning preferences with `apt-get`'s `--target-release` option (synonyms are `-t` and `--default-release`):

```
# apt-get install -t testing kword
```

Another method, which is handy if you are installing packages from multiple distributions in the same install session, looks like this:

```
# apt-get install kdelibs4 kword/testing kdm
```

In this case, `kdelibs4` and `kdm` will come from stable, while only `kword` will come from testing.

These methods can be used to remove packages too.

Installing from a specific site

The `origin` variant of the pin field in `/etc/apt/preferences` can be used to ensure packages have a higher priority if they come from a particular place. Use a stanza like this:

```
Explanation: packages from my own site
Package: *
Pin: origin "src.braincells.com"
Pin-Priority: 999
```

Installing (or keeping) a specific version

Sometimes you might want to ensure that a package *doesn't* get upgraded. Maybe you have a local package that you've tweaked and don't want overwritten with a generic version. Or maybe you are relying on the functionality of one particular version of the package. Again, pinning can help. This time the `version` variant of the pin field is used. A specific package name is also used:

```
Explanation: bash 2.* only
Package: bash
Pin: version 2.*
Pin-Priority: 999
```

This allows upgrades of any new 2.* versions of the `bash` shell, but it keeps you from any nasty surprises when `bash` 3 comes out. (This is just an example. Usually in Debian, packages that are significantly different from their earlier versions are given different names, such as `bash` 3.) Note that the comparison of version numbers is done alphabetically, not numerically.

You can also override version preferences on the `apt-get` command line like this:

```
# apt-get install kword=1:1.3.4-1
```

And once again, this works for package removals too.

Caution `apt` pinning is a very powerful tool that gives you a lot of control over the shape of your system, but it can be dangerous, too. The consensus among savvy Debian users is that it should be used very sparingly and certainly not for important system libraries and other core packages. If you absolutely must have a newer version of one of those and you just can't upgrade your entire system, you should try rebuilding the packages instead.

Summary

I covered a lot of material in this chapter, running the gamut from packaging concepts to using unofficial Debian package repositories. Having read this chapter, you should be perfectly capable of handling software management on your Debian installation, including such tasks as finding, examining, installing, removing, purging, configuring, and upgrading packages. You should also be familiar with the concept of pinning.

✦ ✦ ✦

Basic System Administration

Modern systems administration is a complex topic, but the basic idea is easy to understand: Do no harm. The devil is in the details.

This chapter covers many basic concepts relevant to modern systems administration, with a particular focus on Debian systems. The principles you learn here should apply to every other GNU/Linux system, even if the details differ. If you don't manage, take care of, or administer any systems, not even your own desktop, you may want to skip this chapter; however, with the basic knowledge gained here you'll be able to understand some of the decisions your system administrator makes, and perhaps you'll be able to suggest a few things every now and then.

Much like a doctor, a system administrator can be responsible for the welfare of others. In the case of a company, a system administrator may be charged with ensuring the integrity and privacy of confidential client and customer data. Alternatively, a poorly functioning critical electronic infrastructure essential to business operations might cost people jobs because the business won't be able to maintain its customer base. It goes without saying that a system administrator in a life-or-death environment such as a hospital or a military installation can make mistakes that cost lives — or decisions that save them.

Most system administrators, luckily, don't have such serious pressures put upon them. However, system administrators should approach their duties with a degree of professionalism that might seem overblown at first. Poor-quality systems administration can result in the silent hijacking of computer resources that can then be used for any number of nefarious purposes; it's this possibility of silent infiltration that requires system administrators to be vigilant and skilled.

User, Group, and root Account Management

At the heart of a multi-user system like Debian GNU/Linux is the concept of *privilege separation*. Though it's possible for every process running on the system to be able to access and modify every other part of the system, this model is fraught with difficulties. In this model, a bug in even the smallest, most innocent application can totally wipe out all the data on the system. Any user would be able to access the files of any other user. By default in Debian GNU/Linux, the access model is that of users and groups. Access to resources is based on the user account and the groups that account is a member of. Every process the user runs has the same privileges as the user, including group membership. With a few special exceptions, the user can't run applications as another user.

Linux actually supports multiple privilege-separation schemes, and one of the more popular ones today is SELinux, the United States National Security Agency's Security Enhanced Linux. SELinux takes privilege separation even further, and in addition to traditional user/group identities, it allows administrators to specify in detail which operations an application can perform on which resources. See www.nsa.gov/ selinux/ for general information, and https://sourceforge.net/docman/ display_doc.php?docid=20372&group_id=21266 for a HOWTO that covers using SELinux on a Debian system.

This privilege separation is apparent in all parts of a Debian system; long-running processes such as a Web server have their own user account and group, as do many others. Access to hardware is controlled by group membership, allowing you or your users to access hardware such as sound or video cards directly, while disallowing unrelated applications.

The root account

The *root* or *superuser* account has been the system administrator account on GNU/Linux systems since the beginning. This account has the ability to inspect and modify any part of the system. With privilege, however, comes responsibility: When using the root account it's easy to accidentally damage or even destroy a system, including potentially irreplaceable user data. On your home system, you are likely going go to be your own sysadmin and in charge of the root account. At work, you may or may not occupy this role.

Generally speaking, the root account should be used only when it's absolutely necessary. Reducing the need for the root account in day-to-day operations is a common goal of many GNU/Linux projects. Nevertheless, the root account is still commonly used for a variety of purposes. Safety is a major consideration, but being able to do your work conveniently and easily is also important. Whenever you get an error saying you don't have permission to perform some operation or other, chances are you will want to use the root account.

When you do need to use `root` privileges, try to keep a written narrative audit trail in a file so that if you make a mistake, you can find out where you made it at some point in the future. On machines with multiple administrators, this audit trail is even more important: It allows other administrators to see what you've done.

Quick access to root privileges

There are basically two forms of `root` access available to you: a full login session, covered in the "Full sessions as root" section, or a command-by-command elevation of privileges, which this section addresses. The command-by-command elevation of privileges form allows for myriad features such as a good audit trail, per-administrator configuration files, X11 session sharing, and more.

Installing and configuring sudo

`sudo` allows the system administrator to provide herself (via her regular user account) and others fine-grained access to run particular programs as `root`. It also logs all the command lines that are run, providing an excellent audit trail. Lastly, `sudo` is easy to use. Thanks to its default preservation of environment variables like `$HOME` and `$XAUTHORITY`, which improve the consistency of programs run as `root`, it's actually one of the most convenient ways to run programs as `root`.

Go ahead and run `apt-get install sudo`, as `root`, to install it. `sudo`'s installation is noninteractive, so the output of the command isn't reproduced here. One message of interest, however, is that it should tell you that it's creating a default `/etc/sudoers` file. `/etc/sudoers` is the `sudo` configuration file, and it controls who can access `sudo` and what commands they're allowed to run. Since an error in this configuration file can be considered a security risk, it isn't normally editable.

You will probably want to edit `/etc/sudoers` so that your user can run `sudo`, which the system will not be configured to do by default. To edit `/etc/sudoers`, run `visudo` as `root`. `visudo` will use the `$VISUAL` and `$EDITOR` environment variables to determine which editor to run. Try running `export EDITOR=nano` to change the default editor. It will then copy the file for editing. When you've finished editing the file and you've exited your editor, `visudo` will check the syntax of the temporary file to ensure it's valid. If the syntax of the temporary file is valid, it will be moved to `/etc/sudoers` and the process will be complete; if it's invalid, you'll be prompted to either discard your changes or reedit the temporary file.

The default configuration file should be identical (or nearly so) to the following:

```
# sudoers file.
#
# This file MUST be edited with the 'visudo' command as root.
#
# See the man page for details on how to write a sudoers file.
#
```

```
# Host alias specification

# User alias specification

# Cmnd alias specification

# User privilege specification
root    ALL=(ALL) ALL
```

For the most part, the default configuration consists of a bunch of comments and blank lines. As in many other configuration files in Debian, all lines that begin with #, or anything that follows a # on any line, is a comment and is discarded by the program. The first three substantive comments should be self-explanatory. The next three, the Host, User, and Cmnd specifications, just provide some suggested structure to the file. The last line is more interesting; it's the entirety of the effective default configuration. It allows root to execute all commands, on all hosts, as any user. This type of line, the privilege specification, defines which users are allowed to do what and where. See Figure 5-1 for a quick breakdown of what each component of that line means.

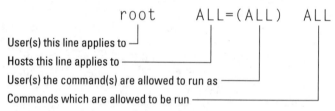

Figure 5-1: sudo privilege specification.

A few secrets are revealed implicitly by the components of this line of the specification file. Though the first component, (User_Alias), isn't remarkable, the three that follow it are. The second component, the host specification, (Host_Alias), indicates that it's common for a single /etc/sudoers file to be shared among many machines. The hostnames of those machines are checked by sudo, and with that you can allow restricted access on one machine but more flexible access on others. The third component indicates the name of the user that commands are allowed to run as (Runas_Alias). It indicates if you can use sudo to run commands as users other than root. This is particularly helpful when troubleshooting permissions problems reported by users. The fourth component, the command specification (Cmnd_Alias), allows you to restrict elevated privileges to only some commands. This is a safe way to give some users limited elevated privileges; perhaps a shared machine with a dial-up Internet connection will have numerous users who can cause the computer to establish the dial-up connection. Briefly, the privilege specification lines can be summarized as follows:

```
  User_Alias      Host_Alias=(Runas_Alias) Cmnd_Alias
```

These are referred to as aliases because they can refer to users, hosts, and commands directly — or they can refer to special configuration tokens such as ALL (which is self-explanatory), or they can refer to lists. You can also assign keywords to commonly used lists. For example, the following line would allow the user foobar to use the commands /bin/ls and /bin/cp as the users root or daemon on hosts quux and quuux:

```
foobar   quux, quuux = (root, daemon)   /bin/ls, /bin/cp
```

For our purposes, we're enabling your unprivileged user account to access full root privileges via sudo. Since you're able to log in as root anyway, you don't need to restrict your access in any way. Add a line similar to the following, but replace *user* with your username. Remember to edit the file using visudo, which must be run as root:

```
user    ALL=(ALL) ALL
```

Save and exit the file, and your unprivileged user account should now be able to access root privileges via sudo. If you wish to create a more complex /etc/sudoers file, for instance to allow restricted root access to some of your users, I encourage you to read the sudoers manpage, in section 5, by running man 5 sudoers.

Using sudo

Now that sudo is installed and configured, you can use it for day-to-day administration. Log out of the root account and log into your regular, unprivileged account. Just for an introduction, run sudo whoami:

```
user@hostname:~$ sudo whoami

We trust you have received the usual lecture from the local System
Administrator. It usually boils down to these two things:

        #1) Respect the privacy of others.
        #2) Think before you type.

Password:
```

Log in at this prompt using your user's password. After you have logged in correctly, sudo will run the command, whoami in this case, with root privileges.

Note   From this point forward, it's assumed that you're logged in via your regular user account — not the root account. If you're ever expected to run a full shell as root, it will be explicitly reintroduced.

sudo is meant to be run often, as an alternative to logging in as root, but security isn't sacrificed. The first time you run sudo, and whenever you run it after having not run it for a period of time (10 minutes by default), sudo will ask you for your

password. This is like a screensaver in some respects: It's meant to prevent somebody from sitting down at your workstation while you're away (but still logged in)
and getting full root access. Note that the password sudo is asking for is your own
unprivileged account's password — not root's. In this manner you can safely give
sudo access to individuals without sharing the root password (which would allow
them to do anything).

sudo accepts a number of options that are covered in its manual page, and I encourage you to read it if you're interested in running commands as users other than
root, or in exploring some of the extra functionality offered. Aside from these
options, sudo simply accepts a command-line as arguments. For instance, sudo
ls -lh --color will run the command ls -lh --color as root. In a shell-based
administration environment, this convenience is unmatched.

sudo, by default, preserves environment variables. This means that your $HOME
and other environment variables will remain the same. When you run any applications that look for configuration files in $HOME — your home directory — as root via
sudo, they will read your user account's own configuration files instead of those
contained in /root/ (the normal home directory for the root user). This is a boon
to systems with multiple administrators because it allows each to keep their own
configuration files instead of having to suffer with whatever the primary administrator has created. Additionally, your $XAUTHORITY and $DISPLAY settings will be preserved. This means that when you're running a desktop environment, you'll be able
to use graphical applications as root without any extra effort — and in a secure
manner, without needing to allow every local user on the system to connect to your
desktop environment (which would let every user steal your passwords).

Auditing sudo logs

sudo records all the commands the user runs directly with sudo to syslog by
default, and on a Debian system the messages will go to /var/log/auth.log. Be
warned, however; sudo logs only the commands it runs directly. It will log the user
starting a root shell by running sudo su -, for instance, but it will not log any of the
commands run within that full root session. An example log line is included here:

```
Apr 18 23:11:53 hostname sudo: user : TTY=tty1 ; PWD=/home/user ; USER=root
; COMMAND=/bin/su -
```

The first part of the line, everything up to sudo:, is the log's timestamp. After
sudo:, the fields are (in their order of appearance): the user who ran sudo, the terminal the user was logged into, the user's working directory at the time, the user
the command was run as, and the command that ran.

Full sessions as root

Even though sudo is secure, fast, and convenient, it isn't perfect. Occasionally
you'll still need to run a full login session as root. The most common reason for

running a full session as `root` is to explore directories that aren't readable by your regular user. As an example, observe the following session:

```
user@hostname:~$ cd /var/spool/exim4/
bash: cd: /var/spool/exim4/: Permission denied
user@hostname:~$ sudo cd /var/spool/exim4/
sudo: cd: command not found
user@hostname:~$
```

As you can see, `/var/spool/exim4/` isn't accessible by our regular user, and `cd` is a shell built-in command, so there's no way to easily explore it without logging in as `root`. One way to get around this is to simply log in as `root` on a spare virtual console. Alternatively, you can launch a new `root` shell with the `sudo -s` command. For the sake of completeness, you can also run a shell in the more traditional way with the `su` command. Running `su` without any options or arguments runs a nonlogin `root` shell, which means that not all the shell's initialization files will be processed. Providing the `-` option, as in the following example, causes `su` to instead run a full login session; it's as if you just logged in as `root`. `su` also accepts a username as an argument; the default is `root`, but you can, for instance, run `su - user` to run a shell as if `user` had just logged in. Whatever you choose, you'll be prompted for the password of the user you're switching to. Since you shouldn't know a random user's password, and since you may not know the `root` password, you can use `sudo` to get around this requirement (`su` doesn't ask for the password if you're already running as `root`, which is what `sudo` gives us). Observe the following session:

```
user@hostname:~$ sudo su -
hostname:~# whoami
root
hostname:~# exit
user@hostname:~$ sudo su - user
user@hostname:~$ whoami
user
user@hostname:~$ exit
user@hostname:~$
```

The session should be pretty self-explanatory: The first call to `su` ran a `root` login shell, we checked that we were `root`, and we exited. The second call to `su` ran a login shell as `user`, and then we double-checked, and we exited. Note that at any point that you invoke `su`, you normally are asked for a password by `sudo`.

Adding users and groups

If you're the only human user on your system, you won't have much need for creating new users. System users (used by long-running daemons or operationally distinct subsystems) are created in package installation scripts. Even if you are the only user, though, you may occasionally have use for a throwaway account for testing purposes. Because access to hardware for certain devices, like sound and printers, is often given to special groups like audio and lpadmin, and because it's recommended that you not change the ownership of device nodes in /dev/ to give access to your normal user to play sounds and print files by creating and maintaining groups, it goes without saying that an administrator of a system shared among multiple users will need to be familiar with account maintenance.

Adding users with adduser

The adduser script, part of the adduser package, is the most convenient way to create new users, and it does a list of things necessary to get the system set up for a new user. adduser creates the new user entry in /etc/passwd, adds the user's initial password to /etc/shadow, creates a personal group for the user in /etc/group, creates the user's home directory, and populates that home directory with a set of skeleton files. Try adding a test user to the system with the following command:

```
user@hostname:~$ sudo adduser testuser
Password:
Adding user testuser...
Adding new group testuser (1001).
Adding new user testuser (1001) with group testuser.
Creating home directory /home/testuser.
Copying files from /etc/skel
Enter new UNIX password: ********
Retype new UNIX password: ********
passwd: password updated successfully
Changing the user information for testuser
Enter the new value, or press ENTER for the default
        Full Name []: Test User
        Room Number []:
        Work Phone []:
        Home Phone []:
        Other []:
Is the information correct? [y/N] y
user@hostname:~$
```

Those bolded stars for the password will not be displayed on your terminal but should be typed. UNIX and Linux do not normally give any feedback while a user is entering a password. That's pretty much all there is to it. In the previous session, sudo asked for my password before it continued. adduser gave some descriptive output, and then asked for (and set) the new user's password. It then asked me to fill out some basic information about the user; be certain to fill out at least the user's full name.

The new user is now ready to log in and interact with the system. It's worth noting that the default in Debian is to create a new group with every new user; the new group's name will be the same as the new username. This effectively allows files from the user to be owned totally by themselves; if every user was in a single default group (historically on systems where this is the default, that group name is users), then all their files would be group-owned by a group that included all members.

Adding groups with addgroup

addgroup works much the same way as adduser; simply supply a group name:

```
user@hostname:~$ sudo addgroup testgroup
Adding group testgroup (1002)...
Done.
user@hostname:~$
```

After this addgroup invocation, you have a new group named testgroup with no members. The "Managing group membership" section later in this chapter explains how to add users to a group.

Removing users and groups

Removing users and groups needs to be done with somewhat more care because there may be files around that are still owned by those users and groups. What's more, these files may contain important data that the user being removed will want.

Removing users with deluser

Before removing any users or groups, you should be familiar with a few deluser options that aid in cleaning up after a user removal: --remove-all-files and --backup. Those two options together cause deluser to back up copies of all the user's files into a single archive and then remove them from the filesystem. Use these options with deluser to remove the account you added in the last subsection, testuser. Because you're using --remove-all-files and --backup, the procedure may take a minute or two.

Using these commands requires that the package perl-modules be installed. Install perl-modules with sudo apt-get install perl-modules.

With the dependencies involved, you will be able to run the following command:

```
user@hostname:~$ sudo deluser --remove-all-files --backup testuser
Looking for files to backup/remove...
Backing up files to be removed to . ...
/bin/tar: Removing leading `/' from member names
Removing files...
Removing user testuser...
done.
user@hostname:~$
```

You may receive errors about being unable to open files and directories in /proc/; you can safely ignore those. /proc/ is a virtual filesystem that simply exports information from the kernel. By default, deluser backs up the user's files to the current working directory, with a basename of username.tar.gz. Look at the file created when you removed the user in the preceding step:

```
user@hostname:~$ ls -lh testuser.tar.gz
-rw-r--r--    1 root      root          1.1K Apr 19 20:43 testuser.tar.gz
user@hostname:~$
```

Now you've got an archive that can easily be transmitted to the user, should they request it, or that can easily be restored if you decide you want to re-add the user.

Deleting groups with delgroup

Deleting groups is more involved than deleting users. First and foremost, there may still be members in the group you want to delete. Passing delgroup the --only-if-empty option will cause it to abort if there are any members remaining in the group. delgroup also doesn't remove or back up files that are group-owned by the group that's about to be deleted. If you later add another group and it gets the same numeric group ID as the one you deleted, all those files will be group-owned by the new group—a potential security risk because the new group might be entirely unrelated to the old group. Thus there are three steps to take whenever you're going to remove a group:

1. Remove any users who are a member of the group.

2. Delete and back up, or change the group-ownership, of files that are group-owned by the group you're about to remove.

3. Remove the group with delgroup.

I discuss removing users from groups in the next subsection, but since the test group, testgroup, has no members, you don't need to worry about it at the moment. However, let's create a test file that is group-owned by testgroup so you can address that issue later in the example. We'll also set the permissions on that file to be group executable and setgid:

```
user@hostname:~$ touch testgroupfile
user@hostname:~$ sudo chgrp testgroup testgroupfile
user@hostname:~$ sudo chmod g+xs testgroupfile
user@hostname:~$ ls -l testgroupfile
-rw-r-sr--    1 user      testgroup        0 Apr 19 22:03 testgroupfile
user@hostname:~$
```

Now we have an example group we want to remove, with no members, and a file that is group-owned by that example group. First we want to take care of files that are group-owned by the group targeted for removal. There are multiple approaches to this problem, but it's my experience that the best approach is to simply change the group-ownership of the relevant files to the root group. Later, the files' owners can change the ownership to a group they're still a member of, if they so choose. Changing the group-ownership to root is good because nobody other than the administrator will be a member of this group; thus it's a pretty safe option. If you remember from Chapter 3, files can be setuid or setgid, which means that executable files are run as the user or group that owns them, regardless of who executes the file. The file you are trying to remove might be executable and setgid, so it's important to remove the setgid bit before you change the file's group-ownership. Otherwise, if somebody executed it, they'd have partial root privileges. You can find all files with a group of test group and then change the permissions to remove setgid with the following bit of shell scripting (don't worry if you don't follow it completely):

```
sudo find / -group testgroup -print0 2> /dev/null | xargs -0 sudo chmod g-s
```

You can go through and find the same files and change their ownership with the following slightly modified bit of shell script:

```
sudo find / -group testgroup -print0 2> /dev/null | xargs -0 sudo chgrp
root
```

See the following example session to see it all in action:

```
user@hostname:~$ ls -l testgroupfile
-rw-r-sr--   1 user     testgroup       0 Apr 19 22:03 testgroupfile
user@hostname:~$ sudo find / -group testgroup -print0 2> /dev/null
| xargs -0 sudo chmod g-s
user@hostname:~$ ls -l testgroupfile
-rw-r-xr--   1 user     testgroup       0 Apr 19 22:03 testgroupfile
user@hostname:~$ sudo find / -group testgroup -print0 2> /dev/null
| xargs -0 sudo chgrp root
user@hostname:~$ ls -l testgroupfile
-rw-r-xr--   1 user     root            0 Apr 19 22:03 testgroupfile
user@hostname:~$
```

Now that you've taken care of files that were group-owned by the group targeted for removal, go ahead and remove the group:

```
user@hostname:~$ sudo delgroup --only-if-empty testgroup
Removing group testgroup...
done.
user@hostname:~$
```

Managing group membership

By default on a Debian system, every user has a group of his own, but there are a number of other standard groups that control access to various resources such as log files and hardware devices. Additionally, if you are administering a multi-user system, chances are you will want to logically group users for access control. See Table 5-1 for a description of some of the more interesting standard groups.

<table>
<tr><td colspan="2" align="center">Table 5-1
Standard Groups</td></tr>
<tr><td>**Group Name**</td><td>**Description**</td></tr>
<tr><td>adm</td><td>Users in the adm group are typically administrators. Many log files are readable only by users in this group.</td></tr>
<tr><td>lp</td><td>Users in the lp, or *line printer*, group are allowed to use the system's printer.</td></tr>
<tr><td>mail</td><td>Users in the mail group are considered mail administrators and are allowed to perform a variety of special mail-related tasks (including reading the mail of other users).</td></tr>
<tr><td>dialout</td><td>Users in the dialout group are allowed to initiate remote connections via a modem—for instance, to an ISP.</td></tr>
<tr><td>cdrom</td><td>Users in the cdrom group are allowed to access any CD drives directly, for example to play or extract audio or to burn writable CDs.</td></tr>
<tr><td>floppy</td><td>Users in the floppy group are allowed to access any floppy disk drives directly.</td></tr>
<tr><td>audio</td><td>Users in the audio group can access audio hardware such as sound cards to either play or record audio.</td></tr>
<tr><td>video</td><td>Users in the video group can access video cards directly, as well as record images off a video capture device such as a Web cam.</td></tr>
</table>

It may seem like overkill to have so many groups, but if all the devices listed previously were readable and writeable by everybody, then anybody could (for instance) record or play audio in the CEO's office, or perhaps watch a system administrator type in passwords in a server room.

Adding users to a group is simple: Just run adduser *username groupname*. For example, you probably want your regular user account to be able to read various log files without needing to use sudo or su, so add it to the adm group:

```
user@hostname:~$ sudo adduser user adm
Adding user user to group adm...
Done.
user@hostname:~$
```

However, note that the additional privileges don't take effect immediately:

```
user@hostname:~$ groups
user
user@hostname:~$
```

For the new group membership to take effect, you must log out or otherwise reinitialize your session. I suggest logging out because it's often the simplest solution and will be required for any session in a graphical desktop interface. When you've logged back in, run the groups command again:

```
user@hostname:~$ groups
user adm
user@hostname:~$
```

To remove a user from a group, run deluser *user group*. Observe the following session:

```
user@willow:~$ sudo deluser user adm
Removing user user from group adm...
done.
user@willow:~$ groups
user adm
user@willow:~$
```

Note that like adding a user to a group, removing a user from a group will take effect only when the user's session is restarted. Any background processes that were running previously need to be killed and restarted from the new session for the new group membership settings to take effect.

Basic Networking

In Chapter 2, you had the option of connecting your computer either to the Internet or to your internal network as part of the Debian installation process. The short treatment of networking concepts given in that chapter, however, doesn't do justice to the rich natures of today's interconnected networks.

In this section, you learn to use a number of low-level network utilities to examine these networks closely. You'll look at your Debian machine's relationship to these networks, and how it interoperates with them.

This section doesn't describe networking in all its gory details. It's a pretty high-level overview. Networking, as I said, is an extremely rich topic owing mainly to its long history and the complexity of interoperating with many different types of machines. A full treatment of networking is available in the Linux Networking HOWTO, located at `www.tldp.org/HOWTO/Net-HOWTO/`.

The Internet Protocol

The Internet, or *inter-network*, is simply a vast collection of smaller networks linked together at many points. These smaller networks, sometimes called *intranets*, are separate from each other mainly due to who's responsible for them; you're responsible for your network, your ISP is responsible for its network, a company is responsible for its network, and so on. This separation of responsibility means that there needs to be some basic agreement on how these networks interoperate, and that's what *protocols* are. Protocols and standards define how computer A communicates with computer B.

TCP/IP

All communications over the Internet or a modern intranet are encoded to match the Internet Protocol (IP) specification. The specification itself is quite large and extremely detailed, but it's also built so that anything can be put on top of it — any application for any use. The basic units of communication over the Internet Protocol are *packets*. Each stream of data is split into very small chunks, and these packets are then sent on their way to their destination. Basic Internet Protocol packets contain information detailing where the packet is coming from and where it's going to, as well as the packet's *payload*. The packet's payload is free-form as far as the Internet Protocol is concerned — anything can be in the payload. However, other protocols and standards exist to define the contents of payloads, such as the *Transmission Control Protocol* (TCP).

IP itself is quite basic, and it doesn't provide any guarantee that the packet will get to its destination. The TCP, or rather, TCP over IP (TCP/IP) is the most widely used network protocol today, and almost every service you use over a network uses TCP/IP as its transmission method. TCP/IP allows computers to reliably send packets over the Internet.

Addresses

Each computer on an IP network has its own IP address, but there's more to a network than simple IP addresses. Though each packet sent has an originating IP address and a destination IP address, figuring out where to send the packet is a bit more involved. There are three important configuration items on every normal network-connected computer: the IP address, the *netmask*, and the *gateway*. The netmask allows your computer to determine which computers it may address locally. If your computer is part of a local area network (LAN), then it can access other machines on that particular segment of the network directly. It can communicate with them without a middleman, so to speak. To converse with computers that aren't on the local network, the packets must first be sent to a *router* or a gateway, which will then forward the packets to the next router, or *hop*, on its way to its eventual destination.

IP addresses, or specifically IP version 4 addresses, are expressed in *dotted quad* notation. This simply means that an IP address has four numbers separated by periods. For instance, 1.2.3.4 is a valid IP address. The numbers between periods can range from 0 to 255.

For more information about netmasks, visit www.computerhope.com/jargon/ n/netmask.htm.

Ports

In addition to source addresses and destination addresses, there are also *ports*. Since any one computer can host a large number of services (Web, FTP, mail, and so on), it's important that each service have a well-known port. The port is used in addition to the Internet address when your computer tries to contact another for a particular service. For instance, if you're browsing a Web site, your browser will attempt to contact the server's port 80, which is the standard port Web servers respond to. Whereas an IP address can be thought of as a street address, a port can be thought of as a room number. In GNU/Linux, the ports of every known service are listed in /etc/services.

Mapping computer names to computer addresses

Computers know only about numbers—or letters that translate into or are represented internally by numbers. This holds true with all things the computer understands—including other computers. When you visit http://www.debian.org/, your computer doesn't magically know what computer to talk to. You and I can read that address and know that we're trying to contact Debian's Web server. For the computer, figuring out which of the billions of accessible computers is www.debian.org is a far more involved task.

Hostname resolution

First install the host package with the sudo apt-get install host command. Next, run the following command and examine its output:

```
user@hostname:~$ host www.debian.org
www.debian.org          A       192.25.206.10
user@hostname:~$
```

In network terminology, every node on a network — every computer, in other words — is a *host*. The `host` command allows you to reproduce what the computer does every time you try to access a host by name. In this case, you're attempting to contact `www.debian.org`. `host` tells you that `www.debian.org` is really `192.25.206.10` — this is the Debian Web server's numeric address or IP (Internet Protocol) address.

The process of turning these human-readable hostnames into computer-addressable numbers is called *hostname resolution*.

Cross-Reference

For a complete treatment of the Domain Name System (DNS), see Chapter 17, "The Domain Name System." In it, you'll not only learn more gory details about how your computer turns hostnames into IP addresses via DNS, but you'll also learn how to set up your own DNS server.

Hostname resolution configuration files

Let's look at which configuration files on your machine affect hostname resolution. Table 5-2 shows the three that are pretty much standard on any GNU/Linux system, including Debian.

Table 5-2 Hostname Resolution Configuration Files	
Configuration File	**Description**
`/etc/nsswitch.conf`	Name Service Switch configuration file (*Switch* is another term for resolution.)
`/etc/resolv.conf`	Hostname resolver library configuration file
`/etc/hosts`	Local database of hostnames and IP addresses

When your computer attempts to contact a named host, for example `www.debian.org`, the first file it looks at is `/etc/nsswitch.conf`. The format of this file is simple, and I invite you to open it in your favorite editor. Though this configuration file describes the behavior of all types of name-to-number resolution, you're learning at the moment about hostnames. In your copy of the file, you should have a line identical to the following:

```
hosts: files dns
```

This line tells your applications that when they want to resolve a hostname, they must first contact the *files* database. This database is `/etc/hosts`, and it is a simple text file that contains static definitions of what IP address belongs to which hostname.

`/etc/hosts` is a very, very old tradition. Decades ago, before the Domain Name System was implemented, every single host on the Internet was listed in each and every computer's `/etc/hosts`. If you didn't have a given host listed in that file, you weren't able to contact it by its name. However, despite the age of this file, it's still used in every network-aware computer today—some names must be known to the computer even if the network isn't available for a real hostname lookup via the Domain Name System. Specifically, the computer's own name must be available for it to function at even a basic level.

Let's take a look at `/etc/hosts`. Your file (and mine) has a line at the very top:

```
127.0.0.1        localhost
```

As I said previously, the format of this file is simple—first the IP address you're giving a name, followed by one or more names. In the example here, there's only one name—`localhost`. `localhost` is a special name; it always refers to your own computer. Even without an Internet connection or an intranet network, your GNU/Linux machine is a full-blown network-capable operating system. Even individual portions of the machine itself are addressable as part of a network internal to the machine. What's more, not only does `localhost` always refer to your own computer, but it also always has the IP address `127.0.0.1`.

Because `localhost` is listed in `/etc/hosts`, when your application tries to contact `localhost`, it doesn't need to look up the IP address via DNS, which may not even be available when the application is running.

When the hostname you're trying to resolve isn't listed in `/etc/hosts`, the next keyword from `/etc/nsswitch.conf` is used. That's the `dns` keyword on our systems. When you need to look up a regular hostname (that is, one that's not already listed in `/etc/hosts`), you need to look it up in the Domain Name System. This requires contacting a Domain Name System server. This is where `/etc/resolv.conf` comes into play. Your `/etc/resolv.conf` won't be identical to mine because you're on a different network, but go ahead and open it in your text editor. You'll have one or more `nameserver` lines similar (but not identical) to my own:

```
nameserver 10.0.0.1
nameserver 10.0.0.2
```

When your computer gets an IP address assigned to it (either automatically via DHCP or statically by an administrator), you also get the IP addresses of the name server(s) you're supposed to use. That's what those lines in `/etc/resolv.conf` are for. When I want to contact `www.debian.org`, my computer will first look to see if it's in `/etc/hosts`. When it's not in `/etc/hosts`, it will talk to the DNS server(s) listed in `/etc/resolv.conf`—in my case, `10.0.0.1` and `10.0.0.2`.

You may have another line in `/etc/resolv.conf`: the `search` line. For simplicity, I said earlier that `/etc/resolv.conf` is used when you try to do a hostname lookup and the host isn't in /etc/hosts. That wasn't entirely correct. The nameserver lines are used only when you're trying to look up a host via DNS, but the search line is always used if it is included in /etc/resolv.conf. Let's look at an example. Again, yours will almost certainly look different than mine if you have one:

```
search debian.org
```

The search keyword tells your applications that if they can't find the hostname at all (via /etc/hosts or via DNS), they should try looking it up again, this time with the domain(s) listed attached to the end of the given hostname from the search line. Observe the following log:

```
user@hostname:~$ cat /etc/resolv.conf
nameserver 24.153.23.66
nameserver 24.153.22.67
user@hostname:~$ host www
www does not exist, try again
user@hostname:~$ editor /etc/resolv.conf
... add a "search" line
user@hostname:~$ cat /etc/resolv.conf
search debian.org
nameserver 24.153.23.66
nameserver 24.253.22.67
user@hostname:~$ host www
www.debian.org          A          192.25.206.10
user@hostname:~$
```

You can see that without a search line, your computer tries to look up the name www and fails. This isn't surprising; there's no Internet host whose full name is www. However, when you add a search line to /etc/resolv.conf, your application will first try to look up the name on its own, and then it will try to look up the name with the domain specified. So it'll look for www first, and if it fails, it then will try to look up www.debian.org (which succeeds).

You can specify multiple domains in a single search line; they'll be tried in order until one succeeds or they all fail.

Network interfaces

During the Debian installation process, you configured a network connection. This process configured a network *interface*, which is jargon for a class of devices in a Linux system that allows it to communicate with other computers. Being able to identify, evaluate, and troubleshoot network devices is an essential building block to network communication. To view the network interfaces you have available on your machine, run sudo ifconfig:

```
user@hostname:~$ sudo ifconfig
eth0      Link encap:Ethernet  HWaddr 00:00:21:6D:4B:BE
          inet addr:192.168.1.1  Bcast:192.168.1.255  Mask:255.255.255.0
          UP BROADCAST RUNNING MULTICAST  MTU:1500  Metric:1
          RX packets:3425824 errors:0 dropped:0 overruns:0 frame:0
          TX packets:2140112 errors:0 dropped:0 overruns:0 carrier:0
          collisions:0 txqueuelen:100
          RX bytes:672077051 (640.9 MiB)  TX bytes:1358539190 (1.2 GiB)
          Interrupt:10 Base address:0xfc80

eth1      Link encap:Ethernet  HWaddr 00:80:C8:F9:F6:AB
          UP BROADCAST RUNNING MULTICAST  MTU:1500  Metric:1
          RX packets:2465422 errors:0 dropped:0 overruns:0 frame:0
          TX packets:2009695 errors:0 dropped:0 overruns:0 carrier:0
          collisions:3530 txqueuelen:100
          RX bytes:1778125589 (1.6 GiB)  TX bytes:260135783 (248.0 MiB)
          Interrupt:9 Base address:0xfc00

lo        Link encap:Local Loopback
          inet addr:127.0.0.1  Mask:255.0.0.0
          UP LOOPBACK RUNNING  MTU:16436  Metric:1
          RX packets:12627 errors:0 dropped:0 overruns:0 frame:0
          TX packets:12627 errors:0 dropped:0 overruns:0 carrier:0
          collisions:0 txqueuelen:0
          RX bytes:1252184 (1.1 MiB)  TX bytes:1252184 (1.1 MiB)

ppp0      Link encap:Point-to-Point Protocol
          inet addr:65.93.139.76  P-t-P:64.230.254.205 Mask:255.255.255.255
          UP POINTOPOINT RUNNING NOARP MULTICAST  MTU:1492  Metric:1
          RX packets:2405279 errors:0 dropped:0 overruns:0 frame:0
          TX packets:1950198 errors:0 dropped:0 overruns:0 carrier:0
          collisions:0 txqueuelen:3
          RX bytes:1721557756 (1.6 GiB)  TX bytes:215446634 (205.4 MiB)

user@hostname:~$
```

The output you see on your machine will almost certainly differ because we're on
different networks. In my case, I have four network interfaces: eth0, eth1, lo, and
ppp0. You will have a lo interface, too; the lo interface is the *loopback* interface,
which is a virtual network interface that different portions of the operating system
use to communicate with one another. Your loopback device always points back to
your computer. You should also have an eth0 (Ethernet device) or a ppp0 (point to
point protocol) interface, though you won't necessarily have an eth1 interface
(which is simply a second Ethernet interface). There's a lot of information in the
previous output, but you need to be interested only in the first two lines from each
paragraph at the moment; those lines describe the type and major configuration of
each interface.

Ethernet interfaces

The most common type of network interface in computers today is the *Ethernet* interface. Ethernet is an *encapsulation* mechanism and doesn't specify a particular form of wiring of electrical interface. Most Ethernet hardware, however, uses simple cabling called *unshielded twisted pair*, or UTP. In my last example, I had two Ethernet interfaces, and the lines from each that you're interested in are reproduced here:

```
eth0      Link encap:Ethernet   HWaddr 00:00:21:6D:4B:BE
          inet addr:192.168.1.1  Bcast:192.168.1.255  Mask:255.255.255.0

eth1      Link encap:Ethernet   HWaddr 00:80:C8:F9:F6:AB
```

Note that only one of my Ethernet interfaces has a line that starts with `inet addr`. That means only `eth0` can be used directly to communicate with remote machines because an Internet address is required for such communication. The first field in that line, `inet addr`, is the interface's own Internet protocol address. Whenever a packet is sent from my computer to another on that particular network interface, its *source address* will be the address listed there. In addition to the `inet addr`, there is also the `Bcast` field. This is the *broadcast address*, and any packets sent to this address will be received by every computer on the local network. Lastly, there's the `Mask` field, which defines the boundaries of the network. In my case, with a network mask of `255.255.255.0` and an IP address of `192.168.1.1`, the network that this particular Ethernet interface connects to is made up of computers with IP addresses between `192.168.1.0` and `192.168.1.255`.

Every Ethernet card has a *hardware address*, or more commonly, a *MAC address (media access control)*. In the previous output, this is denoted by `HWaddr`. The MAC address is only used on a local *Ethernet segment*. Whenever your communications are forwarded by a router or a gateway, the router takes over the packet and the router's own MAC address is used when speaking to the next router along the path towards the packet's final destination.

On a Debian GNU/Linux system, your Ethernet network interfaces are configured via `/etc/network/interfaces`. For more information, see the manpage at `man 5 interfaces`.

PPP interfaces

Point to Point Protocol (PPP) interfaces are usually used to communicate over a dial-up modem, but they are also used by many DSL Internet service providers. My PPP interface has the following configuration:

```
ppp0      Link encap:Point-to-Point Protocol
          inet addr:65.93.139.76  P-t-P:64.230.254.205 Mask:255.255.255.255
```

PPP interfaces are generally much simpler than Ethernet interfaces because PPP interfaces are almost always point-to-point. This means that there's no local network; all packets are simply sent to the other side of the link (the address in P-t-P here, and in most cases, your ISP) and processed there. My PPP interface's Internet address is `65.93.139.76`, and the computer on the other end of the link is `64.230.254.205`.

On Debian, PPP interfaces are configured in `/etc/ppp/peers/`. Each PPP connection that you've set up will have a separate file in that directory. PPP connection configurations are, as such, named entities. To start a given PPP connection, run `pon` *connectionname*. To end it, run `poff` *connectionname*. If your connection is through a DSL provider, during installation, the file `/etc/ppp/peers/dsl-provider` would have been created. Thus to initiate the connection to your ISP, you would run `pon dsl-provider`.

Summary

This chapter focused mainly on user and group management, but with an overall theme of good administration policy and security. Having read this chapter, you should have a comfortable, safe, and secure interface to use `root` privileges. You should be able to create and delete users and groups, and maintain the membership of groups. You should have enough of a working knowledge of networking and the way it works under Linux to understand a bit of how your computer is interacting with others on the Internet, and you will be ready to move on as I discuss other types of networking in more depth.

✦   ✦   ✦

Performing Backups

It may come as a surprise, but very few people begin backing up their workstation data regularly until they have lost something important. In enterprise computing environments, backing up servers is mandatory insurance that protects against a major financial blow to the institution in the case of data loss. In the desktop world, people seem to wait until they have been bitten before they consider backups as something important.

Don't trust your hardware to preserve your important documents, e-mail, projects, and data. No matter how long the warranty on your hard drive is for, it doesn't cover the data on the drive. Drives fail at any time, sometimes slowly corrupting sectors randomly over days before you realize what is happening, and sometimes refusing to spin-up the morning your project is due. Even the best drive manufacturers make bad batches of drives, and every drive will fail at some point in its life. I've had drives fail two months after they were purchased, and drives that are still spinning from 1992.

Even if drive technology advanced to a point where it was possible to have hard drives that never fail, this still does not protect you against fires, robbery, or the more threatening specter of accidental deletion. Backups are necessary to recover from loss, drive failure, human error, and security problems. Unfortunately, backups cannot save you from every problem. It is possible that you backed everything up last night, did some work today, and then a few hours later your drive failed. You will have most of your data saved, but not the work you did today.

Are you prepared for the worst? Its not just drives that fail; faulty wiring in your house could cause a fire, or a pipe could burst in your basement and flood everything, including your computer. Nobody should live in fear of these things, but everyone should be prepared and do what they can to protect their valuable data.

Backups for the workstation should be easy to do; if not, they discourage users from doing them and make it difficult to restore when the time comes. They should also be inexpensive. In this chapter, I attempt to demystify backing up your desktop so that you will do it before it is too late. Don't wait to lose your data before you think about backing it up.

Analyzing Backup Needs

Before deciding on a backup strategy, you need to figure out what you want out of a backup system. Here are some things to consider:

✦ How much history should be kept? Put another way, how far back do you need to be able to go to retrieve old data? If you need to keep a great deal of history, you may need backup capacities much larger than the actual storage capacity of the systems being backed up. If you keep little or no history, you run the risk of not detecting problems before the backups of the originals are overwritten.

✦ How often do you want to back up? Changes that occur since your most recent backup are at risk of being lost if a catastrophe should occur.

✦ How much data is being backed up?

✦ How frequently does the backed-up data change? If it changes frequently and you are keeping a history, more storage space will be required since the changes from one backup to the next will require more space to represent.

✦ How much can you afford to spend on backups? This is often a critical point that forces compromise on most of the others. At the same time, you should not be too cheap; the consequences of losing data due to insufficient backup methods could be far more expensive than putting a proper backup system in place.

✦ How many machines will you be backing up? If you are backing up several machines, you will probably want to consider a centralized backup solution such as Amanda.

✦ Are you willing to do some scripting to make your backups work as desired? If not, you will want to use a backup system such as Amanda that already has support for tasks that otherwise require scripting.

✦ Do you want to use compression? There's a discussion of compression in the next section.

✦ Will you be present while backups run? If not, some sort of automated scheduling system will be a must.

Designing Your Backup Strategy

Your backup strategy should reflect your answers to the preceding questions. Primarily, you will be concerned with: (1) what you need to back up, (2) where to put those backups, (3) when to do them, and (4) how to do them. I explore each of these four questions in depth to help guide you through making these decisions, avoiding some of the most common problems. When considering your answer to each of these questions, different factors will affect your decisions: the costs involved, the difficulty, the relative recoverability of your backups, and what you can afford to lose. Nobody wants to lose anything, but the cost and complexity of creating an environment that ensures absolutely no data loss can, in some cases, be more trouble than it's worth.

What to back up

It is very important to decide what you want and need to back up and how much space that data takes up. Knowing this will help you decide what kind of media requirements you have for performing backups; limiting what you back up to only the essentials saves you space, time, and hassle in completing your backups. However, when you cut out things that you don't think you will need, you are taking a risk that you may neglect to include important data, which you may discover only when you need to restore that particular file. Also, limiting what you back up can increase the hassle of recovery. If resources permit, you can back up everything so you don't have to concern yourself with potentially omitting valuable information, but even then there are some things you won't want to back up.

You should carefully consider what data you have that is not easily replaceable. All the data included with packages is easily replaceable on Debian, but the configuration changes you may have made, your home directory, e-mail, pictures, and documents are not. If you are concerned only with your personal data and local configurations to your system and have a limited amount of available backup space, then you may consider backing up only critical data: your /home partition, the /etc directory, the /var/backups directory, and any other location outside of these that you may have created. Critical to the Debian package subsystem (see the related sidebar) is the file /var/lib/dpkg/status. If you can, back up /var/lib/dpkg and everything underneath, but if this is too much data, be absolutely sure you get both /var/lib/dpkg/status and the corresponding status.old file if you want any hope of reconstructing your installed packages. If your e-mail is stored locally, and if you have created cron jobs, then be sure to also back up /var/mail and /var/spool/cron. You may just want all of /var/spool. Another directory that can have important data is /root. (It also might be completely empty, so there is no harm in backing it up.) If this is all you decide to back up, then you must be aware that you are limiting your ability to recover. If your drive fails, you will need to reinstall a base Debian system, and then recover over the top of your fresh installation your /etc directory and your /home directory, and then use your /var/backups directory to reconstruct your installed packages and your account information. If you are comfortable with this, you will use much less storage in your backup media than if you simply backed up everything you have, but you will encounter more work when the need for recovery rears its ugly head.

Backing Up Debian's Package Subsystem

Debian's core is the package subsystem. If the files representing what is installed on your system are lost, you will have a hard time installing new packages and removing or upgrading packages. This results in a serious mess. The most important information about packages you have installed on your system lies in the /var/lib/dpkg/status file; without this file you may be faced with the harsh reality of a complete reinstallation.

If you have backups of this file or one of the backups that are regularly created in /var/backups/dpkg.status, then there is hope. The latter file is created every day at 6:25 a.m. through the /etc/cron.daily/standard cron job, but beware because simply copying /var/backups/dpkg.status.0 to /var/lib/dpkg/status may not accurately represent your system if you installed or removed anything since that backup was made. If you copy this file into place, you will need to reinstall any package that you might have installed or removed since that backup to get the status file back into synchronization. If you've lost all of your /var partition, then restore your backup of /var/lib/dpkg/status rather than the status file from /var/backups because it will contain newer information. Debian automatically makes a backup of the status file each time a change is made to the package subsystem. If you don't have /var/lib/dpkg/status, see whether you have the backup, located in /var/lib/dpkg/status-old.

There are some clever, albeit unreliable, ways of reconstructing things if you don't have any of these status files, such as reinstalling every package that you find in /usr/share/doc. This is assuming you have a backup of that file, because Debian policy mandates that all installed packages create an entry in that directory, using the name of the package. You might also bootstrap a /var from a similar system. These methods cannot be covered here, due to length, but if you are stuck in such an unfortunate situation, you can find techniques online that people have used in such a scenario.

If you have enough available space on your backup media, you can simplify your decision and recovery procedure by backing up everything on your system. You can specify with your backup software to back up everything under /, but if you do this you will need to specify to the software to exclude certain key directories. The entire /proc directory should be excluded; this is a virtual interface to kernel data. If you back this up, you will back up /proc/kcore, which is the current in-memory snapshot of the kernel and can be quite large. You do not need to back up /tmp because this is flushed by the system each time you reboot. You should carefully exclude any secondary mount points, such as /mnt, because this may be where you have a CD-ROM or other removable media mounted, and you do not want to back that up. There are parts of /var that are very useful, and parts that are a waste of backup space. In /var, the Debian package state directories, mail, and crontabs are important, and some system configuration backups reside in /var/backups. Some people may find it valuable to back up log files in /var/log, but carefully consider this because these can be very large. You can pick specific log files if you need to. Databases tend to live in /var/lib; if you are running a database, such as MySQL, on your desktop system, you will need to take extra precautions in backing these up because you cannot simply copy the files; consult the appropriate documentation to determine the safe way to back these up.

Where to back up

Deciding where to back up your data is an important decision. Making this decision depends on how much data you will need to back up, how much money you are willing to spend, and how easy your backup mechanism is to use. An additional consideration for where to back up is if your media is removable or not. You should be able to easily store your backups in a different physical location from your originals. Although nobody wants to believe it could happen to them, you should plan for catastrophe; if your basement floods or your house catches fire, your backups are worthless if they were in the same location.

Most backup software will compress your backups and be intelligent about not making multiple copies of the same data. Additionally, what you will need to back up will change over time, making exact projected calculations of what you will need in the future akin to black magic. Unless you are doing full images of your partitions, having media that fit approximately three times what you will be backing up in its uncompressed size is a good rule of thumb. A reasonable rotation program should need approximately 1.5 to 3 times the space of the original data to be backed up. This depends a lot on the rate of change of your data and the length of time that you wish to keep older backups. Often your /home directory doesn't have a high rate of change, although it does experience occasional spikes, and that data is important enough to retain for long periods of time. Other data, such as logs in /var, have a very high rate of change and the data isn't very valuable beyond a day or two. In this case, you would want to budget three times the space of /home to hold data from one to three months or longer, while /var may only need 1.5 times more space and would go away after a couple days.

Once you have a rough idea of how much data you will need to back up, you can use that information to consider how the different media options will or will not fit your requirements. Don't forget that the amount of data you need to back up will grow over time, and you should plan accordingly.

Although most desktop users do not have large amounts of data to back up, the amount generally exceeds the CD-ROM limits. Even the 9 gigabytes you can store on new DVDs might be too small, and burning DVDs can be unreliable. That said, if your data will all fit on a single CD or DVD, either can be a good way to store your data.

Tape drives are another popular backup medium. However, most home desktop users do not have a tape drive system and, due to the cost, are unlikely to purchase one for backup.

For the price (between $100 and $300), speed, compatibility, and ease of use, an externally attached hard drive is one of the most attractive options available for desktop backup media. Easily detached and put in another location, a hard drive is probably the best solution for encouraging regular data backups. However, hard drives have problems as much as other media; for a full discussion of the benefits and problems of hard drives, see the "Disk drives" section later in this chapter.

There are many different choices available for where to put your backups, and more are becoming available every year. Because not everyone will find the external drive solution to be the best for them, this chapter covers the different removable media options and discusses their relative benefits and shortcomings as backup media in terms of cost, long-term reliability, and ease of use.

CD-RW

In recent years it has become common for computers to come standard with a CD burner. There are two types of CD burners: CD-R (Recordable) and CD-RW (Rewritable). Most systems come with CD-RW drives, and the CD-R has mostly been phased out. The time it takes to burn a full 650 megabytes onto a CD can be between 9 and 40 minutes, depending on the CD's rating. Burning CDs can be prone to error, causing you to have to throw away ruined media. The discs can hold up to 650 or 700 megabytes, and the media are available at very low costs.

Caution

If you buy a new machine that has a CD burner included, it will probably be a CD-RW, but it would be wise to make sure it is a CD-RW and not a CD-R. You can burn data onto CD-R media only one time; they are not re-recordable as CD-RWs are. This can be a problem with backups because you will go through media very quickly. CD-R drives and their media are cheaper than CD-RWs, but for a reason. Be sure that you are getting a drive (and media) that will let you use it over and over, rather than only once.

CD-RW drives allow you to write over previous data approximately 1,000 times, which is when their material structure begins to degrade. CD-RW media are rated for a specific write speed; this value represents the upper limit, even if your drive is rated to go faster.

CD-RW drives read faster than they write. Because they have the rewrite capability, they also write faster than they rewrite. The x ratings for CD-RW drives are rated for how fast they can perform each operation; the standard way of writing these values is write/rewrite/read, so if your drive is rated as 8x/2x/32x it can write at 8x, rewrite at 2x, and read at 32x. The x indicates the multiplying factor over the original first-generation CD-ROM drives. For CD drives, both writable and rewritable, the original transfer rate is 150 kilobytes per second; this means that a 8x/2x/32x drive writes at 1.2 megabytes per second, rewrites at .300 megabytes per second, and reads at 4.8 megabytes per second. This is the maximum rated speed of the drive; to achieve those speeds you will need to have the appropriately rated CD media. If your drive says it can write at 52x, you will need a 52x-rated CD to get anywhere near that speed. Even with the appropriate media, your transfer rate may never reach the maximum rating. CD-RW drives start writing slower and incrementally increase their speed until they are writing at full speed, so the drive does not write at the maximum speed during the entire process.

CD-R discs can be read in most ordinary CD drives; however, only drives with MultiRead capability can read CD-RW media. This is important if you plan on reading your burned CD on a different reader.

To write to CD burners, special software is required, in addition to properly configured kernel modules. The most common software used to burn CDs is mkisofs combined with cdrecord, k3b, arson, and eroaster.

CDs are sensitive to light and can degrade quickly if left in the sun. Even without sunlight, you should not trust that your CDs are indestructible or will last forever. Remember to replace frequently written-to CDs because there is a limit to the number of times that each can be written to.

DVD

DVDs are very similar to CDs, except that they hold considerably more data. DVD technology is more confusing than CD technology, due to industry fighting over standards. This has resulted in a number of incompatibility issues due to the four different types of writable DVDs: DVD-R, DVD-RW, DVD-RAM, and DVD+RW. Within each of these formats are different generations, which indicate what type of media they can use and what other types they can read and write to. Although the cost of DVD writers is more than their CD counterparts, the price is coming down quickly, and considered by price per megabyte, DVD media is cheaper than CD.

The incompatibility issues around writable DVDs settled on multiformat drives, which were developed to solve this problem. Multiformat DVD drives are able to handle all the different formats and remove the headache of needing to know which formats your drive can handle.

The speed of burning DVD media is not as fast as CD burning yet. Writing to DVD-RAM media is much slower, at roughly 300 to 475KB/s; write speed on a CD-RW is approximately 730KB/s. To back up approximately 15 gigabytes of data on a DVD-RAM would take approximately an hour and would require you to change the media at least once, which means your backups cannot go unattended. To back up the same amount on a CD-RW would take about half as long, but it would require you to insert approximately 22 blank CDs.

Unlike CD-RW media, DVD-RAM discs can be rewritten up to 100,000 times. Double-sided discs are in sealed cartridges, called Type 1, and must be manually flipped to use both sides. The single-sided media come in removable Type 2 cartridges, also known as *caddies*, or as bare discs. The single-sided bare discs can be read only by later-model DVD-ROM drives, and double-sided discs can be used only in DVD-RAM drives due to the cartridge.

Although DVDs can hold up to 9 gigabytes of data, this may be too small to put all your backup data on one disc. For incremental backups, DVDs are too much hassle; however, if your backup requirements are not that large, DVDs are great for periodic archival, for example once-a-month off-site backups. As of this writing, 9-gigabyte dual-layer media is not on the market yet, although it is expected soon. The 9-gigabyte double-sided DVD-RAM exists, but it is also relatively new.

As with CDs, DVDs are sensitive to light, so they should be kept away from direct sunlight. As with burning CDs, burning DVDs can be prone to failure, which can result in wasted media. The long-term viability of this media is uncertain, and you should not trust that a DVD backup you make will be readable 10 years from now. Remember to replace frequently used writable DVDs because there is a limit to how often they can be written to.

Disk drives

Disk drives are much cheaper than tape drives, and as the price per megabyte continues to drop, separate disk drives are quickly becoming the preferred media of choice for backups. The capacity of the media, the ease with which it can be used and managed, and its speed all contribute to making disks an attractive option.

With separate disk drives, you eliminate the hassle of swapping tapes or loading more CD-Rs and waiting. Instead, with a backup drive you can do much more frequent snapshots of your entire system without the deterrent of having to mess with media.

Getting a separate drive for your backups can mean either getting another internal drive for your system, using an externally attached FireWire or USB drive that can be easily removed, or having a separate disk drive on a completely separate machine, which is accessible over a network. An internal drive gives you the backup security only from accidental file deletion or your main drive failing. While these are protections, an easily detached drive or one available in another machine located elsewhere provides for a greater level of data security that an internal drive cannot. With an externally attached drive that is easily removable, such as a FireWire drive, you will need to be careful to detach it and store it somewhere safe regularly. For example, you might bring it to work with you.

Disk drives have disadvantages over other media. For one thing, you must resist the urge to use that extra storage for things other than your backups. Also, it is much harder to use disk drives than other media for archival purposes. Many companies need data archives for record keeping, and though this isn't as frequent a requirement in a desktop scenario, this might be a consideration if you are in need of longer term records of your data. Some users argue that you can't do incremental backups with disk drives without a high cost, but if you use software that is intelligent about its usage of space, through using hard links, you can achieve this. This becomes problematic if you have a database that changes often, but this is not a common problem on a desktop machine.

As with other media, hard drives can fail, and external drives that you frequently move from one place to another are at a higher risk of being dropped. Optical media tends to be more resistant to shocks (although this is not true of DLT tapes), and you can wipe off liquid from a CD, but you can only panic when you drown your hard drive in coffee. As with other media, you should give consideration to how long you might use your backup drive for backups before it might fail. If you have been making incremental backups for years on a backup drive and then it fails, it may not seem so bad because it is only backups, but if archives over time matter for your data, you no longer have that older data.

Tape drives

Tape drives are a popular way to back up data. Tape drives themselves can cost anywhere from around $1,000 (or even less) to many times that, depending on their features. However, the tapes themselves are cheap — usually a fraction of the cost of the hard disks they're backing up. Because tapes are popular and complex, they're treated with more detail in this section than the other forms of media, and some tricks with using tapes are explained.

Tapes are a sequential medium. That means that you have to read them in order. Disks and CDs, on the other hand, are *random access*, which means that you can easily jump around and read whatever data you like. While many modern tape drives can take you to a specific place on the tape, this operation can take minutes or even hours. The same operation on a disk takes a tiny fraction of a second.

That may sound bad, but for backups, it's not really an issue. Most Linux backup programs will generate a long stream of bytes anyway, and tape drives work well with that sort of program.

Because tapes are cheap, many people who use tape backups have a tape rotation. For instance, let's say you have 10 tapes on hand and you run backups 5 nights a week. You would switch tapes before each night's backup runs, always putting in the oldest tape. In that way, you preserve two weeks worth of history. This is a nice benefit; if you don't notice a problem right away, you can still restore files from old backups as long as you catch the problem within two weeks.

Some people that need to store large volumes of data use devices known as robotic changers. With a robotic changer, you can supply your drive with many tapes. As the backups run, the backup software can have the drive automatically cycle between these tapes as necessary. This is a good solution if your backups can't fit on a single tape.

There are many different types of tape technology available. Different drives may require different types of tape. You can't assume that a tape purchased for one drive can be read on another unless you have verified they can read the same media.

Tapes also have a limited life span. Tapes that are used frequently can wear out. It's important to carefully watch backup logs and note any errors. You should also periodically test your tapes or simply discard old ones to help prevent media errors.

SCSI drives

Most tape drives in use today are SCSI (pronounced *skuzzy*) drives. If your computer does not already have a SCSI controller compatible with your chosen drive, you'll need to purchase one. Your tape drive manufacturer can help you identify the type of controller you need. A general rule of thumb is that, if you can't find out how to plug the tape drive into your computer, you probably need a SCSI controller.

Linux has a generic SCSI tape driver that works with almost all SCSI drives out of the box. Certain drives may use a proprietary protocol or require other drivers, but these are not the norm. SCSI controller cards are also well supported in Debian; most controllers made by Adaptec, BusLogic, and Symbios/NCR/LSI are fully compatible with Linux. Even if your controller doesn't list one of those names, chances are it is actually made by one of those companies.

In the past, other methods of interfacing with tape drives were common. These methods included IDE tape drives, parallel port drives, and drives that communicated using the floppy disk controller. While some of these drives are still supported by Linux, they are rare today. Therefore, this chapter focuses on SCSI drives. Certain commands may not apply if you are not using SCSI drives, but most of the concepts will be the same regardless of the type of drive you use.

Also, most drives come with a cleaning cartridge and a recommended cleaning schedule. Make sure you follow the manufacturer's recommendations. This will help preserve the life of both your drive and your tapes.

On-tape layout

A data tape, at its most simple, stores a continuous stream of bytes. However, most modern tapes are capable of storing multiple files. While this sounds similar to files you might store on a disk, there are some important differences. Files on a tape do not have a name, only a sequence. You can refer to the "first file" or "two files after the current one," but not `letter.txt` or `program.c`. Once written, files on a tape cannot be expanded without corrupting data written after them on the tape. They also usually cannot be shrunk without corrupting the file sequence on the tape. If hardware compression is in use, files cannot be reliably modified at all. But these are not really serious problems for backups; most users simply overwrite an entire tape each time a new backup is written to it.

When the tape device is opened for writing, the tape drive will simply copy bytes to tape. When the device is closed, the tape drive writes a special end-of-file (EOF) marker to tape. This marker serves two purposes: First, when the tape is later read back, the drive can signal the operating system that the end of a file has been reached. Second, it makes it possible to quickly wind the tape past an entire file.

Remember that a file on a tape is a specific stream of bytes. Tape backup programs will often store an entire disk's contents in a single file on a tape, and on restore, that tape file is restored into its component disk files.

Tape operations

Modern tape drives can perform a variety of operations, which are detailed in the following list. Note that some older or less-capable drives may not be able to perform all of these tasks:

- ✦ **Write data:** A drive can write out a sequence of bytes to a tape. When the write operation is complete, an EOF marker will be written to the tape.

- ✦ **Read data:** A drive can read a sequence of bytes from a tape. When the physical end of the tape is reached or an EOF marker is encountered, the operating system will be informed that the end of a file has been reached.

- ✦ **Rewind:** This will cause the tape to be rewound to the very beginning.

- ✦ **Eject:** An eject operation will cause the tape to be physically ejected from the drive. On many drives, an eject request will cause a rewind to occur before the tape is actually ejected.

- ✦ **Forward space:** This will run the tape forward, stopping at the next EOF marker.

- ✦ **Backward space:** This will run the tape backward, stopping at the next EOF marker. This can be used to return to the start of the current file.

✦ **Seek:** Some tape drives are capable of winding the tape to a specific location, even if it occurs within a file. The location is usually given as a block number.

✦ **Tell:** On tape drives capable of seeking, one can also ask about the current position of the tape.

✦ **Compression toggle:** Tape drives can have hardware compression adjusted.

✦ **Media load/unload:** Robotic tape units can support commands to move tapes between the drive and storage bays, or, in some cases, between storage bays directly. Depending on the capabilities of a robot, you may also be able to specify a specific storage location, or you may simply have to use the next tape in the lineup.

Tape device names

There are two device entries under /dev for each tape drive on your system. One entry (/dev/st) represents an automatic rewinding device. When you access a tape drive through the automatic rewinding device, the tape will automatically rewind to the beginning after your read or write operation is complete. The second entry (/dev/nst) is the nonrewinding device, which performs no rewinding automatically.

Tape devices are numbered starting with zero. Thus, the first drive on your system would have the names /dev/st0 (rewinding) and /dev/nst0 (nonrewinding). The second drive would be called /dev/st1 (rewinding) and /dev/nst1 (nonrewinding).

I usually recommend the use of the nonrewinding device. Nasty surprises can sometimes occur when the autorewinding devices rewind a tape at an unexpected time. They also make it impossible to work with more than one file on a tape.

Tape manipulation

The mt (magnetic tape) command lets you control your tape drives in Linux. It is included as part of the cpio package, so you would use apt-get install cpio to install it if it's not already available on your system. The mt command performs virtually all of the tape operations I listed above, aside from actually reading or writing data. You will normally want to run mt as root, though you can access most commands as other users if the permissions on the devices are set appropriately.

When running mt, you should always specify your device on the command line with the -f parameter. Thus, if you want to rewind your tape, you could say:

 # mt -f /dev/nst0 rewind

In this example, rewind is an mt operation. There are several different operations. Some of them also take a count, which has a different meaning depending on the operation. Table 6-1 summarizes the most common mt operations.

Table 6-1
Common mt Operations

Operation	Count	Description
asf	File number to seek to, 1 or more	Absolute space to the beginning of the file number given by the count. This command is the logical equivalent of a rewind followed by an fsf with the given count.
bsf	Number of files to skip, 1 or more	Backward space to the beginning of a previous file.
eof	Number of marks to write, 1 or more	Writes an end of file marker at the current position. If the count is greater than 1, multiple markers will be written. When multiple markers are read back, the effect will be empty files.
eom	N/A	Position the tape at the end of media, immediately after the last recorded data.
datcompression	If 0, disable hardware compression. If 1, print current compression status. If any other value, enable compression.	Enable, disable, or inquire about hardware compression as listed with the count. Despite its name, this command often can work with non-DAT drives.
fsf	Number of files to skip, 1 or more	Forward space to the beginning of tape files. A count of 1 means to go to the start of the next file.
offline	N/A	Rewind and eject the tape.
rewind	N/A	Position the tape at the beginning.
seek	Block number	Position the tape at the absolute block number given by count, winding backwards or forwards as necessary.
status	N/A	Display information about the drive's status.
tell	N/A	Display the absolute block number for the current tape location. Useful for a subsequent call to seek.

Reading and writing data

To read or write data to the tape, you simply direct input or output for a program to the tape's device. For instance, if you are using `tar` (see the following section), you could back up your `/etc` directory with the commands:

```
# mt -f /dev/nst0 rewind
# tar -cvf /dev/nst0 /etc
```

To restore from the tape, you would rewind it with:

```
# mt -f /dev/nst0 rewind
```

and then use:

```
# tar -xvf /dev/nst0
```

Note that some tape drives require data to be read or written in blocks of a specific size. Programs such as `tar` will do this for you. However, some programs cannot do this automatically. For those programs, you can use `dd` to reblock the data to the correct size for the drive. In general, you will see this problem only if you try to use programs not specifically designed for use with backups.

When to back up

Deciding when and how frequently to do your backups is important. Depending on your backup media, you may need to be present when you do backups to put in new media because the data won't all fit on one tape, CD, or DVD. You may also not want to be around when your backups happen because they can slow your machine down as they crawl through your system looking for changed or new data, compress that data, and then send it to your backup media. Depending on the relative power of your machine, the amount of data you will be backing up, and how you will be backing up that data, your machine may be otherwise unusable during the backup window.

At any time you may achieve a significant milestone in your work, and it would be catastrophic if you were to lose your data at that point. This is why you save frequently, and it's useful to have programs like OpenOffice that perform autosaves. You should always be able to initiate a backup of your data at any point if you feel it is necessary. After how many e-mails or how much time will you be uncomfortable if you were to lose everything that you've done since your last backup? Ask yourself whether you can manage if you lose an hour of data at any point? What about a day, or a week? Where do you become uncomfortable? Use this question to help guide you in deciding how frequently you need to make backups.

Testing your backup

Your backups should not be trusted if you never test them. Ideally, you should verify every backup because an unverified backup is potentially useless. If you are putting the time and money into making and keeping backups, you should make sure that they are usable. If you only occasionally verify your backups, you must be comfortable with the fact that the unverified backups could be useless. Verifying your backups means confirming that files have been backed up to your backup media properly and that you can restore them; it also means verifying that you are backing up important files and not backing up useless data.

To verify your backups, you should make sure that you can restore the files you have backed up. It's nice to see that your backup software lists your important files as being backed up, but it might not have been able to actually back up anything more than the filename because of permissions. Test restoring files before you need to; fix the problems before they hurt you. Verifying the ability of the restoration procedure to restore the files with the original ownership, permissions, and timestamps may also be critical to you, so you should test this.

You should also occasionally verify that the files you are backing up are the files that you should be backing up. Because people's data usage patterns change, what is important one week may change significantly the next. If you reorganize where you put your files or add another drive for your MP3s, you may not remember that you need to add these new locations to your backup. You should review these changes through verifying what you are backing up.

The converse is also true; you should look for things that you are backing up that you don't need. You can save valuable backup media space if you find a giant log file that you don't need to save, or that you happen to be backing up /proc/kcore. (A snapshot of your system memory at the time of backup is pretty worthless and a large waste of space.)

All backup media has a shelf life. When verifying your backups and restores, consider how long you have been using that particular piece of media for recording backups. Rewritable optical media can be written to only a finite number of times before the structure of the media breaks down; magnetic media can only be spun and unspun, fast-forwarded, rewound, and written to so many times before they too can fail. As with everything with moving parts, anticipate and prevent failures by changing your media periodically.

Backup Fundamentals

Evaluating backup software can be difficult; there's a lot to choose from. Knowledge and familiarity of some important concepts will help make evaluating the different pieces of software much easier and will ultimately lead to a better decision.

Compression

Compression is a way to make data more compact. It typically has two phases. The compression phase reads normal data and generates the compressed output. The decompression phase reads the compressed output and generates the normal data.

Compression is frequently used as part of a backup system to reduce the storage requirements on the backup device. Well-known compression programs on a Debian system include gzip and bzip2. Both are highly regarded and trusted.

When working with backups, which can be so critical in an emergency, it's important to consider what can happen when the backup medium develops a physical problem. CDs can get scratched, tapes can get worn spots, and hard disks can develop bad sectors. These are the most common problems to afflict backup media, and usually render only a small part of the media unreadable.

Some compression techniques, such as the one used in gzip, rely on earlier parts of a file to be able to access later parts when decompressing. For instance, if you have a 600MB file with 2K corrupted 10MB into the file, the remaining 590MB will be unreadable. For this reason, you should try to avoid gzip for backups when possible.

The bzip2 program resets itself every 900K. In this example, the 2K of corruption would result in a total unreadable area of approximately 1MB. However, after that, the data could be read unharmed. Thus, bzip2 is more robust in the face of physical media problems and is usually preferred to gzip for that reason. The bzip2 program is not installed by default in Debian; you'll need to run `apt-get install bzip2` to install it on your system.

Many tape drives have the ability to perform transparent compression in hardware. These drives compress data as it's being sent to them; the operating system and backup software do not even have to be aware that this is happening. They typically have a much smaller window than even bzip2, and thus are very resilient in the face of media problems. However, they also do not get very good levels of compression compared to a program like bzip2. Also, some tape backup programs can become confused, especially if they rely on modifying files at particular locations on the tape. Thus, if possible, it's usually best to use a program such as bzip2 for your tape compression rather than your drive's built-in compression support.

 Caution   Using both the tape drive's built-in support and a software compression tool such as gzip or bzip2 at the same time can actually reduce the efficiency of the drive.

Incremental backups

People that perform regular backups (mainly system administrators), perhaps on a daily basis, often don't need to back up every file every day. For instance, if you back up the entire system to tape on Monday and you save that tape, on Tuesday you only back up the things that have changed since Monday. Such a backup is called an *incremental backup*. To restore from this sort of backup, you would need two tapes: Monday's full backup and Tuesday's incremental backup. It's important to remember to periodically run full backups since recovery from a disaster will require one (and all the incrementals since that full backup).

Some setups take this a step farther and have backup levels. A *level 0 backup* is a full backup. A *level 1 backup* is the same as an incremental backup in the example above, storing only the files that have changed since the most recent level 0 backup. A *level 2 backup* will store only the files that have changed since the most recent level 1 backup, and so on. If you need to perform regular backups, it's a good idea to have a set schedule. For instance, a full backup happens Monday, and incrementals each working day after that. This will help you know when to change tapes and exactly what tapes are required to perform a full restore. Programs such as Amanda (discussed later in this chapter) will schedule your backups for you to optimize tape usage.

Network backups

Many people have multiple machines that need to be backed up. While it would be possible to back up all of these machines individually, it often makes sense to establish some sort of centralized backup system that can back up multiple machines at once. The Amanda system, described later in this chapter, provides all the tools to accomplish this. However, with some scripting, you can also do that with many of the other techniques described here.

There are some issues to consider with network backups. First, if you are backing up a large number of machines at the same time, it is possible that all the traffic could flood your network. You'll want to make sure to schedule things during times of low network usage or make sure your network is capable of handling the load. Amanda has built-in network load limiting. Also, it's important to keep an eye on backup results. Machines may be powered down or network cables unplugged, which could prevent backups from occurring.

Backing up in-use files

A common problem for users of backup technologies of all types revolves around files that are in use at the time the backup runs. If applications are actively writing to files while the backup software is reading them, inconsistent backups could be generated. In many cases, this does not pose a huge problem, since files are not likely to be in use in the first place, and the set of in-use files likely varies from day to day.

However, with some applications, it's almost impossible to obtain backups of data files that are in use. The most common application to cause this problem is an SQL database server. Most SQL servers include commands that will generate a stable backup from a given point in time. Alternatively, a technology such as LVM can generate a stable snapshot of an entire filesystem, which can then be backed up.

Backup Software

There is an unbelievable array of backup software available. Each program does different tasks in different ways for different purposes. Most backup software is written for backing up many machines, generally servers, and there is not much available to Debian that is tailored specifically to the desktop user. Backup software needs to be easy to use for the average desktop user or it won't be used at all. Unfortunately, there is no perfect backup software, and the variety of options available doesn't necessarily mean convenience or easy use.

In this chapter, I present the backup software programs tar, rsync, rdiff-backup, Amanda, rsnapshot, backuppc and Unison, going over their features and benefits, and how to install, configure, and use them. At the end of the chapter, I mention some other options if none of these fits your needs.

Using tar

One of the most well-known backup programs is tar. It can be used as a component of a larger backup system (Amanda, discussed later in this chapter, is one such system). It can also be used as a backup program on its own and is installed by default on every Debian system.

At its most basic level, tar is a program that generates a stream of bytes representing the files and directories on a disk, or generates files and directories from that stream of bytes. The stream of bytes it works with can be stored on disk, tape, CD-R, or just about any other medium. It is frequently compressed when stored, and you've probably seen files like that already: tar.gz files contain a tar stream compressed with gzip, and tar.bz2 files contain a tar stream compressed with bzip2.

tar can back up directly to a tape. Or since it can create a file, that file can be stored on a CD, hard disk, or other device.

Some people compare tar to a program like ZIP. That is not an accurate comparison. Both tar and ZIP are *archivers*; that is, they both aggregate many files into a single file. However, ZIP is also a compressor, while tar is not. On the other hand, tar can be streamed to devices such as tapes, while ZIP cannot. (ZIP requires random access to its output file.) Although tar doesn't do compression itself, it is, of course, possible to compress tar's output stream or file using various compression tools. This is so frequently used that GNU tar, the version of tar used in Debian, includes options to help do this for you.

Running tar

`tar` is operated via a variety of command-line switches. They can be combined, so instead of saying `tar -c -v -S -p -f /dev/nst0 /etc`, you can say `tar -cvSpf /dev/nst0 /etc`. Note that in this case, `/dev/nst0` is a parameter to `-f`, so saying `tar -cvSfp /dev/nst0 /etc` would not generate the result you desire.

`tar` has three commonly used operation modes: create, extract, and list. The create mode is used to create a new archive, putting files from disk into the archive. The extract mode reads an archive and extracts files from it. Finally, the list mode simply displays information about the files. The create mode is selected with `-c`, the extract mode with `-x`, and the list mode with `-t`. Whenever you run `tar`, you must always specify exactly one operation mode.

You can also specify files or directories to operate on, and these typically go at the end of the command line. If you are using create mode, you must specify at least one file or directory. (`tar` will not create an empty archive.) If are using extract or list mode, the file/directory list is optional. If not specified, these modes operate on every entry in the archive. If you do specify one or more files/directories, `tar` will operate on only those archive entries.

In addition to the mode selectors, `tar` supports a wide variety of features. Table 6-2 is a summary of the ones most commonly used for backups. Debian's `tar` supports even more; you can consult the tar(1) manpage for all the esoteric options.

Table 6-2
Common tar Options

Option	Description
`-C directory`	Change to the specified directory prior to performing any actions.
`-f filename`	Read or write (depending on the mode) from the specified filename. If `-f` is not specified, will read or write using standard input or standard output.
`-g filename`	Create incremental backup using the specified filename to determine differences since the last run.
`-j`	In create mode, compress the output stream using bzip2. In extract or list mode, decompress the input stream using bunzip2.
`-k`	When extracting, do not overwrite files that already exist. Not valid in other modes.
`-l`	Do not traverse onto filesystems other than the starting filesystem. Valid only in create mode.
`-p`	Preserve permissions as much as possible when creating or extracting an archive.

Continued

Table 6-2 *(continued)*	
Option	**Description**
-S	Enable code to reduce the output size of sparse files when creating, and to attempt to re-create sparse files when extracting.
-v	Be verbose; display information about what file is being processed in create or extract mode, or show more details about each file in list mode.
-z	In create mode, compress the output stream using gzip. In extract or list mode, decompress the input stream using gunzip.

Backing up with tar

tar enables you to back up to various media: tape, files, CD, or DVD.

✦ **Backing up to tape:** Since tar can generate a stream of data, backing up to tape is a simple operation. The following example would back up /usr and /var, preserving permissions, showing status updates as it goes along:

```
tar -cvSpf /dev/nst0 /usr /var
```

To restore from that backup, you could use this:

```
tar -xvSpf /dev/nst0
```

✦ **Backing up to a file:** tar can, of course, generate a file in much the same way as it would back up to tape. If you simply substitute a valid filename for /dev/nst0, tar will access that file instead of the tape device. People generating a file frequently use -z or -j to compress the output stream.

✦ **Backing up to a CD or DVD:** While most people do not use tar to generate backups to a CD or DVD, it is certainly possible. You may wish to do that if you want to use tar's incremental backup features. Or you might wish to take advantage of tar's ability to back up just about every attribute of each file and every file type. While the most common way to back up a tar file on CD is by burning that file to a CD with an intermediary program, you can also burn your tar output to the CD directly. Here's an example:

```
# tar -cvSpf - /usr /var | cdrecord -v dev=0,0,0 -pad
```

The resulting CD-R or DVD-R cannot be mounted and read as a usual filesystem. However, you can extract files from its tar image in the same way you would for a tape. Assuming your CD burner is at /dev/hdc, your command would be:

```
# tar -xvSpf - /dev/hdc
```

Backing up to a hard drive with rsync

One way to perform backups is by using a hard drive to store your files. You can use `rsync` to accomplish that. The `rsync` program is used to copy entire directory trees over a network. It features a way to detect which files or portions of files have changed and transfer only the changed portions. This means that less network bandwidth is used compared to other network-based backup options, and in most cases, backups finish faster. You will need to run `apt-get install rsync` before you can use `rsync`. Note that both your client and server machines will need to have `rsync` installed, which means you'll need to install it on the remote server as well, or have the administrator of that machine do it for you.

By itself, `rsync` does not provide support for keeping track of history. If you need those features, you should instead consult `rdiff-backup`.

Before starting with `rsync`, you need to have a way to be able to run `rsync` on the remote system. Many people use `ssh` for that, since `ssh` will provide encryption for the connection as well. That permits backups over the Internet or other insecure networks.

Chapter 18 on remote access goes into detail on SSH: what it is and how it is used. It provides useful background for anyone using `rsync` over SSH.

Here's a command you can run to copy a local directory tree to a remote host:

```
# rsync -avz -e ssh --delete /usr remote.example.com:/bak/usr
```

The `--delete` flag can destroy files if not properly used.

This will copy `/usr`, preserving as much information as possible, to `/bak/usr` on the remote system. If any files exist in `/bak/usr` on the remote that do not exist in `/usr` on the local machine, they will be deleted. That's important, since otherwise your backup would contain files that may have been deleted remotely.

To restore from an `rsync` backup, you can simply copy the file using normal methods. Alternatively, you can reverse the direction of the `rsync` by reversing the last two parameters on the command line.

Using rdiff-backup

Like `rsync`, `rdiff-backup` is a tool for performing backups to a hard disk. It can run on the local machine or over a network. And it has mechanisms to detect what portions of files have changed, transmitting only the changes.

Unlike `rsync`, `rdiff-backup` maintains a history of your files. With this history, you can retrieve a file's or directory's contents as of a specific date. In a sense, you are simulating what you would get from incremental backups using a tape system.

The `rdiff-backup` program stores the current versions of files in a directly accessible tree, similar to `rsync`. So if at any time you want to retrieve a file as it existed as of the most recent backup, you can just copy it out of the `rdiff-backup` storage area like any other file.

However, `rdiff-backup` extends this scheme to include history. When a file changes, `rdiff-backup` stores enough information to be able to reconstruct the old file. It does this in a space-efficient way, again noting only the changes to the file. Using `rdiff-backup` commands, you can retrieve a file, directory, or entire system as of a specific date.

The `rdiff-backup` program also provides commands to remove old history from your backup storage area to save space.

Backing up files with rdiff-backup

Before using `rdiff-backup`, you'll need to install it on both your client and server machines. You can do that with `apt-get install rdiff-backup`.

To back up with `rdiff-backup`, you first need to create a backup storage area. That's a simple directory, so a command such as `mkdir /bak` can do the job for you.

Now, you just run `rdiff-backup`. Here's a sample invocation: I've created a `data` directory containing three files — `12345`, `abcd`, and `efgh`. When run with `-v5`, `rdiff-backup` becomes fairly verbose and displays the name of each file as it's being processed. If you want quieter output, you can omit the `-v5`.

```
$ rdiff-backup -v5 data /mnt/bak/data
--------------------------------------------------------------
--
Detected abilities for source (read only) file system:
  Access control lists                      Off
  Extended attributes                       Off
  Mac OS X style resource forks             Off
  Mac OS X Finder information               Off
--------------------------------------------------------------
--
Warning: ownership cannot be changed on filesystem at
/mnt/bak/data/rdiff-backup-data
--------------------------------------------------------------
--
Detected abilities for destination (read/write) file system:
  Characters needing quoting                     ''
```

```
Ownership changing                               Off
Hard linking                                     On
fsync() directories                              On
Directory inc permissions                        On
Access control lists                             Off
Extended attributes                              Off
Mac OS X style resource forks                    Off
Mac OS X Finder information                      Off
------------------------------------------------------------
--
Starting mirror data to /mnt/bak/data
Processing changed file .
Processing changed file 12345
Processing changed file abcd
Processing changed file efgh
```

First, `rdiff-backup` displays information about the filesystems being backed up and used for storage. In my system, I do not use access control lists or extended attributes, so `rdiff-backup` notes that there is no need to back these up. Also, this is not a Mac, so it will not be backing up Mac metadata.

Then, since I'm not running as root, `rdiff-backup` notices that it cannot change ownership values on the files it creates in the destination filesystem. This will not prevent you from obtaining a full restore later; `rdiff-backup` will simply store this information in a special file that it can use later.

Next, the output tells you about the abilities of the destination filesystem. Some filesystems supported by Linux do not fully support all features of normal Linux filesystems. One popular example is `vfat`, the filesystem used on many Windows installations. This isn't a fatal problem for `rdiff-backup`; it again can work around this by storing information in special files. In this case, the destination filesystem is the same as the source, and it supports everything except ownership changing (which it would support if `rdiff-backup` were run as root).

Finally, `rdiff-backup` performs the actual backup itself. Any file that is new or modified shows up as `changed`.

Now, let's say I modified the file `data/abcd`. When I run `rdiff-backup` again, it looks like this:

```
$ rdiff-backup -v5 data /mnt/bak/data
...
Starting increment operation data to /mnt/bak/data
Processing changed file .
Incrementing mirror file /mnt/bak/data
Processing changed file abcd
Incrementing mirror file /mnt/bak/data/abcd
```

I've left out all the startup information here since it's the same as last time. This time, only one `changed` file was processed: `abcd`. The lines noting a mirror file being incremented are `rdiff-backup` saving the history for the file or directory.

You can run `rdiff-backup` in this manner as often as you'd like. It will note the time you run each backup for later restores.

Restoring files with rdiff-backup

You can easily restore the latest backup using `rdiff-backup -r`. Here's an example:

```
$ rdiff-backup -r now -v5 bak restoredir
...
Starting restore of bak to restoredir as it was as of Sat Jul
17 00:00:33 2004.
Processing changed file .
Processing changed file 12345
Processing changed file abcd
Processing changed file efgh
Restore finished
```

This command creates a directory named `restoredir` containing a restored version of the latest backup in `bak`. You can specify older backups, too. For instance, `-r 2D` would restore as of two days ago. You can also use m, h, D, W, M, and Y to refer to minutes, hours, days, weeks, months, and years, respectively. They can also be combined; 1M2D would mean one month and two days ago. You can also specify a date in the format MM/DD/YYYY to restore as of a specific date. `rdiff-backup` also supports other formats; see its manpage for more details.

Removing old history with rdiff-backup

If you have been running `rdiff-backup` for quite a while, you'll notice that your backup area may begin to consume a large amount of disk space. That's because `rdiff-backup` never deletes old data unless you explicitly tell it to. So in most cases, you'll periodically want to tell it to remove old data. To do that, you use `--remove-older-than`. This option operates on a backup area and takes a date or time in the format specified earlier. Here's an example:

```
$ rdiff-backup -v5 --remove-older-than 1m bak
...
Deleting increment(s) before Sat Jul 17 00:05:26 2004
Deleting increment at time:
Fri Jul 16 23:51:22 2004
...
```

`rdiff-backup` will then proceed to list the files it's deleting. In this case, it found one backup more than one minute old and proceeded to remove the old data corresponding to that session.

Remote usage with rdiff-backup

Like `rsync`, `rdiff-backup` can work over a network. Anywhere that you can specify a path on the local machine, you can also specify a path on a remote machine. To do that, simply add the remote machine name and two colons before the path. Thus, to back up /usr on `somehost`, you could run:

```
rdiff-backup -v5 somehost::/usr /bak
```

`rdiff-backup` defaults to using `ssh` to contact the remote host. You will be asked for a password by `ssh`.

Using Amanda

Amanda is one of the most advanced backup solutions available for Debian. It is designed for situations in which a tape device is used to perform backups. It also assumes that you perform regular backups and that you rotate your tapes.

At the heart of Amanda is the scheduler. When you configure Amanda, you tell it information about your tape drive, the number of tapes available in the rotation, and how frequently each disk must be backed up with a full (level 0) backup. As it runs, Amanda will automatically develop, and continually refine, a backup plan that meets your criteria using as few tapes as possible. It will automatically adjust its backup plans in response to changing circumstances, doing the best it can when faced with unexpected situations.

Amanda can be used to back up anything from a part of a single computer to an entire network of computers. It will send backup data over your network to the machine containing the tape backup device. In short, Amanda is a useful tool for automating your tape backups.

As Amanda runs, it can back up multiple machines simultaneously. As it backs up a disk, it will write a backup file to a holding area. Once the disk is completely backed up, the file is written out to tape. This is done for several reasons. First, some disks, networks, or computers may be slower than your tape device. In those instances, more efficient use of the tape can be made if the file is spooled first. Also, in the event of a tape problem, you can still write out these holding area files later.

Amanda is smart about the holding area; it can back up one disk to the holding area and write another backup to tape simultaneously. Also, if space on the holding area is exhausted, Amanda can automatically fall back to a mode where it backs up directly to tape. You can limit the amount of space Amanda uses for its purposes to prevent it from filling up a disk that's also used for other purposes.

Amanda components

Amanda is split into three packages: amanda-server, for machines that have a tape backup device; amanda-client, for machines that get backed up; and amanda-common, for both machines. Any given machine may have both, and that makes sense for situations where the tape drive is on a machine that is itself backed up.

Most commands on either side are run as the user backup on the system. You should run all Amanda commands as that user unless noted otherwise.

There are several commands to be familiar with:

✦ amdump is used to start the backup process.

✦ amflush is used to write to tape any backups that were done to disk but not written to tape due to an error.

✦ amcleanup is used to clean up status areas after an aborted backup.

✦ adadmin is used to perform administrative tasks.

✦ amrecover and amrestore are used to restore from a backup set.

✦ amtapetype is used during configuration to analyze your drive.

First-time configuration

The first thing to do when setting up Amanda is to generate the tape type information for your drive. Make sure a blank tape is in your drive, and then, as the user backup, run /usr/sbin/amtapetype-f /dev/nst0. Of course, substitute your own tape device name for /dev/nst0. Note that the tape you supply will be erased!

This command can take quite some time to complete, depending on the speed and capacity of your drive. Execution times of an entire day are not unheard of. Don't be alarmed; this does not reflect the time that a normal Amanda run will take. The system simply must measure the exact capacity of your drive to make accurate plans.

Next, it's time to configure your backup set in /etc/amanda. An example set named DailySet1 is there for you to start with, and I suggest using it. There are several files there. First is amanda.conf. You'll need to set up this file according to your environment, following the comments in the file and the Amanda documentation. When it's time to define the tape types, use the output from amtapetype above. Then you'll set up the disklist file. This defines which filesystems on which machines are to be backed up.

Now, for each client machine, you need to allow connections from the server as user backup. To do that, create a file named /etc/amandahosts on each client. It needs two lines for every backup server. Here's an example:

```
bkupsrvr.example.com root
bkupsrvr.example.com backup
```

The two lines are necessary because most operations are taken care of as the user backup, but restoration is often done as the user root.

Once you've set everything up, you can run /usr/sbin/amcheck DailySet1. You'll get some warnings about index files not yet existing; that's normal until you run your first backup. If you get any other warnings or errors, something is wrong with your configuration. The error messages will usually point you in the right direction.

Daily backups
You can run your daily backups simply by running this command as the backup user:

```
$ /usr/sbin/amdump DailySet1
```

This will start the backup procedure. When it's finished, a report will be e-mailed to you detailing the actions it performed and the result, if any. The report also tells you which tape Amanda will want to use next. Most people will want to schedule backups to run automatically every day and should use cron to schedule the amdump command to do that.

Restoration
I recommend the amrecover utility to perform a restore. It requires several arguments to start. Here's an example:

```
/usr/sbin/amrecover -C DailySet1 -s localhost -t localhost -d /dev/nst0
```

The -s and -t options tell Amanda where to find the backup server. Since you'll normally run amrecover from the backup server itself, you can just say localhost here (as long as it's in /etc/amandahosts). Once started, amrecover presents an FTP-like interface. Using the sethost, setdisk, setdate, and add commands within this interface, you can specify exact files to restore from exact dates. When you've selected all the files you want, use the extract command. Amanda will tell you which tapes will be necessary to carry out this action and prompt you to insert them as necessary.

Backing up with rsnapshot
rsnapshot is a good backup program for the desktop user who doesn't have a tape drive, but has either a removable external drive or a second computer connected on a network. rsnapshot gives you satisfyingly simple access to your backups; you simply go to the snapshot directory and find your backed up files as if they were normal files on your system. rsnapshot is tricky because it makes it seem like you've taken multiple full backups of your system, while only taking up the space of one full backup, plus any incremental changes. It does this through the use of *hardlinks* (see the related sidebar). rsnapshot makes it possible for you to go back in time to a complete image of your filesystem (made at semi-hourly intervals all day long), and retrieve a copy of something you accidentally deleted without a complex recovery procedure.

Hardlinks

A *hardlink* is basically another name for an already existing file. Normally, a file contains information and has a name; however it is possible, through hardlinks, to create a number of different names that all refer to the same contents, without using very much space. Although hardlinks appear to be separate files, they are simply different names for the same contents. As long as there is a link to a file, it continues to exist; if you remove the original, you have not really removed the contents. They are still available, referenced by the link.

Hardlinks have a negligible overhead, taking up a tiny amount of space, but it is insignificant compared to how much would be taken if the entire contents were duplicated. Through using hardlinks, `rsnapshot` makes it possible to store several weeks' worth of regular snapshots of your system without using several weeks' worth of space.

Installing and configuring rsnapshot

To install `rsnapshot` is, as usual, simple on Debian. All of the dependencies are taken care of when you get the program using `apt-get`:

```
# apt-get install rsnapshot
```

While installation is simple, the configuration is where things matter. Fortunately, configuration is relatively easy as well, and in no time you will be taking regular snapshots. The first step is to configure what you want to back up and to where. This is done by editing the file `/etc/rsnapshot.conf` and setting the appropriate configuration parameters. The most important thing to note about this configuration file is that fields are separated by tabs, not spaces. If you use spaces, things will not work as you expect. There are a few very important configuration parameters that must be carefully set, and the rest can be left as their defaults.

The `snapshot_root` variable is where your snapshots will be stored; this needs to be set to where your backup device is mounted once it is attached to your machine. If you mount an external drive on `/mnt/backup`, you would change the configuration file `/etc/rsnapshot.conf` from:

```
snapshot_root    /var/cache/rsnapshot/
```

to the location of your mounted drive:

```
snapshot_root    /mnt/backup
```

If you are doing your snapshots to external removable media, which is recommended, you need to enable the parameter `no_create_root`. When this is enabled, `rsnapshot` will not try to create the `snapshot_root` directory because this already exists. When mounting your drive, you do not want `rsnapshot` to do this. In the Debian configuration file, this is commented out and you simply need to remove the hash.

Set your backup intervals to how frequently you wish to make snapshots, which will specify how much data to save. You do this by indicating which "intervals" to keep, and how many of each. If you want to make a snapshot of things every four hours, you will be retaining the six most recent snapshots, so your hourly interval is set to six. If you want to also keep a second set that is taken every day and store each of those for a week, then the daily interval is set to seven. The defaults are pretty decent for most desktop use, and you can start with those and later modify them if you feel they are happening too frequently, or not often enough. However, it is important that the first interval line be the smallest unit of time, with each successive entry getting longer. You could add a yearly interval, but it should be added at the end, not at the beginning. Conversely, you could add a minutes interval, and this should be the first line, that is, before hourly.

To enable the defaults of a snapshot done every four hours, six times a day; one snapshot every day of the week, each stored for a week; a snapshot three times a week, each stored for three weeks; and a snapshot three times a month, stored for three months, uncomment the following so that they look like this:

```
interval        hourly   6
interval        daily    7
interval        weekly   3
interval        monthly  3
```

As the final configuration variable, you must tell rsnapshot what files you want to back up. This is done by specifying paths to the backup parameter. For example, to back up the /etc directory to your snapshot directory, you would specify:

```
backup      /etc/         localhost/etc/
```

localhost/etc/ simply indicates the directory inside the snapshot_root where the snapshots will be put. It is very important that directories have a trailing slash. To back up a regular Debian desktop system, the following would suffice, unless you have essential data in other directories, which you would then need to specify:

```
backup      /home/                  localhost/home/
backup      /etc/                   localhost/etc/
backup      /var/spool/mail/        localhost/var/spool/mail/
backup      /var/spool/cron/        localhost/var/spool/cron/
backup      /var/lib/dpkg/          localhost/var/lib/dpkg/
backup      /var/backups/           localhost/var/backups/
```

That's all that needs to be configured. Now check to make sure the syntax of your configuration file is correct by running the following command:

```
# rsnapshot configtest
```

If the syntax is correct, the output should read Syntax OK.

Once everything is fine, you only need to enable the cron entries and your snapshots will begin. To do this, uncomment the following in /etc/cron.d/rsnapshot:

```
0 */4    * * *            root     /usr/bin/rsnapshot hourly
30 3     * * *            root     /usr/bin/rsnapshot daily
0  3     * * 1,3,5        root     /usr/bin/rsnapshot weekly
30 2     1,11,21 * *      root     /usr/bin/rsnapshot monthly
```

If you are using an external hard drive to attach to your system for backup snapshots, you will either need to tailor these times so that they will occur when you have your drive attached, which may be tricky, or not use the cron entries and simply initiate the commands yourself when you want to do a snapshot. If you work at your computer at regular times during the day, you could attach your drive during those hours, set an hourly cron job to run only during those hours, and then before you go home for the day, perform a daily backup by running /usr/bin/rsnapshot daily. At regular intervals throughout the week, manually perform the weekly snapshots, as well as a number of times throughout the month. Another good option is to create a reminder cron that will nudge you by e-mail to do your regular backups.

Another good way to use rsnapshot for backups is to make your snapshot backup directory on a drive in a remotely accessible machine. Ideally, for true fault tolerance, you should use a machine located in a different physical location. The backup occurs over a network, which can take some time depending on the amount of data and your network speed. The first backup tends to take the longest because there is absolutely no data recorded on the remote machine. If your data doesn't change frequently, the following backups will happen with much greater speed.

This requires a few preliminary steps to set up: The sshd and rsync packages must be installed on both machines and running on the remote machine; you need to have access to the remote machine through an account that can write to the directory that you specify; and you must have ssh key–based logins enabled for that user without passphrases. Instead of specifying the local machine in your rsnapshot.conf file, specify the remote machine, with user login:

```
backup        user@domain.org:/etc/    domain.org/etc/
```

Restoring with rsnapshot

Restoring files with rsnapshot is as simple as copying files from one directory to another. You only need to find the snapshot of the file that you want to restore. If you browse the directory that you set for your snapshot_root in the /etc/rsnapshot.conf file, you find a number of snapshot directories that contain what appears to be a full backup at the time the backup was run. The lower the number, the more recent the backup; the highest number contains the oldest backup of the set:

```
# ls -l /man/backups
drwxr-xr-x    7 root     root      4096 Jul 30 00:00 daily.0
drwxr-xr-x    7 root     root      4096 Jul 29 00:00 daily.1
```

```
drwxr-xr-x   7 root     root           4096 Jul 28 00:00 daily.2
drwxr-xr-x   7 root     root           4096 Jul 27 00:00 daily.3
drwxr-xr-x   7 root     root           4096 Jul 26 00:00 daily.4
drwxr-xr-x   7 root     root           4096 Jul 25 00:00 daily.5
drwxr-xr-x   7 root     root           4096 Jul 24 00:00 daily.6
drwxr-xr-x   7 root     root           4096 Jul 31 00:00 hourly.0
drwxr-xr-x   7 root     root           4096 Jul 30 20:00 hourly.1
drwxr-xr-x   7 root     root           4096 Jul 30 16:00 hourly.2
drwxr-xr-x   7 root     root           4096 Jul 30 12:00 hourly.3
drwxr-xr-x   7 root     root           4096 Jul 30 08:00 hourly.4
drwxr-xr-x   7 root     root           4096 Jul 30 04:00 hourly.5
drwxr-xr-x   7 root     root           4096 Jul 28 03:00 weekly.0
drwxr-xr-x   7 root     root           4096 Jul 26 03:00 weekly.1
```

You simply need to step into the appropriate directory and find the file or files that you want to recover. Recovering the file is simple; just copy the files you need into the locations that you need, using standard UNIX commands. There is no special restore command needed.

Backing up with backuppc

Like rsnapshot, backuppc is a disk-based backup program that intelligently handles data to maximize your backup media capacity through hardlinks. A feature of backuppc that is missing from rsnapshot is optional compression, which can significantly decrease the amount of storage needed for backups even further, at a slight CPU hit. Another feature of backuppc is its Web interface, which both allows some administrative overview of the backups (although you cannot configure backuppc through the interface yet) and gives the user the power to initiate and cancel backups and restore files. With little configuration, backuppc can be used to back up your home Linux machines, as well as your Windows machines, over Samba. A good feature in backuppc, and really in any backup software, is that it uses standard GNU/Linux utilities to restore files.

backuppc requires a bit more software, including a working Web server on your machine, and more configuration than rsnapshot, but it provides some advanced features and user interface improvements. Overall, it is a great solution for a home network that has a number of machines and people.

Installing and configuring backuppc

Install backuppc, its various dependencies, and a handful of peripheral necessities via apt:

```
# apt-get install backuppc rsync libfile-rsyncp-perl ssh sudo
```

The next step is to set a new password for the Web interface. Do this by running the following command:

```
# /usr/bin/htpasswd /etc/backuppc/htpasswd backuppc
```

After you have set a new password, launch your Web browser and go to the URL `http://localhost/backuppc/`. You will be presented with an authorization prompt; use the username `backuppc` and the password that you just set. Once in, you will be at the BackupPC main status page, shown in Figure 6-1.

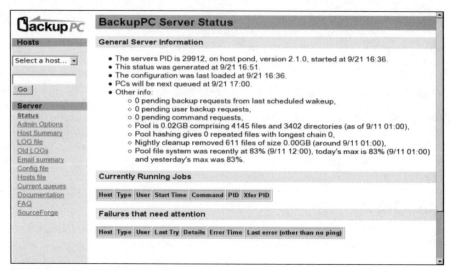

Figure 6-1: The backuppc main status page.

The main status screen, also known as the Server Status, is a summary of the current state of all of `backuppc`'s operations. It will show currently running backups, and it has links in the left bar to your configured clients, additional status pages, log files, and configurations.

The documentation included with `backuppc` is very well done and is provided as a link off the front page of the interface. However, this section covers what you need to get off the ground with a basic configuration.

The main `backuppc` configuration file is `/etc/backuppc/config.pl`. It contains a significant number of configuration parameters. However, the defaults that are set by the Debian package are good to start with.

Each machine that will be backed up is defined in the `/etc/backuppc/hosts` file. The Debian package installation will be set up to back up your desktop already, however if you want to add another machine to be backed up, you simply edit this file to include your changes and then save it. `backuppc` will notice the modified time has changed on the file the next time it "wakes up" and will add this host to its list. The format of the file is simply three fields, separated by white space. For example, if I add a machine called laptop, the file would look as follows:

```
host     dhcp   user    moreUsers   # <--- do not edit this line
localhost 0     backuppc
laptop   0     backuppc
```

The first field is the hostname of the machine, which must also be listed in your system's /etc/hosts file with an IP address. The second field is the DHCP flag. According to "Step 4: Setting up the host file" in the manual, accessed through the link "Documentation" in the left-hand navigational bar of the Web interface, "starting with v2.0.0, the way hosts are discovered has changed and now in most cases you should specify 0 for the DHCP flag, even if the host has a dynamically assigned IP address." Finally, the third field is the username of the person who "owns" the machine being backed up. This user will receive an e-mail about the machine, and the user will have permissions to start and stop backups and initiate restores of files for themselves. This username must be the same that is used to authenticate with Apache.

The default configuration that comes with the Debian package is set up to back up the /etc directory as an unprivileged user, so it cannot back up all the files. Additionally, the backups are put in /var/lib/backuppc. To make backuppc useful for a Debian desktop backup, you need to edit /etc/backuppc/localhost.pl so it looks somewhat similar to the following:

```
$Conf{XferMethod} = 'rsync';

$Conf{BackupFilesOnly} = ['/home', '/var/spool/mail',
'/var/spool/cron', '/var/lib/dpkg', '/var/backups', '/etc'];

$Conf{RsyncClientCmd} = '$sshPath -l backuppc $host nice -n 19
 sudo $rsyncPath $argList+';
```

You should add any additional directories that you need to back up. If you decide to back up the entire /var partition, you need to additionally set the following:

```
$Conf{BackupFilesExclude} = ['/var/lib/backuppc']
```

The backuppc programs run as an unprivileged user, so you need to provide some manner of elevated privileges. An easy and relatively secure way to do this is to configure the sudo package for backuppc. Simply install sudo via apt-get and then as root run the command visudo to edit the sudo configuration file to include the following line:

```
backuppc  ALL=NOPASSWD: /usr/bin/rsync
```

This will enable the backuppc user to be able to run only the rsync command as root.

Next you need to set up ssh keys for the `backuppc` user:

```
# su - backuppc
$ ssh-keygen -t rsa
$ cp .ssh/id_rsa.pub .ssh/authorized_keys2
$ ssh -l root clientHostName whoami
backuppc
```

If this final command does not report `backuppc`, or if you encounter other problems, see Chapter 18 for more details on SSH-key authorization.

The Debian package of `backuppc` is set up to pool all its backups and data about backups in `/var/lib/backuppc`. On a desktop system with only one drive, this directory is probably on the hard drive that is being backed up. This is not a very good backup because it protects you only from accidental file deletion and not against drive failure or worse catastrophes.

There are a few options to make this a viable backup solution. One is to use `backuppc` only on a machine that is specifically dedicated as your backup machine for all the desktop backups in your house or office. Another is to have attached to your system a separate hard drive that holds this pool of data. This can be done with an external drive mounted in another location. To accomplish this, follow the directions indicated in the `README.Debian` file in `/usr/share/doc/backuppc`, which states:

```
If you do not like the default data directory (/var/lib/backuppc/), you
should move this directory where you want and make a symbolic link from
the new directory to the default one (all paths are hardcoded so it's the
easiest way to change the data directory).
```

Another method is to periodically archive your `backuppc` pool directory to removable media, such as a tape drive, CD-R/CD-RWs, or writable DVD media. `backuppc` has an archive mechanism built in to create archives that can be sent straight to your tape device, or it can create files of the necessary size that can fit onto CD or DVD media.

To archive your pool directory using `backuppc`'s archive mechanism, add a line to your `/etc/backuppc/hosts` file with a host that identifies the type of archiving you are doing. For example, if you are creating archives that you write to a tape drive, add something like the following:

```
tapearchive    0    backuppc
```

Then create a file `/etc/backuppc/tapearchive.pl` and put the following lines in it:

```
$Conf{XferMethod} = 'archive';
$Conf{ArchiveDest} = '/dev/nst0';
```

If you write your archives to CDs or DVD media, set the $Conf{ArchiveDest} parameter to a directory that the images should be written to, and when it has completed archiving, burn those to your media.

Once this is set, you can start an archive by visiting the Web interface and selecting the archive name that you provided in the host file (in this case, it was tapearchive). You are presented with a list of any previous archives that were made and summaries of each one. Click the Start Archive button, and select which hosts you wish to archive. At this point you can fine-tune some parameters, such as setting how big to make each archive (the maximum size that your backup media can hold).

Restoring with backuppc

backuppc has a number of different ways to restore files. The most convenient by far is the Web interface, but it is possible to restore through command-line utilities if you choose. Unfortunately, covering the command-line restore utilities is outside the scope of this chapter; consult the manual if you would like to use these. If you use the Web interface, backuppc will automatically complete incremental backups by restoring the corresponding full backup. This eliminates the need to restore both manually to get a full restore.

To restore through the Web interface, click on the host that you want to restore files for. Clicking on the host will bring up a list of all the backups that have been made for that machine, as shown in Figure 6-2.

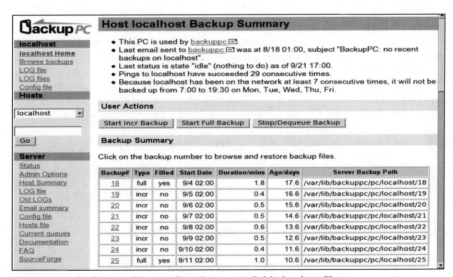

Figure 6-2: backuppc shows a list of your available backup files.

Select the specific backup number you want, and you are presented with a directory tree for that backup, as shown in the example in Figure 6-3. Here you simply select the files and directories you want from the backup, either by clicking on the files individually, or by selecting a number of them and then clicking the Restore Selected Files button.

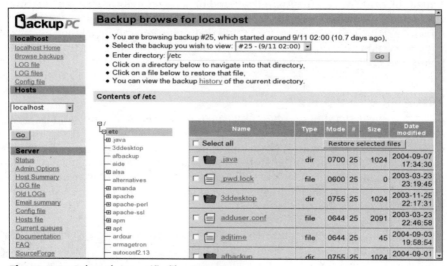

Figure 6-3: Select the specific files to restore.

After you've selected the files to restore, you are presented with three options. The first is to do a Direct Restore; with this option, all the files and directories that you've selected to restore will be put back on the host in their original location. You can change the location of the restore if you prefer to put the files elsewhere. The second option is to Download Zip Archive; this will create a zip file with the selected files and directories, and you will then be allowed to download it through your browser. The third and final option, Download Tar Archive, is essentially the same as the previous option, except that the file created is a `tar` archive, rather than a zip file. This option will not compress the files that you will download.

Caution   Using the Direct Restore option, any old files that have the same name in the original directory as the ones you are restoring will be overwritten!

File synchronization backups with Unison

If you have a laptop and a desktop that you want to keep in sync, you can use the synchronization process as a method of backup. If you regularly perform file synchronization from your desktop to your laptop and experience a catastrophe on your desktop, you will have a copy on your laptop that you can use to recover from. The package `unison-gtk` is a file-synchronization tool that intelligently brings files and directories that may have been modified separately up-to-date. Unison can synchronize between Windows and GNU/Linux, can synchronize in both directions across a network, and is easy to use.

Unlike the other backup software covered in this chapter, Unison can handle updates to both replicas of a directory structure. The other backup software discussed in this chapter assumes that you do not modify your backups, but simply write them periodically. Unison is designed to allow you to make modifications to both copies of your data. It does this by automatically distributing files and directories that do not conflict between the two copies, and displaying those that do conflict for you to resolve.

Unison can be used to synchronize locally between two directories on the same machine; for example, you could synchronize your `/home` directory with your mounted removable drive on `/mnt/backups/home`. Additionally, Unison works between two machines connected via a network, either over an encrypted ssh connection or through direct socket connections. Unison is conservative with its bandwidth usage and can run well over slow dial-up PPP links.

Partition Imaging

It's often useful to make an image of either an entire hard disk or an entire partition. One reason is to duplicate an installed system onto another PC (probably over a network connection); another is to make a backup of your complete hard disk, including every aspect of the installed operating systems, which you can restore if you have to replace your hard disk or if you manage to scramble the bits. Typically, it's useful to be able to transfer these images over the network to another machine, although you may want to save images onto a different partition or hard drive.

One useful utility for making partition images is named rather pragmatically: `partimage`. This software is intelligent about copying data from only the used portions of the partitions, which speeds things up and saves a lot of space. It will also compress your images, which makes putting those images on backup media much easier. Compression always depends on the data itself, but it is possible to take a 1 gigabyte partition and compress it down to 400 megabytes. `partimage` comes with an intuitive curses-based GUI and also has built-in network support to save your partition image to another machine over a secure connection.

The problem with partition imaging, and not `partimage` itself, is that when you image a partition, that partition cannot be mounted or in use. This makes it impossible to image many of your partitions while booted into your normal system. To use `partimage` to image partitions you would generally be using, boot from a CD, such as Knoppix or SystemRescueCd, and run `partimage` from there.

Other software

Table 6-3 provides a list of some of the other Debian packages that can be used for backups and a short description of them to whet your appetite.

Table 6-3 Other Debian Backup Utilities	
Name	**Description**
backup2l	Low-maintenance backup/restore tool for mountable media
multicd	Easy way to back up a large number of files to multiple CDs
cdbackup	CD-R(W) backup utility that uses dump and restore
storebackup	Nice package that does disk-based backup in intelligent ways
dirvish	Filesystem-based backup system using rsync
pdumpfs	Simple daily backup system that works similar to rsnapshot
flexbackup	Flexible backup tool for small- to medium-sized installations
hdup	Filesystem duplicator and backup; relatively easy to set up
faubackup	Very similar system to rsnapshot
mondoarchive	Disaster recovery tool that makes a bootable image of your system

Summary

This chapter showed you the importance of backing up your data and doing so in a regular and systematic way. It provided an overview of the important aspects that should be considered in designing a backup strategy that fits your needs, such as discussing what is important to back up on a Debian desktop. There are several different backup storage technologies available, and the right choice depends on your needs and budget. Tape drives are high capacity and are inexpensive for adding capacity, but have a high setup cost. CD and DVD drives are low capacity but popular and cheap. Hard disks are fast and cheap, but nonportable.

The chapter also went into depth on the different software backup solutions available on Debian systems. The information in the chapter should encourage you to make backing up your Debian desktop system a regular task because your data is important and protecting it should be easy.

✦   ✦   ✦

The Linux Desktop

Configuring Graphics and Sound

◆   ◆   ◆   ◆

In This Chapter

Installing and
configuring graphics
drivers

Installing and
configuring sound
drivers

◆   ◆   ◆   ◆

Debian offers a rich selection of graphical user interfaces
and applications. However, Debian doesn't sacrifice its
utility in one area (such as a server) to better serve another
area (in this case, a desktop). By default, Debian doesn't
require the installation and configuration of the graphics and
sound subsystems that those graphical interfaces and applications require. While most other distributions provide such
things "out of the box," you're required to explicitly request
them in Debian. Adding them to your installation list doesn't
need to be hard; in a production environment, you can simply
select the `Desktop environment` task in `tasksel` during the
installation procedure. In this book, however, I walk through
each subsystem in some detail to familiarize you with their
installation, configuration, and operation.

Note   If your desktop is being maintained by a system administrator, you may choose to skip this chapter and move on to
Chapter 8, which introduces the more popular desktop
environments available in Debian GNU/Linux.

In GNU/Linux, the standard graphics subsystem is XFree86.
XFree86 is a full implementation of the client/server X11 protocol. The X11 protocol allows applications to display graphical interfaces in a device- and network-independent fashion.
An application running on a large mainframe that doesn't have
a keyboard or monitor can display its interface on a computer
hundreds of miles away that does have the hardware to handle it. Aside from this network transparency, XFree86 provides
a full set of drivers for all sorts of video hardware and input
hardware.

Note   Recently, much attention and work has gone into a replacement for XFree86 called X.Org. Debian will, in all likelihood, switch to X.Org, but not until after the release of sarge.

There are two standard sets of GNU/Linux audio drivers: Open Sound System (OSS) and Advanced Linux Sound Architecture (ALSA). OSS is currently being phased out, but that's a multiyear process, and OSS is still supported in Debian. This book focuses on the use of ALSA, though.

This chapter walks you through the installation of X and Sound onto a bare system. For users who install X as part of the initial Debian install, most of the information here still applies. The installation of X Windows still asks the same questions in the same order. I've tried in this chapter to point out where the step-by-step installation method diverges from the all-at-once method.

Introducing XFree86

Because X11 is a client/server protocol, applications initiate a connection to the X11 server. The X11 server (XFree86) runs wherever the input and display hardware is. Applications can run on any machine, but they all initiate a connection to your desktop system for user input and display output. This might seem a bit counterintuitive at first because the applications themselves may be running on very large, shared systems (what you'd normally call a server), while your desktop computer might be a simple thin client with no hard drive and limited resources of its own. Nevertheless, in the scope of X11, applications are the clients, and the desktop is running the server software.

You might think this flexibility causes a performance problem. Quite the opposite: This separation of systems allows for a great deal of optimization to be done centrally in XFree86, while the applications you can run don't need to worry about such things. It's worth noting that X11 as a protocol is around 20 years old now, and it's a testament to its good design that it's still in very wide use today and meets the needs of every conceivable user. Though XFree86 is much younger than the X11 protocol, it is today one of the most, if not the most, mature X11 implementations, and it's certainly the most widely used.

XFree86 provides a number of functions: It provides the X11 server, which includes drivers for input and graphical output devices; it provides shared libraries that allow applications to easily use the X11 protocol for their graphical interfaces; and it provides a central means of sharing small amounts of data among applications (for instance, copy and paste buffers).

Preparing to install XFree86

Configuration of XFree86 on Debian can be somewhat involved, depending on your hardware. Debian has come a long way with respect to hardware autodetection, although there is still work to be done. During the installation and configuration of XFree86, you may need to answer some lower-level questions about the sort of hardware you have. This isn't always the case; it depends primarily on how exotic your hardware is. To be on the safe side, though, and for those cases where you're dealing with a computer that has some unusual hardware, the following subsections cover all the important bits you might need to worry about — namely, specifications for your monitor, mouse, and video card.

If you're more familiar with Windows administration and configuration, this phase is roughly equivalent to finding drivers for your hardware, or installing such drivers off of a CD provided by the vendor. Unlike Windows, it's perfectly legal to redistribute the lion's share of drivers available under GNU/Linux, and distributors such as Debian include every single one they can. The instructions in this section tell you how to find out which driver to use. The drivers themselves will already be available; you simply need to select them.

Finding monitor specifications

Whether your monitor is a CRT (TV-style) or LCD (laptop-style), you need to know its *refresh rates*. The refresh rates, sometimes referred to as *scanning rates*, specify how many times per second the monitor draws the screen. Your monitor does this constantly, and the rate at which it can draw data on the screen controls both the resolution and the quality of the display. There are two separate refresh rates: the horizontal rate and the vertical rate. The horizontal rate is represented in Hz (number of refreshes per second) and the vertical rate is represented in kHz (thousands of refreshes per second). Each rate, horizontal and vertical, will be provided as a range — for instance, 30kHz to 120kHz for the vertical rate. The best places to find this information are in the manual for your monitor, on the manufacturer's Web site, or occasionally, on the back of the monitor itself.

If you can't find this information, there's no need to worry. Chances are you won't need to enter it anyway. If the autodetection fails, however, you'll have to settle for an approximate configuration by simply specifying the size of the monitor, which, while easy, may not allow you to use your monitor at its best settings. If you have this information, the performance will be more closely optimized for your hardware.

If you have an LCD display, it's also important to know its *native resolution*. If your LCD has a native resolution of 1,600×1,200, you can still use it at 1,024×768, but the image quality will be subpar. For a standard CRT display, you'll want to make note of its maximum resolution. You should be able to find native resolution at the same sources as the refresh rate information.

Determining mouse types and connectors

Mouse autodetection is pretty mature and is painless for the common cases — USB and PS/2 mice. USB mice have rectangular connectors about ½ inch wide and ¼ inch tall. PS/2 mice have round connectors approximately ½ inch in diameter, with six pins inside. USB mice have a standard device node, regardless of type, in addition to a standard API/protocol to access them: /dev/input/mice is the device node, and ImPS/2 is the protocol. In the case of PS/2 mice, the device will be /dev/psaux, and the protocol may vary; ImPS/2 and Logitech are the most common protocols.

The less common case these days, serial mice, are tougher to deal with. Serial mice have a trapezoid shape. The connectors are about an inch wide and ½ inch tall. Standard serial devices in Linux are accessible via the /dev/ttyS0, /dev/ttyS1, /dev/ttyS2, and /dev/ttyS3 device nodes. To discover which one your mouse uses, run the cat /dev/ttyS0 command and then wiggle the mouse. If you don't see any garbage characters on the screen, press Ctrl+C and move on to the next device node. Repeat this as necessary until you get an on-screen response from the mouse. (You may have to run the reset command to restore your screen because those binary characters can play havoc with terminal emulation.)

Finding video card information

Most manufacturers use chips from a small number of vendors, such as ATI and NVIDIA, and drivers care about the chipset — not the packaging or the brand name. To discover which chipset your video card uses, install the pciutils package with the sudo apt-get install pciutils command, and then run lspci. Examine the output for a line that contains the text VGA compatible controller. Following is one example from my workstation, and another from my laptop:

```
0000:01:00.0 VGA compatible controller: ATI Technologies Inc Radeon RV100
QY [Radeon 7000/VE]

0000:00:0c.0 VGA compatible controller: Cirrus Logic GD 5430/40 [Alpine]
(rev 47)
```

The most important point to note is the manufacturer — typically the first words after the VGA compatible controller text. Most drivers in XFree86 are named after a manufacturer and are compatible with all the cards using any chipset from that manufacturer.

Installing hardware detection utilities

Hardware detection is handled by a number of programs in Debian. There are two major packages in use: discover and hotplug. Both are useful, although using them together can introduce problems. I suggest using three separate Debian packages that control hardware autodetection: discover (a general-purpose hardware autodetection package), mdetect (mouse-specific autodetection), and read-edid (a utility to probe a monitor for its capabilities and refresh rates). Install those packages with the following command:

```
sudo apt-get install discover mdetect read-edid
```

Installing hardware detection software allows your computer to automatically detect the hardware that you have in your computer for configuration the first time you install X Windows. It also means that when you install new hardware or change your hardware configuration, Debian will be able to recognize this on boot and adjust your configuration accordingly.

Installing and configuring XFree86

If you selected to install XFree86 during the installation of your system, skip down to the sections on configuration later in this chapter. If you are installing it on a minimal or preinstalled base system, the following paragraphs will walk you through the installation of those packages.

Like most other major subsystems in Debian, XFree86 is split into many small packages for maximum flexibility and ease of maintenance. There are two XFree86 *meta-packages* (packages that have dependencies on large numbers of smaller packages): `x-window-system-core` and `x-window-system`. Metapackages allow the maintainer of a given subsystem to provide one or more fake packages that have nothing but dependencies on the parts of their subsystem that most people are interested in. The XFree86 metapackages make XFree86 easy to install. In Debian, installation and configuration are often performed in a single step. To install the first metapackage, run the following command:

```
sudo apt-get install x-window-system-core x-window-system xterm
```

The `x-window-system-core` metapackage contains the basic XFree86 drivers, applications, and libraries, as well as numerous display fonts. With the previous command, you also installed `xterm`. `xterm` is a terminal emulator — like the Linux console — that allows you to run a shell in X11 and perform diagnostics.

When the packages have been downloaded, you'll be presented with a number of questions to determine the correct configuration for your computer.

Configuring XFree86

`fontconfig` is a package used for managing fonts, and it's installed as part of the `x-window-system-core` installation. `fontconfig` is also responsible for drawing (or *rendering*) fonts to the computer's display. The first question asks whether you should enable sub-pixel text rendering. As the explanatory text of the question implies, this is useful only if you have an LCD display. Answer appropriately for your display type.

`xserver-xfree86` is the primary XFree86 package. It contains all the drivers and the XFree86 binary itself, which uses those drivers and implements the X11 protocol. The following steps lead you through the configuration process:

1. The first question asks whether you would like `debconf` to autodetect your video card:

Accept this option if you would like to attempt to
autodetect the recommended X server and driver module for
your video card. If autodetection fails, you will be
asked to specify the desired X server and/or driver
module. If autodetection succeeds, further debconf
questions about your video hardware will be pre-answered.

If you would rather select the X server and driver module
yourself, decline this option. You will not be asked to
select the X server if there is only one available.

Attempt to autodetect video hardware?

Answer **Yes**. debconf asks this first because hardware detection can be a hit-or-miss affair—and it's possible that a miss will cause your computer to hang. That's quite rare, however. If it should happen, just reboot your computer and restart the installation with the command:

```
sudo apt-get install x-window-system-core xterm
```

When debconf asks this question again, answer **No**, and proceed to configure XFree86 manually using the information gathered in the first subsection of this chapter.

If video hardware autodetection fails, you will be asked to manually select the driver you need to use. Simply select the driver that matches the name of your video card's manufacturer. For instance, if you have a video card with an ATI chipset, you select the ati driver. If you have a video card using an NVIDIA chipset, you select the nv driver. Failing that, a quick Google search for "XFree86 driver" followed by your video card model should be fruitful.

2. The next question is related to your keyboard (specifically, the type of keyboard hardware you have):

Please select the XKB ruleset to use.

Unless you're running on a Sparc workstation from Sun, answer **xfree86** at this prompt. All standard PC-compatible keyboards use the xfree86 XKB ruleset.

3. The next question continues to probe for your keyboard information:

Please select your keyboard model.

Though the electronics are virtually identical in all PC-compatible keyboards, their placement, type, and number of keys differ. If you have a keyboard without special keys for Windows and menus (in other words, if there is an empty space between the Ctrl and Alt keys), choose **pc101** here. If your keyboard *does* have those keys, choose **pc104**.

4. The next question addresses the keyboard layout:

Please select your keyboard layout.

Your keyboard layout refers primarily to the characters that appear on the keys themselves. If you're using a standard U.S.-style keyboard, simply choose us. If you're using a keyboard designed for a different nationality, instead choose your two-letter ISO 3316 country code here—for instance, fr for France, de for Germany, and ca for Canada (though only use ca if you have a mixed French/English keyboard).

5. The next question is more hardware autodetection:

   Attempt mouse autodetection?

   The answer you want to try first, as with video autodetection above, is **Yes**. If you don't have a USB mouse, this might fail; in this case, refer to the information you collected earlier to answer the following question:

   Please choose your mouse port.

6. After you've chosen your mouse port (most likely /dev/psaux for a standard PS/2 mouse), you'll be asked for the protocol that the mouse speaks:

   Please choose the entry that best describes your mouse.

   If you have a Microsoft IntelliMouse or a non-Logitech mouse with a scroll wheel, chances are it speaks the ImPS/2 protocol. If you have a Microsoft Explorer mouse, you want to choose the ExplorerPS/2 protocol. If you have a Logitech mouse with a scroll wheel, you likely want MouseManPlusPS/2. If you're unsure of which to use, simply select PS/2. It's a basic protocol that all PS/2 mice speak.

7. The next question is another autodetection question:

   Attempt monitor autodetection?

   Answer **Yes**. This will almost certainly function properly, unless you have a 15-year-old monitor. If it fails, however, you will be asked a few extra questions:

   Is your monitor an LCD device?

   That question you can answer on your own, I'm sure. The next question asks you to specify how you will choose your monitor's properties:

   Please choose a method for selecting your monitor characteristics.

   If you were able to find the refresh rate ranges for your monitor, select Advanced. You'll be asked to enter the vertical and horizontal refresh rates (don't supply kHz or Hz in your responses, and specify ranges like 30-120, with a single dash between the numbers and no spaces). If you were unable to determine the refresh rates for your monitors, I strongly recommend you select Simple. You will be asked for the size of your monitor; answer appropriately.

8. Having configured your monitor's properties (whether automatically or manually), you'll be asked to set the resolution for your display:

   Select the video modes you would like the X server to use.

   Applications can tell XFree86 to change the resolution of your display on-the-fly; for instance, a movie player will do so in fullscreen mode to provide better-quality video. You can limit which resolutions XFree86 will switch your display to. This is especially useful for LCD devices, where the native resolution should always be the only resolution used. If you exceed your monitor's maximum resolution, XFree86 will pan the display based on your mouse movement. Not all areas of your desktop will be visible at once.

9. The last question refers to how many colors you would like displayed on the screen at once:

```
Please select your desired default color depth in bits.
```

Unless you're using a very old computer with limited video memory, select **24** bits. 24 bits is full or *true color*, and the only reason to use fewer colors is if your hardware can't support it (which is unlikely).

That concludes XFree86 configuration. The packages will be unpacked, and when the installation is finished you'll be ready to test your new software. If you later find that you dislike anything about this configuration, or if something does not work, you can always run the command `sudo dpkg-reconfigure xserver-xfree86` to reselect the resolutions you'd like to use.

Testing and troubleshooting XFree86

Now that you have XFree86 installed and configured, you can test whether it works. To do this, use the command-line XFree86 session starter, `startx`. Run that command, and hopefully XFree86 will start, and you'll have a screen similar to the one shown in Figure 7-1.

Figure 7-1: XFree86 test session.

This screen is from a system installed in a step-by-step manner. As a result, it appears very anemic and ugly, but that's just because it is not running on a desktop environment (covered in the next chapter). What you should see is the standard XFree86 stipple background (useful for noticing defects in monitors), as well as a running xterm instance. Without a desktop environment telling it otherwise, XFree86 defaults to *focus-follows-mouse*. This means that wherever your mouse cursor points, that's where your keyboard input goes. At this point you have a single window, but if you move the cursor outside that window, the window will lose keyboard focus. Simply return the cursor to the xterm window to have it regain focus. Exit xterm (and since it's the only application running, your entire X session) by typing **exit** into your bash shell and pressing Enter.

If for some reason XFree86 fails to start, closely examine the last screen of its output. Chances are you see one of two common errors:

✦ **Fatal server error: no screens found** — If you receive the error message no screens found, it almost certainly means a misconfiguration of the video card or monitor settings. Run the command:

```
sudo dpkg-reconfigure xserver-xfree86
```

to redo your configuration, and be sure that each question is answered correctly. If you still receive the error, try foregoing video hardware autodetection and manually selecting the VESA driver. If this XFree86 fails to work, the best course of action would be to get a local GNU/Linux expert to help you out; problems related to hardware are difficult to troubleshoot remotely, so somebody helping in-person is invaluable.

✦ **Fatal server error: failed to initialize core devices** — If you receive the error message failed to initialize core devices, the problem likely lies in your mouse or keyboard configuration. Run the command:

```
sudo dpkg-reconfigure xserver-xfree86
```

to walk through the configuration again, and double-check that all the answers you give are correct. If it still fails and you're using a PS/2 mouse, then forego mouse autodetection and instead manually specify /dev/psaux as the device to use and PS/2 as the protocol to use. If it still doesn't work, I would suggest (as with the previous error) finding a local GNU/Linux expert to lend a hand. There's nothing like live tech support from an experienced user to make all problems seem trivial.

For further support options, visit Debian's support portal: www.debian.org/support.

Installing and Configuring Sound Drivers

As I mentioned earlier, there are two sets of sound drivers available in Debian: OSS and ALSA. This book covers only ALSA. OSS is only of use for those who have extremely ancient hardware, such as some very old ISA sound cards. (They are, quite frankly, extremely difficult to get working.)

If you have an ISA sound card (if you don't know if you do or not, then it's safe to say that you don't, unless your computer is at least 10 years old), check out the full Linux Sound HOWTO available at `http://en.tldp.org/HOWTO/Sound-HOWTO/index.html`, which covers ISA sound systems.

Installing and configuring ALSA

Before configuring ALSA, you should add to the `audio` group any users to whom you want to grant access to sound. If those users are already logged in, they must log back in again for the change to take effect.

To install the ALSA drivers that match your kernel, you need to first determine your kernel version with the `uname` command, like so:

```
user@hostname:~$ uname -r
2.4.25-386-1
user@hostname:~$
```

If you are using an official Debian 2.6 kernel, the ALSA drivers are already included in it as modules, so you can skip this next part. If you are using an official Debian 2.4 kernel, you can install an `alsa-modules` package for your specific kernel. For example, if you are using 2.4.25-1-i686, you should install `alsa-modules-2.4.25-1-i686`.

Next, you should install the `alsa-base` and `alsa-utils` packages. `alsa-utils` contains a program called `alsaconf`, which you should run as `root`. It will make an attempt to autodetect your sound card, but if that doesn't work, you can manually select it from a list of cards.

As a final step, you should go into your desktop's control panel and configure your sound server to use ALSA.

When you've rebooted with the ALSA modules in place, the drivers will be loaded. This reboot isn't strictly necessary because you can poke about to get the drivers loaded manually, but rebooting is the simplest way to do that.

Setting up sound, with a bit more of an application-oriented focus, is covered again in Chapter 11, "Digital Photography and Mutlimedia."

Setting volume levels

With sound drivers loaded on your computer, the first thing you want to do is raise the volume on the sound card's channels. Most sound cards default to a muted state to avoid any noise coming from the speakers as the system is being initialized. Volume levels will be saved each time you shut down your computer and will be restored after sound system initialization on the next boot, so you only need to jump through this particular hoop once.

To start the process, run the `alsamixer` command. If you get a `Permission denied` error, add yourself to the `audio` group with `sudo adduser user audio`, log out, log back in, and try again. When you've started `alsamixer`, you can see a text-based representation of your sound card's channels. The channels you wish to unmute and increase the volume of are `Master`, `PCM`, `Line`, `CD`, and `Aux`. (Your sound card may not support all of these channels, so don't worry if some are missing.) Use your up and down arrow keys to decrease or increase the volume; set the channels as high as they'll go for the time being. Press the M key to unmute each relevant channel. Use the left and right arrow keys to select different channels; note that not all channels can be displayed on one screen, so if you keep pressing the right arrow you'll find more channels. When you're done, press Escape twice to exit `alsamixer`.

Testing and troubleshooting sound drivers

Now that your sound drivers are installed and configured, it's time to play a test audio file. Use the `play` command from the `sox` package to play a sound file from the `sound-icons` package. First, run the following command to install the packages you need:

```
sudo apt-get install sox sound-icons
```

Then run the following command:

```
user@hostname:~$ play /usr/share/sounds/sound-icons/prompt.wav
playing /usr/share/sounds/sound-icons/prompt.wav
user@hostname:~$
```

You should hear a pleasant tone come from your speakers — though it may be unbelievably loud. At this point you can run `alsamixer` again to adjust the volume levels. If you don't have adequate sound after working through the previous steps, it's time to troubleshoot. Troubleshooting sound problems can be much more challenging than troubleshooting XFree86-related problems. Start with the simple steps: The first thing you should do when facing a sound problem is make sure that your speakers are plugged into the right port on your computer, and that the speakers are turned on and functional. (I've spent at least 10 hours of my life troubleshooting sound problems whose solutions were "plug in the speakers.") Checking that channels are unmuted and that volumes are set high in `alsamixer` is also a first line of defense.

Failing those simple (but often successful) checks, it's hard to offer detailed advice, given the range of potential problems with sound drivers. A full list of possible problems and their solutions is beyond the scope of this book. Refer to Debian's support forums at `www.debian.org/support` for advice on handling your specific sound problem.

Summary

This chapter provided instructions to help you achieve working sound and graphics. It covered the basic concepts behind X11 and the installation and configuration of XFree86, GNU/Linux's X11 implementation. The chapter also covered installing sound drivers and using hardware autodetection software to get your sound and graphics going.

Sound and graphics can be difficult to get working correctly under any system and can be especially difficult and frustrating on GNU/Linux systems. This chapter tries to give a good "from scratch" description of how to get this working on many systems, but it's not perfect. If you've done this and are still having trouble, it may be time to find a local GNU/Linux expert or to turn to one of the Debian support forums.

✦   ✦   ✦

The KDE and GNOME Desktop Environments

A common misconception about Linux (and indeed, all UNIX and UNIX-like systems) is that it's solely command-line based, or that what graphical interfaces it has are subpar. Today this couldn't be farther from the truth. You have not one, but *two* full-featured desktop environments to choose from. In addition to the two most popular desktop environments discussed in this chapter, there are myriad leaner environments that are usually intended for more modest computers — for example, PDAs.

Which desktop environment you use depends very much on personal taste. They act similarly in many respects, providing the same basic facilities such as application-launching menus, desktop panels, *applets* (very small utilities that are displayed within a panel and are meant to be viewable at all times, such as e-mail monitors), window borders and dressings, and so on. The differences lie primarily in relatively minor behavioral details and appearance.

Choosing one particular desktop environment doesn't preclude you from running any applications you wish. There is no desktop lock-in to speak of; you can run (for example) the KDE Web browser Konqueror in a GNOME environment, instead of GNOME's default browser, Mozilla.

If you don't want to try out both desktops covered here (to say nothing of the large number not covered), I would suggest the GNOME environment. It's an attractive-looking desktop written by developers who value simplicity. The end result is an environment that is pleasing to the eye and easy to learn.

The GNOME Desktop Environment

One of the most popular desktop environments available for GNU/Linux, GNOME has a large following among both home and business users. The GNOME project (www.gnome.org) was started by Miguel de Icaza in August of 1997, mainly due to the subpar or nonfree nature of the alternatives at the time. Since then, the GNOME project has grown substantially. One of GNOME's longtime supporters, Red Hat, Inc. (www.redhat.com), was instrumental in this growth because it provided a number of paid engineers to the project who helped to smooth out the many rough (some might say jagged) edges that existed at the time. GNOME continues to gain wide acceptance in large part due to its licensing; not only is the GNOME desktop's source code free for modification and redistribution, but application developers also can choose whichever license they prefer; they aren't restricted to licenses that require them to release their own source code.

The term *GNOME desktop* really refers to two separate entities. The first entity is the official GNOME desktop, which includes the basic libraries that all GNOME applications use, as well as the standard set of GUI interfaces such as the file manager, the window manager, the desktop panels, and so on. In addition to this official definition, the term is often used to refer to those base components just mentioned as well as the more popular applications that run atop them, such as spreadsheet applications, Web browsers, e-mail and calendaring software, and so forth.

This section walks you through installing the packages most Debian GNOME users choose, and describes the configuration and use of the GNOME display/login manager. Additionally, I provide a simple tour of the GNOME desktop, and provide some pointers on some desktop configuration settings that many users like to adjust to their own preferences.

Installing GNOME

As part of the GNOME installation, you install the standard Debian GNOME desktop packages. These include the desktop environment, a number of common applications, many utilities, and a graphical login manager or *display manager*. Integrated desktop environments in GNU/Linux typically offer a display manager, which presents a pretty login window at system startup instead of the standard text-based login prompt. If you installed a desktop environment during installation, GNOME and the display manager will already be installed and you can skip this section.

The primary GNOME package in Debian is named gnome. The gdm package provides GNOME's display manager, which is (by default) started when your computer boots. Run this command:

```
sudo aptitude install gnome gdm menu
```

You should see many packages to be installed. This is quite normal; the GNOME packages are heavily split, allowing system administrators to install only what they require. The `gnome` metapackage is also quite complete: It results in the installation of a full GNOME desktop environment. You can press Ctrl+C or press the N key to abort the installation, and use `apt-cache show packagename` to view the details of any package that catches your eye. Many of the packages are relatively uninteresting, however, since they're libraries and other infrastructure components. The more interesting packages are covered in the rest of this chapter as well as in later chapters.

Follow the steps below to complete the GNOME installation. Note that the configuration questions on some machines may appear in a slightly different order than shown in the steps here. Additionally, depending on the versions of the software you are installing, some questions might be slightly different or not asked at all.

1. If you exited `aptitude`, rerun the following to continue with the installation:

   ```
   sudo apt-get install gnome gdm menu
   ```

   Press the Y key to start the package download part of the installation. When the download is completed, you'll be presented with a number of `debconf` configuration prompts.

2. The first configuration prompt is as follows:

   ```
   Do you want to entrust font management to defoma?
   ```

   `defoma` is Debian's font manager. GNU/Linux is often used as a platform for professional publishing and typesetting, and those users typically prefer to use an alternative form of font management. Answer Yes here unless you expect to need special fonts.

3. The next prompt is as follows:

   ```
   Which paper size should be the system default?
   ```

   Myriad GNU/Linux applications relate to printing or viewing documents intended to be printed. To render documents correctly on-screen or to print them, these applications need to know the normal paper size you use. If you're in North America, you almost assuredly want to select letter for standard letter-sized (8½-x-11-inch) paper. If you're in Europe, the standard paper size is usually A4.

4. The next question is as follows:

   ```
   Do you want cdrecord binaries to be installed SUID root?
   ```

   SUID is an acronym for setuid, a concept introduced in Chapter 3. In this instance, you're being asked whether you want `cdrecord` (a CD burning utility) to be installed such that any users in the `cdrom` group can run it as `root`. The default is No for security reasons, but answer Yes here. The only individuals in the `cdrom` group are those users whom you yourself add to the group, so answering Yes is a pretty safe option.

5. The next prompt is as follows:

```
Print paper size
```

Here is another printing-related question, in this case to deal with a particular documentation format (docbook). The question is somewhat redundant; just select the default value, which tells the docbook utilities to automatically use the paper size appropriate for the region you live in.

6. The next prompt reads as follows:

```
Please choose your sound daemon's dsp wrapper.
```

This request relates to Mozilla, the default GNOME browser. Many plugins for Mozilla use an outdated sound system interface, and as such require special handling. This question asks which type of handling to use; enter **1** to have it autodetect which workaround is appropriate. Answering incorrectly can cause Mozilla to crash with old plugins, so if you see that happen at a later time, one of the first things you should do is run `sudo dpkg-reconfigure mozilla` to twiddle with this setting.

7. The next prompt asks the following question:

```
Use nautilus-media as default video thumbnailer?
```

Nautilus is GNOME's file manager and includes several components related to viewing multimedia. Answer Yes here to enable Nautilus' video thumbnailing capabilities.

8. The final query is as follows:

```
Default backend to use for TrueType handling on X:
```

There are several different utilities available to handle TrueType fonts (a particular type of font used for both on-screen display and printing). The default value is acceptable for most purposes. That corresponds to the freetype engine, which is quite capable and mature.

That should complete the package-configuration phase of GNOME's installation. The rest of the installation should be noninteractive, but it might take a few minutes. When it's done, you can move on to the next subsection, which describes how you can use and configure the GNOME Display Manager.

The GNOME Display Manager

The GNOME Display Manager (the gdm package) is a program that will come up on your computer's screen at startup and allow you to log into the system through a graphical interface. GDM doesn't start automatically as soon as you've installed it. If it started while you were in the middle of an installation process, your virtual terminal would be switched to the one the GNOME Display Manager (GDM) uses, and you'd need to press Ctrl+Alt+F*x* (F1, F2, or F3) to get back to your text-based terminal. To start it, run the following:

```
sudo /etc/init.d/gdm start
```

After a few moments, the GNOME Display Manager will launch XFree86 and display a login window. Note that starting GDM manually is only required immediately after you've installed it; otherwise GDM will start automatically at boot-time.

With GDM started, you should see a screen similar to that shown in Figure 8-1.

Figure 8-1: The GNOME Display Manager.

With GDM installed and running, you can configure and use it, as discussed in the following sections.

Configuring the GNOME Display Manager

While you may choose to simply accept the default configuration, GDM is quite configurable. To see what you can do with GDM, go to the Actions menu and choose Configure Login Manager. Type in the root password and press Enter. You need to type in your root password at this point because only privileged users should be able to change the configuration of anything that relates to user authentication.

Within the GDM Configuration dialog box, there are all sorts of options. Table 8-1 gives an overview of the various terms and concepts included in the labels of the options.

Table 8-1
GDM Terms and Definitions

Term/Concept	Definition
Standard Tab	
Greeter	The greeter is the graphical/visible portion of the display manager.
Local versus remote	X11 can be used over a network, such that lightweight computers can run full graphical sessions on central servers. Part of that technology includes logging in to the server, and as such display managers must be able to run on a server and provide login windows to remote computers (in this case, the lightweight computers).
Automatic/timed login	For the case where the display manager is running on a standalone computer with only a single user, it may be convenient for the display manager to automatically assume a particular user is going to log in, and thus log them in automatically. These options entail a security risk because no password would be required to access (possibly private) user data.
Standard Greeter Tab	
Face browser	Many display managers are able to read a picture for each possible username somebody can log in as, and display it in a nice graphical box for selection. If this option is enabled but the username doesn't have a picture associated with it, a generic image will be displayed instead.
Security Tab	
root logins	Given the philosophy that only those operations that *must* be performed as `root` should be, most display managers disallow direct root logins (because running a full desktop environment as root means running a huge amount of unnecessary code as root).
Actions menu	The Actions menu (described in the following subsection) allows the user to perform various operations like rebooting the computer or shutting it down. When Secure Actions Menu is enabled, most of these operations will require the root password.
XDMCP	XDMCP, or the *X11 Display Manager Control Protocol*, is used solely for logging in to shared servers. The XDMCP chooser allows the user to view a list of servers that allow logins and select a particular server.

Term/Concept	Definition
TCP connections	By default, X11 will only display programs running on the same computer as the display hardware (which is where the X11 server runs). If you want to run programs on a remote computer and have them display locally, you'll need to allow remote TCP connections to the X server.
XDMCP Tab	
Enable XDMCP	Enabling GDM's XDMCP support will let other machines run graphical sessions on the machine where GDM is running. This option should be left unchecked unless you use X11 terminals (typically lightweight computers designed solely to log in via an XDMCP-enabled display manager, thus running their entire desktop session on the server where the display manager is running).

When you've finished playing with configuration settings, exit the GDM Configuration Wizard.

With everything configured the way you like it, you should be able to just log in now with the default settings.

Using the GNOME desktop

Having logged into your GNOME desktop, you should see a screen similar to the one shown in Figure 8-2. Note that all GNOME screenshots in this book won't look identical to your own because I'll be changing some colors and fonts (as discussed in the "Personalizing GNOME" section).

Panels and windows

Probably the first notable things in your new GNOME desktop are the icons on the desktop and the two panels (top and bottom). Assuming you've used computers before, the operation of these controls (or *widgets)* should be pretty intuitive. Left-clicking your mouse while it's over a particular widget generally activates said widget, and right-clicking will usually pop up a new menu full of actions related to that widget. The GNOME desktop provides a great deal of basic functionality. In this section, I cover the use of all the basic functionality such as using the GNOME panels, the window manager, the file manager, and so on.

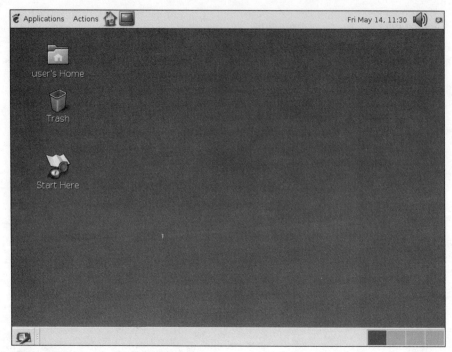

Figure 8-2: Post-login GNOME desktop.

The GNOME panels

GNOME panels are multipurpose and provide a great deal of functionality. Basically, anything that is provided via a panel is meant to be visible at all times. Windows don't cover panels.

Cross-Reference For a full treatment of configuring GNOME panels, see the "Personalizing GNOME" section of this chapter.

The default top panel contains the Applications menu, the Actions menu, two basic *launchers*, and a number of miscellaneous *applets*. Launchers are simple buttons that run applications. In this case, the icon of a house launches the GNOME file manager to view your home directory when it is single-clicked with the left mouse button. The launcher with the monitor icon launches a terminal emulator, giving you access to your shell. Applets are small programs that usually exist to display system information. There are three applets included in the top panel by default: a time-displaying applet, an applet to control speaker volume (the speakerlike icon), and an applet in the far right, which provides a drop-down menu of windows.

The Applications menu provides access to the lion's share of graphical programs available on your system. Open the menu by left-clicking it. The first portion of the menu contains all the GNOME-related applications on the system. The last menu item, titled Debian Menu, contains all the applications on the system, GNOME-related or not. Close the menu by clicking anywhere outside the menu. The Actions menu contains miscellaneous menu items that affect your session. These include menu items to log out and lock your screen.

The bottom panel contains three applets by default. The first is the Show Desktop applet, which simply hides all windows to make the desktop visible in its entirety. The second is the Workspace-Switching applet, explained later in this section. If you have any windows running, you will see a third applet: the Window List applet, which displays all the currently open windows. In all, the default bottom panel is something of a navigation panel; it allows you to quickly and easily access your desktop, your windows, and your workspaces, similar to Microsoft Windows' bottom taskbar.

Open a window by clicking the Home icon in the top panel. When that's open, click the Monitor icon in the top panel as well.

With those two windows open, you should see some changes in the appearance of some of the applets. Most notably, the rightmost applet in the top panel is no longer grayed out. Left-click it, and you'll see the list of open windows. The bottom panel has also undergone some changes; the Window List bar that was previously empty now contains buttons for both windows. Clicking one of those buttons raises the corresponding window to the foreground. To hide the windows and view your desktop in its entirety, click the leftmost applet on the bottom panel. Click it again to unhide your windows. Last, on the far right of the bottom panel, you should note that the first of those four boxes now has a little picture in it. This is a depiction of your *workspace*. Workspaces are common in GNU/Linux, and provide a means for organizing large numbers of open windows. Click on the second box to switch to your second workspace. Your windows will disappear from the Window-List bar in the bottom panel, as well as from the screen itself.

Managing windows

Managing windows in GNOME should be pretty intuitive if you've used Windows or any other common GUI system previously. Take a look at Figure 8-3, a screenshot of my home directory, which has been opened in the GNOME file manager from the Home icon on the top panel:

The Window menu button lets you activate all common window operations, which are described in Table 8-2.

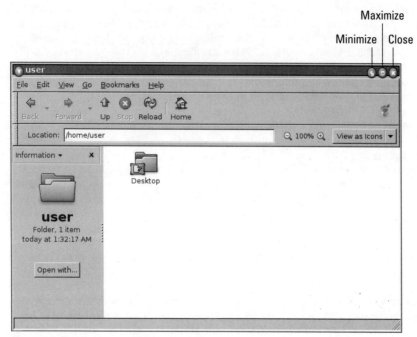

Figure 8-3: Typical window in GNOME.

Table 8-2
Window Operations

Window Operation	Description
Minimize	Hides the window. The window can be restored by clicking on its entry in the bottom taskbar or its entry the Window List menu.
Maximize	Expands the window to fill the entire screen (minus panels). Selecting this item again will restore the window to its original size.
Roll up	Hides the contents of the window and leaves only the title bar visible. Selecting this item again will restore it to its regular dimensions. Note that this function can also be activated by double-clicking any nonbutton part of the title bar.
Move	Enables window movement with either the mouse or keyboard. You can set the window in its place by pressing Enter or single-clicking the left mouse button.

Window Operation	Description
Resize	Enables window resizing with either the mouse or keyboard. Pressing the arrow keys will resize the window in large increments; holding down Ctrl while pressing the arrow keys will allow for more fine-grained resizing. Press Enter or single-click the left mouse button to finish resizing.
Close	Closes the window.
Put on All Workspaces	Makes the window *sticky*; it will appear on all workspaces.
Move to Workspace x	Moves the window to the given workspace.

The Window menu can also be activated by right-clicking any portion of the window frame, including the title bar.

Dedicated icons exist on the title bar for closing, maximizing, and minimizing the window, as seen in Figure 8-3. You can also move the window by clicking and holding down the left mouse button on a nonbutton portion of the title bar and then dragging the mouse. You can resize the window by clicking and holding down the left mouse button on any edge of the window (the mouse cursor will change to indicate when it's over an appropriate location) and then dragging the mouse.

In addition to using the various menus, buttons, and panel applets to navigate through your windows and workspaces, GNOME provides a number of keyboard shortcuts (sequences of keys pressed at the same time) to allow users to more quickly navigate without needing to reach for the mouse. Table 8-3 summarizes the main keyboard shortcuts.

Table 8-3 Window Management Keyboard Shortcuts	
Operation	**Shortcut**
Pop up window menu	Alt+Space
Maximize window	Alt+F10
Unmaximize window	Alt+F5
Minimize window	Alt+F9
Toggle window shade/rollup state	Alt+F12
Close window	Alt+F4
Move window	Alt+F7

Continued

Table 8-3 *(continued)*	
Operation	**Shortcut**
Resize window	Alt+F8
Move window one workspace to the right	Shift+Alt+→
Move window one workspace to the left	Shift+Alt+←
Move window one workspace up	Shift+Alt+↑
Move window one workspace down	Shift+Alt+↓
Cycle through windows	Alt+Tab
Switch to the next workspace to the right	Ctrl+Alt+→
Switch to the next workspace to the left	Ctrl+Alt+←
Switch to the next workspace upwards	Ctrl+Alt+↑
Switch to the next workspace downwards	Ctrl+Alt+↓

Using the GNOME file manager

While many Debian users strongly prefer a command-line interface to file management, there are many reasons to use a graphical file manager. One of the most notable is the ability of a graphical interface to present a great deal of information on-screen at a single time. This section focuses on navigating the file system with the GNOME file manager and manipulating individual files and directories.

Cross-Reference

Before proceeding, you may want to review the first half of Chapter 3, specifically the section "Filesystem Structure." It provides a great deal of background information about the structure and properties of files in a GNU/Linux system, which will aid you when examining files via the GNOME file manager. As a reminder, you can launch a shell by clicking the Monitor icon of the top panel.

Navigating and examining files and directories

You should already have a window open for your home directory, but if you don't, click the house icon in the top panel. The interface presented is similar to that of a browser, including Back and Forward buttons in the toolbar. Opening files and directories is accomplished by double-clicking them with the left mouse button. To move upwards in the filesystem hierarchy, press the Up button on the toolbar.

Note

The desktop part of GNOME, the area of the screen that's mostly blank and has only a few icons in it by default, is actually just an extension of the file manager that's visible at all times. Everything discussed in this section is applicable to the desktop as well as individual file manager windows.

For every file or directory, you can right-click its icon and pop up a context menu of available functions. Right-click the Desktop directory and select Properties from the popup menu to open the Desktop Properties window, shown in Figure 8-4. Within the Desktop Properties window are four tabs: Basic, Emblems, Permissions, and Notes. The Basic tab allows you to rename the file or directory you're viewing, as well as set a special icon for that particular object. The Emblems tab allows you to add small icons to the object. Note that emblems are viewable only within the GNOME file manager. The Permissions tab lets you change the group-ownership and permissions set for the given object. Finally, the Notes tab lets you assign small textual notes to a given object. Close the Desktop Properties window by clicking the Close button (see Figure 8-4).

Figure 8-4: Desktop Properties window.

The left pane of the file manager window is a multipurpose sidebar. By default it displays information about the directory or file you're currently viewing. If you left-click on the Information text, which has a small downward-pointing arrow beside it, you can select different sidebar functions. The Emblems function gives you an easy way to drag emblems to given filesystem objects without needing to go into the Properties window for that object. Note, however, that to remove an emblem you need to turn it off in the Properties window. The History function lists all the recent locations or directories you've viewed in the file manager. The Notes function displays (and lets you edit) notes for the object you're viewing. In most cases this will be a directory. Lastly, the Tree function provides a hierarchical display of directories for easy navigation across different parts of the filesystem. To view a given directory in the main display, click it. To expand the list to view subdirectories in the sidebar, double-click the parent directory.

If you'd like to see more detail about the files and directories in the currently viewed directory, you can increase the zoom by clicking on the magnifying glasses in the second toolbar of the file manager window. The higher the percentage of the zoom, the more details will be shown.

Moving, copying, deleting, and linking files

Moving, copying, deleting, and linking files and folders can be done in several ways using the GNOME file manager.

First, create a sample folder by right-clicking on an empty portion of the file manager's directory display and clicking the Create Folder item. Type in **Test Folder** to give it a name. Right-click on your new folder and choose Cut File (cutting and all the other actions described here can be executed on both files and directories). The folder will remain in place until you paste it somewhere. Double-click on the Desktop folder. Right-click a blank area of the display and click Paste Files. Test Folder now appears in your Desktop folder (and on the desktop itself, if you click the button at the bottom-left of your screen), and is no longer in your home directory. Right-click Test Folder again and select Copy File. Click the Up button in the toolbar to return to your home directory. Right-click an empty area and select Paste Files. There are now two folders named Test Folder, one on your desktop and one in your home directory. Right-click the Test Folder in your home directory and select Move to Trash from the menu. Click the Show Desktop button on the far left of the bottom toolbar to display your desktop. Right-click on the Test Folder on your desktop and select Move to Trash. You'll note that the Trash icon on your desktop now displays a full wastebasket.

In the bottom panel, click on the button that corresponds to the file manager window displaying your home directory. (It has a folder icon with the same name as your username.) Resize the window so that it doesn't take up the whole screen; you want some of your desktop background to be visible. Right-click on a blank area and select Create Folder. This time, name it Test Folder2. Now click and hold the left mouse button on Test Folder2, and drag it to your desktop. Dragging a file or folder with your left mouse button will move it, and now you should see Test Folder2 gone from your home directory but present on your desktop. Drag it back to your home directory with your left mouse button.

Now, instead of dragging it with your left mouse button, drag it with your middle mouse button from your home directory to the desktop (for a two-button mouse, hold down both buttons simultaneously and drag). A menu will appear with the options Move Here, Copy Here, and Link Here. If you choose Link Here, a symbolic link (think of a pointer or a shortcut in Microsoft Windows) will be created. This lets you refer to the same file or directory in multiple locations. Perhaps you'd like to keep a file /home/user/data/notes.txt, but you'd like that file to be accessible directly from the desktop. A link is what you're after. Click on the Link Here menu item. The icon will be created, and it will have a blue arrow indicating that it's a symbolic link. Right-click on the new icon and select Move to Trash.

Note that dragging works between any two file manager windows and remember that the desktop is nothing more than a constantly available file manager window. You can drag and drop files and directories to and from regular file manager windows to your heart's content. For now, close the window that displays your home directory.

Using the Trash bin

You can't actually delete files outright with the GNOME file manager; the most you can do is move them to the Trash bin. The Trash bin should be familiar to you if you've used any other mainstream platform like Windows or Mac OS. It's a step between deciding that you want to remove a file and actually removing it (thus making it totally inaccessible). Care should be taken when emptying the Trash bin because that truly deletes the files, and there's no way to get them back.

To restore files from the Trash bin, double-click the icon on your desktop and use it like you would use any other file manager window. Copy files from it, move them, and so on.

When you right-click a file in the Trash bin, you have an additional menu item available: Delete From Trash. This will delete the file completely. If you'd like to empty the Trash bin entirely, you can select File ⇨ Empty Trash, or right-click on the Trash icon on your desktop and select Empty Trash.

Personalizing GNOME

Since the GNOME philosophy is that of simplicity, configuration options may be more limited than what you're used to. This scarcity of options can be a boon to system administrators and support technicians, however, because there are fewer places where the user may have inadvertently changed the behavior of an application such that they're no longer able to use it. Some GNOME developers refer to GNOME as "the desktop environment for the adult in you," referring to its relative simplicity and blandness. Nevertheless, GNOME doesn't do away with all options, and those that exist tend to be quite heavily used. This section isn't meant to be exhaustive coverage of every option available in every GNOME application, but rather limits itself to the more common configuration options available for panels and the desktop environment in general.

Personalizing desktop panels

A great deal of the GNOME desktop environment is extremely flexible; the GNOME panel is one of the most flexible subsystems. This is largely due to the flexibility inherent in the use of panel applets, which allow for quick addition and removal of additional panel functionality. In fact, the greatest degree of desktop personalization results from the user's choice of applets.

Adding and removing panels

GNOME, by default, contains two panels. Panels are simply the blank spaces on any side of the screen upon which you can add tools that you want easy access to.

Adding panels is quite easy: Simply right-click an empty area of an existing panel and click New Panel. Removing a panel is just as easy. Right-click on an empty area of a panel and click Delete This Panel.

Changing a panel's properties

If you right-click on an empty portion of your new panel and select Properties, a new Properties dialog box will pop up with two tabs, General and Background.

The General tab contains the most interesting settings. The Name setting isn't normally used; it's primarily intended for visually impaired users, who can't navigate through the different panels based on sight. The Orientation setting allows you to specify which edge of the screen the panel is displayed on. Note that you can also drag the panel around the screen with your middle mouse button to place it wherever you'd like. (For a two-button mouse, hold down both buttons simultaneously and drag.) The Size setting is expressed in pixels. New panels have a default size of 48 pixels, but both the default panels included in the GNOME desktop are only 32 pixels high and wide. If Expand is enabled, the panel takes up the full width or height of the screen. If Expand is disabled, it will only take up as much space as is required to display the applets contained within the panel. The Autohide setting tells the panel to hide itself; to make the panel visible, you move your cursor to the edge of the screen which that panel occupies and wait a moment for it to appear. The Show Hide Buttons option, which is enabled for the top panel by default, adds one button on either end of the panel. Clicking on one of these buttons causes the panel to withdraw, leaving only a single button on-screen, which can be clicked to reexpand the panel.

The Background tab allows you to control, to some degree, the appearance of the panel. The default value of None makes the panel appear like everything else on the desktop, using the desktop or system theme. Selecting Solid Color lets you make the panel a particular color, and you can also make the panel opaque in this mode. If you'd like, you can find a picture to use as the panel's background, and set it using the Background Image setting.

After you've finished exploring the various settings, close the Panel Properties window.

Adding, removing, and configuring panel launchers and applets

Panels are useless without content, and the content available for panels comes in one of four forms: drawers, menus, launchers, and applets. You can add new items to a panel by right-clicking an empty portion of the panel and using the Add to Panel submenu.

Launchers are simple buttons you place on panels to launch applications. You can create launchers to run explicit commands, or you can easily add launchers from the menu. Launchers exist primarily to provide easy access to frequently used applications. To add a Calculator icon, for example, right-click on your new panel, highlight Add To Panel, and click Launcher ⇨ Accessories ⇨ Calculator. The new icon will appear on your panel. Click it to start the Calculator if you'd like, and then close it.

You can also add a new launcher without using the Launcher from the panel submenu. Right-click an empty portion of the panel, highlight Add To Panel, and click the Launcher item. A new dialog box will appear, asking you to enter details for your new, custom launcher. For Name, type **Test Launcher**. Leave the Generic Name and Comment fields blank, but type **sudo aptitude update** in the Command field. Click the No Icon button, and select any icon you'd like from the resulting window. Having selected the icon, enable the Run In Terminal option. Then click OK. Now click on your new launcher, and a terminal emulator will be displayed, running the command `sudo aptitude update`. You can run any command via a launcher, but be sure to enable the Run In Terminal option if it's a terminal or console tool.

Applets aren't explicitly marked as such, but you add them in the same manner you add launchers and menus. Right-click an empty portion of your panel, and highlight the Add To Panel submenu. There are six submenus at the top of the Add To Panel submenu: Accessories, Actions, Amusements, Internet, Multimedia, and Utility. Highlight the Amusements submenu and then click on the Eyes item. A pair of eyes will appear in your panel. Move your mouse around, and the pupils will follow the cursor. Applets differ from other types of panel content in that they tend to be active; they often gather data from the system or the Internet and display it in a concise manner. For instance, add the System Monitor applet from the Utilities submenu. This will display your current CPU usage in a moving-graph/histogram format.

Add a drawer to your empty panel by right-clicking on the panel and selecting Add To Panel ⇨ Drawer. A new icon will appear, in the shape of a wooden box. Left-click on the box and a new drawer will slide out. This drawer is, in many respects, identical to a regular panel — a sort of panel within a panel. While the drawer's panel is visible, you can right-click it to add content or manipulate applets, launchers, and menus directly within it. You can even add drawers to drawer panels, for multiple levels of nested drawers.

If you'd like to reposition your applet, either within the panel or to another one, you can either right-click it and select Move from the submenu, or drag it around the screen with your middle mouse button. To remove an applet, right-click it and select Remove From Panel. If you right-click an applet and select Lock, it can't be moved or removed without explicitly unlocking it first. This is handy to prevent accidental removals or movement.

Many applets (or drawers, or menus, or launchers) have individual configuration dialog boxes. Right-click on the Geyes applet, for example, and select Preferences. Within the Geyes preferences window, you can select the appearance of the eyes. As you can see, Geyes is a very simple applet; most applets provide far more options. For example, open the Preferences window for the System Monitor applet for a richer set of choices.

When you're finished playing with applets and panels, you can remove any unwanted experiments by highlighting the panel, right-clicking an empty area, and selecting Delete This Panel. If the panel has any content, a dialog box will appear asking you to confirm the deletion.

Using the Desktop Preferences menu

At one point, GNOME had a monolithic preferences manager that was accessible from a central application, the GNOME Control Center. However, in keeping with the mantra of simplicity that is deeply ingrained in the GNOME desktop, preference windows can now be started like any other window, via the Applications menu.

File management preferences

Open the File Management Preferences window by selecting Applications ⇨ Desktop Preferences ⇨ File Management. There are four tabs: Views, Behavior, Icon Captions, and Preview. The Views tab sets the defaults for any directories you view; whenever you change a setting while viewing a directory (its zoom, for instance, or its display mode), those settings are remembered for that directory only. To change them globally, set them here in the Views tab. Of particular note is the Show Hidden And Backup Files setting. This causes the file manager to display files that begin with a period; it wouldn't otherwise do so. The most interesting setting in the Behavior tab is the Single-Click/Double-Click setting. If you prefer a more Web browser–like interface (in that you dislike double-clicking files and directories to view them), enable the Single Click To Activate Items option. The Icon Captions tab lets you set what information is displayed in the icon view when you zoom in on a group of files. The Preview tab lets you fine-tune preview behavior in the file manager, such as allowing larger images to be thumbnailed and displayed as the file's icon (instead of a generic image-file icon).

Keyboard shortcut preferences

If you'd like to set keyboard shortcuts for functions that don't have them, or if you'd like to change the default shortcuts, you can do so in Applications ⇨ Desktop Preferences ⇨ Keyboard Shortcuts. To add or change a keyboard shortcut, simply click the function from the list and select your new shortcut. If that particular shortcut is being used by another function, a dialog box is displayed. To remove a shortcut, click it in the list and press the Backspace key.

Multimedia key preferences

So-called "multimedia" keys common on newer keyboards provide dedicated buttons for specific functionality, such as volume changes or Web browsing. The Applications ⇨ Desktop Preferences ⇨ Multimedia Keys window works in the same way as the Keyboard Shortcuts window described in the previous subsection. Click on a function and press the appropriate multimedia key, or press Backspace to remove the shortcut.

Setting a network proxy

Settings for network proxies are stored globally in GNOME in Applications ⇨ Desktop Preferences ⇨ Network Proxy, so that these settings don't need to be reset for each new GNOME application you use. Unless your system administrator has told you to set a proxy (and has provided you with instructions on doing so), it's important to leave this set to Direct Internet Connection.

Setting a different screen resolution

Screen resolution in GNU/Linux is often a source of complaints. A regular user can't simply set any arbitrary resolution, as they might in Microsoft Windows. There are good reasons for this: If you can change a setting like that, a virus or a worm can change it, too. Unfortunately, it's possible for your monitor to become damaged if given improper settings. As such, the only resolutions you can change to are those that have been approved by the system administrator, typically during XFree86 installation. During that configuration, or reconfiguration, you'll be able to copy settings from the documentation or technical specifications of your monitor and be able to choose from a range of appropriate and safe resolutions, which you can then make available to your users. Users will be able to change to those resolutions via Applications ⇨ Desktop Preferences ⇨ Screen Resolution.

Sound preferences

If you'd like to assign sounds to GNOME events, such as windows opening and closing, as well as sounds from applications themselves, you can do so in Applications ⇨ Desktop Preferences ⇨ Sound. Note that you need to check the Enable Sound Server Startup check box in the General tab of the Sound Preferences window if you want to use sound events.

Setting a theme

Themes are like skins or customized views you can place on GNOME and other applications that change behavior and appearance in a consistent way. Themes in GNOME can be quite amazing, as is the case with the theme capabilities in most GNU/Linux applications. I encourage you to explore the various preinstalled themes available in the Applications ⇨ Desktop Preferences ⇨ Theme window. There's nothing more impressive to a potential GNU/Linux user than a professional, snappy-looking desktop theme.

Window management preferences

Window management within GNOME is one of the simplest subsystems, and as such there are very few preferences of note. However, if you're migrating from another platform, you may be used to double-clicking a window's title bar to maximize said window. If you prefer this behavior, open Applications ⇨ Desktop Preferences ⇨ Windows and set Double-Click Title Bar to perform this action.

The K Desktop Environment

The K Desktop Environment, or KDE for short, was the first large-scale desktop environment created for GNU/Linux computers. KDE was started in 1996 primarily as a response to the rapid adoption of Windows 95, with its reasonably well-integrated graphical interface. Today, KDE has jumped ahead of much of its competition by leaps and bounds and offers a flexible desktop that almost anybody can feel at home in. This section assumes you've read the GNOME portion of this chapter, which introduces a fair number of important concepts. Here I cover installing KDE, basic KDE usage, managing files with the KDE file manager, and personalizing your KDE desktop.

Installing KDE

This section walks you through installing the most common KDE packages. I'm going to assume that you've also installed GNOME (covered in the first half of this chapter). If you opted not to, however, you may want to occasionally refer to the "Installing GNOME" section to look up appropriate answers to debconf questions, which won't all be covered in this section.

1. First, in a shell, run the following command:

   ```
   sudo apt-get install kde
   ```

   KDE weighs in at a hefty 200 or so megabytes. This is primarily due to KDE's large application base. The kde metapackage in Debian installs virtually every KDE application available. Press Enter or the Y key at the apt-get prompt, which asks whether you'd like to continue.

2. debconf will ask the first question:

   ```
   Use debconf to manage permissions of ls-R files?
   ```

   ls-R files are indexes of directories that can contain thousands of files. The use of these indexes speeds up access to the files within those directories for applications that support them. Say Yes here.

3. The next debconf prompt is as follows:

   ```
   Which group should own the ls-R files?
   ```

   ls-R files need to be writable by a fairly large number of applications and users. Press Enter here for the default value of users.

4. The next debconf question is as follows:

   ```
   Manage language.dat with debconf?
   ```

   language.dat is used to store preferences with respect to hyphenation patterns in the TeX typesetting system. Answer Yes here so you don't need to manually edit a configuration file to load the appropriate hyphenation patterns for your language.

5. The next prompt is as follows:

   What hyphenation patterns to load?

   Enter the numbers for the hyphenation pattern(s) that most closely match the languages you use.

6. The next question is as follows:

   Which communication port to use with the Palm?

   If you have a PalmOS-powered device, you may want to run sudo dpkg-reconfigure kpilot at a later time to see this question again. For the time being, select None.

7. The final prompt is as follows:

   Select the desired default display manager.

   KDE includes its own display manager, KDM. I prefer GDM myself, and this book only documents its use, so I would recommend you choose GDM here. If you know what you're doing and you'd like to give KDM a try on your own, however, feel free.

Using the K Desktop Environment

If you're currently logged into GNOME, log out. Alternatively, if you haven't started GDM, start it now by running the following:

    sudo /etc/init.d/gdm start

If you opted to use KDM instead and you haven't started it, start it now by running:

    sudo /etc/init.d/kdm start

If you're using GDM, select KDE from the Sessions menu. If you're using KDM, click the Menu button, highlight the Session Type item, and then click KDE in the sub-menu. When you've selected the KDE session, log in normally with your username and password.

Upon logging into KDE for the first time, you'll be presented with a new-user wizard that walks you through a rather high-level KDE configuration routine. The first screen is displayed in Figure 8-5.

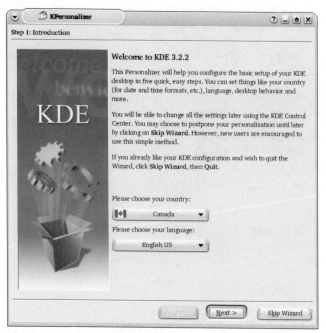

Figure 8-5: KDE first-time configuration wizard.

Read the on-screen instructions and use the buttons to choose an appropriate country and language. Chances are the defaults are correct for you; they're based on answers you've given during Debian installation. When you've answered, click the Next button to move onto the next screen, titled System Behavior. I suggest you leave the default (KDE) in place and click the Next button. The instructions in the rest of this section assume you've answered in that manner. The next screen, Eyecandy-O-Meter, allows you to specify how many special effects will be enabled by default in the environment. If you have a slow computer, say one that was brand-new five years ago, slide the indicator to the far left. When you're done, click Next. This screen, the Theme Selection window, lets you pick from a few predefined themes. Clicking on a theme from the list provided will give you a preview of the theme. Choose one and click Next. The last screen is just an information dialog box. Click Finished.

Having completed the first-time configuration wizard, your desktop should look like the one in Figure 8-6.

As with the treatment of GNOME in the first part of this chapter, all screenshots following this paragraph may appear different than your own desktop.

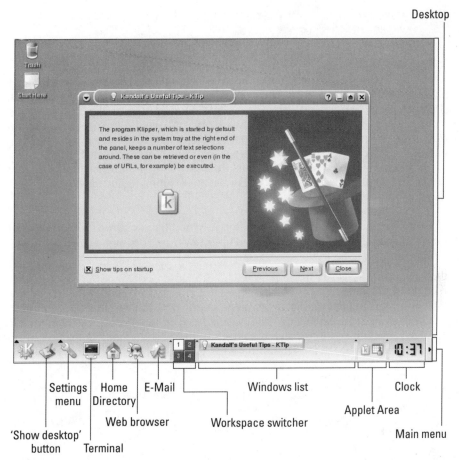

Figure 8-6: KDE desktop.

The main menu in KDE is referred to as the K Menu and is accessed by clicking the K icon in the bottom-left corner of your screen. Unlike the GNOME menus, which are segregated, the KDE menus are merged. All applications on the system are available directly from the K menu. The K menu also includes the standard logout/ screen lock items. By default, the very top of the K menu is reserved for applications that are run often. You won't see anything in that area yet because you haven't run many applications. The K menu also incorporates a simplistic filesystem browser, labeled Quick Browser. Lastly, the K menu includes the bookmarks menu, as seen in the Konqueror application (discussed later in this chapter).

Using panels and windows

As with GNOME, the most-used portions of KDE are its panels. Unlike GNOME, KDE defaults to having a single all-purpose panel at the bottom of the screen. Figure 8-6 has labels to identify all the parts of the default panel.

Cross-Reference   For a full treatment of KDE panel configuration, see the "Personalizing the K Desktop Environment" section of this chapter.

Using KDE panels

There are a few notable differences between GNOME's panel and KDE's panel. KDE panels tend to be less flexible than GNOME panels. They're not made up of distinct, separate parts so much as a single monolithic but feature-rich utility. Additionally, there is no "KDE menu" and no "Debian menu"; it's one large, merged menu. Aside from these points, using the KDE panel should be as simple as using the GNOME panels. Left-click to activate items, drag with your middle mouse button to move items around (for a two-button mouse, hold down both buttons simultaneously and drag), and right-click to view a context-sensitive submenu for each part of the panel.

If you're curious about the functionality provided by any given icon on the panel, hold your mouse cursor over the icon for a few moments and a tooltip will be displayed.

Managing windows

Window management in KDE is virtually identical to window management in GNOME, so refer to the "Using the GNOME desktop" section of this chapter for details. However, keyboard shortcuts differ. Table 8-4 documents the KDE window management keyboard shortcuts.

Table 8-4
KDE Window Management Keyboard Shortcuts

Operation	Shortcut
Cycle through windows	Alt+Tab
Cycle through workspaces	Ctrl+Tab
Pop up window menu	Alt+F3
Close window	Alt+F4
Hide all windows (Show Desktop)	Ctrl+Alt+D
Switch to workspace 1	Ctrl+F1
Switch to workspace n	Ctrl+Fn

Using Konqueror

Konqueror, the KDE file manager, is sometimes called the KDE Swiss Army Knife. Konqueror is one of the greatest examples of the basic differences in design philosophy between KDE and GNOME. As opposed to GNOME's simple file manager, which presents limited options and display mechanisms, Konqueror is a flexible tool for data representation—namely, the data in your filesystem. Though this added flexibility also entails added complexity and a steeper learning curve, the results can be quite rewarding, as you can configure Konqueror to closely match your own work habits. Open a Konqueror window to your home directory by clicking the house icon in your KDE panel. You should see a window similar to Figure 8-7.

Figure 8-7: Konqueror displaying a home directory.

Navigating and examining files and directories

First and foremost, be aware that Konqueror defaults to using single clicks to open files and directories. In fact, virtually everything in KDE is accomplished by single clicks, in an effort to ensure consistency across the entire environment. In that vein, when managing files, Konqueror acts very much like a Web browser. See Figure 8-8 for an explanation of the toolbar.

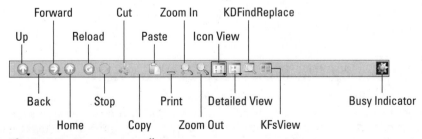

Figure 8-8: Konqueror toolbar.

You don't need to consult documentation whenever you want to know what a button does; you can pop up a tooltip by holding your mouse cursor still over a button for a few moments. Both the Icon View button and the Details View button have submenus; to activate them, click and hold your left mouse button on one of those buttons.

The sidebar in Konqueror is a multipurpose tool that can display everything from Web pages to a media player to a hierarchical representation of the filesystem. As you click icons on the far left of the window, the icon expands to include a full textual label. Click each of the icons in turn and examine the contents. The Services sidebar (denoted by a piece of paper with its bottom-right corner folded upward) is the default sidebar view. Clicking items in the sidebar will cause the main display area to change appropriately; for instance, if you select `bin` in the Root Folder sidebar, the `/bin/` directory will be displayed.

Since items in Konqueror are activated by single left-clicks, you need to hold down the Ctrl key while left-clicking to select an item (as opposed to activating/opening it). Right-clicking an item in Konqueror will bring up a context menu much like in the GNOME file manager (though with many more options), including the object's properties.

Modifying a file or directory's properties

Right-click on the Desktop icon in your home directory and select the Properties item. A window similar to the GNOME File Properties window will be displayed. Konqueror doesn't support emblems, nor does it support file-specific notes. Additionally, the Permissions tab is quite different. Instead of providing a matrix of permissions bits, it provides textual representations of the possible combinations in a drop-down list. If you click the Advanced button in the Permissions tab, a more conventional check box–laden window appears to modify the file's permissions.

Moving, copying, and linking files

Managing files is what a file manager is all about, and Konqueror allows you to perform standard file management operations in a familiar way: right-clicking objects and selecting Cut, Copy, or Paste functions identically to the GNOME file manager.

A few differences exist, however. First, you cannot drag items with the middle mouse button. Instead, with Konqueror, dragging items with the left mouse button always pops up a menu of available operations; there is no default. Additionally, Konqueror by default offers a Delete option in its right-click menu for items, bypassing the Trash bin completely.

Personalizing the K Desktop Environment

While KDE doesn't try to be everything to everybody, the developers go to some length to make the environment flexible enough to support most users. It's more than just making sure people can use the environment; they also try to make sure that people can use the environment *comfortably*. KDE provides a large set of configuration options that allow you to tailor the environment to your own tastes.

Personalizing desktop panels

As I mentioned earlier, KDE's desktop panels are rather more monolithic than GNOME's. In practice, this doesn't mean much, especially for regular use. However, it's worth bearing in mind when changing the panels. You may find that customizing KDE panels is somewhat clunkier than customizing GNOME's panels.

Adding and removing panels

Access to most panel operations is available through right-clicking a blank area of an existing panel. Right-click a blank area of your current panel, then highlight Add, and then highlight Panel.

Note   You can also right-click on the arrow icon on the far right of the panel if you can't find any blank space. Likewise, right-clicking on any occupied part of the panel will pop up a menu that contains a Panel Menu submenu; this is the same menu that appears when right-clicking an empty area of the panel.

There are five different types of panels in KDE:

✦ **Child panel:** In all respects, a child panel is equivalent to the main panel. Anything you can put in the main panel, you can put in a child panel. Add a new child panel by clicking the Child Panel item in the menu.

✦ **Dock application bar:** Before panels were common, many small applications called *dockapps* were created. They served much the same purpose as applets do today. Run `apt-cache search dockapp` in a terminal window to see a list of a few of the `dockapps` that are available in Debian. The dock application bar in KDE holds these `dockapps` in place. They're actually full-blown utilities in their own right and would normally have window borders and take up a great deal of screen real estate. With the dock application bar, they take up significantly less room.

✦ **External taskbar:** The external taskbar is a dedicated panel that displays buttons corresponding to windows. It's comparable to the portion of the Windows taskbar that displays window names.

✦ **KasBar:** The KasBar is a special type of panel that displays a large icon for each type of application on the screen. When there are multiple applications of the same type open (for instance, multiple Konqueror file management windows), clicking on the icon will open a drawerlike panel that shows icons for each individual window of that type.

✦ **Universal Sidebar:** The Universal Sidebar panel is identical to the sidebar in the Konqueror file manager windows. Putting the sidebar directly on your desktop lets you access all sorts of information quickly and easily. For instance, you may keep the Bookmarks sidebar open at all times.

Changing a panel's properties

To change a panel's properties, right-click your new panel and select Configure Panel. The window that appears lets you adjust all sorts of panel properties. The Arrangement tab contains, notably, the Position setting. Use the 12 buttons in that part of the dialog box to set the position of the panel. Note that unless the length of the panel is set to less than 100 percent of the screen width/height, there are effectively only four positions (top, bottom, left, and right). It's worth noting that if you set Length to 1% and enable Expand as Required to Fit Contents, the panel will be the minimum size possible to accommodate its contents; this allows for more application screen real estate. The Hiding tab lets you fine-tune any autohiding behavior, as well as the animation that occurs when the panel is hidden (either automatically or manually, by clicking the arrow-labeled buttons on the panel).

The Menus and Appearance tabs affect all on-screen panels, not just the one you right-clicked. In these tabs you can control the display and behavior of the primary KDE menu (indicated by a large white K with a gear behind it, the leftmost icon on the bottom panel), as well as various cosmetic settings that apply to panels.

Exit the panel configuration window by clicking OK or Cancel.

Adding, removing, and configuring panel components

Right-click your child panel and highlight the Add submenu. Within this submenu you can add applets, launchers, and special buttons.

Add a System Monitor applet by highlighting Applet and clicking System Monitor. To move the System Monitor applet around, right-click its *Handlebar* and select Move from the submenu. The Handlebar is a subtle separator bar with a small black arrow pointing outwards, away from the panel. Panel components with their own right-click menus will have Handlebars displayed so you can invoke the standard right-click menu. You can't move applets between panels in KDE. To move an applet from one panel to the other, you need to remove the first one (by right-clicking and selecting Remove), and then re-create it elsewhere. You can have the same applet appearing in multiple panels, or even multiple times in the same panel. Configuration is specific to each applet (right-click and select Preferences, typically), so you can have one applet that displays information in one way, and a second that displays information in a different way.

To add a launcher, right-click on an empty portion of the panel, highlight Add, and then highlight Application Button. This displays the applications portion of the K menu, and you can add the launcher by simply clicking on the relevant menu item. If you want to add a custom launcher, right-click on an empty portion of the panel, highlight Add, then highlight Special Button, and then select Non-KDE Application.

Note   When in doubt, right-click screen objects. I've never known it to cause any harm, and the resulting submenu is usually full of interesting functionality.

If you'd like to remove your new panel, right-click its Hide button (the button at the top with the arrow on it) and select Remove. Be warned that KDE doesn't ask for confirmation on panel removal, even if it has applets and buttons.

Using the KDE Control Center

Comprehensive documentation of the KDE Control Center, including an explanation of every option, could easily fill a 500-page book. This section is intended to familiarize you with basic operation of the KDE Control Center, and to highlight some of the more commonly changed settings.

Open the KDE Control Center by clicking the Preferences button on your main panel (the icon with the wrench on it), and then clicking the Control Center item. This launches the full KDE Control Center window, which allows you to navigate all of the environment's settings in a single window. If you'd like a shortcut to a particular page of settings, select it from the appropriate submenu in the Preferences menu.

The KDE Control Center window is divided into two parts: a navigation pane on the left, and the content area on the right. As you select items in the navigation pane, the content area will change to display the settings available for the given item. Changed settings in the KDE Control Center don't take effect immediately. After you make a change to any setting, you must click the Apply button in the bottom right of the content area.

Configuring appearance and themes

Left-click on the Appearance & Themes item in the Navigation pane. There are many separate configuration modules for Appearance & Themes, and the full list should now be expanded. You can collapse the list by clicking Appearance & Themes again, but for now select Background.

The background configuration module is pretty mundane in general terms; changing desktop backgrounds is a common occurrence. Note, however, that you can set a different color or background image for each individual workspace (*desktop* in KDE parlance). If you keep all your e-mail–related programs on workspace 2, for instance, it may be worth your effort to change its background color to draw special attention to it.

The Colors module of Appearance & Themes lets you set colors for specific portions of applications — buttons, for instance. Most KDE styles respect these color preferences, allowing you to have a desktop whose buttons not only are shared the way that you want, but also are colored as you want. In the bottom-right portion of the Colors module, just below the Widget Color section, there's a setting for Contrast. The Contrast setting, roughly, corresponds to the "3D-ness" of the widgets; if you set Contrast to its lowest setting, the controls on your screen will appear rather flat. Not all styles respect the Contrast setting, however, because it doesn't always make sense given the way some styles render on-screen controls. The B3/KDE style is a good example of a style that respects the Contrast setting.

The Icons module lets you change the icon theme for your desktop. The Style module lets you select styles that modify the basic properties of widgets, such as buttons and menus; for instance, you can select the Plastik style for a relatively subtle but nevertheless fancy style, as opposed to the default Keramik style, which is quite flashy.

You can download themes, styles, and backgrounds from `www.kde-look.org/`.

Configuring the desktop

The Desktop category of the left-hand navigation pane refers to the desktop that holds icons and is hidden behind application windows, as well as settings for panels and windows. In these modules, you can fine-tune the behavior of desktop icons, configure the number of workspaces you have, access panel settings, and control to a very fine degree the behavior of window controls — to the point of deciding what each different click does.

Network settings

Click on the Internet & Network category in the left-hand navigation pane. Within this category is a plethora of settings for anything network- or Internet-related. These include e-mail and identity settings, local network browsing settings, proxy settings, network connection preferences, Web browser settings (also accessible via the Settings menu in Konqueror), and wireless network settings. In some cases, you'll need to contact your network administrator to set these configuration values correctly.

Security and privacy settings

If you're worried about other people accessing your computer, the best way to keep your information private is to not record it at all. Failing that, you can encrypt your data. The Security & Privacy category in the Navigator pane lets you specify what information is recorded to disk, and in what manner it can be accessed.

Summary

Having read this chapter, you should feel reasonably comfortable working in both the GNOME and KDE environments. If you've used other graphical interfaces in the past, chances are you were already at home as soon as the desktop environments discussed in this chapter were started. There are some pretty standard features across modern graphical environments, and these conventions can help ease a user into a new one. If you didn't read both halves of this chapter and instead decided on a particular environment, I'd like to take a moment to encourage you to try the other when you get some time. I recommended GNOME at the very start of this chapter for those who simply want to get going in their new GNU/Linux system, and I stand by that recommendation. However, some people feel that by investing a little time into KDE to make it behave in a manner that best suits your work habits, you can increase productivity and reduce frustration at having to adapt to GNOME's "one way and only one way" of doing things.

✦   ✦   ✦

Internet Applications

GNU/Linux has, from the very start, been a network operating system. Even its development model is heavily
dependent on cheap network access to its developers. This
rich heritage of network interoperability translates to a
plethora of options for using network services on your
GNU/Linux desktop. In this chapter, I present three competing
options for Web browsing, and three for e-mailing.
Competition is almost invariably good for the user. In the
beginning of each section, I quickly compare the highlights of
each of the three options presented and make some suggestions on which might best suit your needs. For the most part,
though, functionality is close enough across the options that
you can choose based on a purely cosmetic basis — perhaps
one option has prettier buttons or a more pleasing layout. For
each application covered in this chapter, I describe its installation, its main features, and its configuration. For instant
messaging (IM), I focus solely on the Gaim instant messaging
client because it's by far the most mature and capable.

All the applications covered here — Web, e-mail, and IM — use
Internet standards to communicate with servers. (Later chapters in this book, notably those in Parts III and IV, cover
installing server software with which these clients can communicate.) Though a regular home user doesn't *need* to run
her own server, having both client software and server software included in the Debian GNU/Linux distribution allows
individuals to take control of their network environment and
provide services to friends, families, or even customers.

Browsing the Web

Web browsing is, without a doubt, one of the largest uses of
computers today. It's so popular that some mistakenly believe
that Web browsing *is* the Internet. There's no doubt that Web
browsing for education, business, and entertainment is an

important part of many people's daily lives. This section assumes that you're already familiar with Web browsing to some degree; you're familiar with Web pages and how to use them. To add to your basic understanding, I cover following links and filling out Web forms in this chapter.

There are three mainstream browsers available in GNU/Linux:

✦ **Firefox** is the replacement for the popular Mozilla Web browser — the descendent of Netscape Navigator. Mozilla is a famous project and is used by many users on different platforms. Mozilla's developers, however, decided that the browser had become too complex and bloated, and thus started the Firefox project. Firefox is a trimmed-down, streamlined version of Mozilla, built using the same technology. Compliance with standards and compatibility with Web pages is one of the primary goals of the Mozilla (and hence the Firefox) project. Firefox's full name is actually *Mozilla Firefox*.

✦ **Epiphany** is the default GNOME Web browser. As with most things GNOMEish, Epiphany espouses simplicity over virtually every other attribute. Epiphany uses Mozilla technology to render Web pages for on-screen viewing and manipulation.

✦ **Konqueror** is the KDE browser, and is also used for file management. Started from scratch, Konqueror is homegrown, so to speak, for KDE. Konqueror is fast and stable and is of such high quality that Apple decided to use Konqueror's rendering engine in its own browser for OS X, Safari.

Though perhaps a bit premature since we haven't launched any browsers yet, the Web sites for the browsers are `http://conqueror.kde.org/` (Konqueror), `www.mozilla.org/products/firefox/` (Firefox), and `www.gnome.org/projects/epiphany/` (Epiphany).

While the choice of a browser is ultimately a matter of personal preference, I can offer a few quick guidelines. If you're using KDE, you'll almost certainly prefer Konqueror. Konqueror is quite capable as a browser, and its integration with KDE is above par. Konqueror's standards compliance isn't the best of the three browsers (both Firefox and Epiphany, based upon the extremely standards-compliant Mozilla framework, beat Konqueror in this regard), but it's a rare Web page that isn't usable with Konqueror. If you value simplicity above all else, you're probably most interested in Epiphany. There isn't much to say about Epiphany otherwise. It's worth noting that Epiphany uses Mozilla technology, however, and as such it renders Web pages excellently. Firefox is something between Konqueror and Epiphany. Out of the box, it's quite simple but not restrictively so. There is a huge library of extensions available for Firefox, which lets you round out any functionality you might find missing. Firefox renders pages very faithfully according to standards, and in my opinion it does an excellent job. Firefox also has the advantage of being available for many platforms, so if you're stuck using another platform, you can download and install Firefox and use a browser you're already familiar with.

Installing and using Epiphany

This section covers the installation and use of Epiphany. Epiphany is currently the default GNOME browser. GNOME has gone to great lengths to provide a desktop that is easy to learn, and it presents the simplest possible interface to the user. A major reason Epiphany is the default GNOME browser is its adherence to those ideals. As such, Epiphany doesn't offer a lot of the bells and whistles present in other browsers.

Epiphany uses the Mozilla framework for rendering Web pages. The Mozilla project was started years ago to create a standards-compliant platform for Web application development. Mozilla technology isn't the fastest around, but it's arguably the best. Web developers in particular tend to like anything that uses Mozilla technology because very little else in the field renders their Web pages exactly as they intended, the first time around. Since Epiphany uses this technology, it gets standards-compliant Web page rendering for free. A modern Web page–rendering engine is a massive piece of code, and a very complex one at that. There are many complex standards to follow, and even more non-standards-compliant Web pages to deal with. Historically, anything based on Mozilla technology (including Mozilla itself) was considered quite slow, but the continual march of computing technology has made most such concerns irrelevant on modern computer hardware. Mozilla-based applications such as Epiphany feel quite snappy even on relatively low-end (by today's standards) computers such as an 800MHz Pentium-III with 128MB of memory.

If you installed GNOME, you'll already have Epiphany installed. Otherwise, install the package `epiphany-browser`. If you're asked any `debconf` questions, read the "Installing GNOME" section of Chapter 8, which will give you some insight into the answers.

Using Epiphany features

Once installed, Epiphany should appear in your menus. In GNOME, you can start it by selecting Applications ➪ Internet ➪ Web Browser. In KDE, you can start it via the K Menu ➪ Internet ➪ Web Browser. If you're using GNOME, you'll need to log out and log back in to have the icon appear in your menus. Otherwise, you can simply run the command `epiphany` from any terminal emulator. When you start Epiphany, you should see a window similar to the one shown in Figure 9-1 but showing the home page set for your browser.

If you've ever used a browser before, the window layout should be familiar to you. Along with the standard set of toolbar buttons, you have a URL location bar where you can type in Web addresses and other URLs.

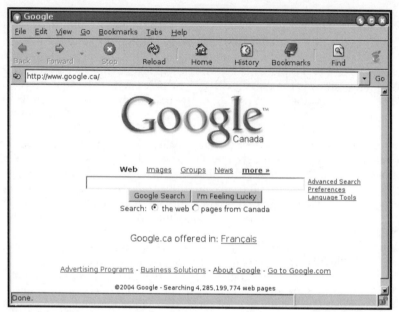

Figure 9-1: Epiphany main window.

Using bookmarks

Bookmarks in Epiphany may be different than what you're used to. Instead of having a hierarchical menu of folders and bookmarks, with each bookmark in one folder, Epiphany instead has *topics*. Each bookmark may appear in one or more topics, or it may be in none at all. There are six topics by default: Entertainment, News, Sports, Shopping, Travel, and Work. Go to the URL bar and type **www.debian.org**, and then either press Enter or click the Go button on the far right side of the URL bar. Add a bookmark for the displayed page by selecting Add Bookmark from the Bookmarks menu. Check the boxes for News, Shopping, and Work. Now open the Bookmarks menu again and view the contents of the News, Shopping, and Work topics to see that the page has been added under those topics. You can also add a bookmark for the current page by right-clicking on a nonlink, nonimage portion of the page. You can add a bookmark for a link by right-clicking on the link and selecting Bookmark Link. To add or remove topics, or to change the topics for an existing bookmark, open the Bookmarks menu and click Edit Bookmarks. A window similar to the one shown in Figure 9-2 is displayed.

The left-hand navigation pane displays all the currently defined topics, as well as the pseudotopics All, Most Visited, and Not Categorized. To rename or delete a topic, right-click on it in the navigation pane and select the appropriate item. To create a new category, click File ⇨ New Topic.

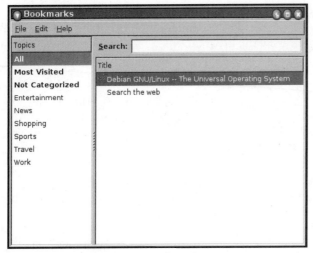

Figure 9-2: Epiphany bookmarks editor.

When you click a topic in the navigation pane, the display area on the right side of the window will display all the bookmarks in that particular topic (or, in the case of the All or Not Categorized topics, all bookmarks or those that haven't been put in any topics, respectively). Within that pane you can change the properties of a bookmark by right-clicking on it and selecting the appropriate item from the submenu (such as Delete, Rename, or Properties).

Using multiple windows and tabs

All the browsers discussed in this chapter support what's called *tabbed browsing*. Instead of opening links in the current window or in a new window, you can opt to open links in a new *tab* of the current window. A tab is like a new window, but instead it looks like the top of a file within one window. I strongly recommend trying this model of browsing for a few weeks; chances are you'll find it very difficult to live without afterwards.

For Epiphany, as with all other browsers discussed here, you can open links in new windows simply by clicking them with the middle button on a three-button mouse. Alternatively, you can right-click on the link and select Open Link In New Window. The next section, "Configuring Epiphany," documents how to make Epiphany open links in new tabs by default when the links are middle-clicked. For now, if you want to open a link in a new tab, right-click it and select Open Link In New Tab. The only reason this isn't the default is because users have come to expect new windows to be opened by middle-clicking a link — in time, we can expect middle-clicking to open links in new tabs by default. Middle-clicking, whether it opens a new window or a new tab, is a great shortcut. Many people find themselves opening new views more often simply because they don't need to go through a right-click menu to do it.

Configuring Epiphany

Epiphany doesn't have a lot in the way of configuration variables, but this section covers the basics of configuring the program. Open the Epiphany preferences window by going to the Edit menu and selecting Preferences. There are four tabs: General, Fonts And Colors, Privacy, and Language.

✦ **General** — There are two settings in the General tab: the Home page (the page that is opened when you first open the browser), and the Tabs setting. With the Open in Tab by Default option enabled, middle-clicking a link opens the link in a new tab instead of a new window. Enable this option; you'll almost certainly come to love that behavior.

✦ **Fonts And Colors** — A standard font selection dialog box, the Fonts And Colors tab lets you pick which fonts (and at what sizes) you prefer Web pages to use. Note, however, the Web pages have the capability to override these settings. If you want Web pages to be forced to use the fonts you've chosen, then enable the Always Use These Fonts setting. The Minimum Font Size setting is also useful; if you find that many pages are using fonts that are too small for you to comfortably read, set the minimum font size to something larger.

✦ **Privacy** — The Privacy tab lets you disable both Java and JavaScript, which some users find intrusive. Cookies are used by Web sites to store information about your visits, such as any preferences you set for that Web site, so you probably shouldn't disable them. The capability to choose whether you want to allow popup windows is a much-lauded feature of GNU/Linux Web browsers. Popup and popunder ads are offensive to many and irritating to most. By disabling this option, most of these intrusive advertisements will be blocked. If you click a link that is meant to pop up a new window, the window will open. Only automatically popped-up windows will be disabled.

✦ **Language** — The Language tab includes places for manipulating encodings and system languages and the default encoding system. In most cases, you can safely leave these as the system default.

Note　If you like the look of Epiphany but find its simplicity overbearing, you should consider Galeon. It uses the same GNOME libraries and the same Mozilla rendering engine as Epiphany, but includes a more feature-rich interface. The package name for Galeon is `galeon`.

Installing and using Firefox

Firefox is a descendant of the famed Mozilla browser and uses much of the same technology. Firefox and Mozilla are the kings of standards compliance and correctness. I personally like the way they render Web pages, too — nice and clean, not too much whitespace, and everything where it's supposed to be. Mozilla started out as a monolithic application; it was a browser, an e-mail client, an IM client, and a few other things. Firefox is the first component to be split out into its own application. It's not an e-mail client. It's not an IM client. It's not a kitchen sink. It's a browser.

Firefox probably isn't installed on your computer; you will need to install the `mozilla-firefox` package. `mozilla-firefox` asks no `debconf` questions, so the installation should be noninteractive. As with Epiphany's installation, however, you may want to consult the "Installing GNOME" section of Chapter 8 if you see any deb-conf questions.

Using Firefox features

With Firefox installed, it's available in GNOME via Applications ➪ Internet ➪ Mozilla Firefox. In KDE, you can run it via K Menu ➪ Internet ➪ Mozilla Firefox. If you're using GNOME, you'll need to log out and log back in to have the item appear in your menu. If you aren't launching it from a menu, simply run `mozilla-firefox` or `firefox` from a terminal emulator. When you start Firefox, you should see a window similar to the one in Figure 9-3 pop up with the following page, or whatever your default home page is set to.

Figure 9-3: Firefox main window.

Firefox's activity indicator, the little icon that shows that it is downloading a Web page, is on the far right of the menu bar. The main toolbar, from left to right, includes icons for Back, Forward, Reload, Stop, and Home. After the buttons, there's an URL entry bar and then a quick-search bar. Firefox also displays a bookmark toolbar by default, which contains Firefox Help, Firefox Support, and Plug-In FAQ buttons.

Navigating Web pages with Firefox is similar to pretty much every other graphical browser. Left-click links to load them, and right-click links to get a menu of other operations. Firefox defaults to opening links in new tabs when you middle-click them, a convention that you can expect other browsers to adopt as time goes on. Middle-click any random link of the default home page; a tab bar will appear, and you'll have a new tab in the process of loading. Close the tab by first clicking on it, and then by clicking the icon marked with a red X to the far right of the tabs.

Using the quick-search bar

The quick-search bar is a handy way to perform Web searches. You can either click on the quick-search bar directly, or use the keyboard shortcut Ctrl+J. The quick-search bar, by default, searches using the Google search engine. The Debian package also includes an additional search engine: Deb Search. To try a different search engine, click on the G (for Google) icon in the quick-search bar, and you'll get a popup menu displaying the other search engines available. Click Deb Search, type your term into the quick-search bar, and press Enter. Firefox loads the Debian Package Search page, with the results for the search term you entered.

Using bookmarks

You can add bookmarks by either using the Add Bookmarks item of the Bookmarks menu, by right-clicking links, or by right-clicking any nonlink portion of the current page. When you add a bookmark, you'll have the opportunity to name it and put it in a bookmark folder. If you click the down arrow at the far right of the dialog box, to the right of the Create In box, you can create new folders right in the Add Bookmark dialog box. Any bookmarks added to the Bookmarks Toolbar folder will be displayed in the bookmarks toolbar in the main browser windows.

To edit or reorganize existing bookmarks, you can use the Bookmarks menu, highlight the bookmark you're interested in, and then right-click it (yep, right-click a menu item). If you want to change the folder a bookmark resides in, open the Bookmarks menu and click Manage Bookmarks. Within the Firefox bookmark manager, you can drag and drop bookmarks to rearrange them, edit their properties, add separators, and create and delete folders.

Configuring Firefox

To configure Firefox, open the Options window by clicking on the Tools menu and selecting the Options item. Firefox occupies, in my mind, a nice medium in terms of configurability. There are seven configuration categories in Firefox: General,

Privacy, Web Features, Downloads, Themes, Extensions, and Advanced. I cover the more commonly used ones but omit Advanced, which is covered in the Firefox documentation:

✦ **General** — In the General tab of Firefox's options window, you can set all the basic configuration items: home page, fonts, and so on. Notably, the Connection Settings button configures any network proxies you may need or want to use. Firefox keeps its own record of which proxies you use, so be sure to set them here.

✦ **Privacy** — The Privacy category controls any data that is stored on disk by Firefox. The same rules apply here as with any sensitive information; the best way to keep it private is to not store it at all. In this tab you can disable the storage of most types of data that Firefox can store. You can also fine-tune the list of sites for which Foxfire will remember information. For instance, you may want Firefox to remember your username and password for a favorite weblog site, but you may not want it to save the username and password you use to access your bank account.

✦ **Themes** — Firefox is fully themeable, meaning every portion of its interface can be customized. A link at the bottom of the Themes category, Get New Themes, lets you easily preview and install new themes at Firefox's Web site. Note that for a theme to be available for selection, you must install it, close all Firefox windows, and start it again.

✦ **Extensions** — Extensions are what make Firefox a real gem in the browser world. Unlike plug-ins, which usually just display particular Web formats on-screen, Firefox extensions can modify the way the browser behaves. Perhaps you'd like to wiggle your mouse to reload a page? There's an extension for that (it's called mouse gestures). There are extensions for almost every conceivable use. Click on the Get New Extensions link at the bottom of the Extensions category in the Firefox options editor to find and install new extensions. The changes won't take effect until you've restarted Firefox.

Installing and using Konqueror

Konqueror, living up to its reputation as the Swiss Army Knife of KDE, is not only a file manager. It's also a Web browser. Konqueror uses its own Web-rendering engine, which is very fast. It isn't known for its stunning standards compliance, but it's better than most commercial browsers available. Konqueror integrates very well into the K Desktop Environment. Its bookmarks appear in the K menu, and you can seamlessly move from viewing Web pages on remote servers to manipulating the local filesystem. With a few exceptions, any file type that a KDE application understands can be viewed directly within the Konqueror window.

If you installed KDE, Konqueror is already available. If you didn't, however, you can install it by installing the package `konqueror`. If you see any debconf prompts you can't answer on your own, read the "Installing GNOME" and "Installing KDE" sections of Chapter 8, where many debconf prompts are discussed.

Using Konqueror features

Konqueror isn't available in the GNOME menu. If you're using GNOME and want to try Konqueror, you can run it by running the command `konqueror-profile web-browsing`. You can use the Actions ⇨ Run Application menu item, you can create a custom launcher for it, or you can run it from a terminal emulator's shell prompt. If you're using KDE, the easiest way to launch Konqueror as the Web browser is to click the blue globe icon in your main panel. Having launched Konqueror, you should see a window similar to the one in Figure 9-4.

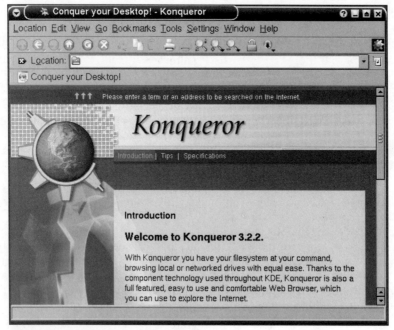

Figure 9-4: Konqueror main window.

Using Konqueror is pretty much identical to using Epiphany or Firefox. Take some time to familiarize yourself with the interface, click some buttons, and explore the menus. Konqueror, by default, opens links in new windows when you middle-click them; that can be changed in the configuration window, as discussed below.

Configuring Konqueror

Like much of KDE, Konqueror is very configurable. To open its configuration window, click the Settings menu and select Configure Konqueror. There are far too many settings to cover here, so I'll just point out some of the more interesting ones. In the Web Behavior category, you can set links to open in new tabs when middle-clicked by unchecking the Open Links in New Window Instead of New Tab setting.

You can set the minimum font size in the Fonts category. You can add shortcuts to often-used search engines and the like in the Web Shortcuts category; defaults exist for many search engines. For example, typing **gg linux** in the URL bar will search for the term *linux* via the Google search engine. Storage of privacy data is controlled by the History Sidebar, Cookies, and Cache categories. You can mask the browser you're using (to appear as Internet Explorer, for example) in the Browser Identity category—useful for sites that behave differently depending on the browser you're using.

Sending and Receiving E-Mail

Historically, e-mail has been the driver of Internet adoption. Browsing the Web is certainly convenient, but there were preexisting alternatives: books, libraries, television, and other information sources. However, before the Internet, there was no cheap and easy way to communicate with people at long distances. Telephone conversations could be expensive, and the quality of the audio could suffer terribly. It's also turned out that people *like* e-mail as a communications method, even when giving somebody a voice call costs little or nothing. Many people in modern offices would sooner send an e-mail to a co-worker than walk across the office to speak to them face-to-face. E-mail gave people the ability to more easily manage their time and effort; you can send an e-mail and then forget it. You needn't wait for a response. Likewise, if you receive an e-mail, no doubt you respond to it when you have the time, as opposed to immediately (which is expected of face-to-face communication).

The three e-mail clients discussed in this section are all graphical and full-featured. They all communicate using industry-standard protocols like POP3 and IMAP (for receiving mail) and SMTP (for sending mail):

✦ **Evolution** is the standard GNOME e-mail client. It also supports extensive groupware and personal information management functionality, such as calendaring and an address book, in an integrated package. Evolution supports using Microsoft Exchange as the server, a widely deployed enterprise mail and groupware package. Evolution is polished, fast, and flexible.

✦ **KMail** is the standard KDE e-mail client, and as such integrates well with the rest of the KDE desktop. KMail has companion applications for its address book, KAddressBook. KMail has excellent cryptography support, letting you assure those who are receiving your e-mails that the e-mails arrived unmodified.

✦ **Thunderbird** is the Firefox companion that handles e-mail. Thunderbird has excellent antispam facilities; you can train it to recognize the type of spam *you* receive and don't want, which allows for very accurate categorization. That makes it very easy for new users to start filtering their mail, a task that normally needs to be done by the system administrator with other e-mail clients. Thunderbird also uses the same Mozilla technology as Firefox, which means that its support for HTML e-mail is excellent, and you can rely on Thunderbird being available to you regardless of the platform you use.

Installing and configuring Evolution

Evolution is an excellent all-in-one personal information manager, e-mail client, and calendaring application. This section focuses on the e-mail capabilities of Evolution, rather than the other functionality. I encourage you to read Evolution's online help (via the Help menu, once it's installed and running) for details on Evolution's additional features.

If you installed GNOME following the directions in Chapter 8, Evolution is already installed and available. If you didn't install GNOME, you can install Evolution by installing the evolution package. Once installed, Evolution can be run from the GNOME menu by selecting Applications ➪ Office ➪ Ximian Evolution. If you use KDE, you can run it by selecting K Menu ➪ Office ➪ Ximian Evolution. If you use GNOME, you'll need to log out and log back in before it's available in your menu. Also, you can start Evolution by running the command evolution. The first window you see should look similar to Figure 9-5.

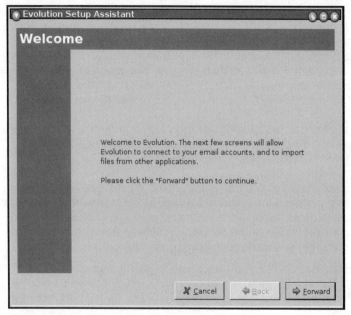

Figure 9-5: Evolution first-time startup window.

When Evolution is started for the first time, you'll be presented with this setup assistant (more commonly known as a *wizard*). Click the Forward button in the bottom-right of the window after you've read the introductory text. In the next screen, Identity, enter your full name, your e-mail address, and if you'd like, your organization. Leave the Reply-To field empty unless you know you need to set it to something specific. When you're done, click Forward again. The next screen is the mail reception configuration screen. Enter information about your ISP's mail server here. More than likely, it's a POP (Post Office Protocol) or POP3 server. If that's the case, click the Server Type button and select POP from the menu. The Host is the name of the server; it's usually something like `pop.isp.com`, `pop3.isp.com`, or `mail.isp.com`; check your ISP's online documentation or ask your network administrator. Enter your username, and consult your ISP's documentation (or your network administrator) for the rest. Specifically, you want to know whether you're supposed to use SSL or not (likely not), and what sort of authentication type you need (probably "plain," which in this case means "password"). When you're finished filling out the mail reception server information, click the Forward button. At the next screen you can set some options for your mail server; if you're using multiple e-mail clients, you may want to enable the Leave Messages on Server setting. When you're done, click Forward.

The next screen is for sending mail. In most cases, the Server Type should be set to SMTP, and the server's name (or Host) will likely be smtp.*isp.com* (where *isp.com* is your ISP's address). Check your ISP's documentation or ask your network administrator. You'll also need to know whether you need to log into the mail server to send mail; this usually isn't the case, however. When you're done, click Forward again. Evolution now asks you to name this account; Evolution can support multiple accounts. This account name can be anything you'd like; it's strictly for your own benefit. The default (your e-mail address) should be fine. Click Forward.

Evolution keeps its own time zone setting so you can change it easily as you travel. It comes with many predefined cities, which are the red dots on the map. Select the one that's closest to you, but still in the same time zone as yourself. Click Forward again.

Evolution configuration is completed, at least the basics. Click Apply to save the settings and open the main Evolution window. It should appear similar to Figure 9-6.

Note   Evolution's manual is very complete. If you want more information, you can view the manual by clicking the Help menu and selecting Contents.

Installing and configuring KMail

KMail is the standard KDE mail client, and it integrates well with the rest of the KDE desktop. Other than that, KMail isn't as full featured as Evolution, though its support for personal cryptography (such as digital signatures and the like) is quite good. Nevertheless, KMail is a good basic e-mail client that provides all the functionality almost every user needs.

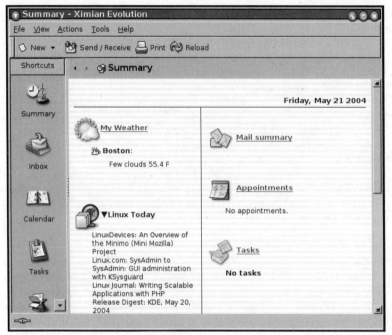

Figure 9-6: Evolution main window.

If you installed KDE as directed in Chapter 8, KMail will already be installed. If not, you can install it by installing the package kmail. Once installed, KMail can be run in KDE by selecting K Menu ➪ Internet ➪ Mail Client (KMail). KMail is not accessible from the GNOME menu, but you can run the command kmail manually, via either a terminal emulator or by making a custom panel launcher. KMail's initial screen should be similar to Figure 9-7.

KMail doesn't provide a wizard for initial setup, so you need to open the Configure KMail window from the Settings menu. That window opens initially to the Identity configuration category; click the Modify button to double-check that all the details for your identity (such as full name, e-mail address, and so on) are correct.

Figure 9-7: KMail main screen.

From the main configuration screen, click the Network category in the left-hand navigation pane to configure the details for the mail servers you use. The first tab, Sending, configures the server you use to send mail. Click the Add button to add a new account. It will ask you which *transport* (or protocol) you'd like to use. You almost certainly want to use SMTP, but you may want to check your ISP's documentation or ask your network administrator for confirmation. When you are done, click the OK button. The window that appears is for configuring the details of your server. First, fill out the Name field to something useful or memorable like the name of your ISP. The Host field should be filled with the hostname of your ISP's SMTP server; it's usually smtp.*isp.com* or mail.*isp.com* (where *isp.com* is your ISP's address). Check your documentation or ask your network administrator to make sure. Leave the Port field alone unless the documentation tells you to use a specific port number other than 25. Also leave the Server Requires Authentication option unchecked unless you know your outgoing mail server needs you to log in. If your outgoing mail server requires you to use encryption, click on the Security tab and change None to SSL or TLS. (Which one depends on the mail server's configuration; again, the documentation here is useful, but you can try sending mail with either one, and if it doesn't work try the other.) When you're done, click the OK button.

Next, click the Receiving tab. Click the Add button again to add a new server, this time for retrieving e-mail. When you click the Add button, a window titled Account Type appears; in most cases, you should answer POP3 here. Double-check with your ISP documentation or your network administrator. Click OK when done. The next window is similar to the window you got when you configured a server for sending mail. Fill out the Name, Login, Password, and Host fields as is appropriate for your ISP's mail server. The server's hostname will likely be `pop.isp.com` or `pop3.isp.com`. If you're using multiple e-mail clients on different computers, you may wish to uncheck the Delete Message from Server After Fetching option. When you're done, click OK.

Finish your configuration by clicking the OK button in the Configure KMail window.

Installing and configuring Thunderbird

Thunderbird is the e-mail client companion to the Firefox Web browser, and as such the two have much in common. They're both built atop the cross-platform, standards-compliant Mozilla framework. Thunderbird isn't the fastest e-mail client available, but it's certainly capable, and its spam filtering is quite well respected. Thunderbird, however, only does e-mail. It doesn't do calendaring, and its address book is simplistic. If you need something very full-featured, Evolution would be a better choice. But if you'd like to use an e-mail client that is available on multiple platforms, and whose support for HTML is unrivaled, Thunderbird is for you.

Thunderbird likely won't be installed on your system already. Install it from the `mozilla-thunderbird` package. Once installed, you can run it from KDE via the K Menu ➪ Internet ➪ Mozilla Thunderbird. If you're using GNOME, it's available via Applications ➪ Internet ➪ Mozilla Thunderbird. Note that if you're using GNOME, you need to log out and log back in before Thunderbird is available in your menu. Otherwise, you can start Thunderbird by running the `mozilla-thunderbird` command.

When Thunderbird is run for the first time, it provides a wizard for easy initial configuration. The first question it asks is whether you're setting up an e-mail or a newsgroup account. Make sure Email Account is selected, and then click the Next button. The next screen in the wizard asks you for your full name and your e-mail address; answer appropriately and click the Next button. The next screen is for your mail servers; Thunderbird supports only POP and IMAP servers for receiving mail and SMTP for sending, but you probably need only POP and SMTP. Fill out the appropriate values for your ISP's mail servers. If in doubt, talk to your network administrator or ISP. Click Next when you're done. Thunderbird will now ask for your username; enter it as appropriate for your server and click Next. Lastly, Thunderbird will ask you to name the account; this name is for your eyes only, so you can answer whatever you'd like. Click Next. Thunderbird will ask you to review the answers you've given. If all is well, click Finished; otherwise, click Back to adjust any of the answers you gave.

Instant Messaging with Gaim

With the advent of always-on home Internet connections, high-speed Internet connections, and the growing problem of junk e-mail, IM (instant messaging) has become a popular medium for personal communication. Though IM will likely never replace e-mail as a means of doing business (though it may complement it), IM nevertheless has many advantages: It's faster than e-mail, for one. IMs sent to others are usually received within seconds, as opposed to the minutes or hours it might take for somebody to check their e-mail. A great deal of IM's popularity comes from the applications themselves, though. Full-featured, they present communications in a line-based interface that's easy to understand and use. Click on a person's name, type in a message, and press Enter. When that person responds, type in your reply and press Enter. This quick back-and-forth exchange allows for very lifelike conversations: People tend to respond quickly and easily instead of mulling over a 10-page-long e-mail.

There are many different types of IM. The most popular include AOL Instant Messenger and ICQ, Microsoft's MSN Messenger, Yahoo! Messenger, IRC, and Jabber.

Gaim is not only available in GNU/Linux, but also in Windows. Its popularity has grown by leaps and bounds because many people find it preferable to the IM platform's native client (such as MSN Messenger). Gaim has been around for years and is quite mature. It's simple and stable and has all the features most people want.

Installing Gaim

Gaim isn't installed as part of GNOME, nor does it "belong" to any other desktop environment, so you need to install the `gaim` package to use it. Once it's installed, you can start Gaim in KDE by clicking K Menu ➪ Internet ➪ Gaim. In GNOME, you can start Gaim via Applications ➪ Internet ➪ Gaim. If you're using GNOME and you just installed Gaim, you'll need to log out and log back in before it appears in your menu. Without the menu, you can start Gaim by running the command `gaim` from a terminal emulator.

Configuring Gaim

When you first start Gaim, two windows will appear — one titled Login, the other Accounts. Start with the latter window because you need to create an account before you use Gaim. Follow these steps to create an account and begin messaging:

1. Click the Add button in the Accounts window.
2. Click the Protocol button and select IRC.
3. Type in whatever you'd like for your Screen Name, but pick something at least six characters long so as to avoid picking a name that's already in use.

4. Leave the Server and Password fields as they are, and click the Save button to save your new account and close the window.

5. Click the Auto-login check box for your new IRC Gaim account in the Accounts window and then click Close.

6. You're now left with the original Gaim window titled Login. Click the Sign On button to connect to the IRC server.

Using Gaim

Before you can send messages to anybody, you need to first add them as a buddy. Click on the Buddies menu and select Add Buddy. The window that pops up will ask you for the person's Screen Name, an optional Alias (this is what will be displayed in the Gaim window), the group you want to put them in (at the beginning you have only one group defined), and the account that person is accessible from (you only have one account defined, so there's not much choice there). Type the name of a person you want to contact here.

To send a message, simply double-click the intended recipient in your buddy list, wait for the window to appear, and start typing. If the recipient is online and paying attention, he'll respond.

To remove a buddy, right-click on the entry and select Remove. To add a new group for organizing your buddy list, click the Add Group item in the Buddies menu; after you've added a new group, you'll want to click Buddies ➪ Show Empty Groups, at which point you can drag buddies from your preexisting groups to your new group.

Summary

This chapter certainly doesn't do full justice to the rich nature of Web, e-mail, and IM clients available in GNU/Linux, but it allows you to take a tour of each. When you've decided you like a particular application more than the others, take the time to explore the functionality it offers; even the most basic applications discussed here have enough utility to each fill an entire chapter.

✦   ✦   ✦

Publishing

Computers were supposed to give us the "paperless office," but it seems we're exchanging bits of paper with each other more than ever now. Luckily, your Debian system is capable of everything from dumping out source code to preparing eye-catching reports, newsletters, and even books. In this chapter, I look at some of the word processing systems available in Debian, ranging from simple text and command-line-based formatters to sophisticated graphical page layout programs.

Using Markup Languages

The original purpose of the UNIX operating system was to provide a system for writing technical documentation at AT&T's Bell Labs. (It was also to play the game Space Travel, but you can't get funding for that.) Linux has inherited its ancestors' rich collection of tools for formatting and publishing text. Because even the biggest machines of the '70s and '80s were rather underpowered and displays were limited to green screen terminals, most of these tools were designed to operate on plain text files "marked up" with special formatting codes to indicate things such as font changes, pagination, and indentation. A set of such codes is called a *markup language*. All you really need to use a markup language is the text editor of your choice, though there are fancier tools available for most of them, with features that may make creating marked up text easier.

In this day and age, are markup languages still useful? They still have some benefits your typical word processor cannot provide. Marked up text is easy to create and edit. Any text editor will do — for that matter, so will simple command-line tools such as grep, awk, and diff. Marked up text is human readable. While the "tag soup" of HTML and similar languages may seem a little daunting to the inexperienced, you've got to admit it is easier to read than a sequence of 1s and 0s. A consequence of this is if you want to tweak it just a little bit, marked up text is easier to work with than a binary format like the ones you might be familiar with from Microsoft Word, which may become unreadable if you get one byte wrong. For these reasons, no matter how fancy word processors may get, markup languages are here to stay.

groff

A popular program of the markup language type was *roff* (and its variants *nroff* and *troff*). Debian contains the GNU implementation of roff and company, called *groff* (in the groff package.) To simplify use, groff commands can be bundled into macros. One such set of macros is *man*, which is used to write manpages. This is now the main use of groff, though many Unix old-timers still swear by it for all kinds of text processing. The following code shows a short manpage written in groff. Each of the letter sequences beginning with a period is a groff macro that causes a particular formatting effect. .B, for instance, indicates the following text on the line is bold. .SH indicates a section heading.

```
.\" This page is in the public domain
.TH LINE 1 "2002-07-07" "" "User Commands"
.SH NAME
line \- read one line
.SH SYNOPSIS
.B line
.SH DESCRIPTION
The utility
.I line
copies one line (up to a newline) from standard input to standard output.
It always prints at least a newline and returns an exit status of 1
on EOF or read error.
.SH "SEE ALSO"
.BR read (1)
```

The following code shows what the output of the preceding code might look like:

```
LINE(1)                 User   Commands                      LINR(1)

NAME

line - read one line

SYNOPSIS

       Line

DESCRIPTION

       The utility line copies one line (up to a newline) from standard
       input to standard output.  It always prints at least a newline and
       returns an exit status of 1 on EOF or read error.
```

```
SEE ALSO

       read(1)

                              2002-07-07                        LINE(1)
```

TeX and LaTeX

Another popular markup language with an emphasis on typographical accuracy is *TeX*. Pronounced *tech*, it was invented by Professor Donald Knuth for typesetting his books on computer science, which included equations and other types of scientific notation. TeX is a full programming language, and a layer built on top of it, called *LaTeX*, makes complex typography even easier. TeX and LaTeX are still widely used today, particularly in the academic and scientific communities. In fact, many scientific journals will accept articles only in TeX format. The following code shows a simple LaTeX document, and Figure 10-1 shows the rendered output. Debian includes a popular distribution of TeX and LaTeX called *teTeX*. To use it, download the `tetex-bin` package, and optionally the `tetex-extra` and `tetex-doc` packages.

```
\documentclass{article}
\title{A Simple \LaTeX Document}
\author{Prof. A.U. Thor}
\begin{document}
\maketitle
\center Did you know the chemical formula for Sulfuric Acid is
{\bf H$_2$SO$_4$}?
\end{document}
```

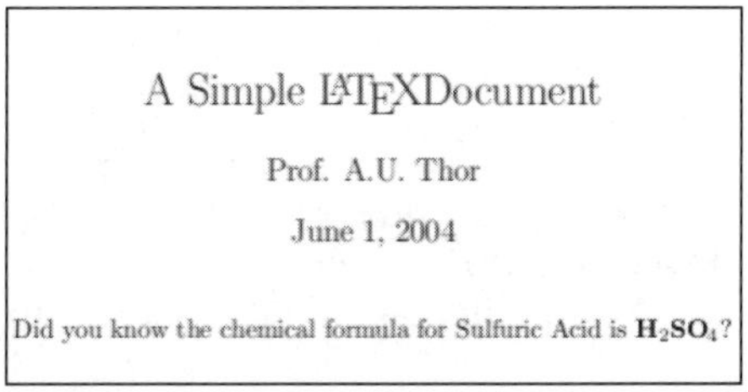
A Simple LaTeX Document

Prof. A.U. Thor

June 1, 2004

Did you know the chemical formula for Sulfuric Acid is $\mathbf{H_2SO_4}$?

Figure 10-1: LaTeX output.

HTML, SGML, and XML

Thanks to the World Wide Web, the most popular markup language by far is *HyperText Markup Language* (HTML). HTML was a particular application of SGML (Standard Generalized Markup Language), which you can think of as a markup language for creating markup languages. SGML is rather complicated to program and use, so experts in the field got together and pared down its less-used features and simplified its syntax. The resulting subset is called *XML* (*eXtensible Markup Language*). XML-based markup languages are widely used throughout the computing world. HTML itself has been redefined as an XML-based language called XHTML. Debian contains everything you need to process HTML, SGML, and XML documents.

Word Processing with OpenOffice.org

Perhaps the thought of manually adding markup to a text file in vi does not thrill you and you want a nice graphical word processor capable of WYSIWYG (What You See Is What You Get) display. Don't worry; Debian has that covered too. Both the GNOME and KDE desktop environments feature word processing programs as part of their application suites (called *Abiword* and *Kword*, respectively). The premier application of this sort, however, is *OpenOffice.org* (*Ooo* for short).

OpenOffice.org, originally a suite called StarOffice, has its roots in an Office suite made by a German company called Star Division. OpenOffice.org contains all the applications for today's business needs:

- ✦ A word processor — Writer
- ✦ An HTML editor — Writer/Web
- ✦ A spreadsheet — Calc
- ✦ An equation editor — Math
- ✦ A presentation tool — Impress
- ✦ A graphics tool — Draw
- ✦ A database program — Adabas D

Star Division was later acquired by Sun Microsystems, which generously made the StarOffice suite open source, except for Adabas D and some minor accessories (such as fonts and filters that legally belonged to third-parties and thus could not be freed). The name StarOffice was kept for the commercial version and is supported by Sun.

Installing OpenOffice.org

Using apt-get (or a front end), install the openoffice.org package. This will give you the main parts of its functionality. You can install additional packages to enhance its functionality:

✦ **myspell-dictionary:** This package adds spell-checking to the OpenOffice.org applications. There are dictionary packages for several languages. Each has the language's two- or three-letter standard code as a suffix; for example, the Italian dictionary package is called `myspell-dictionary-it`. In cases where a language has spelling variants, the standard code for the country is added to the suffix. For example, `myspell-dictionary-en-us` is the dictionary package for American English and `myspell-dictionary-en-gb` is the one for British English.

✦ **openoffice.org-help:** This package is the extensive online help for the OpenOffice.org suite. It is also available in several languages and uses the same naming convention as the dictionary packages.

✦ **openoffice.org-hyphenation:** Breaking long words correctly requires sophisticated hyphenation algorithms, which are implemented in this package. Each language has different rules for where to place hyphens, so there are separate packages for each language.

✦ **openoffice.org-l10n:** L10n is a compression of the word localization (there are 10 letters between the *l* and *n* in "localization"). It refers to features specific to a particular culture or nation, such as currency symbols, units of measurement, and so on. The name of the package for each language has its standard code suffixed to it.

✦ **openoffice.org-thesaurus:** This package adds a thesaurus to OpenOffic.org applications. Currently only a thesaurus for en-us (American English) is available.

✦ **oooqs-kde and oooqs-gnome:** These packages install an applet to the panels of KDE or GNOME that, when run, preloads OpenOffice.org into memory. This makes start-up substantially faster when you need to use one of the apps, at the cost of taking up a good chunk of memory even if you're not using any of them.

✦ **openoffice.org-mimelnk:** To know which program should be launched when you click on a particular file type, KDE uses special files. This package sets up those files so that when you click on the icon for an OpenOffice.org document in KDE, the appropriate application is launched.

✦ **openoffice.org-crashrep:** In the event an OpenOffice.org app crashes, you can use this package to send the developers a bug report.

Using OpenOffice.org Writer

Explaining everything about the OpenOffice.org suite would require an entire book in itself, so this section offers a brief look at the Writer application. When you start Writer, it will look something like Figure 10-2.

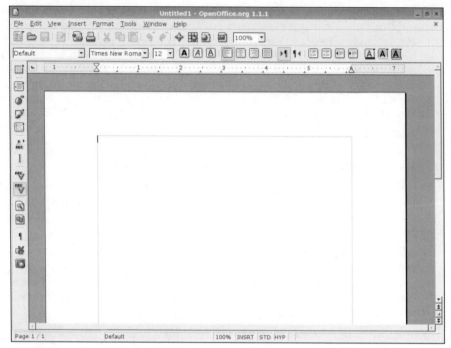

Figure 10-2: OpenOffice.org Writer.

If you've used a word processor on other platforms, you'll instantly be at home. If you've installed the Help package, you can get comprehensive online help by pressing F1. Moving the mouse over the toolbar buttons on the top or the left shows a "tool tip," which explains what the button does. The black rectangle in the middle of the window is a *frame,* a logical unit on a page that can contain text or pictures, or can even embed other OpenOffice.org documents such as a spreadsheet from Calc. In a typical letter or other short document, you will have only one frame, which extends to the margins of the page. But more complicated layouts like a three-column newsletter will use more frames.

You can customize the font, margins, and other layout features to suit your needs by using styles. You can apply a style to each page, frame, paragraph, list, or sequence of characters. If you use a particular style often, you can save it with a descriptive name using an interface called the *stylist*. Press F11 to access the stylist. Figure 10-3 shows the stylist open to the default list of character styles.

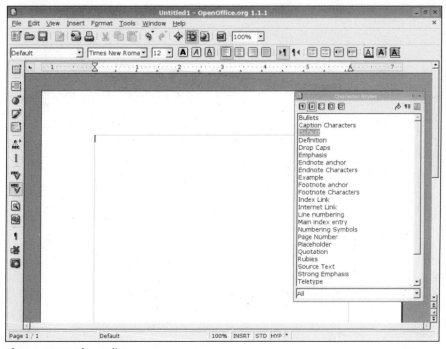

Figure 10-3: The stylist.

You can create a new style by right-clicking on the stylist window and selecting New for a brand-new style or Modify to tweak a few aspects of an existing style. When you create or modify a style, you see a window like the one shown in Figure 10-4. (The exact number and type of tabs will depend on the type of style you are editing.)

When you save your document, the styles will be saved with it. If you want to use the same set of styles in more than one document, you can save them as a template. You do this by selecting Templates from the File menu and clicking Save. The next time you want to create a document, you can select File ➪ New ➪ Templates and Documents and your template will be listed.

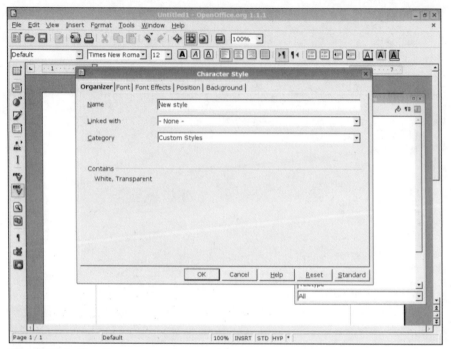

Figure 10-4: Creating a new style.

Exchanging documents with OpenOffice.org

It's a fact of life that people who use Linux and OpenOffice.org are not (yet) in the majority. Sooner or later you're going to have to exchange documents with users of other word processors. Openoffice.org can help with its export filters. When you are ready to save your document, click on File ⇨ Save As. From the File Type drop-down menu, you will be able to choose from several formats:

✦ **.sxw:** OpenOffice.org's native format.

✦ **.sxt:** OpenOffice.org's template format.

✦ **.doc:** The format Microsoft Word uses. Word 6.0, 95, 97, 2000, and XP are supported.

✦ **.sdw:** The format for StarWriter, the predecessor to OpenOffice.org Writer. Versions 3.0, 4.0, and 5.0 are supported.

✦ **.vor:** StarWriter's template format.

✦ **.txt:** Plain text.

✦ **.html or .htm:** Selecting this format will save your document as an HTML Web page.

You can also open documents created in these formats and import them into OpenOffice.org. Beware! Conversions from one format to another may not be exact. In particular, Microsoft Word documents that contain Visual Basic for Applications (VBA) macros will not work. The VBA code will, however, be transferred intact when imported or exported.

Desktop Publishing with Scribus

OpenOffice.org Writer is capable of many tasks that fall under the rubric of desktop publishing, but when you want to deal with very complex layouts or large documents, it falls a little short. Enter Scribus. Scribus has a number of advanced features needed for professional publishing, such as the following:

✦ Full support for Unicode fonts: Unicode is a way of encoding all of the world's languages in one format. Using Unicode means you can use Scribus to publish text in any language, even right-to-left scripts like Arabic and Hebrew.

✦ Color models used by printing presses: Scribus supports the CMYK (Cyan, Magenta, Yellow, and Key, which is what printers call black) and RGB (Red, Green, and Blue) models so the colors in your document are matched and printed to the exact shade. Color separations using these models can also be made.

✦ Accurate kerning (spacing) of text.

✦ Embedding and subsetting of fonts in PostScript Type 1 and TrueType formats.

✦ Support for industry-standard file formats such as PostScript level 2 and a large subset of level 3 EPS (Encapsulated PostScript); PDF (Portable Document Format) 1.4 and X-3; TIFF (Tagged Image File Format) graphics; and SVG (Scalable Vector Graphics).

✦ Powerful scripting in the Python programming language so repetitive tasks can be automated.

Install the `scribus` package and run it from the Start menu. Figure 10-5 shows the main Scribus screen. There is extensive documentation available at the project's Web site: `www.scribus.net`.

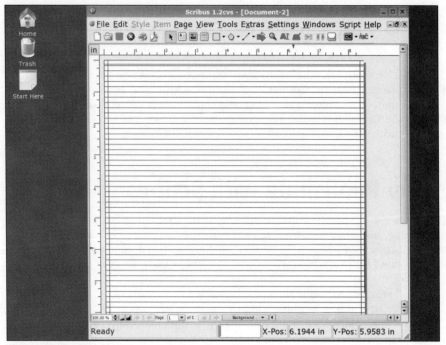

Figure 10-5: Scribus.

Web Authoring with Quanta+

As a simple text-based markup language, HTML doesn't really need any authoring tools beyond a text editor. But these days everyone wants to have a Web page, and they don't necessarily want to have to learn a lot of esoteric markup. Openoffice.org Writer and Writer/Web can help them here. For those users who become more familiar with HTML but still need a little hand-holding, a good tool is Quanta+. Install the `quanta` package with `apt-get` or a front end. Figure 10-6 shows the Quanta+ main screen.

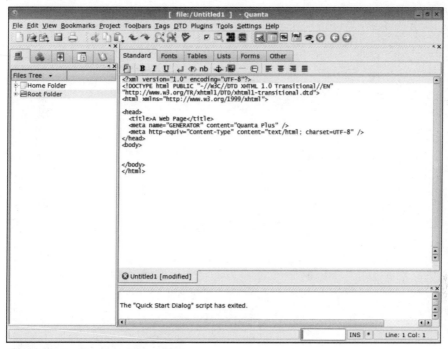

Figure 10-6: Quanta+ code editor.

As well as the code-based editor shown in the figure, Quanta+ has a visual editor (see Figure 10-7) that can help you see what your Web page will look like. You can change between the code and visual editors from the View menu. But bear in mind that HTML doesn't guarantee an exact visual representation. Every browser will implement HTML and display it slightly differently, so don't assume this view is exactly what a visitor to your Web page will see. Instead, try to test your pages with as many different browsers as you have access to. Sticking to Web standards and avoiding browser manufacturers' proprietary features will help you ensure maximum compatibility.

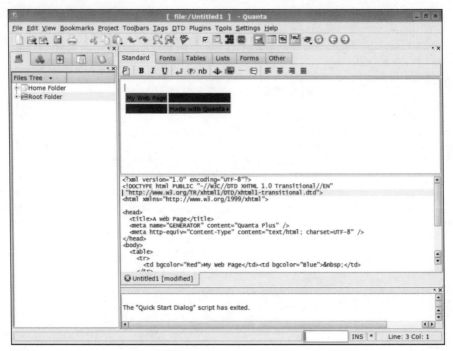

Figure 10-7: Quanta+ visual editor.

You can also use Quanta+ to edit files for other Web technologies, such as PHP (a server-side scripting language), CSS (Cascading Stylesheets), and XSL (eXtensible Stylesheet Language). HTML and other code, images, and the other elements of a Web site can be gathered into a project for easy management. Quanta+ even handles uploading your completed Web pages to a server.

Scanning and OCR

A picture, they say, is worth a thousand words. Scanning pictures into your computer is another task you can achieve with Debian. Scanner support in Linux has been unified into one method called *SANE (Scanner Access Now Easy)*. SANE splits up the task of scanner access into two parts. The front end is implemented in an application and contains all the buttons and windows needed for the user to control the scan. The back end is specific to each model of scanner and contains the code necessary to talk to it.

Installing SANE

To get started with SANE, install the `libsane`, `libsane-extras`, and `sane-utils` packages. These contain the various back ends SANE supports as well as a simple front end for testing called *scanimage*. When you have them installed, turn on your scanner and make sure it is properly connected to the right port on your computer and the cables are inserted tightly. Then, using `sudo` (or some other way of getting `root` privileges), run the `sane-find-scanner` command from a shell prompt. This should give you some information about your scanner, its type, and what port it is connected to. Armed with this information, go to the `/etc/sane.d` directory. You will see a number of files named after scanner types and ending in `conf`. Find the one that matches what `sane-find-scanner` said was your scanner type. In most cases you can leave it as is but you may want to tweak some options in it. The exact set of options offered by the configuration file will depend on the type of scanner but may include such things as scan buffer size and gamma correction.

Now you are ready to test the scanner. Run the `scanimage` program from the command line like this:

```
$ scanimage -format tiff > out.tif
```

This should create a scanned image in TIFF format that you can inspect with any graphics program.

If `sane-find-scanner` fails to find your scanner, there is most likely a cabling problem. Particularly for the old SCSI interface scanners, having the scanner at the right place in the device chain (multiple SCSI devices can be connected to one port) makes all the difference. If the scanner is found but a scanned image cannot be created, the problem could be due to incorrect SANE configuration settings. The best course of action at that point would be to compare notes with other users who have that model of scanner to see how they have configured it. The Debian-user mailing list (`debian-user@lists.debian.org`) is a good place to ask this type of question.

Some SANE front ends

The simple scanning program included with SANE, *scanimage*, is not the friendliest program to use. The SANE packages also contain a basic GUI front end called *xscanimage*, but it isn't much better. Luckily, there are some better ones.

Xsane (in a Debian package called `xsane`) is by the authors of SANE and supports it well. Another nice feature is that it can act as a plugin to The GIMP graphics program. (Install the `xsane-gimp1.2` package for this.) This means you can scan a picture and instantly edit it to change the brightness, remove red eye, and so on.

Kooka is a SANE front end for KDE. It doesn't integrate with The GIMP like Xsane, but it does have a built-in Optical Character Recognition (OCR) facility to convert scanned words into digital text. You need to install the `kooka` and `gocr` packages for this. While `gocr` is adequate, it doesn't match the quality of commercial OCR packages. Unfortunately, this is a field where free software has to compete with proprietary trade secrets and patents, which make it hard to provide high-quality free solutions.

Both Xsane and Kooka can save scanned images in standard graphic formats. From there, you can easily edit them and import them into other applications like OpenOffice.org and Scribus.

Summary

In this chapter you took a whirlwind tour of some of the ways you can use Debian to prepare documents. Whether you want to have precise typographic control or to quickly type a letter, and whether you prefer the elegant simplicity of plain text in vi or a grandiose WYSIWYG environment, Debian has the text processing system for you. You also learned how scanners work in Linux and how to set them up.

✦   ✦   ✦

Digital Photography and Multimedia

With a flock of impressive tools for multimedia projects, Debian lets you learn to become an artist, photographer, composer, or movie producer. In this chapter, I show you how to use and create sights and sounds with Debian.

In this chapter I also introduce you to tools for downloading pictures from digital cameras (gPhoto2, kamera, and Digikam), creating and editing images (the GIMP and Inkscape), playing and recording music (XMMS, Timidity++, Rosegarden, and Ardour), watching video files (xine), and creating movies of your own (dvgrab, kino, and CinePaint).

Note There is a huge amount of activity going on in the field of Linux multimedia, and the limited space available doesn't permit full coverage of this topic, so consider this only a sample of the things you can do. Throughout the course of this chapter, I give pointers to other sites and projects that deal with some of these topics in greater detail.

Using Digital Cameras with gPhoto2

Digital cameras have become so popular that they now outsell the traditional film-based variety. So naturally, adding Linux support for them was a task the community approached with enthusiasm. Some cameras simply act as USB or SCSI storage devices with a typically Windows-compatible (VFAT) filesystem.

These devices can be mounted just like any other filesystem, and listing and downloading images from them is as simple as using the `ls` and `cp` commands. Other cameras are not so simple, and access to them is centralized through the gPhoto2 library, which currently supports about 400 different models. To use it with Debian, install the `gphoto2` package and its dependencies. Then plug in your camera per the instructions that came with it and from a `bash` prompt, start the gPhoto2 command-line interface. The first command to try is `gphoto2 -auto-detect`, which will attempt to find which port your camera is on and load a driver for it. The results may look something like this:

```
$ gphoto2 --auto-detect
Model                      Port
-----------------------------------------------------------
HP PhotoSmart 715 (PTP mode)   usb:
```

Now you can access the camera with `gphoto2 -shell`.

Setting Up On-Demand Access to a USB Camera

If you have a USB camera, you might find that `gphoto2 -shell` works only for the root user. Others get a "permission denied" message. This is because access permissions for USB devices are set only for `root` by default. Savvy Linux users know that the `root` account should be used as sparingly as possible and certainly not for mundane activities like accessing pictures in a camera. The simplest way to rectify this situation is to install the `hotplug` package. This installs a daemon that watches for USB events such as devices being attached and detached from the system and performs user-defined actions in reaction to them. After `hotplug` is installed, any users in the group `camera` will have the necessary permissions to use the camera. (You will have to add the group `camera` if it doesn't already exist and add the users you want to grant access to it. See Chapter 5 to learn about adding users and groups.) If you want to use a different group, you can change the `GROUP=` line in the `/etc/hotplug/usb/libgphoto2` script to an already existing group. If you change this script you must restart `hotplug` for the changes to take effect. Do so by running this command as `root`:

```
# /etc/init.d/hotplug restart
```

The gPhoto2 shell

When you run gphoto2 -shell, you are placed at a prompt much like the one you get at a command-line. From here you can run a number of commands to control the camera:

✦ cd <*directory*> — Changes to a directory on the camera.

✦ delete <*filename*> — Deletes a picture from the camera.

✦ exit, quit, or q — Leaves the gPhoto2 shell.

✦ get <*filename*> — Downloads a picture to the PC.

✦ get-thumbnail <*filename*> — Downloads a scaled-down preview of a picture.

✦ get-raw <*filename*> — Downloads a picture as a raw stream of bytes.

✦ lcd <*directory*> — Changes to a directory on the PC.

✦ ls <optional *directory*> — Lists the files in the current or named directory.

✦ show-exif <*filename*> — Shows any EXIF tags in the picture. EXIF (Exchangeable Image File format) is a standard format for exchanging metadata about an image such as a caption, date produced, resolution, or the like.

✦ show-info <*filename*> — Gives some basic information about an image such as its size in bytes, height, and width.

Note   If you get an error such as Could not claim the USB device when you try to use the gPhoto2 shell, it is most likely a permissions problem. After adding your account to the Camera group, make sure you log out and log in again. The group membership won't come into effect until you do so.

Graphical front ends for gPhoto2

If the command-line gPhoto2 shell emulates a filesystem, it seems to be a logical progression to give graphical file managers the ability to access the camera, too. That's precisely what the authors of KDE's Konqueror thought when they created kamera. After installing the `kamera` package, you can use a pseudo-URL of `camera:/` to access your digital camera and then drag and drop pictures to the desktop or other file manager windows (see Figure 11-1).

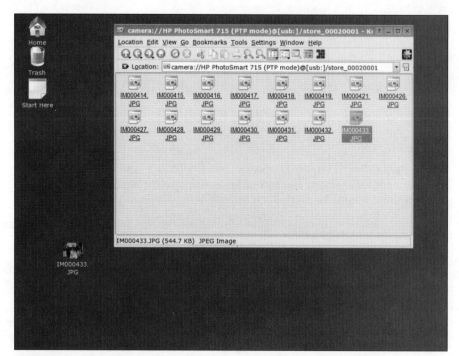

Figure 11-1: Konqueror copies a picture from a camera to the desktop.

Digikam is another KDE application for handling digital cameras, and it does kamera one better by providing a full photo management solution. Not only can you view, delete, or download pictures from your digital camera, you can add captions and other information to them (using EXIF tags), index them, and organize them into albums. You can even convert the albums into HTML and upload them to a Web site (see Figure 11-2).

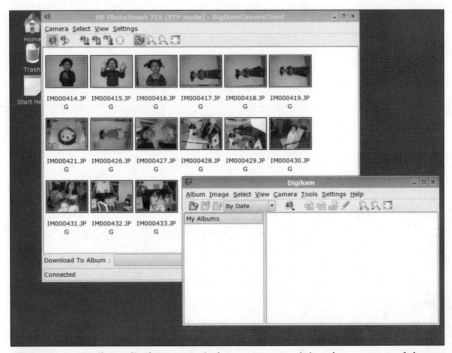

Figure 11-2: Digikam displays two windows, one containing the contents of the camera and the other an empty album ready to receive pictures.

Using Graphics Applications in Debian

Whether you are just touching up a photo from your digital camera, creating a chart for a report, or just expressing your artistic yearnings, Debian can help with sophisticated tools for creating and editing images.

The GIMP

The GIMP is a program to create and manipulate bitmap images, similar to Adobe Photoshop. The GIMP is actually one of the most venerable Linux graphical applications. The first version came out in 1995. Since then it has become only more impressive in terms of its functionality and popularity. The GIMP has had even greater influence due to the GTK+ programming toolkit, which was designed for it and is the basis for GNOME and many other Linux programs. (GTK originally stood for GIMP ToolKit.)

Start using the GIMP by installing the `gimp` and `gimp-help` packages. If you also want to be able to print, install `libgimpprint1` and `cupsys-driver-gimpprint` and set up CUPS. (See Chapter 23 for details on printing.)

The GIMP interface

Figure 11-3 shows the GIMP with one image open. The window on the left contains tools for drawing, painting, and erasing. These can be applied to all or part of the image. The window on the right displays the image itself. You can open as many image windows as your PC's memory will allow. The menus above the image provide all sorts of options for cropping, scaling, and otherwise transforming the image.

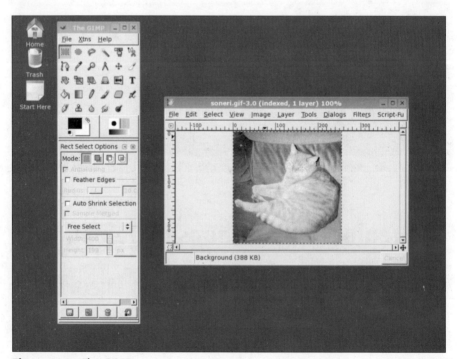

Figure 11-3: The GIMP.

Like Photoshop, the GIMP uses the concept of *image layers*, each of which can be independently manipulated. By treating an image this way, sophisticated effects can be achieved. The GIMP can save images in all the major image formats, such as BMP, TIFF, JPEG, and PNG. It also has its own native format called XCF.

Notice that the rightmost menu above the image window has the curious name of Script-Fu. This is one of the most powerful features of the GIMP. Script-Fu is an interpreter for the Scheme programming language embedded into the GIMP, making it fully scriptable. Or if you don't like Scheme, you can use Perl or Python by installing the `libgimp-perl` or `gimp-python` package, respectively. Scripts can automate much of the tedious work involved in common tasks. The scripts in the Script-Fu menu do such things as create buttons for Web sites and logos, make the corners of an image rounded, or even add an "alien glow" to images.

GIMP add-ons

Several other packages in Debian can enhance the functionality of the GIMP. In Chapter 10, I mentioned how Xsane could be used to transfer scanned images directly into the GIMP. `gimp-data-extras` is another package, which contains extra brushes. Finally, in the non-free section is `grokking-the-gimp`, which is the HTML version of the book *Grokking the GIMP* by Carey Bunk. It is an extensive beginners' tutorial on how to use the full power of the GIMP.

Note   Late-breaking news: The GIF patent has expired and the version of GIMP that will be included in sarge will have GIF support in the main package. So `gimp-nonfree` is obsolete.

Vector graphics with Inkscape

A bitmap-based program like the GIMP edits every pixel of an image. An alternative graphics program, GNOME's Inkscape, is vector based. A vector-based image is made up of points and lines. This makes it very complicated to use to describe, say, a photograph, but much more compact when representing a graph or cartoon. Inkscape uses the SVG (Scalable Vector Graphics) format, which is an industry standard. Figure 11-4 shows the main Inkscape screen. The tools along the left let you draw different types of lines and shapes. Inkscape is under rapid development. As I write this, it doesn't support the entire SVG feature set, though this is a goal for the project. It already has most of the features the average user will want, however.

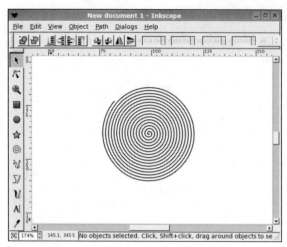

Figure 11-4: Inkscape.

Using Debian for Sound

Linux has had support for sound cards for a long time, but it is only relatively recently that the support has become high quality. The story starts in the kernel, where device drivers talk to the actual sound card hardware. The first Linux device drivers were followed an API (Application Programming Interface) called OSS (Open Sound System) created by a Finn named Hannu Savolainen in 1992. Following a common API was a good move because it meant that applications wanting to utilize sound had to deal with only one target instead of including special case code for the quirks of each sound card. Some years later, Hannu formed a company called 4Front Technologies to commercialize the OSS system. While the existing OSS drivers remained in the kernel under the name OSS/Free, new development was centered on the proprietary commercial version. In the late '90s, that and some dissatisfaction with the technical merits of OSS led some Linux developers to create another API called ALSA (Advanced Linux Sound Architecture). ALSA also includes OSS emulation, so it will at some point replace OSS/Free altogether. As of now though, both systems are available in the kernel.

Because Linux is a multitasking operating system, it is quite possible that two users — or two processes run by a single user — may want to play sounds at the same time. Some cards operate on a first-come, first-served basis, in which case one sound will play and the other will not. Sometimes the card may attempt to play the two sounds together, with grating results. To arbitrate between contending demands for the sound card's resources, a program called a sound server should be run. The sound server can route different sounds to different channels and mix them together on a multichannel sound card. Or it can place one "on hold" while the other plays. Both GNOME and KDE have their own sound servers called aRts (analog Realtime synthesis) and ESD (Enlightened Sound daemon), respectively. A third sound server is JACK (Jack Audio Connection Kit), which is optimized for low-latency professional quality sound. GStreamer is yet another general-purpose audio toolkit with a special emphasis on streaming audio and video.

Another important use for sound is to provide accessibility software. Screen readers, for example, enable visually impaired people to use a computer by reading text out loud to them. Because nearly every feature of Debian can be used via the command line, and graphical interfaces are optional, Linux is a very good choice for the visually impaired.

Last, there are the sound-using applications themselves. Debian contains a full complement of MP3 players, jukeboxes, mixers, and recording tools. This chapter assumes that you were successfully able to set up sound in Chapter 7.

Applications requiring direct sound card access

Some of the older and more primitive Linux applications may try to access the sound card directly (for example through `/dev/dsp` or `/dev/audio`). As you can imagine, in the presence of a sound server this is either going to fail altogether or succeed and lock other applications out. You can get around this by temporarily suspending the sound server from the sound section of the GNOME or KDE control panel while you use the application. Or you can run it through a program like `artsdsp` (or `esddsp`) that intercepts any calls the application makes to sound devices and reroutes them to the sound server.

A Few Words about Latency

UNIX was designed in the days when all that people did on their computers was type away on simple terminals. From the computer's point of view, even the fastest typist spends an eternity between key presses, so the computer can use that time to service other users and do a pretty good simulation of instant interactivity. The time gap between when a human asks a computer to do something and when the machine actually gets around to doing it is called *latency*. Multimedia output requires very low latency, and a kernel optimized for high-latency tasks like typing can't cut it. Our senses can easily detect even tiny hiccups and stutters in audio and video playback, and we find such things annoying.

If you are using version 2.4 of the Linux kernel, you can apply patches to lower the latency of the kernel. (See the `kernel-patch-lowlatency-2.4` **and** `kernel-patch-preempt-2.4` packages.) With kernel 2.6, latency isn't as much of a problem. The JACK sound server mentioned in this section attempts to reduce latency at the application level.

Troubleshooting

Problems can occur at several different stages of the sound output, so often it isn't easy to solve problems without a lot of trial and error. But here are a few common situations that account for a good percentage of audio problems:

✦ First look at the hardware itself. Is the sound card properly installed? If it requires cables to, say, the CD-ROM drive, are they properly connected? If your sound card is attached to powered speakers, are they switched on? Are the speakers plugged into the output socket on the card? (As opposed to the microphone socket. I've made this mistake many times!)

✦ Is the right kernel device driver for the card loaded? (You can find which drivers are currently in memory by running `/sbin/lsmod` from the command-line.) Does the driver need any particular IRQ or port settings? Are two sound servers running at once? Is the volume set to 0? (I've wasted hours with that mistake too!) If the application you are running gives a choice, is it configured for the sound server you are actually running?

In the event that none of these suggestions solves your problem, I suggest you bring it up on the Debian-user mailing list (`debian-user@lists.debian.org`). To help others help you, provide as many details as possible about your setup and what you've done to try and solve the problem so far.

The XMMS media player

GNOME has rhythmbox, KDE has noatun, and there are many other MP3/ogg players available in Debian. But X MultiMedia System, or XMMS, is one of the most popular. It has a plugin-based architecture, which means all aspects of it can be changed and extended. Begin using it by installing the `xmms` package and one or more plugin packages. At least one of these is necessary to actually play sounds:

✦ `xmms-arts` — allows XMMS to work with KDE's aRts sound server

✦ `xmms-esd` — allows XMMS to work with GNOME's ESD sound server

✦ `xmms-jack` — does the same for the JACK sound server

The Debian convention is for the names of XMMS plugin packages to start with `xmms-` so you can easily search for them with `apt-cache` or `aptitude`. The available plugins do everything from changing the "skin" or appearance of the player, to adding a psychedelic visual display along with the music, to providing lyrics to sing along to.

XMMS is fully scriptable. The `libxmms-perl`, `python-xmms`, and `libxmms-ruby` packages provide scripting support for the Perl, Python, and Ruby programming languages, respectively. XMMS can even be controlled by remote control if your computer has an infrared port and the `lirc` and `xmms-lirc` packages are installed.

Playing Music — The Legal Issues

The most popular format for digital music is MP3. Thanks to services like Napster, even the mainstream nontechnical population has gotten used to the idea of downloading music in MP3 format from the Internet. While the Recording Industry Association of America (RIAA) has made the legality of the content of pirated MP3's clear, many people assume that the MP3 format, especially when used to distribute music with the permission of the copyright holders, is perfectly legal. In fact, the MP3 format is patented and under the tight control of the Fraunhofer Institute of Erlangen, Germany. Theoretically, every MP3 should be made with software licensed from the Institute and royalties must be paid. In practice, this rule is widely ignored, and the vast majority of MP3s found on the Internet are not created with legal software. Furthermore, downloading copyrighted songs without permission deprives the record companies and artists who own the copyrights on those songs of royalties. The industry has reacted by creating a massive (though so far not very effective) legal and public relations campaign to have downloading suppressed even for legitimate uses such as backups of music already purchased and for trade in public domain recordings.

Supporters of free downloading often have the impression that the Debian Project, which talks so much about freedom, will be a kindred spirit. They are surprised to find that Debian actually prohibits MP3 creation software and unauthorized copyrighted material from entering the distribution. This is because although most developers may disapprove of the heavy-handed tactics of the recording industry, we recognize that they are within their legal rights. The correct way to solve the problem is to lobby your government representatives to fix the laws that are being abused by greedy intellectual property holders. Another tactic is to discourage the use of MP3s. The ogg (Ogg Vorbis) format is a possible replacement. It is freely licensed and unencumbered with patents, and yet it doesn't stint on sound quality, even outperforming MP3s in some tests. You can find out more about this new format at `www.vorbis.com`. This site has some links to music you can download in ogg format.

MIDI

The Musical Instrument Digital Interface (MIDI) is a standard way of connecting computers to musical instruments such as keyboards and drum machines. If your sound card has MIDI capability, ALSA detects it and configures the necessary kernel drivers and devices. To play MIDI files, you can install Timidity++ (Debian package: `timidity`). It also has GNOME and KDE front ends. There is also a MIDI plugin for XMMS.

Rosegarden is a MIDI sequencer and music composer with a KDE interface. It uses the JACK sound server. As you play your MIDI instrument, Rosegarden will transcribe the notes into musical notation. Or you can go the other way and write a score, which can then be played on the instrument. MIDI tracks can be sampled, edited, or mixed together in various ways. Ardour (package: `ardour-gtk`) is a similar type of program but with a GNOME interface. You can use Rosegarden, Ardour, and MIDI instruments to create a full-scale recording studio on your PC. A good site that deals with MIDI is www.midi.com.

Using Debian for Video

The field of digital video is much more fragmented than audio. Of the major video formats, Microsoft's Windows Media, Real Network's Real Video, and Apple's QuickTime are proprietary or bedeviled by restrictive licensing. AVI and MPEG are open, so they have the best support under Linux.

There are some efforts underway to clone or reverse engineer the proprietary formats. They do work in some cases, but you have to experiment because they are inconsistent. If you're willing to compromise free software purity a little bit, Real's closed-source Real Video Player for Linux is downloadable from their Web site. The QuickTime and Windows Media players for Windows will also work in Linux using WINE (see Chapter 12).

Another approach is to simply emulate enough of Windows to be able to make use of codecs (coder/decoders — the software libraries that actually handle the details of each video format) designed for that operating system. This turns out to be not that difficult and is how one of the best video players for Linux, mplayer, handles it. However, it is not quite clear whether a non-Windows user is legally allowed to use these codecs. This, along with a history of licensing irregularities, means mplayer is not distributed as part of Debian yet, although that may change soon.

Christian Marillat to the Rescue

While the Debian Project is constrained from offering software of disputed legality, individuals can decide for themselves whether they want to take the risk. French Debian developer Christian Marillat has decided to create an independent archive of multimedia software. It contains mplayer, Windows codecs, rippers and encoders for creating MP3 files from CDs, and a wide variety of DVD-related software, all in high-quality Debian packages. You can use this archive by adding a line like the following to /etc/apt/sources.list:

```
deb ftp://ftp.nerim.net/debian-marillat/ stable main
```

Replace stable with unstable or testing if you are using one of those distributions. Then update apt-get or the front end of your choice, and you should be able to install and remove the new packages as easily as any other.

DVDs are another popular type of video where the reasons for poor Linux support are legal rather than technical. Support should be perfect. After all, many DVD players are actually running Linux inside. DVD video is basically just a variant of the MPEG format, which is well supported. But the DVD industry refuses to legally license Open Source DVD software. Most DVDs have what is called *region encoding*, which restricts their use to players from a certain geographic region. An Open Source player would easily get around this restriction. Of course, one can argue that region encoding is a dumb idea and easy to circumvent anyway, not to mention an egregious violation of consumer rights, but corporate types seem rather unmoved by such sentiments.

The xine video player

A competitor to mplayer that is included within the main Debian distribution is xine, which can be found in the `xine-ui` package. Its default interface looks like a video player, but you can alter the appearance with different skins. There are front ends to xine called totem and kaffeine, which respectively integrate into the GNOME and KDE desktop environments. Figure 11-5 shows kaffeine embedded in the Konqueror Web browser playing a QuickTime format movie.

Figure 11-5: kaffeine playing a QuickTime format movie.

Watching TV

There are a number of add-on cards you can buy for your PC that can turn it into a cable box or satellite receiver. Many of these cards are supported in the Linux kernel by the Video4Linux project, which, like ALSA does for sound, provides a common API for programs that wish to make use of video input. You can find out more about Video4Linux, including a list of supported cards, at `http://linux.bytesex.org/v4l2/`. With the ability to receive video input and play it back on your machine, you can create your own digital VCR, just like the commercial ones sold by TiVo and DirectTV. A fascinating Web site that deals with this topic is `www.byopvr.com`. There you will find discussion groups, HOWTOs, and reviews from a thriving community of DIY video enthusiasts, several of whom run Debian.

Burning CDs and DVDs

If your computer is equipped with an appropriate recorder, you can easily make your own CDs and DVDs. The basic packages required for CDs are `mkisofs`, which creates the special filesystem used on a CD, and `cdrecord`, which actually transfers media to the filesystem. For DVDs, a package called `dvdrtools` contains all you need. These tools are command-line based. For an easier graphical interface, try the K3b package. When run for the first time after installation, K3b will ask some questions to configure itself for your hardware. As shown in Figure 11-6, K3b lets you create projects that represent a CD or DVD. Files or directories can be graphically dragged and dropped into the project, and special options such as spacing between tracks can be added. When the layout is satisfactory, all you have to do is press a button and your project is copied to the CD or DVD.

DeMuDi — A Debian Multimedia Distribution

Although it is not part of Debian itself (it may become so in the future), it would be remiss not to mention DeMuDi, a Debian-based distribution dedicated to the needs of artists. It got its start with a project called AGNULA, which was funded by the European Commission to develop a Linux-based system for multimedia development. The AGNULA project developed two Linux distributions: RehMuDi, based on Red Hat, and DeMuDi, based on Debian. When the funding period was finished, the work was continued by volunteers. If you are interested in a distribution tightly focused on multimedia or you just want some extra multimedia packages, this might be a project worth keeping an eye on.

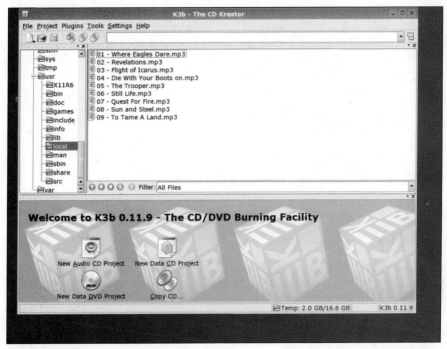

Figure 11-6: The K3b package.

Making videos of your own

Linux is playing an increasingly large role in the production of Hollywood films. Blockbusters including *Titanic* and the *Lord of the Rings* trilogy are only a few of the many films that were edited or had their special effects rendered using Linux. Of course, the needs of a big studio are quite different from those of a family that just wants to edit the camcorder footage of their vacation in Hawaii, but Linux can serve them both. Debian lets you use several tools to create your own videos:

✦ dvgrab (in the package of the same name) transfers video from a FireWire- or USB-connected camcorder or other video device and converts it into an AVI or QuickTime file.

✦ kino (package: kino) is a GNOME editor for digital video. It lets you slice and dice frames from a video file with a fast keyboard interface. You can add subtitles and fades and other special effects. The kinoplus and kino-timfx packages add extra special effects. The kino-dvtitler package adds the capability to create titles and menus like those found on professional DVDs.

✦ When you need really heavy-duty editing capabilities, why not use a program designed in part by professionals from Rhythm & Hues, Sony, DreamWorks, and ILM? CinePaint is capable of frame-by-frame editing of high-intensity color (32 bits per channel) images and saving them in industry-standard formats such as Cineon, OpenEXR, and IFF. It can be found in the `cinepaint` package.

✦ Another heavy-duty piece of video software from the big studios is Cinelerra. Cinelerra is a very complex piece of software for video editing, but it is extremely powerful. The project's Web site (`http://heroinewarrior.com/cinelerra.php3`) says, "If you want to make movies, you just want to defy the establishment, you want the same kind of compositing and editing suite that the big boys use, on the world's most efficient UNIX operating system, it's time for Cinelerra. Cinelerra is not for consumer use."

Summary

This subject is so huge that one chapter can't do it justice. But you've learned how sound works in Linux. You had a quick glimpse of some of the many available programs for viewing and creating audio and video, and you learned about some of the legal issues involved.

✦   ✦   ✦

Games

I f you think about it, Linux itself is the ultimate Linux game.
After all, Linus Torvalds has said that he started the project just for fun. Many Linux developers will agree that hacking on free software is a pleasurable hobby. But Debian has a wide range of more conventional games and pastimes too. In this chapter, I walk you through a small sample. In addition to presenting games designed especially for Linux, the chapter covers *retrogaming*, that is, using Linux to play the beloved games of the past. Although they were not designed for Linux, these games can be played on Linux, and this chapter shows you how.

Note   Due to space restrictions, the games mentioned in this chapter aren't covered fully. Information is given on which packages you need to install. With the exception of the commercial games mentioned at the end of the chapter, all of these games are available in the Debian distribution. With the exception of pydance, none of these games requires special equipment. However, many will benefit from joysticks, modern video cards, and other such peripherals. Consult the documentation of each package in /usr/share/doc/<packagename> to find out if there are any other requirements or hints.

Classic UNIX Games

From the beginning, UNIX was designed for play as well as work. When the influential BSD (Berkeley Software Distribution) of UNIX was created (during the late '70s/ early '80s), a good selection of games was included. These classic games are available on your Debian system in the bsdgames and bsdgames-nonfree packages. While they are limited to the ASCII terminals that were the typical display systems in those days, some of these games are surprisingly addictive.

First Things First

The various varieties of Microsoft Windows come with some games, such as the familiar Minesweeper and Solitaire. (Some Linux fans think that they are the only worthwhile parts of Windows.) Can Debian beat that? Sure it can! The following figure shows the KDE versions of solitaire and minesweeper, which can be found in the `kmines` and `kpat` packages, respectively. As the `kpat` menu shows, it can actually play 18 different solitaire games.

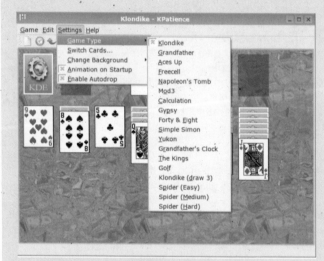

KDE's solitaire and minesweeper games.

Rogue-like games

One of the most popular of the classic games was Rogue. Rogue is a fantasy role-playing adventure in the style of Dungeons and Dragons. As the player, you are an inexperienced hero eager to prove your mettle by descending into the Dungeons of Doom and returning alive with the mystical Amulet of Yendor.

Initially you start in level 1 of the 20 levels that make up the Dungeons of Doom. The room you are in is displayed but the rest of the screen is blank except for the status line at the bottom. As you explore, more of the map is revealed. The dungeons are randomly generated each time you play.) You and all the monsters and objects in the game are represented by ASCII characters. In the following code illustration, you can see your adventurer (the @ sign) doing battle against a fearsome Ice Monster (represented by the I). As you can see, playing Rogue requires some imagination, but that hasn't dampened its popularity. Commands to the game are given as one- or two-letter sequences. Like the vi text editor, the h, j, k, and l keys are used to move left, up, down, and right, respectively. You fight a monster or pick up an object by moving over it. The other two essential commands to know are the ? character, which gives you the online help, and the / followed by a character, which tells you what that character represents.

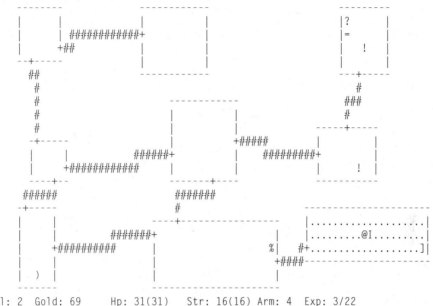

```
Level: 2  Gold: 69     Hp: 31(31)   Str: 16(16) Arm: 4  Exp: 3/22
```

Rogue inspired many similar games. In fact, the dungeon-crawling, monster-slaying, and treasure-collecting game genre is known as *roguelike*. Other roguelike games in Debian include NetHack (a cult favorite in its own right), Angband, Crawl, Crossfire, Egoboo, Falcon's Eye, Moria, Omega, Slash'EM, ToME, and Zangband. All of these have the same basic style as Rogue but add extra features such as multiple-player character classes and races, fancier visuals (such as graphics and even 3-D views), and more involved story lines.

/usr/games

While most Debian programs are installed into the /usr/bin directory, you'll notice that games are installed into /usr/games. This is a long-standing UNIX convention. It dates back to the day when only powerful mainframe computers used for very important purposes ran UNIX. It wouldn't do, for instance, if a corporation's accounting system ground to a halt because all the CPU time was being used up playing Tetris. Having all the game programs in one directory made it easier for system administrators to restrict access to after-hours or to certain users only. Now that everyone can install Linux on their own PCs, this is no longer a big deal, but the tradition continues.

Adventure games and interactive fiction

An even less visual fantasy game is adventure. Again you are a bold explorer, this time spelunking through the Colossal Cave. Unlike Rogue-style games, adventure is purely text-based. You are given descriptions of what's going on, and you type in simple English responses. Here's a sample session:

```
Welcome to Adventure!! Would you like instructions?
no

You are standing at the end of a road before a small brick
building.
Around you is a forest. A small stream flows out of the
building and down a gully.
enter building

You are inside a building, a well house for a large spring.

There are some keys on the ground here.

There is a shiny brass lamp nearby.

There is food here.

There is a bottle of water here.
take keys

OK
eat food

Thank you, it was delicious!
drink water

The bottle of water is now empty.

rub lamp

Rubbing the electric lamp is not particularly rewarding.
Anyway, nothing exciting happens.

take lamp

OK
go east

There is no way to go that direction.

You're inside building.

There is an empty bottle here.
go west
```

```
You're at end of road again.
go west

You have walked up a hill, still in the forest. The road
slopes back down the other side of the hill. There is a
building in the distance.
quit

Do you really want to quit now?
yes

OK


You scored 27 out of a possible 350 using 10 turns.

You are obviously a rank amateur. Better luck next time. To
 achieve the next higher rating, you need 9 more points.
```

Adventure was the prototype for Infocom's best-selling adventure games such as the Zork trilogy.

Note   Speaking of Infocom, if you have copies of any of their games (the Zork trilogy can be downloaded for free from `http://infocom.gerf.org/`), you can play them under Debian by installing the `frotz` package. In fact, you can even create your own Infocom-type games by installing the `inform` package from the non-free section of the archive.

Avant-garde authors created the idea of interactive fiction where the reader can make choices that affect the plot. They soon realized that it was easy to create such interactive fiction on the computer using the Infocom format, and today there are many such works available via the Internet. The Internet Fiction Archive (`www.ifarchive.org/`) is a good place to find examples. Installing the `int-fiction-installer` package makes it easy to download and read them.

Emulators

For many people, their first introduction to the idea of a personal computer was a small plastic box connected to a TV set and a tape recorder with an 8-bit processor and 64K or less RAM. Despite their limited capabilities, some excellent games were created for these platforms. The Commodore 64 and Sinclair Spectrum (sold in the U.S. and Canada as the Timex Sinclair 2000) were two of the most popular, and controversy over which one was better was the subject of many playground discussions in the early '80s. Other systems such as the Atari 2600 also have their votaries, and let's not forget the standalone arcade games such as Pacman, Space Invaders, and Q*Bert.

Abandonware

A term you often hear in the context of retrogaming is *abandonware*. This refers to commercial games and other software whose original owners have gone defunct without a successor taking over ownership of copyrights or to software that is out of print or can no longer be used on modern machines. The rise of emulation and the possibilities of making the most esoteric old stuff widely available over the Internet have made abandonware a hot topic, but many people are unaware of the legal questions involved.

From the legal point of view, copyright remains with the grantee for their lifetime plus 70 years unless it is assigned to another company or specifically authorized for release to the public. This remains true even if the copyright holders are nowhere to be found, though of course a bankrupt or otherwise defunct company is not going to be in a position to sue anyone for using its wares. Abandonware sites take advantage of this lack of enforcement to operate openly on the Internet. Also, many game companies turn a blind eye to third-party noncommercial redistribution of their older, out-of-production games as long as their current, profitable titles are not offered. But be careful. Some of the less-reputable sites use the idea of abandonware to make flimsy justifications for what is unambiguously software piracy. If you are involved in such an activity, whether as a distributor or recipient, don't expect any sympathy from the Free Software community or Debian. Free Software is about working within the law to convince proprietary software vendors to make their software 100 percent free to use and does not support stealing their property.

None of this applies if you legally own a copy of a game. Then you are well within your rights to make a copy to play on an emulator.

If all this talk makes you feel nostalgic, there's no need to rummage through the closet for that plastic box. As even today's low-end computers have several orders of magnitude more power than those '80s machines, it is now feasible to completely emulate every aspect of their hardware and software within the PC.

Here are some of the emulators available in Debian (presented in order of awesomeness).

Sinclair Spectrum

An emulator for the Sinclair ZX Spectrum/Sinclair and clones can be found in the `spectemu-x11` package. The program itself is called xspect. Start it from the command line. The virtual Spectrum will initialize and take you to a BASIC prompt just like on a real Spectrum. Pressing Ctrl+H will show help on the functions of the emulator. This program has a rather odd interface. You press function or control keys to do things such as load or save virtual "tapes," but interaction takes place in the window from which you started xspect. This is why I suggest starting it from the command line rather than from the menus.

In the absence of a real tape recorder to load programs from, Spectrum emulators use several different binary formats. xspect supports all the major ones. You can find many Spectrum programs including games at a wonderful Web site called The World Of Spectrum (`www.worldofspectrum.org/`).

Atari 2600

You can play games for the Atari 2600 by installing the `stella` package. A huge selection of games can be found at Atari Age (`www.atariage.com`). The Debian package already has a good set of defaults, but if you want to change things, you can set options on the command line or in a configuration file as described in the `stella` Manpage.

Nintendo Entertainment System

There are several emulators for the Nintendo Entertainment System (NES) and Super NES. Snes, znes, and FCE Ultra are three that have been packaged for Debian. FCE Ultra (in the `fceu-sdl` package) seems to be the most feature rich. As with the other emulators mentioned here, finding legal ROMs can be a problem. One is packaged for Debian, a simple Pong-type tennis game called Escape From Pong. Install the `efp` package and look for it in `/usr/share/nes/efp-rev.nes`. A comprehensive source of ROMs on the Internet can be found at `www.theoldcomputer.com/Libarary's/Emulation/NES/ROMs`.

Nintendo's Gameboy handhelds also have emulators. The original Gameboy is represented by the `Gnuboy` emulator. There are two packages: `gnuboy-x` for standard X Windowing System libraries, and `gnuboy-sdl` for the accelerated SDL libraries. The Gameboy Advance is emulated by `visualboyadvance` in the package of the same name.

Commodore computers

VICE, the Versatlle Commodore Emulator, is a collection of emulators that can run programs from the whole line of Commodore computers, from the VIC20 to the Commodore 64 and beyond. In order for it to actually be usable, you will also have to install ROMs that Debian cannot include in the package for licensing reasons. But you can download them yourself; `www.c64.com/` is a well-organized and comprehensive site dealing with all aspects of Commodore 64 culture.

DOS games

The reign of the 8-bit machines was finally ended by the PC, which, though not initially intended as a gaming machine, quickly amassed a large number of titles. The

PC's original operating system was Microsoft DOS. Even Windows in its first few incarnations was just a shell on top of DOS. Because DOS was rather anemic in terms of the systems services it offered, game developers often bypassed it completely and wrote their own routines for things such as memory management. This makes it hard to emulate old DOS games without also emulating the quirks of the environment in which they were written. DOSbox is such an emulator. It tries to mimic not just the DOS operating system, but also an entire virtual PC. Although it is still under heavy development, it is already capable of running many games. You can find a list of games along with their status at `http://dosbox.sourceforge.net/comp_list.php?letter=a`.

After installing DOSbox, which is in the package of the same name, you need to configure it. A sample configuration file is provided along with the package in `/usr/share/doc/dosbox/dosbox.conf.example.gz`. At the command line, copy it to your home directory, gunzip it, and rename it as `.dosboxrc`. Each option in the sample configuration file is annotated, but you'll find that you can leave most of the configuration as is. The major exception is in the section called `[autoexec]`. As the annotation says, lines in this section will be run at start-up, just like the `autoexec.bat` file in a real DOS installation. In the following example, you use a DOSbox built-in command called `mount` to make your games visible to the emulator. It might look something like this:

```
mount C /usr/local/share/dosgames
c:
```

Assuming your DOS games are in directories under `/usr/local/share/dosgames`, they will show up in DOSbox as directories under `C:`.

Windows games

The first fully featured operating system for the PC from Microsoft was Windows 95. Another big change occurred in Windows NT. All subsequent Microsoft operating systems have been based on one of these two. With the advent of Windows 95, game developers could at last rely on the system rather than doing everything themselves. The flip side was that Windows 95 and subsequent Windows operating systems were a lot bigger and more complicated. This meant that emulating Windows was a much tougher job. Nevertheless, some Linux developers are trying, and they have organized their efforts in the WINE project (`www.winehq.com`).

WINE stands for WINE Is Not an Emulator. Unlike the previous programs mentioned, WINE is an API (Application Programming Interface). What is being emulated is not the Windows code itself but the way a Windows program calls into the operating system in order to get some task done, such as drawing a window on the screen. Behind the scenes, WINE converts these calls into native Linux APIs such as X or ALSA, but the program is none the wiser. The application thinks it is running under Windows.

To use WINE, first install the `wine` and `winesetuptk` packages and any of these optional packages:

✦ `libwine-alsa` — A plugin to play Windows sound through ALSA.

✦ `libwine-arts` — A plugin to play Windows sound through aRts. If you are using KDE, you should install this instead of one of the other sound server modules.

✦ `libwine-jack` — A plugin to play Windows sound through the JACK audio server.

✦ `libwine-nas` — A plugin to play Windows sound through the Network Audio Server.

✦ `libwine-print` — A plugin to allow Windows print functions to work through CUPS. (See Chapter 23.)

✦ `wine-doc` — Documentation for the WINE system.

✦ `wine-utils` — Some utilities that come with WINE. They are mainly of use to programmers.

From the command line, run the `winesetup` program and it will take you through the steps to create a working WINE configuration. Many parameters are automatically configured to sensible values, so you can just accept the default choices if you like. You can also press the Help button at the bottom for a brief description of an option if you get stuck.

The first thing to decide is where you want to keep the configuration. The suggested choice, `wine/config` in your home directory, should be fine for almost everyone. Then you choose to edit a number of options grouped into basic and advanced categories.

The basic options are as follows:

✦ **Look & Feel** — Do you want programs running under WINE to look like the style of Windows 3.1, Windows 95, or Windows 98?

✦ **Window Mode** — This determines how windows created by WINE will interact with X. In managed mode, the X Windows manager takes care of everything, so the program running under WINE will appear to be more integrated into the desktop. The value you specified for Look & Feel will be ignored. This mode can cause problems for a few Windows programs that do things such as draw on the title bar, which is considered a job for the application in Windows, but a job for the window manager in X. In unmanaged mode, Windows Look & Feel is used and each window draws itself. In desktop mode, WINE provides one root window in which all WINE-using programs are displayed. This in turn is managed by X. The window mode can be set for all programs running WINE in general or on a per-program basis using application profiles (with the Apply To button).

The advanced options are as follows:

✦ **Drives** — You can make peripherals or file systems on Debian look like Windows-compatible drives to programs running under WINE.

✦ **Paths** — Windows programs need to know the location of certain directories in order to run. If you changed drives, you may need to edit this.

✦ **Look & Feel** — Here you will find some advanced options for translating Windows graphics calls. These are especially important for running games at a decent speed. Read the help text for each feature to learn more about it. As with the basic Look & Feel option, you can set these options on a per-program basis if needed using application profiles from the Apply To button.

✦ **DLLs** — The Windows operating system is made up of Dynamically Linked Libraries, or DLLs. WINE provides its own, but you can also use the ones from a copy of Windows itself. You might think you are better off using the ones native to Windows, as after all, what could be more compatible with Windows programs? But this is not always the case. Because WINE is still a work in progress, there may be bad interactions with native DLLs that can cause instability. Most users should stick to the defaults here.

✦ **Ports** — These options specify how calls that WINE-using Windows programs make to serial, parallel, and printer ports will be translated to their native Linux equivalents.

✦ **Registry** — Windows programs store their settings in a binary database called the registry. These options control how and where registry data will be stored under Linux. Most users will not need to change the defaults.

After you have tweaked the options to your satisfaction, press the Finish button to save the configuration file. You can run a Windows program now by typing

```
wine <name of program>
```

on the command line. Remember, UNIX filenames are case sensitive and do not automatically recognize extensions, so if your Windows program is called PROGRAM.EXE, use exactly that and not program.exe or PROGRAM. If you run into problems (and bear in mind that WINE is still under heavy development and doesn't claim perfect emulation of every Windows feature), check Frank's Corner (www.frankscorner.org/), a Web site with many helpful tips for running popular programs. Figure 12-1 shows WINE running Windows Solitaire and DOSbox running PC*Bert.

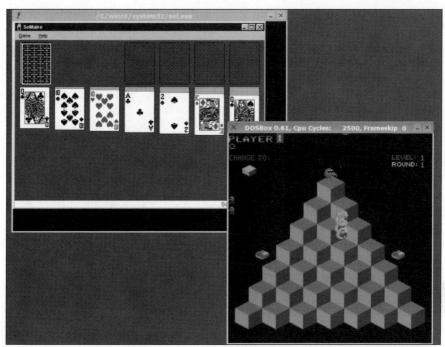

Figure 12-1: WINE running Windows Solitaire and DOSbox running PC*Bert.

TransGaming's Cedega

WINE is designed to be a general-purpose tool for running Windows programs and emulating the entire Windows API, but unfortunately the demands of reverse engineering closed-source software and reimplementing it in a compatible way, plus the fact that most WINE developers are volunteers working in their spare time, have resulted in gaps in functionality. Modern Windows games typically mainly use a subset of the Windows API called DirectX, but unfortunately this is one area that is not well covered by WINE. Also, games often have "features" such as copy protection that simply cannot be included in an Open Source project. A company called TransGaming Technologies saw this as an opportunity to produce a variant of WINE as a commercial product (which was allowed by the WINE license) that would concentrate on enhancing game compatibility. This product, formerly known as WineX, is called Cedega, and it can be purchased on a subscription basis for $5 per month with a minimum of three months. A subscription entitles you to download Cedega and receive any updates during the subscription period. Cedega fully supports Debian, and a .deb package is available, which you can install like any other. An impressive list of Windows games work with Cedega; you can search TransGaming's compatibility list at www.transgaming.com/searchgame.php.

Games Designed for Linux

So far, I may have given you the impression that Linux games all come from elsewhere. The problem is that game development doesn't lend itself very readily to the Open Source development model. Today's top-selling games are incredibly complicated from a programming point of view, even more so than a C compiler or a word processor. Although a word processor can still be usable when half-complete, a game that is only 50 percent implemented is unplayable. Commercial games are produced by teams of artists, animators, and musicians that rival those of a Hollywood film. Open Source software is typically developed by lone programmers or small teams as a hobby and with limited resources.

Despite these drawbacks, there is in fact a lot of interest in game development in the Linux community. A good place to find out about what's new is the Linux Game Tome (www.happypenguin.org/). This site offers a forum for programmers to announce their latest creations and for users to discuss the games and rate them. Many of the games have been packaged for Debian. Here's a brief look at a selection of them.

Games for kids

My two-year-old daughter loves a KDE game called Ktuberling, or in English, Potato Guy. It's a computerized version of the Mr. Potato Head doll. You have a cartoon picture of a potato on which you can drag and drop different facial parts and accessories. Two other scenes are included, one featuring Tux the Linux Penguin and the other an aquarium in which you can place fish and other undersea creatures. The Ktuberling manual also includes instructions on how to create your own scenes (or "playgrounds," as the program calls them). You can install this program from the ktuberling package. Figure 12-2 shows Ktuberling.

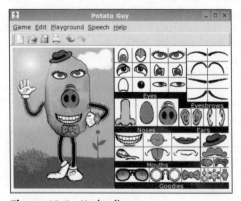

Figure 12-2: Ktuberling.

Debian Jr.

Debian Jr. is a subproject within Debian whose mission is to provide a complete desktop for children. It is implemented as a set of metapackages, each covering a particular topic. Each of these will pull in a selection of Debian packages pertaining to that topic deemed suitable for children. You can install Debian Jr. through the `tasksel` program or by installing each package individually. Here is a list of the games-related packages:

✦ `junior-arcade` — Arcade games

✦ `junior-games-card` — Card games

✦ `junior-games-gl` — Games that require an OpenGL accelerated video card

✦ `junior-games-net` — Games that can be played over a network or the Internet

✦ `junior-games-sim` — Simulation games

✦ `junior-games-text` — Games that require only text mode

✦ `junior-puzzle` — Puzzles and other games of logic

✦ `junior-toys` — Frivolous and fun amusements

And for the sake of completeness, here are the other Debian Jr. packages:

✦ `junior-art` — Painting programs

✦ `junior-doc` — Documentation for Debian Jr.

✦ `junior-gnome` — A selection of GNOME programs for children

✦ `junior-internet` — Internet programs such as a Web browser

✦ `junior-math` — Programs for learning math

✦ `junior-programming` — Programs for learning programming

✦ `junior-sound` — Music programs

✦ `junior-system` — Some programs that allow children to administer their computers in a safe and educational way

✦ `junior-typing` — Programs for learning typing

✦ `junior-writing` — Word processor, dictionary, spell-checker, and other writing tools

✦ `junior-kde` — A selection of KDE programs for children

The Debian Jr. Web page is at `www.debian.org/devel/debian-jr`. Parents, educators, and anyone else interested in helping make Debian more useful for children are invited to help out.

For slightly older children, gcompris, in the package of the same name, is a unified shell for many small educational games that teach the rudiments of using a computer, reading, shapes, simple math, and even how to play chess (for this you need the GNU chess program, described later in this chapter).

Puzzles and logic games

Tetris is probably the leader in the category of puzzles and logic games. A search of the package database will show several versions and variants on the Tetris theme. A text-mode version is included in the `bsdgames` package mentioned previously. The `sirtet` package contains a version for KDE. A version for GNOME is included in the `gnome-games` package.

If you liked the classic game Oxyd or Marble Madness, you'll enjoy Enigma, which not only is a faithful remake but also adds some twists of its own. Install the `enigma` package to play this game. For those who are not familiar with Oxyd, you control a marble, which you maneuver around trying to uncover matching pairs of colored stones. This can get quite tricky as the marble will ricochet off walls and can fall into holes. Success requires careful planning and problem solving. Figure 12-3 shows Enigma's level selection screen.

A game so addictive that Debian developers claim it almost derailed the woody release is Frozen Bubble. To play this game, install the `frozen-bubble` package and either `fb-music-high` or `fb-music-low` depending on whether you want high-quality or low-quality music. The low-quality music, as the name suggests, doesn't sound as good but it takes up a lot less space. The goal of Frozen Bubble is to pop all the bubbles. You can pop bubbles only if they are of the right color and there are three or more of that color in a clump. Figure 12-4 is a screenshot of Frozen Bubble.

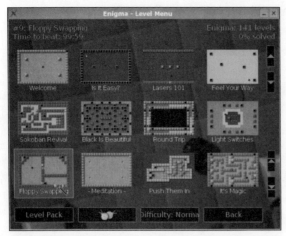

Figure 12-3: Enigma's level selection screen.

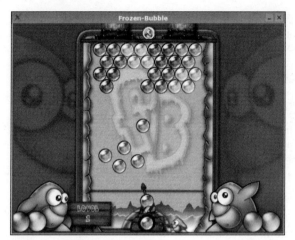

Figure 12-4: Frozen Bubble.

Board games

Naturally, Linux developers love intellectual pursuits, and the game of chess is the first thing that comes to mind when you think of intellectual pursuits, so there are several chess-playing programs. The oldest, which is still strong enough to give the average player a good challenge, is GNU chess. You will need to install the gnuchess package to play it. A separate package called gnuchess-book should also be installed as it gives GNU chess a bigger database of openings, which makes it a stronger player. Although GNU chess has its own simple interface, it is usually played through a graphical interface called xboard (in the package of the same name). Using xboard also gives you the capability to play head-to-head with another person over the network or via the Free Internet Chess Server (www.freechess. org/). A more modern variation on this theme is found in the eboard package. eboard allows you to use different themes for the chess pieces and sounds. Some extra themes can be found in the eboard-extras-pack1 package. An alternative chess engine, which is even stronger than GNU chess yet still compatible with xboard and eboard, is called crafty (in the package of the same name). Figure 12-5 shows GNU chess and xboard.

A rather less taxing but still fun board game is Monopoly. A text mode version of Monopoly is monop in the bsdgames package. A more graphical version designed for KDE is Atlantik (atlantik package). You can play with other people over the Internet, and if you install the monopd package, you can even run your own server for people to play on. Atlantik comes with several boards representing properties in various world cities, but if you want to design your own, you can install the atlantikdesigner package.

Figure 12-5: GNU chess and xboard.

Strategy games

Lincity is a clone of the popular *SimCity*. You are the mayor of a fledgling town. You must build homes and businesses to attract people (and their tax revenue) to your town. But you cannot allow runaway growth or your town will be affected by pollution and other disasters. Install the `lincity` package to play this game.

Sid Meier's classic *Civilization* also has a clone called Freeciv. This game takes the idea of Lincity a step farther and puts you in charge of an entire civilization that you must guide from a primitive state to high culture while also fighting off rival civilizations. To play this game, install the `freeciv-client` package. To run your own server so that other people can play Freeciv with you over the Internet, install the `freeciv-server` package.

Battle for Wesnoth is an original turn-based strategy game. You play the general of one of several armies of fantasy creatures. The other armies are controlled either by the computer or by other players. It is possible to play this game with others over the Internet by connecting to a special server. See `www.wesnoth.org/` for more information about this. You then fight in different scenarios, each with its own objectives and conditions for victory. To play this game, you should install the `wesnoth` package and optionally the `wesnoth-music` package if you want in-game music. If you want to create your own custom scenarios, install `wesnoth-editor`, and if you want to run your own server, install `wesnoth-server`.

Pydance

This one deserves a category of its own. Pydance is a dancing game like Dance Dance Revolution. Yes, that's right, a dancing game. Armed with a special pressure-sensitive mat, the game tells you a sequence of dance steps that you must perform correctly. Given the stereotype of the overweight and uncoordinated Linux geek, this seems like an unlikely game to be a hit, but it is. It can provide good aerobic exercise too. The only problem is finding the mat. The typical mats you find were designed to interface with the Sony PlayStation gaming console. You will need to buy an adapter to allow the mat to plug into a USB port on your PC. You will also need to compile a special kernel module found in the `ddrmat-source` package so that Linux can communicate with the mat.

Shoot-'em-ups

From time to time, even the most cerebral person feels the elemental urge to just blow things up. Debian will come to your assistance here too.

One of the seminal games in the "first-person shooter" genre, where you take the perspective of the character blowing things up, was ID Software's Doom. Its dark, eerie atmosphere and scary ambient sound were groundbreaking. I still vividly recall almost falling out of my chair the first time a demon crept up behind me. The story line puts you in the role of a tough space marine sent to investigate a research base on one of the moons of Jupiter whose staff has inadvertently opened the gates of hell. Your job is to close them again. But story line shmory line. Your real job is to blow things up, a task that you can accomplish with a wide variety of exotic weaponry. Figure 12-6 shows Doom.

Figure 12-6: Doom (the lxdoom version).

When Doom stopped selling commercially and was replaced by newer titles that refined the "blow things up" idea to even greater degrees, ID could have easily just buried it like so many other commercial games have been buried in the past, at best surviving in the gray status of abandonware. But ID very generously decided to free the source code instead. Doom was originally written for DOS, but very quickly, a port was made to Linux, and Doom is available in Debian today. Actually, several different versions are available. The `lxdoom` package contains a version close to ID's original version. You will also need `lxdoom-sndsrv` and `lxmussrv` to hear sound and music. Doom Legacy is an enhanced port. It has a version for standard X API (in the `doomlegacy-x11` package) and the SDL API (in the `doomlegacy-sdl` package). Prboom (in the `prboom` package) is another SDL port. Regardless of which version of Doom you install, you will also need what is called a WAD file. The WAD contains maps and other level data for the game. ID's original WAD for Episode 1 of Doom has been packaged in the `doom-wad-shareware` package. As the name suggests, this WAD is shareware. Although you can use it without charge, you are honor-bound to pay ID Software $25 for it. As an incentive, they will send you Episodes 2 and 3. Some of ID Software's other games such as Hexen and Heretic also use this WAD format, so if you own them (they also have Linux ports, but no one seems to have packaged them for Debian), you can play them under Linux with one of the Doom ports mentioned previously. Another ID first-person shooter, Quake 2, is also available in the `quake2` package.

A few more games

I can't resist mentioning a few more Open Source games from different genres that are really fun to play. Tuxkart is an entertaining go-cart racing game featuring Tux the penguin along with other Open Source mascots. Pingus is a clone of Lemmings. In this game, you have to guide a group of penguins through obstacles without getting them killed. Flightgear is a flight simulator. All three of these games can be found in packages under their respective names. Lbreakout is, sure enough, a Breakout remake. It is found in the `lbreakout2` package. FreeCraft (in the `freecraft` package) is a clone of Warcraft 2 from Blizzard Entertainment.

Commercial Linux Games

I'd like to wrap up by discussing a new trend that is very exciting for the Linux gamer. Increasingly, the most eagerly awaited new games are being ported directly to Linux. No emulators. No reverse engineering by unpaid volunteers. These are full versions of the games equal to Macintosh and Windows ports. To be sure, there have been some bumps in the road. Loki Games, a company that was a pioneer in bringing top games to Linux such as Civilization: Call To Power, Quake3 Arena, and Soldier of Fortune, among others, fell victim to a bad business plan and closed down in 2002. Some of their games are still available from other retailers, sometimes for as little as $10. Their Web site at `www.lokigames.com/` is still around for downloading patches and updates. Loki's noble work has been continued by such companies as Linux Game Publishing (www.linuxgamepublishing.com/) and independent developers such as Ryan "Icculus" Gordon (www.icculus.org/).

Even the U.S. Army has gotten in on the act. They have released two no-cost games called America's Army: Operations and America's Army: Special Forces, which put you in the persona of an American soldier. They are not Open Source, but they are supported on the same level as the Windows versions, and that is quite an achievement. The games have been controversial not for their content but for their source. Critics wonder whether they are just propaganda. The Army readily admits that it has produced the games to give people a realistic glimpse of what their missions are like with a view to persuading people to enlist. But regardless of motive, they are good action-packed games and have become very popular as a result. You can find out more about these games and how to download them from www.americas army.com/.

Ironically, one factor that might be holding back the growth of Linux gaming is the eagerness of Linux enthusiasts themselves. Often publishers will include the Linux version of a game in the same box as the Windows version. Or they may offer it as a free download after purchase of a boxed version. You may purchase the game intending to play it on Linux, but the trouble is that to the corporate bean counters at the publisher it looks like you just bought a Windows version. At the end of the day, they will conclude that people are not interested in a Linux port, and this will dampen future efforts to bring their titles to Linux. If you wish to support the cause, bide your time and wait for the Linux version of the game to come out. Or buy it through Linux-friendly online retailers such as Tux Games (www.tuxgames.com/).

Summary

In this chapter, you saw that Debian is not just for serious purposes. Linux has a large complement of games of its own, and through the use of emulators, it has many of the games from other platforms as well. You learned how to set up these emulators and where to find games for them. Debian's games cover every genre and appeal to all age levels. Debian Jr. is a subproject aimed at small children. Many Linux games are produced by Open Source developers, but slowly commercial developers have been getting in on the act.

✦　　✦　　✦

The Internet Server

Network Security

The processes and tools that protect computer systems are many, but first and foremost are proactive planning, proper implementation, secure coding, testing, and treating the Internet as it should be treated — a hostile environment that must be mitigated as much as possible while still allowing you to get work done. But ultimately, you're going to have security holes in your system. Often, you're going to have someone exploiting them.

Security problems are systemic. In almost all real-world conditions, your systems will interact with other systems. You must be mindful of these interactions. To make a system totally secure is a noble goal, but no general security magic will make you completely secure. Your first question should be, "What is secure enough?"

Some 30 years ago, when the Internet was first taking shape, the electronic world was a very different place than it is today. Most networks were trusted and network administrators knew everybody who could access their networks. Most users didn't access the network directly, either; they used large central machines, which in turn spoke with other large machines.

Today, millions of unaccountable computers are connected to the same Internet your servers are connected to, and you can't be too careful. Understanding security implications on the modern Internet is a fundamental requirement before you place your systems online. Not only is your own data at risk, but a compromised server — regardless of whose server it is — can serve as a springboard for attacks on other computers. It's a harsh reality, but administrators need to worry not only about flaws in their own security policies but also about flaws in their neighbors' security policies. If your upstream router can monitor your traffic, you'd better be using encryption. Never trust the network.

In the first part of this chapter, I discuss the theory behind many security policies and some of the basic techniques and principles that are useful in approaching security. The policies themselves are mostly quite simple, but understanding them is essential to implementing them correctly. As the administrator of a Debian system, you'll regularly be faced with situations that require reasoned and rational responses — something a cookie-cutter approach can't provide. This chapter focuses on security for a larger network of computers — in particular for a corporate network — and speaks of attack vectors in that context. That said, most of the principles illustrated in these examples will also be applicable in home or other noncorporate spheres.

If you skipped Chapters 3 and 5 and are at all confused or uncomfortable with the information in this chapter, you may want to return to those chapters for background information. Many of the examples in this chapter build from concepts covered in those chapters.

A Theoretical Overview

This section provides an overview of the basic tenets that make up a modern security and administration policy. I include a discussion of user identity and access and the contingencies you need to cover whenever you're running a network-connected computer.

Granting Access: Identification, Authentication, Authorization, and Auditing

The example of creating a new user on your machine can illustrate some of the types of thinking that a security-conscious Debian administrator must go through. Before you give access to your machine to any individual, it's almost always a good idea to ask the following questions:

✦ Is the user who he claims to be? If ever there's a problem, will you know whom to contact?

✦ How secure is that user's computer? Will she always log in from her own computer or does she use public workstations? Do you know within reason that somebody can't impersonate her?

✦ Does the user understand and observe good security policies? The user may have a crack security expert administering his computer, but if the user does not properly protect his username and password, the security of his computer is irrelevant.

✦ Can the user be trusted? If she's given access to a particular service or some data, can you trust the user not to misuse that access? What about accidental damage? Are you making sure you have backups in the event of damage?

Can you trust your users not to make mistakes that will compromise the security of the entire machine?

These questions touch on four tenets of security-minded administrative behavior that should be addressed in a range of administrative issues from a security standpoint. These four pillars are identification, authentication, authorization, and auditing.

✦ **Identification** — *Identification* means that administrators should identify the users they allow to access their systems. This might include knowing the names and "identities" of the people who use the system. Identification in this security context means that you are able to name and group users — even if it is in large, impersonal swaths — and then make security policies with your users in mind.

For example, if you're running a public Web site, a large amount of your traffic may be made up of requests and responses to and from anonymous users. If that's the case, identify those users as such: Your users are anonymous, unknown, and untrustworthy. This group of users should be highly restricted in the way that they can access your server. People you know and trust highly may be able to access your server in much more powerful ways. Many others will fall somewhere between these two extremes. Identification is the important first step of identifying where your users fall on this spectrum of trust. This step is largely nontechnical.

✦ **Authentication** — The second pillar is *authentication*. The individual you're giving access to may be highly trusted, but you need to be sure that any person, program, or computer that claims to be an individual, a program, or a computer on the network is truly who they claim to be. Most forms of identification in the setting of a computer network rely on a secret of some form. This secret most commonly takes the form of a *password*. The user states her username and then provides her password as proof that she is who she claims to be.

Passwords have historically been one of the weakest points of any system's security. Passwords that are easy for a human to guess are truly trivial for the advanced password-breaking tools available to malicious crackers today. A good policy for using complex nondictionary passwords is required for any password-protected service. Because security is a balance, you can't force your users to use horribly long, difficult-to-remember passwords. If you do, they'll write down the passwords, making it more available to a malicious cracker. Tools like `pwgen` in the `pwgen` package let you (or your users) create passwords that are reasonably easy to remember but very difficult for password-cracking programs to guess. However, such password programs should be treated with caution, as they may not be using a sufficiently random source of data to generate the passwords.

Of course, passwords need to be sent to the server over a network. You can **never, never, never** trust the network. Under no circumstances can a password be sent unencrypted and be considered a secret suitable for authentication. As such, the first precaution to take is to make sure that all passwords are sent only over encrypted channels. SSL or TLS (two different names for the same technology) is the most common cryptography standard in use today, and most daemons support it. SSH, discussed in the chapter on remote access, provides other secure methods of authentication. Nor should these passwords be left in a state on a system where they are in an unencrypted format or a reversible hashing format. In order to make sure that the user is in fact setting a strong password, take a look at the `cracklib-runtime` package. Enabling that is much more effective than only auditing the `/etc/shadow` files (the file where the passwords are stored) later. If you're interested in auditing your users' passwords, take a look at the password-cracking utility `john`. `john` can be run from `cron` to automatically attempt to crack the system passwords. It's a good idea to make use of those facilities.

✦ **Authorization** — *Authorization* is the act of granting user access to specific resources or services on your system. Best security practices include limiting access for each user to only the services he or she requires. Giving all authenticated users full access to everything on your system may be easier, but it can be a recipe for disaster. A user should have to show good cause to require elevated privileges; the system administrator should not have to prove how this is a security risk.

For example, you may have multiple people accessing login shells on a shared Internet machine for collaborative purposes. You might give each user the root password so that they don't need to bother you to install new software, but spreading this very sensitive and powerful information can be a very dangerous route. A good rule of thumb is that unless a user asks for access to something or unless you know that they'll need it, don't give them access to it. When a user asks for access to something, weigh the risks and the benefits of granting this access. By most accounts, giving out the root password is a very bad idea and should never be done unless it's a matter of sharing administrative roles between trusted individuals.

✦ **Auditing** — Having given access to your system, to anybody and through whatever means, you will need to have an audit trail for those cases when things go wrong. If something unpleasant happens on a system that you are responsible for, you will need to find out who is responsible and how they did it in order to keep it from happening again. Personally, I keep a very extensive audit trail, including every action I take as administrator on my systems. I use the program `sudo` to help me do this. You can set this type of audit trail up easily by installing and configuring the `sudo` package and then using it instead of `su` to gain superuser access. `sudo` logs every command issued and, in the process, creates an audit trail that you can consult later. Using one of many different system integrity-checking programs can be a lifesaver. Such packages can be installed very easily, but depending on the scale of your monitoring activities, you may need more planning than you would normally expect. Some packages to inspect for those needs include `aide`, `integrit`, `osiris`, `samhain`, and `tripwire`. However, only `osiris` and `samhain` are really up to snuff when it comes to monitoring more than a single host, and depending on your threat model, even that much might be too much for `aide` or `integrit`. There are many different levels of compromise; a factor in fixing problems is knowing what levels have been breached. If your system is compromised, the difference between an irritation and a disaster can be in the forensics.

Making sure the worst doesn't happen

The adage "an ounce of prevention is worth a pound of cure" applies to computer security. When formulating a security policy, your first goal should be to prevent any successful attacks from occurring. This means that you should limit access, encrypt communications, and limit access some more. It also means that you should make an effort to keep your software up-to-date. This should be done for all the systems on a network, whether it's a router, a firewall, a bridge, a switch, a workstation, or even a coffeepot controlled by TCP/IP.

The notion of a perimeter creating security as a panacea is invalid. A firewall is an important step to securing a network. However, if your workstations aren't secured in any manner, if your servers don't have the most recent patches, what will happen when an attacker gets in? The intruder can wreak havoc on your network. Treat every asset on your network as if it's a target, both for attack and for hardening. It's better to be proactive about your security than to call it "secure" because you have a firewall. Unknown exploits occur in the wild every day, some more prolific than others. Known exploits aren't even kept at bay on most networks or systems. So ask yourself, how do you know no one has hacked you? If you're not checking the integrity of your systems, the bottom line is that you do not know whether you have been hacked. You can be reasonable about it; if the risk is low (it's not directly connected to the Internet, for example), it is reasonable to assume it hasn't been attacked by an unknown person. But if you're connected to the Internet, it's unreasonable to think you remain untouched.

Compromise can occur from either remote or local sources. The main forms can be broken down into three main categories: malicious users abusing access privileges, nonmalicious users accidentally compromising a system's integrity, and malicious users gaining access to privileges they shouldn't otherwise have.

✦ **Malicious users abusing access privileges** — The only way to prevent malicious users from abusing their access privileges is by making sure they don't have them in the first place. Be careful about whom you give access to and what access you give. One example of this is carefully auditing permission settings, groups, and ownership on sensitive files on shared hosts. And don't forget about physical access: Simply because you, as a legitimate user, have to prove who you are to get access to your company collocation facility does not mean that others will have trouble getting in. Most collocation facilities have locks on their cabinet doors, but in many companies, the cameras aren't watching you when you're in the cabinet space.

✦ **Users or administrators accidentally compromising the system**—This is a rare case, but it happens nevertheless; occasionally a user will quite honestly stumble upon a flaw in your security. Strictly speaking, the user didn't compromise the system; the compromise was in the flawed security. However, take advantage of a user's honesty wherever possible. Unless you think they were being malicious, thank them for telling you about the breach. And, of course, correct the flaw so that it doesn't happen again.

More commonly, the user may have misunderstood (for instance) the importance of keeping a password secret. If a legitimate user's password falls into the hands of an attacker, steps need to be taken to ensure that the attacker can't use those credentials anymore. Changing the user's password is the first step, but ensuring that the accident doesn't happen again is at least as important. If an attacker finds an easy way to compromise the system, he'll try doing it again the same way later.

✦ **Malicious users gaining access**—This is, by far, the most common form of security compromise. Whether exploiting a bug in the software or a flaw in your security policies, malicious users may be able to gain access privileges you didn't expressly give them. These are the most difficult compromises to deal with; you can't count on knowing that a violation ever happened. Only luck will help you, as a skilled cracker will leave nearly no trace whatsoever. The only way to prevent somebody from gaining unauthorized access is to make sure they can't. It may sound simple, but it's not easy. Your software needs to be vulnerability-free, and since that's not going to happen, you need to update any vulnerable software as soon as there are new versions available or disable any known vulnerable services until an update is available. Your system's locations need to be secured as well. You need to double- and triple-check your security policies to make sure there are no unacceptable flaws. Preferably you'll have a colleague well-versed in security practices examine your systems and critique your policies. Don't decide that because you can't break into it, it cannot be broken into. It isn't secure necessarily because you or your colleague cannot figure out how to circumvent it.

Tip

To stay up-to-date with security vulnerabilities in Debian and with updated packages that fix these, you should sign up on the Debian Security Announce mailing list at `http://lists.debian.org/debian-security-announce`.

Make sure you're getting the most recent security updates by adding a line similar to this to your `/etc/apt/sources.list` file (all code should be on one line):

```
deb http://security.debian.org/ stable/updates main
contrib non-free
```

Or if you're running testing:

```
deb http://security.debian.org/ testing/updates main
contrib non-free
```

See Chapter 4 for more details on configuring `apt`.

Awareness and Education

A key term in dealing with security is *awareness*. Before any effective security can be put into place, you as an administrator should be aware of a great deal of information. You should know what software is being used, how it's used, and who is accessing it. The real point to having this information available isn't so that you know when somebody is doing something bad, but rather so that you can design your systems such that *only* the appropriate access methods are available. If possible, you should also be aware of your own users on a personal level so that you can work with them to implement any security measures you decide on.

When planning any broad security-related strategy, it's important to keep in mind that the devil is in the details. Knowing the ins and outs of your software and your users *before* you make any plans is required. Even if you don't consciously examine every single piece of the system during the planning stages, you'll be far better equipped to come up with a workable plan if you're at least ready to deal with the details.

A second key term is *education*. Often the easiest way for an intruder to gain access to an intranet is to pretend to be somebody who *should* have access to it and then get somebody else to give it to him. (This is often called social engineering.) There are any number of ways this can be done, and often the simplest methods work best: faked employee badges or random telephone calls to office workers to get their passwords. To prevent this, make sure that all the users on your network understand that their access is *their own*, not to be shared with anybody else for whatever reason. Make sure that they understand that any administrator is capable of logging in to any part of the system as any user, so they should never need to give away their password. It may seem harsh, but if the data you're protecting is particularly valuable (say, credit card numbers for customers, which can be used to defraud them), it may help to let your users know that giving out account details is grounds for dismissal.

Probably the best education you can give your users is an understanding of the consequences of any security breaches: Real people can get hurt in real ways, and sometimes that isn't apparent when somebody's just sitting at a desk doing their routine work. In a corporate environment, it may mean loss of jobs (because a secret was lost), a company embarrassment (private e-mail sent across the network without encryption), stock drops, brand loyalty drops, and so on.

Other networks your users may have access to may be set up incorrectly, so it's important that your network is as secure as possible by default because even though you try, not all users are going to listen or understand. Education of your users is a very important step, but it's your job to be a technical translator. That means your users will need help along the way.

Making sure the worst isn't so bad

Short of cutting its wires, you can't guarantee that your system will never be compromised; you need to plan for the day when a compromise happens. Your second goal in preparing any security system is to ensure that when a compromise happens, it's limited in scope. Just because an attacker can compromise the Web server doesn't mean he should be able to compromise the entire operating system or internal network. Likewise, even if an attacker manages to get a working user-name and password pair to log in to a shell, she shouldn't be able to fiddle around with the Web server. Reducing the scope of compromises is all about another security concept: segregation and separation into compartments.

By *segregation* and *separation*, I mean that each part of your system should be identified as separately as possible from each other part. User accounts are the most common form of separation; two users should never share a single account. Likewise, two services/daemons should not run under the same accounts. Most daemons of note drop their elevated privileges as soon as they possibly can; if the service is compromised, the attacker will only have privileges equal to the lesser account, not the root account. Depending on what the service offers, this may or may not matter. If it's a Web server and you're trying to protect the database, it doesn't matter if this resource is isolated and locked down, as a legitimate use of the server is to connect to the database.

A good mantra is to compartmentalize your system to the best extent possible and to be watchful. There is a program in Debian called *chroot* which can perform a certain type of compartmentalization that is often used for daemons.

Making sure you can recover

You can't even reasonably guarantee that an attacker will have only limited access after they break in. You can do your best, which may be good enough, but you never know for sure. Part of being a responsible administrator is ensuring that no matter what happens, it could have been worse. For a professional administrator, being able to say, "Yeah, they destroyed six years of financial data and it'll take us a month to restore from backup — but at least I pushed and pulled to get our backup system in place," could save your job. Though recovering from a compromise isn't a security measure per se, it's worth mentioning in the same context, as it needs to be planned in advance and *with a possible compromise in mind*.

In the context of security, there are two primary reasons for keeping backups: tracking down any security breach and restoring service after a breach. If you're backing up to a hard drive or other read-write media, *never* leave the backup media in the restored machine unless you know with certainty that the vulnerability has been fixed. If you're using backups to determine what an attacker did, it goes without saying that the systems you're working with to reconstruct the sequence of events aren't network-connected in any manner.

 The mechanics of doing backups are described in Chapter 6.

Border security versus pervasive security

Because many crackers attack computers over networks, another good technique in evaluating and planning network security involves an analysis of the network itself. A common theme in many network security policies is that of *border security* or *perimeter security*. The idea is to prevent external attacks from gaining any access at all to intranet resources by stopping them at the intranet/Internet border. This can be a cheap way to gain some security, but the end result is more superficial protection than can be otherwise achieved. *Border security* is important, but when it's the sole layer in the security policy, it's referred to as *eggshell security* or *Tootsie Pop security*: superficially hard on the outside, very honestly soft inside. When relying solely on border security, most system administrators become very lax in handling the security of their intranet hosts, and a single crack in the border can result in the full compromise of every machine on the intranet. You need *pervasive security* — security measures that address both external and internal network security concerns. Treat all networks as if they are untrusted, granting only the needed privileges that are required to use the systems for their intended purposes. This of course means that you have a firewall on every machine. With logging and monitoring of logging, you can detect port scanning and other activity without even resorting to having an IDS.

The distinction between your intranet and the Internet is primarily one of convenience; both networks run the same software using the same protocols. The software vulnerabilities that affect Internet hosts affect intranet hosts as well. The primary differences between intranet and Internet hosts, in a security context, are the vectors through which attacks may come. Some of these vectors are outlined in the next section.

Types of Attacks

In the following list, I outline some of the more common vectors used when attacking a network:

✦ **An internal user deliberately misusing valid intranet access** — One of the more obvious ways an attacker can gain illegitimate access to network resources is by gaining legitimate access to network resources and then misusing that access. In many cases, their access is legitimate simply because the particular intranet resource — a sensitive client list, perhaps — is available to all members of the organization. In my own experience, I've seen at least one employee burn an entire client directory to a CD and take it home; his contract was expiring in the following week, and he wanted a contact list to help find new work.

Perhaps more common is the misuse of computer resources, though some might not call that a *security* problem. Specifically, this is the issue of employees using an organization's network facilities for their own personal business. In most cases, this is harmless; after all, nobody wants to work in an environment where they're not allowed to call their family to tell them they're on the way home. There's no reason why this courtesy can't also be extended to network resources such as e-mail or instant messaging.

Unfortunately, there are always people who take such privileges too far — perhaps they use the company phone to make long, expensive overseas calls of a personal nature. A careful balance must be maintained such that people using an organization's resources for their own purposes are free to do so in a responsible manner, while at the same time providing the administrators with the ability to take measures should abuses become apparent. One would argue that this is most obvious in the case of blatant file sharing that uses all the network bandwidth.

✦ **An internal user elevating her intranet access illegitimately** — Although many intranet services are generally provided to all users on the network, there are common cases where information isn't provided to all users, such as detailed personal information of other members of the organization. Most organizations these days keep directories of all employees and their personal information (mailing addresses, telephone numbers, tax identification numbers, insurance numbers, medical records, and so on), but for obvious reasons access to that information is restricted.

In this scenario, a user deliberately seeks to elevate her privileges beyond normal means. In a lax environment, a user doesn't really need to elevate her privileges in a technical sense; she can simply access information or services that she knows she's not supposed to be accessing. It's a sad state of affairs when the electronic equivalent of a cheap five-dollar, file-cabinet lock isn't put in place. Unfortunately though, even with technical measures, individuals are still often able to elevate their privileges, often by innocuous methods such as borrowing somebody else's computer for a seemingly everyday purpose.

✦ **An external user gaining intranet access** — Although internal users abusing intranet access is certainly cause for concern, it's generally less scary than an anonymous external user gaining access to intranet resources. Unfortunately, internal users aren't the only ones who may potentially have access to your intranet. External users from the Internet may very well be able to access all of your intranet resources as they please.

For all intents and purposes, you should consider it a given that if intranet host A can connect to intranet host B, then any hosts that can connect to intranet host A can also connect to intranet host B. For example, if you provide Internet access to your users, you'll need a gateway that is connected to both your intranet and the Internet. Should that gateway ever be compromised, the attacker on the Internet at large will be able to access any hosts the gateway can contact — in other words, your intranet hosts.

This is one place where the border-security model breaks down; it relies on a single class of machines being invulnerable. The instant any of those Internet-connected hosts are compromised (user workstations that have access rights to both, for example), access is gained to all the poorly secured intranet hosts. I can't stress the danger of this enough, as I've seen security breaches of this nature happen many times. Also, for a real-world example, consider misconfigured proxy servers. The use of proxy servers as the source of attacks on organizational intranets is a very common issue. This is one method successfully used by noteworthy ex-hacker turned critical-thinking journalist Adrian Lamo. He was able to gain access to the internal networks of *The New York Times*, MCI WorldCom, Microsoft, Yahoo!, and many others.

✦ **Viruses and worms** — Unlike individual attackers who have names and faces, viruses and worms are largely not targeted. They usually aren't designed to cause your specific network and the computers on it any harm. Viruses don't usually target networks, but rather individual computers (most commonly Windows workstations). Unfortunately, the sophistication of such attacks is high enough that even these nondirected attacks can cause serious harm to your network. Many viruses and worms have payloads designed to cause outages by rendering the infected hosts inoperable. Some collect username and login information when one of your users logs in to Web sites. Still others mean to do no outright harm but nevertheless render entire networks inoperable due to traffic congestion.

Most viruses can't propagate on their own from the start; they need human interaction of some form. Once they run, most other things on the system will be "infected" and the host is compromised. These days, viruses are most commonly distributed via e-mail — specifically, e-mail attachments that are executable and (when run by the user) send copies of themselves to any e-mail address they can find on the infected computer.

Worms, on the other hand, are self-propagating. They use vulnerabilities in network-aware applications and services to spread from host to host. Since worms require no human interaction to spread, they're often devastatingly effective, spreading from vulnerable host to vulnerable host faster than any human could hope to stop them manually. In the cases of both worms and viruses, the only effective defense is prevention.

The idea of border security can fail here too. In a modern office, many people enjoy the use of laptop computers. They can take these computers home with them, get infected with a virus or worm, and return to work the next day and infect all the vulnerable machines on the internal and "secure" network. A very effective use of resources is to make sure that these mobile machines are locked down very tightly. In addition, make sure that any machines that are vulnerable to such infection have firewalls and are patched or updated as soon as possible. This goes double for servers over workstations. A virus may use the permissions of the user when he signs on to the network and may delete all of this user's files or any files the user can access. If this happens, making sure that computer is disconnected and isolated for forensic analysis is a very important step.

✦ **Physical and social vectors** — The attack vectors discussed so far all occurred over the wire, so to speak. They're all electronic in nature. An often-overlooked part of network security is simple physical security. It's important to make sure that nobody can walk into your building, calmly place a very expensive server on a trolley, walk out with it, and drive away. Likewise, it's very important that not just anyone who can walk into your building can have tours of your server rooms. Nor can they simply plug in their laptop or any other networked device.

Perhaps more important, however, is the ever-present risk of a *social* attack. This is a favorite of seasoned crackers and is often used in lieu of some of the more computationally intensive remote attacks. Social attacks can be as simple as phoning a user, pretending to be acting on behalf of an administrator, and asking for the user's password. Or pretending to be the lead system administrator's manager's assistant. Or being dressed as a delivery person. Social engineering brings all the threats down to the common elements: access and people. They may employ phone tactics, Web sites with exploits, or e-mails with viruses. Just being helpful to someone may compromise security, as in holding the door open for someone who has one too many packages. All of a sudden that carefully placed border security is totally irrelevant; for all intents and purposes, a random person has intimate access to the network. Not only do you need to make sure that your users can't gain unauthorized access to parts of your intranet resources, but you also need to be sure that users don't inadvertently give their own access away to others. Social engineering is a very large topic that can basically be summed up best by the people who are known for this craft.

Note If you're interested in some real-world examples of security being broken by social engineering, pick up a copy of Kevin Mitnick's *The Art of Deception*, Wiley Publishing, 2002.

Security Tactics

Now that you've identified the theoretical security concerns, it's time to address some measures you can take to make your network more secure.

Isolation

Isolation plays an important part in reducing the effects of any given security compromise. By isolation, I mean setting up your network so that compromising one system doesn't immediately result in the compromise of all systems. This isn't a realistic approach for many parts of an intranet; for instance, if an attacker can breach the security of an authentication service, he'll be able to masquerade as any user on the network and subvert those services. Despite the inability to isolate all systems from every other system, it's worth doing what you can do to isolate those services that you can.

✦ **Isolate the network**—Securing your network's borders, while not sufficient in and of itself, is still useful. All entry and exit points should be well defined and carefully crafted. Any software configuration relevant to your gateways should be as simple as possible, in order to reduce the chance of any operator error introducing vulnerabilities. If you employ virtual private network software, don't treat end points of a VPN as if they are part of the local intranet; treat each differently and craft access controls that meet each particular network's needs.

Isolating adjoining networks as much as possible — especially VPNs — also serves a benefit secondary to your own security. While such isolation can certainly benefit you, it also benefits your neighbor. A close relationship with a client might result in the implementation of a VPN between your two intranets, but that client won't be very happy at all if a worm that has infected your network travels through the VPN and proceeds to infect their intranet. Aside from VPNs to partners and clients, your ISP may not take it kindly if, for instance, you're the source of a great deal of spam e-mail due to a poorly secured intranet e-mail server.

✦ **Isolate the hosts** — The concept of border security isn't bad in and of itself; it's usually just poorly implemented. Specifically, the borders are usually made too large and there aren't enough of them. If each host on the network has its own "border," if each piece of equipment has its own layers of protection, you can greatly reduce the chances and effects of any breaches of security. Arguably, *all* security measures are implemented at borders of one form or another, logical or physical; it's just important to make sure there are enough of them to protect all your systems.

In the case of workstations, for instance, make sure each has its own firewall. Workstations rarely need to actively respond to network traffic; they almost exclusively make outgoing connections (as opposed to responding to incoming connections). If your workstations are running a GNU/Linux distribution, such as Debian, it's relatively easy to remotely administer thousands of workstations in a homogeneous manner, allowing each to have its own standard firewall configuration. Should a laptop ever get infected with a worm, the worm's ability to propagate can be severely hampered if there aren't any other machines that accept the worm's connection attempts.

✦ **Isolate the software** — Isolating software can be reasonably easy. Running daemons under their own accounts is a good first step. In Debian GNU/Linux, most daemons that have been designed to operate under their own account(s) do so out of the box. Going further than this requires careful examination of the software in question and developing a solution that's appropriate for your particular uses of the software.

Reducing intersoftware complexity can also be helpful in this regard. It's also a good idea to disable unessential features whenever they are found.

✦ **Isolate the hardware** — If you have any data that could be used when physically stolen (credit card numbers, valuable databases, source code for a proprietary application, what have you), it makes sense to segregate the hardware as well. All that data stored in a single server box would be relatively easy to steal physically; if you spread the data over a dozen servers, anybody physically stealing them would be far more conspicuous.

Additionally, if the machines in question aren't administered centrally (for instance, if each is administered as if it was entirely separate, not standardized in any way), having multiple installations reduces the risk of a single configuration error resulting in a catastrophic vulnerability.

Fault tolerance

Aside from theft of data and resources, simple denial of service attacks can be devastating to a business. Denial of service attacks can take many forms but they typically involve crashing software through a flood of otherwise legitimate traffic. Alternatively, some worms and viruses take up so much network bandwidth that they make legitimate communications impossible. Being able to deal with these outages is part of your response to a security incident and, combined with an effective backup strategy (discussed in Chapter 6), can reduce the effect of any compromise.

In an ideal world, you would keep two of each server you operate — one connected and operational, the other disconnected and "cold." When the first server is compromised, you would take it off-line, examine it to determine the cause of the compromise, discover the cause, make it impossible to exploit the vulnerability again *on the backup server*, bring that backup server online, and retain the original for further forensics (perhaps to determine who, exactly, compromised the machine). This level of redundancy is difficult to achieve in practice; the best most administrators can hope for is a rapid-response procedure that involves keeping one or two spare general-purpose machines handy. When a host is compromised, its last backups are restored to a general-purpose spare machine, the vulnerability is fixed, and the new machine is placed online — again, keeping the original for forensic purposes.

In the case of network-level breaches, where the network itself is inoperable, it's best to be able to quickly segregate the source of the problem (if there is one). For instance, if your workstations are all infected with the latest worm, it would be prudent to disconnect them from the network. In such a situation, unplugging your intranet servers wouldn't be a problem, as your pool of users is off-line, while your Internet servers would need to remain functional. How you choose to implement this sort of policy depends largely on the design and the hardware that your network uses.

These approaches can allow for reasonably rapid responses to any denial of service and can help reduce the effect of such types of security breaches.

Getting help

Although you should take every possible technological and internal measure to protect your systems, you shouldn't overlook the value of having a support community to learn from and help you. This community isn't simply composed of peers within your organization but should also be composed of engineers from your software provider, researchers in the larger community, and the authors of the software itself (should that differ from the group you actually get your software from).

Working with your service and software providers

Your first point of contact when dealing with any security issue—whether planning, response, or simply curiosity—should be the service or software provider you use. Your best source of information about specific vulnerabilities that affect the software you use will likely come through your service/software provider channels. If your service/software provider offers dedicated security communications channels (such as e-mail notification or telephone notification), avail yourself of them if feasible. In the case of software vulnerabilities, a vendor's notification will often contain information that's more reliable than the general alert sent out by the software's author. A case in point is a vulnerability in OpenSSH a couple of years ago; the author of the software instructed everybody to upgrade to the newest version, but it turned out that many distributions (Debian included) weren't vulnerable. Software authors are rarely able to keep track of myriad software vendors and the way that they've changed the software.

Mailing lists

The canonical mailing list for UNIX and Linux security issues is BugTraq. The BugTraq mailing list is run by SecurityFocus (`www.securityfocus.com`), a company that specializes in security research and information dissemination. This mailing list is more frequently a venue for releasing rather than strictly a discussion list. You can subscribe to BugTraq by filling out the form available at `www.securityfocus.com/subscribe`.

Most vendors post security advisories to BugTraq as well as to their own mailing lists, so expect to see duplicated advisories. Upstream authors also use BugTraq to inform administrators about flaws in their software. Lastly, security researchers often post very well-written dissertations on various security-related topics.

A great place to find additional mailing lists is by searching MARC (Mailing list ARChives) at `http://marc.theaimsgroup.com/`. I highly recommend Full Disclosure, at `http://lists.netsys.com/mailman/listinfo/full-disclosure`.

For Debian-specific lists, try `www.debian.org/MailingLists/`, or check out some of these sites:

- ✦ `http://lists.debian.org/debian-announce/`—Used for major announcements regarding Debian.
- ✦ `http://lists.debian.org/debian-user/`—Aimed at beginning users.
- ✦ `http://lists.debian.org/debian-security/`—For security discussions.
- ✦ `http://lists.debian.org/debian-security-announce/`—If you're on only one list, this is the one you want to be on. It includes security advisory posts about Debian packages.
- ✦ `www.debian.org/security/audit/`—If you're interested in proactive security, check out this Debian audit project started by Steve Kemp.

Gray Hat Hackers

In security parlance, there are three types of hackers: black hats, gray hats, and white hats. *Black hats* use their skills for their own personal gain, cracking into other people's systems for their own purposes. *White hats* perform research to benefit the community as a whole and use the information they garner responsibly. White hats never break into other people's systems; they use their own for testing. *Gray hats* are similar to white hats, except that they *do* break into other people's systems. Most gray hats honestly mean well and choose a method of education that's hard to ignore—education by example. It's a rare system administrator who will refuse to even acknowledge a security flaw when somebody anonymous has demonstrated its existence. Gray hats inform the administrators of the systems they crack about how they broke in and often how to fix the problem (if they don't inform the proper administrators, they're not gray hats, they're black hats).

If any of your systems are ever cracked by a gray hat, consider them compromised for all intents and purposes. You can't know that they didn't do something truly bad (such as altering data or stealing sensitive information) without going through the entire process as if the compromise had been performed by a truly malicious individual. That said, it may not be in your best interest to react with hostility to the gray hat. If somebody broke into your house and installed an alarm system that would have prevented the break-in, you would rightly feel that your privacy was invaded. And indeed it was—but the intruder honestly wanted to help, and did so. In the case of your servers, the gray hat has performed some auditing and analysis that you might otherwise have had to do yourself. By contacting you, gray hats put themselves at risk; their actions are illegal in most parts of the world, and if they care enough to let you know about the problem despite the personal risk to themselves, it may be worth holding back on a lawsuit. Lastly, the gray hat broke into your systems once, without any harm to you other than a bruised pride. If he did it once, he might be able to do it again if he sets his mind to it.

It's worth noting that many security professionals would still push for contacting law enforcement. Depending on whom the system belongs to, what type of data is exposed, and who the system users are, it may be absolutely required to disclose the break-in. In California, it is state law that any company that is broken into must disclose that such an event occurred.

Ultimately, you're responsible for the system as set forth in employment or volunteer documents and verbal contracts that were agreed on. Your responsibility ultimately lies with the group that asked for your experience as a system operator. You should always default to protecting your users, your organization, and yourself before an intruder.

You should also look for a local GNU/Linux user group. For example, in the northern California area, I attend NBLUG, the North Bay Linux Users Group. Its mailing list is open to everyone: www.nblug.org.

If you're in North America, the North American Network Operators Group (NANOG) mailing list can also provide a source for early-warning information about general Internet security issues (which may, of course, affect your intranet). You can subscribe to the NANOG mailing list by following the instructions detailed at `www.nanog.org/email.html`. Administrators from outside North America are welcome to join the NANOG mailing list, though some of the routing issues discussed therein are specific to North America.

Both BugTraq and the NANOG mailing list are high-traffic; BugTraq sees dozens of messages a day, and NANOG can see hundreds.

> **Note** These communities work two ways. Not only should you depend on resources such as the authors of software and BugTraq for information about bugs in your software, but you can also send bugs to them when you find them. If your system is compromised in a way that is not a previously published vulnerability, you may be able to work with these communities to help others avoid your fate.

It's important to find a list that has the right topical approach and level of interest for your needs. If you're going to subscribe to a number of mailing lists, make sure you take the time to read them. Choose them carefully and don't ignore the threads that may teach you things about the system you're already running.

Example Security Procedures

So far, this chapter has been largely doom and gloom. Security isn't a trivial thing to worry about, and sometimes administrators need to adopt an attitude of professional paranoia. A serious compromise usually isn't outside the realm of possibility when a computer is connected to the Internet. It's important for administrators to take every precaution they can reasonably take. Being *secure enough* is a moving target. It should vary project to project with a strong default baseline. You need to consider the potential for damage on your particular network; Web sites that accept credit cards are routinely broken into and those credit cards are abused, which can leave real people with poor credit ratings in their wake. Entire businesses rely on their ability to send and receive e-mail, and a day's outage while the administrators restore from backups can mean a real loss in sales.

The rest of this chapter is devoted to some concrete technical measures you can take to reduce the chances of compromises happening in the first place and to reduce the damage done by those compromises, should they happen.

The first line of defense: Your baseline system software and exemplary planning practices

Keeping your software up-to-date is essential to a secure system. Though Debian goes to great lengths to make sure that the compromise of one subsystem doesn't mean a compromise of them all, any crack in the security of your computer can lead to a full-blown compromise. Unfortunately, Debian doesn't guarantee the kind of unattended security updates that an administrator can set up and leave alone.

However, when Debian updates a package in its stable branch, *only* the code that is vulnerable is changed. In this way, the impact of a security bug is kept to a bare minimum. This is somewhat ironic, as these noninvasive security updates are far more reliable than many vendors' practices of upgrading entire software packages to deal with a bug in a single line of code. Nevertheless, Debian still doesn't guarantee noninteractive updates, so instead of risking a nonfunctional system, we'll bite the bullet and add some due diligence to the mix.

To have your stable Debian system automatically check for updates and then upgrade automatically, create a new file in /etc/cron.daily/ named update-check. In that file, put the following contents:

```
#!/bin/sh

aptitude -yy -d upgrade
```

After saving the file, make it executable by running

```
sudo chmod +x /etc/cron.daily/update-check
```

Passing aptitude the -yy parameter tells it to assume "yes" for any questions it may have (such as whether to continue with the download or not). Passing -d tells it to just download the new packages, not actually upgrade them. Now, once daily, you'll be sent an e-mail containing the output of that command, which will let you know if you have any package upgrades available. If there are any, log in as soon as you can and upgrade those packages, as they may have important security fixes. (apt-cron may also be suited to this need.)

Caution   Keep in mind that automatic fetching and patching of a system is very reasonably considered a possible security vulnerability. Doing anything automatically should be treated with extreme caution.

Some packages will have requirements that exacerbate the number of running services on your system in nonobvious ways.

The second line of defense: Your firewall

Generally speaking, an Internet-connected machine faces greater security threats from anonymous attackers coming from outside the network than from users who have privileged access to the network. Given that, it's important to make as few services as possible available to those anonymous attackers. Aside from not running the services at all, which isn't usually an option given the interconnected nature of a modern GNU/Linux system, you can use Linux firewalling capabilities to erect a first barrier against these attackers.

Most end-users do not need to run any software on their local system. As a system administrator, you obviously provide those facilities to your users.

Internet Protocol Basics

If you're already well-versed in the operation of a modern IP network and how packets are addressed to computers, skip this sidebar. If you're not, here's a quick rundown. Whenever an IP packet is sent from one computer to another, it has a *source address*, a *destination address*, a *protocol*, and in some cases, a *source port* and a *destination port*. When I say *protocol,* I don't mean like DNS or SMTP, but rather TCP or UDP or ICMP. When dealing with the firewall on an Internet server, the attributes you're most interested in are the protocol and the port attributes. Specifically, you want to block certain ports in certain protocols, so that *nobody* from the Internet can access them. However, it's worth noting that firewalls are not the be-all and end-all of access controls. If you use a firewall to control access to otherwise vulnerable software, it may come back to bite you. Also, it's worth noting that it's a matter of filtering not only incoming traffic but also outgoing traffic.

Network basics and the mechanics of setting this all up are described in Chapter 5.

This section is meant to get you up and running with a firewall. It allows for all data that passes into your network interfaces to be categorized and filtered. This allows for superior control over the way data is handled. Firewalls can block traffic in polite ways, and in other ways, they can be used to make a computer quite stealthy. Depending on the threat model of your systems, you must make the appropriate choices in how to configure your firewall. The firewall simply carries out your orders. In this section, I show you how to order it to be quite overzealous so as to err on the side of blocking, as opposed to traditional open-to-the-world systems with a basically disabled firewall.

One method of building a firewall with Debian is by using a prepackaged firewall script or program. While you can roll your own script, in this chapter I assume that you're looking for a ready-to-go solution. Writing your own firewall script is beyond the scope of this book.

If you're using a package from Debian, I suggest using the `shorewall` package. It's a set of scripts that reads some configuration files you write and then sets up the firewall for you. By configuring it, you tell it what you want it to do by default, what you want it to make exceptions for, and what you want it to do when it takes an action, such as logging or dropping a packet. It's run on boot, and it simply acts as a front end to the `iptables` and `ip` programs (as well as a few others).

Firewalls work by having support in the kernel and userspace applications that configure the supported features in the kernel normally loaded as modules. If you're using the 2.4 or 2.6 kernel images that come with Debian, the required modules for firewalling will be ready for use.

Installing the firewall package

To build your firewall, start by installing the required package, as root:

```
# apt-get install shorewall shorewall-doc
[...]
The following extra packages will be installed:
  iproute libatm1
[...]
The following NEW packages will be installed:
  iproute libatm1 shorewall
[...]
```

Select Y and press Enter.

You should see a message similar to this at the end of the install:

```
Setting up shorewall (2.0.9-1) ...
#### WARNING ####
the firewall won't be started/stopped unless it is configured

please configure it and then edit /etc/default/shorewall
and set the "startup" variable to 1 in order to allow
shorewall to start
##################
```

Configuring the firewall

As the message indicates, next you need to configure the firewall. This section walks you through setting up shorewall from its configuration files.

First, read the /etc/shorewall/shorewall.conf file. This file sets all the reasonable defaults. It's a very well-commented file. Depending on your tastes, you might want to change things around. By default, you only need to change something in that file if you absolutely want to.

However, at this point, you have simply configured the defaults that shorewall needs once you have explained what the rules are. The next step is to define some rules.

There are currently three locations for configuration files:

✦ /etc/shorewall/ — This is where all your configuration files should go after you edit them.

✦ /usr/share/shorewall/ — This is where many *actions* or nonuser configuration files are kept (you don't need to edit these normally).

✦ /usr/share/doc/shorewall/ — The thoughtful people that packed the Debian package have left the default configurations in /usr/share/doc/shorewall/default-config/.

Follow these steps to configure shorewall:

1. To set up your default rules, simply copy over the rules file:

```
cp /usr/share/doc/shorewall/default-config/rules.gz /etc/
shorewall/
```

2. Next, uncompress it:

```
gzip -d /etc/shorewall/rules.gz
```

By default, it's simply a heavily commented file. In fact, no rules are actually defined in this file unless you decide to define them.

3. Shorewall does most of its important logic by dividing network traffic into hosts and zones, so you need to copy over the default zone file:

```
cp /usr/share/doc/shorewall/default-config/zones
/etc/shorewall/
```

Take a look at this file. It shows the default zones; they should be just fine for your use.

4. Next, set up the default policy:

```
cp /usr/share/doc/shorewall/default-config/policy /etc/
shorewall/
```

The three lines by default in the policy file are the following:

```
loc          net            ACCEPT
net          all            DROP           info
all          all            REJECT         info
```

This means that all local network traffic is accepted, traffic from the Internet is dropped and logged at a syslog level of info, and by default, everything else is rejected with a syslog level of info.

5. To allow traffic from the host `fw` to all users, you need to add a single line to this file:

```
Fw      all     ACCEPT
```

This means that incoming traffic is blocked, but it allows for all outgoing traffic.

6. Now you simply need to tell shorewall which network interfaces are to be configured and how to configure them:

```
cp /usr/share/doc/shorewall/default-config/interfaces.gz
/etc/shorewall/
gzip -d /etc/shorewall/interfaces.gz
```

This file is actually the one that will take the most effort to configure.

7. I assume that this is a networked computer and that network is 10/100BaseT Ethernet with a dhcp server providing addresses when they are requested. This should be a safe assumption for most new setups. If these conditions

don't fit your situation (for example, if you're a PPP user), reading the comments in each file should help you. The shorewall documentation is really excellent; use it!

If your system matches these conditions, simply add this line to the /etc/shorewall/interfaces file:

```
loc     eth0    detect  dhcp
```

This sets up the interface eth0 to be in the local zone; it detects your broadcast address and allows for requesting an IP address via dhcp.

At this point, you have all the configuration files you need to connect to your local network resources. Start using shorewall like so:

```
shorewall start
```

To stop the firewall, use this command:

```
shorewall stop
```

Note   This command doesn't actually stop the firewall entirely; it puts shorewall into a stopped state. Refer to the shorewall documentation for more detail.

To restart and reload the configuration files, use the following command:

```
shorewall restart
```

To make sure that shorewall starts at boot each time, simply edit the file /etc/default/shorewall and change the value of startup from 0 to 1, like so:

```
startup=1
```

Logging with shorewall

By default, shorewall is configured to log messages to /var/log/messages. If you're looking for something that should be logged or something seems to be blocked, take a look there first.

The following code is a log sample of a single packet being blocked:

```
Shorewall:net2all:DROP:IN=eth0 OUT=
MAC=00:0c:76:14:01:cb:00:0e:39:0c:fc:00:08:00
SRC=201.124.21.220 DST=62.147.123.29 LEN=48 TOS=0x00
PREC=0x00 TTL=111 ID=25761 DF PROTO=TCP SPT=4892 DPT=9898
WINDOW=16384 RES=0x00 SYN URGP=0
```

This example shows the log prefix of Shorewall and the chain and the policy that it had applied to it. It also shows the interface it was received on, eth0, as well as the MAC address. Its source IP address is shown in the SRC field. Its destination IP address (generally the one assigned to eth0 but not always) is shown following the DST. For now, the other things that matter are the PROTO, SPT, and DPT fields. Those specify what the protocol, source port, and destination port are in the packet.

This is a half-open model for a firewall. It's useful, but it's not as security-conscious as what you may want. It's your choice how you want to allow access to the Internet with this type of firewall. You can alternately add rules in /etc/shorewall/rules to allow only certain traffic, but this can be a gotcha if you don't know what you need to allow out. Reading the shorewall documentation will give you some idea of the direction you need to take.

Note   For an example of how packets pass through the system, take a look at the diagram on the shorewall Web site: www.shorewall.net/NetfilterOverview.html.

The preceding firewall, basic though it may be, is adequate for most uses. I use a firewall very similar to that on all of my servers except that I lock down the outgoing policy to be default deny, allowing only the things I want out to get out. Keeping security as simple as possible is an advantage. The simpler your security policies are, the easier they are to understand, implement, explain, and audit.

I highly suggest you learn how the underlying firewalling actually works. While front ends like shorewall are great, knowing how the kernel portion (netfilter) and the userspace portion (iptables, iproute2) are configured by shorewall is really useful. This firewall should be sufficient on a personal workstation, but it's not ready to be deployed on a server, so don't try that just yet with the given configuration.

Visit the netfilter/iptables project at www.netfilter.org/ to learn more.

The third line of defense: Your daemons

Because most of your risk comes from crackers attacking from the Internet, those daemons that are accessible to the public Internet need to be secure, well-configured, and up-to-date. When possible, rely on widely used daemons that have a history for good security. It can be a sensible position to never use a daemon that always runs as root unless it has good reason to be root (sshd, for instance, needs to run as root so as to change its privileges to those of the user logging in).

There is no other documentation that can surpass and help you to secure your Debian machine like the documentation provided by Debian itself. For the Debian documentation, refer to www.debian.org/doc/manuals/securing-debian-howto/. This document covers all the Debian-specific methods for securing a system. Follow all of the steps that you can manage, and remember which ones you haven't performed.

The following list provides some general rules of thumb that can make your life much easier:

✦ Always set a BIOS password; change the boot order of your devices to boot only from your hard drive/raid array.

✦ Always set a boot loader password.

✦ Always comment out the line in /etc/inittab that allows for a local reboot if someone simply has a keyboard. To do this, change the lines

```
# What to do when CTRL-ALT-DEL is pressed.
ca:12345:ctrlaltdel:/sbin/shutdown -t1 -a -r now
```

to

```
# What to do when CTRL-ALT-DEL is pressed.
# ca:12345:ctrlaltdel:/sbin/shutdown -t1 -a -r now
```

✦ Any user that should reboot the system should be able to log in to do so. It's very rare that they cannot do so; if that's the case with your systems, try to find a better key combo so that not every person on the planet knows it.

✦ Install and run integrity-checking software: aide, osiris, samhain, integrit, or tripwire. This allows you to have a baseline of checksums and lists of files on your system. It also allows for (not foolproof) detection if a user starts messing around with the system; if they break root, it's possible to tamper with these logs, so be careful.

✦ Selecting software that leaves your users less open to nonintrusive monitoring is always the best choice. Encrypt everything, always.

✦ Provide HTTPS whenever you can. There is no reason to provide only basic HTTP if there is any sort of login procedure.

✦ When running mail systems (POP, SMTP, IMAP), don't allow your daemons (such as those that provide POP3 or IMAP service) to allow logins without using SSL. Never let users check their e-mail and have their passwords in the clear.

If you want to see this problem at work, install a packet sniffer such as ethereal and watch the network traffic as you check your own mail. If it's not encrypted, you're going to see yourself authorize and request mail. If you have new mail, you will see the mail as well when you pull it down. This is obviously a problem; if you're the administrator, you should fix that as soon as possible. If you're not, you should request secured access to those services. This doesn't make e-mail secure, but it does make your e-mail experience more secure from the server to your MUA.

✦ Ensure that your SMTP server provides extensions for communication with servers that are aware of cryptography (STARTTLS). This means that communication to the mail server and to other mail servers may be encrypted. The e-mail message itself isn't encrypted, but the SMTP transaction may be. Due to the nature of SMTP, not all such communications will be encrypted, as not all mail servers support this. This is sometimes considered a Band-Aid solution, but when you have no choice but to offer a particular service (e-mail is a requirement), it's best to provide at least limited node-to-node security.

✦ Never let a user have telnet access to any system. Always use SSH. Even modern switches these days have SSH. It's important to implement it correctly (using protocol 2 only). It's very nice to use; it supports all the features of rsh and telnet, with the added benefit of being encrypted. Granted, SSH has had its share of security vulnerabilities, so firewall zealously. Use nonstandard port numbers if you're going to not bother firewalling. This will at least stop a random script kiddie who is simply scanning for servers listening on port 22.

✦ Always disable all software that is enabled by default if it's a listening network service. To check for running software, simply look at the output of the command `netstat -tuanp` as root. It should look something like this:

```
Active Internet connections (servers and established)
Proto Recv-Q Send-Q Local Address Foreign Address State  PID/Program name
tcp     0      0 127.0.0.1:8001  0.0.0.0:*       LISTEN  3206/ssh
```

In this case, ssh is listening on port 8001. This is a local port forward, so it's actually the ssh client, not sshd listening.

Notice that the process name is the last entry on the right-hand side. If you don't want it to run on boot anymore, take a look at your startup scripts. Find the master script in `/etc/init.d/*` and then run the following (for example, to disable `xinetd`):

```
update-rc.d -f xinetd remove
Removing any system startup links for /etc/init.d/xinetd ...
```

Do this for each service that is running that you don't actually want running. See the Securing Debian HOWTO for more examples of this (`www.debian.org/doc/manuals/securing-debian-howto/`).

✦ Hardening the systems-critical daemons is a very important part as well. For each service you're going to implement, learn as much about it as possible. Seek out guides that teach you how to harden whatever obscure or very well-known software project you're running.

✦ Try to build chroots as often as possible. Most of the time, these can be used to thwart even a semiskilled cracker. Remember: The really talented hackers will not leave a trace. It's possible to root a box without ever writing your rootkit to the disk. It's possible that, upon reboot, it could be gone (all of this can be done in memory). But you can't protect against everything all of the time. Try to harden every aspect of the system, not just one part of it.

✦ A killer firewall won't help you if Apache has an exploit in it and you just happen to serve Web pages to the world. The firewall will be happy to let the exploit packets in.

✦ If you want to take a crack at giving yourself a quick and effective security
scan, take a look at the `nessus` package.

✦ If you're looking for automated hardening, take a look at the `bastille` package. It will walk you through hardening a system and teach you while you go.
It's written by a very smart fellow by the name of Jay Beale.

Summary

After reading this chapter, you should have some basic ideas about how security
processes *should* work and some tools to help you reduce obvious insecurity.
You should also have a solid grasp of the common vectors used to compromise a
network and the hosts contained therein. You should have a good understanding
of the higher-level concepts such as awareness, education, and isolation. Lastly,
you should know when to contact the community for assistance and how to best
use that community's support. You should have some idea of what security looks
like when it's being applied, as in a firewall. In the rest of this book, I'll often touch
on the security implications of particular daemons, applications, and administration tasks.

✦   ✦   ✦

E-Mail Servers

E-mail has become a mission-critical application for almost every Internet user. Whether you're a business or an individual, you rely on an e-mail system for communication with the outside world. The simple interface presented by your e-mail client, however, can hide the underlying complexity of the system — now more than 20 years old.

The fundamentals of e-mail are reasonably simple, and the first section of this chapter provides you with an introduction to those basic concepts. By far the most complex parts of the global e-mail system (and your part of it) are in the software and in the interactions between the millions of e-mail servers. The rest of this chapter provides a hands-on walk-through of installing and configuring a number of e-mail servers.

This chapter, however, will limit itself mainly to *public* e-mail servers. E-mail systems are actually composed of many different layers to serve local and remote users and to accept e-mail from (mostly) anonymous remote users and systems. E-mail is as ubiquitous as it is largely due to the ability of any system administrator to set up a public e-mail server that accepts mail from any other e-mail server and can send mail to any other e-mail server. When somebody sends you an e-mail, the first place where that e-mail comes into contact with your network will be your MTA, or *mail transport agent*. The MTA is responsible for receiving mail from remote systems and processing it for delivery, as well as collecting e-mail from your users and sending it to remote MTAs. Your MTA either stores received e-mails for user retrieval or passes the e-mails onto a separate delivery system (an MDA, or *mail delivery agent*) for further processing. Users read their e-mail with MUAs, or *mail user agents*. The public layer is the MTA, which must accept connections from remote systems and initiate connections to remote systems to send e-mail.

In This Chapter

E-mail composition

E-mail transmission and reception

Exim installation and configuration

Exim mail delivery

Other mail transport agents

E-Mail Basics

The foundation architecture of e-mail is really quite simple. Though the software that works with e-mail can be quite complex, this complexity is simply the result of a simple system being built upon to fit the needs of its users 20 years after its creation. This chapter focuses on MTAs, and MTAs follow standard rules when dealing with the transmission, reception, and routing of e-mail. This section covers those rules in an MTA-agnostic fashion; you'll learn what particular bits of an e-mail message mean, how e-mail is routed, and so on.

If you're interested in the technical details concerning the formatting and transmission of e-mail, read RFCs 2821 and 2822 at www.faqs.org/rfcs/rfc2821. html and www.faqs.org/rfcs/rfc2822.html, respectively. Most Internet standards are codified in RFCs, which stands for *Request For Comments*. This section is a very short distillation of some of the more salient parts of those RFCs.

Standard e-mail composition

Each e-mail message is composed of two broad parts — the headers and the body. The headers aren't usually displayed by mail-reading applications, though they're read and interpreted by those applications. For instance, the sender of the e-mail is recorded in the e-mail's headers. The body of the e-mail is the content area, the part of the e-mail that is free-form. The body may contain a simple plaintext message written by the user, a complex HTML message generated by an automated service, a single large binary file (perhaps a tarball or a zip archive), or all of the above. There are standards defining how multiple parts and subparts of the body can be encoded, allowing for cross-client compatibility, but as far as your MTA cares, the body of the message is just the body.

Though the body of an e-mail is free-form and can be encoded such that any data can be transmitted, that isn't to say that e-mails are wholly without structure — quite the opposite, in fact. Outside of the body, there are many strict rules defining what the parts of the e-mail mean and how they're to be represented.

The anatomy of an e-mail address

The part of the global e-mail system most visible to users tends to be its addressing method — that is to say, e-mail addresses. E-mail addresses are ubiquitous today, appearing on business cards, Web pages, cellphones, sticky notes, letterhead, and marketing materials. There are a couple of basic properties common to every valid e-mail address:

✦ Every valid e-mail address is globally unique. Barring software misconfiguration, every e-mail server in the world will know exactly where to send messages addressed to any given e-mail address.

✦ Each e-mail has a *domain* part and a *user* part. The user part is also often referred to as the *local* part. For instance, the fictitious e-mail address user@domain.com refers to the local user user at the site domain.com. When communicating with a remote system, your e-mail server concerns itself primarily with the domain part; it's up to the receiving end to do something appropriate with the local part.

Sometimes, especially in your mail client, you'll see an e-mail address of the form
Joe User <joe.user@domain.com>. In such cases, the e-mail address is contained within the angle brackets — joe.user@domain.com in our example. The rest
of the address is ignored by the server software; it exists solely for humans to read.
Generally speaking, the valid characters for the local part of the e-mail address are
letters, numbers, a hyphen (-), an underscore (_), or a plus symbol (+). Using characters other than these, while officially allowed by the specification, can result in
compatibility problems with other e-mail servers (typically those that are badly
configured).

Headers in an e-mail

Second to e-mail addresses in importance, headers provide gobs of machine-
parseable data, which is used by e-mail servers and clients to make e-mail more
generally useful. For instance, the subject of an e-mail, which is displayed by virtually every e-mail client, is set using the Subject: header. The following is a simplified e-mail in its source format, as it would be transmitted from system to system:

```
From: dbharris@debian.org
To: fake.user@domain.com
Subject: Example e-mail

This is the body of the example e-mail.
```

In this example e-mail, the headers are in bold whereas the body of the e-mail is
not. In the example e-mail, you see three headers: the originator of the e-mail
(dbharris@debian.org), the destination (fake.user@domain.com), and the subject (Example e-mail). The message body contains a single line: This is the
body of the example e-mail. Note that both the headers and the body are
human-readable. The body is distinguished from the headers by a single blank line;
there are no blank lines between consecutive headers. A more realistic e-mail follows; I sent this e-mail to myself from a remote system:

```
Return-path: <dbharris@andromeda.oftc.net>
Envelope-to: dbharris@willow.eelf.ddts.net
Delivery-date: Tue, 25 May 2004 02:18:15 -0400
Received: from oak.eelf.ddts.net ([192.168.1.1])
        by willow.eelf.ddts.net with esmtp (Exim 4.34)
        id 1BW81l-00014S-H1
        for dbharris@willow.eelf.ddts.net;
        Tue, 25 May 2004 02:18:05 -0400
Received: from andromeda.oftc.net ([80.190.233.18])
        by oak.eelf.ddts.net with esmtp
        (TLS-1.0:RSA_ARCFOUR_SHA:16) (Exim 4.24)
        id 1BW81l-0003Bs-4p
        for dbharris@eelf.ddts.net;
        Tue, 25 May 2004 02:18:05 -0400
Received: from dbharris by andromeda.oftc.net with local
        (Exim 4.33) id 1BW81h-0003Ay-B8
        for dbharris@eelf.ddts.net;
        Tue, 25 May 2004 06:18:01 +0000
```

```
To: dbharris@eelf.ddts.net
Message-Id: <E1BW81h-0003Ay-B8@andromeda.oftc.net>
From: David B Harris <dbharris@andromeda.oftc.net>
Date: Tue, 25 May 2004 06:18:01 +0000
X-Spam-Checker-Version: SpamAssassin 2.63 (2004-01-11) on
        willow.eelf.ddts.net
X-Spam-Level:
X-Spam-Status: No, hits=-2.3 required=5.0 tests=AWL,BAYES_01
        autolearn=ham
        version=2.63

Test e-mail's body.
```

As you can see, there's a great deal of information included in the headers of a *real* e-mail. Many headers include too much information to fit onto one line. When a header is too long for a single line, it's continued by starting the next line with a single tab character. See Table 14-1 for a description of each header in the example e-mail. Be aware, however, that there are many more standard headers than are covered here, and there is an infinite number of nonstandard headers used by various mail clients and servers for their own purposes.

Table 14-1
Standard E-mail Headers

Header	Description
Return-path:	When a server is unable to deliver a message it has accepted for delivery, it needs to send a *bounce* message. The address to which to send this bounce message is provided by the server that sent the message and is stored by many receiving servers in the e-mail using the Return-path: header.
Envelope-to:	Because e-mails can be forwarded from one address to another, and because the To: header contains only what the original e-mail author entered, some MTAs store the address the e-mail was actually delivered to in the Envelope-to: header.
Delivery-date:	Some MTAs record the date and time of delivery in the Delivery-date: header.
Received:	An e-mail can pass through many MTAs before reaching its final destination. A standards-compliant MTA will add a Received: header indicating that it handled the mail at one point; this is often used for debugging.

Header	Description
`To:`	The `To:` field doesn't necessarily mean anything. When you receive an e-mail, the `To:` field can be any e-mail address at all; it doesn't need to be your own. This is because e-mail servers tell other e-mail servers the address to which to deliver the e-mail via the SMTP dialogue (discussed subsequently), not via the message itself. In the real world, the only place the `To:` field is respected is in the sending user's e-mail client, which then tells their MTA where to send the e-mail based on what the user supplied in the `To:` field.
`Message-Id:`	Each e-mail message *should* have a globally unique `Message-id:` header, which is often quite similar in form to an e-mail address. The `Message-id:` is used in debugging, in tracking, and by some e-mail clients to display replies to e-mails specially.
`From:`	Much like the `To:` header, the `From:` header doesn't necessarily have any real meaning. It is, however, the header most often used by mail clients when choosing an address to reply to.
`Date:`	The `Date:` header is inserted by the e-mail client at the time it sends the e-mail (which may be quite different from when the e-mail is delivered at its destination).
`X-Spam-Checker-Version:`	A common Internet convention among protocols and file formats that have headers and bodies (like e-mail) is to allow custom headers. Typically, these headers are distinguished by starting with the character `X`, and e-mail is no different. In our example, `X-Spam-Checker-Version:` is a nonstandard header inserted by the SpamAssassin spam-filtering software, which contains SpamAssassin's version and other miscellaneous information.
`X-Spam-Level:`	SpamAssassin also inserts an `X-Spam-Level:` header, which contains zero or more asterisks (*). The more asterisks there are, the more likely it is that the e-mail is a spam message (according to SpamAssassin).
`X-Spam-Status:`	Another SpamAssassin-inserted header, `X-Spam-Status:` provides detailed information about the message, such as its spam score (the higher the score, the more likely it is that it's a spam message) and the specific tests that it passed or failed.

The body of an e-mail

Though e-mail headers are interesting to any MTA administrator, the body of a message is without doubt what most people are interested in when they're reading an e-mail. Within some broad limits, the format of the body of a message is free-form as far as the MTA is concerned. The body can be (and often is) plaintext, without any special formatting. It's simply transmitted as the user typed it. Another popular body type is HTML, which can be used by some clients to display fancier messages.

Even if the body of the message is free-form as far as MTAs are concerned, clients still need to be able to read them. As such, there exists a standard for formatting the body as well. The standard is called MIME, or *Multipurpose Internet Mail Extensions*. MIME is, in some ways, a metaformat. It doesn't specify the format for the content of the message, but it provides a framework for telling other mail clients about which formats are used within the body. When you attach a file to a message, for instance, you're using a multipart MIME message. Your mail client provides the file type and its name in MIME formatting headers, and it's up to the receiving client to deal with the file itself (for example, if it's an image, it may be displayed within the mail client).

Roughly speaking, MIME provides an e-mail body the structure required for sending complex data. MIME messages can have multiple parts, and each part is labeled with the file format contained within that part. For instance, a commonly seen form of e-mail is a multipart plaintext/HTML e-mail; MIME constructs specify that there are two alternative parts, both having the same content. One part has the content in plaintext, and the other part has the content in HTML. The mail client can then choose which of these two alternatives it will process and display for the user. In cases where the mail client is unable to display any of the formats contained within the e-mail, it will typically ask the user to save the MIME part as a file (at which point it's up to the user to do something with it).

It's worth noting that MIME works within the confines of regular e-mail. MIME uses standard plaintext to represent the data contained within the message, even if that data is binary in nature.

MIME is a very complex standard, and it is made even more complex by its flexibility; using MIME, a client can send information in whatever form it pleases. For example, a client can send an HTML message, but the receiving client needs to understand HTML as well. A full description of MIME is beyond the scope of this book, but MIME is documented in five RFCs — 2045, 2046, 2047, 2048, and 2049. If you'd like to learn more about MIME, you can start by reading RFC 2045 at www. faqs.org/rfcs/rfc2045.html.

E-mail transmission and reception

While the headers and body of an e-mail are obviously instrumental in the processing and reading of e-mail, this chapter concerns itself mainly with the actions that are taken in the process of delivering the e-mail to its intended recipient. This section provides an introduction to those actions in a general sense. The topics discussed here apply equally to all the MTAs covered in the rest of this chapter.

The Simple Message Transport Protocol

While I've examined the format of an e-mail message in some detail, the messages themselves are only part of the equation. The communications that occur between e-mail servers aren't in the form of raw e-mail messages; there's actually a dedicated language called SMTP, or the *Simple Message Transport Protocol*. SMTP is arguably the simplest part of modern e-mail. Though it's been extended occasionally throughout the years, the flexibility of the e-mail message format itself has meant that fewer changes needed to be made to the underlying transport protocol (SMTP) in order to adopt new uses. Simple protocols and complex contents is a theme that's repeated in many standard Internet protocols, and it has very distinct advantages; for instance, as large portions of the Internet-using community adopted HTML e-mail, servers didn't need to be upgraded to handle the new content.

SMTP, at its core, is a command/response protocol. Commands are issued serially (one at a time) from the client, which then waits for the server's response. In this context, the *client* is the piece of software that initiated the SMTP connection. The *server* is the piece of software that listened for remote connections. In the case of e-mail, MTAs are both clients and servers; they typically send outbound e-mail to other servers and wait for connections from remote MTAs in order to receive e-mail.

SMTP is described fully in RFC 2821; go to `www.faqs.org/rfcs/rfc2821.html` for a complete reference. I'll go over some of the basics here, though, because I think it can be enlightening.

Note   In the transcripts that follow, and in all further transcripts of over-the-wire network protocol sessions, the text that the client sends is in bold, and the server's responses are not.

Upon first connecting to an SMTP server, the server sends the client its *banner*, just a general-purpose string containing some information about the server. Its primary purpose is to tell the client that the server is running and responsive and that the client may begin issuing commands. For SMTP, it's illegal for a client to send a command before it has received the server's banner. By default, your SMTP's banner will be similar to the following:

```
220 localhost ESMTP Exim 4.33 Tue,  25 May 2004 23:33:26 -0400
```

Note the number at the very start of the line. In many cases, a server's response to a command will be an error or warning of some sort, which is intended to be displayed by the mail client for a user to read. As such, the language of the response may not be English, and it certainly won't be consistently machine-parseable. The number at the start of each response is what daemons and e-mail clients actually use to distinguish different responses, not the text that follows the number. In the case of the banner, the numeric code is 220 — the greeting numeric.

After receiving the greeting banner, the client then sends the EHLO command. Originally the first command sent by a client was HELO (a play on "hello"; most SMTP commands are four letters), but the protocol was extended some time ago, mandating the use of EHLO to indicate that a client supported the extensions. The EHLO command requires a single parameter, the hostname of the client. In response to the EHLO command, the server prints some information about some of its configuration options (the maximum message size it will accept, for instance), as well as any features it supports. The following session shows the reply from the default Debian MTA, Exim:

```
220 localhost ESMTP Exim 4.33 Tue,  25 May 2004 23:33:26 -0400
EHLO fake.mail.server.hostname.com
250-localhost Hello localhost [127.0.0.1]
250-SIZE 52428800
250-PIPELINING
250 HELP
```

Unlike most server responses, the text in the 250 response (the standard "OK" response) is meant to be machine-parsed. With the server's affirmative reply to the EHLO command, the initial handshake is complete; the server is ready to accept SMTP commands related to mail transmission, and the client knows enough about the server to do so confidently. At this point, the client will typically either authenticate itself (typically done by a user's e-mail client in order to get the MTA to accept mail destined for remote systems) or begin the process of sending the mail by telling the server whom the mail is from and where it's going. This is done with the MAIL FROM and RCPT TO commands, respectively. After the server accepts those commands, the client sends the DATA command to start transferring the e-mail itself (headers and body). The following transcript demonstrates this conversation:

```
220 localhost ESMTP Exim 4.33 Tue,  25 May 2004 23:33:26 -0400
EHLO fake.mail.server.hostname.com
250-localhost Hello localhost [127.0.0.1]
250-SIZE 52428800
250-PIPELINING
250 HELP
MAIL FROM: <user@localhost>
250 OK
RCPT TO: <user@localhost>
250 Accepted
DATA
354 Enter message, ending with "." on a line by itself.
X-HeaderTest: This is a header test.

This is the body.

.
250 OK id=1BW6V1-0000Fr-AQ
QUIT
```

When the client is done sending messages (it can send many in a single connection, by sending `MAIL FROM/RCPT TO/DATA` commands again), it closes the connection with the `QUIT` command. In the preceding transcript, I provided the source address for the message (and the server responded with the "OK" numeric — `250`) and the destination of the message, and then I started the `DATA` portion of the dialogue. The server sends the `354` numeric, which tells the client to send the message and end it by sending a line containing nothing but a single period. The client then sends the full e-mail (both headers and body, separated by a single blank line) and sends the line containing only a period. The server then responds with the `OK` numeric and optionally includes the `Message-id` header (if one was added).

The full text of the e-mail, as delivered and stored on disk, follows:

```
From user@localhost Tue May 25 00:40:24 2004
Return-path: <user@localhost>
Envelope-to: user@localhost
Delivery-date: Tue, 25 May 2004 00:40:24 -0400
Received: from localhost ([127.0.0.1] helo=fake.mail.server.hostname.com)
        by localhost with esmtp (Exim 4.33)
        id 1BW6V1-0000Fr-AQ
        for user@localhost; Tue, 25 May 2004 00:40:24 -0400
X-HeaderTest: This is a header test.
Message-ID: <E1BW6V1-0000Fr-AQ@localhost>

This is the body.
```

Note in the preceding e-mail the lack of headers. There's no `From:` header and there's no `To:` header. Both of these headers are added by a user's e-mail application, and the MTA uses only the `MAIL FROM` and `RCPT TO` commands from the SMTP dialogue to determine whom the mail came from and where it's going. Note that the `From` header, without a colon, is not the `From:` header. Strictly speaking, `From` without a colon isn't a header at all; it's actually part of the on-disk message format used, and it isn't sent between MTAs. The only header supplied by the client in the preceding transcripts was the `X-HeaderTest:` header (which dutifully appears). The rest of the headers (`From`, `Return-path:`, `Envelope-to:`, `Delivery-date:`, and `Message-ID:`) were added by the MTA.

The entirety of the last transcript, from the server's banner greeting to the client's `QUIT` command, is referred to as the *SMTP dialogue*.

Relaying, forwarding, and storing

When an MTA receives an e-mail, it can be for a *local user*, or it could be destined for a *remote user*. This differentiation between addresses is vital within an MTA, as misconfigurations abound on the Internet and mail is sometimes sent to inappropriate servers. Your MTA, thus, has a list of domains for which it accepts mail and a list of users within those domains for whom it accepts mail. The actions the MTA can take when receiving a message for a user, whether remote or local, are varied. They all fall into three categories, however — relaying, forwarding, and storing:

✦ **Relaying** — Roughly speaking, relaying involves accepting a client's message and then sending it on its way toward its destination. An MTA needn't accept mail destined only for its own users; it also needs to accept mail *from* its local users and make sure that mail gets to the recipient's MTA. This act is called relaying, and it can be a potentially dangerous behavior if uncontrolled. Many misconfigured MTAs exist, which will accept mail from any client on the Internet and relay it to any recipient. These are referred to as *open relays*, and they are the source of a great deal of the spam you receive. When you configure your MTA, you'll need to be careful to control the access to any relaying functionality, such that your MTA accepts only mail destined for remote users from those local users you trust.

✦ **Forwarding** — In the case of the message being destined for a local user (or more generally, a user the MTA will accept mail for), the MTA accepts the message from the client and takes charge of its delivery. This delivery doesn't necessarily mean that the mail is stored on disk, waiting for your user to retrieve it. Many users have multiple e-mail addresses but prefer retrieving their mail from a single server. This is accomplished via *forwarding*. With forwarding, your MTA accepts an e-mail destined for a local user, sees that that local user wishes to forward the e-mail, and then contacts that e-mail address's MTA for final delivery. Of course, that MTA in turn may forward the message to another MTA, and so on.

✦ **Storing** — When the message accepted by the MTA will be neither forwarded nor relayed, it's generally meant to be stored in some way or another. On GNU/Linux systems, there are several ways to store e-mail. Some are faster than others, some more flexible than others, and some more stable than others. Which storage method you choose doesn't need to be the user's only option; there also exists a large number of MDAs (Mail Delivery Agents), which abstract mail storage away from the MTA and toward a user-configurable application. The most popular MDA on GNU/Linux systems (aside from MTAs themselves) is `procmail`. `procmail` knows how to store messages in a variety of formats and is also capable of filtering, forwarding, and sorting e-mail according to the user's wishes. Many MTAs in Debian automatically use `procmail` if it exists on the system; without a user configuration file, `procmail` stores messages using the standard mbox file format, which is understood by most MUAs.

The two main on-disk storage formats used in GNU/Linux systems are the *mbox* format and the *Maildir* format. The mbox format is a single-file format; every message is stored in one monolithic file. mbox has a number of advantages — it's old and well supported, reading the whole thing from start to finish is quite fast, and given its single-file nature, it's generally pretty easy for the user to work with. Maildir is newer (though still a number of years old) and has a number of advantages of its own. In Maildir, each e-mail is stored in its own file. The mailbox is split into three separate directories: one for mail that's been read, one for mail that's in the process of being stored, and one for mail that's unread. This makes checking for new mail a very fast operation, since the entire mailbox doesn't need to be processed. Maildir is also a very sturdy format; in the case of mbox, a program crashing halfway through modifying the single file can break the entire mailbox. Because each e-mail message is stored in its own file with Maildir, such problems are far less common (and when they happen, they're usually limited to a single e-mail). These days, Maildir is the most commonly used format for new installations. It tends to be more disk- and processor-intensive, but its technical advantages tend to outweigh the performance loss.

Failures and bounces

There are times when an MTA accepts a message for delivery but isn't able to actually deliver it in the end. Likewise, during the SMTP dialogue, the MTA may know that it's unable to accept a message (whether for security reasons or because there's no disk space to store the message). When an MTA doesn't accept the message at all, it's referred to as a *failure*. When the MTA accepts the message but eventually gives up on delivering it, it sends a message back to the sending user in what is called a *bounce*.

✦ **Failures**—More common than bounces, failures can result from any number of conditions. If the mail is destined for a nonexistent local user, the MTA won't accept the message for delivery. If the user exists, but there's no disk space available to store the message, the MTA won't accept the message. Another case where the MTA will send a failure notice is when the mail is destined for a remote user, but the client isn't authorized to use the MTA as a relay. Failures are part of the SMTP dialogue, and there are two types: *permanent* failures and *temporary* failures. In the previous examples, a nonexistent local user is a permanent failure. The MTA will tell the client that delivery can't be made. The MTA will *not* accept the message on the assumption that a user of that name will eventually be created; that'd be silly. If the client is trying to use the MTA as a relay, but the MTA isn't configured to do so (or if the user isn't authorized to use the MTA as a relay), that's another permanent failure. If the MTA doesn't have enough disk space to store the message, but it would otherwise accept the message for delivery, then it's a temporary failure. It's reasonable to assume that a mail server that has run out of disk space will be fixed.

It's relatively rare to get an immediate failure notice when using a regular e-mail client. MUAs are generally configured to contact an MTA that will relay mail for them; thus, all messages destined for remote users will be accepted. When such a message is accepted, but eventual transmission fails (perhaps because the remote server says the remote user doesn't exist), a bounce is sent back to the originating user.

✦ **Bounces**—A bounced e-mail is just like a regular e-mail in most respects. All that's different is its purpose; it indicates that an MTA has accepted the mail for delivery, but that the delivery failed for whatever reason. The reason is generally included in the body of the bounce message. Most often, you receive bounce messages from your own MTA, which accepted a message for relaying but was unable to transmit the message properly. If the local MTA gets a temporary error from the remote MTA (or if it isn't able to contact the remote MTA for reasons of temporary network outages and whatnot), then it will continue trying to send the message for a preconfigured amount of time, usually somewhere in the range of 4 to 5 days. When that time passes and the message still hasn't been transmitted, a bounce is sent to the originating user. Alternatively, the local MTA can accept the message for relaying, try to relay it, and then get a fatal error (permanent failure) from the remote MTA — for instance, if the remote MTA doesn't accept mail for the user the mail is destined for (perhaps because the user doesn't exist). In these cases, the bounce message will often arrive quickly in the sending user's mailbox.

The Exim Mail Transport Agent

Exim is the default mail transport agent in Debian. Exim is venerable but not ancient. It remains a valuable software package today thanks to its active development cycle, meaning support for newer technologies is typically quickly available. Exim is a monolithic MTA; it's a single binary that can support a huge number of features. As such, its performance is middle-of-the-pack; it's neither so slow as to be useless, nor so fast as to be usable in every conceivable situation. This is reflected in the Debian Exim packages: `exim4-daemon-heavy` and `exim4-daemon-light`. The former has all the heavy features and library support enabled; the latter (which is the default) contains only the most commonly used features.

Exim's configuration file syntax can be difficult to get used to, but it's very expressive. Exim is often used as a glue layer between wildly different systems, as the administrator is able to specify all sorts of flexible statements for such things as authentication and delivery. For example, Exim is capable of communicating with MySQL, PostgreSQL, and OpenLDAP databases to retrieve whatever information it requires; a modern MTA can take advantage of a great deal of information from a great many sources in order to decide how to deliver messages and where to deliver them to.

Exim is a sensible default for Debian; there's virtually nothing that can't be done with Exim, and the basic setup is quick and easy with some help from debconf. When a new GNU/Linux user asks me which MTA they should use, I generally recommend Exim, as they'll be able to easily expand their skill set *and* their installation as time goes on and they need more advanced functionality. Exim has a good security history, and its support for relatively painless authentication configuration makes it reasonably easy for administrators to require their clients to authenticate before they can relay mail.

Note Exim is one of the best-documented mail transport agents available on any system, GNU/Linux or otherwise. The manual is included in text form as `/usr/share/doc/exim4-base/exim4-base/spec.txt.gz`. I refer to sections of this manual occasionally for further information later in this section. The full manual is also available in HTML form by installing the `exim4-doc-html` package and looking in `/usr/share/doc/exim4-doc-html/html/` or online at `www.exim.org/exim-html-4.30/doc/html/spec.html`.

Exim is installed by default in Debian GNU/Linux. In this section, I review the Exim configuration and explain in more detail how each question affects the MTA. This serves as a good introduction to some of Exim's basic functionality. Given that there are multiple Exim daemon packages (lightweight and one heavyweight), the common parts of these packages have been split into two other packages: `exim4-base` and `exim4-config`.

Configuring Exim

The questions in this section refer to the questions that you will be asked when you install or reconfigure the Exim package. Exim is installed by default onto a Debian system, so these questions will be asked whenever you install your system. If you have already installed Exim (with the default or most simple configuration, for example) and would like to reconfigure, you can start Exim's configuration now with the `sudo dpkg-reconfigure exim4-config` command. In the following pages, I'll treat each question in turn, beginning with this one:

```
Split configuration into small files?
```

Debian's Exim packages are pretty complex, and configuration is always a place where a package's complexity is most apparent. In order to facilitate simple debconf-based configuration for the majority of users, the Exim packages in Debian create (at time of install or reconfiguration) a configuration file based on the answers given to debconf questions. However, due to the complexity of Exim's configuration file, this operation is write-only. When Exim starts at boot time, if a standard configuration file (created by you) doesn't exist, the debconf-generated configuration is parsed and placed in `/var/lib/exim4/config.autogenerated`. The debconf-generated configuration can be stored in two forms: as a monolithic configuration file (`/etc/exim4/exim4.conf.template`) or in little snippets (stored in `/etc/exim4/conf.d/`).

Splitting the configuration file into little snippets makes it easier to manage small changes to the debconf-generated configuration file. When you upgrade Exim, it will prompt you only when you've changed a snippet that has also been changed in the latest package. There are dozens of these configuration snippets, which provides some degree of granularity. However, splitting the configuration into many snippets makes it more difficult to conceptualize the actions Exim takes, and that schema is totally inappropriate for making large-scale changes to the debconf-generated configuration.

Alternatively, a monolithic configuration template can be generated. This is quite robust, but if you need to make any changes to the configuration template, you'll have to manually merge them during upgrades. This can be a tedious task given the size of the default Exim configuration. Truth be told, neither of the debconf-generated configuration options is extremely well suited for making local changes. This isn't surprising, as the entire point of them is to provide easy configuration for users with common needs, not MTA administrators. Given the complexity of Exim's configuration, these options are simply the best available.

For the time being, answer no to the question, so that a single monolithic configuration file is created. You can copy this template and modify it, so that future Exim upgrades don't affect it.

The next question is

```
General type of mail configuration:
```

The answer to this question tells exim4-config's debconf scripts which questions to ask for the rest of the configuration routine. Some questions are only applicable to one usage type, and this question allows the elimination of many needless questions. Table 14-2 describes each usage scenario in turn.

Table 14-2 Exim Usage Types	
Internet site	This usage type corresponds to most Internet MTAs; mail destined for remote systems is sent directly to those systems' MTAs via SMTP, and the local MTA accepts mail via SMTP.
Mail sent by smarthost	Another common Internet MTA configuration, mail is accepted via SMTP as normal. However, all outbound mail is sent via a relay MTA (or *smarthost* in Exim parlance).
Mail sent by smarthost; no local delivery	This configuration is suitable for workstations that are part of a larger network, typically a corporate network; no mail will be delivered locally, and all mail will be forwarded to a relay for delivery.

Local delivery only	When the computer in question isn't connected via a network or isn't expected to either send or receive e-mail via the MTA, this usage type applies. Mail will be accepted only when it's locally generated, and no mail will ever be sent to another MTA. This is a safe default to use; there's a fair bit of locally generated e-mail from daemons and such, which provide status updates, and not allowing any network connections reduces the risk of security problems.
Manually convert from Exim3	Because your installation is new, this option isn't useful. It's used by people who are upgrading from previous versions of Debian, where Exim version 3 was used. Sarge uses Exim version 4.
No configuration at this time	This option is typically selected by system administrators who have their own configuration file prepared. The MTA won't be usable until it's configured properly; thus, this should be chosen only if one of the first things you're ready to do after installation is configure the MTA manually.

At this point, select `Internet site`. The rest of this chapter assumes you're setting up an Internet server, but later in this section I revisit this portion of the configuration and document how to use a relay (typically provided by an ISP).

The next prompt is

```
System mail name:
```

Today, many Internet MTAs serve multiple domains, so a single system name doesn't make as much sense as it used to. However, the system name (a fully qualified hostname) still has use; most locally generated mail is sent with only the local part as the originating e-mail address, for instance, `user` instead of `user@domain.com`. Such addresses are referred to as *unqualified* addresses. Before the MTA can process the mail or send it on to another system, the unqualified address must be *qualified* by adding a fully qualified hostname—usually the system's mail name. It makes sense to ask this question in the context of debconf, because many Internet servers do only serve a single domain's mail, even if it's more the exception than the rule these days. For now, the default value of `localhost` is acceptable, so leave it and press Enter. Any mail destined for the domain `localhost` will be accepted, and any unqualified addresses in locally generated mail will be qualified by adding `@localhost`.

The next item in the debconf list is

```
IP-addresses to listen on for incoming SMTP connections:
```

Because your server can have numerous IP addresses, most daemons have the ability to limit those on which they accept connections. In the case of an MTA, limiting the network interfaces from which it accepts connections is a common way to make sure that nobody other than the users on your internal network can use the MTA as a relay. However, disallowing connections from a given interface not only stops people from using it as a relay, but also stops them from sending mail to your users. The default is 127.0.0.1, which is very strict: Only locally generated mail (mail generated on the server itself) will be accepted. Press Backspace to clear out the answer to this question; you want to leave it blank. Exim's debconf scripts interpret that to mean that you want it to listen on all available interfaces. Press Enter.

The next question is

```
Other destinations for which mail is accepted:
```

This question asks you to enter a space-separated list of *other* domains that your MTA should consider local. This doesn't include localhost and your system mail name (which we've set to localhost too); mails to those domains are always accepted. This question, then, provides a quick way to set up any other domains you're receiving mail for. You'll configure virtual domains in detail in the next section, so for the time being, leave the answer blank and press Enter.

The next question is

```
Domains to relay mail for:
```

E-mail is supposed to be a reasonably reliable form of communication, and as such, redundancy is built into the basic behavior of all MTAs. This includes functionality to run *secondary* MTAs. When your primary MTA can't be contacted, a remote MTA will then try to contact one of your secondary MTAs, which has been configured to relay mail for your domain. The secondary will then store the e-mail temporarily until your primary MTA is available, at which point it will send them all. For now, leave the answer to this question blank and press Enter. You won't be using your MTA as a secondary for anybody else's domains at the moment.

The next debconf prompt is

```
Machines to relay mail for:
```

If you run an intranet that has a large number of machines that use your MTA as a relay for outgoing mail (again, a smarthost in Exim parlance), you want to put in their IP address ranges here. For now, leave the answer blank and press Enter.

The next question is

```
Keep number of DNS-queries minimal (Dial-on-Demand)?
```

If your system is connected via an expensive dial-up connection, Exim can reduce the number of external connections it tries to make on a semirandom basis. Instead, all these outgoing connections will be saved so that they're all performed one right after another. This has the advantage of cooperating well with dial-on-demand systems, which dial up the ISP whenever an outgoing connection is made. The default answer of no is suitable here, so press Enter.

That completes Exim's detailed debconf configuration. Next, we'll examine the configuration file it generates.

The Exim configuration file

Exim's configuration file format is very flexible and is capable of expressing virtually every conceivable variation on MTA behavior required. The advantage of having a flexible configuration file format is that potentially less code is required in the daemon itself; what used to be done in code can now be done in the configuration file. This provides a more accessible interface for customization, as relatively few system administrators these days feel comfortable creating local forks of software for every minor change in behavior they require. So instead of having a huge amount of code within Exim to deal with every corner-case configuration, and instead of making system administrators add custom code themselves, Exim supports a flexible configuration file that is capable of dealing with virtually every scenario. The main disadvantage of putting much of the work into the configuration file is that many housekeeping tasks need to be repeated in each configuration file. For instance, there are some characters that aren't allowed to appear in the local part of an e-mail address. Exim doesn't include code to reject mail that breaks this rule by default; instead, it provides a flexible access control mechanism to deal with such mail.

Exim's debconf scripts generate a template configuration file, /etc/exim4/exim4. conf.template. Ignore that for now; the real configuration file is generated from that file and stored in /var/lib/exim4/config.autogenerated. Open that file in your editor of choice. There isn't enough room in this book to go over the entire default configuration file, unfortunately. The default configuration file is pretty huge; it's meant to provide enough functionality for almost every common-use case. However, in the following few pages, I'll give an example of each different type of configuration format available in Exim; there are several.

Variables

Exim's configuration file format supports setting and referencing variables. This is used to reduce the number of places you need to change in the configuration file to

effect a large-scale change in the MTA's behavior. Near the start of /var/lib/
exim4/config.autogenerated, at line 38 or so, the following line appears:

```
LOCAL_DELIVERY=mail_spool
```

This variable, LOCAL_DELIVERY, is set to mail_spool. It's used later in the configuration file to control how mail is stored on disk for local users. The value of
mail_spool refers to an Exim *transport*, discussed later, which controls the transmission or storage of a message.

Sometimes variables aren't just simple strings; they can be lists of hosts or domains.
For instance, the domains you accept mail for are expressed in a list of domains.
List variables are set specially. In the configuration file, at around line 26, the follow-
ing appears:

```
domainlist local_domains = @:localhost:localhost
```

The variable in this case is local_domains. It's preceded by the keyword
domainlist to denote that the contents of the variable are a list of domains. Items
in the list are separated by colons. The first item, @, is shorthand for the system's
mail name. The second item will always be localhost in any debconf-generated
configuration; mail for localhost *must* be accepted. The third item is simply an
artifact from the complex debconf configuration system.

Just below the preceding example, the following line appears:

```
hostlist relay_from_hosts = 127.0.0.1 : ::::1 :
```

Again you see a keyword at the start of the line, in this case hostlist, denoting
that the variable (relay_from_hosts) contains a list of hosts. The value of the
variable is again colon-separated. However, this list contains an IPv6 address, ::1.
Because Exim uses colons for list separators, and IPv6 uses colons in addresses as
well, the colons in the IPv6 address are doubled. So ::1 becomes ::::1. Both
127.0.0.1 and ::1 refer to the localhost, and Exim will thus accept locally generated mail.

Access control lists

Exim includes a very flexible, programmable, access control mechanism. The access
control list (ACL) portion of the configuration file is started by the line containing
only begin acl, at approximately line 69 in the debconf-generated configuration
file. The ACL portion of the configuration file continues until the next begin statement. This holds true for other sections of the Exim configuration file as well. ACLs
are documented in Chapter 38 of the Exim manual.

Exim has a number of predetermined points at which it will process an access control list. Access control lists can be arbitrarily named, and Exim lets you specify

which named ACL to use at which point by setting various variables. For instance, the value of `acl_smtp_rcpt` should be the name of an ACL to process when the RCPT command has been received. `acl_smtp_data` does the same, but it does so when a DATA command has been received. The full list of available ACL processing points is available in the Exim manual, section 38.2.

Each ACL may contain multiple stanzas corresponding to multiple conditions. A single ACL must be able to accept or deny a command or message for any number of reasons. Each condition begins with one of four keywords: `accept`, `deny`, `defer`, or `discard`. These are the ACL return codes. `accept` means that the command or message is accepted, `deny` means that the client will be sent a fatal error (at which point it should generate a bounce message), `defer` will send a temporary error, and `discard` causes Exim to tell the client that it's accepted the message, but Exim will then discard the message. In order for a command or message to be accepted, at least one and possibly many `accept` conditions within the ACL must be satisfied. Any condition that specifies that the mail be denied, deferred, or discarded will return the appropriate response to the client. Optionally, some condition stanzas may also specify a message to return to the client. In the following paragraphs, I'll dissect the default `acl_check_rcpt` ACL, which is used by setting `acl_smtp_rcpt = acl_check_rcpt` earlier in the configuration file:

```
acl_check_rcpt:
```

This line indicates the start of the `acl_check_rcpt` ACL. Like many multiline or multistanza Exim configuration parts, the part starts with a name followed by a colon. Everything following that line is part of the named entity until another named entity is started via the same method.

```
  accept hosts = :
```

This stanza will accept the mail if it's generated locally. Providing an empty host list tells Exim that you mean "any connection not received over TCP/IP." This is done by using the standard command-line interface for sending mail, `/usr/sbin/sendmail`. `/usr/sbin/sendmail` is used by many daemons to send mail to the system administrator for reporting purposes.

```
  deny local_parts = ^.*[@%!/|] : ^\\.
```

This means that if the message isn't being received locally, deny any mail that is addressed to an e-mail address that either ends in one of @, %, !, /, or | or starts with a single period. These characters are illegal in an e-mail address.

```
  accept local_parts = postmaster
         domains = +local_domains
```

If the recipient domain is a local domain (that is, one we process mail for locally, as opposed to a domain we simply relay mail for), then *always* accept the mail if it's addressed to `postmaster`. MTAs absolutely *must* accept mail to the postmaster address; critical errors and other MTA administrators use the `postmaster` address to inform you of any problems.

```
deny message = sender envelope address $sender_address is \
               locally blacklisted here. If you think this is \
               wrong, get in touch with postmaster
     !acl = acl_whitelist_local_deny
     senders = ${if exists{CONFDIR/local_sender_blacklist}\
                          {CONFDIR/local_sender_blacklist}\
                          {}}
```

This ACL checks to see whether the sender's address has been blacklisted (that is, you don't accept any mail from them whatsoever, except of course to the `postmaster` address). First, the stanza specifies the message that will be sent to the client if the conditions match. Then, the stanza checks to see whether the sender is in the local whitelist (a list of e-mail addresses you always accept mail from) with `!acl = acl_whitelist_local_deny`. After that, it checks to see whether the sender is listed in `/etc/exim4/local_sender_blacklist`. If the sender's e-mail address is listed there, the condition is satisfied and the mail is denied.

```
deny message = sender IP address $sender_host_address is \
               locally blacklisted here. If you think this \
               is wrong, get in touch with postmaster
     !acl = acl_whitelist_local_deny
     hosts = ${if exists{CONFDIR/local_host_blacklist}\
                        {CONFDIR/local_host_blacklist}\
                        {}}
```

This stanza functions similarly to the last stanza, with the exception that the source hostname or IP address is checked, instead of the sender's e-mail address.

```
accept domains = +local_domains
       endpass
       message = unknown user
       verify = recipient
```

In this stanza, you see the first use of the `endpass` keyword. If a condition in the stanza below the `endpass` keyword fails, then the message is denied. If any conditions before the `endpass` keyword fail, then the next stanza is checked instead. In this particular case, the stanza first checks to see whether the recipient domain is in one of your locally served domains. If it is, then the stanza will verify that the recipient exists locally. If the recipient doesn't exist, the message will be denied and the client will receive the error message `unknown user`.

```
accept domains = +relay_to_domains
       endpass
       message = unrouteable address
       verify = recipient
```

This stanza deals with accepting or rejecting e-mail for domains you relay for. If Exim can verify that the remote user exists, then the mail is accepted. If it can't (it does this because `verify = recipient` is specified), then the mail is denied, as the failure occurs after the `endpass` keyword.

```
accept hosts = +relay_from_hosts
```

This stanza tells Exim that if the mail is destined for neither a locally served domain nor a domain that you relay mail for, then accept the mail only if it's coming from a host that you allow relaying from. This may be a workstation on your network, for instance.

```
accept authenticated = *
```

This stanza is similar to the previous stanza, but instead of checking for the host that the mail is coming from, it checks to see whether the user has authenticated himself. This is covered in more detail later.

```
deny message = relay not permitted
```

This is the final stanza in `smtp_check_rcpt` ACL, and it serves as a stopgap. If no other stanzas told Exim to accept the message, then the message shouldn't be accepted. It's not destined for a local user, it's not destined for a remote user, the client hasn't authenticated himself or herself, and the client machine isn't allowed to use your MTA as a relay in an unauthenticated manner. Mail reaching this ACL will be rejected with the error message `relay not permitted`.

Routers

Routers in the Exim configuration file define, broadly, how incoming mail should be handled. Within the `routers` section of the configuration file, items such as e-mail aliases, forwarding, and filtering are handled. When a message arrives, each router is examined in turn. Each router may specify one or more conditions; if the conditions are true, the *transport* that that router specifies is invoked. The transports themselves are responsible for calling programs or providing the details for particular transport methods (such as sending the message to a remote MTA). Routers are covered in detail in Chapters 15 through 22 of the Exim manual.

A good example router is the router that deals with a user forwarding his mail elsewhere. In the following paragraphs, I examine it in detail.

```
userforward:
```

As with ACLs, discussed previously, a new router is specified by including a line containing just the arbitrary name followed by a colon. Everything following this line is part of the named router, until another router is named.

```
debug_print = "R: userforward for $local_part@$domain"
```

During mail processing, if Exim is in debug mode, this message will be printed when Exim reaches this router. It will reach this router only if all the previous routers didn't handle the mail.

```
driver = redirect
```

Each router has a predetermined type: one of `accept`, `dnslookup`, `iplookup`, `ipliteral`, `manualroute`, `queryprogram`, or `redirect`. This router forwards a user's mail to another address and so uses the portion of Exim router code named `redirect`.

```
domains = +local_domains
```

Mail forwarding is done only for local domains. Mail destined for remote domains will be handled at that domain's MTA.

```
check_local_user
```

`check_local_user` is a condition. It returns `true` if the recipient exists as a local user, and `false` otherwise. If the condition fails, then this router will be skipped and the next will be examined.

```
file = $home/.forward
```

This is both a condition and a command; it checks to see whether a file named `.forward` exists in the user's home directory. Generally, a user's `~/.forward` file contains a single line: the destination e-mail address. If the user doesn't have a `~/.forward` file, it's assumed that either they don't want their mail forwarded or they handle it via other means. If the file exists, its contents are read and the e-mail address is used as the new address for the message. The contents of the file can also be the full path to another file, the path to a directory, or a command that takes the message on the standard-in interface (in this case, the command is preceded by the | character).

```
no_verify
no_expn
```

These two options are used during debugging. They cause the router to be skipped if the address is being verified.

```
check_ancestor
```

The `check_ancestor` condition causes Exim to check to see whether the new e-mail address has been redirected already. This prevents mail loops. Two users could have `.forward` files that point to each other; without this condition, mail would loop between the two indefinitely.

```
allow_filter
```

Exim has its own filtering language. It's not used very often, as most users tend to prefer an MTA-agnostic filtering solution. This command tells Exim that the user is allowed to use Exim's built-in filtering capabilities within their .forward file.

```
directory_transport = address_directory
file_transport = address_file
pipe_transport = address_pipe
reply_transport = address_reply
```

These four commands set the various transports that will be used to direct the message, if the destination isn't a simple e-mail address. A different transport can be set for each type of data that the user can have in her .forward file. Transports are covered in more detail in the next section.

```
skip_syntax_errors
syntax_errors_to = real-$local_part@$domain
```

These two lines direct Exim to send e-mail in the case where the user's .forward file has a syntax error. The destination address is set by syntax_errors_to and is set to send the mail to the user's mailbox, which bypasses the .forward file (which is known at this point to be broken). It does this by appending a real- prefix to the address, which is in turn handled in the real_local router.

```
syntax_errors_text = \
  This is an automatically generated message. An error has\n\
  been found in your .forward file. Details of the error are\n\
  reported below. While this error persists, you will receive\n\
  a copy of this message for every message that is addressed\n\
  to you. If your .forward file is a filter file, or if it is\n\
  a non-filter file containing no valid forwarding addresses,\n\
  a copy of each incoming message will be put in your normal\n\
  mailbox. If a non-filter file contains at least one valid\n\
  forwarding address, forwarding to the valid addresses will\n\
  happen, and those will be the only deliveries that occur.
```

This variable sets the text for any errors that are sent to the user. When creating your own messages, being reasonably verbose can save you a follow-up e-mail.

Transports

Transports perform the actual mail transmission or delivery. The order in which they appear in the configuration file doesn't matter, as they're referred to directly from the routers section. Various settings can be tweaked in each transport to match your particular needs, but most transports are simple in nature. One of the reasons for this simplicity is the requirement for interoperability; mail may be stored or sent to any number of applications or other MTAs, and as such, flexibility is limited. In the following paragraphs, I examine the mail_spool transport, which stores mail in the traditional mbox format.

```
mail_spool:
```

As with ACLs and routers, transports are started by a single line containing the transport's name and a colon. Everything up to the next transport declaration is part of this transport.

```
debug_print = "T: appendfile for $local_part@$domain"
```

As with routers, when Exim uses this transport in debugging mode, it will print the preceding message. Unlike routers, only one transport is ever touched. They're called directly from the routers.

```
driver = appendfile
```

The appendfile transport driver is the standard driver for storing messages on disk. Its name doesn't mean that it can't use the Maildir format (which also contains directories); keep in mind that messages within a Maildir archive are still stored in individual files.

```
file = /var/mail/$local_part
```

The file variable defines which file the message will be stored in. All messages in an mbox-format archive are stored in a single file. You see in the previous example some variable expansion; mail to the user testuser will go to /var/mail/testuser. You could set file to /var/mail/$domain/$local_part, and the mail would be stored in the file /var/mail/testdomain.com/testuser. This is used later in the chapter to provide easy segregation of many virtual hosts.

```
delivery_date_add
envelope_to_add
return_path_add
```

These three commands tell Exim to add the Delivery-date:, Envelope-to:, and Return-path: headers, respectively.

```
group = mail
```

The group variable controls the group ownership of the destination file. In the case of mbox-formatted archives, the file must be writable by the user that Exim runs as. In Debian, all MTAs run as the user mail. The user ownership of the file is, by default, the recipient. This too can be set, however, allowing multiple mailboxes to be owned by a single user (helpful with virtual domains).

```
mode = 0660
```

This sets the file's permissions to 0660, which is the numeric representation of the permissions u+rw,g+rw,o=.

```
mode_fail_narrower = false
```

If the file's permissions are more restrictive than u+rw,g+rw,o=, this won't cause an error to be produced. Normally, permissions that are more restrictive simply cause Exim to stop delivery and defer the message.

Rewriting addresses

Occasionally, you'll want to rewrite addresses from received messages. This is most commonly done by qualifying an unqualified address. Additionally, rewriting is used to regularize e-mail addresses. For instance, you may have numerous internal mail servers used to balance the load among a large number of users, such that you have user1@host1.domain.com, user2@host2.domain.com, and so on. Externally, however, you want to present all users under a single domain; you would then want to rewrite user1@host1.domain.com and user2@host2.domain.com to user1@domain.com and user2@domain.com, respectively. The debconf-generated configuration file you're examining includes a default rewrite rule, examined in the following paragraphs.

```
begin rewrite
*@+local_domains ${lookup{${local_part}}lsearch{/etc/email-addresses}\
                {$value}fail} Ffrs
```

The syntax for rewriting rules is quite compact, as you can see. The first field (fields are space-separated) is the address to rewrite. Wildcards, variables, and lists can be used (as with virtually all portions of Exim's configuration). In the example here, all local parts of all local domains will be rewritten according to the rule, which is the second field. The second field is an example of an Exim lookup. The local part is searched for in /etc/email-addresses. If it's found, the value from that line in the file takes the place of the e-mail portion of the e-mail address that was to be rewritten. The last field of the line, Ffrs in the example, is a collection of single-letter flags denoting which field(s) should be rewritten. F is the From line (as seen in mbox files), f rewrites the From: header, r rewrites the Reply-to: header, and s rewrites the Sender: header.

```
*@+local_domains "${if exists {CONFDIR/email-addresses}\
                {${lookup{${local_part}}lsearch\
                {CONFDIR/email-addresses}\
                {$value}fail}}fail}" Ffrs
```

As with the first rewrite rule, this preceding rule rewrites entire e-mail addresses in the same fields. This particular rewrite rule exists only for backward compatibility, which reads the file at /etc/exim4/email-addresses instead of /etc/email-addresses (the latter being the standard location).

The rest of the debconf-generated configuration file revolves around authentication (both for clients authenticating to your MTA and for your MTA authenticating itself to other MTAs).

Mail delivery with Exim

This section is intended to provide a high-level overview of the process of mail delivery when using the Exim MTA. Because Exim is controlled pretty much entirely from its configuration file (some might say Exim is programmed via its configuration file, given the wealth of constructs available), this section is largely an overview of all the features enabled in the default debconf-generated Exim configuration file in Debian GNU/Linux. Changes to the configuration file can change any of the processes described in the following sections.

Upon receiving an incoming connection via either TCP/IP or the local command-line interface (`/usr/sbin/sendmail`), Exim will first look to see whether the recipient's domain is a locally served domain, a remote domain for which your Exim has been configured to unconditionally relay, or a remote domain for which Exim *hasn't* been configured to unconditionally relay.

Relaying mail to explicitly configured remote domains

If the recipient's domain is in the Exim variable `relay_to_domains`, Exim will attempt to verify that the recipient user exists. Exim verifies that the recipient user at the remote domain exists by opening a connection to the remote domain's MTA and beginning the process of sending an e-mail (using the `EHLO`, `MAIL FROM`, and `RCTP TO` SMTP dialogue commands); Exim will abort the process, however, so that no mail is actually sent. The result of this check is cached so that it isn't repeated for every e-mail received. If the recipient exists at the remote domain, the message is accepted for delivery from the client. Exim then stores the message temporarily, and as soon as the mail queue is flushed (this happens periodically), the message will be sent to the remote domain's MTA. If the recipient doesn't exist, then the message will instead be refused.

Relaying mail to domains in the `relay_to_domains` variable does not require that the client has authenticated itself; it's performed unconditionally (except as noted previously). The following snippets from `/var/lib/exim4/config.autogenerated` are relevant to the preceding mail delivery process; each line is preceded by the line number:

```
28: domainlist relay_to_domains =

79: acl_check_rcpt:
110:   accept domains = +relay_to_domains
111:          endpass
112:          message = unrouteable address
113:          verify = recipient

129: begin routers
133: dnslookup_relay_to_domains:
134:    driver = dnslookup
135:    domains = ! +local_domains : +relay_to_domains
```

```
136:    transport = remote_smtp
137:    same_domain_copy_routing = yes
138:    no_more
```

Relaying mail to otherwise anonymous remote domains

You may have one or more users or machines from which you'd like to accept mail
destined for any remote domain. Typically these are users who use your MTA as
their outgoing SMTP server. There are two default conditions in which these users
can send mail through your MTA: either the IP address of their computer is in the
`relay_from_hosts` variable, or the client has authenticated itself with a password.
In either case, the mail is accepted, stored temporarily, and eventually sent to the
remote MTA's domain. No verification is done on the recipient's address; should it
fail, the user who sent the mail will receive a bounce message. The following snippets from `/var/lib/exim4/config.autogenerated` are relevant to authenticated
users (either via source IP address or password) sending mail to random remote
domains; each line is preceded by the line number:

```
30: hostlist relay_from_hosts 127.0.0.1 : ::::1 :

79: acl_check_rcpt:
115: accept hosts = +relay_from_hosts
117: accept authenticated = *
```

Mail sent to a locally served domain

When the message is intended for a locally served domain, the processing is rather
more involved. This is mainly due to the authority the system administrator has
over his own namespace. Additionally, at least in the default Debian GNU/Linux
Exim configuration, users are given a fair degree of control over what happens to
their mail. There are multiple possible paths a given message can take, but they all
generally end up in one of three places — either redirected to another address,
delivered to a local user, or fed into an application.

Mail forced to real users

Because mail can be redirected in a variety of fashions, there exists in the default
Debian Exim configuration the provision for forcing mail to go to a real user. By
sending mail to *real*-user@localhost, all aliases, forward files, and redirections
are bypassed. The mail will be stored, on disk, in user@localhost's mailbox. The
relevant stanza from Exim's configuration file follows, each line prefixed with the
line number:

```
175: real_local:
176:    debug_print = "R: real_local for $local_part@$domain"
177:    driver = accept
178:    local_part_prefix = real-
179:    check_local_user
180:    transport = LOCAL_DELIVERY
```

If the destination e-mail address begins with `real-`, and the rest of the address corresponds to a real local user with an account, then the preceding router will be used.

Redirecting mail at the system level

In Debian, the standard location for e-mail aliases is `/etc/aliases`. Open that file in your favorite editor. The format is simple: Blank lines and lines that begin with the comment character (#) are ignored. All other lines have a local mailbox name, a colon, and then the destination. Take, for example, the following line:

```
root: user
```

That line would redirect all mail sent to `root` to `user` instead. Alternatively, the mail could be sent to `user@remote.domain.com`. By default, a dozen or so system mail accounts are redirected to `root`, which is in turn redirected to the user created during Debian's installation process. Mail can also be sent to a command, by using the pipe character:

```
destination: |/path/to/command
```

Note that the command being called must be specifically written to read e-mail and process it. The e-mail message is sent to the command via standard in. Aside from commands and plain e-mail addresses, mail can also be redirected to a plain mbox-formatted file. To invoke that behavior, make the destination the full (absolute) path to the file; it must start with a slash. The following snippet of the default Exim configuration file controls system-wide aliases:

```
183: system_aliases:
184:    debug_print = "R: system_aliases for $local_part@$domain"
185:    driver = redirect
186:    allow_fail
187:    allow_defer
188:    data = ${lookup{$local_part}lsearch{/etc/aliases}}
189:    file_transport = address_file
190:    pipe_transport = address_pipe
```

Mail redirected by users

If the message was neither forced to the local user's own mailbox nor aliased in the system-wide `/etc/aliases` configuration file, then the local user's home directory will be checked for a `.forward` file. The format for a user's `.forward` file is identical to the right-hand side of a line in `/etc/aliases`. The user's mail can be redirected to any arbitrary e-mail address, or it can be directed to other commands. It can also be sent to files. The following snippet from the default Debian Exim configuration file specifies that the user's `.forward` files should be respected:

```
202: userforward:
203:    debug_print = "R: userforward for $local_part@$domain"
204:    driver = redirect
```

```
205:    check_local_user
206:    file = $home/.forward
207:    no_verify
208:    no_expn
209:    check_ancestor
210:    allow_filter
211:    directory_transport = address_directory
212:    file_transport = address_file
213:    pipe_transport = address_pipe
214:    reply_transport = address_reply
215:    skip_syntax_errors
216:    syntax_errors_to = real-$local_part@$domain
217:    syntax_errors_text = \
218:      This is an automatically generated message. An error has\n\
219:      been found in your .forward file. Details of the error are\n\
220:      reported below. While this error persists, you will receive\n\
221:      a copy of this message for every message that is addressed\n\
222:      to you. If your .forward file is a filter file, or if it is\n\
223:      a non-filter file containing no valid forwarding addresses,\n\
224:      a copy of each incoming message will be put in your normal\n\
225:      mailbox. If a non-filter file contains at least one valid\n\
226:      forwarding address, forwarding to the valid addresses will\n\
227:      happen, and those will be the only deliveries that occur.
```

Mail filtered by users

If the user doesn't have a .forward file but *does* have a .procmailrc file, and the procmail package is installed, then the message will be passed to procmail for filtering. procmail is a command-line application that allows for very flexible filtering under the user's control. It can deliver mail to a variety of storage formats and can also forward mail to other addresses or pass them to other applications. procmail is well supported by most MTAs, and its configuration file format is reasonably simple and easy to learn, so it's quite popular among users who like to use server-side filtering. If you'd like to learn more about procmail, install the package and run man procmail. Note that users can also run procmail explicitly from their .forward files by putting |/usr/bin/procmail into them. The following snippet from the Exim configuration file calls procmail when the preceding conditions are met:

```
229: procmail:
230:    debug_print = "R: procmail for $local_part@$domain"
231:    driver = accept
232:    check_local_user
233:    transport = procmail_pipe
234:    require_files = ${local_part}:${home}/.procmailrc:+/usr/bin/procmail
235:    no_verify
236:    no_expn
```

Mail sent to a local user normally

If the user's mail wasn't redirected from the system aliases file, and she didn't redirect it herself, then it's delivered normally to her mailbox. The definition of "her mailbox" can vary from system to system. In Debian's case, the default is to deliver a user's mail to `/var/mail/username`, in standard mbox format. This is done via the `mail_spool` router and transport.

Using virtual domains with Exim

One of the more common uses of an MTA today isn't to serve a single domain but to serve *many*. The term *virtual* in *virtual domain* doesn't really have as much significance as it once did; at one point, a domain or server was considered virtual if it didn't have its own hardware and IP address. Now that computing power is abundant and cheap, the distinction between a virtual domain and a regular domain doesn't make much sense — except that perhaps somebody is paying for way too much hardware.

Exim isn't the most lightweight MTA around, but it's still well suited to high-volume traffic, more than anybody reading this book (or writing it — I certainly don't run a server that receives tens of millions of messages a day) would likely ever see. Exim is often used in situations where ongoing administration overhead must be kept to a minimum. A single person-hour invested in configuring Exim well can save person-years in ongoing maintenance costs. The primary reason for this, in my opinion, is the dynamic nature of Exim. The configuration file can be full of variables expanded whenever a message is received. These variables make it very easy for an administrator and can offer a convenient way to, for instance, add new virtual domains and users.

Since Exim is so flexible, I cover only the most common form of virtual domain hosting with Exim here. It's rather simplistic in that domains aren't differentiated between each other; they all share the same user base and settings.

Adding a simple virtual domain to Exim is a matter of editing a single line in the configuration file. You can do this directly, or you can change it via debconf. If you want to edit the configuration file manually, copy `/var/lib/exim4/config.autogenerated` to `/etc/exim4/exim4.conf`, open that file in your editor, and locate the line that begins with `domainlist local_domains`. Change that line from `domainlist local_domains =` to `domainlist local_domains = @:domain1.com:domain2.com:domain3.com`, and so on. Note that after copying the file from `/var/lib/exim4/config.autogenerated`, any changes you make via `dpkg-reconfigure` will be totally ignored; you need to update the configuration file manually.

To change the list of local domains with debconf, run `sudo dpkg-reconfigure exim4-base`. Answer the questions as you answered them previously, with the exception of the question titled `Other destinations for which mail is accepted:`. To that question, answer with a list of the domains you'd like to consider local. Separate them with spaces (you might answer *domain1.com domain2.com domain3.com*).

Domains added in this manner are *simple* virtual domains. They all share a single username database and a single alias database: Everything is shared between them. For more advanced virtual hosting, consult the Exim manual.

Other Mail Transport Agents

Exim is the default MTA in Debian for good reason: It's flexible, it's reasonably fast, and you can learn Exim inside out and know that in all likelihood, that's all you'll ever need to learn for your own systems. That said, Exim isn't the only option by any measure; there are many other capable MTAs available in Debian. Choosing which to use is often as much a matter of policy as it is of taste. If you're working at a company that already has a hundred installations of Sendmail, then that's certainly the MTA you should be focusing your efforts on. This section provides a brief introduction to the mainstream MTA options aside from Exim.

Sendmail

Sendmail is the granddaddy of MTAs, at over 20 years old (though those early versions bear nearly no resemblance to the modern Sendmail code base). Sendmail's tradition can be seen in virtually any MTA in Debian today; the standard command-line interface for sending mail is `/usr/sbin/sendmail`, which is typically a compatibility wrapper that provides the same interface Sendmail always has.

Sendmail's architecture is monolithic in a way that is similar to Exim's architecture. Sendmail is even more flexible than Exim, but many find that it suffers from extremely difficult-to-maintain configuration files. Sendmail also has a history of security vulnerabilities.

Sendmail is typically discouraged for new installations, but there are still some extremely rare cases where only a special Sendmail configuration can do the job. What's more, there are so many active Sendmail installations around the world that there remains a strong demand for administrators knowledgeable in Sendmail lore. The Sendmail package in Debian is named `sendmail`.

Postfix

Postfix is a relatively new MTA, and it has a more modern design. With more than three dozen separate binaries, Postfix is a very modularly designed system. Its main goals are security, stability, and speed. The Postfix project was started largely in response to growing discontent with Sendmail and its security issues. Postfix's modular design isn't modular for flexibility (there are no alternative modules for the various Postfix parts), but rather for fault isolation; a single module being exploited doesn't necessarily bring the whole system down.

Postfix supports as many external lookup mechanisms as Exim, including OpenLDAP, MySQL, PostgreSQL, and simple text files. Its configuration file format is quite clean and friendly; it lies somewhere between Exim's near programming language and an inflexible static keyword-driven configuration. Postfix is popular with many system administrators, mainly for its excellent security track record. The Postfix package in Debian is named `postfix`.

ssmtp

`ssmtp` is a very simple MTA designed only to forward mail to a relay. If you have a large number of workstations, you should consider installing `ssmtp` on them instead of a full-featured MTA such as Exim. `ssmtp` does absolutely no local delivery whatsoever; all mail is instead sent to the configured relay. This allows `ssmtp` to run as the user invoking it at all times, reducing the chances of a catastrophic security breach. Other MTAs such as Exim, Sendmail, and Postfix all need to run as `root` in order to deliver mail locally.

Summary

Having read this chapter, you should have a grasp of a great deal of e-mail system fundamentals. Additionally, you should feel comfortable at least reading Exim's configuration file and making simple changes. Exim's documentation is without equal, so if you ever need to seriously modify its configuration (which can sometimes be a daunting task), avail yourself of that great documentation.

✦   ✦   ✦

Web Serving

It should surprise no one that Debian GNU/Linux is widely
used as a Web server platform. The underlying operating
system is rock solid, the associated utilities are plentiful, and
the Web server of choice, Apache, is the most popular Web
server on the planet and another premier example of Free
Software at its best. This chapter describes how to install and
configure Apache on your Debian GNU/Linux system. It also
describes how to use some popular tools with Apache; when
combined with Perl, Python, and PHP, Apache enables you to
create highly customized, dynamic Web sites. The final section shows you how to install and configure Boa. The section
on Boa addresses the sizable minority of you who don't need
a big, feature-rich Web server, just a fast, resource-stingy
HTTP server that excels at serving static Web pages.

Apache

The Apache HTTP server, colloquially known as Apache, is
the dial tone of the World Wide Web. As of June 2004, Apache
was the most widely used HTTP server in the world, running
on more Web sites than any other Web server software for
over eight consecutive years (see the June 2004 Netcraft Web
Server Survey at `http://news.netcraft.com/archives/`
`2004/06/06/june_2004_web_server_survey.html` for
more details). Why? Doubtless there are many reasons, some
of the most important being the following:

- ✦ Like everything else in Debian, it is available as Free
  Software and Open Source.

- ✦ It runs on most operating systems, including GNU/Linux,
  UNIX, Windows NT, and OS X.

- ✦ It is secure, efficient, and extensible.

- ✦ It is standards-compliant, supporting the current HTTP
  standards.

- ✦ It has a cool name.

This section describes how to install and use Apache. As it happens, the Apache HTTP server is currently available in two versions, 1.3.x and 2.0.x; this section covers both versions. The 1.3 series, which is still widely used, is more directly related to the original NCSA HTTP server that formed the base of the original Apache Web server and so also shares some of that code's shortcomings. Apache 1.3 is no longer actively *developed*, meaning that no or few new features are being added, but it is actively *maintained*, which means that bug fixes and security patches continue to be produced as necessary.

The 2.0 series reflects a redesign of the core Apache architecture that enables Apache to run on more platforms, to run faster, and to be more extensible. The 2.0 series also attempted to simplify building and configuring Apache. At the time this chapter was written, the newest release in the 2.0 series was 2.0.49.

New features in Apache version 2.0 include the following:

✦ Support for POSIX threads on UNIX and UNIX-like systems that have a POSIX threads implementation enables Apache to scale more efficiently on a variety of common large-site Web server configurations.

✦ The build system is based on the standard GNU build tools, `autoconf` and `libtool`, which simplifies compile-time configuration and places the Apache build system on equal footing with other Open Source and Free Software projects.

✦ Apache now uses native operating system APIs, encapsulated in platform-specific multiprocessing modules (MPMs), rather than POSIX emulation layers, on non-UNIX platforms, which significantly improves Apache's performance and stability on operating systems such as BeOS, OS/2, and Windows.

✦ Thanks to enhancements and changes to Apache's API, loadable modules are much less sensitive to load order, simplifying runtime configuration and eliminating an entire class of headaches for Apache administrators.

✦ IPv6 support is built into the server if Apache's underlying runtime library supports IPv6 on that host system.

✦ Configuration directives have been simplified, and some directives (such as `Port` and `BindAddress`) have been removed entirely.

✦ Apache's regular expression handling now uses the more powerful (and arguably more standard) Perl-Compatible Regular Expression (PCRE) library, which uses the regular expression syntax from Perl 5.

Which version should you use? My recommendation is to use Apache 2.0 whenever possible. While Apache 1.3 still has the larger installed base, 2.0 gets the most developer attention, is gaining in popularity, runs faster and more efficiently, and is marginally easier to configure. The reality, though, is that either one will probably suit your needs. Perhaps the most compelling reason to use version 2.0 is that, at some point, maintenance on 1.3 will come to an end, so you can save some aggravation by moving to 2.0 now.

For more information about the Apache Web server, visit the Apache HTTP Server Project Web page at `http://httpd.apache.org/`.

Installing and Configuring Apache 1.3

This section gets you up and running with Apache 1.3. One compelling reason to use Apache 1.3 is its much larger installed base and the resulting community familiarity with Apache 1.3. It is a known quantity; there are few problems with Apache 1.3 that have not already been solved and even fewer configuration and usage questions that have not already been answered.

Installing Apache 1.3

As usual, installing a binary version of Apache on a Debian system is delightfully simple:

```
# apt-get install apache apache-common apache-doc
```

The `apache` package installs the core HTTP server; `apache-common` installs support files needed on all platforms; and `apache-doc` installs the documentation that you will almost certainly want at some point.

If you want Secure Sockets Layer (SSL) support, you should install the `apache-ssl` package. You might also want the `apache-utils` package, which includes helpful utilities such as a benchmarking tool (`ab`), authentication tools (`htpasswd`, `htdigest`, and `dbmmanage`), a log file rotation utility (`logresolve`), and a tool to extract IP addresses from Apache's log files and resolve them to hostnames (`logresolve`). You can install it with the following command:

```
# apt-get apache-utils
```

Configuring Apache 1.3

Despite the cryptic-looking contents of Apache's configuration file, most of the configuration has already been done for you. To get a functioning, no-frills Apache server, you need only make a couple of changes to the stock configuration file and it will work. With only a few additional edits, you will have a moderately customized server. Most of Apache's configuration directives address specific requirements that might not apply to your situation.

The default location of the Apache configuration file is `/etc/apache/httpd.conf`. The stock configuration file created by Debian will work, but I suggest making sure that the configuration directives `User`, `Group`, `ServerAdmin`, and `ServerName` are set and that their values make sense for your system.

`User` and `Group` identify the user and group names that the server uses. By default, both values are set to `www-data`. Make sure that the listed user and group exist in `/etc/passwd` and `/etc/group`. `ServerAdmin` defines the e-mail address shown in error messages. This e-mail address, usually `webmaster@your.domain`, should be aliased to the root user in `/etc/aliases`. If it isn't, add the following line to the bottom of `/etc/aliases`:

```
webmaster: root
```

You must then execute the command `newaliases` to update the alias database used by the mail server:

```
# /usr/bin/newaliases
```

`ServerName` tells Apache the hostname that connecting machines will see. For example, if the hostname of the Web server is `webbeast.kurtwerks.com`, but you want browsers to display `www.kurtwerks.com`, edit the `ServerName` directive so that it looks like the following:

```
ServerName www.kurtwerks.com
```

The server name you specify *must* exist, however. You cannot just make one up and expect it to work. Rather, the specified server name must have a valid DNS A (address) record or be aliased using a `CNAME` record.

After you have confirmed that these configuration options are set appropriately, you can start the Apache Web server using the following command:

```
# /etc/init.d/apache start
Starting web server: apache.
```

To test the configuration, point your favorite Web browser at `http://localhost/index.html`. If everything works according to plan, you should see a figure resembling Figure 15-1.

The four directives just mentioned—`User`, `Group`, `ServerAdmin`, and `ServerName`—hardly exhaust the list of Apache knobs you can turn. Table 15-1 briefly describes additional options available to you. The default values for some of these directives are also shown in the table. These directives control the behavior of the Apache server as a whole. The directives listed in Tables 15-1 and 15-2 apply to both Apache 1.3 and 2.0, except as described in the next section, "Installing and Configuring Apache 2.0."

Figure 15-1: The home page of a newly installed Debian Apache Web server.

Table 15-1
Apache Global Configuration Directives

Directive	Description
AddModuleInfo *module*.c	Activates the built-in but inactive module *module*.c
KeepAlive On	Permits multiple requests on the same connection, speeding up delivery of HTML documents
KeepAliveTimeout 15	Sets the number of seconds (15 by default) permitted to elapse between requests from the same client on the same connection when KeepAlive is On
Listen *[ipaddress:]*80	Determines the combination of IP address and port (80 by default) on which Apache listens for connections; multiple Listen directives may be used
LoadModule *modname filename*	Links the module or library *filename* into the server and adds it to the list of active modules using the name *modname*

Continued

Table 15-1 *(continued)*

Directive	Description
MaxClients 150	Sets the maximum number of simultaneous connections (child servers) supported (150 by default)
MaxKeepAliveRequests 100	Sets the number of requests permitted per connection (100 by default)
MaxRequestsPerChild 100	Sets the maximum number of requests each child server fills before terminating (100 by default)
MaxSpareServers 10	Defines the maximum number of spare (idle) child servers the master server spawns (10 by default)
MinSpareServers 5	Defines the minimum number of spare (idle) child servers permitted (5 by default)
PidFile /var/run/ apache.pid	Defines the file containing the PID of the master server process
ServerRoot /etc/apache	Defines the top-level directory for Apache's configuration files and log files (including error logs)
StartServers 5	Defines the number of child servers created when Apache starts (5 by default)
Timeout 300	Defines the maximum time in seconds Apache waits for packet send and receive operations to complete (300 by default)

The names of log files or additional configuration files are appended to ServerRoot unless they begin with /. That is, if ServerRoot is /etc/apache and a log file is specified as logs/somelog.log, the complete name will be /etc/apache/logs/somelog.log. /logs/mylog.log, on the other hand, will be interpreted as an absolute pathname.

Specifying KeepAlive On results in significant performance improvements because it eliminates the overhead involved in initiating new HTTP connections between clients and the Web server. The MinSpareServers and MaxSpareServers directives enable Apache to self-regulate by adding and deleting child processes as Web server usage fluctuates. When more clients than the value specified in MaxClients attempt to connect, each connection request is put onto a queue, in particular, a FIFO (*first-in, first-out*) queue, and serviced in the order received as current connections close. If the value of MaxClients is too low, however, users of your Web site will have to wait too long to load a page. As a result, they will either send another request or disconnect and go somewhere else. Busy Web sites may need to increase this value to accommodate heavy traffic.

Caution

Apache 1.3 is very sensitive to the order in which its modules are loaded and activated. The order listed in the configuration file is known to work, so do not modify the order in which modules are loaded and activated using `LoadModule` and `AddModuleInfo`. Some modules depend on other modules in order to function properly. Apache will not start if problems occur when loading modules.

The *default* or *primary* server denotes the server (more precisely, the master server process) that responds to all HTTP requests not handled by virtual hosts, also known as *virtual servers*. A *virtual server* or *virtual host* is a Web server that runs on the same machine as the default server but that serves different content, is distinguished from the default server by its different hostname or IP address, and uses different log files. Despite the distinction between the default server and virtual servers, the configuration directives are the same. Directives defined for the default server apply to virtual servers unless specifically overridden. Conversely, directives used to configure the default server can also be used to configure virtual servers.

Table 15-2 lists directives used to configure the default server.

Table 15-2 Default Server Configuration Directives	
Directive	**Description**
`AccessFileName .htaccess`	Lists filenames in the path to requested document that control access to documents in each directory or subdirectory at the same level as or below the topmost directory where the file(s) specified by `AccessFileName` (if any) is found
`AddDescription str file`	Defines the string `str` as the description for one or more files named `file` (used with the `FancyIndexing` directive)
`AddEncoding mimeencoding ext`	Adds the MIME encoding specified by `mimeencoding` for files ending with `ext`, overriding previous encodings for `ext`
`AddIcon icon ext`	Causes `icon` to be displayed next to files ending with `ext` (used with the `FancyIndexing` directive)
`AddIconByEncoding icon mimeencoding`	Causes `icon` to be displayed next to files with the MIME encoding of `mimeencoding` (used with the `FancyIndexing` directive)
`AddIconByType icon mimetype`	Causes `icon` to be displayed next to files with the MIME type of `mimetype` (used with the `FancyIndexing` directive)

Continued

Table 15-2 *(continued)*

Directive	Description
AddLanguage *mimelang* *ext*	Maps the filename extension specified by *ext* to the MIME language *mimelang*, overriding existing mappings for *ext*
AddType *mimetype* *ext*	Adds the specified *mimetype* for files ending in *ext* to the list of MIME types read from the TypeConfig file
Alias *urlpath* *dirpath*	Links the directory *urlpath* (relative to DocumentRoot) to the filesystem directory *dirpath*, which might be outside DocumentRoot
CustomLog /var/log/httpd/access_log combined	Defines the name of Apache's access log file and the log format used when logging requests to the server (disabled by default)
DefaultIcon /icons/unknown.gif	Sets the default icon (/icons/unknown.gif by default) displayed next to files whose content type cannot be determined (used with the FancyIndexing directive)
DefaultType text/plain	Defines the default MIME type used when a requested document's MIME type cannot be determined using the TypesConfig or AddType directives (text/plain by default)
DirectoryIndex *filename*	Specifies one or more *filename*s that serve as a directory index when a request does not specify a particular file or document
DocumentRoot "/var/www"	Sets the base directory of the server's document tree (/var/www by default); URLs (filenames) are interpreted relative to DocumentRoot; see also UserDir
ErrorLog /var/log/apache/error _log	Defines the name of Apache's error log (/var/log/apache/error _log by default), relative to ServerRoot if the filename does not begin with /
HeaderName HEADER	Defines HEADER as the file whose contents will be inserted at the top of a directory listing
HostnameLookups Off	Controls whether Apache performs DNS lookups on connecting hosts in order to log hostnames (off by default)
IndexOptions Fancy Indexing NameWidth=*	Specifies the behavior of Apache's directory indexing feature

Directive	Description
LogFormat *formatstr*	Defines *formatstr* as the format Apache uses for messages it logs in the access log (see also TransferLog and CustomLog)
LogLevel warn	Sets the amount and type of information Apache records in its error log (see the ErrorLog directive); the default log level is warn
ReadmeName README	Defines README as the file whose contents will be appended to the end of a directory listing
ScriptAlias *urlpath dirpath*	Maps *urlpath* to *dirpath*, telling Apache where to find CGI scripts
ServerSignature On	Appends the ServerName and version number to server-generated documents, such as error message and FTP file listings (on by default)
TypesConfig /etc/mime.types	Defines the location of the MIME types configuration file (/etc/mime.types by default) that maps filename extensions to content types (see also AddType)
UserDir public_html	Defines the subdirectory in a user's home directory that is used when clients request documents belonging to a specific user (public_html by default)

If you look at the default configuration file, you will notice that it does not use the BindAddress or Listen directives. As a result, the Port 80 directive indicates that the server listens on port 80 for incoming requests. Port 80 is the default port, so the Port 80 directive is redundant, but its presence makes the configuration explicit and easier for less-experienced administrators to understand.

If you use a port numbered below 1024, that is, a privileged port, the root user must start the master server. You can configure Apache to listen on an unprivileged port (for example, with a Port 8080 directive), though, which would allow normal users to run the master server. In order to run the child servers under less-privileged users in this fashion, the master server *must* be started by the root user because only processes running with root permissions can change their UID and GID at run-time. This restriction exists because of the Linux security model.

Each <Directory></Directory> block configures access information for the named directory (or directories) and its subdirectories. The first block sets the default permissions for all directories:

```
<Directory />
    Options SymlinksIfOwnerMatch
    AllowOverride None
</Directory>
```

In this case, the applicable directory is the server's root directory, /. Other `<Directory></Directory>` blocks apply to the server's document root, /var/www; user's personal HTML directories, /home/*/public_html>; the server's default icon directory, /usr/share/apache/icons; and the directory of CGI scripts, /usr/lib/cgi-bin.

The `Options` directive lists server features that apply to the named directory. Values for the `Options` directive can be a space-delimited list of one or more of the following:

✦ `All` — Enables all options except `MultiViews`. `All` is the default `Option`.

✦ `ExecCGI` — Enables execution of CGI scripts.

✦ `FollowSymLinks` — Enables the server to follow symbolic links in this directory.

✦ `Includes` — Enables server-side includes (SSI).

✦ `IncludesNOEXEC` — Enables SSI but disables the SSI #exec command and the use of #include for CGI scripts.

✦ `Indexes` — Enables the server to generate a formatted directory listing automatically if no directory index, such as index.html, exists.

✦ `None` — Disables all special directory features in this directory and any of its subdirectories.

✦ `SymLinksIfOwnerMatch` — Enables the server to follow symbolic links only if the link target has the same UID as the link itself.

Options prefixed with + are added to `Options` currently in force; those prefixed with - are removed from `Options` currently in force. If multiple `Options` can apply to a directory, the most specific one is applied. If *all* of the options in an `Options` directive are prefixed with + or -, the options are merged.

So the only option enabled for all of the directories under the server root (/) is the `SymLinksIfOwnerMatch` option. From this point forward, to add directory features, these features must be activated specifically. Consider the following directory block:

```
<Directory "/var/www">
    Options Indexes Includes FollowSymLinks MultiViews
    AllowOverride None
    Order allow,deny
    Allow from all
</Directory>
```

The `AllowOverride` directive tells the server which directives declared in access files specified by the `AccessFileName` directive (`AccessFileName .htaccess`, in this case) it should honor. If set to None, the server ignores the access files. If set to All, any directive valid in the current context is enabled. For the server's root directory and its subdirectories, therefore, the server ignores access files unless AllowOverride All is specifically set for a given directory under the server root.

The Order directive controls the default access policy for various resources, such as files and directories, and the order in which the server evaluates Allow and Deny directives for those resources. Order can be one of the following:

✦ Order Deny,Allow — Evaluate Deny directives before Allow directives and enable access by default. Clients not matching a Deny directive or matching an Allow directive are allowed access.

✦ Order Allow,Deny — Evaluate Allow directives before Deny directives and deny access by default. Clients not matching an Allow directive or matching a Deny directive are denied access.

✦ Order Mutual-failure — Only clients appearing in the Allow list and not appearing in the Deny list are permitted to access the server. This ordering has the same effect as Order Allow,Deny. Apache's documentation states that Order Allow,Deny should be used instead of Mutual-failure.

For example, all clients are permitted to access the server root directory, and Allow directives are evaluated before Deny directives. However, the <Files> </Files> block denies access to all files beginning with the pattern .ht. As well it should, because htaccess files can contain security-sensitive information (a Files directive has the same effect for files that a Directory directive has for directories).

All directives inside an <IfModules></IfModule> block are evaluated only if the indicated module is loaded. The default configuration file has a number of such blocks. For example, consider the following IfModule directive:

```
<IfModule mod_mime_magic.c>
    MIMEMagicFile share/magic
</IfModule>
```

If the mod_mime_magic module is loaded, the MIMEMagicFile directive causes Apache to read the contents of the configuration file named magic (/etc/apache/ share/magic in this case). Apache uses this file to determine file types. First, Apache reads the first few bytes of a file (mod_mime_magic works much like the Linux file command works and is, in fact, based on an older version of the file command), and then it uses the magic file to determine the type of file by comparing the read pattern to the contents of magic.

Table 15-3 lists directives that control the configuration and behavior of virtual servers.

Table 15-3
Virtual Server Configuration Directives

Directive	Description
`NameVirtualHost ipaddr[:port]`	Defines the IP address `ipaddr` (listening on `port`, if specified) for a name-based virtual host
`ServerAlias altname`	Enables the virtual server to respond to one or more alternate hostnames `altname` when used with name-based virtual hosts
`ServerName fqdn`	Sets the name of the virtual server to the FQDN `fqdn`
`<VirtualHost ipaddr[:port]> directives </VirtualHost>`	Defines a virtual host whose IP address is `ipaddr` (listening on `port`, if specified); `directives` are one or more of the directives listed previously and override the directives listed for the default server

Virtual servers enable a single system to support multiple domains. For example, the single host `webbeast.kurtwerks.com` might function as the Web server for `www.kurtwerks.com`, `www.sendmemoney.net`, and `www.whereiswaldo.org`, but they can also be used to enable multiple workgroups or departments on the same network to maintain independent Web sites without overburdening system administrators or requiring dedicated departmental Web servers.

Installing and Configuring Apache 2.0

Apache 2.0's installation and configuration process is quite similar to Apache 1.3's. The most noticeable differences are slight changes to the package names, the necessity to select a server processing model, and some updates and deletions in configuration file directives. As noted earlier in the chapter, Apache 2.0 adds features that 1.3 did not support, removed some of the more confusing directives that typically confounded novice Apache sysadmins, and significantly reduced the fragility of module loading.

Installing Apache 2.0

To install Apache 2.0.x, use the command `apt-get install to` to install one of the following packages:

✦ `apache2-mpm-prefork`—Installs the standard Linux MPM

✦ `apache2-mpm-worker`—Installs the multiprocess, multithreaded MPM

The prefork MPM implements the standard Apache parent-child server process model in which a single master server process spawns several spare or idle child server processes to handle incoming requests. As incoming HTTP requests consume the idle child server processes, the master server process spawns additional child server processes. This MPM is referred to as a *prefork MPM* because the master server forks (spawns) child server process before they are used. Preforking child servers was the method used by Apache 1.3 and is used in Apache 2.0 to provide both stability and continuity with 1.3.

The worker MPM, on the other hand, implements a hybrid multiprocess, multi-threaded server model that is appropriate for busy, high-volume Web servers. It is described as a *multiprocess, multithreaded server* because, although the worker MPM uses multiple child server processes, each child server creates multiple threads to process incoming requests. The design favors creating additional threads (up to a limit configured at runtime) *before* spawning another process. Using threads results in lower system resource consumption because all threads share the same address space, whereas processes each have their own address space and incur startup overhead that threads do not.

Regardless of which MPM you choose, the dependencies include a number of additional packages. Of these, the ones that bear directly on the current discussion are `apache2-common`, `libapr0`, `openssl`, and `ssl-cert`.

✦ `apache2-common`—Installs important Apache 2.0 support files required on all platforms

✦ `libapr0`—Installs the Apache Portable Runtime library, the interface between the Apache API and the platform-specific MPM

✦ `openssl`—Installs the OpenSSL libraries and utilities, needed for creating a secure Web server using the Secure Sockets Layer

✦ `ssl-cert`—Installs a `debconf`-compatible wrapper script around the `openssl` command installed by the `openssl` package

Tip   You might also want to install the `apache2-doc` package if you want to be able to read the documentation that comes with Apache 2.0.

As with Apache 1.3, after you have installed the binary packages, you have a functioning server. In fact, APT will try to start the server at the end of the installation process. If it fails to start, continue reading with the section titled "Configuring Apache 2.0." If the server does start, make sure you can view the default server home page by pointing your browser at `http://localhost/index.html`.

Tip   Make sure to shut down any other Web server that might be running on your system before starting Apache 2.0. All sorts of interesting things can happen if two HTTP servers try to bind to the same IP address and port. Most often, though, the second server will simply refuse to start and complain that the address it wants to use is already in use.

Configuring Apache 2.0

The default Apache 2.0 configuration file, `/etc/apache2/httpd.conf`, resembles the version 1 configuration file (big surprise, eh?). There are some new and changed directives that regulate the size of the server pool, that is, the number of servers that start, how many spare servers are preforked, and the maximum size of the server pool. These directives are described in the following section, "Controlling the Apache 2.0 server pool." In addition to the new and updated directives, however, Debian's Apache 2.0 configuration scheme has changed significantly. The section titled "Managing Debian's Apache 2.0 configuration system" describes the new configuration system and how to use it.

Controlling the Apache 2.0 server pool

Under Apache 1.3, the server pool was regulated globally. Under Apache 2.0, the directives that control the server pool depend on the type of MPM. For example, the following two sections from `/etc/apache2/httpd.conf` show server pool regulation for the prefork MPM and the worker MPM:

```
<IfModule prefork.c>
StartServers         5
MinSpareServers      5
MaxSpareServers      10
MaxClients           20
MaxRequestsPerChild  0
</IfModule>
```

This section should seem vaguely familiar, because it is almost exactly like the server pool regulation used in Apache 1.3, as described in Table 15-1. The directive you haven't seen before is `MaxRequestsPerChild`. This directive defines the maximum number of connections a server process will handle before the process is killed and a new one spawned. If `MaxRequestsPerChild` is set to 0, the server process never dies.

```
<IfModule worker.c>
StartServers         2
MaxClients           150
MinSpareThreads      25
MaxSpareThreads      75
ThreadsPerChild      25
MaxRequestsPerChild  0
</IfModule>
```

This section controls the worker MPM. It looks different, but the principle is the same: Carefully control the number of server processes running, setting upper limits that ensure that an increased workload is spread evenly over all Apache processes and setting lower limits that force Apache to give resources back to the system during quiescent periods.

✦ `StartServers` defines the initial number of server processes that should be running at all times.

✦ `MaxClients` sets the maximum number of server processes permitted to start.

✦ `MinSpareThreads` sets the minimum number of spare worker threads that must be running in each server. If the number of unused worker threads in a server process falls below this value, additional worker threads will be started.

✦ `MaxSpareThreads` sets the maximum number of unused worker threads that must be running in each server. If the number of spare worker threads in a server process exceeds this value, the excess threads will be terminated.

✦ `ThreadsPerChild` defines the number of threads to run in each server process.

✦ `MaxRequestsPerChild` defines the maximum number of connections a server process will handle before the process is killed and a new one spawned. If set to 0, the server process never dies.

From a practical perspective, the level of control you can exercise over Apache's resource consumption has been increased and made more finely grained. You can still add server processes as needed, but each process has been given its own pool of resource-stingy threads with which to handle HTTP requests. The net effect is to limit the number of processes while expanding each server process's ability to serve incoming connections.

Another significant change between Apache 1.3 and Apache 2.0 is that the `Port` directive, which told Apache 1.3 which port to listen to for incoming HTTP requests, does not work for Apache 2.0. Instead of `Port`, use the `Listen` directive. For example,

```
Listen 80
```

Why the change? To reduce confusion. Both the `Port` and `Listen` directives could tell Apache 1.3 which ports to listen on, but the `Port` directive defined only Apache's default port. The `Listen` directive defined additional ports. The semantics of the `Listen` directive have been changed such that it alone controls the ports to which Apache listens.

Managing Debian's Apache 2.0 configuration system

Debian's default Apache 2.0 installation attempts to take advantage of the reduced fragility of Apache's module handling and also to make Apache server configuration more modular, easier to automate, and simpler to manage. To this end, the installation uses the files and directories shown in Table 15-4 to control the configuration. All the configuration files are situated in `/etc/apache2`.

Table 15-4
Debian's Apache 2.0 Configuration Structure

File/Directory	Description
apache2.conf	Replaces httpd.conf as Apache 2.0's primary configuration file
conf.d/	Stores additional files containing configuration directives not used elsewhere in the new configuration system
httpd.conf	This file is empty and not used with Apache 2.0
magic	Contains the MIME magic data for mod_mime_magic (see htdocs/manual/mod/mod_mime_magic.html)
mods-available/	Contains a set of module.load and (if necessary) corresponding module.conf files that load the specified module and provide module's configuration directives
mods-enabled/	Contains symbolic links to the module.load and module.conf files in mods-available/ for each module that Apache 2.0 should load when it starts
ports.conf	Consists of configuration directives for the IP addresses and ports to which Apache 2.0 should listen
sites-available/	Serves as an analog to mods-available/ for virtual hosts that are available but not necessarily enabled (yet)
sites-enabled/	Serves as an analog to mods-enabled/ for virtual hosts that are both available and that should be accessible from the server

As you can see, Debian's Apache 2.0 configuration system is significantly different. The venerable httpd.conf configuration file has been superseded by apache2.conf, which is considerably smaller than its predecessor. This size reduction and consequent simplification is possible because the bulk of the old configuration file, which consisted of LoadModule statements followed by configuration directives applicable to the loaded module, has been moved to the mods-available directory.

Files in the conf.d directory should be used to store additional configuration directives that aren't present in the default apache2.conf file. These additional configuration snippets get included in the configuration by the line

```
Include /etc/apache2/conf.d in apache2.conf.
```

The ports.conf file is, happily, pretty straightforward. It contains a list of Listen directives that define the ports on which Apache 2.0 listens for incoming connections. The default entry is

```
Listen 80
```

In `mods-available`, you will find a set of files whose names end in `.load` and `.conf`. The `.load` files contain directives that load a module. For modules that require or that can use configuration directives, a corresponding `.conf` file contains the associated configuration directives. For example, the `cgid.load` file contains the line

```
LoadModule cgid_module /usr/lib/apache2/modules/mod_cgid.so
```

The corresponding configuration snippet, `cgid.conf`, contains the following lines:

```
# Socket thingy for CGI
ScriptSock /var/run/apache2/cgisock
```

Gotta love that technical language!

The modules in `mods-available`, as the directory name suggests, are only available. They are not (necessarily) enabled. To enable a module, you have to create a symbolic link in `mods-enabled` to the appropriate `.load` file and the `.conf` file (if it exists) in `mods-available`. So, for example, to enable the `cgid` module, execute the following commands from the `/etc/apache2/mods-enabled` directory:

```
# ln -s ../mods-available/cgid.load
# ln -s ../mods-available/cgid.conf
```

As an alternative to manually creating and deleting symbolic links as you enable and disable modules, you can use the scripts `a2enmod` and `a2dismod` to enable and disable modules, respectively. To enable a module, use the following syntax:

```
# a2enmod module
```

Replace *module* with the name of a module in `mods-available`. For example, to enable the `cgid` module, use the command `a2enmod cgid`, as shown here:

```
# a2enmod cgid
Module cgid installed successfully; run apache2ctl graceful
to enable.
```

The output message tells you to execute the following command to persuade Apache 2.0 to reload its configuration and pick up the newly enabled module:

```
# apache2ctl graceful
```

Likewise, use `a2dismod` to disable a module. The syntax is the same as for `a2enmod`:

```
# a2dismod cgid
Module cgid disabled successfully; run apache2ctl graceful to
fully disable.
```

Tip   If you don't know the name of the module, just execute `a2enmod` or `a2dismod` with no arguments. They will display a list of modules and then prompt you for the name. If no modules are available to enable or disable, you will see an error message.

The `sites-available` and `sites-enabled` directories function for virtual hosts as the `mods-available` and `mods-enabled` directories function for Apache 2.0 modules. `sites-available/` contains a set of files consisting of configuration directives for different virtual hosts that might be served by your Apache 2.0 server. While the hostnames needn't correspond exactly to the filename, choosing mnemonic filenames for your virtual hosts would be a great way to preserve your sanity. To enable a virtual host, create a symbolic link in `sites-enabled` to the virtual host configuration file in `sites-available`. Unfortunately, there are no scripts, yet, for managing virtual hosts. You'll have to do it the old-fashioned way using `ln` to create symbolic links and `rm` to delete the links.

In the default configuration, one "virtual" host is enabled, the default server. The relevant file is `sites-available/default` and the associated symbolic link is `sites-enabled/default`. From the administrator's point of view, the default server isn't really a virtual host at all, but rather the primary or main server. From Apache's point of view, though, the default server is just one of potentially many server configurations it *could* serve.

Apache and Perl, Python, and PHP

One of Apache's greatest attractions is its extensibility. Almost any sort of functionality can be added to Apache by creating an Apache module, or Dynamic Shared Object (DSO), that provides the desired functionality and then loading that module into Apache at runtime. Three of the most popular modules to use with Apache are Perl, Python, and PHP. The next three sections describe how to add support for these modules to Apache 1.3 and also provide short examples of using each module.

Using Perl with Apache

Perl is the long-preferred Web programming language of the World Wide Web (the claims of Java's creators notwithstanding) because it has an enormous and easy-to-use toolkit for writing CGI scripts, gluing Web-based applications to databases, providing dynamic content, and performing almost any other task you can imagine via a Web browser and a Web server. For more information about Perl, see the Perl Web pages at `www.perl.org/` and the huge collection of Perl software and documentation at the Comprehensive Perl Archive Network, more generally known as CPAN, at `www.cpan.org/`.

To use Perl with Apache, you have (at least) three options. First, you can install an Apache binary file that has Perl support compiled into it (the `apache-perl` package). Second, you can install `mod_perl`, an Apache module that provides

Perl support in an Apache DSO. If you need to squeeze every inch of performance out of a Perl-enabled Apache server, use the statically linked `mod_perl`. The downside of this approach is that your server becomes bigger and consumes more resources because Apache cannot unload Perl support when it is no longer needed.

The `apache-perl` package installs a statically linked Perl. Install it using the following command:

```
# apt-get install apache-perl
```

To install the `mod_perl` DSO, use the following command:

```
# apt-get install libapache-mod-perl
```

The third alternative, and the method used in this section, is to enable Apache's CGI (*Common Gateway Interface*) support and invoke Perl scripts directly. CGI is the protocol that Apache uses to invoke external programs (such as Perl scripts) and display the results in a Web browser. You might need to make one modification to Apache's configuration file, but the default Debian configuration enables CGI by default. You will also need to put the Perl scripts you want to run in a directory where Apache can find them.

The configuration file edits, if necessary, are simple. The line in the `httpd.conf` that tells Apache where to find Perl scripts is `ScriptAlias /cgi-bin/ /usr/lib/cgi-bin/`. This directive maps the "physical" or filesystem directory `/usr/lib/cgi-bin` to the directory component `/cgi-bin` used in URLs. For example, if the URL is `http://localhost/cgi-bin/some_script.pl`, Apache looks for `some_script.pl` in `/usr/lib/cgi-bin/some_script.pl`. Immediately following the `ScriptAlias` directive is the directory configuration section, reproduced here for reference:

```
ScriptAlias /cgi-bin/ /usr/lib/cgi-bin/
<Directory /usr/lib/cgi-bin/>
    AllowOverride None
    Options ExecCGI
    Order allow,deny
    Allow from all
</Directory>
```

The key directive is `Options ExecCGI`, which permits Apache to execute CGI scripts found in this directory. If you modify the configuration file, restart Apache using the `apache` initialization script:

```
# /etc/init.d/apache restart
```

To test the configuration, create the script in Listing 15-1, `hello.pl`, place it in `/usr/lib/cgi-bin`, make it executable (`chmod 755 hello.pl`), and then point your Web browser at `http://localhost/cgi-bin/hello.pl`. You should see a screen resembling Figure 15-2.

Listing 15-1: A Simple Perl CGI Script

```
print "Content-type: text/html\n\n";

print "<html>\n";
print "<head>\n";
print "<title>Apache Perl Test Page</title>\n";
print "</head>\n;"
print "<body>\n";
print "<center>\n";
print "<h1>Apache Perl Test Page</h1>\n";
print "<hr width='50%'>\n";
print "<h2>Hello, Apache/Perl World</h2>\n";
print "<hr width='50%'>\n";
print "</center>\n";
print "</body>\n";
print "</html>\n";
```

hello.pl prints very basic HTML to standard output, which Apache captures and renders properly. The first line, print "Content-type: text/html\n\n";, is very important because it tells the Web browser (and Apache) to treat all of the output as HTML. The two newlines (\n\n) are also very important because they are required by the CGI specification. The balance of the script prints the HTML necessary to display two centered horizontal lines half the width of the browser screen and the message "Hello, Apache/Perl World."

Tip   To see the HTML output without the Perl encumbrances, you can execute hello.pl at the command line.

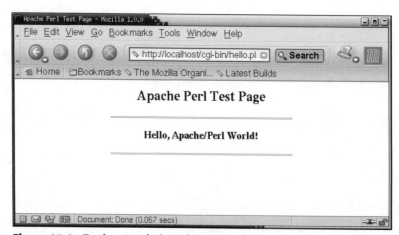

Figure 15-2: Testing Apache's Perl support.

This is not the place to go into the finer points of CGI or Perl; there are fine books available that cover both subjects in considerable detail. But you should have the idea that persuading Apache and Perl to play together nicely is relatively simple.

Using Python with Apache

Python is quickly growing in popularity. Python appeals to those who prefer a neat, tidy, object-oriented language to Perl's deliberate, studied eclecticism. Language wars notwithstanding, Python already has a strong following. The major Python Web site is `www.python.org/`.

At the moment, the only way to get Python support into Apache 1.3 is to use `mod_python`, an Apache DSO. That is, you can't compile Python support into Apache the way you can with Perl. Use `apt-get` to install `libapache-mod-python`, as shown in the following example:

```
# apt-get install libapache-mod-python
```

When the installation completes, `apt-get` offers to reconfigure Apache because a new module was installed (duh!). Type y and press Enter to go through the short reconfiguration process and then follow the prompts. You should allow `apt-get` to save the changes to the configuration file, too, but there is no reason to restart Apache (yet) because you have to edit `httpd.conf` manually to enable `mod_python`.

First, find the line in `/etc/apache/httpd.conf` that reads

```
# LoadModule python_module /usr/lib/apache/1.3/mod-python.so
```

As you might guess, the hash sign disables loading the Python module, so remove the hash sign, which will enable Apache to load the Python module. The edited line should look like the following:

```
LoadModule python_module /usr/lib/apache/1.3/mod-python.so
```

Next, add the following directives to the configuration file. I suggest putting them under the directory configuration directives for CGI (mentioned in the previous section):

```
<Directory /var/www/pytest>
    AddHandler python-program .py
    PythonHandler hello
    PythonDebug On
</Directory>
```

These directives configure a directory named `/var/www/pytest`. The `AddHandler` line tells Apache that files in this directory that end in `.py` should be handled, or executed, by `python-program` handler, which means that Apache will hand requests for .py files off to mod_python for processing. The PythonHandler line tells mod_python that it should execute the Python program named hello.py (the .py extension is implied). The final line, PythonDebug, turns on the Python module's debugging routines. Save your changes and exit the configuration file.

Before you get started, though, you need to create the directory /var/www/pytest and create the hello.py program in this directory (see Listing 15-2). To create the directory, the command mkdir /var/www/pytest should do.

Listing 15-2: A Simple Apache/Python Script

```
from mod_python import apache

def handler(req):
    req.content_type = "text/html"
    req.send_http_header()
    req.write("<html>")
    req.write("<head>")
    req.write("<title>Apache Python Test Page</title>")
    req.write("</head>")
    req.write("<body>")
    req.write("<center>")
    req.write("<h1>Apache Python Test Page</h1>")
    req.write("<hr width='50%'>")
    req.write("<h2>Hello Apache/Python World!</h2>")
    req.write("<hr width='50%'>")
    req.write("</body>")
    req.write("</html>")
    return apache.OK
```

Without going into detail about Python's innards, the first two lines of this script provide the information the Python interpreter needs to execute the rest of the script. As with hello.pl in the previous section, the output from this script needs to begin with the proper content type for HTML (req.content_type = "text/html"). After invoking mod_python's built-in method for sending HTTP headers, the balance of the script consists of displaying the same information as hello.py: a proper title, two centered horizontal rules that are half the width of the browser's window, and the text (also centered) "Hello Apache/Python World!" The final line of the script returns an "error" code to the Python interpreter indicating that the script completed successfully.

After you create the hello.py script (in /var/www/pytest), restart Apache using its initialization script and then point your Web browser to http://localhost/pytest/hello.py. You should see a screen resembling Figure 15-3.

Figure 15-3: Testing Apache's Python support.

The output might not win any Web design awards, but it does demonstrate that the configuration works. mod_python comes with a very good documentation set that describes its configuration and use in great detail. It is in HTML format, of course, so you can view it by opening the file /usr/share/doc/libapache-mod-python/ doc-html/index.html in a Web browser.

Using PHP with Apache

PHP is an HTML scripting language. You embed PHP code in HTML files or write pure PHP programs that create HTML output. All that is required is to load a PHP interpreter into Apache. The beauty of PHP is that it generates HTML output for you, saving you the time and effort of writing (sometimes tedious) HTML yourself. PHP makes it a snap to create a dynamic, active Web site with all the bells and whistles and chrome you can stand. PHP has many features built into the core language and provides numerous additional features through an extensive collection of pre-built modules. If you are inclined, you can create your own PHP modules to implement missing functionality because PHP includes an easy-to-use module API. To learn more about PHP, visit the PHP Web pages at www.php.net/.

To get started, you need to install PHP support, which involves installing the PHP DSO. Right away, though, things get complicated, because two versions of PHP are available in Debian's stable distribution, PHP3 and PHP4. PHP3 is simpler, but PHP4 has more features and is also the focus of current development. Review the PHP Web site and make your own decision. This section illustrates PHP4.

A simple `apt-get install php4` command should suffice, unless you want to install the documentation, in which case, add the `phpdoc` package to your `apt-get` invocation:

```
# apt-get install php4 phpdoc
```

As you saw when you installed `mod_python`, the PHP4 installation modifies `httpd.conf` and offers to reconfigure Apache for you. As before, type y and press Enter to proceed with the reconfiguration. Allow `apt-get` to update the configuration file, but don't restart the server because you need to enable the PHP4 module first and make some additional modifications to Apache's configuration file.

To enable the module, open `/etc/apache/httpd.conf` in a text editor, and remove the hash sign at the beginning of the line that reads

```
# LoadModule php4_module /usr/lib/apache/1.3/libphp4.so
```

You also need to let Apache know that two new MIME types exist so that files of those types will be handled by the proper application (`libphp4.so`, in this case). So, scroll down in `httpd.conf` until you get to the following lines:

```
#AddType application/x-httpd-php .php
#AddType application/x-httpd-php-source .phps
```

Remove the hash marks from the front of these two lines.

These directives associate files with the extensions `.php` and `.phps` with the MIME types `application/x-httpd-php` and `application/x-httpd-php-source`, respectively. They have the same effect, although using a different method, as the `AddHandler` statement did for the Python configuration. In this case, though, Apache's plumbing is set up to handle PHP files by passing files with the PHP MIME type to the PHP module (`libphp4.so`). Restart Apache using the initialization script and you're ready to write a little bit of PHP code to test the configuration. Listing 15-3 shows `hello.php`, a cognate in PHP of the `hello.pl` and `hello.py` scripts shown in the previous sections.

Listing 15-3: **A PHP4 Script**

```
<html>
<head>
<title>Apache PHP4 Test Page</title>
</head>
<body>

<?php
include 'funcs.php';
?>
```

```
<center>

<?php
hdr("Apache PHP4 Test Page");
rule();
msg("Hello, Apache/PHP4 World!");
rule();
?>

</center>
</body>
</html>
```

This "script" is really an HTML file that contains embedded PHP code. The embedded PHP code exists between special start tags, `<?php`, and end tags, `?>`, that delimit code the PHP interpreter must process. The first block of PHP code includes the contents of a file named `funcs.php` (more about that in a moment). The second block of PHP code calls some PHP functions defined in the include file that create the HTML output. The `hdr()`, `rule()`, and `msg()` functions are defined in `funcs.php`, which is shown in Listing 15-4.

Listing 15-4: **PHP4 Functions Used in hello.php**

```
<?php
function rule()
{
    echo "<hr width='50%'>\n";
}

function hdr($title)
{
    echo "<h1>$title</h1>\n";
}

function msg($message)
{
    echo "<h2>$message</h2>\n";
}
?>
```

The first function, `rule()`, draws a horizontal rule that is half the width of the browser window. The second function, `hdr()`, takes one argument, `$title`, and then displays that argument between `<h1>` and `</h1>` HTML tags. The last function, `msg()`, also takes a single argument, `$message`, and displays that argument between <h2> and </h2> HTML tags. Notice that the functions are defined between the special start and end tags that indicate PHP code. If you accidentally omit these tags, your PHP code won't work and will spew an error message out instead of the HTML you were expecting.

Create these two files and place them in the root of your Apache document tree, which is /var/www by default on Debian systems. Point your Web browser at http://localhost/hello.php and you should see a page resembling Figure 15-4.

Figure 15-4: Testing Apache's PHP4 support.

As you can see in Figure 15-4, the output PHP4 creates is identical to the output created by Perl and Python, save for the difference in the message displayed. If you want to learn more about PHP, you can start with the documentation installed by the phpdoc package in /usr/share/doc/phpdoc/html. It is in HTML format, so you can view it using a Web browser. For more information, see the PHP Web site at www.php.net.

Serving Static Content with Boa

The previous sections showed you how to use Apache together with Perl, Python, and PHP, but face it, not every Web site needs Apache's features and configurability. Moreover, as you add feature support to Apache, its resource requirements and its maintenance load — that is, the amount of time and effort you spend on Apache's care and feeding — increase. Of course, Apache's place as one of Free Software's poster children is rightfully secure and certainly deserved, but there are other HTTP servers available that might better suit your needs. Boa is an example of a Web server that you can use when Apache's capabilities exceed your needs.

Boa is a lightweight, high-performance Web server. It is well suited for systems that have minimal RAM or CPU resources, sites that serve only static content, low-volume Web sites, and any situation in which Apache's feature set is overkill. Boa is a single-tasking HTTP server. This simply means that Boa, unlike Apache, does not fork a child process to handle incoming connections, nor does it spawn multiple copies of itself to serve multiple simultaneous connections. Rather, Boa internally *multiplexes* (switches between) all active HTTP connections using a single process, and it forks only under the following limited conditions:

✦ To execute CGI programs, which must be spawned as separate processes

✦ To generate directories automatically

✦ To decompress gzipped files automatically

Boa's maintainers claim that it can handle "several thousand hits per second on a 300 MHz Pentium and dozens of hits per second on a lowly 20 MHz 386/SX" (www. boa.org/documentation/boa-1.html). One of the reasons lightweight HTTP servers such as Boa are popular is that they are quite compatible with small, resource-constrained embedded systems, such as PDAs, cellphones, and other consumer electronic devices, an increasing number of which use versions of Linux customized for low-resource environments.

Note   For more information about Boa, visit the project home page at www.boa.org/. Although the Boa project has a SourceForge page (https://sourceforge. net/projects/boa/), it did not, at the time this chapter was written, have the most recent releases or seem to be actively maintained.

Installing Boa

As usual, the easiest way to install a binary version of Boa is to use apt-get:

```
$ apt-get install boa
```

That's all there is to it. Except, of course, for the niggling configuration details, addressed in the next section.

Figure 15-5 shows a simple index page served by Boa displayed in a browser. This is not the default index page you will see if you've just installed Boa, however, because the default behavior is to show the standard Debian home page (see Figure 15-1). The next section shows you how to customize the server using the configuration directives in the boa.conf configuration file.

Figure 15-5: The Boa Web server serving a simple index page.

Configuring Boa

After you have a functioning Boa installation, you will likely want to customize it. Befitting Boa's slimmer, trimmer profile, it lacks the multitude of configuration directives that characterize Apache. Nevertheless, Boa is configurable enough to suit the majority of the Web sites that need it. Table 15-5 lists Boa's configuration options.

Table 15-5 Boa Configuration Directives	
Directive	*Description*
AccessLog	Specifies the location of Boa's access log (`/var/log/boa/access_log` by default)
AddType	Adds MIME types without editing the MIME types file (see the `MimeTypes` directive)
Alias	Maps one document or directory to another document or directory, respectively
CGIPath	Controls the value of the `PATH` environment variable passed to CGI scripts (`/bin:/usr/bin:/usr/local/bin` by default)
DefaultType	Defines the default MIME type used if `MimeTypes` is unset, a MIME type is unrecognized, or a file lacks an extension

Directive	Description
DirectoryCache	Specifies the location of directory indexes created by Boa when both DirectoryIndex and DirectoryMaker are disabled
DirectoryIndex	Names the HTML file that lists the contents of a directory (index.html by default)
DirectoryMaker	Names the program that creates directory listings dynamically (disabled by default)
DocumentRoot	Points at the root directory of all non-user-specific HTML documents
ErrorLog	Specifies the location of Boa's error log (/var/log/boa/error_log by default)
Group	Identifies the server process's group name or group ID (GID)
KeepAliveMax	Sets the upper limit to the number of KeepAlive requests permitted per client connection (1,000 by default)
KeepAliveTimeout	Sets the number of seconds before a KeepAlive connection times out (10 seconds by default)
Listen	Defines the IP address on which Boa listens
Port	Defines the port on which Boa runs (80 by default)
MimeTypes	Defines the location of the MIME types file (/etc/mime.types by default)
Redirect	Maps documents that no longer exist on the server to another document on another server
ScriptAlias	Maps a virtual path to an actual directory containing CGI scripts
ServerAdmin	Defines the e-mail address where problems should be sent
ServerName	Defines the name Boa displays to clients
SinglePostLimit	Limits the maximum size of POST requests (1 MB by default)
UseLocaltime	Instructs Boa to report time using local time instead of Universal Coordinated Time (UCT)
User	Identifies the server process's username or user ID
UserDir	Defines the directory name appended to requests that include a username of the form ~username
VerboseCGIlogs	Causes Boa to log the start and stop times of CGI scripts
VirtualHost	Maps requests to a given name to a directory name

The good news is that almost all of Boa's configuration directives share the syntax and semantics of similarly named Apache directives. Moreover, as you can see in Figure 15-6, a lot of Boa's functionality is the same, too. Figure 15-6 shows the output of a Perl CGI script, `hello-boa.pl`. As remarked at the beginning of this section, Boa is well suited for Web sites for which Apache would be overkill and that serve only static content or use only CGI functions to present dynamic content. If these characteristics describe your Web site, give Boa a try. You will be pleased with its speed and small resource appetite.

Figure 15-6: Testing Boa's Perl support.

Summary

Providing Web services is widely acknowledged, even by Linux opponents, as one of Linux's strengths. Debian GNU/Linux is no exception. As you have seen in this chapter, installing and configuring a Web server is quick and relatively easy. Apache 1.3 and Apache 2.0 provide full-featured Web servers for those Web sites that need rich functionality, such as built-in Python or PHP interpreters. You've also seen that getting Apache to support Perl, Python, or PHP scripts is as easy as installing Apache itself. For some Web sites, though, Apache might not be appropriate. If your Web site is running on an underpowered system or doesn't need the extensive support that Apache excels at providing, a smaller HTTP server like Boa is worth a look. It is easy to install and easy to configure and maintain. Boa is also considerably less resource-intensive than Apache. Which one you choose is up to you and your analysis of your Web site's needs.

✦   ✦   ✦

File Transfer Services

Although lacking the glamour of the World Wide Web, the ubiquity of e-mail, and the immediacy of Internet Relay Chat, FTP (the File Transfer Protocol) is an essential pillar of the Internet. Perhaps everyone, at one time or another, has used FTP to transfer a file to their local machine, whether they realized they were using FTP or not. Although you don't have to set up an FTP server to provide file transfer services (RSYNC, RDIST, and file transfers via HTTP come to mind), FTP is certainly the simplest file transfer service to configure, the most straightforward to maintain, and the most common solution to the problem of providing centralized access for downloading files. This chapter discusses using FTP to offer file transfer services and shows you how to provide FTP services using two popular FTP servers, vsftpd and ProFTPD. It also discusses how to use SFTP, Secure FTP, to permit secure file transfer services via the SSH protocol.

Running an FTP Server

FTP servers vary widely in their purpose, usage, and configuration. FTP servers can be large and busy, such as the Metalab site at the University of North Carolina (`ftp://metalab.unc.edu/`), or they can be small, low-traffic servers, such as the KurtWerks FTP site (`ftp://ftp.kurtwerks.com/`). They can be public download sites that are accessible to anyone with an Internet connection, or they can be private, intended only for use within an organization's intranet. FTP servers can permit anonymous FTP, that is, allow anyone to download files, or they can require a valid FTP or login account before you are permitted to download files. FTP servers can permit users to upload files, or they can allow only downloads.

The Risks of Anonymity

Unless absolutely necessary, avoid allowing anonymous uploads on your FTP site. Sites that allow anonymous file uploads always run the risk of becoming a dumping ground for so-called *warez*, which are illegal, unlicensed, or bootlegged copies of software, music, and movies. Unless you like lawyers and courtrooms, you do not want your FTP server to become a warez site.

A second risk of permitting anonymous uploads is that unless you continually monitor the upload volume, you might run out of disk space, which can have, well, unpleasant consequences. In fact, one way to attack an FTP server is to cause a denial-of-service (DoS) attack by deliberately filling up its disk space with uploaded files. A related problem is that uploaders might inadvertently, or deliberately, consume your network bandwidth with multiple, high-volume uploads. When done deliberately, this is another type of DoS attack.

Another risk is that some ne'er-do-well will upload some type of *malware*, a file or program that contains a trojan, virus, or other malicious code, such as a packet sniffer, root kit, or backdoor. When you install or execute the program, your server has been compromised. Even if you don't install it on your own system, you don't want to help spread malware to other people's systems. In short, the risks associated with anonymous uploads are high and impose significant burdens on the server administrator to protect and maintain the FTP server and to protect other users of the server. Just say "No!" to anonymous uploads.

Depending on your situation (whether you are running your own FTP server or administering someone else's), your task as system administrator is to decide which FTP services you will provide (if any) and to whom you will provide them. As a general rule, you will want to avoid permitting anonymous uploads if at all possible because of the security risks that anonymous uploads represent (see the related sidebar).

The most typical usage and configuration of an FTP server is to provide anonymous download services, that is, *anonymous FTP*. Historically, software, especially Free or Open Source software, has been distributed via FTP. To a considerable degree, FTP is still the preferred distribution method for Free and Open Source software. An anonymous FTP server allows unauthenticated users to connect to the server and download files from a carefully limited set of directories (or a specially designed directory tree). The users are "unauthenticated" in that they do not need to have login accounts on the server. Rather, they typically use a login name such as `ftp` or `anonymous`. When prompted for a password, the convention is to provide a valid e-mail address (this convention can be enforced, to some degree, by the FTP server daemon).

Obviously, allowing unauthenticated access to a system is inherently risky. To address this risk, most FTP servers, including the three discussed in this chapter, are written and configured in such a way that anonymous users do not have access to system directories. The only files and directories anonymous users see are those that exist in the FTP server's directory tree. The FTP servers discussed in this chapter include a variety of features that make it possible to run a very secure server that poses minimal risk.

To further mitigate potential security breaches and enhance the server's security, most FTP servers execute client sessions in a *chroot* environment (either implicitly or explicitly). A chroot environment is one in which the process's root directory is changed to a directory other than the system root. Changing a process's root directory to, for example, /var/ftp/pub means that the only files and directories the process knows about are those at and below /var/ftp/pub. It is as if, for example, /usr and /bin do not exist.

As a final security measure, you, as the administrator, need to make sure the anonymous FTP is adequately logged and, even more importantly, that you routinely review the logs for any sign of attack, compromise, or even an attempted attack or compromise. As you will see in the sections that follow, vsftpd and ProFTPD can log a great deal of information that facilitates monitoring. With a little scripting moxie, you can even automate some or most of the monitoring to weed out the uninteresting or routine log activity and draw attention to signs of untoward activity.

Users routinely use FTP to transfer files to and from their accounts on a system, a configuration referred to as *authenticated access*. Authenticated access often exists side by side with anonymous FTP. In authenticated access, users log in to the FTP server using their system login name and password. The drawback to this approach is that FTP is a so-called *clear text* or *plaintext* protocol, which means that authentication information is passed without being encrypted or obscured in any meaningful way. As a result, someone can capture FTP packets with a packet sniffer, decode the packets, and extract from the network traffic both valid usernames *and* valid passwords. *Voilà*! Your system has just been compromised!

The moral of this story is just this: Authenticated FTP access is a *really bad idea*. The good news, though, is that SFTP — FTP over SSH (Secure Shell) — is available, is brain-dead simple to configure, and addresses the problem of plaintext authentication by using an encrypted connection. See "Using Secure FTP" later in the chapter to learn how to use SFTP for *secure* authenticated FTP access.

With the foregoing caveats in mind, the next two sections, "Providing FTP Services with vsftpd" and "Running an FTP Server on ProFTPD," make the following assumptions:

✦ You are setting up an anonymous FTP server.

✦ Anonymous uploads are not permitted.

✦ Authenticated FTP access will be handled by SFTP.

Providing FTP Services with vsftpd

vsftpd (Very Secure FTP Daemon) is a small, high-performance FTP server with the stated goal of being the most secure FTP daemon available. Small, fast, and secure, vsftpd has the added benefit of being easy to configure and even easier to maintain. In fact, once you have it installed and configured to your liking, vsftpd is effectively a *set-and-forget* program; install it, configure it, test it, and then get on with more scintillating administrative duties such as pruning your Web server's log files, validating your last backup, and, of course, checking the FTP log files for signs of attack.

Note   vsftpd's home page on the Web is http://vsftpd.beasts.org/.

Installing vsftpd

To install vsftpd, the appropriate apt-get command is:

```
# apt-get install vsftpd
```

There is no configuration performed during the installation, so vsftpd is not ready to use after the installation is complete. vsftpd expects a user named ftp whose home directory will be used as the root directory for anonymous FTP. Accordingly, create a directory named /var/ftp using the following command:

```
# mkdir /var/ftp
```

Now, create a user named ftp whose home directory is /var/ftp:

```
# useradd -d /var/ftp ftp
```

You also need to enable the FTP service in /etc/inetd.conf. Open /etc/inetd.conf in a text editor and find the line that reads

```
#<off>#ftp        stream  tcp     nowait  root    /usr/sbin
/tcpd  /usr/sbin/vsftpd
```

Note that the preceding code line wraps here due to page width restrictions. The initial text might read #<disabled># instead of #<off>#. Remove the text between and including the hash (#) marks. The edited line should resemble the following:

```
ftp           stream  tcp     nowait  root    /usr/sbin/tcpd
/usr/sbin/vsftpd
```

Again, the preceding code line wraps due to page width limitations. Save your changes and exit the editor.

This modification is necessary because vsftpd runs as an inetd service, so inetd needs to be configured to start vsftpd when an FTP connection is requested. To make the change take effect, restart the inetd daemon using the `inetd` initialization script:

```
# /etc/init.d/inetd reload
Reloading internet superserver: inetd
```

Now you can test the FTP server by opening an FTP session to localhost. The following example illustrates the testing process:

```
# ftp localhost
Connected to localhost.
220 ready, dude (vsFTPd 1.0.0: beat me, break me)
Name (localhost:kurt): ftp
331 Please specify the password.
Password:
230 Login successful.
Remote system type is UNIX.
Using binary mode to transfer files.
ftp> ls
200 PORT command successful.
150 Here comes the directory listing.
-rw-rw-r--    1 0           0              136041 Jun 27 22:11
  vsftpd-1.2.1.tar.gz
-rw-rw-r--    1 0           0              136669 Jun 27 22:11
  vsftpd-1.2.2.tar.gz
226 Directory send OK.
ftp> close
221 Goodbye.
ftp> bye
```

In this example, I had copied two versions of vsftpd's source code archives into the download directory (`/var/ftp` in this particular case) for purposes of the illustration. As you can see from the example, the default installation almost works "out of the box" and meets most of the requirements discussed in the previous section. The next section describes how to customize vsftpd if the stock Debian configuration doesn't meet your needs or requirements.

Configuring vsftpd

If you installed vsftpd using `apt-get`, the default configuration as defined in `/etc/vsftpd.conf` might well be sufficient for you:

✦ It runs in standalone mode, as a daemon, rather than being executed by the TCP superserver, `inetd`.

✦ Anonymous FTP is enabled.

✦ Local users are *not* permitted to log in.

✦ Uploads are disabled.

✦ Downloads are logged.

✦ The server emulates ASCII (text) mode downloads but uses only binary downloads.

Tip Unlike many GNU/Linux programs, `vsftpd` accepts only one command-line argument, the name of a file that will be used as an alternative configuration file. By default, `vsftpd` looks for `/etc/vsftpd.conf`. To use the configuration file `myvsftpd.conf` in `/usr/local/etc`, start `vsftpd` with the command:

```
/usr/sbin/vsftpd /usr/local/etc/myvsftpd.conf
```

All other `vsftpd` features are controlled by compiled-in defaults and by entries in the configuration file.

The configuration file has a simple format. Each line is either a comment — which begins with the nearly universal comment delimiter, # — or a *directive*. A directive controls a single vsftpd characteristic and takes the form

```
option=value
```

option is the characteristic to configure and *value* is, well, its value. For example, the following configuration entries correspond to the behavior described as the default configuration:

```
anonymous_enable=YES
#local_enable=YES
#anon_upload_enable=YES
xferlog_enable=YES
#ascii_download_enable=YES
```

Configuration entries beginning with a hash mark are commented out, which means that vsftpd will fall back on its default behavior. As the name suggests, `anonymous_enable=YES` enables anonymous FTP (set it to NO to disable anonymous FTP). The next two entries, `local_enable` and `anon_upload_enable`, are commented out, which is the same as setting them to NO. `local_enable` controls whether local users are permitted to log in to the server (the default is not to permit local users to connect). `anon_upload_enable` (disabled by default) controls whether anonymous file uploads are permitted. `xferlog_enable=YES` means that file downloads (and uploads, if you permit file uploads) will be logged to `/var/log/vsftpd.log`. You should enable logging so that you can keep track of how your FTP server is used.

The last directive, `ascii_download_enable`, is unusual and bears some explanation. Most FTP servers allow clients to specify whether to download (and upload, when permitted) files in ASCII (text) format or binary format. Using ASCII format, however, poses a security risk because if you have large files on your FTP site, a malicious user can issue the FTP command `SIZE /some/really/big/file`, which will consume I/O resources. Moreover, the FTP server must take into account the conversion between line-end conventions between platforms when transferring files. Binary format, on the other hand, disregards line-end conventions; the server simply transfers the file image byte for byte.

The point is that vsftpd emulates ASCII mode transfers unless specifically instructed not to do so, which closes the security hole. If you want vsftpd to honor requests for ASCII transfers (which are used for features such as directory listings and any display of information between the server and FTP clients), set `ascii_download_enable=YES`.

What can you configure in vsftpd? Almost everything. Table 16-1 lists many of the most common configuration options. For the complete list, review the `vsftpd.conf` manual page (`man vsftpd.conf`).

Table 16-1
Common vsftpd Configuration Options

Option	Type	Description	Default
`anon_max_rate`	N	Defines the maximum permitted transfer rate in bytes per second (0 for unlimited transfer rate)	0
`anon_root`	S	Identifies the directory to which vsftpd will chroot for anonymous connections	NONE
`anon_upload_enable`	B	Specifies whether anonymous uploads are permitted	NO
`anonymous_enable`	B	Specifies whether anonymous FTP is enabled	YES
`banned_email_file`	S	Names the file containing a list of e-mail address passwords that are denied login permission (see `deny_email_enable`)	`/etc/vsftpd.banned_emails`
`chroot_list_file`	S	Contains a list of users that will be chrooted to their home directory after logging in	`/etc/vsftpd.chroot_list`
`deny_email_enable`	B	Activates a list of e-mail addresses (`/etc/vsftpd.banned_emails`) that result in denied logins (see `banned_email_file`)	NO

Continued

Table 16-1 *(continued)*

Option	Type	Description	Default
dirmessage_enable	B	Enables display of directory-specific messages (.message) when users first enter a new directory (see message_file)	NO
ftp_username	S	Specifies the username used for handling anonymous FTP and whose home directory is the root of the anonymous FTP area	ftp
ftpd_banner	S	Contains the string used as a greeting when clients initially connect	NONE
idle_session_timeout	N	Sets the maximum number of seconds a connection can be idle before the client is disconnected	20
message_file	S	Lists the filename that contains the message displayed when users first enter a new directory (see dirmessage_enable)	.message
pasv_enable	B	Enables use of passive mode data connections	YES
port_enable	B	Activates use of the FTP PORT command to open a data connection	YES
sylog_enable	B	Redirects log file output from /var/log/vsftpd.log to the system log	NO
tcp_wrappers	B	Routes incoming connections through TCP wrappers access control	NO
vsftpd_log_file	S	Specifies the file to which vsftpd-style log entries will be written (see xferlog_enable, xflerlog_std_format, dual_log_enable, and syslog_enable)	/var/log/ vsftpd.log
xferlog_enable	B	Enables logging of file downloads and uploads to /var/log/vsftpd.log	NO

Option	Type	Description	Default
xferlog_file	S	Specifies the file to which WU-FTPD-style log entries will be written (see xferlog_enable and xferlog_std_format)	/var/log/ xferlog
xferlog_std_format	B	Creates standard (WU-FTPD-style) transfer log file entries, if xferlog_file is set (see xferlog_file)	NO

The Type column in Table 16-1 specifies the type of value to use for the option in question. B indicates that the option expects a Boolean value, N specifies a numeric value, and S means that the option requires a string value. Boolean options may be either YES or NO, numeric options take nonnegative integers (octal numbers may be used if the first digit is a zero), and string options can contain spaces if the option is surrounded by quotes.

Configuring download options

If your FTP server has a low-bandwidth Internet connection or if you want to prevent a single FTP client from consuming all of your available bandwidth, use the anon_max_rate option. For example, to limit outbound bandwidth consumption to 1 kilobyte per second (1,024 bytes per second), use the directive anon_max_rate= 1024. You really don't want to use such a low value, though, or downloads from your server will be excruciatingly slow.

A second useful directive for limiting resource consumption is idle_session_ timeout. Set this value to the maximum number of seconds permitted to elapse between FTP commands issued by an attached client. If an attached client's session is idle for more than this amount of time (the default value is 20 seconds), the session will be closed. This is a good way to reclaim client slots that appear to be in use but that show little or no activity. idle_session_timeout is especially useful in conjunction with the max_clients directive.

Using the banner and message options

There are a number of directives that you can use to customize your FTP server, including the following:

✦ ftpd_banner

✦ dirmessage_enable

✦ message_enable

`banner_file` specifies the name of a file whose contents will be displayed when an FTP client connects to the server. `ftpd_banner`, on the other hand, specifies the greeting string vsftpd displays when someone connects. If neither of these options is specified, vsftpd displays the following greeting:

```
220 ready, dude (vsFTPd 1.0.0: beat me, break me)
```

If you specify `ftpd_banner`, it overrides vsftpd's default banner message. `ftpd_banner` is best suited if you have a short, one-line banner message to display. If the banner message contains spaces, you do not need to quote it, unless you want the quote marks to appear in the banner message. The following directive shows a sample banner message:

```
ftpd_banner=Welcome to the KurtWerks FTP Server!
```

Use `dirmessage_enable` and `message_file` to show users a message the first time they enter a directory. If `dirmessage_enable` is set to `YES`, the message file, which defaults to the hidden file `.message`, will be displayed. You can use `message_file` to change the default name of the message file. The KurtWerks FTP server, for example, uses message files to tell users the contents of each directory. In one case, the message file contains a disclaimer about the files provided, as shown below:

```
ftp> cd pub/docbook
250-This is the KurtWerks DocBook Repository. The files in this
250-directory support the DocBook Toolchain Installation HOWTO at
250-http://www.kurtwerks.com/software/docbook_install.html. They are
250-unmodified, meaning that they (should) be identical to their twins
250-at their home repositories. They are here solely as a convenience for
250-netizens.
250-
250 Directory successfully changed.
```

Setting logging options

The logging-related directives in Table 16-1 are potentially confusing, so some explanation might be in order. The directives in question are the following:

- ✦ `xferlog_enable`
- ✦ `xferlog_file`
- ✦ `xferlog_std_format`

By default, if `xferlog_enable=YES` is set (which is the default), vsftpd logs file downloads and uploads to `/var/log/vsftpd.log` using its own format. The following short listing illustrates vsftpd-style log entries:

```
Mon Jun 28 00:32:47 2004 [pid 8806] CONNECT: Client "127.0.
0.1"
Mon Jun 28 00:32:53 2004 [pid 8805] [ftp] OK LOGIN: Client
"127.0.0.1", anon password "gnuser@localhost"
Mon Jun 28 00:35:12 2004 [pid 8807] [ftp] OK DOWNLOAD: Clie
nt "127.0.0.1", "/vsftpd-1.2.1.tar.gz", 136041 bytes, 1.04K
byte/sec
```

xferlog_std_format=YES causes vsftpd to create standard WU-FTPD-style file
transfer log files and to store the log in /var/log/xferlog. WU-FTPD-style log
entries are "standard" because WU-FTPD, the Washington University FTP Daemon,
predates vsftpd by a considerable period of time, its log file format has been copied
by other FTP server implementations, and numerous tools and utilities have been
created that parse WU-FTPD-style log files. The following listing illustrates WU-
FTPD-style log entries for the same download demonstrated earlier with vsftpd:

```
Mon Jun 28 00:50:43 2004 69 127.0.0.1 136041 /vsftpd-
1.2.1.tar.gz b _ o a gnuser@localhost ftp 0 * c
```

The format of WU-FTPD-style logging is clearly more compact, but it is also
markedly more difficult to read. You can change the log file used when xferlog_
std_format is set using the xferlog_file directive, which has the same syntax
as vsftpd_log_file.

To recap vsftpd's rather confusing log file handling:

✦ If you want logging in vsftpd format, set xferlog_enable=YES and look for
the log messages in /var/log/vsftpd.log.

✦ If you want logging in vsftpd format and you want to change the default log file
location, specify the new path with vsftpd_log_file.

✦ If you want logging in WU-FTPD format, set xferlog_std_format=YES and
look for the log messages in /var/log/xferlog.

✦ If you want logging in WU-FTPD format and you want to change the default log
file location, specify the new path with xferlog_file.

Running an FTP Server on ProFTPD

ProFTPD, which stands for Professional FTP Daemon, is a secure and highly configurable FTP server. Like vsftpd, ProFTPD is designed with security in mind. ProFTPD
surpasses vsftpd in terms of configurability, however, and it builds on and extends
the feature set of WU-FTPD. Although ProFTPD shares similarities with WU-FTPD,
ProFTPD shares no code with WU-FTPD and, as a result, lacks WU-FTPD's security

problems. ProFTPD has also adapted some features from Apache, such as per-directory `.ftpaccess` files that control directory access for FTP clients in much the same way that Apache's `.htaccesss` files control directory access for HTTP clients. ProFTPD is also, like vsftpd, largely a set-and-forget program that requires little ongoing care and feeding aside from routine monitoring.

Note   ProFTPD's home page on the Web is `www.proftpd.org/`.

ProFTPD's features include the following:

✦ Uses directives and a configuration syntax familiar to anyone who has worked with the Apache Web server

✦ Runs either as a standalone server or via `inetd` or `xinetd`

✦ Executes as an unprivileged user in standalone mode to limit the impact of attacks that attempt to exploit root access

✦ Permits per-directory access control using `.ftpaccess` files

✦ Requires no specific directory structure and uses no system binaries to support anonymous FTP

✦ Supports virtual FTP servers and anonymous FTP services

✦ Executes no external programs (via the FTP protocol's `SITE EXEC` command)

✦ Supports both WU-FTPD-style logging and ProFTPD-specific log extensions

✦ Incorporates support for the shadow password suite

As you can see from the list of features, ProFTPD starts with the good qualities of WU-FTPD, adds some features from Apache, and incorporates 30 years of accumulated security experience to create a feature-rich and, admittedly, complex FTP server that might well be the only FTP server you will ever need.

Installing ProFTPD

If it isn't already installed, you can install ProFTPD using the following `apt-get` command:

```
# apt-get install proftpd
```

In addition to installing ProFTPD, this command will also install `proftpd-common`. The initial configuration screen you encounter should resemble Figure 16-1, which simply tells you that you have some configuration to do. Select Yes and press Enter to continue.

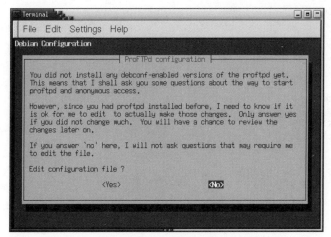

Figure 16-1: Starting the ProFTPD configuration.

As part of the installation, you will be prompted to choose between running ProFTPD as a standalone daemon and invoking it from `inetd` (see Figure 16-2). If you have or anticipate having a busy FTP site, run ProFTPD as a standalone daemon; this reduces the overhead of spawning a new FTP server process each time an FTP connection occurs. For simplicity's sake, it is probably easiest to run ProFTPD as a daemon rather than as an `inetd` (or `xinetd`) service.

Select Standalone (if it isn't already selected) and press Enter to continue.

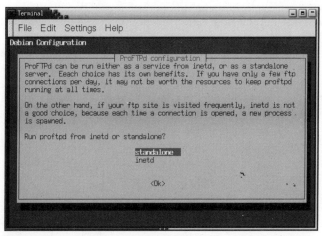

Figure 16-2: Selecting ProFTPD's execution style.

On the next screen (see Figure 16-3), you see the obligatory warning about running an anonymous FTP server and are given the choice to enable anonymous FTP access or not.

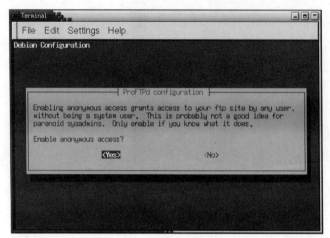

Figure 16-3: Choosing whether to provide anonymous FTP services.

Select Yes and press Enter to continue.

The last screen you see, shown in Figure 16-4, enables you to activate your configuration options by replacing an existing ProFTPD configuration file, /etc/proftp. conf, with a new version. You might not see this screen, but if you do, select Yes and press Enter to finish the installation.

When the installation completes, you will have a running FTP server that supports a single anonymous user. This configuration, although seemingly crippled, is perfect for testing the server and provides a simple, known base from which you can customize ProFTPD to your needs. You can test the server by FTPing to localhost, as shown in the following example:

```
$ ftp localhost
Connected to localhost.
220 ProFTPD 1.2.5rc1 Server (Debian) [luther.kurtwerks.com]
Name (localhost:kurt): ftp
331 Anonymous login ok, send your complete email address as your password.
Password:
230 Anonymous access granted, restrictions apply.
Remote system type is UNIX.
Using binary mode to transfer files.
ftp> bye
221 Goodbye.
```

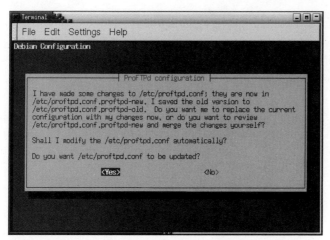

Figure 16-4: Choosing to update the configuration file.

If you are satisfied that the server is working, you can get started configuring and customizing it, as described in the next section.

Configuring ProFTPD

One of the handiest features ProFTPD offers is that you can invoke it in syntax-only mode to validate the syntax of the configuration file, which is /etc/proftpd.conf by default. To test configuration file changes, invoke ProFTPD (/usr/sbin/proftpd) with the -t or --configtest option, as shown below:

```
# /usr/sbin/proftpd -t
Checking syntax of configuration file
Syntax check complete.
```

In this example, there are no syntax errors. The following example shows what happens if the syntax check reveals an error:

```
# /usr/sbin/proftpd -t
Checking syntax of configuration file
 - Fatal: ServerType: type must be either 'inetd' or 'standalone'
```

You will quickly come to appreciate the syntax-checking option.

Another useful command-line option is -n, which prevents ProFTPD from putting itself in the background when you run it in standalone mode and forces error messages out to stderr (the screen) rather than dumping the errors into the log. If you are having problems with the configuration that the syntax check doesn't uncover, it is quite handy to have error messages displayed on the screen *and* to be able to press Ctrl+C to kill the server.

Examining the default configuration

The stock Debian ProFTPD configuration file is simple and serves as a good starting point for describing ProFTPD configuration. Listing 16-1 shows the installed /etc/proftpd.conf, with comments and whitespace removed.

Listing 16-1: Debian's Default ProFTPD Configuration

```
ServerName                "Debian"
ServerType                standalone
DeferWelcome              off
ShowSymlinks              on
MultilineRFC2228          on
DefaultServer             on
AllowOverwrite            on
TimeoutNoTransfer         600
TimeoutStalled            600
TimeoutIdle               1200
DisplayLogin              welcome.msg
DisplayFirstChdir         .message
ListOptions               "-l"
DenyFilter                \*.*/
Port                      21
MaxInstances              30
User                      nobody
Group                     nogroup
<Directory /*>
  Umask                   022  022
  AllowOverwrite          on
</Directory>
# <Anonymous ~ftp>
#   User                  ftp
#   Group                 nogroup
#   UserAlias             anonymous ftp
#   DirFakeUser           on ftp
#   DirFakeGroup          on ftp
#   RequireValidShell     off
#   MaxClients            10
#   DisplayLogin          welcome.msg
#   DisplayFirstChdir     .message
#   <Directory *>
#     <Limit WRITE>
#       DenyAll
#     </Limit>
#   </Directory>
# </Anonymous>
```

As you can see in Listing 16-1, ProFTPD's configuration directives are mostly self-documenting in that the directive names, if sometimes long, suggest their purpose and use. If you read Chapter 15, "Web Serving," you will also notice that the syntax and structure of /etc/proftpd.conf resemble Apache's configuration file syntax and structure. As noted at the beginning of this section, the similarity is deliberate; it is intended to make administrators familiar with Apache more comfortable with ProFTPD. Table 16-2 lists and describes the directives shown in this listing.

Table 16-2
Basic ProFTPD Configuration Directives

Directive	Description
`<Anonymous>` `</Anonymous>`	Creates a block that defines an anonymous FTP server
`<Directory>` `</Directory>`	Groups directives that specify a per-directory configuration
`<Limit>` `</Limit>`	Defines a set of commands or actions that are permitted, denied, or otherwise controlled
`AllowOverwrite`	Permits files to be overwritten (if uploads are permitted)
`DefaultServer`	Identifies the server used when incoming connections don't connect to the server's IP address of a virtual FTP server
`DeferWelcome`	Delays showing `ServerName` and the server IP address until after users have logged in
`DenyFilter`	Defines a regular expression that matches commands that cannot be executed
`DirFakeGroup`	Changes the group name displayed for files and directories
`DirFakeUser`	Changes the username displayed for files and directories
`DisplayFirstChdir`	Names the file whose contents are displayed when users first enter a new directory
`DisplayLogin`	Names the file whose contents are displayed after users successfully authenticate
`Group`	Identifies the group name under which the server daemon runs
`ListOptions`	Defines the options used for FTP commands that generate directory listings (`NLST`, `LIST`, and `STAT`)
`MaxInstances`	Sets the maximum number of server processes spawned
`MultilineRFC2228`	Enables multiline response codes consistent with RFC 2228

Continued

	Table 16-2 *(continued)*
Directive	**Description**
Port	Configures the port number on which ProFTPD listens when running in standalone mode
RequireValidShell	Allows or denies logins to users whose shells are not listed in /etc/shells
ServerName	Defines the server name shown as part of the login greeting
ServerType	Specifies whether ProFTPD runs as a daemon in standalone mode or as an inetd (or xinetd) service
ShowSymlinks	Enables the display of symbolic links in the FTP directory tree
TimeoutIdle	Defines the amount of time, in seconds, that clients can receive no data before the session will be closed
TimeoutNoTransfer	Sets the amount of time, in seconds, a client can be connected without receiving (or sending, if uploads are permitted) a file transfer or directory listing before the session will be closed
TimeoutStalled	Specifies the amount of time, in seconds, a transfer can be stalled (a data connection exists, but no data is transferred) before the session will be closed
User	Identifies the username under which the server daemon runs
UserAlias	Creates an alias from a ProFTPD username to a system username

Although most of these options are self-explanatory, a few require additional explanation. ServerType can be either standalone or inetd, which you might expect. The subtlety in this case is that inetd can refer to an FTP server that is run by inetd *or* by xinetd.

DeferWelcome is one of many directives that provide a measure of security. When set to on, no information identifying the server is displayed to connecting clients until (or unless) they successfully authenticate. The rationale behind this setting is to show as little server identification information as possible to incoming clients to deter, or at least make more difficult, subsequent attempts to attack the server. Setting this option to off causes ProFTPD to display the standard greeting banner.

There are two more security-related directives in Table 16-2, MaxInstances and RequireValidShell. MaxInstances specifies the maximum number of ProFTPD processes that can execute simultaneously. MaxInstances is one defense against DoS attacks that attempt to swamp the FTP server with active connections.

Obviously, `MaxInstances` also serves to limit the FTP server's resource consumption. `RequireValidShell` simply requires users logging in to the system to have a valid shell, that is, a shell listed in `/etc/shells`. If set to `on` and a user's shell is not listed in `/etc/shells`, the user will be denied permission to log in; if set to `off`, a valid login shell is not required.

The `DefaultServer` directive determines the server to which incoming connections are routed. If the requested FTP server is unknown — that is, the IP address is neither the FTP server's primary IP address nor an IP address specified in a `<VirtualHost>` `</VirtualHost>` block — and `DefaultServer` is set to `on`, requests for unknown servers are routed to the default server. Only a single server configuration can be set as the default configuration.

`UserAlias` simply creates an alias from a name used by ProFTPD to a username in `/etc/passwd`. This allows the ProFTPD name to be treated as though it were a valid system name. The complete syntax is

```
UserAlias fake_name system_name
```

Replace `fake_name` with the alias you want to use (`anonymous` in Listing 16-1), and replace `system_name` with the name of a valid user listed in `/etc/passwd` (`ftp` in Listing 16-1). So `UserAlias anonymous ftp` allows clients to use either the login name `anonymous` or the login name `ftp` when connecting to your FTP server to use anonymous FTP.

The directives `<Anonymous></Anonymous>`, `<Directory></Directory>`, and `<Limit></Limit>` create configuration blocks, sets of configuration entries that apply to one server or directory or that set security policy for sets of commands. They are some of ProFTPD's directives and are discussed in the next section, "Advanced ProFTPD configuration," in greater detail. For purposes of this discussion, and to pique your curiosity, `<Anonymous></Anonymous>` makes it possible to create multiple anonymous FTP servers, `<Directory></Directory>` specifies per-directory access and privilege settings (in much the same way that Apache handles per-directory configurations), and `<Limit></Limit>` defines actions or commands that are subject to some type of control or limitation.

Without going into greater detail, the first directory configuration block applies to the FTP server's entire directory tree:

```
<Directory /*>
   Umask               022  022
   AllowOverwrite      on
</Directory>
```

The `Umask` directive sets the default umask applied to files and directories. A umask of 022 prevents new files and directories from being world or group writable. The second directive in the global block, `AllowOverwrite on`, allows uploaded files to overwrite existing ones. Frankly, this is a significant security risk and should be changed to `AllowOverwrite off`.

The `<Anonymous></Anonymous>` block configures an anonymous FTP server that is rooted at, in this case, `/home/ftp`. The configuration directives inside this block apply to only the `/home/ftp` root directory and its subdirectories and to only the anonymous FTP account named ftp (and aliased, as you can see, to the ProFTPD username `anonymous`). In case it isn't clear, this method of creating anonymous FTP servers makes its possible, and trivial, to create additional anonymous FTP servers by specifying a different root directory and a different `User`. Thus, you can set up multiple anonymous FTP servers that have different characteristics.

The anonymous FTP server configured in Listing 16-1 (notice that it is commented out, and so disabled) is configured as follows:

✦ It supports a maximum of 10 simultaneously connected clients (`MaxClients 10`).

✦ It does not use `RequireValidShell` (the `ftp` user does not have a shell listed in `/etc/passwd`).

✦ It displays the contents of the file `.message` the first time a user enters a new directory (`DisplayFirstChdir .message`).

✦ It displays the contents of the file `welcome.msg` after the `ftp` (or `anonymous`) user successfully authenticates (`DisplayLogin welcome.msg`).

✦ It denies all FTP protocol `WRITE` commands (`Limit WRITE`) to all users (`DenyAll`) for all directories in the tree (`Directory *`), effectively preventing anonymous uploads.

Advanced ProFTPD configuration

The list of ProFTPD configuration directives in Table 16-2 should make clear that ProFTPD has lots of knobs and dials you can use to configure its behavior. For example, you can heavily customize the user experience, that is, the messages users see when they log in to the server and navigate the directory tree, and you can control the manner in which information about the files residing on the server is presented. ProFTPD's per-directory configuration permits you to allow actions in one directory tree that you would otherwise disallow in other directory trees, such as deleting files or changing filenames. Using the `<Virtual>` directive permits you to create one or more virtual FTP servers that reside on the same physical server, which makes it trivial to use your Debian GNU/Linux system as an FTP hosting server (in much the same way that you can configure Apache to run multiple Web sites on the same physical system using Apache's virtual host capabilities).

Customizing the user experience

The configuration directives discussed in this section allow you to control the banners and messages that users see when they log in to the server and navigate the directory tree, and they also enable you to configure how directory and file listings are displayed. Table 16-3 lists the directives this section describes.

Table 16-3
ProFTPD Directives Controlling Banners, Messages, and Listings

Directive	Description
AccessDenyMsg "msg"	Defines msg as the string displayed when login authentication fails
AccessGrantMsg "msg"	Defines msg as the string displayed when login authentication succeeds
DirFakeGroup On|Off [name]	Controls the display of group ownership in directory listings
DirFakeUser On|Off [name]	Controls the display of user ownership in directory listings
DisplayConnect file	Defines the file to display after users connect to the server but before they log in
DisplayFirstChdir file	Defines the file to display when users first enter a directory
DisplayGoAway file	Defines the file to display when connections to the server are rejected
DisplayLogin file	Defines the file to display when users first log in to the server
DisplayQuit file	Defines the file to display when users disconnect from the server
ListOptions ["opts"] ["strict"]	Specifies the options used to display directory listings
ServerIdent Off|On [string]	Defines the server identification string shown when users connect
ShowSymlinks	Specifies whether to show symbolic links in directory listings
UseGlobbing On|Off	Enables the server to support wildcard characters for file and directory operations

In Table 16-3, arguments separated by the pipe character (|) indicate that one of the options *must* be used if the directive is used. Directive arguments enclosed in brackets ([ ]) indicate optional arguments that can be omitted.

The `AccessDenyMsg` and `AccessGrantMsg` work for both anonymous and authenticated access. The message string should be surrounded by double quotes. These messages are displayed after a connection is initiated (that is, after the banner message controlled by `DisplayConnect` is displayed). Both `AccessDenyMsg` and `AccessGrantMsg` support a variable, %u, that is replaced by the username used during the authentication attempt. The following list shows example authentication message directives:

```
AccessDenyMsg "Bummer! Access for %u is denied. :-("
AccessGrantMsg "Dude! Access for %u is granted."
```

The %u variable is one example of a *magic cookie*, tokens that are replaced with other text when displayed. Using magic cookies is a powerful way to give your FTP server a customized appearance. ProFTPD supports magic cookies in a number of directives, but not all of them, and some directives support only a limited subset of magic cookies. For complete details, refer to the `proftpd.conf` Manpage (`man proftpd.conf`). The following list shows the magic cookies that ProFTPD supports:

✦ %C — Current working directory

✦ %E — Server administrator's e-mail address

✦ %F — Amount of filesystem space available, in bytes

✦ %f — Amount of filesystem space available, with units

✦ %I — Number of files uploaded

✦ %L — Local hostname

✦ %M — Maximum number of connections permitted

✦ %N — Current number of connections

✦ %o — Number of files downloaded

✦ %R — Remote (connecting) hostname

✦ %T — Current time

✦ %t — Number of files uploaded and downloaded

✦ %U — Username used to log in

✦ %u — Username as reported by the IDENT protocol

✦ %V — Name of the virtual host (if any)

✦ %x — Name of the user's class

✦ %y — Current number of connections from the user's class

✦ %z — Maximum number of connections from the user's class

The various `Display*` directives are easy enough to understand. Bear in mind, though, that *file* can be specified using a relative path or an absolute path. If you use a relative path, such as

```
DisplayConnect welcome.txt
```

ProFTPD looks for `welcome.txt` relative to the home directory of the username under which it is running. In the default Debian configuration, ProFTPD runs as `nobody`, so the complete path would be `/home/welcome.txt` because the user `nobody`'s home directory is listed as `/home` in `/etc/passwd`. However, the anonymous FTP user, `ftp`, has a home directory of `/home/ftp`. This is a potential source of confusion, so it is far simpler and easier to understand if you specify absolute paths for the message files. Thus, the `DisplayConnect` directive might be

```
DisplayConnect /home/ftp/welcome.txt
```

The `ServerIdent` directive controls the server identification string shown after a connection starts (and after the file specified by `DisplayConnect`, if any) and before authentication. If set to `On` and *string* is not specified, the default is to display the message `ProFTPD` *version* `Server (`*server_name*`) [`*host_name*`]`, for example, `ProFTPD 1.2.5rc1 Server (Debian) [luther.kurtwerks.com]`. To suppress any sort of server identification, use the following directive:

```
ServerIdent On ""
```

Suppressing all server identification is one way administrators attempt to limit disseminating information that might be used to compromise the server. In this case, though, the effort is nearly futile because a person is already logged in to your system, albeit as an unprivileged user with limited access.

The file specified for `DisplayFirstChdir`, however, should always be a relative path, because the named file is looked for in the directory to which the user is logging in. The following directives show some example `Display*` directives:

```
DisplayConnect /home/ftp/.connect.txt
DisplayFirstChdir .message
DisplayGoAway /home/ftp/.goaway.txt
DisplayLogin /home/ftp/.login.txt
DisplayQuit /home/ftp/.quit.txt
```

The idea behind `DirFakeGroup` and `DirFakeUser` is to control the ownership and permission information displayed when users use the `ls` command (which corresponds to the `LIST`, `NLIST`, and `STAT` commands in the FTP protocol). If `DirFakeGroup` or `DirFakeUser` is simply turned on (`DirFakeGroup On` or `DirFakeUser On`), the group or user ownership that is displayed will be `ftp`. If *name* is also specified, the group or user owner displayed will be *name*. You can use the tilde character (~) to cause the displayed owner to be the current user.

These changes are strictly cosmetic, though. That is, these two directives affect only the displayed ownership. The actual ownership is not affected. A somewhat whimsical example might be the following:

```
DirFakeGroup On pyle
DirFakeUser On gomer
```

The following code shows an FTP session that uses all of the directives just discussed:

```
$ ftp localhost
Connected to localhost.
220
Name (localhost:kurt): bubba
331 Password required for bubba.
Password:
530 Bummer! Access for bubba is denied. :-(
Login failed.
ftp> user ftp kurt@localhost
331 Anonymous login ok, send your complete email address as
 your password.
230 Anonymous access granted, restrictions apply.
Remote system type is UNIX.
Using binary mode to transfer files.
ftp> cd /pub
250-Files in this directory:
250-    big.tar.gz - a medium-sized tarball
250-    little.tar.gz - a diminutive tarball
250-
250 CWD command successful.
ftp> ls
200 PORT command successful.
150 Opening ASCII mode data connection for file list.
-rw-r--r--   1 gomer     pyle           751616 Aug  8 21:58 big.
tar.gz
-rw-r--r--   1 gomer     pyle             8347 Aug  8 21:58 litt
le.tar.gz
226-Transfer complete.
226 Quotas off
ftp> close
221
ftp> bye
```

The output wraps in several places due to page width restrictions of this book. When the user named bubba attempted to log in, the attempt failed and the AccessDenyMsg was displayed. Because the anonymous user is treated specially, the successful login does not trigger display of the AccessGrantMsg. If a normal user with an account on the system had logged in, the output would have looked like the following:

```
Name (localhost:kurt): kurt
331 Password required for kurt
Password:
230 Dude! Access for kurt is granted.
```

Upon entering the `pub` directory, ProFTPD displayed the contents of a file named `.message`, which listed the contents of the directory. Notice how the `ls` command showed `gomer` and `pyle` as the user and group names for the two files in the directory.

Using per-directory configurations

As noted in the previous section, ProFTPD supports Apache-style per-directory configuration, which makes it possible to create an FTP server with tightly controlled access, depending on who is logging in and the directory in which they are working. The key directive that makes this possible is, not surprisingly, `<Directory>`. All configuration statements in a directory block apply to only the named directory and its subdirectories. For example, suppose you have the following directory block:

```
<Directory ~/ftp>
  HideNoAccess On
  <Limit WRITE>
    AllowAll
  </Limit>
</Directory>
```

This configuration applies to all users with system accounts that have subdirectories named `ftp` at the top level of their home directories (`/home/kurt/ftp`, for example). The `HideNoAccess On` statement prevents logged-in users from listing files and directories in this directory tree to which they do not have access. The `<Limit WRITE>` block allows logged-in users to upload files to this directory tree, provided they have write permission based on their login name and normal Linux file and directory permissions.

Creating a virtual FTP server

A virtual FTP server is trivial to set up using ProFTPD, but it requires some help from Linux to do so. You have to configure your Debian system to handle multiple IP addresses, such as using IP aliasing or, of course, via additional Ethernet interface cards. After you have the host IP address issues worked out, use ProFTPD's `VirtualHost` directive to configure a virtual FTP server on the additional IP address.

Consider the following example:

```
<VirtualHost 192.168.0.40>
  ServerName "PossumHoller"
  ServerIdent On "PossumHoller Virtual FTP Server"
  DefaultRoot /home/ftp/pub/possumholler
</VirtualServer>
```

This block of directives creates a virtual FTP server on the IP address 192.168.0.40 (you can also use hostnames if they resolve to valid IP addresses). The server's name is `PossumHoller` and the identification string displayed immediately before login is `PossumHoller Virtual FTP Server`. The `DefaultRoot` statement causes all users connecting to this server to be jailed (chrooted) into the directory `/home/ftp/pub/possumholler`. No one can use the `cd` (or `cdup`) commands to navigate higher in the directory tree; from the user's point of view, the root directory is `/`, not `/home/ftp/pub/possumholler`.

Within a `VirtualHost` block, you can add any sort of configuration directive that suits your needs. All directives in that block will apply to only the specified host or IP address and override like-named directives inherited from the enclosing context (that is, from ProFTPD's default server configuration). It is even possible to create an additional anonymous FTP account for the virtual host. A virtual host is, in general, regarded as a separate entity from the default FTP server and from other virtual hosts.

This section has hardly scratched the surface of ProFTPD's capabilities. It just isn't possible to cover all 256 configuration directives in this chapter, but you should have a sense of the possibilities. The manual page for ProFTPD's configuration file (`man proftpd.conf`) is very well written, and the example configuration files provided with the package should give you additional ideas for configuring and tweaking the server.

Using Secure FTP

As remarked earlier in the chapter, authenticated or nonanonymous FTP is fundamentally insecure because it is a clear text protocol; authentication information is passed unencrypted, making it trivial to snoop and intercept. This section shows you how to set up secure FTP services. For the purposes of this section, *secure* means that the FTP session is encrypted, which makes it harder to pull username and password information out of the packets transmitted across a network connection. There are several ways to arrange for secure FTP. This section goes over the most straightforward way using the secure FTP subsystem in the SSH suite.

Using SSH's sftp-server

`sftp-server` is a program that is part of the SSH (Secure Shell) suite of client and server programs. It provides the server portion of the FTP protocol; it is not invoked directly but is called by the SSH daemon, `sshd`. There is little to configure on the server side for secure FTP. Of course, you need to have the `ssh` package installed. In most Debian installations, it is part of the base installation, but on the off chance that you did not install it, the following `apt-get` command should do the trick:

```
# apt-get install ssh
```

Cross-Reference   See Chapter 18 on "Remote Access" for an in-depth discussion of SSH and other ways to transfer files securely to and from remote machines.

After SSH is installed, make sure the following line appears in `/etc/ssh/sshd_config`:

```
Subsystem          sftp     /usr/lib/sftp-server
```

This directive tells `sshd` to execute the program `/usr/lib/sftp-server` to service the SFTP subsystem. Again, this entry should be part of the stock installation, but if it isn't, add it to the configuration file and then restart the SSH daemon using the following command:

```
# /etc/init.d/ssh restart
```

From the client's perspective, very little changes. The client command to execute is `sftp` rather than `ftp`, and the set of support commands is slightly different from the standard FTP commands. One important difference is that `sftp` does not support anonymous FTP; users will always be prompted to provide a password. However, this should not be a problem, because you can configure ProFTPD to provide only anonymous FTP and then use SFTP to provide secure, authenticated FTP service for users that have valid accounts on the system. The two services can exist side by side.

Summary

FTP services are one of the Internet's most fundamental services, and most administrators running Internet servers eventually find it useful, if not necessary, to set up an FTP server. Given the importance of FTP, it should come as no surprise that software developers and Linux distribution builders have gone to the trouble to ensure that FTP servers are easy to install, relatively uncomplicated to configure, and reasonably secure. vsftpd requires a little more work than ProFTPD to configure, but the small amount of postinstallation configuration you have to do is more than balanced out by its simple configuration and first-class performance. ProFTPD, conversely, provides administrators with much more flexibility in creating and configuring FTP servers, but the tradeoff for this flexibility is the proportionately greater number of knobs to turn. Given that FTP is inherently insecure because it is a clear text protocol, SFTP is growing in popularity. Its greater security is well worth the added aggravation of having to learn still more configuration directives.

✦   ✦   ✦

The Domain Name System

In this chapter, you take a look at how to set up a Domain Name System (DNS) server and how to set up the Berkeley Internet Name Domain (BIND) for your Debian system. You will need BIND installed on Debian to run a DNS server.

Think of a DNS server as a telephone book of devices that are connected to the network. Each device on the network has a unique Internet Protocol (IP) address much like a telephone number. This is true regardless of whether the network is an intranet within your organization or the Internet.

Unfortunately, IP addresses aren't easy to remember because an IP address seems to be a meaningless series of numbers, such as 192.168.100.10.

Because of DNS, few of us need to remember an IP address. Generally, network-accessible machines are assigned a unique hostname in addition to being assigned an IP address. A host-name is easier to remember than an IP address. A hostname can be any name, although most conform to a widely accepted style such as www.mycompany.com for a Web server or mail.mycompany.com for a mail server. A DNS server associates a hostname with an IP address.

Each time that you need to communicate with a machine on a network, you need to refer to the machine's IP address. For example, if you want to access a page of a Web site, you'll need the IP address of the Web server that hosts the Web site in order to retrieve the page.

This is similar to if you wanted to call your friend Bob Jones on the telephone. You would need to know Bob Jones's telephone number in order to make the call. If you don't remember Bob Jones's phone number, you would look up the name "Bob Jones" in your personal telephone directory, where you'll find Bob Jones's telephone number listed alongside his name.

This same basic process occurs when accessing a machine on the Internet. However, instead of looking up the IP number of the machine, you simply reference the hostname in the software that you use to communicate with the machine, such as a browser. The software then looks up the hostname in files on the DNS server and retrieves the IP address that is associated with the hostname. The IP address is then used to communicate with the machine.

DNS and BIND

DNS is a system for naming domains; it is a convention used to convert a hostname to an IP address and an IP address to a hostname. The DNS is implemented in Debian by using Berkeley Internet Name Domain (BIND). BIND consists of software used to set up and manage DNS on a Debian-based server.

As you'll learn later in this chapter, you need to create and modify the following three kinds of files to install DNS:

- ✦ `named.conf` — This is the main configuration file for BIND, and it is created during the Debian installation process. Although the default configuration settings are adequate for many installations, you need to modify the `named.conf` file to reflect zone files for each hostname/IP relationship that is used in the DNS for your network. This modification tells the DNS that a relationship exists between a hostname and an IP address. (You learn how to do this later in the chapter.)

- ✦ Zone files — A domain is something like `mycompany.com` or `columbia.edu`. Within a domain, there are hostnames such as `www`, `mail`, and `dns` that identify a type of network service, which is located on a server. For example, `www` is a Web server, `mail` is an e-mail server, and `dns` is the server that contains the DNS files. Each domain can have many hostnames, and each hostname is associated with an IP address of the machine that hosts the hostname. This means that `www.mycompany.com` is a hostname that is associated with an IP address of a Web server that hosts Web files for the domain `mycompany.com`.

  For each domain on your network, you must create two zone files. One zone file relates hostnames to IP addresses. This lets the system use a hostname (such as `mail.mycompany.com`) to look up the IP address of the machine that hosts the service. The other zone file relates IP addresses to hostnames. This enables the system to use an IP address to look up a hostname that is hosted by the machine assigned to the IP address. (You'll learn how to create both types of zone files later in this chapter.)

- ✦ `resolv.conf` — The `resolv.conf` file contains instructions for your system to use DNS to retrieve IP addresses and hostnames. As you'll see later in this chapter, these are very basic instructions; they simply tell Debian the domain name and IP addresses of machines that host the primary and secondary DNS.

Primary and secondary DNS servers

Networks typically have multiple DNS servers. The first, or *primary*, DNS is referenced to resolve a hostname to the corresponding IP address. A *secondary* DNS server is referenced if the primary DNS server is unavailable, and a *tertiary* DNS server is referenced if the secondary is unavailable.

Think of secondary and tertiary DNS servers as a copy of the same telephone book. If you can't access the first telephone book because someone else is using it or you can't reach it or get to it, you will use another copy of the telephone book.

It's best to set up at least a primary and secondary DNS server, as this enables you to keep hostname referencing operational should the primary DNS server go offline. Furthermore, this architecture enables you to keep the network running while you maintain the primary DNS server.

IP Address Refresher

A large network is organized into smaller networks in order to efficiently transport information between devices that are connected to the network. Each smaller network is a segment of a larger network and is called a subnet. Devices that connect to a network actually connect to a subnet.

Each device that is connected to a subnet is uniquely identified by an IP address. An IP address is a 32-bit number that is split into four decimal numbers each representing 8 bits such as 192.168.100.10. This is referred to as the dotted quad notation.

Each of the four decimal numbers represents either a network address or a local address. A network address is an address of the segment of the larger network (subnet), and the local address is the address of the device that is connected to the subnet.

Whether the decimal number represents a network address or a local address depends on the class of the IP address. There are four IP address classes, each representing one of the four types of networks. These are Class A (large networks), Class B (medium-size networks), Class C (small networks), and Class D (multicast networks).

In a Class-A IP address, the first number represents a network address and the last three numbers represent a local address. In a Class-B IP address, the first two numbers are the network address and the last two numbers are the local address. In a Class-C IP address, the first three numbers are the network address and the last number is the local address. And in a Class-D IP address, all the numbers represent the network address.

IP addresses are assigned either statically or dynamically. A static IP address is an address that is assigned to a device by the network administrator. A dynamic IP address is automatically assigned from a pool of IP addresses when a device connects to the network.

For large corporate networks that provide the highway for many mission-critical applications, and networks that must be fully operational 24/7, consider setting up a tertiary DNS server. The tertiary DNS server gives you a third level of protection should the primary and secondary DNS servers fail.

Surveying your network

You need to develop a DNS server file before you set up a DNS server. A DNS file lists the hostname for each network device and its corresponding IP address. Think of the DNS file as pages of the telephone book.

Survey the network and identify each machine that is connected to the network. All those machines have an IP address. Many of them also have a hostname, although some may not because an operator rarely directly accesses them.

Create a three-column table that you can use to list these machines. The first column should contain the machine's hostname. The second column should contain the machine's IP address. The third column should contain general comments, such as the machine's function and its physical location.

For the examples in this chapter, I use a small network that contains four network devices, all of which are servers. The first server is `www.mycompany.com`, which is a Web server that hosts a company's Web sites. The second sever is `mail.mycompany.com`, which is a company's mail server. The last two servers are `dns.mycompany.com` and `dns2.mycompany.com`, which are the primary and secondary domain servers for the company. The network setup is illustrated in Figure 17-1.

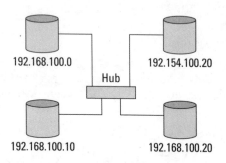

Figure 17-1: The sample network consists of four servers that are connected together through a network hub.

www.mycompany.com	192.168.100.0
mail.mycompany.com	192.154.100.20
dns.mycompany.com	192.168.100.10
dns2.mycompany.com	192.168.100.20

Table 17-1 contains detailed information about the example machines on the network.

Table 17-1 Survey of Machines on the Network		
Hostname	*IP Address*	*Comment*
www.mycompany.com	192.168.100.0	Web server, eighth-floor server room
mail.mycompany.com	192.154.100.20	Mail server, eighth-floor server room
dns.mycompany.com	192.168.100.10	Primary DNS server, seventh-floor server room

Installing BIND

Now that you have a good idea of what you need to do, it's time to get started with the BIND installation. There are two files that you must install and several other files that are optional. I suggest that you install both the required and optional files.

The best way to install these files is to use apt-get. Use the following command to install the files:

```
# apt-get install bind9 dnsutils bind9-doc bind9-host
```

Note The 9 in bind9 refers to the version of BIND. As you might expect, a lower number signifies previous versions. Use bind9 because this is the latest version.

During the installation of BIND, you will be prompted to answer several questions. You can accept the default values by pressing the Enter key. The default settings are sufficient for most setups. However, there are a few default settings that you might want to alter.

The first of these is Forwarder Hosts. A *forwarder host* is an outside server that can respond to DNS queries. It is advantageous to use forwarder hosts in a large network to distribute queries in an effort to maintain adequate response times. You won't need forwarder hosts in small networks or networks where there isn't heavy traffic.

Another question you'll be prompted to answer is the question regarding Localhost Entries. You can have BIND contain entries for the localhost by typing Y. By responding with N, the localhost will not be contained in BIND. We suggest that you answer Y and include the localhost in BIND.

Creating zone files

You'll need to create two files called zone files. A *zone file* is a database file that contains information about hostnames and related IP addresses. The first file is for your domain name information and the other is for your network information. The domain zone file contains hostnames and corresponding IP addresses. The subnet zone file contains IP addresses and corresponding hostnames. Think of the domain file as the traditional telephone book, and the zone network file as a reverse telephone book (that is, you look up a telephone number to find the person associated with the telephone number).

Creating the domain zone file

Begin by creating the zone file for your domain, which is mycompany.com. Create the following file called mycompany.db in your /var/named directory.

```
; BIND data file for mycompany.db
; /var/named/mycompany.db
;
@ IN SOA mycompany.com. root.mycompany.com. (
  2005100801; Serial (date + two digit serial)
  10800 ; Refresh (3 hours)
  3600 ; Retry (1 hour)
  86400 ; Expire (1 day)
  3600 ) ; Default TTL  1 hours
  IN NS dns.mycompany.com.
  IN MX 10 mail.mycompany.com.
  www  IN A 192.168.100.5
  mail IN A 192.168.100.20

  dns IN A 192.168.100.10
  dns2 IN A 192.168.100.20
```

The first few lines of mycompany.db identify the file as being BIND data for mycompany.com and give the location of the file. The SOA line identifies your zone, which is mycompany.com, and also identifies who is responsible for the zone, which is root.mycompany.com. (Writing root.mycompany.com has the same effect as writing root@mycompany.com.) The first number in the SOA line is the serial number for the file, and it references the date the file was created. This states that the file was created October 8, 2005, and it is the first (01) version created that day.

Caution   It's important to increase the serial number of the zone file each time that the zone file is changed in order to identify the version of the zone file. This seems obvious, but some developers simply modify the zone file without changing the serial number. This could result in two or more zone files having the same serial number but different content.

Below the serial number are lines that specify the refresh period, retry period, the expiration of the zone information, and the default time to live (TTL). These values are given in seconds.

The next few lines that begin with `IN` are referring to `mycompany.com` without any prefix. The `NS` line identifies the primary DNS, which is `dns.mycompany.com`. The `MX` line identifies the mail server. You'll notice that there is a `10` in front of the mail server. The `10` expresses a priority. Although we use only one mail server in this example, you can have multiple mail servers each having a different priority value. The mail server with the lowest priority value is used first. If this fails, the mail server with the next lowest priority is used.

Note   Make sure that you place a period at the end of each `IN` statement, otherwise an error will occur. This is very easily overlooked.

The remaining lines identify the specific machines on the network and their corresponding IP addresses. When matching names to IP addresses, you use what are called "A" records, as you can see from the `A` in the middle of the line. Include as many lines as needed for your network. This example illustrates the machines included in Table 17-1.

Creating the reverse zone file

Next, you need to create a reverse zone file. A reverse zone file is a reverse of the domain zone file, in that the focus is on the IP addresses rather than on the hostnames. The name of the file must be the IP address subnet of the network. The subnet is the first three sets of numbers in the IP address. In our sample network, the subnet is 192.168.100.

The first few lines of the reverse zone file are similar to the first few lines of the domain zone file. Subsequent lines identify the segment of the IP address that uniquely identifies each machine on the network. For example, `10` is referenced as `192.168.100.10` and is associated with the hostname `www.mycompany.com`. The reverse zone file can then be used to look up an IP address to determine the hostname that is associated with the IP address.

```
; BIND reverse data file for 192.168.100.0
; /var/named/192.168.100.db
;
@ IN SOA mycompany.com. root.mycompany.com. (
  2005100801;
  10800 ;
  3600 ;
  86400 ;
  3600 ) ;
  IN NS dns.mycompany.com.
  10 IN PTR www.mycompany.com.
  20 IN PTR mail.mycompany.com.
  30 IN PTR dns.mycompany.com.
  40 IN PTR dns2.mycompany.com.
```

Once the zone files are created, you need to update the BIND configuration file with the new domain. The BIND configuration file is /etc/named.conf, which can be directly edited using any text editor.

The named.conf file is the main configuration file for BIND and is created automatically during the Debian installation process. The following code shows what the named.conf file looks like after installation and before you update it with information about your new domain:

```
options {
    directory "/var/named";
};
// Name server boot file
zone "." {
    type hint;
    file "named.root";
};
zone "localhost" {
    type master;
    file "named.local";
};
zone "127.in-addr.arpa" {
    type master;
    file "named.rev-local";
};
```

Enter the following zone references to the bottom of the named.conf file. The first reference is to the domain file and the second reference is to the reverse file.

```
zone "mycompany.com" {
    type master;
    file "mycompany.db";
};
```

```
zone "100.168.192.in-addr.arpa" {
   type master;
   file "192.168.100.rev";
};
```

The type of each zone file can be either master or slave. A *master* type is used when the DNS does not rely on other servers for information about the domain. If the DNS depends on another server, then the type must be changed from master to slave. This requires a *zone transfer* from a master DNS server in order to provide information about a domain. Most times, the DNS server will not depend on another server; therefore, it is best to set the type as master.

Think of a zone transfer as referencing another server when there is a need to relate a hostname with an IP address. The other server has the zone file that is necessary to resolve a hostname with an IP address and vice versa.

Here's what the /var/named.conf file should look like after you update it with the domains from the example in this chapter:

```
options {
   directory "/var/named";
};
// Name server boot file
zone "." {
   type hint;
   file "named.root";
};
zone "localhost" {
   type master;
   file "named.local";
};
zone "127.in-addr.arpa" {
   type master;
   file "named.rev local";
};
zone "mycompany.com" {
   type master;
   file "mycompany.db";
};
zone "100.168.192.in-addr.arpa" {
   type master;
   file "192.168.100.rev";
};
```

Plugging security holes
Information contained in zone files is the roadmap to machines on your network. To protect the security and integrity of your system, this information should

be accessed on a need-to-know basis, such as when resolving a hostname or an IP address.

Let's say a server has a hostname and needs the IP address that is associated with the hostname. The first step is to run `host`, passing it the hostname. Next, the `named.conf` file is accessed to learn the identity of the zone file that contains the hostname. The last step is to search the zone file of the hostname and then return the IP address that corresponds to the hostname. The same basic process is followed when using an IP address to look up the hostname that is associated with the IP address.

You don't want to give anyone unbridled access to a zone file because that gives the hostnames and IP addresses for everything on your network.

By default, nothing prevents access to the zone file. However, you can limit who can set restrictions by inserting the following line in the options section of the `named.conf` file:

```
allow-transfer "192.168.100.60";
```

This line should specify the IP address of the device that can access the zone file and therefore have complete access to the contents of that file. You can have multiple allow-transfer lines as is necessary for your network.

Devices whose IP addresses are not listed in an `allow-transfer` line can still resolve a hostname or an IP address, but the device cannot transfer the entire contents of the zone file.

Here's how the `named.conf` file looks once you use the allow-transfer line to plug the security hole:

```
options {
    directory "/var/named";
    allow-transfer "192.168.100.60";
};
// Name server boot file
zone "." {
    type hint;
    file "named.root";
};
zone "localhost" {
    type master;
    file "named.local";
};
zone "127.in-addr.arpa" {
    type master;
    file "named.rev-local";
};
```

```
zone "mycompany.com" {
  type master;
  file "mycompany.db";
};
zone "100.168.192.in-addr.arpa" {
  type master;
  file "192.168.100.rev";
};
```

Allowing recursion

It is best to restrict multiple access to zone files to prevent someone from freely searching the file. A good way to do this is to set the `allow-recursion` option to the IP address of the device that can freely access the zone files.

You do this by inserting the `allow-recursion` option attribute within the options section of the `named.config` file and then associating the IP address(es) of the device that can access the zone files recursively, as shown here:

```
options {
    directory "/var/named";
    allow-transfer "192.168.100.60";
    allow-recursion "192.168.100.60";
};
```

Reloading configuration

The final step after modifying the `named.conf` file or any of the zone files is to reload the file into memory. Each time you start your primary server, the `named.conf` file along with other files are loaded into memory. Changes made to the `named.conf` file and the zone files take effect only if you restart your primary server or reload the `named.conf` file into memory.

Note   Whenever you modify the `named.conf` file or any zone files, you need to increase the serial number of the file in order to distinguish the file from previous versions.

You reload the `named.conf` file by calling the following program at the command prompt:

```
/etc/init.d/bind reload
```

The secondary DNS server

Previously in this chapter I explained that many networks have more than one DNS server. The primary DNS server is the first DNS server accessed to resolve host-name and IP addresses. If the primary DNS server is unavailable due to heavy demand or the server is off-line, the secondary DNS server is used to resolve host-name and IP addresses.

You must set up a secondary and subsequent DNS server in order for those servers to be available to machines on the Net. You do this by modifying entries in the zone files and the `named.conf` file. You also need to install `bind` on this server (see the "Installing BIND" section earlier in the chapter).

Begin by editing the `mycompany.db` file that you created previously. Insert a reference to the `dns2` below the `dns.mycompany.com` line in the file, as shown here:

```
; BIND data file for mycompany.db
; /var/named/mycompany.db
;
@ IN SOA mycompany.com. root.mycompany.com. (
  2005100801;
    10800 ;
    3600 ;
    86400 ;
    3600 ) ;
  IN NS dns.mycompany.com.
  IN NS dns2.mycompany.com.
  IN MX 10 mail.mycompany.com.
  www IN A 192.168.100.5
  mail IN A 192.168.100.20
  dns  IN A 192.168.100.30
  dns2 IN A 192.168.100.40
```

Next, modify the `192.168.100.db` file to include the secondary DNS server. You do this by placing a new line containing `dns2.mycompany.com` below the `dns.mycompany.com` line as shown here:

```
; BIND reverse data file for 192.168.100.0
; /var/named/192.168.100.db
;
@ IN SOA mycompany.com. root.mycompany.com. (
  2005100801;
  10800 ;
  3600 ;
  86400 ;
  3600 ) ;
  IN NS dns.mycompany.com.
  IN NS dns2.mycompany.com.
  10 IN PTR www.mycompany.com.
  20 IN PTR mail.mycompany.com.
  30 IN PTR dns.mycompany.com.
  40 IN PTR dns2.mycompany.com.
```

Next, you need to modify the `named.conf` file to include the secondary DNS server. There are three modifications that you need to make to identify the secondary DNS server in each of the zone files as slaves. You also need to enable the secondary DNS server to zone transfer files.

 Note   It's important to remember that the slave definitions are in the secondary DNS server's `named.conf` file. The master entries remain in the primary DNS server's `named.conf` file.

Start by inserting the following lines at the end of the `named.conf` file on the secondary DNS server. These identify the secondary DNS server as a slave to the primary DNS server. They also state that zone information must be acquired from the primary DNS server at 192.168.100.30.

```
zone "mycompany.com" {
    type slave;
    file "mycompany.db";
    masters {
        192.168.100.30;
    };
};

zone "100.168.192.in-addr.arpa" {
    type slave;
    file "192.168.100.db";
    masters {
      192.168.100.30;
    };
};
```

The final step is to give the secondary DNS server rights to zone transfer. You do this by inserting the following line under the `options` section of `named/conf` of the primary DNS server. The `192.168.100.40` is the IP address of the secondary DNS server (see Table 17-1).

```
allow-transfer "192.168.100.60";
```

Here is what the `named.conf` file should look like after you made modifications for the secondary DNS server:

```
options {
    directory "/var/named";
    allow-transfer "192.168.100.60";
    allow-transfer "192.168.100.40";
};
// Name server boot file
zone "." {
    type hint;
    file "named.root";
```

```
};
zone "localhost" {
   type master;
   file "named.local";
};
zone "127.in-addr.arpa" {
   type master;
   file "named.rev-local";
};
zone "mycompany.com" {
   type master;
   file "mycompany.db";
};
zone "100.168.192.in-addr.arpa" {
   type master;
   file "192.168.100.rev";
};
```

If you require additional DNS servers, you can insert references to those servers into the named.conf file in the same way as you inserted a reference to the secondary DNS server. Remember that after the named.conf file is modified, you need to either restart the primary server or reload the named.conf file.

Modifying resolv.conf

We have not yet introduced the idea of using DNS. Debian needs to know how to perform the DNS server lookup, and it learns how by following instructions in the /etc/resolv.conf file. You must modify the /etc/resolv.conf file to include instructions on how to look up the DNS server on your network.

Here is the resolv.conf file:

```
domain mycompany.com
search mycompany.com
nameserver 192.168.100.30
nameserver 192.168.100.40
```

The domain line is your domain name. The search line specifies the search pattern used to look up an IP address. This enables a DNS query to search on a partial hostname. For example, a query might be mail. The search combines mail with the search pattern mycompany.com to create the final query mail.mycompany.com.

You can include multiple hostnames for the search line, as shown in the following code. This causes the query to be combined with both search patterns. For example, mail would be combined with mail.mycompany.com and mail.yourcompany.com.

```
search mycompany.com yourcompany.com
```

The domain line and the search line are optional, although it makes sense to include them in the resolv.conf file. If you exclude the search line, the original query must be fully qualified. For example, mail must be mail.mycompany.com.

The nameserver lines contain the IP addresses of the primary, secondary, and subsequent DNS servers. The first nameserver listed is the primary DNS server, and the second nameserver is the secondary DNS server. IP addresses for subsequent DNS servers could be listed below the second nameserver line.

Testing your setup

Now it's time to make sure that DNS and BIND are working correctly. The first step is to reload BIND by executing the following command at the operating system prompt:

```
/etc/init.d/bind reload
```

Next, type the following command to look up www.mycompany.com:

```
~# host www.mycompany.com
```

You should see the following output, assuming that you used the IP address that is shown in Table 17-1. If you see this, then DNS and BIND are installed properly. If you don't see this, then review each step in this chapter to make sure that you haven't overlooked a step.

```
dns.mycompany.com
192.168.100.30
```

Maintenance

It is critical that the named.conf, resolv.conf, and zone files be updated each time a change occurs to the relationships between hostnames and IP addresses, otherwise the system won't be able to resolve hostnames. The result is that some services (such as Web pages) will be inaccessible by using the hostname. However, you still can access the machine on the network by referring to the device's IP address.

Here are some simple tasks that will help you avoid DNS problems after DNS is installed on your network:

✦ Always review the log file after reloading BIND to be sure no errors occurred. If you don't and an error occurs, then the error will affect your DNS.

✦ Maintain an inventory list of networked devices and their IP addresses outside of the DNS. Use this list as a roadmap for updating the DNS.

✦ Update the DNS *immediately* whenever a hostname or IP address is added, changed, or removed from the network. Don't postpone updating DNS.

✦ Always reload files whenever they are changed. Remember, there are two copies of each file. One copy is on disk and the other is in memory. Changes made to the file on the disk don't take effect until the file is loaded into memory. This means that you might have pointed the mail to a different IP address (mail server) by changing the related IP address in the file, but those changes don't take effect until the file is reloaded into memory.

✦ Maintain backup copies of `named.conf`, `resolv.conf`, and zone files and use them as references when modifying and restoring DNS.

Summary

In this chapter, you learned how to set up a Domain Name System (DNS) server and how to set up the Berkeley Internet Name Domain (BIND) for your Debian system. A DNS server associates a device name called a hostname with an IP address. A hostname can take any name, although most conform to a widely accepted style such as `www.mycompany.com` for a Web server and `mail.mycompany.com` for a mail server.

The DNS is implemented in Debian by using BIND. BIND consists of software used to set up and manage DNS on a Debian-based network. You need to create and modify the following three kinds of files to install DNS:

✦ `named.conf`, which is the main configuration file for BIND and is created during the installation process.

✦ Zone files, which are files that associate hostnames with IP addresses and vice versa. Two are needed for each domain.

✦ `resolv.conf`, which contains instructions for Debian on how to use the DNS to retrieve IP addresses and hostnames.

✦   ✦   ✦

Remote Access

UNIX — and GNU/Linux as a derivative — was originally designed as a multiuser operating system. While it's amusing to imagine 15 geeks fighting for space around a single keyboard, the way that multiple users manage to use a single machine is in almost all cases via remote access — whether across the room or across the world. As a result, Debian comes with a strong suite of tools for a variety of different types of remote access. With the proper knowledge of and experience with these tools, a user can work remotely to do *anything* that he could do while sitting at the computer.

Any tool that allows a computer user to access or manipulate information on a computer from a remote location can be accurately described as a remote access tool. In other chapters, this book goes into detail about a number of these tools (Web, DNS, e-mail, and so forth). This chapter focuses on tools that allow one to "use" a computer remotely in a way that is similar to, and in some cases even indistinguishable from, the way it would be used locally.

Remote access, as it is presented in this chapter, can be broken down into two major types: shell access and desktop access. *Shell access* is the type of access you can receive when you launch a terminal on your desktop or log in without the computer in X mode. In fact, accessing a remote machine via shell access is often done *from* a shell on the local machine. When you access a machine remotely, the commands that you enter in the terminal are run on the remote machine. Unless you are launching graphical applications from the shell, the experience is not only *like* running a terminal on the machine; programmatically, it is exactly equivalent. The input and output are just being directed differently.

Desktop access is easier to define and understand: It is access that gives you a picture of the desktop running on a remote machine and lets you use it, remotely, as if it was the local machine.

Over the life of UNIX, GNU/Linux, and Debian, these remote access tools have risen, fallen, and been replaced. As network and Internet security has become increasingly important, many older utilities have been deemed insecure and replaced.

This chapter gives a brief overview of the most widespread remote access tools. It then focuses its analysis on SSH, the secure replacement for many historically used tools and the modern Swiss Army knife of remote access on a GNU/Linux system.

Users setting up their computers to be accessed remotely, even with secure tools such as SSH and VNC, should always remember that allowing a computer to be accessed by its owner or administrator opens the possibility that it could be accessed remotely by others with nefarious purposes. This chapter describes steps that users can take to minimize the possibility of this, but the user must always be aware of the risk. Users should be aware that powerful remote access means that they can do anything on their computer from anywhere, but it also means that unless they are careful, anyone, anywhere, might be able to do the same.

As a word of advice, it's also worth noting that a nefarious individual who compromises one machine may be able to use that machine to attack other machines and work through a user's group of trusted machines as easily as pushing over dominoes.

Remote Access in the Past

Many users at universities, at work, or in other environments may have used the program *telnet* to connect to a computer to check e-mail or to run programs. Telnet is the venerable grandfather of remote access on UNIX and Linux, and Debian includes both server and client versions of the program — although they are not installed by default, for reasons I will explain shortly.

Telnet is a tool and a protocol for interactive shell-style communication with another machine. Users invoke the command

```
telnet host
```

to connect to a remote machine. Once connected to a remote machine, users are prompted for a username and password and are logged in to the computer and given a shell as if they had launched or logged in from a local terminal. From that prompt, they can use all of the commands they could invoke on a local machine.

Rlogin (remote login) and RSH (remote shell) are two other tools, and they are similar to telnet in many respects. Rlogin operates in a way nearly identical to telnet. Unlike telnet, RSH was designed to be a more flexible protocol for remote access that included the possibility of sending files and using other programs to access files and programs running on a remote host.

While powerful and well established, both RSH and telnet pass all the data — both the username and passwords necessary to log in to the system and the data of the connection—over the network, be it Internet or LAN, unencrypted. This means that any user along the way can simply listen to the traffic and read any sensitive information that travels back and forth and, more importantly, the username and login data that the user used to authenticate the connection. FTP, popular for sending and receiving files, suffers similar shortcomings and also passes information in a purely transparent manner. Because the login data is sent unencrypted, any nefarious interceptor can record the login information and use it to access information, wreak havoc, and invade privacy.

As a result, new tools were created to protect both login data and the remote access sessions themselves. Foremost among these is SSH, which aims to be a flexible, secure replacement for RSH.

SSH—Secure Shell

SSH's (Secure Shell) history is somewhat long and torturous. SSH was first developed as a secure replacement for RSH in the mid-'90s. While early versions of SSH were freely available, it quickly became proprietary. As a result, SSH was included in the Debian archive in a special nonfree section but was not included in Debian proper. Because it was extremely important, and basically irreplaceable, it was one of the first tools that every new Debian user installed. Developers for a proactively secure UNIX-like operating system called OpenBSD kick-started a development project to develop a freely available replacement for SSH; they called the project OpenSSH. OpenSSH was released to the world on December 1, 1999, and quickly was included in Debian, the nonfree version being removed from the archives altogether at a later point. OpenSSH is the version included in Debian and other versions of Linux and is the one described in this section.

However, by the time of OpenSSH's release, a second secure protocol, dubbed SSH2, had been built into the proprietary SSH servers and clients. SSH2 is viewed as a more cryptographically secure protocol for a number of reasons. While the original OpenSSH release supported only the first version, OpenSSH now supports both versions of the protocol. SSH2 is the default behavior, although both clients and server will default to trying the older versions if necessary. For most purposes, the different versions of SSH are interchangeable.

Getting started

Normally, an SSH connection is invoked from a terminal to a remote host by running the `ssh` command. To log in to `master.debian.org`, for example, you type the following:

```
ssh master.debian.org
```

If your computer does not have a registered DNS address, you can also connect to a machine over SSH by specifying its IP number.

By default, this command will attempt to log in to the remote system with the user-name being that of the user invoking the program. If you need to specify the user-name as something other than the name you are logged in with, you can do it with either of the following two commands:

```
ssh -l mako master.debian.org
ssh mako@master.debian.org
```

As you initiate a connection, SSH will connect to the remote machine first and create a secure tunnel. The first step of this process is a cryptographic exchange that verifies that the host you are connecting to is indeed the host you are trying to connect to. Unlike secure connections on Web pages, which rely on paid third parties to vouch for the identity, SSH connections must be verified one at a time. If you have never connected to a machine before, it will announce that the authenticity of the host being connected to cannot be established with a message like the following:

```
The authenticity of host 'master.debian.org (146.82.138.7)'
can't be established.

RSA key fingerprint is
fa:03:0e:e1:7b:52:d5:58:32:c0:39:14:05:d5:cc:97.
Are you sure you want to continue connecting (yes/no)?
```

To verify that you are not subject to someone intercepting and monitoring your connection, it's a good idea to check this fingerprint against one given to you by the administrator of the machine you are trying to connect to. If you are the administrator, you can use the command

```
ssh-keygen -l
```

to list the fingerprint on the public host key. The program will ask for the location of the key. The public host key on a Debian system is normally generated when you first install the SSH server and is located at /etc/ssh/ssh_host_rsa_key.pub.

After you have typed yes at the prompt in the previous code block, SSH will cache the key in a file in your home directory and you will never be asked to verify it again. Each time you connect to a server, it will make sure that the "host key" on the host you are connecting to matches the key given the first time you connected. You will be alerted if there are any changes that suggest either a nefarious interceptor or a careless administrator. If you need to change or remove a cached key, you can view or edit the file ~/.ssh/known_hosts.

Once your client is confident that it is connected to the server you are trying to connect to, it will create a secure tunnel. When you are prompted for your password, it passes within this secure tunnel; your connection is secure from eavesdroppers even before you authenticate. This is shown in Figure 18-1.

Figure 18-1: Shell connections and login information pass through a secure tunnel that SSH creates through the Internet to connect the two computers.

Authentication

SSH supports authentication through a handful of different methods including certificates and Kerberos. This chapter covers the two simplest methods: passwords and authentication keys.

Passwords

When you log in to a machine for the first time, SSH prompts you for your password:

```
ssh mako@master.debian.org
mako@master.debian.org's password:
```

Simply type the password for your user account on that machine and press Enter to log in to a machine.

Passwords are the simplest type of authentication because they need no additional setup. If you are using passwords to log in to different computers, it's highly recommended that you create different passwords for each computer you have an account on. It's also recommended that you do not normally use SSH from one computer through another. Often, when a machine is compromised by an attacker, the attacker will install software on the compromised machine that will listen in on all incoming and outgoing connections. Therefore, if you use machine A to connect to machine B and then connect again to machine C from machine B, your account on machine C — and the entire machine — can be compromised as soon as machine B is. If you have the same password on all three machines, a compromise on any machine will compromise all others. Connect to all machines from your workstation or workstations. When using passwords, use different passwords for different machines.

> **Note** A good password for a machine you will be accessing remotely is one that is not based on a dictionary word and that contains capital and lowercase letters, numbers, and symbols if possible. There are many pieces of software in Debian to help generate secure passwords, including pwgen, gpw, and makepasswd.

Clearly, remembering many passwords can be very difficult. If you are accessing enough machines remotely, it will be impossible. As a result, Debian includes a wide number of tools to make storing passwords in a secure way possible, including `gringotts` and `makepasswd`. They often are described with the metaphor of a password "safe."

Authentication keys

SSH includes the option to authenticate in several ways other than passwords. Once set up, using key-based authentication can be both more convenient and more secure.

Authenticating with SSH using keys is very similar to the way that SSH determines the identity of hosts using public key encryption. Using public key encryption, you generate a pair of keys. In SSH, you do this with the command

```
ssh-keygen -t rsa
```

In this example, you are using the `-t` flag to generate an RSA SSH2 key. RSA is the type of encryption key and the name of the encryption protocol into which the key fits. Other types that you can specify include DSA and RSA/SSH1 (RSA1) style keys. Because SSH2 using RSA is the default protocol, choosing the type `rsa` is a safe choice. If you want to generate a DSA key or an RSA key for SSH1 connections, simply run the command again and replace RSA where appropriate. SSH prompts for a name for the key:

```
Generating public/private rsa key pair.
Enter file in which to save the key (/home/mako/.ssh/id_rsa):
```

Press Enter to choose the default, which will be the best option unless you already have a key with that name. `ssh-keygen` will then prompt you for a passphrase to block access to the key. Pick a good passphrase that you will be able to remember and type it in. Repeat it when prompted to confirm it as your choice.

Your key will now be placed in the `.ssh` directory in your home directory. Along with the private key will be a second file with the same name followed by `.pub` (in this example, it would be `id_rsa.pub`). This is your public key. By placing this public key on servers you want to connect to, you will be able to connect based only on the possession of the corresponding private key and the passphrase necessary to unlock it.

To place your key on a server, you must connect to the remote server using your password on that machine and copy the contents of your public key file (`id_rsa.pub`) into the file `~/.ssh/authorized_keys`, creating that file and the parent directory if they do not already exist.

Because typing in your passphrase each time you connect is really no more convenient (and, if your passphrase is longer, might even be *less* convenient) than using passwords, SSH includes a set of programs to help store SSH private keys called `ssh-agent`.

The SSH agent stores keys that are added and then allows SSH to use these keys when connecting. This means that once you have added a key to the agent, you can log in to machines that have a copy of your public key installed on them without typing in your passphrase. To add your key to the `ssh-agent`, run the command

```
ssh-add
```

After your key is installed in the agent, you should be able to connect by invoking SSH as you would normally. You will notice that you are able to log in without being prompted for your passphrase or password. When you are done using SSH, you can remove the key from the agent with the command

```
ssh-add -D
```

It's always a good idea to remove keys when you are not actively using them. There is no problem with placing the same public key on multiple hosts, although you should realize that anyone who is able to gain access to the private key will have access to every machine upon which the public key has been placed.

Transferring files

While using a machine remotely is one of the most common ways of accessing machines, it's also useful to be able to move files. SSH comes with a handful of applications to make transferring files between different machines very easy and more convenient.

SCP — Secure Copy

The most commonly used tool for copying between machines over SSH is SCP (Secure Copy). SCP is similar to the `cp` command. SCP uses the same authentication methods as SSH and asks you for passphrases or passwords where appropriate, or it uses key-based authentication when a key is present or in `ssh-agent`. SCP uses the same "command source destination" syntax common in other commands such as `cp`. Remote hosts are specified in the following way:

```
user@remotehost:file
```

Remote files that do not begin with a backslash (/) are interpreted as relative to the user's home directory. To copy a file `foo` from `master.debian.org` to the current directory on my local machine (`mako`), I would type

```
scp mako@master.debian.org:foo ./
```

To copy a local file `foo` to the remote location, I reverse the order:

```
scp foo mako@master.debian.org:
```

Other applications

There are a number of other applications that use SSH for transferring files.

Just as SCP can be thought of as an SSH-enabled version of the `cp` command, SFTP is an SSH-enabled way of transferring files through an interface that is very similar to the popular FTP command. Copying files with long or complex names, or copying multiple files, can be difficult or unruly with SCP. SFTP provides an easily available way to avoid many of these problems. SFTP is part of the SSH package in Debian and should be installed on your system by default.

Cross-Reference   SFTP is discussed in some depth in Chapter 16 on "File Transfer Services."

Additionally, both KDE and GNOME include systems for accessing files over SSH through their respective file browsers. Prefixing a URL with `fish://` in KDE will allow users to browse files on remote hosts over SSH. In the GNOME file manager, users can prefix URLs with `sftp://` to browse remote files over SSH. Many of these systems were designed to access files over RSH, but they work with SSH as a drop-in replacement.

The exciting world of port forwarding

A final, and less understood, strong point of SSH is the ability to do what is called *port forwarding*. While the concept is relatively simple, the technology opens up a wide range of possibilities.

All Internet services run on ports, which can be thought of as doors. Different services run on different ports. Mail traditionally runs on port 25, the Web runs on port 80, and SSH itself runs on port 22. Ports under 1024 are considered registered or reserved ports, whereas ports over 1024 are unreserved. Normal (nonroot) users often cannot start services running on the low-numbered ports.

SSH allows users to listen to a port and to forward all traffic, incoming or outgoing, to a port on the other end of an SSH connection. Because SSH is encrypted, users can tunnel unencrypted and insecure network protocols and connect over these protocols securely.

Creating a tunnel is like creating an SSH connection, except that in addition to the normal shell connection, a secure TCP/IP stream running on a single port is opened as well. Figure 18-2 shows a graphical depiction of what is going on.

SSH tunneling is not unlike Virtual Private Networking (VPN) technology, although it's much simpler and less intrusive and it only works for ports that are explicitly forwarded. The most difficult thing about port forwarding is deciding how you want to forward ports.

Figure 18-2: Tunnels secure unsecured TCP/IP traffic over an authenticated SSH.

Forwarding local ports

Forwarding a local port means that you will invoke SSH to listen to a port on the local machine and to forward all of that traffic across the network to a specified port on the specified host relative to the SSH connection. Forwarding a local port is done using SSH's `-L` option. You will use this, for example, if you want to deliver mail securely from your machine to a remote machine that you have SSH access to over an SSH tunnel:

```
ssh -L 2525:localhost:25 remotehost
```

The first number is the port on the machine on which you are invoking SSH, or the local port. The term after the colon is the name or IP address of the host to which you are trying to open a tunnel *relative to the host to which you are connecting*. The third term is the remote port to which you are aiming to connect. The final argument is the host to which you are opening up an SSH connection, just as it is any time you invoke SSH.

In this example, you are opening port 2525 on your local machine and forwarding all contents to port 25 on localhost relative to the machine to which you are connecting. With this port forwarded, if you connect to port 2525 on `localhost` from the machine where you invoked this connection, you will, in fact, be connecting to port 25 on the remote host.

Port 25 is the standard mail port. Because on many networks port 25 is blocked altogether to prevent spam, mail needs to be delivered to the remote host over some protocol other than port 25. By opening a port 2525 that is in fact simply an alias to port 25 (the real mail port on the trusted `localhost` interface on a remote server), you can configure your mail software to deliver to port 2525 on your local machine and your mail will be transferred, encrypted over your SSH connection, to the internal (`localhost`) mail port on the remote machine, where your mail can then be relayed.

Forwarding remote ports

Forwarding remote ports is almost identical in syntax to forwarding local ports:

```
ssh -R 2222:localhost:22 remotehost
```

However, instead of forwarding traffic from the local port to the given remote port on the given remote host, you are forwarding traffic from the given port on the remote side to the given port on the given host relative to the localhost. I'll go over that a little more slowly.

The first number always is the number of the new port that will be opened up, and the rest is the host and the port number where the data will be forwarded. When creating a tunnel with -L, the port being created (the first number) is on the local computer — that is, the computer on which you are invoking the command. With -R, the first number is still the port you are opening, but it will be on the remote host that you are connecting to with the ssh command (the argument you give on the command line separated by a space). With -L, the host between the colons is relative to the remote host. In this case, it is relative to the local computer. Although localhost was used in both examples, it referred to the computer that you are connecting *to* in the first example and the computer you are connecting *from* in the second example. The final number after the colon in the second example refers to the port on the computer directly before the colon — as it did in the earlier example.

In this example, you have opened up a tunnel from the host you are connecting to, leading *back* to port 22 on the machine you are running the command on. Because port 22 is the SSH port, people can now connect to port 2222 on the remote host and get to your machine; their traffic is being forwarded over the secure encrypted SSH tunnel. Because SSH is already encrypted, it will be encrypted twice.

Proxying

SSH port forwarding and tunneling is a type of *proxying* that works on the TCP/IP port level. With this dynamic ability to forward data over a secure connection, SSH can be made to proxy and forward other types of data.

A common Internet proxy is the SOCKS proxy. There are two common versions of SOCKS in use, SOCKS4 and SOCKS5. SOCKS5 is primarily distinguished in that it forwards domain name requests over the tunnel and is in this way more similar to Virtual Private Networking. The version of SSH in Debian includes a simple ability to create a SOCKS4 proxy over a secure SSH connection. To do this, invoke SSH with the -D option and the number of the port on the local machine on which you want your proxy to run. For example,

```
ssh -D 8080 remotehost
```

This command opens up a SOCKS4 proxy on port 8080. To browse the Web, go to the proxy setting for your Web browser in the Options or Preferences dialog box and find the field to enter a SOCKS proxy name and port. For name, enter local-host, and for port, enter 8080. This proxy will run as long as you keep the SSH connection open. When the SSH connection is dropped, your proxy will move off-line and you will no longer be able to visit Web pages until you either reestablish the connection or reconfigure your Web browser to not use the proxy. This simple command is a good way to tunnel your unencrypted and insecure Web traffic out of untrusted networks and into a machine on a trusted network.

Accessing a remote machine behind NAT/firewalls

A complex, but impressive, demonstration of the power of SSH tunneling involves the need to connect two machines that are each inaccessible from the outside world.

Increasingly, machines are not accessible from outside their network. Often this is due to firewall rules that block SSH, but it can also be an unintended side effect of NAT (Network Address Translations), when many computers are given non-Internet-routable IPs and all traffic appears to be coming from a single or small number of Internet IPs. Although a computer or router doing NAT can route outgoing traffic and keep track of existing connections, it cannot usually direct incoming traffic. SSH port forwarding can provide a solution for remote access between two computers that are both on NAT-enabled networks. Figure 18-3 documents the process by which this tunneling can occur.

Caution

In no way should this be interpreted as encouragement to bypass security firewalls that have blocked incoming SSH for security reasons. Creating a tunnel from a remote machine into a network can compromise network security and should be done carefully and only where appropriate and approved by network administrators. An incoming tunnel bypassing a firewall blocking such traffic for network security purposes can be a violation of a company network security policy with negative consequences for both network security and one's continued employment.

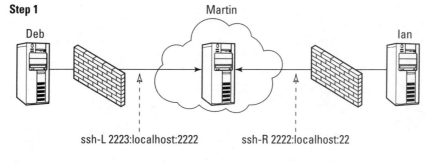

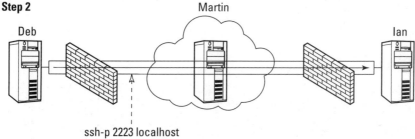

Figure 18-3: This figure details the two-step procedure by which Deb can access Ian's computer while both of them remain behind firewalls blocking incoming SSH traffic or doing NAT.

In the scenario documented in the figure, Deb, at work, wants to access her husband Ian's computer at home to download a plane ticket receipt she left on his desktop and forgot to print. However, both Deb's and Ian's computers are on networks that are using NAT and cannot be accessed remotely.

To do this, Deb makes an SSH connection to a third computer owned by Martin, which has an Internet-accessible IP address and, as a result, is accessible to both her and Ian. To initiate the connection, she uses the following command:

```
ssh -L 2223:localhost:2222 martin
```

This command forwards port 2223 on Deb's computer to port 2222 on localhost relative to Martin's computer — or to be more specific, to port 2222 on Martin's computer, because localhost relative to martin would be martin. Of course, there is nothing at port 2222 on Martin's computer yet.

Now, Deb coordinates with Ian so that Ian also connects to Martin's computer but with a slightly different SSH command:

```
ssh -R 2222:localhost:22 martin
```

When Ian runs this command, he also opens up a connection to Martin's computer. In doing so, he starts listening on port 2222 on Martin's computer (the one where Deb is forwarding traffic) and forwarding all traffic to port 22 on localhost relative to his computer — which, in this case, is his own machine. The pieces are in place.

Leaving all those connections open, Deb connects to port 2223 on her own computer with the following command:

```
ssh -p 2223 localhost
```

Because of the command she ran earlier, SSH is listening on that port and forwarding all traffic to port 2222 on Martin's computer. Her SSH connection is forwarded over the port to Martin's computer. Now, on Martin's computer, port 2222 is itself a tunnel over to port 22, or the SSH port, on Ian's computer because of the command Ian ran. By connecting to port 2223 on her own computer with all this in place, Deb is connected directly to Ian's computer.

X-Forwarding

In the past, shell-based access over SSH and its predecessors was a powerful tool to access computers and was sufficient for most users. As increasing numbers of users use Debian in a graphical or X Windows–based interface, the demand for graphical forms of remote access has grown.

XFree86, the X Windowing System shipped with Debian, is based on an old UNIX architecture that was modeled after and built on the text-based access methods popular under UNIX. Many users used cheap clients, often called "dumb terminals," to access a single powerful server. In a bout of somewhat confusing terminology that came about when we entered the graphical world, the graphical terminals or client machines each run what is called an *X server*. Each application run by a user at a terminal would connect — from the server or host — as a client to the server running on the user's terminal. The program memory, processor, and disk space needed to run the program would be on the server or host, but the output of the program and the input from the users would be transferred and mediated by the X server running on the client.

While this method of using X Windows is being used less frequently, the basic architecture still remains. The immediate benefit is that any X Windows, and Debian, user can take advantage of this to run graphical programs remotely using a straightforward system called X-forwarding.

General X-forwarding

X-forwarded traffic is, by default, unencrypted and insecure. It is also very high bandwidth and can be relatively slow. It should not be attempted on publicly accessible networks or with secure data. If you are concerned about this, skip to the next session covering secure X-forwarding over SSH.

Although the subject of remote X is a complex one, a simpler subset is that of running individual applications from a remote machine onto a local display. In the X Windowing System, the display on which a program should run is specified with the DISPLAY environment variable. This variable is set to host:*D*, where *host* refers to the host and D refers to the sequence number of the display. If omitted, host refers to localhost. Unless there is more than one display connected to a host, D will be 0. Because DISPLAYs can have multiple screens, 0.0 would, for example, refer to the first screen on the first display on the given host.

To run a program remotely, you must specify an alternate DISPLAY by setting the environment variable in the following way:

```
DISPLAY=remotehost:0.0 program
```

Of course, if every remote host allowed anyone, anywhere, to run applications on a display, this might be problematic. As a result, X comes with access control measures that are designed to disallow this by default. There are two major ways to change the access control configuration: Xhost and Xauth.

Xhost changes configuration on a host-by-host basis. If you want to allow clients from my.remote.host to connect to your machine, you would run the following line from the machine running the X server on which you want to launch the application:

```
xhost +my.remote.host
```

To remove it, you use the complementary command:

```
xhost -my.remote.host
```

Of course, this means that *any* application launched from that host would be able to connect to the display. A better solution can be Xauth, which allows authentication to anyone who knows a secret phrase or word. Because this is much more complex and not as secure as X-forwarding with SSH, it is not detailed in this chapter. More information on X-forwarding, and Xauth in particular, is available in the Remote X Apps HOWTO at `www.tldp.org/HOWTO/Remote-X-Apps.html`.

Secure X-forwarding with SSH

The final, most simple, and most secure way to forward X traffic is built into SSH itself. Just as you are able to tunnel TCP/IP traffic over SSH, you can also tunnel X traffic from applications running on one machine to a display on another machine using SSH.

However, the SSH client on Debian is configured to not forward SSH sessions by default. To turn it on, you should include a -X option in your SSH command like this:

```
ssh -X remotehost
```

Once you have logged in, you should be able to run X programs as you would normally. Instead of starting on the remote host, however, the output from the connection will be tunneled over your SSH connection, and the application will launch on the screen of the computer where you ran SSH.

Keep in mind that even a simple application in X Windows is extremely bandwidth intensive and is not intended for or optimized for Internet connection; if the application doesn't pop up immediately, be patient.

If X-forwarding over SSH is proving problematic, you should make sure that X-forwarding is enabled in your SSH daemon or server. Check to see that the line `X11Forwarding` is not commented out from the `/etc/ssh/sshd_config` file on the server.

VNC Graphical Remote Access

VNC stands for Virtual Network Computing. According to the Web site of its authors (`www.realvnc.com`),

> VNC software makes it possible to view and fully-interact with one computer from any other computer or mobile device anywhere on the Internet. VNC software is cross-platform, allowing remote control between different types of computer.

VNC was released as Free Software/Open Source software in 1998 and has been downloaded more than 20 million times. Perhaps most important, both client and server software exist on a wide array of operating systems including Linux, UNIX, Mac OS, and Microsoft Windows.

A user on a computer launches a VNC server. With this server running, he can connect to his computer using his IP and a VNC client from a remote machine and by providing requested authentication information such as a username and password.

The VNC client application will open a window that contains a snapshot of the desktop. The user can use the mouse and keyboard on the local machine to manipulate the mouse and keyboard on the remote computer and can do anything that he would be able to do while sitting at the computer.

There are several pieces of VNC server software in Debian, including the following packages:

- ✦ vncserver
- ✦ tightvncserver
- ✦ rfb
- ✦ krfb
- ✦ x11vnc
- ✦ linuxvnc

Notable among this list are vncserver, the original VNC server, and tightvncserver, a version of the same code base that is optimized for a low-bandwidth connection. Recently, the encoding on the standard VNC server has improved, making TightVNC somewhat less useful. RFB and x11vnc are unique in that they export the currently running display to any VNC client, so you do not have to launch another session as the VNC user, as the regular VNC server requires. KRFB is the KDE version of RFB. Finally, linuxvnc allows you to export your currently running text sessions to any VNC client. It is similar to the UNIX program screen in this regard.

Similarly, there is a long list of VNC clients available:

- ✦ xvncviewer
- ✦ xtightvncviewer
- ✦ krdc
- ✦ directvnc
- ✦ svncviewer
- ✦ tightvnc-java
- ✦ vnc-java

Most of these clients are complementary to an application in the preceding list of VNC server software. This is the case with xvncviewer and xtightvncviewer, which are the standard and low-bandwidth-optimized versions of VNC, respectively. KRDC is the KDE-based graphical client for the RFB protocol used by VNC. DirectVNC is another VNC client meant to run using a frame buffer as a display, whereas svncviewer takes advantage of SVGA libraries and can run without X. The final two in the list are both Java applets that are functional VNC clients.

VNC clients are not only useful in connecting to servers running on Debian or Linux computers. They are equally useful for connecting to systems running VNC servers on Windows or Mac OS operating systems. Each of the packages comes with documentation on the usage of the program in /usr/share/doc/packagename.

Summary

In this chapter, I introduced the concept of remote access and differentiated different types of remote access as shell-based and desktop-based access. I reviewed the history of remote access and introduced some of the older tools used for remote access on UNIX and its derivatives that can still show up from time to time. I introduced SSH, the Swiss Army knife of remote access for most Linux users, and described a range of ways that it can be put into use. Finally, I introduced the concept of remote desktop access and explained how this can be done using X Windows. I closed with a brief pointer to VNC, a cross-platform way to get desktop access to your Debian machine remotely.

✦   ✦   ✦

The Intranet Server

Workstation Network and Internet Access

Most organizations have many workstations on their network. These workstations are generally network client machines, running applications such as Web browsers, mail clients, and office tools. In this chapter, I look at different services you can provide on your server running Debian.

 Cross-Reference Chapter 5 gives an in-depth introduction to configuring your computer on the network. This chapter assumes that you have already been able to get your computer on the network and gives information on installing and using applications in the role of *network administrator*.

Assigning Addresses with DHCP

One problem facing many companies is that of assigning IP addresses for desktop and mobile machines. There are often many of these machines, and keeping track of all of their IP addresses manually can be trying. IP address conflicts, which occur when more than one machine has the same IP address, can be difficult to track down and easy to cause (a simple typo can cause mysterious problems). Laptop users may frequently shift from one network to the next, and adjusting network settings can be cumbersome.

DHCP, the Dynamic Host Configuration Protocol, can be a way to help address these dilemmas. DHCP can be used to provide PCs with an IP address dynamically chosen out of a pool of available addresses. Alternatively, you can use DHCP to hand out static IP addresses based on the PC's Ethernet card MAC address.

Dynamic allocation means that a given machine may not always get the same IP address. For desktops and workstations, that usually doesn't matter; nobody needs to know their IP address.

A popular misconception is that DHCP is always used to provide dynamic IP addresses. That's not true; DHCP can be configured to always give the same IP address to a particular machine. In effect, it is providing a static IP address for that machine.

DHCP can also give out more than just IP addresses. It can give out information about DNS servers, default gateways, and proxy servers on the network. This chapter covers using DHCP from a network administration perspective.

Installing DHCP

To get started with DHCP, you first need to install the DHCP server somewhere on your network. The command `apt-get install dhcp` will do that for you. DHCP works by sending broadcasts across the network. You can place it anywhere on your network as long as traffic doesn't have to cross a router to reach it. Switches and hubs pass DHCP traffic with no problems.

Configuration for DHCP is done in `/etc/dhcpd.conf`. After modifying this file, you should run `/etc/init.d/dhcp restart` for the changes to take effect. Many options can be set either globally or in a clause for a particular machine or subnet. This lets you establish useful defaults for your network, and override them for a certain group of machines or even individual machines. Here's an example of a global configuration section at the top of a `dhcpd.conf` file:

```
option domain-name "lan.example.com";
option domain-name-servers 192.168.0.1, 192.168.0.32;
option subnet-mask 255.255.0.0;
default-lease-time 600;
max-lease-time 7200;
```

These lines define four basic configuration items. First, the nameserver search path is `lan.example.com`. This means that attempts to look up unqualified hostnames will attempt to find them in that domain. Second, the DNS servers for the network are defined to include two machines, residing at 192.168.0.1 and 192.168.0.32. Third, the default netmask is set to 255.255.0.0. Finally, clients are asked to renew their DHCP information every 10 minutes (600 seconds) and will be granted a DHCP lease for a maximum of two hours. (This is primarily of interest to people using dynamic IPs, where machines will be guaranteed the same static IP for up to two hours in this case.)

Now, you need to define one or more `subnet` clauses. The method for doing this depends on whether you will be giving out dynamic or static IP addresses with DHCP, as explained in the following sections.

Providing static IP addresses

Static IP addresses can be easily configured with DHCP. First, add lines like this to set up your subnet (or subnets) in `dhcpd.conf`:

```
subnet 192.168.0.0 netmask 255.255.0.0 {
   option broadcast-address 192.168.255.2;
   option routers 192.168.0.1;
}
```

This simply defines some basic information about your network — the broadcast address and the routers on the network. Next, add a `host` section for each machine on your network. You need the MAC address for each network card (you can find the MAC address by running `ifconfig` in Linux, or under the Network section in the Control Panel in Windows). Here's an example of the `host` section:

```
host jon-doe-pc.lan.example.com {
   hardware ethernet 0:0:c0:5d:bd:95;
   fixed-address 192.168.1.55;
}
```

You need to create a clause like this for every machine on your LAN with a static IP address.

Providing dynamic IP addresses

You can also provide dynamic IP addresses for your machines. With this method, new PCs do not require any configuration at all. However, tracking data back to a particular PC is more complicated.

To set up dynamic IP addresses, you provide only `subnet` sections. Here's an example:

```
subnet 192.168.0.0 netmask 255.255.0.0 {
   option broadcast-address 192.168.255.2;
   option routers 192.168.0.1;
   range 192.168.50.1 192.168.50.254;
}
```

This behaves similarly to the `subnet` section for static IP users. Note the new `range` line. This specifies that IP addresses may be handed out to dynamic DHCP clients — those that are never explicitly listed in a `host` section. Some people run an all-dynamic setup, where they have no `hosts` sections at all. In those instances, the IPs specified in `range` are the only ones the DHCP server makes available.

Assigning Addresses with radvd

The basic protocol at the root of the present-day Internet is known as IPv4. IPv4 has been with us for many years and has some weaknesses. One of the main problems with IPv4 is that its 32-bit address space is becoming a limiting factor thanks to the explosive growth of the Internet. To address this and other problems, researchers have developed a new protocol known as IPv6.

As IPv6 becomes more popular, its new methods for assigning IP addresses will start to gain popularity. Because IPv6 has such a huge address space, IPv6 addresses can be generated that actually incorporate the MAC address of the network card into the IPv6 address itself. Because of this property, it is possible for IPv6 users to obtain static IP addresses while at the same time not requiring any configuration on the server side to support those IP addresses.

IPv6 automatic assignment occurs with the help of a router advertisement daemon, or radvd. To install radvd, you can simply run `apt-get install radvd`. Since radvd supports a simple protocol, configuration also is simple. Here's an example of a fully configured `/etc/radvd.conf` file:

```
interface eth0
{
  AdvSendAdvert on;
  prefix 0:470:1f00:296::/64
  {
  };
};
```

That's it. Make sure that you change the prefix to reflect your particular network. Save this file, run `/etc/init.d/radvd restart`, and everything will be ready to go.

Note that, unlike DHCP, radvd has no way to specify DNS server or DNS information for your clients. That must be configured manually on a per-client basis or, if your clients also use IPv4, obtained via IPv4 DHCP.

Using Web Proxies to Speed Up Surfing

Proxy servers are programs that receive outgoing requests for Web pages, retrieve those pages themselves, and then pass the result back to the original Web browser. They are used for several purposes, the most prominent being speed. Imagine a large company, where hundreds or thousands of machines have Web browsers. Chances are that several hundred machines might access a page such as www. google.com in a day. Rather than downloading the same data several hundred times over your Internet link, a caching proxy server will download it once and give the stored copy to every machine making a request.

Proxy servers can also be used to implement security policies, restricting the sites that users are allowed to visit. Finally, proxies are, in some cases, used to log activity on a network.

By far the most popular proxy program in Debian is Squid. Squid is a well-known proxy server that, together with related utilities, can accomplish all of the uses for a proxy server outlined previously. In its most basic configuration, Squid acts as a caching proxy server. For more information on Squid, you can visit www. squid-cache.org.

Squid can be installed by running `apt-get install squid`. The primary Squid configuration file resides in `/etc/squid.conf`. Debian ships a working default configuration, and the default configuration file contains comments explaining all the options. There are several parameters to immediately consider tuning, however. The first is `cache_mem`, which defines the size of the in-RAM cache. Small systems may wish to reduce this, whereas very large ones will likely want to expand it. The `cache_dir` parameter specifies the location and size of the on-disk cache, and you will also likely want to adjust this for your particular situation. After modifying `squid.conf`, you should run `/etc/init.d/squid restart` to cause the changes to take effect.

To have clients use your new Squid installation, you need to configure the proxy settings in their browsers to access your Squid server at the port specified with `http_port` in the configuration file, which defaults to 3128. Choosing Options ➪ Connection Settings to open a proxy confirmation dialog box in Mozilla Firefox is perhaps the most common example of a place where a client can be configured to use a Squid proxy. It is shown in Figure 19-1.

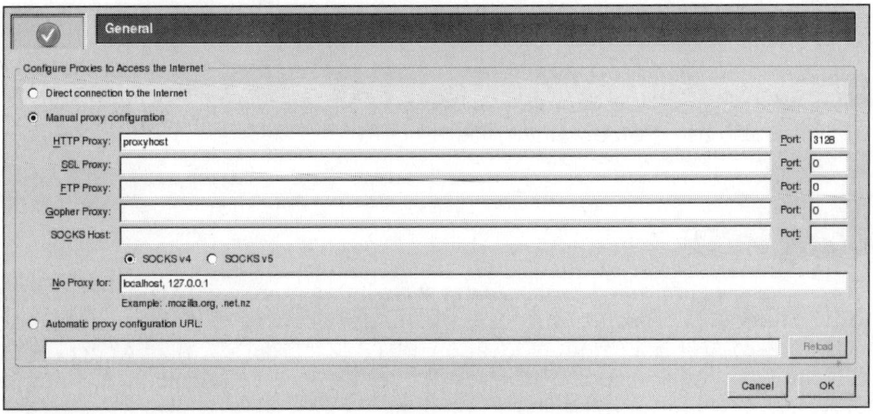

Figure 19-1: Mozilla Firefox proxy configuration dialog box.

There are a number of packages in Debian that enhance Squid in various ways. Table 19-1 is a summary of the most popular Squid-related packages.

Table 19-1 Squid Add-Ons	
Package	**Description**
adzapper	Blocks advertisements on Web pages
calamaris	Generates statistical reports from Squid activity
ccze	Generates statistical reports from Squid activity, viewable from a terminal
chastity-list	Categorizes Web site blacklists for use with SquidGuard
sarg	Generates statistical reports from Squid activity, viewable from a Web browser
squidguard	Filtering, blocking, redirection, and security features for Squid

Virtual Private Networks

Virtual Private Networks are used to securely connect two locations over an insecure network. They are typically used to securely connect two branches of a company over the Internet or to securely connect a remote worker to a company's internal LAN over the Internet. To achieve security, VPN implementations use some form of encryption and authentication.

There are two protocols in wide use today: PPTP, popularized by Microsoft VPN clients, and IPsec, a set of extensions to IP itself to enable encryption and authentication.

Using PPTP

PPTP is less secure than IPsec in many ways but is more easily configured on a wide variety of Microsoft clients. It is often seen as a way to let laptop users access a corporate LAN from a remote location. PPTP essentially works by encrypting a PPP conversation and sending the result over the Internet. As such, it is not particularly fast or robust, but it gets the job done.

To use PPTP, you need several pieces of software:

✦ The PPTP server itself, found in Debian package `pptpd`.

✦ A PPP server, found in Debian package `ppp`. Depending on your version of Debian, you may need to build your own `ppp` package using the information available at `www.chiark.greenend.org.uk/~owend/free/pptp-debian.html`.

✦ Most servers also need MPPE encryption support in the kernel. The Debian package `kernel-patch-mppe` contains the patch necessary to compile a kernel with MPPE support.

Once installed, the PPTP server is configured in `/etc/pptpd.conf` and `/etc/ppp/pptpd-options`. The first file provides some overall configuration parameters, such as IP addresses to hand out. The second behaves as a standard PPP configuration, just as you might configure a PPP server for dial-up users.

PPTP works by establishing an encrypted link over the Internet. Across that encrypted link, standard PPP data is sent. Essentially, PPTP is emulating a modem's PPP connection. This means that performance is not great, but the system works.

Client machines running Windows 98 or newer should have the software necessary to connect to your new PPTP server as a part of the operating system. If you want to configure Debian clients to use PPTP, you can check out the `pptp-client` package.

Using IPsec

IPsec is a relatively new VPN protocol, but it is rapidly gaining popularity. Support for IPsec can be frequently found on routers and less frequently on desktop and server machines. The 2.6.x Linux kernel series includes a fully functional IPsec stack, though it is usually disabled by default.

There are no less than four separate ways to go for IPsec support on Linux 2.6: FreeS/WAN, Openswan, KAME, and isakmpd. Each one is configured differently, though the basic feature set supported is the same with each. More details on each of these can be found at `www.ipsec-howto.org/`.

Table 19-2 shows the most popular Debian packages related to configuring IPsec.

Table 19-2
Debian IPsec-Related Packages

Package	Description
freeswan	Basic FreeS/WAN user-land utilities
ipsec-tools	Basic KAME user-land utilities
isakmpd	Basic isakmpd user-land tools
kernel-patch-freeswan	FreeS/WAN kernel code
kernel-patch-openswan	Openswan kernel code
kernel-patch-usagi	IPv6 kernel code for 2.4.x kernels
openswan	Basic Openswan user-land tools

The configuration method for IPsec varies depending on the tool you have chosen. Consult the documentation for the packages you have installed for configuration details.

Summary

Many administrators find a need to let clients automatically determine their IP address settings. For most networks, DHCP provides a solution that enables both static and dynamic IP configurations. For people using IPv6, a simpler solution is radvd, designed specifically for IPv6 configuration.

Caching Web proxies are useful in large environments to reduce download time for Web sites and decrease bandwidth usage. They work by storing locally content that is requested by multiple computers and by avoiding network access when possible. The most popular Web proxy is Squid, and it also has a number of add-on utilities that provide extra functionality.

Virtual Private Networks (VPNs) permit secure access to a network over an insecure link. The two most popular VPN technologies are PPTP and IPsec. PPTP is commonly used when Microsoft clients connect to a LAN, whereas IPsec is often used to link two LANs together, though both can be used in either configuration.

✦   ✦   ✦

File Serving and Sharing

With apologies to Sun Microsystems, "The network is the disk." Even the smallest home network can make use of networked filesystems to share files between computers and users. This chapter looks at two common methods for sharing files and directories across a network: Samba and the Network File System (NFS). Samba is most often used to share files between Windows and Linux systems. NFS, on the other hand, is used almost exclusively to provide file-sharing services between UNIX and UNIX-like systems, the latter, naturally, including Linux systems.

Understanding Distributed Filesystems

Networked filesystems, or, to introduce the term used in this chapter, *distributed filesystems*, are so named because they provide access to files and directories that are distributed across multiple computers on a network. I prefer the term *distributed* to *networked* because some distributed filesystems continue to function in the absence of a network, whereas networked filesystems, by definition, require a functioning network connection. If that seems unnecessarily pedantic, try accessing a file on an NFS-exported filesystem when the NFS server is down or network service is otherwise interrupted! Truly distributed filesystems, on the other hand, enable clients that are disconnected from the network to continue to access shared files using copies of the shared files maintained in the client's persistent cache.

The distributed filesystems discussed in this chapter are examples of *client/server* computing: a single server system (or a small number of server systems) provides file access services to an arbitrary number of client systems. The *server* system (referred to as the *file server*, even if "the server" is actually multiple systems) performs a number of tasks:

✦ Stores and maintains the files

✦ Manages synchronization when multiple client systems access (and, especially, update) the same files

✦ Maintains the filesystem hierarchy that client systems see

✦ Validates and limits client access to a filesystem

✦ Ensures *consistency*, which means that the server ensures that copies of a file being used by client systems are the same as the master file on the server

Distributed filesystems use both volatile (RAM-based) and nonvolatile (disk-based) caches to reduce I/O load on the server, to speed up client file access, and to limit the amount of network traffic required between the client and server. Samba and NFS both provide some support of RAM-based file caching on the client. When access to a file is requested, the server tries to send the entire file to the requesting client, based on the (reasonable) assumption that the client will, in the short run, probably want to access more of the same file rather than request access to another file. Thus, the server sends the entire file in a single network transaction, rather than dribbling out chunks of it in multiple network transactions.

Because the client stores the file in memory, client-side I/O is also fast. If the file is updated on the server, the server notifies the client and resends the file. Similarly, if the client updates the file, the client notifies the server and sends the updated file to the server so that other clients have access to the latest version of the file.

Note   The book *Linux Filesystems*, by William von Hagen (Sams, 2002), discusses distributed filesystems in detail. Bill deserves special thanks for graciously agreeing to review this chapter.

In today's computing world, like it or not, you will inevitably have to interoperate with Windows systems and will just as inevitably need to share files between your Debian system and one or more Windows systems. The next section, "Windows Networking with Samba," describes how to install and configure Samba, a native Linux and UNIX implementation of the SMB (Server Message Block) protocol that is used to share files between Windows systems. "UNIX File Repositories with NFS" describes how to use the standard Linux system for file sharing, NFS. If you are fortunate enough to work in a Linux-only environment, NFS might well be all you need.

Windows Networking with Samba

It's an unavoidable reality: Most networks are heterogeneous. They usually consist of some number (probably not enough) of Linux systems and some number (probably too many) of Windows systems. Equally unavoidable is the necessity to share files between Linux and Windows systems. All versions of Windows since

Windows 95 have used the SMB (Server Message Block) protocol to communicate with each other and to share services such as files and printers. This section explains how to configure your Debian system to share files with Windows systems using Samba, a free software implementation of SMB. You can use Samba as a Windows file server or you can use Samba to access files that are stored on real Windows systems.

Note Samba also supports CIFS, the Common Internet File System. CIFS is a new version of SMB that extends the original SMB specification to the Internet. For more information about CIFS, see the Samba Web pages that discuss CIFS at www.samba.org/cifs/ and the Microsoft Web pages devoted to CIFS at www.microsoft.com/windows2000/techinfo/reskit/en-us/default.asp?url=/windows2000/techinfo/reskit/en-us/cnet/cnad_arc_endh.asp.

Installing Samba

Of course, you cannot use Samba if it isn't installed. Thus, the obligatory command to install Samba is

```
# apt-get install samba samba-client
```

The samba package installs the Samba server daemons and supporting files. It depends on the samba-common package, which installs files used by both Samba servers and Samba clients. The samba-client package installs the programs necessary to access files and directories on Windows systems.

Note If you use apt-get to install the samba-client package, apt-get will select the smbclient package instead. This is The Right Thing to Do.

After installing the required packages, you need to perform some basic configuration before you can use Samba, as described in the next section.

Configuring Samba

Under normal circumstances, apt-get will start the configuration process automatically while installing the various Samba-related packages. If the debconf configuration screens do not start, you can configure Samba manually after installation using the command dpkg --reconfigure -plow samba samba-common, that is,

```
# dpkg-reconfigure -plow samba samba-common
```

The reason this command uses the -plow option is that debconf's priority setting might be too high to see all of the questions. In addition, if you reconfigure only the samba package, you'll miss some of the original configuration options, so it is important to reconfigure both the samba and samba-common packages.

The first dialog box you see, shown in Figure 20-1, asks you to provide the Windows workgroup or domain name that Samba clients will use when they query your server.

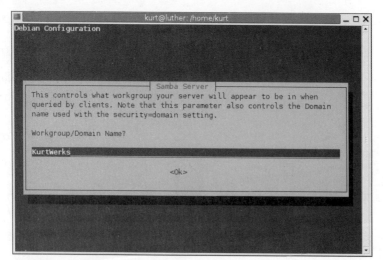

Figure 20-1: Assigning the Windows workgroup Samba will use.

Type the workgroup or domain name (KurtWerks is the workgroup name that I use), and then press Enter to continue.

Figure 20-2 shows the authentication configuration screen. Recent Windows-based SMB clients always use encrypted passwords (unless specifically configured not to). This screen enables you to select whether Samba will use encrypted passwords.

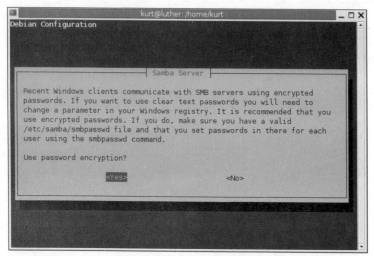

Figure 20-2: Choosing whether to use encrypted passwords.

Unless you know you don't need password encryption, choose Yes and press Enter to continue.

The next screen enables you to configure Samba to play nicely with DHCP (see Figure 20-3). If your system uses DHCP and there are Windows-based servers using WINS (NetBIOS) nameservers on your network, the DHCP server might also provide WINS information.

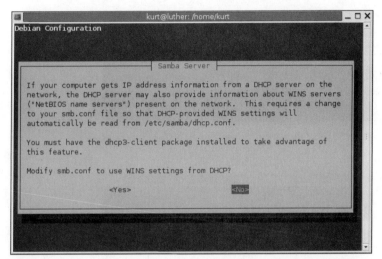

Figure 20-3: Configuring Samba to use DHCP for WINS services.

If your system is also a DHCP client, you might want to modify the Samba configuration to use this information, so select Yes and press Enter. Otherwise, select No and press Enter.

Tip   If you select Yes in Figure 20-3, you must also install the dhcp3-client package.

In the next configuration dialog box, shown in Figure 20-4, you choose whether the Samba daemons, nmbd and smbd, will run under the control of inetd or as normal standalone daemons.

For performance reasons, you should run them as standalone daemons, so select the first entry, daemons, and then press Enter to continue.

If you answered Yes in Figure 20-2 to use encrypted passwords, then answer Yes on the next screen, which offers to create /var/lib/samba/passdb.tdb (see Figure 20-5).

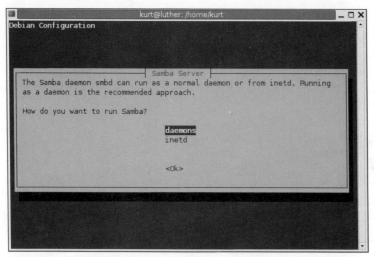

Figure 20-4: Setting Samba to run from inetd or as a standalone service.

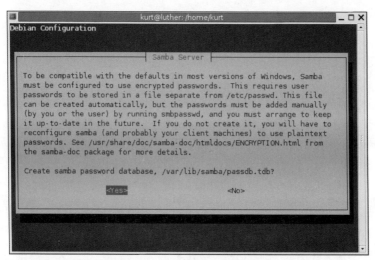

Figure 20-5: Creating the Samba password file, /var/lib/samba/
passdb.tdb.

This file must exist in order to store encrypted passwords. The default answer is
No, so make sure to select Yes before pressing Enter.

Test the initial configuration using the smbclient program. smbclient is a program (client) that can communicate with SMB servers for a wide range of purposes.
In the following example, the -L option instructs smbclient to query the named

SMB server (luther) to find out which services it offers. When prompted for a password, just press Enter to perform an anonymous login.

```
$ smbclient -L luther
Password:
Anonymous login successful
Domain=[KURTWERKS] OS=[Unix] Server=[Samba 3.0.7-Debian]

        Sharename       Type      Comment
        ---------       ----      -------
        print$          Disk      Printer Drivers
        IPC$            IPC       IPC Service (luther server (Samba 3.0.7-
Debian))
        ADMIN$          IPC       IPC Service (luther server (Samba 3.0.7-
Debian))
Anonymous login successful
Domain=[KURTWERKS] OS=[Unix] Server=[Samba 3.0.7-Debian]

        Server                  Comment
        ---------               -------
        LUTHER                  luther server (Samba 3.0.7-Debian)

        Workgroup               Master
        ---------               -------
        KURTWERKS
```

 Note You might need to install the smbclient package to use the smbclient program:

apt-get install smbclient

The output wraps due to formatting limitations of this book. As you can see from the output, there are four SMB *shares* or services running: IPC$, ADMIN$, printers, and print$. Under known servers, only the SMB server luther is listed. Notice also that the authentication process supports anonymous logins. The anonymous mode was invoked by pressing Enter at the Password: prompt without typing a password. The point here was to illustrate that the SMB server is running. The next task will be to add some shared directories (this *is* a chapter about file serving, after all).

Sharing Directories with Samba

To understand how to share directories with Samba, you will need to understand a little bit about the contents of /etc/samba/smb.conf, the Samba configuration file. The configuration file is divided into sections referred to as *shares*, which are shown in the following discussion in brackets, for example, [homes]. The first section or share, [global], configures the server's overall behavior and provides default settings for other shares. It is shown in the following listing, with commented lines removed for brevity (comments can be prefixed with the universal comment delimiter, #, also called the hash sign, or with a semicolon):

```
[global]
   workgroup = KurtWerks
   server string = %h server (Samba %v)
   dns proxy = no
   log file = /var/log/samba/log.%m
   max log size = 1000
   syslog = 0
   panic action = /usr/share/samba/panic-action %d
   encrypt passwords = true
   passdb backend = tdbsam guest
   obey pam restrictions = yes
   invalid users = root
   passwd program = /usr/bin/passwd %u
   passwd chat = *Enter\snew\sUNIX\spassword:* %n\n
 *Retype\snew\sUNIX\spassword:* %n\n .
   socket options = TCP_NODELAY
```

As you can see in the listing, each entry has the form *variable = value*. For example, workgroup = KurtWerks sets the Windows workgroup name to KurtWerks. This is the name shown in the identification tab of the network properties box on a Windows computer. server string = %h server (Samba %v) provides the comment string that Windows computers display (and which is also shown in the smbclient -L output at the end of the previous section). Table 20-1 describes the other directives in the first section.

Table 20-1
Global Samba Configuration Directives

Directive	Description
dns proxy	Determines whether the NetBIOS name will be treated as a DNS name and whether DNS lookups will be performed
encrypt passwords	Indicates whether passwords will be encrypted
invalid users	Specifies users not allowed to log in to the server
log file	Identifies the name and location of the log files
max log size	Sets the maximum size of the log file, in kilobytes (KB)
obey pam restrictions	Tells Samba whether to use PAM for access control
passwd chat	Defines the dialogue used to prompt for password changes
passwd program	Identifies the program used for password management
socket options	Sets TCP behavior for performance purposes
syslog	Controls how much information is sent to the system log daemon, syslogd

You should now be able to decipher the default configuration:

✦ `dns proxy = no` means the server's NetBIOS name will not be treated as a DNS name and so will not cause a DNS lookup.

✦ `log file = /var/log/samba/log.%m` creates a log file for each machine (%m) that connects to the server.

✦ `max log size = 1000` sets the maximum size of each log file to 1,000KB.

✦ `syslog = 0` sends only minimal log information to the system logger.

✦ `panic action = /usr/share/samba/panic-action %d` means this program is to run if something goes wrong. In this case, it is set to an included script that will send an e-mail with some information about the error that occurred.

✦ `encrypt passwords = true` means that the server will use encrypted passwords.

✦ `socket options = TCP_NODELAY` is a default setting used for performance tuning.

✦ `invalid users = root` means that the root user is not permitted to log in (directly) to the server.

✦ `passwd program = /usr/bin/passwd %u` passes the username (%u) to the program `/usr/bin/passwd` when changing passwords.

✦ `passwd chat = *Enter\snew\sUNIX\spassword:* %n\n *Retype\snew\ sUNIX\spassword:* %n\n .` defines the chat sequence Samba uses to communicate with `passwd program` when users change their passwords. `\s` is replaced with a space, `\n` is replaced with a newline, and %n stands for the new password.

The next share, `[homes]`, gives users access to their home directories from Windows machines (these are the default settings):

```
[homes]
   comment = Home Directories
   browseable = no
   writable = no
   create mask = 0700
   directory mask = 0700
```

As it stands, this is a restrictive share:

✦ `comment = Home Directories` is a comment string.

✦ `browseable = no` means that the directory will not appear in Windows' file browser.

✦ `writable = no` means that users cannot write to their home directories.

✦ `create mask = 0700` sets the default permissions files created in the directory (user readable, writable, and executable; no access for group or world).

✦ `directory mask = 0700` sets the default permission for new directories created in the directory.

To make this share less restrictive, use the following settings:

```
[homes]
    comment = Home Directories
    browseable = yes
    writable = yes
    create mask = 0644
    directory mask = 0755
```

You can test the new settings using Samba's `testparm` command, which validates the syntax of the file:

```
# testparm
Load smb config files from /etc/samba/smb.conf
Processing section "[homes]"
Processing section "[printers]"
Loaded services file OK.
Server role: ROLE_STANDALONE
Press enter to see a dump of your service definitions
```

Press Enter to see the contents of the file, or press Ctrl+C to cancel. You should always use `testparm` to validate the configuration file before applying the changes. After you've verified the syntax of your changes, restart the Samba servers using the `samba rc` script:

```
# /etc/init.d/samba restart
Stopping Samba daemons: nmbd smbd.
Starting Samba daemons: nmbd smbd.
```

The next share, `[printers]`, sets the options for printing:

```
[printers]
    comment = All Printers
    browseable = no
    path = /tmp
    printable = yes
    public = no
    writable = no
    create mode = 0700
```

Again, the default settings are fairly restrictive. The following list describes only the options not already discussed:

- ✦ `path = /tmp` defines the location of the printer spool directory.

- ✦ `printable = yes` permits clients to send print jobs to the named directory. This option must be set to `yes` for printing to work.

- ✦ `public = no` means that a password is required before using the printer.

Because `browseable = no` is also set, printers will not appear in the browser list. To make the printer configuration less restrictive, you can use the following settings:

```
[printers]
    comment = All Printers
    browseable = yes
    path = /tmp
    printable = yes
    public = yes
    writable = yes
    create mode = 0775
```

Test the configuration using `testparm` and then restart the server as shown previously. The final share, `[print$]`, defines a share that contains printer drivers. The default settings, shown here, are acceptable.

```
[print$]
    comment = Printer Drivers
    path = /var/lib/samba/printers
    browseable = yes
    read only = yes
    guest ok = no
```

There are no changes to make, so Samba is now ready to use.

UNIX File Repositories with NFS

As remarked previously, you can create a "pure" Linux file-sharing environment using the Network File System (NFS). It is pure because NFS-based file sharing uses a native Linux (and UNIX) approach that has been deployed in literally thousands of networks for years. This section describes NFS, explains how to configure an NFS server, and illustrates setting up an NFS client. You will also learn how to mount remote filesystems automatically, which can simplify administering NFS client systems.

Understanding NFS

NFS is the most widely used network-based filesystem. This is due in part to its relatively simple design and the willingness of NFS's designer, Sun Microsystems, to make both the protocol specification and initial client and server implementations freely available. NFS's popularity is also a result of the fact that NFS makes it possible for file-sharing services to be implemented across heterogeneous networks. An NFS client running on a Solaris system can access files stored on a Linux-based NFS server without needing to take into account the differences between the physical file formats of the client and server systems. This interoperability is the key to providing seamless file-sharing services.

As you can surmise from the previous paragraph, NFS is a client-server system. A server system functions as a central repository for files (rather, filesystems) that need to be shared among a group of client systems. When an NFS server makes a filesystem accessible to NFS clients, the server is said to *export* the filesystem, and the filesystem is commonly referred to as an *export* or an *NFS-exported filesystem*. Client systems mount a remote filesystem on the local filesystem, just as if it was a filesystem on a disk inside the client. When a client system mounts an NFS-exported filesystem locally, the local view of the remote filesystem is referred to as an *NFS mount*. Subject to network availability, NFS client systems manipulate NFS exports in exactly the same way as they would filesystems on local disks.

Without going into the gory details, NFS works because it is based on *remote procedure calls* (RPCs). RPCs enable a local process (the client) to invoke a service on a remote process (the server) as if the client was calling the process locally. NFS is built on top of RPCs. Thus, when an NFS client invokes a filesystem operation, such as reading or writing a file on an NFS mount, a number of calls are made over RPCs to the server translating the operations into the equivalent operations on the server.

As a networked filesystem, NFS is sensitive to network latency. Every file operation has to be transmitted over the network, so it should be clear that NFS filesystem operations are slower than local filesystem operations by several orders of magnitude. NFS attempts to mediate this by maintaining a cache of file handles (pointers to files requested by the client) on the client and by caching frequently requested files on the server. The NFS protocol also permits servers to respond to client requests asynchronously, delaying actual file changes. For example, if an NFS client uses the `write()` system call to save changes to an NFS-mounted file, the server can acknowledge the change to the client before the server actually makes the change to the file on disk. This asynchronous behavior allows client systems to continue without waiting for disk writes on a busy server to complete, resulting in better (perceived) performance.

Note   NFS default protocol reply behavior is synchronous rather than asynchronous. That is, the NFS protocol requires that the server wait for all operations requested by a client to complete before sending a reply to the client.

NFS requires services that run on the server and services that run on the client. NFS clients have the simpler configuration: three daemons (the portmapper, `lockd`, and `statd`) and a configuration file (`/etc/fstab`). On the server side, the daemons include the portmapper, `lockd`, `statd`, `mountd`, and `rquotad`, and the configuration file is `/etc/exports`. In addition, both client and server require kernel support for NFS services. The kernel support can be compiled into the kernel or loaded dynamically using loadable kernel modules (LKMs).

What do all of these programs and files do? Consider first the daemons that run on both the client and the server:

✦ The portmapper, `/sbin/portmap`, maps RPCs (that is, remote procedure calls) to the programs that provide the specific service requested by an RPC. The daemon is almost always running on most Linux systems, so you rarely need to worry about it. For the record, though, you can see whether it is running using the command `pmap_dump`, as shown in the following example:

```
$ pmap_dump
    100000    2    tcp    111    portmapper
    100000    2    udp    111    portmapper
```

If the portmapper isn't running, start it using the initialization script `/etc/init.d/portmap`:

```
$ /etc/init.d/portmap start
Starting portmap daemon: portmap.
```

✦ `lockd` — `lockd`, or `/sbin/rpc.lockd`, is the daemon that implements the NFS Lock Manager (NLM). The lock daemon coordinates file locking between the NFS server and NFS clients, arbitrating lock and write requests to files served by the NFS server. Client systems communicate file lock and write requests to the client's `lockd`, which communicates via RPC to the server's `lockd`, which makes sure that all lock and write requests are handled in an orderly manner. The purpose of the NLM is to prevent multiple NFS clients from writing to the same file or the same part of the same file simultaneously.

✦ `statd` — `statd`, or `/sbin/rpc.statd`, is the daemon that implements the NFS Status Monitor (NSM). `statd` works with `lockd` on both the client and the server, providing lock status information. If an NFS server crashes, it loses any information about locks held by attached clients. At start-up, the server's `lockd` queries `statd` for any known locks (which NSM stores in `/var/lib/nfs/sm`). After learning what locks existed when the server went down, the server's `lockd` and `statd` daemons relay that information to the `lockd` and `statd` services running on any attached clients, bringing the clients into sync with the server.

There are no client-specific daemons required to run NFS. The server-specific NFS daemons are `mountd` and `rquotad`.

✦ mountd — mountd, or /sbin/rpc.mountd, is the mount daemon. Its purpose is to read the contents of the server's NFS configuration file, /etc/exports, and make that information available to potential NFS clients. In addition, mountd authenticates client mount requests and validates a given client's access to a requested NFS export against the contents of /etc/exports.

✦ rquotad — rquotad, or /sbin/rpc.rquotad, implements quota services for NFS. Specifically, rquotad displays filesystem quotas to NFS clients by enabling the quota program, which is ordinarily used to monitor local filesystem quotas, to request and retrieve quota information from the NFS server. It is important to note that rquotad is simply an informational service and does not enforce policy. That is, the kernel enforces filesystem quotas on both local and remote filesystems; rquotad simply displays quota information for NFS mounts.

On the client, the required configuration file is /etc/fstab. The server's NFS configuration file is /etc/exports. As you might remember, /etc/fstab lists any filesystems that should be mounted when the system boots. These filesystems can include network-based filesystems, including NFS mounts. The mount entries for NFS mounts indicate the server on which the filesystem resides, the filesystem exported by the server, where the exported filesystem should be mounted on the client, and NFS-specific mount options. Analogously, /etc/exports lists the filesystems that the NFS server makes available to clients, defines the clients permitted to access that filesystem, and indicates the conditions of the export, such as whether it can be mounted read-write or read-only. The section titled "Configuring an NFS client" discusses the syntax of /etc/fstab entries for NFS mounts; the next section, "Configuring the NFS server," describes the syntax of /etc/exports.

Configuring the NFS server

Before you start configuring an NFS server, you need to do a little planning. In particular, you must do the following:

✦ Select the filesystem(s) to export and the access privileges granted for those filesystems.

✦ Determine the users, hosts, or subnets that will be permitted to mount the exports.

✦ Choose a naming convention and mounting scheme that maintain network transparency and ease of use.

The best candidates for NFS exports are filesystems shared among a large number of users, such as /home; project directories; shared directories, such as /usr/share; the mail spool (/var/mail); and filesystems that contain application binaries and data used by many users on the network. Filesystems that are relatively static, such as /usr, are good candidates for NFS exports because there is no need to replicate the same data and binaries across multiple machines.

Caution

On client systems, mount users' home directories on /home/*username*. This is one of the most fundamental directory idioms in the Linux world. Disregarding it violates the principle of least surprise, antagonizes users, and breaks any software that assumes that user home directories live in /home. On the server, of course, you have more leeway about where to locate the exports.

Servers that store user data are infamously dynamic; disk space consumption only goes up, so design NFS servers with growth in mind. Avoid the temptation to install all third-party software to a single exported filesystem, because that filesystem will inevitably grow to the point that it needs to be redistributed. You will have administrative headaches galore when you have to update client mount tables to reflect a new set of exports. Instead, distribute applications and data across multiple filesystems and export each application and its associated data separately. You might also find it useful to spread NFS exports across multiple disks so that a single disk failure will limit the impact to the affected application.

Likewise, you can improve disk and network performance by distributing NFS exports across multiple servers rather than concentrating them on a single server. If hardware, budget, or other resource constraints make it impossible to use multiple servers, at least try to situate NFS exports on separate physical devices and/or on separate disk controllers. Doing so reduces disk I/O contention.

You cannot export a filesystem that is itself already an NFS mount. Put another way, an NFS client cannot reexport a filesystem it has mounted. For example, if the client system coondog mounts /home from a server named diskbeast, coondog cannot reexport /home to any system. If the client system hounddog wants to mount /home, it must mount /home from diskbeast directly.

A subdirectory of an exported filesystem cannot be exported unless that subdirectory resides on a different physical disk than its parent directory. For example, suppose diskbeast, an NFS server, has the following entry in its /etc/fstab:

```
/dev/sda1 /projects xfs defaults 1 2
```

If you export /projects, which is located on /dev/sda1, you cannot also separately export /projects/net if it is on the same disk as /projects. This restriction applies even if /projects/net is on a different partition of the same disk, for example, /dev/sda2.

Suppose, however, diskbeast's /etc/fstab showed the following disk configuration:

```
/dev/sda1    /projects          xfs defaults 1 2
/dev/sdb1    /projects/net       xfs defaults 1 2
```

In this case, diskbeast can export both /projects and /projects/net because the exported filesystems reside on different physical disks (/dev/sda and /dev/sdb, respectively).

Creating /etc/exports

With the foregoing in mind, you are ready to set up /etc/exports. Its general syntax is

```
fs      client[(opts)] [client[(opts)]] ...
```

fs is the filesystem on the server that will be exported, such as /usr or /projects/net. client identifies the client (or clients) that can mount fs. opts, an optional component, specifies the export options applied to fs. The exports options list the access privileges granted to client and any operational conditions applied to the clients that mount fs. Multiple client/option entries may be specified, separated by white space. Notice, however, that no space is permitted between clients and the parenthesized list of opts, if any.

client can be specified in a number of ways. The most common method is to specify a single host, either by an alias, a fully qualified domain name (FQDN), or an IP address. If you use an alias or FQDN, the resolver library must be able to resolve the hostname to an IP address. The following export statements illustrate each method of specifying a host (disregard the export options for the moment):

```
# a single host specified by alias
/projects     coondog(rw,async)

# a single host specified by FQDN
/projects     houndog.kurtwerks.com(rw,async)

# a single host specified by IP address
/projects     192.168.2.10(rw,async)
```

You can also specify a subdomain of clients by using the familiar shell wildcard characters * and ?, where * stands for one or more characters (including the dot) in a domain name and ? represents a single character. Thus, to specify all of the hosts in the dev.wiley.com subdomain, you could use either of the following export statements:

```
/projects     *dev.wiley.com(rw,async)
/projects     *.dev.wiley.com(rw,async)
```

The next example illustrates how to use address/netmask notation to export a directory to all of the hosts on a network or subnet:

```
/projects     192.168.2.0/24(rw,async)
/projects     192.168.2.0/255.255.255.0(rw,async)
```

The first line specifies a netmask in which 28 bits of the IP address (that is, the first three octets) are used to identify the network. The second line specifies the same subnet, using dotted-quad notation to specify the netmask.

Table 20-2 lists the most commonly used export options.

Table 20-2
/etc/exports Export Options

Option	Description
all_squash	Maps all requests from all UIDs or GIDs to the UID or GID, respectively, of the anonymous user (see no_all_squash)
anongid=gid	Sets the GID of the anonymous account to gid
anonuid=uid	Sets the UID of the anonymous account to uid
async	Allows the server to cache disk writes to improve performance (see sync)
insecure	Permits client requests to originate from unprivileged ports, those numbered 1024 and higher (see secure)
insecure_locks	Disables the need for authentication before activating lock operations (see insecure_locks)
no_all_squash	Disables the all_squash option
no_root_squash	Disables the root_squash option
no_subtree_check	Disables the subtree_check option
no_wdelay	Disables wdelay (must be used with the sync option)
ro	Exports the filesystem read-only, disabling any operation that changes the filesystem
root_squash	Maps all requests from a user ID (UID) or group ID (GID) of 0 to the UID or GID, respectively, of the anonymous user (see no_root_squash)
rw	Exports the filesystem read-write, permitting operations that change the filesystem
secure	Requires client requests to originate from a secure (privileged) port, that is, one numbered less than 1024
secure_locks	Requires that clients requesting lock operations be properly authenticated before activating the lock
subtree_check	If only part of a filesystem, such as a subdirectory, is exported, subtree checking makes sure that file requests apply to files in the exported portion of the filesystem
sync	Forces the server to perform a disk write before the request is considered complete
wdelay	Allows the server to delay a disk write if another related disk write might be requested soon or if one is in progress, improving overall performance (see no_wdelay)

Tip   Recent versions of the NFS utilities now export directories using the `sync` option, as required by the NFS protocol. This is a change from previous versions of the NFS utilities, which exported directories using the `async` option.

Naturally, if client systems mounting NFS exports need to be able to modify files, the filesystem must be exported read-write using the `rw` option. However, to prevent the root user on the client system from having root-equivalent access on the exported filesystem, NFS exports (usually) need to be exported using the `root_squash` option, which maps the client's UID and GID of 0 to the value –2, or 65534. The rationale for root squashing is that root on client systems usually does not need (and should not have) root access to any filesystem on the NFS server.

Note   One exception to root squashing arises when an NFS client mounts its root filesystem from an NFS server. In this case, the client's root user usually *does* need root access to the mounted filesystem. In this case, you should export such filesystems using the `no_root_squash` option because `root_squash` is the default option if neither is specified.

The `subtree_check` option warrants additional explanation. Suppose you export the directory `/projects/net`, where `/projects` is a separate filesystem. Obviously, `net` is a subdirectory of `/projects`. If a client system mounts this export and then tries to access, say, `/projects/net/e100/e100.c`, the server has to verify that `e100.c` resides in the exported filesystem (`/project/net`) *and* that `e100.c` resides in the exported subdirectory (referred to as a *subtree*) of the filesystem. This second access check is called a *subtree check*. For reasons that are unintuitive and not germane to this discussion, the subtree check is more difficult and time-consuming to perform, a situation aggravated if the filesystem is dynamic and undergoing heavy updates. Consequently, you can disable subtree checking using the `no_subtree_check` option. You will usually want to do this on exported home directories and on any shared directory that will see a great deal of file creation, deletion, and modification.

The `async`, `sync`, `wdelay`, and `no_wdelay` options also bear a closer look because of the impact they can have on data integrity and server performance. As briefly explained in Table 20-2, the `async` option permits the NFS server to tell clients that write operations have completed before the server has, in fact, committed the write changes to disk. The default behavior is `sync`, which forces the server to commit changes to disk before communicating a successful write result to NFS clients. The `async` option can significantly improve performance on a heavily used filesystem, but if the server crashes, data not written to disk will be lost because the client flushes its local cache after it receives a successful write result.

The `wdelay` option, which can be used only if the `async` option is set, allows the NFS server to delay disk writes if a disk write is in progress or if the server (heuristically) believes that another disk write request will arrive soon (for some value of "soon"). As a result, the `wdelay` option enables the server to commit multiple write requests to disk in a single operation. Use the `no_wdelay` option to disable this type of caching, but keep in mind that you can use `no_wdelay` only if the `async` option is *not* set.

The following `/etc/exports` file shows the NFS exports used as an example in the rest of this section (note that the last code line is a continuation of the preceding one and should not wrap in the file):

```
/usr/local      192.168.0.0/24()
/projects/kernel    coondog(rw,no_root_squash,async,wdelay,no
_subtree_check)
```

The first line exports the `/usr/local` filesystem to all hosts on the subnet 192.168.0.0, which includes the IP addresses 192.168.0.1 through 192.168.0.254. It does not specify any mount options, so the built-in default mount options will be used (the empty parentheses exist to quiet a warning from the kernel's NFS daemon [`knfsd`] about missing mount options). The second line, which wraps due to this book's formatting constraints, exports the `/projects/kernel` filesystem to the host named `coondog`. The mount options specify the following characteristics:

✦ The filesystem is exported read-write (`rw`).

✦ Root squashing is disabled (`no_root_squash`).

✦ Asynchronous NFS protocol replies are enabled (`async`).

✦ Write delays are enabled (`wdelay`).

✦ Subtree checking is disabled (`no_subtree_checking`).

Exporting the filesystems

After you have edited the NFS server's exports file to your liking, you can start (or restart) the necessary NFS server daemons. As usual, Debian GNU/Linux provides a couple of `rc` scripts to handle the particulars of starting NFS server services, `/etc/init.d/nfs-common` and `/etc/init.d/nfs-kernel-server`. `nfs-common` starts the daemons required for both clients and servers, `rpc.statd` and `rpc.lockd`. As explained earlier in this section, a separate `rc` script, `/etc/init.d/portmap`, starts the portmapper, which should already be running. `nfs-kernel-server` starts the server-specific daemons and exports the filesystem listed in `/etc/exports`. In the interests of being thorough, however, the following example shows the proper order for starting NFS server services, including the portmapper:

```
# /etc/init.d/portmap start
Starting portmap daemon: portmap.
# /etc/init.d/nfs-common start
Starting NFS common utilities: statd.
# /etc/init.d/nfs-kernel-server start
Export directories for NFS kernel daemon...done.
Starting NFS kernel daemon: nfsd mountd.
```

To verify that the exported filesystems are, in fact, exported, use the `exportfs` command as shown here:

```
# exportfs -v
/projects/kernel
                coondog.kurtwerks.com(rw,async,wdelay,no_ro
ot_squash,no_subtree_check)
/usr/local      192.168.0.0/24(rw,sync,wdelay,root_squash)
```

The output of the command wraps due to the width of the displayed information and page layout constraints of this book. The `exportfs` command is the command used to export the filesystems listed in `/etc/exports` and to maintain `/var/lib/nfs/xtab`, which lists NFS-exported filesystems. The first item to notice is that `exportfs` expanded the alias `coondog` to its FQDN, `coondog.kurtwerks.com`. Notice also the mount options listed for `/usr/local`. Even though the `/etc/exports` entry did not list any options, `exportfs` applied the default exports options; the filesystem is exported read-only, and asynchronous replies, write-delay, and root squashing are enabled.

If you want a shorter listing of the current exports, perhaps to use in a script, issue a bare `exportfs` command:

```
# exportfs
/projects/kernel
                coondog.kurtwerks.com
/usr/local      192.168.0.0/28
```

At this point, your NFS server is running and you are ready to configure an NFS client to mount the exported filesystems.

Configuring an NFS client

Setting up an NFS client is remarkably simple. First, on the client system, make sure that the `nfs-common` package is installed:

```
# apt-get install nfs-common
```

Assuming the client has network connectivity to the NFS server, you can mount NFS exports manually using the same command, `mount`, that you use to mount local filesystems. Likewise, if you want the NFS exports mounted automatically when the system boots, you add the appropriate entries to the filesystem mount table, `/etc/fstab`. It is usually a good idea to test NFS mounts by mounting them manually before adding them to `/etc/fstab`. The syntax for mounting NFS exports is only slightly different from mounting local filesystems:

```
mount -t nfs nfs_server:fs mnt_dir -o opts
```

The `-t nfs` argument tells `mount` that you want to mount an NFS filesystem. The construct `nfs_server:fs` identifies the NFS server and the filesystem on the server that you want to mount. `nfs_server` can be specified as an alias name, an FQDN, or an IP address, but if you use an alias name, `mount` must be able to resolve the alias to an IP address. `mnt_dir` specifies the local mount point for the exported filesystem. `opts` defines the local mount options you want to apply (see Table 20-3). So, for example, to mount the `/projects/kernel` served by the NFS server named `grits` on your local filesystem at `/kernel` using the default mount options, you might issue the following command (as root, of course):

```
# mount -t nfs grits:/projects/kernel /kernel
```

To add this entry to the client's `/etc/fstab` file, use an entry such as the following:

```
grits:/projects/kernel /kernel nfs defaults 0 0
```

In many cases, however, you will want to use nondefault mount options. Table 20-3 lists the NFS- and client-specific mount options that you can use.

Table 20-3
NFS-Specific Mount Options

Option	Description
bg	Enables mount attempts to run in the background if the first mount attempt times out (see fg)
fg	Causes mount attempts to run in the foreground if the first mount attempt times out, the default behavior (see bg)
hard	Enables failed NFS file operations to continue retrying after reporting "server not responding" on the system, the default behavior (see soft)
intr	Allows signals (such as Ctrl+C) to interrupt a failed NFS file operation if the filesystem is mounted with the hard option (disable with nointr); This option has no effect unless the hard option is also specified or if soft or nohard is specified
lock	Enables NFS locking and starts the statd and lockd daemons
mounthost=name	Sets the name of the server running mountd to name
mountport=n	Sets the mountd server port to connect to n (no default)
port=n	Sets the NFS server port to which to connect to n (the default is 2049)

Continued

Table 20-3 *(continued)*

Option	Description
retry=*n*	Sets the time to retry a mount operation before giving up to *n* minutes (the default is 10,000)
rsize=*n*	Sets the NFS read buffer size to *n* bytes (the default is 4,096)
soft	Allows an NFS file operation to fail and terminate (see hard)
tcp	Mounts the NFS filesystem using the TCP protocol (see udp)
timeo=*n*	Sets the RPC transmission timeout to *n* tenths of a second (the default is 7); especially useful with the soft mount option
udp	Mounts the NFS filesystem using the UDP protocol, the default behavior (see tcp)
wsize=*n*	Sets the NFS write buffer size to *n* bytes (the default is 4,096)

The background mount option, bg, is useful to use because it allows mount attempts to continue in the background. Background mounts enable the boot process to continue if a given NFS mount isn't available. *Hard mounts* (so-called because they are mounts that use the hard option) force NFS clients to continue trying to mount (or remount) an NFS filesystem even if the specified NFS server is unavailable. As a rule, hard mounts are a bad idea because the continual attempts to access the otherwise unavailable server will cause your machine to appear to freeze. If users need to be able to use a system even when a remote filesystem is not available, you must specifically use the soft or nohard option (creating what is known as a *soft mount*) because hard mounts are the default. Alternatively, if you prefer hard mounts, you can specify intr, which allows signals such as SIGKILL (Ctrl+C) to interrupt a failed mount operation.

Notice that the default amount of time NFS mount operations continue is *10,000 minutes*. It isn't quite infinite, but it is close enough! If you intend to use hard mounts, consider setting the retry option to something more sensible, such as 10 minutes, that is, retyr=10.

The two options that get the most use are rsize and wsize. As their names suggest, rsize and wsize control the size of the buffers, in bytes, that NFS clients use for reading and writing, respectively. The default value is 4,096 bytes, as shown in Table 20-3, but you can increase client responsiveness and assist the server if you increase the size to 8,192. Experiment with the read and write buffer sizes until you find a setting that works for you, but in most situations, 8,192 is ideal.

Tip   As a rule, you want to enable NFS locking, so you can specify the lock option if you wish, but recent versions of NFS enable locking by default.

Example NFS client

The following /etc/fstab entries mount the directories exported in the previous section on the local filesystem:

```
grits:/projects/kernel /kernel rsize=8192,wsize=8192,soft 0 0
grits:/usr/local /usr/local defaults 0 0
```

The first entry mounts /projects/kernel on the mount point /kernel. The mount options specify read and write buffer sizes of 8,192 bytes and indicate that this should be a soft mount. By requesting a soft mount, the mount operation can time out if the host grits is not available for some reason. The 0 0 option is part of the standard fstab syntax indicating that this filesystem should not be dumped and should not be fscked at mount time. The second entry mounts the server's /usr/local export on the local /usr/local directory. It uses the default mount options and the same dump and fsck options as the first entry.

A quick mount command, like the following, will determine at runtime whether these directories were mounted successfully:

```
$ mount -t nfs
grits:/project/kernel on /kernel (rw,addr=192.168.2.10)
grits:/usr/local on /usr/local (rw,addr=192.168.2.10)
```

As you can see from the output, the two NFS exports have been successfully mounted. You can access them just as you would normal filesystem mounts from locally installed disks.

Summary

When you need to create or configure a file server, Debian GNU/Linux gives you a number of options. You can use Samba to share files between Debian and Windows systems (in fact, you can use Samba even if no Windows systems are involved). Debian systems also can be used to create "pure" Linux file servers if you use NFS. Using NFS to share files across a Linux or Linux and UNIX network is by far the most common file-serving model used with Debian systems. This chapter described how to install and configure these file-serving methods, covering both server installation and client-side configuration.

✦ ✦ ✦

OpenLDAP

T his chapter describes creating an OpenLDAP server and
configuring client applications and systems to use
OpenLDAP directory services. After you create the directory
server, you learn how to create a global address book and
how to connect to the global address book.

Unless you're a serious IT infrastructure freak, directory services are a pretty ho-hum subject. A *directory service* is an
intranet-centric function that maintains repositories of information about network-based objects, such as printers, applications, files, servers, users, and e-mail addresses. In addition
to maintaining the repository, a directory service also provides ways for clients to query and retrieve this information.
In a highly integrated intranet environment, applications,
client workstations, and even other servers can be designed
or configured to use the directory service automatically,
resulting in seamless access to network services.

The canonical example of a directory service is a global
address book, an address book accessible to all authorized
users across an intranet. Using a well-maintained and up-to-
date global address book eliminates the necessity for each
user on an intranet to maintain local address books and significantly reduces the likelihood of directory information becoming stale.

Another common use for directory services is to implement
enterprise-wide user authentication and access control.
Rather than controlling users' access to certain servers, applications, or data on a local (per-server or per-application)
basis, the access policy is controlled by a centrally managed
directory service. The goal is to simplify administrative functions, such as adding and deleting users or locating printers,
which is a huge plus for administrators of large networks, and
also to make it possible to implement access and authorization policies at the highest possible level or, to use a common
buzz phrase, *enterprise-wide*.

✦ ✦ ✦ ✦

In This Chapter

Setting up an
OpenLDAP server

Using the directory
with Linux systems

Connecting to the
global address book

✦ ✦ ✦ ✦

What is OpenLDAP?

OpenLDAP is an Open Source implementation of LDAP. *LDAP* stands for Lightweight Directory Access Protocol and is defined in RFC3377 (see `http://www.faqs.org/rfcs/rfc3377.html`). Without descending into a bog of standards and obtuse terminology, LDAP provides a means for accessing X.500-compliant directory information over the Internet (rather, over any TCP/IP network) while minimizing the complexity of both the client and server applications.

OpenLDAP is a suite of servers, client applications, and a library that implements LDAP. The servers include `slapd`, which provides the LDAP services, and `slurpd`, which implements replication services for LDAP directories. The `libldap` library implements the bulk of the functionality used in the client applications and also defines the API that applications can use to incorporate LDAP functionality without needing to invoke external programs. The OpenLDAP project also includes LDAP class libraries for Java, known as JLDAP, and JDBC-LDAP, a Java bridge that enables Java applications to access LDAP data stores using SQL and JDBC (Java Database Connectivity).

The OpenLDAP client applications consist of utilities, tools, and sample clients for interacting with LDAP directories. The sample clients serve both as administrative utilities for working with LDAP directories and as example programs for developers to use when developing their own LDAP-enabled programs. The client programs and utilities, as a group, provide all of the functionality necessary for creating and maintaining LDAP directory data. Table 21-1 lists and briefly describes the key client utilities.

Table 21-1
OpenLDAP Client Applications

Program	Description
ldapadd	Adds a new entry to an LDAP directory
ldapcompare	Compares LDAP directory entries
ldapdelete	Deletes an entry from an LDAP directory
ldapmodify	Modifies an existing LDAP directory entry
ldapmodrdn	Renames an LDAP directory entry
ldappasswd	Changes the password of an LDAP directory entry
ldapsearch	Searches an LDAP directory
ldapwhoami	Performs a whoami search in an LDAP directory
slapadd	Adds entries to a SLAPD database
slapcat	Converts a SLAPD database to LDIF format

Program	Description
slapdn	Validates string-format DNs against a directory schema
slapindex	Converts a SLAPD index to LDIF format
slaptest	Verifies the syntax of the slapd.conf configuration file

OpenLDAP software is provided by a group of developers working under the auspices of the OpenLDAP Project. The OpenLDAP Foundation coordinates the OpenLDAP Project.

 Note For more information about OpenLDAP, the OpenLDAP Project, and the OpenLDAP Foundation, visit the OpenLDAP Web pages at www.openldap.org/.

The OpenLDAP Data Model

To understand most of the discussion in this chapter, you might want a brief overview of the data model that LDAP (and, thus, OpenLDAP) uses, if only to comprehend the odd naming conventions and acronyms that inevitably creep into the text. If you are familiar with LDAP, this section will be review, so you can profitably skip ahead to the next section, "Creating an OpenLDAP Server."

LDAP assumes that one or more servers together provide access to a *directory information tree* (DIT). A DIT is an inverted tree made up of *entries* with the root of the tree at the top. Entries, in turn, have *names* and consist of a set of *attributes*. Attributes, finally, consist of a *type* and one or more *values* associated with that type.

Each entry has a unique name relative to other entries at the same level in the DIT. This name is referred to as a *relative distinguished name* or RDN. The RDN is formed by concatenating one or more of the entry's attribute values. Similarly, if you concatenate all of the RDNs from the root of the DIT to a particular entry, you have that entry's *distinguished name* (DN), which is unique in the DIT. An example of a DN is

```
CN=Kurt Wall, O=KurtWerks, Inc., C=US\
```

LDAP also carries the notion of a naming context, which is analogous to a *namespace* in programming. A programming namespace is simply a domain in which a name assigned to objects such as variables, data structures, or functions is guaranteed to be unique and not to clash with another object with the same name in another namespace. In the LDAP data model, a *naming context* consists of all of the entries that start at an entry that is mastered by one server and traverse down to entries that are mastered by different servers. The root of the DIT is not part of any naming context; each server has different attribute values in the root directory server.

As noted previously, an LDAP entry is made up of attributes, which consist of a type and one or more associated values. The attribute type is identified by a short descriptive name and an *object identifier* (OID). Attribute types define the content of an attribute, whether the attribute can have multiple values, what kinds of searches can be performed on that attribute, and a number of other functions that make the information in LDAP directories useful.

For example, `mail` is an attribute. The `mail` attribute has the following characteristics:

- ✦ You can assign it multiple values (people can have multiple e-mail addresses).
- ✦ The attribute values must be encoded as ASCII strings (`kurt@wiley.com`).
- ✦ Searches on this attribute are case insensitive (`kurt@wiley.com` matches `KURT@wiley.COM`).

To make sense of the contents of an LDAP store, the LDAP protocol defines a *schema* or information map (really, metainformation). The schema is the collection of attribute type definitions, object class definitions, and other constraints that LDAP servers use to determine how to match or filter searches and whether attribute values (or, in some cases, attribute types) can be created, deleted, or modified.

Note The directory service wonks out there might observe that LDAP's data model resembles the X.500 data model. This should be no surprise because LDAP is a low-overhead X.500 directory.

This should be enough information to help you make sense of the terminology and concepts used in the rest of this chapter. If you need an in-depth reference to LDAP, see the excellent reference guide *LDAP Directories: Building an Enterprise Directory* by Marcel Rizcallah (Wiley, 2003).

Creating an OpenLDAP Server

Predictably enough, you have to install OpenLDAP software before you're going to get very far. Install the following Debian packages:

- ✦ `libldap2`—Contains the core OpenLDAP runtime libraries
- ✦ `libldap2-dev`—Installs header files and libraries necessary for developing OpenLDAP applications (optional)
- ✦ `ldap-utils`—Installs the client programs necessary to connect to OpenLDAP servers
- ✦ `slapd`—Contains the OpenLDAP server, `slapd`, and the replication daemon, `slurpd`

To perform the installation, follow these steps:

1. Use the following command to start the OpenLDAP installation:

   ```
   # apt-get install libldap2 ldap-utils slapd
   ```

   In some cases, you might be asked whether you want to omit configuration `slapd`. If you see this dialog box, select No and press Enter to continue.

   Note

   Depending on how your system is configured and the packages you initially installed, some of the configuration dialog boxes you see might appear in a different order or you might see configuration screens not described in this procedure.

2. The first configuration step involves setting the DNS domain name used to construct the base or root DN of your LDAP directory, as shown in Figure 21-1.

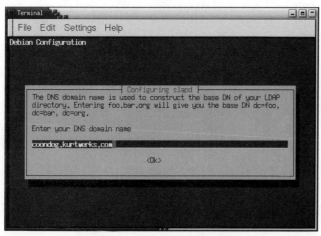

Figure 21-1: Entering the DNS domain name.

In Figure 21-1, the domain name is `coondog.kurtwerks.com`, so the base DN will be `dc=coondog,dc=kurtwerks,dc=com`. Type your domain name and press Enter.

3. The next configuration step is to provide your organization name. Figure 21-2 shows the dialog box. Type your organization's name, if any, and press Enter to continue.

4. One of the improvements of the LDAPv3 (LDAP version 3) protocol over earlier LDAP specifications was the addition of security features and authentication. Figure 21-3 shows the screen on which you provide a password for the LDAP administrator. The administrator adds, deletes, and modifies entries in the data store, updates the schema, and performs all of the other standard administrative tedium.

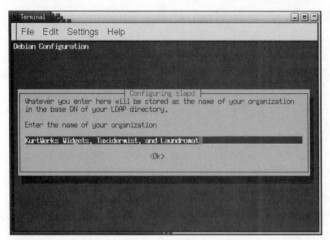

Figure 21-2: Entering the organization name.

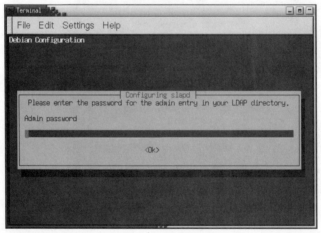

Figure 21-3: Assigning the LDAP administrator's password.

Type a password, press Enter, and then retype the password and press Enter to verify the password and continue.

5. On the next screen, you are presented the option to enable the older LDAP protocol, version 2 (see Figure 21-4). The default is to leave the version 2 protocol disabled and use version 3 exclusively. You should accept the default behavior and stick to version 3, so make sure No is selected and press Enter to continue.

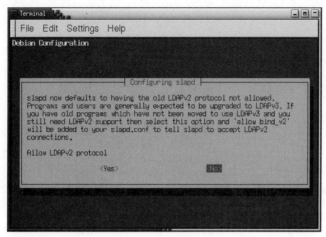

Figure 21-4: Leaving LDAPv2 disabled.

6. Depending on your system's configuration, you might also be asked to select the database back end. The options are BDB, the Berkeley database, and LDBM, the Lightweight Database Manager. You can select either one, but BDB is more well known and better supported, so you would be better off using the Berkeley database.

7. Another question you might be asked is whether you want to remove the LDAP data store if you remove the LDAP packages. This decision is yours, but if you spend time and effort creating the data, you might want to keep it around even if you do remove the LDAP packages.

Testing the installation

When the slapd installation and configuration completes, you should have a functioning OpenLDAP server running on your system. In addition to using the ps command to confirm that the slapd daemon is running, you should also make sure the slapd daemon is properly configured. You can verify the configuration by executing a query using the ldapsearch command. The syntax is awkward and tedious to type, but you will have to type only a few of these commands. The command to execute and typical results are shown in the following example:

```
$ ldapsearch -x -s base namingContexts
# extended LDIF
#
# LDAPv3
# base <> with scope base
```

```
# filter: (objectclass=*)
# requesting: namingContexts
#

#
dn:
namingContexts: dc=coondog,dc=kurtwerks,dc=com

# search result
search: 2
result: 0 Success

# numResponses: 2
# numEntries: 1
```

The `-x` option tells `ldapsearch` to use plain (unencrypted) authentication instead of SASL. The `-s base` option indicates that the search should start at the base object, or root entry, of the directory tree. `namingContexts`, finally, indicates that the search should be limited to the `namingContexts` attribute.

The output you want to see is the distinguished name (dn) entry. Your LDAP server's DN will be different, of course, but you should see the name you provided when asked for the hostname in the configuration screen shown in Figure 21-1. Notice how the hostname typed in Figure 21-1, `coondog.kurtwerks.com`, has been broken up into three components: `dc=coondog`, `dc=kurtwerks`, and `dc=com`. For more information about the `ldapsearch` command, see its Manpage (`man ldapsearch`).

Note   The Linux LDAP-HOWTO at the Linux Documentation Project (`www.tldp.org/HOWTO/LDAP-HOWTO/index.html`) is an excellent resource that provides additional information on setting up an LDAP server. Although not specific to Debian GNU/Linux, the information is generally applicable.

Adding entries to the database

There are various ways to add entries to the LDAP data store. You can add entries manually using an LDIF (LDAP Interchange Format) file and the `ldapadd` command, you can use migration tools that import the system password file, or you can use an LDAP viewer/editor, such as LDAP Explorer, a PHP-based LDAP browsing and editing tool. This section shows you how to add an entry to the LDAP data store using an LDIF file and `ldapadd`.

The LDIF format permits LDAP directory information to be represented in a simple textual form. Each LDIF entry consists of a distinguished name (which is required), an optional entry ID, one or more object classes, and attribute definitions. A blank line separates multiple LDIF entries. Thus, the general LDIF format resembles the following:

```
[entry_id]
dn: distinguished_name
objectClass: object_class
...
attribute_type: attribute_value
attribute_type: attribute_value
...
```

Only the DN and a single objectClass are required. However, any attribute types that are associated with the specified objectClass *must* be specified. There are a large number of object classes and an equally large (if not larger) number of attributes associated with these object classes. To keep things simple, the example presented here uses the object classes Person and inetOrgPerson and the attributes listed in Table 21-2. The class inetOrgPerson is based on the class Person and is used in this example because the inetOrgPerson class includes the mail attribute.

Tip   See http://developer.netscape.com/docs/manuals/directory/admin 30/ldif.htm#1043905 for more information about the attributes and object classes used to create LDAP directories.

Table 21-2
LDAP Attributes

Attribute	Description	Example
cn	A person's first or given name	Kurt Wall
jpegphoto	A photo of the person in JPEG format	Not shown
mail	The person's e-mail address	kwall@kurtwerks.com
sn	A person's last name or surname	Wall
uid	The person's user ID or login name	kwall

The following listing shows the LDIF file, example.ldif, used to add an entry to the directory:

```
dn: cn=Kurt Wall,dc=coondog,dc=kurtwerks,dc=com
objectclass: inetorgperson
objectclass: person
cn: Kurt Wall
sn: Wall
mail: kurt@kurtwerks.com
uid: kurt
```

Create this file, with values appropriate for your directory, using the text editor of your choice. After you've created this file, execute the `ldapadd` command using the syntax shown in the following example to add the new entry to your directory:

```
ldapadd -x -D "cn=admin,dc=domain" -W -f example.ldif
```

The -x option tells `ldapadd` to use plain authentication to connect to the LDAP store. The option -D `"cn=admin,dc=domain "` identifies the distinguished name to use to bind, or log in to, the LDAP store. In this example, cn, which stands for *common name*, is `admin`, the administrative user created when you configured the LDAP server during installation. Replace the `dc=domain` entry with the domain name you selected. -W tells `ldapadd` to prompt you for the password. The argument -f `example.ldif` specifies the file from which to create the new entry. A complete `ldappadd` invocation might resemble the following:

```
$ ldapadd -x -D "cn=admin,dc=coondog,dc=kurtwerks,dc=com" \
> -W -f example.ldif
Enter LDAP Password:
adding new entry "cn=Kurt Wall,dc=coondog,dc=kurtwerks,dc=com"
```

Note   Any user that has the LDAP administrator's password can add, delete, or modify entries in the LDAP data store. It is not necessary to be the root user to do these tasks.

Notice the use of the backslash character, \, to break the command across two lines. A quick `ldapsearch` command shows that the entry was added successfully:

```
$ ldapsearch -x -b 'dc=coondog,dc=kurtwerks,dc=com" \
> '(objectclass=person)'
# extended LDIF
#
# LDAPv3
# base <dc=coondog,dc=kurtwerks,dc=com> with scope sub
# filter: (objectclass=person)
# requesting: ALL
#

# Kurt Wall, coondog.kurtwerks.com
dn: cn=Kurt Wall,dc=coondog,dc=kurtwerks,dc=com
objectClass: inetorgperson
objectClass: person
cn: Kurt Wall
sn: Wall
mail: kwall@kurtwerks.com
uid: kurt

# search result
search: 2
result: 0 Success
```

```
# numResponses: 2
# numEntries: 1
```

As you can see from the output, the entry was added successfully. Notice also that the default configuration permits any user to query the LDAP data store. The query limited the search to the `person` object class using the `'(objectclass=person)'` search predicate (refer to the `ldapsearch` Manpage for more details about this command).

Connecting to the Directory Server from Linux Systems

Connecting to your LDAP data store from Linux systems can be as simple or as complicated as you want it to be. In the simple-but-tedious department, you can use the various OpenLDAP client commands (`ldapadd`, `ldapdelete`, `ldapmodify`, `ldapsearch`, and so forth) with the option `-H ldapuri` that specifies connecting to a remote LDAP server whose URI is `ldapuri`. The following example shows using the `ldapsearch` command on the host `coondog.kurtwerks.com` to connect to the LDAP server running on `luther.kurtwerks.com`:

```
[kwall@coondog]$ ldapsearch -x \
> -H ldap://luther.kurtwerks.com \
> -b 'dc=coondog,dc=kurtwerks,dc=com' \
> '(objectclass=person)' mail
# extended LDIF
#
# LDAPv3
# base <dc=coondog,dc=kurtwerks,dc=com> with scope sub
# filter: (objectclass=person)
# requesting: mail
#

# GNU User, coondog.kurtwerks.com
dn: cn=GNU User,dc=coondog,dc=kurtwerks,dc=com
mail: gnuser@kurtwerks.com

# Tux Penguin, coondog.kurtwerks.com
dn: cn=Tux Penguin,dc=coondog,dc=kurtwerks,dc=com
mail: tux@kurtwerks.com

# Kurt Wall, coondog.kurtwerks.com
dn: cn=Kurt Wall,dc=coondog,dc=kurtwerks,dc=com
mail: kwall@kurtwerks.com
```

```
# Kelly Dyky, coondog.kurtwerks.com
dn: cn=Kelly Dyky,dc=coondog,dc=kurtwerks,dc=com
mail: kelly@kurtwerks.com

# search result
search: 2
result: 0 success

# numResponses: 5
# numEntries: 4
```

This search request looks for the same information as the query at the end of the previous section. This time, however, the query filtered the output on the `mail` attribute, so only entries that have a `mail` attribute were displayed and only the `mail` attribute's values were displayed. Notice the syntax used to specify the remote LDAP server, `ldap://luther.kurtwerks.com`. The `ldap:` portion specifies the protocol, LDAP, to use, and `//luther.kurtwerks.com` specifies the server to which to connect using this protocol (it's the same as `http://luther.kurtwerks.com`, only different — that is, in the standard Web URL, the protocol specification is `http:` instead of `ldap:`).

Using a Global Address Book

Perhaps the most common use of an LDAP directory server is to create a global address book, that is, an address book that has everyone's e-mail addresses and other identifying information in it. Such information typically includes a person's office number, office phone and/or extension, full name, organizational role, and so on. The value of a global address book is that network administrators need to update only a single directory to have the new information immediately available to all users (well, all users who use the global address book). Most of the popular e-mail clients speak fluent LDAP, so they are easy to configure to use a global address book. The trick, of course, is creating the global directory.

In the absence of slick, graphical tools that hide the ugly, obtuse LDIF format behind an attractive, user-friendly interface, the easiest way to create a global address book is to create a text file in LDIF format that contains the information you want to share via LDAP and then load it into the database using the procedure described in the section titled "Adding entries to the database," earlier in this chapter.

To configure the Mozilla mail client (and derivatives of Mozilla, such as Thunderbird) to use the global address book, start the mail client and select Edit ⇨ Mail & Newsgroup Account Settings. Then click the Mail & Newsgroups item under the Category column. This will open the dialog box shown in Figure 21-5.

Click the Addressing label under the Mail & Newsgroups heading to display the Addressing panel (see Figure 21-6).

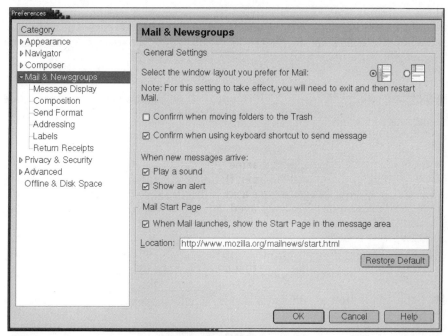

Figure 21-5: Configuring the Mozilla mail client.

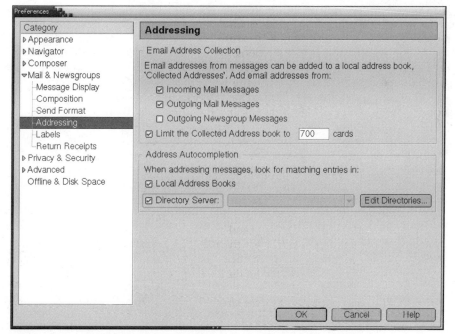

Figure 21-6: The Addressing panel in Mozilla's mail account settings.

At the bottom of the panel, check the Directory Server check box, and then click the Edit Directories button. This button opens the LDAP Directory Servers dialog box, shown in Figure 21-7. Unless you have already selected another LDAP server, this list will be empty.

Figure 21-7: Selecting an LDAP directory server for the Mozilla 1.0 mail client.

Click the Add button to add a new server, which opens the Directory Server Properties dialog box (see Figure 21-8).

Figure 21-8: Adding an LDAP directory server for the Mozilla 1.0 mail client.

The Port Number field will already be filled in for you, so leave this value alone. For the Name field, type a name that identifies this server (KurtWerks in Figure 21-8). For the Hostname field, type the name of the server on which the LDAP server is running (luther.kurtwerks.com in Figure 21-8). In the Base DN field, type the DN (distinguished name) you used in the query examples in the previous section (dc=luther,dc=kurtwerks,dc=com in Figure 21-8). Click OK to close the Directory Server Properties dialog box, click OK to close the LDAP Directory Servers dialog box, and click OK to close the Preferences dialog box.

Mozilla 1.0's mail client is now configured to use the global address book. To see it in action, start a new message and click the Address button on the toolbar to open Mozilla's address book (see Figure 21-9). When the address book opens, type an asterisk (*) in the Search box, as shown in Figure 21-9, and Mozilla's built-in LDAP client will populate the address list on the left-hand side of the address book with the contents of your LDAP directory. *Voilà!* Ain't technology grand!

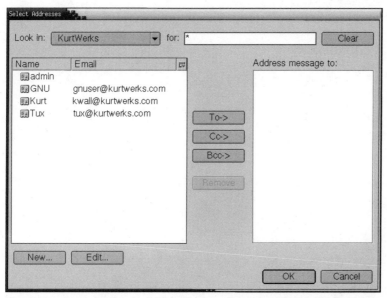

Figure 21-9: Accessing the LDAP directory from Mozilla's address book.

Summary

This chapter provided basic instructions for using OpenLDAP on a Debian GNU/ Linux system. You picked up some fundamental LDAP theory and learned how to create an LDAP data store, how to populate that data store to create a global address book, and how to configure Mozilla Messenger to use that global address book. The chapter also illustrated using OpenLDAP command-line programs to work with LDAP databases and connecting to a remote LDAP data store.

✦ ✦ ✦

Intranet E-Mail Servers

It should surprise no one that e-mail services are one of the most heavily used services on any intranet server (or Internet server, for that matter). If you have any doubt about the importance of a reliable e-mail system, take down your own organization's e-mail server; you can count in seconds the time that elapses before someone, usually your boss, lets you know that e-mail is down and asks when it will be back up. E-mail places especially heavy demands on computing resources and, thus, on the person that administers the e-mail server.

This chapter examines some of the options available to you when setting up an e-mail server and describes some of the issues involved in doing so. It also describes how to install and configure an e-mail server that provides IMAP access and an e-mail server that provides POP access.

Providing E-Mail Services

This section offers an overview of e-mail services. Given space constraints, it simply won't be feasible to discuss every possible mail server application. Moreover, from a pedagogical point of view, it is probably more instructive to show you how to configure one typical POP server and one typical IMAP server. You are more likely to grasp the basic principles if the examples are simple and focused.

Succinctly stated, e-mail just has to work. To keep it working, you need to understand how e-mail gets from one e-mail user to another. The various components are shown in the following list:

✦ *Mail User Agents*, or MUAs, enable users to read and write e-mail. MUAs are what most users generally regard as "e-mail." MUAs can be configured to hand off e-mail to a delivery mechanism on the user's machine or to use another system (the mail server) for e-mail delivery. Similarly, MUAs can be configured to read incoming e-mail that is handled by a local mail server or to read e-mail from another system. Web-based or browser-based e-mail clients also qualify as MUAs, but they can also be considered groupware if the Web-based e-mail client is part of an integrated suite of collaborative tools accessed via a Web browser. Evolution, Mozilla Thunderbird, and my personal favorite, mutt, are examples of MUAs.

✦ *Mail Transfer Agents*, or MTAs, deliver e-mail messages between computer systems but are rarely capable of acting as MUAs. Large sites typically have a centralized MTA, referred to as a *relay host*, that handles all incoming and outgoing e-mail; individual users configure their MUAs to deliver mail to and receive mail from this relay host. At smaller sites, individual users might run MTAs on their own systems. Under most circumstances, MTAs receive and process mail for only the domain in which they reside, but it is possible for MTAs to serve as relays or transfer agents for other mail systems. Exim, Postfix, and Sendmail are examples of MTAs.

✦ *Local Delivery Agents*, or LDAs, are the silent partners of an e-mail system. LDAs receive mail from an MTA and deliver it to users' mailbox files. Procmail and Fetchmail are two popular LDAs.

✦ Optionally, users can use an e-mail notification program (the classic GUI example is xbiff) that informs them when new mail arrives. Many, perhaps most, MUAs include this function, so it is not necessary to use an external program for this purpose.

✦ Various TCP/IP protocols, including SMTP, POP, and IMAP, handle storing and transferring mail across the network.

Figure 22-1 illustrates the general process of e-mail delivery.

The details vary somewhat from site to site, but the principle is the same. The solid arrows trace the primary delivery path. Bubba uses his MUA to compose an e-mail message to Joe Bob. Bubba's MUA sends the message to his MTA. Bubba's MTA then connects to Joe Bob's MTA across the Internet and delivers the message. Joe Bob's MTA hands the message off to the LDA, which delivers Bubba's message to Joe Bob's mail spool. In the last step, Joe Bob uses his MUA to read the message (and, presumably, to reply).

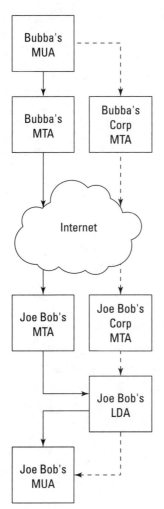

Figure 22-1: High-level diagram of the e-mail delivery process.

Figure 22-1 uses dashed arrows to illustrate an alternative delivery path. This alternate path routes Bubba's message through his company's relay host, which then transfers the message to Joe Bob's company's relay host. From there, Joe Bob's LDA still deposits the message into Joe Bob's mail spool. There are still other variations of the delivery path Bubba's message might follow. As the message crosses the Internet, for example, it might pass through one or more (unspecified) systems. Or, Bubba's local MTA might deliver the message directly to Joe Bob's corporate MTA or Joe Bob's own local MTA. There could also be other systems involved, such as firewalls or systems that check incoming and outgoing messages for viruses. The key point is that at least two MTAs, two MUAs, and, optionally, one LDA are involved in delivering Bubba's e-mail to Joe Bob.

Analyzed in terms of the protocols involved, Bubba's MUA uses SMTP, the Simple Message Transfer Protocol, to transfer his message to the MTA. In turn, Bubba's MTA uses SMTP to transfer the message to Joe Bob's MTA. To read the message, Joe Bob's MUA uses POP, the Post Office Protocol, or IMAP, the Internet Message Access Protocol, to read the message from the MTA. Below SMTP, POP, and IMAP, lower-level TCP/IP protocols handle the nuts and bolts of establishing connections between hosts and transferring data.

Creating an IMAP E-Mail Server

IMAP stands for Internet Message Access Protocol. Unlike the POP3 protocol described in the previous section, IMAP supports a greater range of operations on mailboxes. Whereas POP3 permits storing, retrieving, and deleting messages on only a remote server, IMAP4 enables mail clients to use the remote message store maintained on an IMAP4 server in the same way as they would a local message store. More specifically, in addition to the basic maildrop services provided by POP3, IMAP4 adds the following features:

✦ Creating, removing, and renaming mailboxes ("folders") on the server

✦ Setting and unsetting various status flags on messages

✦ Retrieving subsets of messages based on message attributes (such as their subjects or senders) or the contents of the message

✦ Working off-line and then synchronizing with the server when the client has an active network connection

This section describes installing, configuring, and testing an IMAP4 server.

Note   RFC1730, the RFC that defines IMAP4, contains a much more thorough description of the IMAP4 protocol than provided in this section. If you want to know more about IMAP4, you can read RFC1730 online at The Internet FAQ Archives Web site (www.faqs.org/rfcs/rfc1730.html).

Installing an IMAP4 server

The IMAP4 server installed and configured in this section is the Courier IMAP server. I've chosen Courier IMAP over alternative IMAP4 servers because Courier IMAP has a large installed base, so its care and feeding are well known. The

Debian package for Courier IMAP comes in two varieties: vanilla Courier IMAP (`courier-imap`) and Courier IMAP with SSL flavor crystals (`courier-imap-ssl`). Of the two, the SSL-enabled version of Courier IMAP is preferable because it uses SSL to encrypt communication between the server and IMAP clients. Accordingly, the example IMAP4 server created in this section installs Courier IMAP with SSL support.

For the record, the phrase "encrypt communication" means that all communication between the e-mail client and the IMAP server, such as the authentication exchange (username and password) and the messages themselves, is encrypted using (in this case) SSL as the data travels between the client and server. Like POP3, plain vanilla IMAP4 is an open or plaintext protocol, so it is insecure. Encryption does not make your e-mail (or anything else) invulnerable to malicious ne'er-do-wells, just considerably more difficult to compromise.

Note   For more information than you could possibly want about Courier IMAP, see the Courier Mail Server Web pages at `www.courier-mta.org/`.

To install Courier IMAP with SSL and its supporting packages, use the following `apt-get` command:

```
# apt-get install courier-imap-ssl
```

This command might also install a number of other packages, including `courier-authdaemon`, `courier-base`, and `openssl` because `courier-imap-ssl` depends on these packages for various features and functionality.

Configuring an IMAP4 server

Before users can use your IMAP server, you need to add users to `/etc/courier/userdb`. This file contains a list of accounts that IMAP handles. Each entry in `/etc/courier/userdb` consists of a line that identifies an account, such as `imapuser`, and one or more configuration pairs that define information that governs that account, such as a password, a mail spool directory, and so on. The general format of entries in `userdb` is

```
name         field=value[|...]
```

The *name* field must be a lowercase account name and must be separated from the configuration pairs by *one* tab character; eight spaces (or any number of spaces) won't do. Multiple `field=value` pairs are permitted, separated by the pipe character, `|`. The contents of `field` and `value` cannot contain slashes or control characters. The configuration pairs can appear in any order. Table 22-1 lists the currently allowed fields.

Table 22-1
userdb Configuration Fields

Field	Description
gid	Assigns the group ID (text or numeric) for the *name* account
home	Lists the home directory for the *name* account
mail	Defines the location of *name*'s mailbox
quota	Specifies the Maildir quota assigned to *name*
shell	Identifies *name* account's default login shell
systempw	Specifies the password for *name*
uid	Assigns the user ID (text or numeric) for the *name* account

The maildir quota configuration pair is separate from filesystem quotas you might have configured and is used only by Courier's maildir utilities, which are not described in this book.

Don't panic! You don't have to create this file by hand. You can use a handy Perl script, pw2userdb, to create /etc/courier/userdb for you from the contents of /etc/passwd. pw2userdb writes its output to standard output, so you need to redirect the output to, you guessed it, /etc/courier/userdb, as shown in the following example:

```
# pw2userdb > /etc/courier/userdb
```

Because /etc/courier/userdb contains system and user passwords, delete unnecessary entries from the /etc/courier/userdb file. In this context, *unnecessary* means system users such as daemon, sys, bin, sync, and so forth. /etc/courier/userdb is a text file, so you can edit it with a regular text editor (as the root user, of course). Moreover, due to the sensitivity of the authentication information contained in /etc/courier/userdb, remove any group and world permissions using the following chmod command. This step is necessary because the makeuserdb command discussed next requires that userdb be readable by only the root user.

```
# chmod 600 /etc/courier/userdb
```

The final step is to create a binary database file, /etc/courier/userdb.dat, which is much faster for Courier IMAP to read than a plaintext file. If you have only a few dozen IMAP4 users, the binary file doesn't benefit you much, but if you have several hundred or several thousand, using a binary file makes a significant difference in the IMAP server's performance. Create `userdb.dat` using the `makeuserdb` command:

```
# cd /etc/courier
# makeuserdb
```

After you execute `makeuserdb`, you will see that a binary file named `userdb.dat` has been created in `/etc/courier`. It is group- and world-readable, which at first glance seems to defeat the purpose of making `userdb` accessible only by root. However, you will also notice that a second file, `/etc/courier/userdbshadow.dat`, has also been created and that this file is accessible only by root. `userdbshadow.dat` is to `userdb.dat` as `/etc/shadow` is to `/etc/password`. It contains authentication information that must be protected from prying eyes. In the process of creating `userdb.dat`, `makeuserdb` copies any field in `userdb` that ends in pw, such as `systempw` (see Table 22-1), into `userdbshadow.dat`, not `userdb.dat`.

What Is Maildir?

Maildir is the mailbox format created and popularized by Dan Bernstein, author of QMail, a fast and secure MTA. The traditional mbox-style mailbox format stores all messages in a single spool file (usually `/var/mail/username` or a variant thereof). The primary shortcoming of the mbox format is that using a single file forces MUAs (and MTAs and LDAs, for that matter) to use locks when accessing the file. For example, if an MTA is delivering (appending) new mail to a user's mbox-style spool file, an MUA cannot simultaneously delete or otherwise manipulate messages in that spool file. Maildir, on the other hand, as the name suggests, uses a top-level directory named `Maildir` (by default and by convention) as the primary message store. Each incoming message is stored in its own, uniquely named file in that directory. Maildir also makes it simpler to organize mail into, if you will, submailboxes, by creating subdirectories beneath the top-level directory and storing message files in these submailboxes. As a result, MUAs can read, delete, and move existing messages without needing to worry about bumping into the MTA while the MTA is delivering new mail. Another advantage of maildir is that the mailbox format makes it trivial to use all of the standard Linux text-processing utilities on groups of related messages. It is also easier to manage your mailbox by manipulating maildir mailboxes (that is, directories).

Maildir is not quite as widely supported as the older mbox format, which has been around for a *long* time, but it is widely enough supported; modern MUAs and MTAs either support it natively or can be made to deliver mail in maildir format with minimal fuss. It is the only mailbox format that Courier IMAP supports, so that's why this chapter discusses it.

For more information about maildir, see Dan Bernstein's article "Using maildir format" on the Web at `http://cr.yp.to/proto/maildir.html`.

Configuring Exim to use Maildir

The next step is to teach Exim, the default Debian GNU/Linux MTA, to use Courier IMAP's maildir-style mailbox rather than the standard Linux mbox mailbox format. To do so, edit /etc/exim4/exim4.conf.template and /etc/exim4/conf.d/main/01_exim4-config_listmacrosdefs and find the entry that begins with the LOCAL_DELIVERY= directive. It should look like the following by default:

```
LOCAL_DELIVERY=mail_spool
```

Modify this line so that it reads

```
LOCAL_DELIVERY=maildir_home
```

Next, execute the command update-exim4.conf to update the Exim configuration with the changes:

```
# update-exim4.conf
```

If there are no errors (there shouldn't be), the command produces no output.

This change enables delivery to maildir-type mailboxes. To make these changes take effect, use Exim's initialization script, /etc/init.d/exim4, to reload the configuration file:

```
# /etc/init.d/exim4 restart
Restarting MTA: exim4.
```

Now you need to make sure that new users will have a Maildir directory created when their accounts are created. You can use the maildirmake command to create /etc/skel/Maildir. Courier IMAP requires this directory to exist in order to deliver mail. By creating the directory in /etc/skel, all new users will have a properly configured Maildir delivery directory, where "properly configured" means "Maildir has the correct permissions and certain required subdirectories." The command to execute is

```
# maildirmake /etc/skel/Maildir
```

You need to decide what to do about existing users that do not have a Maildir directory in their home directories. One option is to send an e-mail to each existing user, which will cause Courier IMAP to create the directory on the fly. Alternatively, you can write a script that invokes maildirmake for each user. It is probably easiest just to send an e-mail to each existing user, but it is more fun to write a script to do it.

Console-based applications such as mutt require a modification to `/etc/login.defs`. Find the lines that look like the following:

```
#QMAIL_DIR      Maildir/
MAIL_DIR        /var/mail
#MAIL_FILE      .mail
```

Modify them to look like the following instead:

```
QMAIL_DIR       Maildir/
#MAIL_DIR       /var/mail
MAIL_FILE       Maildir/
```

These entries define the mail environment used by most applications. To receive new mail notification from the shell, you'll also need to modify `/etc/pam.d/login`. Find the line that reads

```
session optional pam_mail.so standard noenv
```

Change it so that it looks like

```
session optional pam_mail.so standard noenv dir=~/Maildir
```

If you permit users to connect to the server using SSH, you'll need to make a similar modification to `/etc/pam.d/ssh`. Locate the line that resembles the following:

```
session optional pam_mail.so standard noenv # [1]
```

Edit it so that it looks like this:

```
session optional pam_mail.so standard noenv dir=~/Maildir
```

At last, the configuration process is complete. The final step is testing the configuration.

Testing the IMAP server

You can test your IMAP4 setup by using telnet (which might need to be installed) to connect to the IMAP4 server and by entering a few IMAP protocol commands. If telnet needs to be installed, the following command should do the trick:

```
# apt-get install telnet
```

After telnet is installed, send an e-mail to a user with an account on the system so that the IMAP server will have something to say. The following command should suffice:

```
# echo 'Didja get it?' | mailx -s 'IMAP test' username
```

Replace *username* with the name of the user you are using to test. Now, use the `telnet` command to connect to the IMAP server and issue some IMAP protocol commands to make sure that the server is working. The following example shows a complete test:

```
$ telnet localhost 143
Trying 127.0.0.1...
Connected to localhost.
Escape character is '^]'.
* OK [CAPABILITY IMAP4rev1 UIDPLUS CHILDREN NAMESPACE THREA
D=ORDEREDSUBJECT THREAD=REFERENCES SORT QUOTA IDLE ACL ACL2
=UNION] Courier-IMAP ready. Copyright 1998-2004 Double Prec
ision, Inc.  See COPYING for distribution information.
aa login imapuser sekritword
aa OK LOGIN Ok.
bb select inbox
* FLAGS (\Draft \Answered \Flagged \Deleted \Seen \Recent)
* OK [PERMANENTFLAGS (\* \Draft \Answered \Flagged \Deleted
\Seen)] Limited
* 1 EXISTS
* 1 RECENT
* OK [UIDVALIDITY 1095996936] Ok
* OK [MYRIGHTS "acdilrsw"] ACL
bb OK [READ-WRITE] Ok
zzzz logout
* BYE Courier-IMAP server shutting down
zzzz OK LOGOUT completed
Connection closed by foreign host.
```

This example used a normal user account, `imapuser`, rather than the root account, to test the server's functionality. You should use the username you used to send the test message. The IMAP commands you enter are the following:

✦ `aa login username password` — Authenticates to the IMAP server. Replace *username* and *password* with the username and password you want to use (and that are listed in `/etc/courier/userdb`).

✦ `bb select inbox` — Opens the named mailbox, inbox.

✦ `zzzz logout` — Logs you out and closes the connection.

The `aa`, `bb`, and `zzzz` (case is insignificant) are required by the protocol. `aa` and `bb` could be any two-letter sequence, but `zzzz` (or `ZZZZ`) is a required part of the logout command.

At this point, you (or your users) can configure e-mail clients to use the newly configured IMAP server.

Setting Up a POP3 E-Mail Server

As suggested earlier in the chapter, POP is an acronym for Post Office Protocol. POP is often referred to as POP3 because the current version of the POP protocol is version 3. POP3 was designed to provide small Internet sites (even single workstations) with reliable mail services even if such sites did not have continuous Internet connectivity or sufficient computing resources to run an MTA continuously. POP3 accomplished this by creating a *maildrop* service. Workstations would access a server system, use POP3 protocol commands to retrieve mail that the server is holding for it, delete the mail from the server, and then disconnect from the server system.

From the administrator's point of view, POP3 is desirable because, by design, it minimizes disk space consumption. Unless specifically configured otherwise, when POP3 clients connect to the server and retrieve mail, the mail is deleted from the server. Deleting mail from the server means it consumes less disk space and doesn't need to be backed up. Storing and accessing retrieved mail locally is also convenient for end-users because it is considerably easier to manipulate e-mail locally than it is over the network.

On the downside, server-based POP3 folders are not visible to POP3 clients, so organizing mail *must* be handled on client systems. POP3 also has a significant disadvantage for the administrator of a mail server: network and I/O overhead. The POP3 protocol, although small and compact, imposes significant burdens on network bandwidth and server I/O because clients can poll the server for new mail frequently, keeping network connections open. Likewise, the I/O involved at the server in checking for new mail can easily bog down an underpowered server.

POP3 is a relatively simple protocol, and the servers that implement the protocol are easy to configure and maintain. The trade-off for this simple design is that POP3 does not provide a rich set of features for manipulating mail on the server system. If you need more than a simple maildrop service, read the earlier section "Creating an IMAP E-Mail Server."

Note   For more information about the POP3 protocol, read RFC1939, the RFC (Request for Comment) that defines the POP3 protocol. RFC1939 can be read online at The Internet FAQ Archives Web site (`www.faqs.org/rfcs/rfc1939.html`).

Note   The following section on installing and configuring POP3 requires a working MTA. If you don't already have Exim or another MTA working on your system, refer to Chapter 14, "E-Mail Servers," to learn how to get your MTA configured.

Installing a POP3 server

As usual, use `apt-get` to install the software you want. For POP3 servers, I strongly recommend the Courier POP3 server, which is installed by the package `courier-pop`. Before installing this package, consider the security implications. POP3 is a plaintext protocol, meaning that all network traffic between the client and server is passed as plaintext, including authentication information. One best practice to start emulating is to use SSL-enabled services, such as POP3 over SSL, whenever network traffic travels over public or untrusted networks. Conversely, you should use only services based on plaintext protocols, such as vanilla POP3, on trusted networks or over encrypted tunnels. As an alternative, you can install the `courier-pop-ssl` package, which installs a version of the Courier POP3 server that uses the Secure Socket Layer (SSL) to encrypt communication between the server and client.

One reason you might *not* want to use the SSL-enabled version of Courier POP3 is that not all e-mail clients are capable of POP3s (POP3 over SSL). Most modern POP3 e-mail clients speak fluent SSL, but, depending on who your users are and how the server will be deployed, you might have to deal with non-SSL-enabled clients.

The example in this chapter uses POP3s. Use the following command to install the Courier POP3s package, which might trigger the installation of several additional Courier-related packages in order to meet package dependencies (the additional packages might include `courier-authdaemon`, `courier-base`, `courier-pop`, and/or `courier-ssl`):

```
# apt-get install courier-pop-ssl
```

In the first screen, debconf prompts you to choose whether to create directories used by a browser-based administration tool (see Figure 22-2). If you intend to install the `courier-webadmin` package, select Yes and press Enter. Otherwise, select No and press Enter.

Tip   To install the `courier-webadmin` **package, use the command** `apt-get install courier-webadmin`.

In the next step, debconf tells you it needs to create an SSL certificate for the POP3-SSL server. Press Enter to acknowledge the message and continue the installation. The actual certificate creation is automated as part of the installation process, so it requires no intervention on your part.

When the installation and certificate creation are complete, the POP3-SSL server is up and running (the daemon is named `/usr/sbin/pop3d-ssl`). To start and stop the daemon, use the initialization script `/etc/init.d/courier-pop-ssl`. Like many of the `rc` scripts described in this book, the `courier-pop-ssl` script accepts the `start` option to start the server, the `stop` option to stop it, and the `restart` option to restart (stop and start) it.

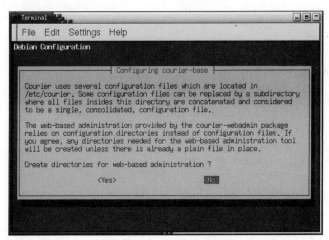

Figure 22-2: Omitting Courier's Web-based configuration tool.

Testing the POP3 server

Before your POP3 server can be used, however, you need to make sure that users who might need to use your server appear in the password database and in Courier's special user database, /etc/courier/userdb and /etc/courier/userdb.dat, as described in the previous section.

In the following example, the guinea pig username is popuser. Now, send some mail to popuser:

```
# echo "This is a test." | mailx -s "Test Mail" popuser
```

Finally, connect to the POP3 server and use the POP3 protocol commands shown in the following example to retrieve the message:

```
# telnet localhost 110
Trying 127.0.0.1...
Connected to localhost.
Escape character is '^]'.
+OK Hello there.
USER popuser
+OK Password required.
PASS sekritword
+OK
STAT
+OK 1 465
RETR 1
+OK
```

```
Return-path: <root@.kurtwerks.com>
Envelope-to: popuser@luther.kurtwerks.com
Received: from root by luther.kurtwerks.com with local (Exi
m 3.35 #1 (Debian))
   id 1Bn9N8-00000E-00
   for <popuser@luther.kurtwerks.com>; Wed, 21 Jul 2004 01:1
0:30 -0400
To: popuser@luther.kurtwerks.com
Subject: Test Mail
Message-Id: <E1Bn9N8-00000E-00@luther.kurtwerks.com>
From: root <root@luther.kurtwerks.com>
Date: Wed, 21 Jul 2004 01:10:30 -0400

This is a test.
.
DELE 1
+OK
QUIT
+OK
Connection closed by foreign host.
```

The telnet command opens a connection to the POP3 server on the local system (110 is the port on which POP3 services listen). USER popuser identifies the user to the POP3 server, while PASS sekritword transmits the password. After authenticating successfully, the STAT command indicates that there is one message of 465 bytes waiting. The command RETR 1 retrieves the first message, which is displayed to the screen (the mail server is named, fictitiously, luther.kurtwerks.com). The DELE 1 command deletes the message, and the QUIT command closes the connection and terminates the POP3 session.

After verifying that your POP3 server is functioning properly, any user who can receive e-mail at this machine can retrieve it using POP3. See the section titled "Sending and Receiving E-Mail" in Chapter 9 for instructions on how to configure a MUA to retrieve messages via POP3.

Summary

In this chapter, you took a quick tour of installing and configuring IMAP4 and POP3 e-mail servers. The servers used, Courier IMAP and Courier POP, impose a small amount of additional configuration burden during installation because you have to configure your Debian system to spool mail to users' Maildir directories. This isn't the "standard" mail-spooling method, but it addresses some perceived shortcomings of the traditional file-based mail spool and also permits users to have fuller control over how their e-mail is handled. The servers installed in this chapter's examples also had SSL support, removing a significant security risk.

✦   ✦   ✦

Printing Services

✦ ✦ ✦ ✦

In This Chapter

How to set up a
printing service

Working with print
spoolers

Setting up lpd, lpr,
and CUPS

Managing the CUPS
printing service

✦ ✦ ✦ ✦

An important feature of every Debian installation is a
printing service. A printing service enables computers
connected to the network to print to any network printer.
Printing services also enable the Debian administrator to
manage printing operations.

There are a number of printing services available in the UNIX
world. Debian supports three of them: lpd, lpr, and CUPS. The
lpd and lpr printing services are old-timers and are found in
nearly every flavor of UNIX. CUPS is the relatively new kid on
the block and is based on the Internet Printing Protocol.

In this chapter, you learn the fundamentals of printing services
and how to implement printing services in Debian. I touch
upon setting up lpd and lpr only briefly because CUPS is now
a far more common choice for printing services. The main
thrust of this chapter shows you how to set up and manage a
Debian printing service using CUPS.

What Are Printing Services?

Let's face it. No one wants to wait to have a document printed.
We want to select the Print button and pick up the printed document at the printer. This isn't a problem if a separate printer
is connected to every computer, but that's not economical for
most companies. In the real world, we share computers and
sometimes must wait our turn to have a document printed.

A printing service gives you a feeling that a printer is attached
to your computer, although you have to walk a few steps to
pick up your printed document. A well-designed and well-
managed printing service provides relatively instant printing,
similar to the experience we have when using a dedicated
printer.

When you select the Print button on your software, the document that you want printed is sent to the printing service, not directly to the printer. The printing service then delivers the document to the appropriate printer, which may or may not be connected to the computer that you are printing from. Think of a printing service as a shipping company that queues documents for printing and then transports the document to the correct printer.

Choosing a print service

Debian gives you a choice of at least three printing services: lpd, lpr, and CUPS. There are other printing services that you can acquire (see www.linuxprinting.org), although none is as supported in Debian.

✦ **lpd** — The lpd (line printer daemon) printing service has historically been the standard used by various flavors of UNIX. In fact, lpd is the name given to the network printing protocol, which is recognized by networked print servers, printers, and other printing services. It is for this reason that lpd is the go-to printing service when all others fail to work properly.

There are two important drawbacks to using lpd. The first concern is security. The lpd printing service lacks security features found in other printing services. The other concern is that the lpd printing service requires companion filter scripts and programs for it to be used with most modern printers. Fortunately, many of these scripts and programs are readily available.

✦ **lprng or lpr** — If you're considering the lpd printing service for your implementation, then also consider the lpr (lprng) printing service. The lpr printing service is an enhanced version of the lpd printing service and has improved security and easier setup, while still being compatible with many of the same basic filters used by the lpd printing service.

✦ **CUPS** — The new standard printing service is CUPS. The CUPS printing service uses the Internet Printing Protocol (IPP), which tries to tackle weaknesses found in the lpd network printing protocol while still being backward compatible. Major printer vendors support IPP. However, some Windows clients, especially Windows 2000, work with SMB and not with IPP. On some Windows clients, the printer drivers that are automatically downloaded do not work with IPP. The solution in these cases is to use both CUPS and the Samba print spooler.

Inside print spooling

Before learning how to set up printing services for your implementation, you need to understand how print spooling works. *Print spooling* is a way to print efficiently over a network by sharing printers among multiple clients. Keep in mind that while often useful, a network and multiple clients are not required to use and even to take advantage of a printer spool. There are variations in how printing services handle print spooling, but here's how most work.

PostScript versus Non-PostScript

Whenever you are setting up a printing service for Debian, you're faced with providing access to both PostScript and non-PostScript printers. You may have heard the term PostScript before, but you may not really understand the differences between a PostScript and non-PostScript printer.

PostScript is a printer control language that became the mainstay of desktop publishing in the 1980s with the introduction of the Apple LaserWriter. If you spent time learning PostScript, you could write instructions that control every aspect of how a document is printed. Fortunately, you don't need to become that familiar with PostScript to set up a printing service.

PostScript is usually limited to laser printers. Combined with a PostScript-enabled printer and the right application software, PostScript can produce near-perfect commercial print quality. Furthermore, a PostScript document can be displayed on nearly any kind of printing device, including a fax machine and either a pixel or vector screen using a special program.

However, PostScript ran afoul of Windows. Because Windows did not include a PostScript previewer, PostScript failed to become the standard for electronically exchanging complex documents. Adobe saw this as an opportunity and created its own viewer for a compressed PostScript variant, Adobe Acrobat.

Non-PostScript printers don't understand the PostScript printer control language. If you send a PostScript document to a non-PostScript printer, the PostScript instructions will print.

An alternative to using a PostScript printer is to use a non-PostScript printer that is supported by Ghostscript. Ghostscript is a PostScript interpreter that translates PostScript printer commands into an output that is understood by non-PostScript printers.

The printing process begins when the print option is selected from a client application such as a word processing program. It seems to the user that the document is sent directly to the printer, but in reality the document is sent to the printing service, which in turns sends the document to a print spooler that resides on the print server.

When the document arrives at the print server, the print spooler stores the document in a temporary holding area on a disk or in memory, depending on how the print spooler is set up and how many other documents are waiting to be printed.

The print spooler also places reference to the document on the *print queue*. The print queue determines the order in which documents are printed. Newly arrived documents are placed at the end of the print queue unless the document has priority over the other waiting documents. In that case, the newly arrived document goes to the head of the print queue. (The network administrator sets print priority.) When the document reaches the front of the queue, the print spooler sends the document to the printer.

Sending a document to the printer is a little more involved than streaming bits out of the printer port. The print spooler must apply printing options selected by the client (such as paper size, landscape or portrait orientation, and so on) by translating those options and the document itself into the printer's native language, which will vary among printers. This process is called filtering. The set of rules that determine how to translate print options and the document into the printer's native language is called a filter. The major task of getting a print spooler to work with a printer is to use the proper filter.

Once the document is translated into the printer's native language, the document is sent to the printer. The print spooler monitors the printing process and notifies the client on its status (such as printing completed, printer error). After the document is printed, the print spooler updates the print queue and the next document on the queue is then processed.

Setting Up lpd and lpr

This chapter focuses more on CUPS than on lpd and lpr because you'll likely want to use CUPS. In case you need to use lpd and lpr, this section gives you the basics of how to set them up.

Note   You'll find more information about these printing services at `www.linux printing.org`.

You can set up the lpd and lpr printing services within Debian by using `/etc/printcap`. The `/etc/printcap` command is used for connecting to either a PostScript printer or a text-only printer, although the setup for each is slightly different.

Configuring lpd and lpr

If you are using a PostScript printer, the following configuration instructions will enable you to utilize the lpd and lpr printing services. The file is `/etc/printcap`.

To configure the printing service, you need to adjust four settings:

- ✦ The name of the print spooler
- ✦ The maximum file size of the document that can be sent to the print spooler
- ✦ Whether the burst page header should be suppressed when printing
- ✦ The name of the local printer device

You set the configuration by using the `lp\alias` as shown here:

```
lp|alias:\
               :sd=/var/spool/lpd/lp:\
               :mx#0:\
               :sh:\
               :lp=/dev/lp0:
```

The first line of the configuration is called the headline, identified as `sd`, and contains the name of the spooler and the alias, which is `lp`. Next is the maximum file size, identified as `mx`. I suggest that you set the maximum file size to `#0`, meaning there is an unlimited file size.

The next line is identified as `sh` and is set to suppress printing of the burst page header, which is the setting that you should use to avoid wasting paper. The last line, identified as `lp`, sets the local printer device. In this example, the printer assigned to the spooler is named `/dev/lp0`. If you're using a remote printer, you can change this value to *port@host*, where *port* is the port number of the printer and *host* is the hostname of the remote printing device.

Testing your printer

After everything is installed, you can quickly check to see whether you are able to print by using the `lpr` command. The `lpr` command works with lpd and with CUPS. Simply type `lpr` followed by the name of the file that you want printed. The following command prints the contents of the address file:

```
lpr address.txt
```

Display the print queue by using the `lpq` command. All the waiting print jobs are displayed on the screen. You can remove a print job from the print queue by using the `lprm` command followed by the print job's ID.

The `lp` command also works with CUPS and System V installations. Here's how you print the same address file using the `lp` command:

```
lp address.txt
```

The `lpstat` command is used to display the queue on the screen, and the `cancel` command followed by the print job's ID removes a print job from the print queue. Other commands that might be useful include the following:

✦ `lpq`: Shows what's currently on the print queue

✦ `lprm`: Removes a job from the print queue

Installing and Configuring CUPS

CUPS has features that you won't find in lpd and lpr, including encryption, authentication, and access control.

As a security measure, Debian is set up so that only the root account and members of the group lp have permission to access the printer. So you must add any users that you want to allow to print to the lp group. (See Chapter 5 for more information on adding a user to a group.)

Using your favorite package manager, install the cupsys-client and cupsys packages.

When you install cupsys, you are asked some configuration questions about your printing options. If you are not sure of how to answer, I recommend you accept the defaults.

Using CUPS via the Web interface

With installation and configuration complete, you are ready to use the CUPS Web interface. Open up a Web browser and go to http://localhost:631/. Port 631 is the standard port for IPP (Internet Printing Protocol), which is the basis for CUPS. As a security measure, the CUPS server is initially set up to be accessible only from localhost. If you want to enable the printer to be shared across a whole network, you can loosen this restriction in the /etc/cups/cupsd.conf configuration file. Look for the part that begins with <Location /> and ends with </Location> and change the Allow and Deny directives. The default file provided by Debian is well commented, so this should be straightforward. When you access the Web interface, you are greeted by the screen shown in Figure 23-1.

The links to ESP (Easy Software Products) take you to the home page of the company that created CUPS. In addition to providing the Open Source version, ESP sells a commercial version of the CUPS system.

From the main screen, you can click on the following links:

✦ **Do Administration Tasks** allows the system administrator to add printers to the CUPS system.

✦ **Manage Printer Classes** deals with *classes* or clusters of printers. Imagine a scenario where a company has all the printing done by 20 massive, heavy-duty line printers clanking away in the basement, spewing out reams of green and white striped paper by the minute. (There is probably disco music playing in the background and the operators are discussing President Carter.)

When you send a job to those printers, you don't care which one gets it. By treating them all as one class, the job is sent to the first printer that's free. Nowadays, when most people have personal or at least departmental printers, this is a less useful feature, but the capability is there if needed.

✦ **Online Help** provides extensive help on using CUPS.

✦ **Manage Printers** lets you examine the print queue for a particular printer, remove jobs from it, and check the printer's status.

✦ **Download the Current CUPS Software** takes you to the Easy Software Products Web site, where you can upgrade CUPS to a newer version if it is available.

Caution   Debian users should not download directly from the ESP Web site. Get the latest version via `apt-get` so that you won't have dependency problems.

Adding a printer from the Web interface

To add a printer, from the Web interface's main page, select Do Administration Tasks ⇨ Add Printer. You will see the screen shown in Figure 23-2.

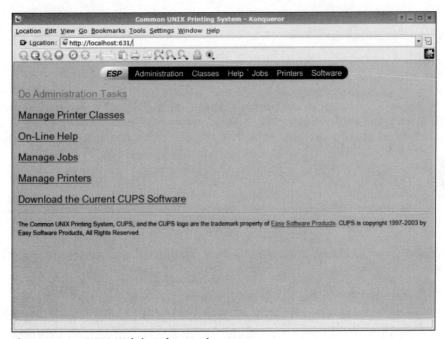

Figure 23-1: CUPS Web interface main screen.

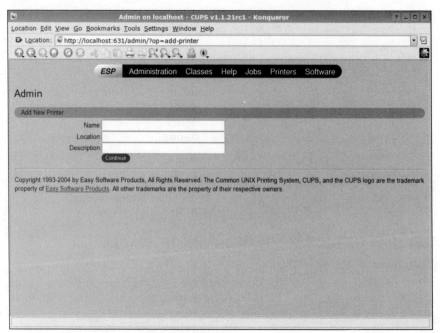

Figure 23-2: Adding a printer to CUPS.

Enter information into the fields as appropriate:

✦ **Name** is the name for the printer that will show up in CUPS-enabled software. This is the only one of the three fields on this screen that is mandatory. The name cannot contain spaces or nonprintable characters and must be unique on the network.

✦ **Location** is an optional field that can contain a value like "Room 432," "7th floor," or "Next to Bob."

✦ **Description** is an optional field that can contain the printer brand and model number or anything else that describes it.

When you are finished with this screen, click Continue. The next screen has a drop-down list for selecting the type of device the printer is connected to:

✦ **AppSocket/HP JetDirect** is a proprietary protocol for connecting printers over a network found in some heavy-duty printers, notably those from Hewlett Packard.

✦ **Internet Printing Protocol** is the open standard protocol for networked printers. There are two choices for using IPP: on port 80 (http) or on port 631 (ipp).

✦ **LPD/LPR Host or Printer** is for networked printers using the BSD print system described earlier.

✦ **Parallel Port** is for local printers connected to a parallel port. There are several choices, the exact number depending on how many parallel ports your computer has. Select Parallel Port #1 if your printer is on /dev/lp0 (what Windows calls LPT1). Select Parallel Port #2 if your printer is on /dev/lp1 (LPT2), and so on.

✦ **Serial Port** is for local printers connected to a serial port. As with parallel ports, there are several choices. Select Serial Port #1 if your printer is attached to /dev/ttyS0 (COM1 in Windows nomenclature), Serial Port #2 if it is attached to /dev/ttyS1 (COM2), and so on.

✦ **USB Printer** is for local printers connected to a USB port. Again, there are several choices. Pick USB Printer #1 if your printer is on /dev/usblp0, USB Printer #2 if it is on /dev/usblp1, and so on.

✦ **Windows Printer via SAMBA** allows you to use the SMB protocol to connect to a printer attached to a Windows machine if you have SAMBA installed (see Chapter 20 for more information on SAMBA).

Select the right choice for your printer and click Continue to go to the next step. In the next two screens, you will pick a driver and a particular model for your printer. The driver types are named after particular manufacturers. Each manufacturer seems to have its own unique way of talking to a printer. The driver is responsible for translating the print request in a way the printer will understand. The only driver that might require further explanation is RAW. This driver just sends the print job to the server without further interpretation. You use this driver with network protocols such as SMB.

When you have selected the right driver, click Continue and you are done. If you go back to Do Administration Tasks and select Manage Printers, you should see your printer listed. From the buttons underneath the printer status, click on Print Test Page. If it displays correctly, you are finished and ready to commence printing.

A Digression on Printer Drivers . . .

What do you do if your printer model is not supported by a CUPS driver? Well, many printers emulate more popular brands, so you might be able to use a CUPS driver for an emulated model. This approach works, but it is suboptimal, as emulation means you might not be able to use all of your printer's features. Another idea is to install GIMP Print. As the name suggests, this is the print system for the popular graphics program The GIMP, but it can also work with CUPS when you install a special driver. The Debian packages to install are libgimpprint1 and cupsys-driver-gimpprint. The hpoj package contains drivers for Hewlett-Packard OfficeJet, LaserJet, PSC, and PhotoSmart printers. You can even install a "virtual" printer that outputs a PDF file with the cups-pdf package. After installing these packages, you should see extra choices in the driver and model selection pages of the CUPS Web interface.

Continued

Continued

Some of the more progressive printer manufacturers have begun providing their own Linux drivers. Take a look at the CD or floppies that came with your printer, or perhaps the manufacturer's Web site, and you might find them. The downside is that most companies think that Linux equals Red Hat, so Debian users might not be able to use the drivers easily or the provided instructions may not be correct. The great thing about the Debian user community is that it is so big that the chances are that someone, somewhere, has managed to get the drivers working under our favorite distribution. It's just a matter of doing some research with a search engine like Google.

If rummaging through the Web hunting down printer setup information sounds a little tedious and haphazard to you, Grant Taylor and Till Kamppeter would agree. They are the founder and current maintainer, respectively, of `www.linuxprinting.org/`, which aims to be the one-stop place for information on all things related to printing on Linux. They have built up a database (shown in the following figure) of every printer known to work with Linux. (If you find one that is not on the list, be sure to tell them.) Each printer is rated on how well it works. What is more, drivers are provided for each one and instructions for integrating the driver into CUPS are provided. They even have forums and mailing lists for printing-related tech support. So if you run into problems, this should definitely be the first place you visit.

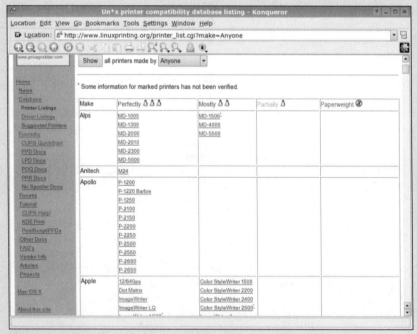

The printer database at linuxprinting.org.

Using CUPS from the command line

You can perform the same tasks from the command line that you can using the Web interface. Some administrators feel the command-line approach gives them more control when adding the printer, while others prefer to press buttons in the wizard in the Web interface. Many configuration changes can be made by entering the following command and then using the appropriate options, shown in Table 23-1:

```
/usr/sbin/lpadmin -p printerName
```

Table 23-1
Options for the lpadmin Program

Option	Description
-c class	Creates a class, if one doesn't exist, and adds the printer to the class
-i interface	Copies the interface script to the printer. An interface script is used if a PPD file is unavailable for a printer.
-m model	Specifies the PPD file (model), which is the printer driver. If no PPD file is specified, then a list of printer drivers (PPD files) is displayed.
-E	Enables the printer
-r class	Removes a printer from the specified class. If the printer is the only printer associated with the class, then the class is also removed.
-v device-uri	Specifies the device/URI for the printer. The print job is restarted on the new device if the print job is being printed when the device/URI is changed.
-D info	Specifies a comment about the printer
-L location	Specifies the location of the printer as a comment
-x printerName	Deletes a printer
-x className	Deletes a class
-u allow:userid	Grants permission to use a printer to a specific user ID. The user ID "all" can be used to permit everyone access to the printer.
-u deny:userid	Denies permission to use a printer to a specific user ID. The user ID "all" can be used to permit everyone access to the printer.

Continued

Table 23-1 *(continued)*	
Option	**Description**
`-o job-k-limit=`	Sets the KB quota for a printer
`-o job-page-limit=`	Sets the page limit quota for a printer
`-o job-quota-period=`	Sets the period quota for a printer
`-P ppd-file`	Specifies the PPD file for the printer driver

Adding a printer from the command line

You add a printer from the command line by running the following program:

```
/usr/sbin/lpadmin - p printerName -E -v deviceName -m PPDfile
```

The `-p` option is followed by the name of the printer that you want to add to CUPS. The `-E` option enables the printer. The `-v` option identifies the device used to communicate with the printer, which is followed by the name of the device. The `-m` option identifies the PPD file that defines the printer's capabilities.

You can add some very commonly used printers with the following commands:

```
/usr/sbin/lpadmin -p DeskJet -E -v Parallel:/dev/lp1 -m deskjet.ppd

/usr/sbin/lpadmin -p LaserJet -E -v socket://180.152.45.10 -m laserjet.ppd

/usr/sbin/lpadmin -p Matrix -E -v serial:/dev/ttyS0?baud=9600+size=
8+parity=none+flow=soft -m epson9.ppd

/usr/sbin/lpadmin -p DeskJet -E -v usb:/dev/usb/lp0 -m deskjet.ppd
```

Notice that to add the Matrix printer in this example requires more information than is supplied for the other printers. This is because the Matrix printer's device is a serial port. When setting up a serial port device, you need to specify the baud rate of the transmission, the size, and whether parity is odd, even, or none. Flow control is an optional setting. If you're unsure of these specifications for your printer, use the settings shown in the foregoing example.

Modifying printer settings through the command line

As with adding a printer, you can modify the settings of a printer that was added to CUPS through the command line. Enter the following command followed by the option that you want to change (see Table 23-1 for a list of options):

```
/usr/sbin/lpadmin - p printerName
```

This program searches for the printer named in the command. If found, existing values are replaced by the new values specified by options on the command line. If the printer is not found, then the program assumes that you are adding a new printer to CUPS.

It is a good practice before modifying the setting of a printer that you make sure the print queue is empty and nothing is being printed. However, should there be a job printing while you are modifying the printer, CUPS restarts the print job using the new settings.

You can remove a printer from CUPS using either the command line or the Web interface. Enter the following command to delete a printer from CUPS using the command line:

```
/usr/sbin/lpadmin - x printerName
```

Caution   You cannot undelete a printer once the printer is removed from CUPS. The only way to restore the printer is to add the printer as if it were a new printer.

Still not working?

If the test page doesn't print out correctly, first check your printer cable. It's amazing how many problems are fixed by tightening a loose connection. Is the user a member of the lp group? Verify that the printer is connected to the port that CUPS expects. Go through the install again and make sure you are entering the right values for the driver. If worst comes to worst, ask on the Debian-user mailing list or at www.linuxprinting.org for advice on how to proceed. There are many knowledgeable users on the list who may have already run into your problem.

In order to help you, people need to know as many details as possible. A simple "It doesn't work" will not cut it, and such messages will most likely be ignored. Provide information such as the exact make and model of the printer you are having trouble with, what version of Debian you are using, the versions of the CUPS packages and others that you are using, any measures you have already tried, and any error messages you are seeing.

Managing Printing

You'll need to perform routine administrative activities once Debian is set up for printing. These include the following:

✦ Starting and stopping the printer queue

✦ Restricting access to the printer

✦ Accepting/rejecting print jobs

✦ Setting the default printer

✦ Setting the printer quota

These routines can be performed either at the command line or through the Web interface. The following sections show you how to perform these tasks at the command line. Once you start using the Web interface, you'll realize that performing these tasks is intuitive, so there is no need to describe those steps in detail.

Starting and stopping the printer queues

As you learned previously in this chapter, each printer has its own print queue. Sometimes printers malfunction and are unable to print jobs on the queue. This causes a backlog of print jobs as new print jobs find their way to the print queue.

You can reduce the backlog by disabling the print queue until the printer is repaired. Once the print queue is disabled, print jobs designed for that print queue are rerouted to another printer within the same class or rerouted to an implicit class.

If a print job is already on the queue when the queue is disabled, the print job is printed once the queue is enabled again.

Here's how to start and stop the print queue:

```
/usr/bin/disable printerName
/usr/bin/enable printerName
```

Granting and restricting access to the printer

You can restrict access to a printer by using the -u option and then specifying the user IDs of users who can access the printer. By default, all users can access a printer. You must explicitly restrict access.

You can explicitly deny a user access to a printer by using the following command-line commands. The first line denies the user IDs john,mike access to the laser1 printer. The second line denies everyone access to the laser1 printer.

```
/usr/sbin/lpadmin -p laser1 -u deny:john,mike
/usr/sbin/lpadmin -p laser1 -u deny:all
```

Let's say that John and Mike want access to the printer named laser1. John's and Mike's user IDs are john and mike, respectively. Here's how you grant them access to the laser1 printer:

```
/usr/sbin/lpadmin -p laser1 -u allow:john,mike
```

If you want to grant everyone access to the laser1 printer, then enter the following at the command line:

```
/usr/sbin/lpadmin -p laser1 -u allow:all
```

Access can also be granted or denied by using the Debian group name instead of individual user IDs. User IDs that are associated with a group inherit all the rights given to the group. Therefore, you might find using group names instead of user IDs a more efficient way to grant or deny access to a printer.

The following lines show the commands you need to grant or deny access to a group. In the first line, the accounting group is allowed access to the laser1 printer, and then it is denied access in the second line. The @ symbol must precede the name of the group.

```
/usr/sbin/lpadmin -p laser1 -u allow:@accounting
/usr/sbin/lpadmin -p laser1 -u deny:@accounting
```

Accepting/rejecting print jobs

You can cause a printer queue to reject print jobs should the printer go out of service. In this way, new jobs are routed to another printer. Once the printer is online again, you can begin accepting new print jobs.

The following are the command-line commands used to accept and then reject print jobs. In this example, the printer queue for laser1 is accepting and then rejecting print jobs.

```
/usr/sbin/accept laser1
/usr/sbin/reject laser1
```

Making the printer the default printer

It is always best to designate a printer as the default printer. If a user fails to select a printer, CUPS will use the printer that you designate as the default printer. Any printer that is set up in CUPS can be selected as the default printer.

You designate the default printer by using the following command. In this example, printer laser1 is becoming the default printer.

```
/usr/sbin/lpadmin -d laser1
```

Setting the printer quota

Organizations that are trying to control the cost of printing will find the quota feature of CUPS a gift from heaven because it places limits on how printers are used. This is especially ideal for expensive color printers.

You can set three kinds of quotas per printer:

✦ Size limit in kilobytes

✦ Page limit

✦ Period limit (hours, days)

Quotas are applied to all user IDs, although each user ID is tracked. This means that you cannot limit Mike to printing 100 pages while John can print only 30 pages. If you set the page quota as 100 pages, then Mike and John can each print 100 pages.

You can combine quotas to limit the use of a printer. For example, you can say that no user ID can print more than 100 pages or more than 40 KB each day. You do this by placing commands to set all three quotas on the same command line.

Quotas are set by using the -o option in the lpadmin program. The -o option is followed by the kind of quota that you are setting and the value of the quota.

The following example shows how to set the size quota. You use the job-k-limit parameter, but you can set the kilobyte value to whatever value you desire. In this example, no user ID can print more than 1,024 KB to the laser1 printer.

```
/usr/sbin/lpadmin -p laser1 -o job-k-limit=1024
```

The next example shows how to set the page limit quota. In this case, the job-page-limit parameter is used and is set with a page value of 100. This means that no user ID will be able to print more than 100 pages on the laser1 printer.

```
/usr/sbin/lpadmin -p laser1 -o job-page-limit=100
```

The next example shows how to set the period quota. The period is measured in seconds. A day is 86,400 seconds, a week is 604,800 seconds, and a month is 2,592,000 seconds. In this example, all user IDs can use the laser1 printer for a month.

```
/usr/sbin/lpadmin -p laser1 -o job-quota-period=2592000
```

You can combine quotas by placing multiple quotas on the same command line, as shown in the following example. In this example, no user ID can print more than 1,000 pages per month on the laser1 printer.

```
/usr/sbin/lpadmin -p laser1 -o job-quota-period=2592000 -o job-page-limit=1000
```

Inside Printer Classes

Printers are organized into groups called printer classes. Typically printers within the same class have the same capabilities and are within the same physical location. For example, all LaserJet printers in the eighth-floor printing room may be designated as members of the same class.

The similarities of printers within a class and their vicinity to each other are critical to how CUPS uses printers because a print job is sent to a class of printers rather than to a particular printer. The print job is assigned to the first available printer within the class.

There are two kinds of classes: explicit and implicit. An *explicit* class is one that you create using the following command:

```
/usr/sbin/lpadmin -c className
```

You can assign a printer to the class by using the following command. This command also creates the class if the class doesn't exist.

```
/usr/sbin/lpadmin - p printerName -c className
```

You can remove a printer from a class by using the following command:

```
/usr/sbin/lpadmin - p printerName -r className
```

And you can remove the class itself by using this command:

```
/usr/sbin/lpadmin -x className
```

An implicit class is automatically created according to existing classes and printers that are currently available when a job needs to be printed. This means that a print job is rerouted automatically to an available printer server, ensuring that the job is printed even if some printer servers become unavailable.

Classes can be created, modified, and deleted by using the Add Class and Modify Class features of the Web interface. The Modify Class feature also enables you to delete a class.

Client Configuration

Finally, if you will be printing from other computers on the network to the printer server that you have set up, you will need to set up client computers to print using CUPS. A client is any computer that generates a print job, including end-user desktop computers and servers connected to the network.

There are five ways to set up a client:

✦ Automatic

✦ Manual

✦ Single-server printing

✦ Multiple-server printing

✦ Relay printing

These methods are explained in the following sections.

Automatic setup

The automatic setup is the easiest way to set up a client for printing because you simply don't have to do anything as long as the client is on the same subnet as the printers.

Here's how the automatic setup works. When a client connects to the network, a search is made for available printers, classes, and servers. The result of the search is compared to the list of printers, classes, and servers that resides with the client. If necessary, the client's lists are updated automatically by adding or removing printers, classes, and servers. This entire process takes about 30 seconds.

If you want the client to have access to printers on a subnet other than the client's subnet, then you'll need to use the `BrowsePoll` directive, which is discussed in the "Multiple-server printing" section of this chapter.

Manual setup

Another approach you can use to set up a client is to use the command line. This is a labor-intensive process and should be avoided at all costs if you are setting up a large network. You really don't want to manually set up each client. Instead, use other methods that are discussed in this section of the chapter.

Manual setup is an acceptable practice in one-off situations whenever the automatic setup process doesn't produce the desired results. You can also use the manual setup to enable a client to access a printer that is not on the client's subnet.

Here's the command to set up a printer for a client:

```
lpadmin -p printerName -E -v
ipp://serverName/printers/printerName
```

Enter this command on the client's computer. The *printerName* is the name of the printer that the client will be accessing. The *serverName* is either the hostname or the IP address of the print server. The IP address can reference a subnet other than the client's subnet.

The drawback of using the manual setup is that you must enter the command for each printer that you want the client to access.

Single-server printing

In a well-designed printing system, a local spooler and a remote spooler are located on the print server. If the print server goes off-line, print jobs remain on the local spooler and can be redirected to another print server.

In rare situations, you might want to avoid having a local spooler, such as when printing a sensitive document where it is desirable to limit the number of electronic copies of the document. Instead of having the document stored in the local spooler and the remote spooler, you can have the document stored on only the remote spooler. This is referred to as *single-server printing*. The drawback of single-server printing is that if the print server goes off-line, then printing stops.

Here's how to set up single-server printing. Create a file named `/etc/cups/client.conf`. Place the following line in the file:

```
ServerName serverName
```

The `serverName` is either the hostname or the IP address of the remote print server. This line overwrites the localhost as the default print server.

Multiple-server printing

Multiple-server printing is a setup that gives a client access to printer servers located on subnets other than the client's subnet. This is accomplished through the technique called polling.

Here's how you set up multiple print servers. Open the file `/etc/cups/cupsd.conf` and enter the following directive in the file:

```
BrowsePoll printServerName
```

The `printServerName` is either the hostname or the IP address of the printer server. Insert a `BrowsePoll` directive for each print server that you want to be polled by the client each time the client prints a document.

Here's how polling works. Before the client sends a job to the printer, the client opens the `/etc/cups/cupsd.conf` file and reads the first `BrowsePoll` directive to locate the print server to use for printing. If that print server is unavailable, the client then uses the next `BrowsePoll` statement in the file. This process continues until either an active print server is found or there are no more `BrowsePoll` directives in the file.

The drawback to using multiple-server printing is that this setup is inefficient when there are multiple clients and print servers located on multiple subnets. A more efficient approach is to use relay printing.

Relay printing

Relay printing is a technique of reducing the amount of polling across the network by having the client that initiates the polling share its polling result with other clients on the client's subnet.

Here's how this works: Client A wants to print a document and polls the network for available print servers as described in the previous section. The poll identifies active and inactive print servers. This information is then relayed to other clients on Client A's subnet. When Client B wants to print, Client B doesn't need to poll to discover the active print server because Client A has already identified the active print server and passed along this information to Client B and other clients on the same subnet.

Here's how to set up relay printing. Open the file `/etc/cups/cupsd.conf` and enter the following directives:

```
BrowsePoll printServerName
BrowseRelay localClient broadcastAddress
```

First is the `BrowsePoll` directive, which you learned about in the previous section of this chapter. You need one `BrowsePoll` directive for each print server that you want the client to poll.

Second is the `BrowseRelay` directive. The `BrowseRelay` directive specifies the hostname or IP address of the client that is conducting the poll and the hostname or IP address of a client that is being relayed the results of the poll. You need a `BrowseRelay` for each client who is to receive the polling results.

Additional CUPS Configuration

Throughout this chapter, you learned how to use CUPS commands to administer the printing service for your implementation of Debian. You can also modify the behavior of CUPS itself by changing directives in the CUPS configuration file and the client configuration.

Changing the directive

A directive consists of a directive name and a value. The directive name is associated with a modifiable feature of CUPS that you can alter by changing the corresponding value of the directive.

For example, CUPS tracks printing activity by recording each time a user ID sends a document to a printer. This information is stored in an activity log. You can tell CUPS which activity log to use and the location of the activity log by inserting a directive in the CUPS configuration file, which is shown here:

```
/etc/cups/cupsd.conf
```

Here's the directive that you would enter:

```
AccessLog /var/log/cups/myaccess_log
```

Notice that there are two parts to this directive. The first part is the directive name, which is AccessLog. The second part is the value assigned to the AccessLog directive, which is the path and name of the access log.

I strongly suggest that you organize the CUPS configuration file by grouping together like directives and identifying each group with a comment. (CUPS treats any line beginning with # as a comment.) After you finish making changes to the CUPS configuration file, you must restart CUPS using the following command; otherwise your changes won't take effect until the next time CUPS is loaded.

```
/etc/init.d/cups restart
```

As you might imagine, there are many directives that can be used to tailor the performance of CUPS. Table 23-2 shows some of the most useful directives. You can find the full list of directives at www.cups.org.

Table 23-2
Directives for CUPS Configuration

Directive	Description	Example
AccessLog	The path and name of the access log. If the path isn't included, then CUPS assumes the file to be relative to the ServerRoot directory.	AccessLog /var/log/ cups/myaccess_log
Allow	Specifies a hostname, IP address, or network that is allowed access to the server	Allow from All Allow from host.domain.com Allow from 180.143.23.*

Continued

Table 23-2 *(continued)*

Directive	Description	Example
AuthClass	Defines what level of authentication is required: Anonymous: Perform no authentication (default) User: Require a valid username and password System: Require that the valid username and password belong to the sys group Group: Require that a valid username and password belong to the group named by the AuthGroupName directive	AuthClass Anonymous
DataDir	Sets the directory to use for data files	/usr/share/cups/data
Deny	Specifies a hostname, IP address, or network that is not allowed access to the server	Deny from All Deny from *.domain.com Deny from nnn.nnn.nnn.* Deny from None
Encryption	Sets the encryption policy; must be placed in the location section of the CUPS configuration file	Encryption Never Encryption Required Encryption IfRequested (default) Encryption Always
ErrorLog	Sets the path and name for the error log	ErrorLog /var/log/cups/myerror_log
PreserveJobFiles	Determines whether all print jobs (completed, canceled, or aborted) are stored on disk	PreserveJobFiles On PreserveJobFiles Off
PreserveJobHistory	Determines whether information about all print jobs is retained	PreserveJobHistory On PreserveJobHistory Off
ServerAdmin	Sets the e-mail address for the system administrator	ServerAdmin root@mycompany.com

Directive	Description	Example
ServerRoot	Sets the absolute path to the CUPS configuration file	ServerRoot /etc/cups
TempDir	Sets the absolute path to the directory used for temporary files	TempDir /var/tmp
Timeout	Sets the interval to wait until a print request is aborted	Timeout 60

Modifying the client configuration

You can also set printing configuration for each client on the network by inserting client directives into the client configuration file named client.conf.

Two of the important directives that you may want to use are Encryption and ServerName. Encryption is the same directive as is used with the CUPS configuration file (see Table 23-2).

The ServerName directive is used to specify the server that will handle the client's request. By default, this is the localhost; however, you can set this to either the hostname or an IP address as shown here:

```
ServerName 180.143.79.102
```

Summary

Nearly every Debian implementation requires that you set up a printing service in order for clients to print to networked printers. A printing service is a feature of Debian that enables the Debian administrator to efficiently manage print operations.

In this chapter, you learned how a printing service works and that Debian supports three printing services: lpd, lpr, and CUPS.

You also learned how print spoolers work. The lpd and lpr printing services are the old-timers and are found in nearly every flavor of UNIX. CUPS is newer and is based on the Internet Printing Protocol. Use lpd or lpr if all else fails, but generally you will want to use CUPS as the printing service for your Debian printing needs.

✦   ✦   ✦

Database Servers

Many programs need to persistently store data. The system's authentication information, for instance, is largely contained in the file /etc/passwd. Customer lists may be stored in a database file on the system. Information for an online shopping site may be stored on a database server.

In this chapter, I focus on SQL database systems. These systems all use ANSI SQL (Structured Query Language) for accessing the underlying data. They also separate the database into two components: a server component, responsible for the storage and retrieval of data; and a client component, responsible for submitting requests to the server and parsing responses. They are also networkable; the server and client components need not be on the same physical machine.

Debian ships with several SQL database systems. The two most popular ones are MySQL and PostgreSQL. Both provide client infrastructures for many of the numerous programming languages represented in Debian, and thus both are widely available to developers. Both also are deployed at many sites and are fairly easy for administrators to set up and maintain.

In this chapter, you learn how to set up and maintain a PostgreSQL (also known simply as Postgres) or MySQL database server. You learn about the initial installation, configuration, backup, and upgrade procedures for both database systems. You also learn a bit about the various clients along the way.

Caution   This chapter does not cover storing or accessing data in a database; only the installation and configuration of a server are discussed. If you are a developer wanting to access a database server, you should obtain an SQL programming book for your chosen database and language.

Choosing a Server

Of course, before you begin setting up a machine, you must choose which server you wish to deploy: PostgreSQL, MySQL, or *both*. It is possible to deploy both on a single system, though this is rarely done in practice.

Both MySQL and PostgreSQL are very capable systems and, in many cases, either of them will serve you well. You should first consider the applications you intend to use with your database server. If your applications support only one or the other, then your choice is easy: use the server supported by your applications.

Many applications will support both. In that case, you'll need to spend a little bit of time deciding what your requirements are.

Historically, MySQL has placed its greatest emphasis on speed, and PostgreSQL has placed its greatest emphasis on features. That's not to say that MySQL is underpowered or PostgreSQL is slow, but it does give an insight into the approach favored by the different database systems.

MySQL is often the database of choice for Web-based applications, partly due to its speed and partly because it held a greater speed advantage over PostgreSQL when Web applications were first starting to mature. PostgreSQL is commonly favored for client/server applications or applications where precise control or advanced features are required. This again has somewhat historic roots: While MySQL's speed was winning Web developers, it lacked certain crucial features that drove others to PostgreSQL. PostgreSQL has also had its own embedded language for quite some time and supports many advanced SQL features.

Today, the two systems have closed the gap in both speed and feature set, but they still maintain some of these differences. However, the rise of database-neutral programming systems has meant that you can freely substitute one for the other in many applications.

If you have some applications that support only MySQL and others that support only PostgreSQL, you can install both. However, I suggest you avoid that situation when possible. It means more work to learn two different ways of administering databases and more effort to maintain two different systems on a single machine.

Using PostgreSQL

PostgreSQL is a robust and stable database system. It is used in a variety of applications from Web services to enterprise databases. It's also fairly easy to use.

Installing PostgreSQL

Like most Debian packages, the first step is to install the server itself. The command `apt-get install postgresql` will accomplish this for you. You can also install the `postgresql-doc` package if you would like to have the optional documentation on your system.

During installation, you may be asked several questions. First, the system may ask you where to store your databases, with a default of `/var/lib/postgres/data`. Databases can grow quite large depending on your application, so make sure the location you specify here has enough room.

Next, you may be asked what to do when the `postgres` package is purged (uninstalled). Either you can have it automatically remove all your databases, or it can leave the databases on-disk even though you no longer have the means to access the data.

Next, you may be asked what character encoding to use for the database. For most, the default `per_locale` will be fine, but if you will be dealing with a specific character set, you can choose a different option. Using Unicode/UTF-8 is a good idea if you plan to store data with multiple scripts in different languages. Finally, you can choose which date format to use by default.

Creating databases and users

As part of the installation, the user `postgres` is created on your system. You should perform most administrative tasks while running as the `postgres` user. If you are already logged in as root, you can change to the `postgres` user by running `su - postgres`. When done, type **exit** to return to your root login.

In PostgreSQL, a database contains tables, which hold the data of interest to you. PostgreSQL does not create databases for you to use by default. You will need to create the databases for your applications.

The `createdb` command is used to create a new database. You simply give it the name of the database to create as a command-line parameter. It must be run as the `postgres` user. Here's an example:

```
postgres@example:~$ createdb testdb
CREATE DATABASE
```

In this example, the database `testdb` was created. Now that you have a database, you'll probably want to create one or more user accounts that can do work within that database. The command to do this is `createuser`. Here's an example that creates the user `testuser`:

```
postgres@example:~$ createuser testuser
Shall the new user be allowed to create databases? (y/n) n
Shall the new user be allowed to create more new users? (y/n) n
CREATE USER
```

The two questions relate to the capabilities of the newly created user. The first question controls whether the user may create new databases with `createdb` or a similar command. The second controls whether the user may create other users with `createuser` or a similar command.

If you are using passwords for users in your setup, you can also specify a password at creation time. To do so, add the `-P` option to the `createuser` command line like this:

```
postgres@example:~$ createuser -P testuser2
Enter password for new user:
Enter it again:
Shall the new user be allowed to create databases? (y/n) n
Shall the new user be allowed to create more new users? (y/n) n
CREATE USER
```

When prompted, supply the new password for the user. If you do not specify `-P`, the user will be created without any password.

> **Note**   If you want to modify the password later, you may use the PostgreSQL command `ALTER USER`. This is an SQL command, not a UNIX command.

Configuring access rules

Now that you have your databases and users configured, you need to configure access rules. The access rules define where people may connect from, which users are allowed in, how they are authenticated, and which databases they may connect to. All of these rules are defined in `/etc/postgresql/pg_hba.conf`. I describe that file as it is used in PostgreSQL 7.4.3. If you use a different version of PostgreSQL, the file may look slightly different. You can use the command `dpkg -l postgresql` to find out which version you have installed.

PostgreSQL access rules are defined in `/etc/postgresql/pg_hba.conf`. Each line in `/etc/postgresql/pg_hba.conf` defines a single rule. The rules defined first in the file have precedence over those defined later. There are four main rule entry types — `local`, `host`, `hostssl`, and `hostnossl`, and each can use one of several types of authentication.

Rule type local

The most basic rule type is `local`. A `local` entry will match a connection established via UNIX domain sockets on the local machine. This will typically match connections for which no hostname is specified. The PostgreSQL documentation defines a `local` entry like this:

```
# local       DATABASE   USER   METHOD   [OPTION]
```

The first field, *DATABASE*, specifies the database to which this rule applies, or `all` to apply to any database. The second field, *USER*, specifies the user to which this rule applies, or `all` to apply to any user. Both fields also support more options as described later in this section. The remaining fields specify the authentication method chosen.

Debian defines two default `local` entries, like this:

```
# Database administrative login by UNIX sockets
local all postgres ident sameuser
#
# All other connections by UNIX sockets
local  all all ident sameuser
```

The first rule provides access to the `postgres` user, and the second applies to all other users. In this case, both rules are the same and use `ident`-style authentication. (See the "Authentication types" section later in this chapter for an explanation of the various authentication types.)

Rule types host, hostssl, and hostnossl

These three rule types apply to connections from local or remote systems using TCP. The `host` type applies to any kind of TCP connection. The `hostssl` type applies solely to SSL-encrypted connections, and the `hostnossl` type applies solely to non-SSL connections. You can use these to define different policies for encrypted or unencrypted connections. PostgreSQL defines these rule types like this:

```
# host DATABASE USER IP-ADDRESS IP-MASK METHOD [OPTION]
# hostssl DATABASE USER IP-ADDRESS IP-MASK METHOD [OPTION]
# hostnossl DATABASE USER IP-ADDRESS IP-MASK METHOD [OPTION]
# host DATABASE USER IP-ADDRESS/CIDR-MASK METHOD [OPTION]
# hostssl DATABASE USER IP-ADDRESS/CIDR-MASK METHOD [OPTION]
# hostnossl DATABASE USER IP-ADDRESS/CIDR-MASK METHOD [OPTION]
```

The database and user fields have the same meaning as they do for `local`. The next part defines an IP address and netmask. You can specify an IP address and mask pair, such as `127.0.0.1 255.255.255.255` to refer to the single machine `127.0.0.1`. Alternatively, you can specify it in CIDR form, such as `127.0.0.1/32` to refer to the same thing. Together, these items specify an IP range that the rule is considered to match. The remaining parameters specify an authentication method and optional arguments for it in the same manner as `local`.

Debian defines the following default `host` rules for PostgreSQL:

```
# All IPv4 connections from localhost
host all all 127.0.0.1 255.255.255.255 ident sameuser
#
# All IPv6 localhost connections
host all all ::1 ffff:ffff:ffff:ffff:ffff:ffff:ffff:ffff ident sameuser
host all all ::ffff:127.0.0.1/128 ident sameuser
#
# reject all other connection attempts
host all all 0.0.0.0 0.0.0.0 reject
```

The first three lines accept connections from the local machine using the `ident` authentication method. The final line rejects all other connections. Since the first matching line defines the policy for any given connections, if a connection matches one of the first lines, it will use that policy. The last line then behaves as a sort of default; if nothing else matches, that line sets the policy. It is always wise to leave this rejection line in place so that connection attempts from unauthorized computers are automatically rejected.

Authentication types

There are eight different authentication types. These can be used as the final component of any rule definition line.

- ✦ The `trust` method will always accept the user the client claims to be without performing any checks. This is dangerous and is usually not recommended. Some administrators that have complete control over all servers and clients may use it to simplify authentication architectures, but even then, its use remains discouraged.

- ✦ The `reject` method will reject any connection, no matter what user or password is supplied.

- ✦ The `pam` option uses the system's authentication system. This is the authentication system used for other services such as SSH, FTP, or telnet. This requires an additional argument, the name of the PAM service to use. To use the Debian defaults, you should set it to `postgresql`.

- ✦ The `md5`, `crypt`, and `password` options use passwords defined when `createuser` is run. These three options refer to different methods of storing the passwords in the PostgreSQL database.

- ✦ The `krb5` method uses Kerberos for authentication.

- ✦ The final method, `ident`, uses the TCP identd service to attempt to detect the username the connecting client is running from. This method should be used only for machines that you (or a trusted person) have direct administrative control over, since the identd service has known vulnerabilities.

Restarting the server

After modifying the `pg_hba.conf` file, you must restart PostgreSQL to have the changes take effect. You can restart PostgreSQL by running `/etc/init.d/postgresql restart`.

Testing access

You should now be able to connect to your new database and user. PostgreSQL supplies a program called `psql` to use for connecting to the database. With `psql`, you can issue arbitrary SQL commands to the system. Because you now have new users created and don't need to perform administration for these commands, you don't need to run `psql` as the `postgres` user in this case.

First, you'll need to make sure that your access rules in `/etc/postgresql/pg_hba.conf` are accurate for your situation. For instance, if you created the `testuser2` account as described in the chapter, you won't be able to connect to it by default. The reason is that PostgreSQL uses ident authentication by default, and unless you happen to be logged in as `testuser2`, it's not going to accept your connection. If you adjust the second `local` line to read like this, your connection will work:

```
local all all password
```

Now, try the connection with `psql`:

```
jgoerzen@example:~$ psql -U testuser2 testdb
Password:
Welcome to psql 7.4.2, the PostgreSQL interactive terminal.

Type:  \copyright for distribution terms
       \h for help with SQL commands
       \? for help on internal slash commands
       \g or terminate with semicolon to execute query
       \q to quit

testdb=>
```

In this case, the `psql` client was able to successfully connect and authenticate to the remote. The `testdb=>` is the `psql` prompt. You can issue SQL commands directly. For instance, you could create a new table like this:

```
estdb=> create table test (
testdb(>    mynum integer,
testdb(>    description varchar(50)
testdb(> );
CREATE TABLE
```

Like most SQL databases, PostgreSQL supports the GRANT and REVOKE commands to adjust permissions on individual tables. By default, users may create new tables in any database they're allowed to connect to, but they are not given access to existing tables. The GRANT and REVOKE commands alter the permissions for an individual table.

Removing databases and users

You can remove databases and users very easily. When logged in as postgres, you can run either dropuser or dropdb to remove users or databases.

 Caution   Beware—neither program asks for confirmation. The effects are immediate. If you use dropdb to drop a database, that database and all its data will be completely lost.

Here's an example of dropping a user:

```
postgres@example:~$ dropuser testuser2
DROP USER
```

And here's an example of dropping a database:

```
postgres@example:~$ dropdb testdb
DROP DATABASE
```

Upgrading PostgreSQL

There are two major kinds of upgrades relevant for PostgreSQL: minor version upgrades and major version upgrades. A minor version upgrade occurs when only the last component of the PostgreSQL version number changes—for instance, an upgrade from 7.4.1 to 7.4.2. A major version upgrade occurs when the first or second component of the version number changes—for instance, 7.3.1 to 7.4.0.

A minor version upgrade usually happens fairly easily. The Debian system will stop and restart the PostgreSQL server, and that's all it takes.

A major version upgrade indicates a change in the on-disk format of the PostgreSQL database. The Debian PostgreSQL package provides a mechanism to automatically upgrade between version numbers. It will perform a full database dump to ASCII from the old server, install the new server, and then restore from the saved backup file.

The backup process will require a lot of disk space if your database is large. Before performing a major version upgrade, keep this in mind. Also, large databases may take quite some time to back up and restore, so if your PostgreSQL server is critical, make sure to schedule major version upgrades for nonpeak times.

Backing up PostgreSQL

PostgreSQL provides a program called `pg_dump` to back up databases. It generates a plaintext file representing the contents of part or all of a database. It can represent a snapshot in time of the database, and it can be used to re-create the database in various versions of PostgreSQL.

The syntax is simple: Just run `pg_dump` and give, as a parameter, the name of the database to back up. It will generate the result on standard output. Here's an example of creating a compressed backup:

```
postgres@example:~$ pg_dump testdb | gzip -9 > bak.gz
```

There is also a script named `pg_dumpall`. This script will back up the entire contents of every database present on your system. It takes no parameters and, like `pg_dump`, it writes its result to standard output.

You should make sure that your backup program backs up the dumped file instead of the database files themselves. To restore from a dumped file, you can use a command such as the following:

```
postgres@example:~$ zcat bak.gz | psql
```

Using MySQL

Like PostgreSQL, the MySQL database has been around for a while and is used for a variety of different applications. MySQL's installation procedure is similar to PostgreSQL's, but its authentication system is rather different.

Installing MySQL

To start the process of installing the MySQL server, simply run `apt-get install mysql-server`. Like PostgreSQL, the MySQL installation procedure asks several questions at install time. The exact questions you see will depend on your `debconf` settings.

You are first asked whether databases should be removed when the MySQL server is removed. If you answer Yes, then when you purge the `mysql-server` package, all the databases on your system will be removed as well. If you say No, then your databases will never be removed automatically.

The next question asks whether to start MySQL at boot time. Usually, you will answer Yes. If you say No, MySQL will not be automatically started. In either case, you can manually start MySQL by running `/etc/init.d/mysql start`.

Configuring MySQL

The primary location for MySQL configuration is /etc/mysql/my.cnf. Between this file and the values that can be set via the mysqladmin administrative utility, the MySQL server can be completely configured.

There are two things that are frequently configured: the password for the root user and whether to enable networking for MySQL.

Configuring the root password

The MySQL administrative user is root. By default, you could log in as any user and connect to MySQL claiming to be root and receive full administrative access. Therefore, one of the first things that you normally do is set up the root password.

First, you'll want to actually change the root password. To do that, you'll use mysqladmin. Here's an example that sets the password to TestPass:

```
root@example:~$ mysqladmin -u root password 'TestPass'
```

Next, you will probably find it convenient to not have to always supply that password when you log in to MySQL using the command-line tools. You can have MySQL automatically supply the password for you by creating the file ~root/.my.cnf~. Here is an example of that file, assuming the password TestPass:

```
[mysql]
user = root
password = TestPass

[mysqladmin]
user = root
password = TestPass
```

Now, you should run chmod 0600 ~root/.my.cnf. This will ensure that no other users will be able to read your MySQL password.

Configuring networking

MySQL does not have the global IP-based restriction system that PostgreSQL does, so the Debian MySQL package disables networking by default. That means that, by default, you will be able to connect to your MySQL server only from the local machine.

If you want to connect to it over the network, you need to enable networking. To do that, simply delete the skip-networking line from /etc/mysql/my.cnf and then restart the MySQL server. You can restart the server by running /etc/init.d/mysql restart.

Creating databases

Before data can be stored or tables can be created, a new database must be created. The database will store all your data. You will need to create the databases that your applications will use.

The `mysqladmin create` command is used to create a database. Given the name of a database, it will create the storage area for that database. Here's an example:

```
root@example:~# mysqladmin create testdb
```

Interactive queries

You can use the command-line tool `mysql` to supply commands directly to the server. Some configuration is done via the interactive command-line tool.

You can simply start it with `mysql`. That will connect to the server using the user you're logged in as. To connect to a server on a remote machine, you can specify the hostname with `-h`. To supply a different username, you can use `-u`. If you need to supply a password, give `-p`, and `mysql` will prompt you for a password. Following is an example command line. At the end of the command line, specify the database you'd like to connect to. If you are accessing databases on a system other than your own, you can use the `-h` option to specify the MySQL server to access, as in the following command:

```
mysql -u user2 -h server -p database
```

Configuring users

All authentication in MySQL is done per table. There is no global authentication system like there is with PostgreSQL, though it's possible to achieve the same effect. You must explicitly set up users for each table.

Basics of granting access

MySQL uses the `GRANT` and `REVOKE` statements to manage access permissions. You can use the `mysql` tool to issue these statements; just follow each statement with a semicolon. The MySQL manual gives the syntax like this:

```
GRANT priv_type [(column_list)] [, priv_type [(column_list)]] ...
    ON {tbl_name | * | *.* | db_name.*}
    TO user [IDENTIFIED BY [PASSWORD] 'password']
        [, user [IDENTIFIED BY [PASSWORD] 'password']] ...
    [REQUIRE
        NONE |
        [{SSL| X509}]
        [CIPHER 'cipher' [AND]]
        [ISSUER 'issuer' [AND]]
```

```
              [SUBJECT 'subject']]
      [WITH [GRANT OPTION | MAX_QUERIES_PER_HOUR count |
                          MAX_UPDATES_PER_HOUR count |
                          MAX_CONNECTIONS_PER_HOUR count]]

REVOKE priv_type [(column_list)] [, priv_type [(column_list)]] ...
    ON {tbl_name | * | *.* | db_name.*}
    FROM user [, user] ...

REVOKE ALL PRIVILEGES, GRANT OPTION FROM user [, user] ...
```

The most basic form of GRANT might look like this:

```
GRANT ALL ON THISTABLE TO testuser@localhost
```

That will allow the user testuser, connecting from the local machine, full access to THISTABLE. The user will not need to supply any password.

You can grant access to the user from all hosts by using the % character, which stands for 0 or more characters. Here's another example:

```
GRANT ALL ON THISTABLE TO 'testuser@%'
```

This is probably not very wise; it will allow the user to connect from any computer without supplying any form of authentication or password. Notice that you must supply quotes if you are going to use the wildcard. You can force a user to supply a password:

```
GRANT ALL ON THISTABLE TO testuser@localhost
    IDENTIFIED BY 'PassWord'
```

MySQL will now refuse access to the user unless the connection comes from local-host and the specified password is given.

You can also grant access system-wide. This will act as a global default. Here's an example:

```
GRANT ALL ON *.* TO testuser@localhost
```

If you don't want to grant access that broadly, you can instead grant access on a per-database basis. Try a command such as this:

```
GRANT ALL ON testdb.* TO testuser@localhost
```

Available access types

In the preceding examples, the special privilege ALL was granted to the user. You can be much more precise and give specific privileges instead. Table 24-1 summarizes them.

Table 24-1
Available Access Types

Access Type	Description
ALL or ALL PRIVILEGES	Behaves as if all access types except GRANT OPTION were set
ALTER	Permits the user to run ALTER TABLE
CREATE	Permits the user to run the CREATE TABLE command. This is most useful when set globally or per database.
CREATE TEMPORARY TABLES	Allows you to run the SQL command CREATE TEMPORARY TABLE. Like the CREATE access type, this is most useful when set globally or per database.
DELETE	Allows the user to delete rows from a table via the DELETE command
DROP	Allows the user to remove tables with the DROP command. Usually set on a per-database or global basis.
FILE	Permits the user to run queries that save or load data directly from a file
GRANT OPTION	Allows the user to alter the permissions for others
INDEX	Permits the creation and deletion of indices
INSERT	Lets the user add new rows to a table
LOCK TABLES	Lets the user run LOCK TABLES. The user must also have the SELECT access type for this to work.
PROCESS	Lets the user see who is connected via the query SHOW FULL PROCESSLIST
RELOAD	Lets the user force MySQL to reload configuration data via the various FLUSH commands
SELECT	Lets the user read data from a table via SELECT
SHOW DATABASES	Allows the user to get a list of databases on the server via the SHOW DATABASES command
SHUTDOWN	Permits shutting down the entire server via mysqladmin
SUPER	The user can run various administrative commands.
UPDATE	The user can alter existing rows in the table via the UPDATE command.
USAGE	Acts the same as if the user has no access at all

Revoking privileges

Any privileges that have been granted can later be revoked with the REVOKE command. The syntax is very similar to GRANT. Here's an example:

```
REVOKE ALL ON testdb.* FROM testuser@localhost
```

This is effectively how users are removed from the MySQL system.

Removing databases

Databases can be removed via the mysqladmin drop command. Given a database name, the command will completely remove that database from your disk. Here is an example:

```
root@example:~# mysqladmin drop testdb
Dropping the database is potentially a very bad thing to do.
Any data stored in the database will be destroyed.

Do you really want to drop the 'testdb' database [y/N] y
Database "testdb" dropped
```

Caution   This command will delete the database and all its data without any further warning!

Backing up databases

MySQL provides a tool called mysqldump to generate a plaintext dump of your database. This is good for backups, since it can be used for many different versions of MySQL and is directly human-readable.

The mysqldump command takes most of the same command-line options as mysql. It requires at least one database, or alternatively, the argument --all-databases to select all databases on the system. The dump is written to standard output. So, the following command would generate a compressed dump of the entire database installation on your system:

```
root@example:~# mysqldump -p --all-databases | gzip -9 > backup.txt.gz
Enter password:
```

The mysqldump command will not honor the password stored in ~/.my.cnf, so you will need to supply it yourself if you have set a root password with mysqladmin.

You'll want to make sure your backup software backs up the output from mysqldump instead of the raw database files. To restore from a backup, you can use a command such as the following:

```
root@example:~# zcat backup.txt.gz | mysql
```

Client-Side Tools

Now that your server is configured, you'll need to configure the clients for your database. Some applications will be tied to a particular database, and they should have information on that database already.

There are several database-independent infrastructures in Debian. To use them, you will usually need a generic driver component and a specific database driver component. Table 24-2 shows you the Debian package names for these infrastructures.

	Table 24-2		
	Database Client Tools		
Infrastructure Name	*Generic Component*	*PostgreSQL Component*	*MySQL Component*
Java JDBC	n/a	`libpgjava` (in `contrib`)	`libmysql-java` (in contrib)
Python DB-API 2.0	n/a	**choice of** `python-pygresql` **or** `python-psycopg`	`python-mysqldb`
Perl DBI	`libdbi-perl`	`libdbd-pgsql` **or** `libdbd-pg-perl`	`libdbd-mysql-perl`
OCaml OCamlDBI	`libdbi-ocaml`	`libpgsql-ocaml`	`libmysql-ocaml`
Ruby/DBI	n/a	`libdbd-pg-ruby`	`libdbd-mysql-ruby`

In addition to these, other database-specific packages exist in Debian as well.

Summary

Debian provides several different database servers for your use. The two most popular are PostgreSQL and MySQL. Installation of both databases is fairly straightforward thanks to Debian's `apt-get`.

If you choose PostgreSQL, you use the `createdb` and `createuser` commands to set up your databases and users. Access rules are defined in `/etc/postgresql/pg_hba.conf` and configure how users are allowed to connect and authenticate. PostgreSQL provides `pg_dump` and `pg_dumpall` commands to back up your database to plaintext files.

If you choose MySQL, you can use `mysqladmin create` to create databases. User access is defined solely via `GRANT` and `REVOKE` statements. MySQL provides the `mysqldump` command to back up your database to plaintext files.

Debian provides client-side tools for various programming languages and databases. Table 24-2 shows you which tools are available.

✦   ✦   ✦

The Developer

The Debian Community

The real power of Debian is not in the software, as great as that may be, but in the people behind it. Amazingly, these people work long hours on Debian without pay and give away the fruits of their labor for free. In this chapter, I explain the history and philosophy of the Debian Project, how it works on a daily basis, and most importantly, how you can contribute to it.

A Brief History of Debian

To understand how Debian got to be the way it is today, you have to start at the very beginning of the computer age. In those days, computers were big hulking monsters requiring entire rooms and a dedicated staff. *Programming* meant manually setting switches and relays on the front panel of one of these computers. A little later, the first programming languages such as COBOL and FORTRAN were created, and it became feasible to store programs for later use and move them to different computers. But there was still a lot of work involved as there were many types of machines, each with different hardware quirks, so software wasn't worth very much in itself. The manufacturers made their money selling big computer systems and maintenance contracts for them, and they threw in some software for free to sweeten the deal. Their biggest customers were universities and other research institutions, and in the academic world, sharing ideas for the advancement of knowledge is a deeply cherished ideal. So in the early years of computing, the idea of selling software would have struck most people as a very strange one.

The UNIX operating system was developed in the early '70s. Some of its most innovative aspects were that it was written in a high-level language called C, which is fairly small and easy to port to new machines, and that it abstracted details of how each computer did things to a common interface so that a program did not have to deal with individual quirks.

Although it was developed in AT&T's Bell Labs to support that company's commercial documentation needs, its authors had the typical relaxed attitude to ownership of the day. Virtually anyone who showed up with some magnetic tapes could get a copy, and the source code with annotations was also available in an unofficial but widely disseminated book (the so-called *Lions* book, after its author, Australian professor John Lions). This meant that programmers could easily fix flaws in the software and contribute enhancements and new programs. All these factors combined made UNIX a big hit, and it spread through the computing world like wildfire. Even other operating systems were heavily influenced by the UNIX style.

By the mid '70s, people (including a young Bill Gates) were beginning to realize that software could become a commercial product. AT&T started charging large amounts of money for a UNIX license and banned publication or copying of the Lions book. UNIX hackers felt betrayed because they felt they were being asked to pay for code they had written in the first place.

Another place where hackers gathered was MIT and its Artificial Intelligence (AI) Lab. When software became commercialized, people who previously had been happy to share code started jealously hoarding it instead. Many left completely to join the business world. A staff member by the name of Richard M. Stallman, known to his friends by his login name RMS, watched the disintegration of the AI Lab in dismay. The final straw came when the lab was given a new printer that didn't work correctly. RMS approached the manufacturer for the printer driver source code, offering to fix the problem himself, and was refused because the code was a trade secret.

At this point, RMS realized that what was going wrong with the computer industry was not the pursuit of money per se, but rather the attending proprietary attitude, which resulted in a lack of freedom and cooperation. He resolved to do something about it, so he left MIT and founded the FSF (Free Software Foundation) with the then rather quixotic-sounding goal of creating a totally free operating system: free as in freedom, not as in cost. Unlike UNIX, the freedom of this new operating system would be explicitly guaranteed by a license that would allow complete rights to free use, distribution, and modification of its source code, if and only if the licensee agreed to the same terms for their copy. Because this was a legal license, it would have the full force of copyright law behind it. This ingenious subversion of copyright is referred to humorously by FSF advocates as *copyleft*. A similar verbal playfulness is shown in the name of the new operating system, GNU, which is a recursive acronym for "GNU's Not UNIX."

Free Software or Open Source?

RMS and his followers refer to the software they create as Free Software. This term emphasizes that the software is without any encumbrances that would prevent its use, distribution, or modification for any purpose. One problem this creates is that *free* has a double meaning in English. In addition to meaning "unrestricted," it also means "no cost," and that's the meaning most people think of when they hear the word. However, the FSF definition of *free* in no way implies that Free Software cannot be bought or sold. (Though realistically, widespread availability does tend to keep prices down.) The FSF itself sells tapes and CDs containing GNU software to raise funds. Still, people hear *free* and think $0.

When Linux started getting popular, companies arose to sell it and related products. Some were hit square in the business plan by this misunderstanding. Linux enthusiasts, trying to get the business world to move away from proprietary operating systems, also had this problem. The business world was potentially interested in the benefits of Free Software, such as lack of vendor lock-in, superior quality, and flexibility in deployment. But they shied away from the notion that their software would have to be given away for nothing. As a result, a group of interested people got together to form the Open Source Initiative or OSI (www.opensource.org/), an advocacy group aimed at popularizing the term *Open Source* instead of Free Software. In order to maintain the clarity of the term, an Open Source Definition was created. Unfortunately, OSI was denied a trademark on the term, so it is unable to force compliance with the Open Source Definition, but it has become widely accepted anyway.

The use of Open Source is meant to be tactical. The Open Source Definition is based on, and is essentially the same as, the Debian Free Software Guidelines. Many Open Source advocates use the terms *Open Source* and *Free Software* interchangeably. However, some advocates of the term *Free Software* feel that soft-pedaling the ethical aspects of their movement in favor of purely pragmatic considerations does a grave disservice to the public. Some of them get rather annoyed at being referred to as Open Source advocates. Many Linux people use both terms interchangeably. Debian has a history of being identified with advocates of both terms.

The FSF began the arduous task of writing new versions of the UNIX utilities, and although they became widely used in their own right, they never finished a complete operating system.

UNIX was very popular in computer science classrooms. The kernel or heart of the system was small and easy to understand for an operating systems course yet powerful enough to be more interesting than a textbook example. So when the prices for UNIX licenses started climbing, educators were not happy.

A Dutch professor named Andrew Tanenbaum decided to create his own UNIX clone called MINIX. It was released in 1987. MINIX became very popular, and suggestions and code for new features poured in. But Professor Tanenbaum resisted adding features. He wanted to keep MINIX nice and simple to fulfill its educational mission.

Linux or GNU/Linux?

One of the disputes that roil the Linux community is whether the system should be known as Linux or GNU/Linux. The FSF and its supporters say that Linux properly refers to the kernel only. As you need GNU tools such as the `bash` shell and the `gcc` C compiler to actually make the Linux kernel usable, it deserves the name GNU/Linux. Using the name GNU/Linux emphasizes the ethical ideal of free software. Detractors point out that the majority of software that a user would consider essential in a modern Linux distribution is not from GNU. Many people refer to the entire system only as "Linux." Debian Developers have, as a group, decided to show solidarity with the FSF and refer to their work as Debian GNU/Linux. So Debian should always be officially referred to that way. As for Linus himself, he is okay with either name.

Meanwhile, in 1991, over in Finland, a graduate student in computer science named Linus Torvalds, who wanted to run UNIX on his brand-new 386 PC, decided to write his own UNIX-like kernel. He made two monumental decisions. The first was that he decided to advertise his project on the Internet, inviting any interested people to contribute. The second was that he decided to license the project under the terms of the GNU General Public License (GPL). The kernel, which Linus's friend (and now Debian Developer) Lars Wirzenius named Linux, together with the GNU utilities, formed a complete, free operating system. This is why many people refer to the combination as *GNU/Linux*. The new operating system took off rapidly, attracting both people who felt held back by the constraints of MINIX and those who were too impatient to wait for GNU.

In the early days, assembling a Linux system required a great deal of time and effort, tracking down bits and pieces of software from here and there. Some enterprising people soon thought of providing prebuilt "distributions" that would provide the Linux kernel, GNU utilities, and various other pieces of software necessary for a fully functional system in a prebuilt, easy-to-install package. These were commercial endeavors and of varying quality. Ian Murdock, who in 1993 was a college student in Indiana, wrote a manifesto calling for the creation of a distribution that would follow the tried-and-true principles that had made Linux a success: open participation, commitment to software freedom, and technical excellence. He named this new distribution Debian, a contraction of his now ex-wife Debra's name and his own.

The FSF took notice of the Debian manifesto, made a grant to fund the initial development of Debian, and for a while sponsored it as the official GNU/Linux distribution. They parted ways in 1996 over organizational and technical disagreements but still continue working together on topics of mutual interest. In order to clearly differentiate Debian's mission from other organizations and to clarify their position in regards to software freedom, the Debian Developers, then led by Bruce Perens, developed two comprehensive documents: the *Social Contract* and *Free Software Guidelines*. Later, Bruce took out the Debian-specific bits from the Free Software Guidelines to form the Open Source Definition mentioned previously.

The Debian GNU/Linux Social Contract and Free Software Guidelines

The Debian Project is an association of individuals who have made common cause to create a free operating system. This is the "social contract" we offer to the Free Software community.

The Debian GNU/Linux Social Contract

1. **Debian Will Remain 100% Free Software.** We promise to keep the Debian GNU/Linux Distribution entirely free software. As there are many definitions of free software, we include the guidelines we use to determine if software is "free" below. We will support our users who develop and run non-free software on Debian, but we will never make the system depend on an item of non-free software.

2. **We Will Give Back to the Free Software Community.** When we write new components of the Debian system, we will license them as free software. We will make the best system we can, so that free software will be widely distributed and used. We will feed back bug fixes, improvements, user requests, etc. to the "upstream" authors of software included in our system.

3. **We Won't Hide Problems.** We will keep our entire bug-report database open for public view at all times. Reports that users file online will immediately become visible to others.

4. **Our Priorities Are Our Users and Free Software.** We will be guided by the needs of our users and the free-software community. We will place their interests first in our priorities. We will support the needs of our users for operation in many different kinds of computing environments. We won't object to commercial software that is intended to run on Debian systems, and we'll allow others to create value-added distributions containing both Debian and commercial software, without any fee from us. To support these goals, we will provide an integrated system of high-quality, 100%-free software, with no legal restrictions that would prevent these kinds of use.

5. **Programs That Don't Meet Our Free Software Standards.** We acknowledge that some of our users require the use of programs that don't conform to the Debian Free Software Guidelines. We have created "contrib" and "non-free" areas in our FTP archive for this software. The software in these directories is not part of the Debian system, although it has been configured for use with Debian. We encourage CD manufacturers to read the licenses of software packages in these directories and determine if they can distribute that software on their CDs. Thus, although non-free software isn't a part of Debian, we support its use, and we provide infrastructure (such as our bug-tracking system and mailing lists) for non-free software packages.

The Debian Free Software Guidelines

1. **Free Redistribution.** The license of a Debian component may not restrict any party from selling or giving away the software as a component of an aggregate software distribution containing programs from several different sources. The license may not require a royalty or other fee for such sale.

Continued

Continued

2. **Source Code.** The program must include source code and must allow distribution in source code as well as compiled form.

3. **Derived Works.** The license must allow modifications and derived works and must allow them to be distributed under the same terms as the license of the original software.

4. **Integrity of the Author's Source Code.** The license may restrict source code from being distributed in modified form only if the license allows the distribution of "patch files" with the source code for the purpose of modifying the program at build time. The license must explicitly permit distribution of software built from modified source code. The license may require derived works to carry a different name or version number from the original software. (This is a compromise. The Debian group encourages all authors to not restrict any files, source or binary, from being modified.)

5. **No Discrimination against Persons or Groups.** The license must not discriminate against any person or group of persons.

6. **No Discrimination against Fields of Endeavor.** The license must not restrict anyone from making use of the program in a specific field of endeavor. For example, it may not restrict the program from being used in a business or from being used for genetic research.

7. **Distribution of License.** The rights attached to the program must apply to all to whom the program is redistributed without the need for execution of an additional license by those parties.

8. **License Must Not Be Specific to Debian.** The rights attached to the program must not depend on the program's being part of a Debian system. If the program is extracted from Debian and used or distributed without Debian but otherwise within the terms of the program's license, all parties to whom the program is redistributed should have the same rights as those that are granted in conjunction with the Debian system.

9. **License Must Not Contaminate Other Software.** The license must not place restrictions on other software that is distributed along with the licensed software. For example, the license must not insist that all other programs distributed on the same medium must be free software.

10. **Example Licenses.** The "GPL," "BSD," and "Artistic" licenses that we consider "free."

It is the Social Contract and DFSG (as the Debian Free Software Guidelines are known for short) that define the policies and future directions of the project. No one agrees with every single stance the Debian Project takes, but the firm foundations set by these documents mean there is no mistaking the project's views on Free Software–related topics. This philosophical consistency has served the project well through the years and enabled it to keep its mission coherent and expand its reach ever further.

The Organization of the Debian Project

The Debian Project itself follows the Free Software/Open Source model very closely. Work in Debian is done by almost a thousand volunteers working as *Debian Developers*. They are led by an elected project leader and his delegates and supported by a nonprofit, Software in the Public Interest. The developers work together under a common set of policies in an often disorganized but extremely effective development model.

The project leader, delegates, and other officers

The Debian Project has a constitution (see Appendix B), which, together with the Social Contract and Debian Free Software Guidelines, makes up the formal rules by which the project operates. The constitution outlines the powers of a project leader (`leader@debian.org`), **secretary** (`secretary@debian.org`), and technical committee (`debian-ctte@lists.debian.org`). Other positions are filled by delegates the project leader chooses. This is the project leader's major power; in other respects, he or she is more of a "first among equals" rather than a CEO. Other than constitutional duties, the leader's chief job is to represent Debian to the world.

Two of the most important delegated positions are the release manager (`debian-release@lists.debian.org`) and the FTP archive maintainers (`ftpmaster@debian.org`). The release manager determines whether the testing distribution is in a fit enough state to be declared stable and whether any packages should be dropped for being too buggy to release. Plus, the release manager has the fun job of picking a code name for the new release. The FTP archive maintainers perform the manual process of adding new packages into Debian for the first time (subsequent versions of the package are installed automatically). At that time, they check each package to make sure the license meets the Debian Free Software Guidelines, if it was uploaded to the main section, or if there are any other problems with it.

Software in the Public Interest, Inc.

In order to do business in an official capacity, the Debian Project has set up a nonprofit corporation registered in New York State called Software in the Public Interest, Inc., or SPI. SPI is the legal owner of Debian's assets and can accept tax-deductible donations on the project's behalf (contact `treasurer@spi-inc.org` for questions related to donations). The exact relationship between Debian and SPI is delineated in the Debian constitution.

Cathedrals and bazaars

A compelling analysis of the organizational methods of Open Source and how groups like Debian have managed to take on large, organized, well-funded companies like Microsoft is contained in an interesting paper by Eric S. Raymond, called "The

Cathedral and the Bazaar" (www.catb.org/~esr/writings/cathedral-bazaar/).
A gothic cathedral such as Chartres, says Raymond, is a mammoth edifice. It has one
goal in mind, the glory of God, and the identities of the builders are subsumed in this
goal. A few master craftsmen, the Masons, whose guild jealously guarded the secrets
of building in medieval times, have total control over the project. A cathedral could
take years and consume vast amounts of money before it was completed. On the
other hand, a bazaar presents a scene of seeming chaos. There are all kinds of merchants selling all kinds of things, some of which are valuable and some of which are
useless junk. A frequent shopper in a bazaar soon learns which merchants are reliable and which ones are fraudulent. He gets to haggle over how much to actually pay,
and there is no ideology beyond buying and selling. Proprietary software is like a
cathedral. It is developed purely for profit and designed in a formal hierarchical way
by people who, as far as the end-user is concerned, are faceless strangers. Releases
are made infrequently and by the vendor's agenda, not necessarily the user's. Open
Source projects, on the other hand, tend to be ad hoc, highly personal creations
made to "scratch an itch" the author had rather than to achieve any particular lofty
goal. They are released early and often — many times before they are even usable —
so they constantly attract scrutiny from other developers and the general public.

Debian operates like a bazaar. You can view all stages of development from the time
a package is first uploaded to unstable to the time it becomes part of the stable
release. Problems are not hidden. Anyone can file a bug, which will be on public display in Debian's bug-tracking system. Each package has the maintainer's name on it
so you know who is responsible. All Debian business is carried out on public mailing lists where any interested person can join in the discussion. Anyone can also
apply to be a developer.

The downside of openness is that the need to establish consensus in a large heterogeneous group can make it frustratingly hard to actually get things moving in Debian
as each topic is talked to death first. And the polish you can get from a single-
minded, sharply focused vision is missing. (Whatever problems cathedrals may
have, you have to admit they sure look pretty!) Still, overall, a policy of openness
has served Debian and its users well, as its continuing rise in popularity attests.

Debian as a platform

If you are a commercial vendor considering targeting Debian as a market or basing
a product on top of it, you should be aware of how bazaar-style organization can
impact your business plans. The safest bet is to support stable, but you should
bear in mind that many people do use testing and unstable. You shouldn't get in
their way if they want to use your product under those distributions, though you
can explain to them that they are on their own, support-wise.

Definitely do provide your software in deb format. Make sure the debs are policy-
compliant and take advantage of Debian features. If you must modify existing

Debian packages, do it in such a way that it is easy for a user to roll back to the standard version. If your product is downloadable, provide your own `apt` archive so that users can take advantage of the powerful features of `apt`.

Debian people expect dialogue. Make sure there is an easy way for users to give you feedback and report problems. Pay attention to the feedback! Don't let it disappear into a black hole.

Be part of the community. If you are taking from Debian, give something back. A commercial company can provide much-needed funds and resources to the project. It can also help by advocating Debian in areas where nonprofit volunteers cannot penetrate. Or it can represent Debian interests in standards bodies or other industry organizations.

Debian policy

The technical decisions made by the project are collected in the Debian Policy Manual (`www.debian.org/doc/policy-manual`, also downloadable in the `debian-policy` package). These policies ensure that packages meet a certain standard of quality and integrate well. Violations of policy are considered to be bugs, and packages with serious unfixed policy violations can be dropped from the distribution.

Debian Developers

With around a thousand developers, Debian has a larger "staff" than most commercial software companies. These developers are not paid a salary. They are located all over the planet and have wildly differing backgrounds, interests, and skill sets. They are united by one thing only, a desire to create the world's best and freest operating system.

Becoming a Debian Developer is open to anyone. There is a rather involved process to go through first, though. Although in an ideal world you could just jump right in, the fact that Debian is so widely used now for so many important tasks means that applicants have to be vetted to make sure they are technically competent and have the interests of the project and users at heart.

There are a few standard terms used to describe the roles of the various people involved in a candidate's attempt to join the project. A prospective applicant is referred to as a New Maintainer. An existing developer who can vouch for the New Maintainer is called an advocate. An existing developer who will vet the New Maintainer's application is called an application manager. And the project administrator who will actually allow the New Maintainer in (or reject him or her) is the Debian account manager.

The steps in the New Maintainer process are the following:

1. Study the Social Contract and Debian Free Software Guidelines. There will be a test!

2. Install the `gnupg` package and create an encryption key. This consists of a public and a private part. The public part should be uploaded to the public key servers (`http://wwwkeys.pgp.net/`). The private part should be kept secret. This will be used as your digital signature, so you should on no account keep your private key on a machine connected to the Internet or any other place where it is in danger of being stolen. At the time you create the key, you should also create a revocation certificate. This can be uploaded to the key servers if you ever need to declare your key invalid. You can learn more about these tasks by reading the documentation in the `gnupg-doc` package.

3. Get the key signed. In order to be useful as a form of identification, someone who already has a trusted key has to vouch for your identity. As existing Debian Developers are deemed to be trusted, you need to find one and prove to him or her that you are the person who has issued your key. You do this by giving the developer a copy of the public key ID and showing an official form of identification such as a driver's license or passport. The developer will then "sign" your public key with his or her own and either upload it to the key servers or give it to you for uploading. Now you are part of Debian's web of trust. The more signatures you get, the stronger your key can be trusted to represent your identity.

4. Read the policy manual and other Debian documentation to familiarize yourself with the techniques of building a high-quality package. Even before you become an official developer, you can build a package and have it uploaded by a sponsor. This is good practice and will give you a good feel for the glamorous life of a Debian Developer (or something like that). You can also file bug reports, fix bugs, and otherwise involve yourself in the activities of the project.

5. Find an advocate. By this time, you should have been involved with the project for a while and other developers should have gotten to know you. You need one of those developers to write a statement vouching for your ability to function as a developer.

6. Now you are ready to make a formal application to become a member of the project at `http://nm.debian.org/newnm.php`.

7. You will be assigned an application manager who will test you on your knowledge of Debian philosophy, procedures, and skills.

8. When the application manager is satisfied, he or she will make a report recommending you as a developer, and after a while, the Debian Account Manager will create an account for you on the Debian servers. (Unfortunately, this has been a bottleneck in the past.) You will now be able to make uploads on your own.

In general, each developer is responsible for one or more packages, though there are some who focus on quality assurance, translations, or other activities. It is their job to interact with the upstream developers of the software if it is not something they have written themselves and with the users of the package who submit bug reports if they discover problems or want new features implemented. Developers also get to vote once a year for the project leader.

Bug Reporting

Practically everyone has spent some time cursing at a computer. It is cathartic but doesn't really do much good. What you really want is to get the problem fixed, but with proprietary software, fixing a problem—sometimes even figuring out what exactly the problem is—is like trying to fix a car whose hood is welded shut. By using Free Software, it is much easier to solve problems because you have all the source code available to you. It's easier if you are a programmer, that is. For the typical user confronted with the gobbledygook of C, the hood may as well still be welded shut. But there's no need to worry; the Debian community can lend a helping hand.

The Seven Habits of Highly Effective Bug Reporters

Whichever avenue you follow to get help, there are a number of things you can do to help maximize your chances of getting prompt and accurate help. These tips are discussed in greater detail in an article by Eric Raymond and Rick Moen called "How to Ask Questions the Smart Way" (www.catb.org/~esr/faqs/smart-questions.html).

Read the documentation. It's not always complete or easy to understand, but most programs do have some sort of documentation. Read it carefully. There may be a work-around for the bug, or it may actually be the way the program is supposed to work. Search engines like Google can also give possible leads.

Check to see whether the bug has already been reported. Look in the archives of debian-user at http://lists.debian.org/debian-user/ or the BTS, http://bugs.debian.org. If you have some extra information to add, join an existing thread or add to an existing bug report rather than create a new one.

Explain your problem clearly and succinctly. "It doesn't work" doesn't give potential helpers enough to go on. Similarly, a rambling digression about the state of the universe in the middle of your report will not make any friends. If you are posting to a mailing list like debian-user, use a specific, descriptive subject. "Please help with Debian problem"—bad. "foo package in unstable causes screen to turn black"—good.

Provide as much information as possible. Include things such as the version and distribution of Debian you are using, the version of the package and any other packages it depends on, any relevant hardware details, or other details that may be relevant. If you're not sure if it's relevant, mention it anyway. Too much information is less of a problem for people giving support than too little. One of the best bug reporters I had was a total Linux novice who felt he couldn't explain the problem he was having so he sent me a screenshot.

Continued

Continued

Don't whine. By the time you ask for help, you may have been trying to solve your problem for a long time and have gotten quite frustrated. But resist the temptation to lash out. It will only antagonize people who might otherwise be of assistance. Another mistake people often make is to treat Debian as a commercial vendor you can demand service from. Debian Developers are volunteers, as are the people who provide help in the Debian-user mailing list and the #debian IRC channel. They resent imperious treatment. Remember that you are getting help for free and show some gratitude. Conversely, if you are being treated rudely (this happens more on IRC than other places), you don't have to tolerate it. Complain publicly and peer pressure will usually take care of it. Do bear in mind that current computer interfaces do not allow for much subtlety of human expression and many Debian people are not native English speakers. So what may seem like a brusque or rude response may just be a misunderstanding. Above all, heed the advice of that sagacious philosopher, Mom: "Everyone play nice!"

Follow through. When you are asked for more information or to perform a test, do it promptly. If by chance you manage to solve the problem yourself, don't just disappear; mention it so that other people don't waste time trying to work it out.

Share your knowledge. After getting your answer, consider giving back to the community by volunteering in the help forums yourself. Or you could put up a Web page. By adding your experience to those of others, Debian moves ever closer to perfection.

Your first stop when you need help should be the Debian-user mailing list (debian-user@lists.debian.org). Here you can get advice from many knowledgeable people. If you prefer more immediate methods of communication, try the Internet Relay Chat (IRC) channel, #debian, on the IRC server irc.debian.org. If other users are unable to help, you can contact the package maintainer via Debian's Bug Tracking System (BTS).

Section 3 of the Debian Social Contract promises that bugs will not be hidden away and that the bug-tracking system will be open to all. You can search the BTS at http://bugs.debian.org/. To actually submit a bug report, though, you have to use e-mail. You send a message to submit@bugs.debian.org with certain special lines at the top of the body of the message:

✦ **Package:** Followed by the name of the package you are submitting a bug against.

✦ **Version:** Followed by the version of the package you are reporting a bug against.

✦ **Severity:** Followed by one of several levels of severity:

- **critical** — A bug so bad that it causes other parts of the system to break, destroys your data, or opens up a security hole on the system.

- **grave** — A bug that makes the package unusable or can potentially cause data loss or weakens security for a user of the package.

- **serious** — File a bug of this level when you notice that a package is severely violating Debian policy in some way.

- **important** — A bug that causes big problems for some users of a package but not necessarily for all of them.

- **normal** — A problem in some feature of a package but nothing so bad that the package cannot be used.

- **minor** — This bug is for things like spelling mistakes that definitely ought to be corrected but don't really impact the use of the package.

- **wish list** — Not a bug per se but a suggestion or a request for a new feature.

If you aren't sure which severity to use, make your best guess. If necessary, the maintainer will adjust it for you.

✦ **Tag:** Followed by one or more special tags separated by spaces. Tags are normally set by the maintainer or other Debian Developers, but there are a couple that the submitter can usefully set:

- **l10n** — This is short for *localization* and indicates that the bug relates to foreign-language translations of the package text.

- **patch** — This tag means that a source code patch that fixes the bug is included along with the report. Needless to say, patches are most welcome.

- **security** — This tag means that the bug relates to security and so should be treated with special scrutiny.

After these special lines, add a blank line and then your report. A sample message might look something like this:

```
From: Joe User <user@example.com>
To: submit@bugs.debian.org
Subject: output of echo omits vowels
Date: Thu, 01 Jan 1970 00:00:00 -0000

Package: coreutils
Version: 5.091-2
Severity: important

Can you help me? When you use the version of echo in this package eg.
echo hello world
you get back
hll wrld
I tried the echo builtin to the bash shell and it doesn't have this problem.
```

After you submit the report, you will receive a response stating that it has been for-warded to the maintainer of the package and providing a reference number for the bug, for example, 123456. Further correspondence concerning the bug can be sent to 123456@bugs.debian.org. You and the maintainer and any other interested parties can continue the dialogue until the problem is resolved, hopefully to your satisfaction.

To simplify the process of submitting a bug, install the reportbug package. reportbug is a program that will ask you a few questions about the bug you wish to report, such as its severity and which package it occurred in. It will add some diagnostic information that would be useful to the package maintainer and then format the report properly and mail it to the bug-tracking system for you.

One of the huge advantages Free Software/Open Source has over proprietary soft-ware is that it has many eyes looking over it, hunting for bugs. Thus, it can improve at a more rapid pace and with more attention to the needs of the user. So please don't just curse at your Debian box when something goes wrong. Report a bug and get it fixed instead.

Summary

In this chapter, I explained to you how the Debian Project was formed and the ideals that keep it going to this day. You learned about the organization of the project and how it functions, both from the human standpoint and in terms of the life cycle of packages. I finished up by showing you how to help improve Debian by reporting a bug.

✦   ✦   ✦

Building Packages

The time may come when you need some software that is not in Debian. Or maybe there is a package, but it isn't the most current version, or you disagree with the compilation choices the maintainer made. In all these scenarios, most operating systems would leave you at the mercy of the vendor. Happily, Debian is completely Free Software, so you can make your own software packages. In this chapter, I show you how.

Essential Tools

Throughout this chapter, you'll make use of some core tools. By installing the `build-essential` package, you can have them all on your system in one fell swoop. Another way is to select the C/C++ development task when installing Debian or afterwards using `tasksel`. This will give you all the tools used in this chapter and more. When you install `build-essential`, it will in turn install the following packages:

♦ gcc, g++ — The GNU Compiler Collection consists of a set of programs for compiling various programming languages into executables. gcc is the C compiler and g++ is the C++ compiler. Although there are graphical front ends to the compilers like those found on Windows or Macs, most Linux programmers invoke them from the command line. A typical use of gcc might look like this:

```
gcc -o hello hello.c
```

This says compile the C source code in `hello.c` and output an executable file called `hello`. g++ works the same way, but for C++ source code (which typically has a .cc or .C extension). You can find out more about the many other options gcc and g++ accept by installing the `gcc-doc` package.

✦ libc6-dev — This package contains the headers and object files needed to compile C programs with the GNU C library. Its documentation is contained in the glibc-doc package. If you want to compile C++ programs that use more than the C-compatible subset of C++, you have to install the libstdc++6-dev package. Its documentation is contained in the libstdc++6-doc package.

✦ dpkg-dev — This package contains the programs needed to create a .deb package.

✦ make — Typing long sets of compiler options at the command line is boring and error-prone. Plus, in a large program, there may be many source code files that need to be compiled in a specific order with specific options. The make utility automates all this for you through a script called a makefile. make has many features. To find out more about them, install the make-doc package.

Together, these packages are sufficient to compile a large majority of the software in Debian.

A Five-Minute Guide to makefiles

You can do a lot with makefiles. In fact, whole books have been written on this topic alone. I can't go into all the details in this short space, but as understanding makefiles is going to be an important part of this chapter, here is a quick overview.

A simple makefile for a program consisting of two source code files producing one executable might look like this:

```
CC=/usr/bin/gcc

hello: hello.o extras.o
  $(CC) -o hello hello.o extras.o

hello.o: hello.c
  $(CC) -c hello.c

extras.o: extras.c
  $(CC) -ansi -pedantic -c extras.c

install: hello
  cp hello /usr/local/bin
  @echo Installation complete.

clean:
  -rm hello *.o
```

The first line defines a variable called CC, which we set to the name of the C compiler. The value of the variable is substituted at various places in the makefile by the $(`variable_name`) notation. Note that make variables are case-sensitive, and if a nonexistent variable is referenced, it will be substituted by empty space, which can lead to unexpected results.

The rest of the makefile consists of "actions" and "targets." Each of these consists of a name followed by a colon and an optional set of prerequisites, which can be files, other targets, or both, followed by a series of lines starting with a tab and containing shell commands. If make is called without any arguments, processing begins with the first target (hello in this case), or if it is given the name of a target as an argument (such as make install), processing begins with that target.

For each target, the prerequisites are checked. If they are files, make checks to see if the file exists or has been modified. If so, it runs the commands associated with this target to bring the file up to date. If the prerequisite is a target, that target is examined in the same way.

You can see in this example that the end product, the hello executable program, depends on two object (.o) files. Each of them has its own target that depends on a corresponding .c file and compiles it with a different set of options. (Admittedly, this is a bit contrived. Normally all your object files should be compiled with the same options or subtle bugs can develop. In this case it's okay because the -ansi and -pedantic options check only syntax and do not affect code output.) So a change to extras.c would trigger a rebuild of extras.o, which would in turn cause hello to be rebuilt. hello.o would be unaffected.

The other two targets in this example are install, which just copies the hello executable to a particular location (it has a dependency on hello, so it will be built first if it doesn't already exist), and clean, which clears up the extra files created by the build process.

As it runs, make echoes each command to the screen. If you want to suppress echoing, typically because you are printing your own message as in the last line of the install target, you can put an @ symbol at the beginning of a line of commands. Normally, if a command fails for some reason, make halts. If you want to carry on regardless, you can put a dash (-) character in front of the line as shown in the clean target.

Non-Debian Packages

Before I get into building Debian packages, here's a brief look at installing software packages that do not come in Debian's own format. In Chapter 1, I mentioned that the lowest-common-denominator package format in the Linux world is the tarball. So if you need a program right away, the path of least resistance may be to just use a tarball. You can install tarballs on Debian the same way as on any other Linux system. Typically it goes something like this:

```
$ ./configure
$ make
# make install
```

Most tarballs are packaged using programs from GNU called `autoconf` and `automake` (though unfortunately some packages choose to reinvent this wheel—badly). The programs create a script called `configure`, which as the name suggests configures the source for building on your system. It also checks whether you have any required libraries and other prerequisites and lets you set any optional features provided by the program. Running `configure --help` will give you all the details.

Configuring the program will create a makefile. You run `make` on the makefile and compile the program, and then as the last step, you install the newly compiled program with the command `make install`. This technique is easy, but the trouble is that the Debian packaging system will not know about the files you installed. This can lead to `.deb`s overwriting files installed by your tarballs, or the files you installed "by hand" can interfere with files managed by Debian. The way to avoid this is to use the `configure scripts --prefix` argument to declare the directory in which the package will be installed. Debian policy guarantees that `/usr/local` and directories under it are off-limits to `.deb`s, so you can safely use `/usr/local` as `--prefix` (it's the default in well-behaved configure scripts) and there won't be any conflict.

Be warned: A big problem with going behind the packaging system's back in this way is dependencies. Suppose that using the aforementioned method, you've installed the popular, but alas, nonfree, qmail MTA (Mail Transport Agent). Many Debian packages depend on the presence of an MTA, so you might think that by installing qmail you can now remove Exim or whatever MTA was previously installed. But you would be wrong. Although, being in `/usr/local`, qmail will not be touched by the packaging system, neither will the packaging system take any notice of it. When you try to remove Exim, `dpkg` will complain that there is no longer an MTA. Your installation of qmail doesn't exist as far as the packaging system is concerned.

One way of getting around this is to keep a real Debian package around but disabled, just to provide dependencies. This is not very elegant or satisfactory and can lead to a whole set of problems. Another way is to keep overriding the packaging system whenever it asks for a missing dependency. This is also unsatisfactory, and a pain in the neck to boot. You can also create a dummy `.deb` to fool the packaging system into leaving you alone. You can do this with the `equivs` package, but as using `equivs` requires some of the same knowledge as creating a full-blown `.deb`, I will suspend discussion of it until after that topic is covered. See the "Creating Dummy Packages" section later in this chapter for more detail.

Packaging the Kernel

The most frequent encounter a Debian user has with package building is compiling a custom kernel or adding modules or patches to the kernel. You can certainly do this the old way, which will be familiar to anyone who has built kernels before:

```
$ make menuconfig
$ make dep
$ make clean
# make bzlilo
# make modules_install
```

The Debian way of building a kernel is easier and results in a .deb! The advantage of this scheme is that you can use the package management utilities to add or remove the kernel .deb. This is handy if, say, you are a tester who needs to switch between different kernel versions, or if you are a system administrator who wants to compile a standard kernel with the same set of options for a whole group of machines. Plus, the package does all the necessary setup work a new kernel needs, so there's no more rummaging around for a boot disk because you forgot to run lilo.

To begin, install the fakeroot and kernel-package packages, plus the kernel source package for the version you wish to install (for example, kernel-source-2.6.8 for Linux 2.6.8). You can also grab the kernel tarball directly from www.kernel.org/ if you want the exact source code Linus Torvalds produces, but like most distributions, Debian enhances its version of the source with patches that did not make it into the official version, so the Debian kernel source package is preferable. I'm going to assume you are using it for the rest of these instructions. I'm also going to assume you are installing version 2.6.8, so you need to substitute a different number if you are using another version (which you probably are).

After you have the right packages installed, change the directory to /usr/src. Except for the final step of actually installing the new kernel, you should follow the good security practice of doing all the compilation as a nonprivileged user. The /usr/src directory is set up to be writable by group src, so if the user ID you wish to use is not a member of that group, you should add it. (You may need to log out and log in again for the new group membership to take effect.) The kernel source you downloaded can be found in /usr/src as a tarball compressed with bzip2 called linux-source-2.6.8.tar.bz2. It is installed this way because the Linux kernel is huge; it's about 50MB uncompressed. So to save space, it is not installed in an uncompressed state; you can do that yourself. Go ahead and uncompress it like this:

```
$ tar xjf linux-source-2.6.8.tar.bz2
```

If you get an error message, you may have to install the bzip2 package.

When you have the source uncompressed, change to the newly created linux-source-2.6.8 directory. Some people suggest making a symlink from linux-source-2.6.8 to /usr/src/linux, but this is not recommended these days as it can cause the compiler and libc to find certain header files in the wrong place.

Next, configure the kernel the same way as you would when building the kernel the classic way, that is, make menuconfig, make xconfig, and so on. A common mistake people who are new to Debian make is not having the right packages installed for their chosen configuration method to work. For `menuconfig`, you need the `libncurses5-dev`, and for `xconfig`, the `libqt3-mt` package. (Older kernel versions used the TK toolkit in the `tk8.4` package for `xconfig`.) If you are merely tweaking an existing kernel and you want to start from its configuration, you can find it in `/boot`. Just copy it to `/usr/src/linux-2.6.7/.config`.

Now you can build the kernel the Debian way with a command like this:

```
$ fakeroot make-kpkg -revision=mykernel1 buildpackage
```

What's going on here? Part of the process of building a `.deb` involves changing file ownership and permissions. Under the UNIX security model, changing ownership to root, for example, requires you to be root. It's not a good idea to grant root privileges to a user just for the purpose of changing files in a package. The `fakeroot` program gets around this problem by running commands in such a way that invocations of system calls such as `chmod` and `chown` are intercepted and redirected to safe, restricted versions. The build process is tricked into thinking it is really changing file attributes while the real system is unaffected.

`make-kpkg` is the program that actually builds the `.debs`. Here it is being called with the `-revision` argument, which allows you to include a custom string as part of the package version number. This can be used to distinguish your custom kernel from others. The last part, after any options, is called the target, in this case `buildpackage`. The target specifies the action that `make-kpkg` takes. Table 26-1 shows some of the targets you can choose. (You can get the entire current list with the command `make-kpkg -targets`.)

Table 26-1
Some make-kpkg Targets

Name	Builds
`buildpackage`	Builds all four `.debs`: `kernel-doc`, `kernel-source`, `kernel-headers`, and `kernel-image`
`kernel-doc`	`kernel-doc` only
`kernel-source`	`kernel-source` only
`kernel-headers`	`kernel-headers` only
`kernel-image`	`kernel-image` only
`clean`	Removes built files and restores source to unbuilt state
`modules_image`	Builds module packages
`modules_clean`	Removes built files for module packages

`make-kpkg` builds up to four `.debs`:

- ✦ `kernel-doc`—A package containing the kernel documentation only.

- ✦ `kernel-headers`—A package containing only the header files for this kernel. This can be useful if you want to build programs that make use of the kernel data structures directly (such as kernel modules) and don't want to have the entire massive kernel source around.

- ✦ `kernel-image`—The new kernel itself is contained in this package.

- ✦ `kernel-source`—A package containing the kernel source. It's not much use in this case, as it is exactly the same as the source available from Debian, but if you had added your own patches, they would be included here.

The next-to-last target in Table 26-1, `modules_image`, is one you'll use a lot. It is for building third-party kernel modules, which are not distributed as part of the official Linux source. An example would be the hostap drivers for Prism chipset-based wireless network cards. Although you could just download them from the hostap Web site (`http://hostap.epitest.fi/`), Debian already has them in the `hostap-source` package. Installing this package also deposits a gzipped tarball into `/usr/src`. Unpacking it creates a `/usr/src/modules/hostap-source` directory containing the hostap module source code. After changing to the `/usr/src/kernel-2.6.7` directory, you can compile it like this:

```
$ fakeroot make-kpkg –revision=mykernel1 modules_image
```

When compilation has finished, you will find a new `.deb` in `/usr/src`. There are many other module source packages in Debian that work the same way, and `make-kpkg modules_image` will build them all at once. If, however, you want to build only a subset, perhaps because only one or two needed to be updated to new versions, you can use the `–added_modules` option followed by a module package name (or a comma-separated list if there is more than one) to `make-kpkg` like this:

```
$ fakeroot make-kpkg –revision=mykernel1 added_modules=hostap_source \
modules_image
```

Another useful option to `make-kpkg`, particularly when dealing with official Debian kernels, is `–append-to-version`. The problem is this: By and large, Debian packages are not optimized for specific processors, as the speedup is negligible for most programs. The kernel, however, is an exception, as it is one place where every bit of speed can make a difference. Also, separate optimizations have to be done for systems with one processor and those with several (SMP or Symmetric Multi-Processor systems). Official kernels are provided in a variety of flavors and some extra information is added to the version number to distinguish them. For example, the 2.6.7 kernel optimized for Intel Pentium Pro and higher chips on multiprocessor machines is called `2.6.7-1-686-smp`, whereas the same kernel optimized for single AMD Athlon or Duron chips would be `2.6.7-1-k7`. These kernels look for modules in

/lib/modules/2.6.7-1-686-smp and /lib/modules/2.6.7-1-k7, respectively. But if you used make-kpkg in the same way as the previous example, modules you built would be installed to /lib/modules/2.6.7, which could be a problem. So instead you would invoke make-kpkg like this (assuming you were building for the Athlon version of the kernel):

```
$ fakeroot make-kpkg --revision=mykernel1 --append-to-version=-1-k7 \
  modules_image
```

make-kpkg has many other options, which are described in the make-kpkg(1) Manpage and, more extensively, in /usr/share/doc/kernel-package. make-kpkg has a system-wide configuration file called /etc/kernel-pkg.conf that can be overridden on a per-user basis with a file in the home directory called .kernel-pkg.conf. The configuration file is documented in the kernel-pkg.conf(5) Manpage. The behavior of a kernel-image .deb created with make-kpg can also be configured with a file called /etc/kernel-img.conf. It is described in the kernel-img.conf(5) Manpage.

Rebuilding an Existing Package

There are times when you might want to rebuild a Debian package. A typical scenario is when you are using the stable distribution and you want to install a package that is only in unstable. For example, as I write this, there is a newer version of the game Frozen Bubble in unstable than is available for stable. If you were to download and try to install the unstable Debian package for Frozen Bubble, you would have to satisfy many dependencies. The problem in this case is that Frozen Bubble was compiled using the version of perl in unstable. So installing it requires that version of perl, which might cause libapache-mod-perl to need upgrading, which in turn might require apache to be upgraded. Those are rather drastic changes to make just for one game! Perhaps you might be able to live with this, but if you choose to run stable for the, well, stability, it's a problem. A better strategy in this case would be to download the source and build it so that it uses the version of perl currently available on stable.

To download the file, you can go the Web page at packages.debian.org and download the source packages from the links at the very bottom of the page. This source package will be made up of the following files:

✦ frozen-bubble_1.0.0.orig.tar.gz — This is the original Frozen Bubble source as the author distributed it.

✦ frozen-bubble_1.0.0-6.diff.gz — This is a gzipped patch containing all the changes the Debian maintainer made to the original source. Mostly, it will contain the actual scripts and metadata needed to create the .debs, but sometimes the maintainer has to patch the source to fix problems or make it conform to Debian policy.

✦ `frozen-bubble_1.0.0-6.dsc`—This is a small text file containing a description of the package. It also has MD5 sums of the `.orig.tar.gz` and `.diff.gz` and is cryptographically signed by the maintainer. With these two features, you can check to make sure the source has not been tampered with since the maintainer uploaded it.

✦ `frozen-bubble-1.0.0`—This is a directory containing the Frozen Bubble source with the Debian patches applied.

The set of `.orig.tar.gz`, `.diff.gz`, and `.dsc` is collectively referred to as a source package. Download these files. Now, you can unpack the files using this command:

```
$ dpkg-source -x frozen-bubble_1.0.0-6.dsc
```

Change to the `frozen-bubble-1.0.0` directory and open up the file `debian/changelog` in the text editor of your choice. The top of it should look something like this:

```
frozen-bubble (1.0.0-6) unstable; urgency=low

  * c_stuff/lib/FBLE.pm: fix to deal with new SDL_perl (closes: #257749).

 -- Josselin Mouette <joss@debian.org>  Thu,  8 Jul 2004 17:22:16 +0200
```

Copy this block and then change the value between the parentheses to `1.0.0-6.1` and the name and e-mail address to your name and address. The value between the parentheses is the version number of the package. The number before the hyphen is the upstream version, and the number after the hyphen is the Debian version. It is a convention to use a decimal number in the Debian version if someone other than the official maintainer has created a revision of the packages. There are other styles too; some people like `1.0.0-6myorganization1`, for instance, but the key thing is to change the version number to emphasize that this is an unofficial version of the package. The name and e-mail address should also be changed to make clear who created this package, and because Mr. Mouette doesn't want to receive mail about problems that may occur in this version. Please bear this in mind if you are thinking about sharing your modified packages with others. This is the quick and dirty way of changing the version and contact information for a package. Later on in this chapter, I show you how to make a proper entry in `debian/changelog`, but for now it will suffice.

Now run this command:

```
$ dpkg-buildpackage -rfakeroot -uc -us
```

`dpkg-buildpackage` is the program that actually builds `.deb`s. The `-r` option suggests a method for temporarily gaining root privileges during some phases of package building. `fakeroot`, to which you have already been introduced, is a good tool for this. The `-uc` and `-us` options tell `dpkg-buildpackage` not to cryptographically sign the `.dsc` and `.changes` files. (The latter will be explained in a bit.) When I tried this command, I got the following error:

```
dpkg-buildpackage: source version is 1.0.0-6.1
dpkg-buildpackage: source maintainer is Debian Fan <debian@example.org>
dpkg-buildpackage: host architecture is i386
dpkg-checkbuilddeps: Unmet build dependencies: libsdl-mixer1.2-dev (>>
 1.2.2)
dpkg-buildpackage: Build dependencies/conflicts unsatisfied; aborting.
dpkg-buildpackage: (Use -d flag to override.)
```

Whoops, what just happened? Well, like the dependencies you are already familiar with, packages have *build dependencies*. These are packages that must be present in order to build the package, though they may not necessarily be needed to run the package. In this case, apparently I didn't have libsdl-mixer1.2-dev installed. As the error message suggests, you can use the -d option to apt-get source in order to bypass the checking of build dependencies, but this only means that compilation will fail later on when it needs this library. If you want to rebuild this package, you really ought to have all the build dependencies it requires installed first. You could just install libsdl-mixer1.2-dev, rerun apt-get source until you get another error, install the package it is asking for that time, and repeat until you get a successful compile, but that would be tedious. A smarter way would be to look at the frozen-bubble_1.0.0-6.dsc file. Build dependencies are listed there and you could use that list to install them all at once. But there's an even better way than that. The command

```
# apt-get build-dep frozen-bubble
```

will take care of all the build dependencies for you. apt-get build-dep is insufficient, however, when the package you need doesn't exist in the stable distribution or isn't a high enough version. Then you have no recourse except to download the source to that package from unstable and install any build dependencies it might have and rebuild it. And if that can't be done, you must then download *those* packages and install their build dependencies and so on.

After you've got all of the build dependencies all straightened out, you can run dpkg-buildpackage again, and if you go up one directory level, you should see some new .debs. You will also see a file called frozen-bubble_1.0.0-6.1_i386.changes. The .changes file contains the package description from the .dsc file, the latest entry from debian/changelog, and the MD5 sums of the source package and .debs. This file is used only if you upload your .debs to the Debian archives. As you aren't going to be doing that, you can just delete it for this example.

Starting a Package from Scratch

The first step in building a new .deb is to select some program to package. The rest of this chapter uses the example of a game called Aklabeth. It's a role-playing adventure game, the forerunner of the Ultima series of adventure games, originally written in BASIC for the Apple II computer by Richard Garriot. Paul Robson did a port to Linux and C++ that I found at `www.autismuk.freeserve.co.uk/aklabeth-1.0.tar.gz` and downloaded to an empty new directory.

Some additional packages

Download and install the `debian-policy`, `dh-make`, `debhelper`, `devscripts`, and `lintian` packages. Although `dpkg-dev` is the only package you really need to build `.debs`, these additional packages make the process a lot easier. Here is a description of each:

✦ `debian-policy` — The Debian Policy Manual, which is contained in this package, was briefly mentioned in Chapter 25 as the key to well-integrated, high-quality packages. Read it. Memorize it even.

✦ `debhelper` — This package consists of a number of programs that do various common packaging-related tasks. Think of it as a higher-level interface to the package-building process.

✦ `dh-make` — This program will create a skeleton package using `debhelper` that you can customize.

✦ `devscripts` — This package contains scripts to aid the development of Debian packages. Some are useful only to official package maintainers, but others can come in handy for anyone building `.debs`.

✦ `lintian` — This program is used for quality assurance. You run it after you've created your `.deb` and it will warn you if you did anything wrong.

Creating the package infrastructure

If you are not in the directory you downloaded `aklabeth` to, change to it now and unpack the `aklabeth` tarball. Change to the resulting `aklabeth-1.0` directory:

```
$ tar xzf aklabeth-1.0.tar.gz
$ cd aklabeth-1.0
```

Now run the `dh_make` program. (Note that the program has an underscore in the name, whereas the package has a hyphen.) You are presented with a dialog like this:

```
$ dh_make

Type of package: single binary, multiple binary, library, or kernel module?
[s/m/l/k]
```

`dh_make` can create templates for several types of source packages, represented by the choices in the last line:

✦ **single binary** — The source package creates one .deb.

✦ **multiple binary** — The source package creates several .debs.

✦ **library** — Packages that contain shared libraries have to be built in a special way, so there is a separate template for them.

✦ **kernel module** — Packaging a kernel module for use with make-kpkg also requires special handling and so has its own template.

Select s for a single binary package. You are presented with a screen like this:

```
Maintainer name : Debian Fan
Email-Address   : debian@example.com
Date            : Thu, 01 Jan 2004 09:00:00 -0500
Package Name    : aklabeth
Version         : 1.0
Type of Package : Single
Hit <enter> to confirm:
```

If the values above are incorrect, abort by pressing Ctrl+C. Usually the only value that needs to be changed is the maintainer's e-mail address. You can do that by using the -e option of dh_make.

```
$ dh_make -e "Someone Else <other@example.com>"
```

When you are satisfied, press Enter and dh_make will create the package template. There will be a new subdirectory called debian, which I'll describe in a moment, but for now go up one directory level. You'll see that alongside aklabeth-1.0 there is a new directory called aklabeth-1.0.orig. Remember, in a Debian source package the changes the maintainer makes are separated from the original source. The copy in aklabeth-1.0.orig will be kept just as it was. Any changes you make will be in aklabeth-1.0 only.

The Debian Directory

Change back to the aklabeth-1.0/debian directory. It contains a number of files, detailed in the following sections.

The control file

The control file provides the metadata for the package. Here's what the template created by dh_make for the control file looks like:

```
Source: aklabeth
Section: unknown
Priority: optional
```

```
Maintainer: Debian Fan <debian@example.com>
Build-Depends: debhelper (>= 4.0.0)
Standards-Version: 3.6.0

Package: aklabeth
Architecture: any
Depends: ${shlibs:Depends}, ${misc:Depends}
Description: <insert up to 60 chars description>
 <insert long description, indented with spaces>
```

The file consists of two paragraphs or stanzas separated by a blank line. The first stanza describes the source package. The second describes the binary package created by this source. There can be multiple package stanzas if more than one .deb is being built, but Aklabeth produces just one. Each stanza consists of fields made up of a name, a colon, and a value. Where the value of the field is longer than one line (as in Description), successive lines are indented with one space.

The source stanza has the following fields:

✦ **Source** — The name of the source package.

✦ **Section** — The section of the Debian archive the package belongs to. In this example, you are not going to upload Aklabeth so this field could be left as unknown, but that would be bad form. So instead, change it to games.

✦ **Priority** — This is another field that has meaning only in the context of Debian packages. The Policy Manual defines a set of priorities from essential (for packages without which the system could not function) to extra (for packages that are completely redundant). Most packages are priority optional, meaning it doesn't matter whether they are installed or not. So you can leave this field as is.

✦ **Maintainer** — The name and e-mail address of the person responsible for this package.

✦ **Build Depends** — A comma-separated list of packages that must be present in order to build aklabeth. Right now, the list includes just debhelper (version 4.0.0 or above). How do you know what else, if anything, to include here? Well, in this case, you are lucky that the README file in the aklabeth source says that it requires the SDL (Simple DirectMedia Layer) library. In Debian, the development files for SDL are in the libsdl1.2-dev package, so you can just put that in after debhelper. Packages that use GNU autoconf and automake such as this one should build-depend on the autotools-dev package, for reasons explained in the next section. (Take this opportunity to install these packages if you don't already have them.) In other cases, it might be harder to figure out what exactly you need to depend on. One method is to examine the configure script, if there is one, to see which programs it is looking for. Notice that packages such as g++ are not included in the build dependencies. They are already "build-essential," so it is assumed they are already installed by anyone trying to build a Debian package.

✦ **Standards-Version** — This is a declaration of which version of the Debian Policy (the same as the version number of the debian-policy package) this package claims to adhere to. Leave it at 3.6.0 for now.

The package stanza has the following fields:

✦ **Package** — The name of the .deb. For a single binary package, it is usually the same as the name of the source package, but it need not be.

✦ **Architecture** — This field indicates the architectures the package may be built for. Most of the time, you just leave this as any, indicating that the package can be built anywhere. But if the package truly was architecture-specific (such as the silo boot loader, which is designed solely for the sparc architecture), you can indicate it here. The only other exception is for packages that are architecture-independent such as documentation and scripts. For those, set the architecture to all.

✦ **Depends** — These are the packages aklabeth will need to run. There are two values already in place here, ${shlib:depends} and ${misc:depends}. These are macros into which names of packages will be substituted by the debhelper programs. Though they are not used here, there are other control fields than Depends for showing the relationship between packages, as shown in Table 26-2.

<table>
<tr><td colspan="2">Table 26-2
Package Relationships</td></tr>
<tr><td>*Field Name*</td><td>*What It Means*</td></tr>
<tr><td>pre-depends</td><td>Installation and configuration of the pre-depended package must be complete before this one can be installed. Use only sparingly.</td></tr>
<tr><td>depends</td><td>Depended package must be installed before this one can be installed.</td></tr>
<tr><td>recommends</td><td>Installing the recommended package is a good idea but not strictly necessary for this one.</td></tr>
<tr><td>suggests</td><td>Installing the suggested package would increase the functionality of this one.</td></tr>
<tr><td>enhances</td><td>Like suggests but in the opposite direction. This package increases the functionality of the enhanced one.</td></tr>
<tr><td>conflicts</td><td>This file cannot be installed at the same time as the package with which it conflicts. If one package is to be installed, the other must be removed first.</td></tr>
</table>

✦ **Description**—This field consists of two parts, a short description (of 60 characters or less) and a longer description. The short description should not be a full sentence, nor should it repeat the name of the package. The long description should include as many details as you think a user might find pertinent. You can simulate a blank line in the description by placing a . (period) as the only character on the line.

After you have edited and customized the control file, it should look something like this:

```
Source: aklabeth
Section: games
Priority: optional
Maintainer: Debian Fan <debian@example.com>
Build-Depends: debhelper (>= 4.0.0), libsdl1.2-dev, autotools-dev
Standards-Version: 3.6.0

Package: aklabeth
Architecture: any
Depends: ${shlibs:Depends}, ${misc:Depends}
Description: a role playing adventure game
 In this game you wander the world, visit dungeons, beat up monsters
 and perform tasks for the legendary Lord British.
 .
 Aklabeth was the first game designed by Richard Garriot, the author
 of the popular Ultima series.
 .
Homepage: http://www.autismuk.freeserve.co.uk/
```

The rules file

The `rules` file controls the building of the package. Following, interspersed with commentary, is the `rules` template created by dh_make:

```
#!/usr/bin/make -f
```

What Is a Shebang?

In UNIX-based operating systems, if the kernel sees that the first line of an executable file starts with the #! characters, the rest of the line is treated as a program to be run and the rest of the file is a script to be interpreted by that program. The #! characters are known as a *shebang*. The etymology of this word as used in computer jargon isn't precisely known, but it is probably a contraction of *shell* (the shebang mechanism was originally designed for shell scripts) and *bang*, a common nickname for the exclamation mark.

The first noteworthy thing about `rules` is that it is a makefile. You are probably familiar with a shebang line at the beginning of a shell or `perl` script (if not, see the related sidebar), but there is no reason why a makefile can't be made executable and run as a script too. The `-f` option to make is used to specify input that should come from a file named something other than the usual `makefile`. As our file is called `rules`, it is obvious that we need to use this.

```
# -*- makefile -*-
# Sample debian/rules that uses debhelper.
# GNU copyright 1997 to 1999 by Joey Hess.

# Uncomment this to turn on verbose mode.
#export DH_VERBOSE=1
```

If you want to turn on `debhelper`'s verbose mode (handy for debugging), you can uncomment the preceding line.

```
# These are used for cross-compiling and for saving the configure script
# from having to guess our platform (since we know it already)
DEB_HOST_GNU_TYPE   ?= $(shell dpkg-architecture -qDEB_HOST_GNU_TYPE)
DEB_BUILD_GNU_TYPE   ?= $(shell dpkg-architecture -qDEB_BUILD_GNU_TYPE)

CFLAGS = -Wall -g

ifneq (,$(findstring noopt,$(DEB_BUILD_OPTIONS)))
        CFLAGS += -O0
else
        CFLAGS += -O2
endif

ifeq (,$(findstring nostrip,$(DEB_BUILD_OPTIONS)))
        INSTALL_PROGRAM += -s
endif
```

`CFLAGS` is the `make` variable that determines which options to give to the compiler. `-Wall` means turn on all warnings and `-g` means include debugging information. These you pretty much always want to include.

Other options may or may not be wanted by every user. There is a fledgling effort underway to make it possible for the user to specify some options at build time. If the environment variable `DEB_BUILD_OPTIONS` includes the string `noopt`, optimization of the program will be turned off (the `-O0` flag); otherwise it will be turned on (the `-O2` flag). Similarly, if `DEB_BUILD_OPTIONS` contains the string `nostrip`, the program will not be stripped of debugging information when installed; otherwise it will be. Hopefully, one day you will be able to change all kinds of package settings this way.

```
config.status: configure
        dh_testdir
        # Add here commands to configure the package.
        CFLAGS="$(CFLAGS)" ./configure --host=$(DEB_HOST_GNU_TYPE) \
    --build=$(DEB_BUILD_GNU_TYPE) --prefix=/usr \
    --mandir=\$${prefix}/share/man -bindir=\$${prefix}/games \
    --infodir=\$${prefix}/share/info
```

This makefile target is where configuration takes place.

First, a call is made to dh_testdir. This is a debhelper program that merely checks that you are in the right directory to build the package and that the control file exists.

Then, Aklabeth's configure script is run. As you can see, some of its default values are being changed to fit Debian policy. For instance, Aklabeth is being installed into /usr rather than /usr/local. When configure finishes successfully, config. status is created. However, it won't be created if configure fails. So the presence of config.status can be used as a sentinel to confirm that configuration was successful. When any step of the packaging process fails, everything should grind to a halt so that you can fix problems. A package that is subtly broken because one step failed is worse than no package at all.

The next target in the rules file is build.

```
build: build-stamp

build-stamp:  config.status
        dh_testdir

        # Add here commands to compile the package.
        $(MAKE)
        #/usr/bin/docbook-to-man debian/aklabeth.sgml > aklabeth.1

        touch build-stamp
```

Certain targets in the rules file are required. build is one of them. It is the default target run when you invoke dpkg-buildpackage. However, as you can see, the build target merely depends on build-stamp and is otherwise empty. The real work is done in the build-stamp target, which as its last step creates a file called build-stamp. The reason for this seemingly roundabout way of doing things is to once again set up a sentinel so that you can tell whether the target has succeeded or failed.

In the build-stamp target, dh_testdir is run first to make sure you are still in the right directory.

Then make is run on Aklabeth's makefile to actually build the program. make is called as a variable, so if you want to use something other than Debian's standard, GNU Make, you can specify it in the MAKE environment variable.

Other steps can be taken after `make` has been run. For example, look at the commented-out call to `docbook-to-man`. Debian policy requires all programs to have a Manpage, and many people find DocBook SGML an easier format to work with than troff, so if Aklabeth had a manual page in that format, it could be built here. (In that case, you would also have to declare a build-dependency on `docbook-to-man`.)

If all goes well, `build-stamp` gets created.

Next comes the `clean` target.

```
clean:
        dh_testdir
        dh_testroot
        rm -f build-stamp

        # Add here commands to clean up after the build process.
        -$(MAKE) distclean
ifneq "$(wildcard /usr/share/misc/config.sub)" ""
        cp -f /usr/share/misc/config.sub config.sub
endif
ifneq "$(wildcard /usr/share/misc/config.guess)" ""
        cp -f /usr/share/misc/config.guess config.guess
endif
        dh_clean
```

`clean` is another required target. As its name suggests, this is where the package is restored to its prebuild condition.

A call to `dh_testdir` is made once again, followed by another `debhelper` program called `dh_testroot`. As the name suggests, `dh_testroot` makes sure you are running as root or a reasonable facsimile thereof such as `fakeroot`. This is to ensure that you can successfully remove files that may have been created in the build process.

Next, the `build-stamp` file is removed if it exists.

After that, the `distclean` target in Aklabeth's `makefile` is invoked to clean up any files it built.

The next part might be a little hard to understand. GNU `autoconf` uses two auxiliary files called `config.sub` and `config.guess` to do its magic. It is important to keep these as up-to-date as possible to give `configure` the latest information on architectures and features. This is especially important for a project like Debian, which covers so many different architectures. Unfortunately, a program like Aklabeth is not updated upstream that often, so its copies of `config.sub` and `config.guess` are probably obsolete. This code copies these files from `/usr/share/misc` where they were installed by the `autotools-dev` package into the `aklabeth` source. This is done in the `clean` target, as it is actually the first target run when `dpkg-buildpackage` is run.

Finally, a debhelper program called dh_clean is called to remove any files debhelper may have created.

After build and clean, the next rules file target to consider is install.

```
install: build
        dh_testdir
        dh_testroot
        dh_clean -k
        dh_installdirs

        # Add here commands to install the package into debian/aklabeth.
        $(MAKE) install DESTDIR=$(CURDIR)/debian/aklabeth
```

The install target is, naturally, where the program is installed. The build target must have successfully completed first.

dh_testdir and dh_testroot are called. Then dh_clean is called, but this time with the -k option. -k is not so useful in this case, but when building multiple .debs, it cleans up between runs but keeps the files from created packages. Without it, you would end up with only the last created .deb.

The next debhelper program, dh_installdirs, creates the installation directory and any others needed that are not created by the program's makefile. They are defined in a separate file called dirs (or aklabeth.dirs), which I cover later in the chapter.

Finally, the install target of Aklabeth's makefile is invoked. Notice that the DESTDIR variable is being redefined. Although in the configuration phase, the location where Aklabeth is to be installed is defined as /usr, you don't want to install directly into /usr because you want to build a .deb as an intermediate step. Instead, changing DESTDIR results in the program being built in a temporary directory in the debian directory. (CURDIR is a special GNU make variable that refers to the current working directory.) The packaging process will treat this temporary directory as its base, so when the .deb is installed, it will go into /usr.

```
# Build architecture-independent files here.
binary-indep: build install
# We have nothing to do by default.
```

binary-indep is a required target. This is where you would build any architecture-independent (a.k.a. architecture: all) .debs. But you aren't building any such .debs, so this target does nothing. It depends on the build and install targets having successfully completed first.

```
# Build architecture-dependent files here.
binary-arch: build install
        dh_testdir
        dh_testroot
```

`binary-arch` is also a required target. This is where architecture-dependent `.debs` are built. It too depends on `build` and `install` having completed first. Why are there two separate targets, `binary-indep` and `binary-arch`, for building packages? To answer this question, you have to understand how the Debian upload process works. A typical Debian maintainer has access to only one or a few of Debian's many architectures. He builds the source package on his machine for a particular architecture. He uploads the resulting `.debs` to the Debian archive. Any `architecture all` `.debs` from the source package are built and uploaded at the same time. Debian has autobuilders for each architecture. They notice when a new package comes in and try to rebuild it for their architecture. But it would be wasteful for them to build the `architecture all` `.debs`, because their initial upload should suffice for all architectures. Separating the two types enables the autobuilders to pick out only the packages they are interested in.

The standard calls to `dh_testdir` and `dh_testroot` are made next, followed by a series of calls to other `debhelper` programs. I have broken out the remaining calls to explain each in turn. Many of the `debhelper` programs have highly specialized uses and will be used in only a few packages. The ones I describe in detail here are the set typically used for packaging desktop applications. The rest will just be explained briefly and deleted.

> `dh_installchangelogs ChangeLog`

`dh_changelogs` is responsible for installing changelogs into packages. There are two types of changelogs. There is one mentioned as an argument to `dh_install changelog`, which is Aklabeth's own changelog (by the name of `ChangeLog`). This will get installed as `/usr/share/doc/aklabeth/changelog`. Then there is the changelog for the Debian source package. This file is discussed later, but for now, all you need to know is that it will get installed as `/usr/share/doc/aklabeth/changelog.Debian`.

> `dh_installdocs`

`dh_installdocs` installs documentation (except changelogs, examples, info, and Manpages) into the package. How does it know what is documentation? From a file called `docs` or `aklabeth.docs` (described later in this chapter). The documentation is installed into `/usr/share/doc/aklabeth`.

> `dh_installexamples`

Some packages come with examples. If Aklabeth was such a package, you could list them in a file called `aklabeth.examples`, and `dh_installexamples` would install them into `/usr/share/doc/aklabeth/examples`. But there are none, so you can just delete this line.

> `#        dh_install`

If there are other files that you want to install into the package, you can do so using `dh_install`. It looks for a list of files and destinations in `aklabeth.install`. It is commented out with the preceding # because it is not always needed. Aklabeth doesn't need it, so you can just delete it.

```
#        dh_installmenu
```

One of the convenient integration features Debian offers is a menu system unified across all window managers. You create a file called `aklabeth.menu`, and scripts specific to GNOME, KDE, Windowmaker, and so forth will turn it into a menu entry for their respective environments. Uncomment this; it will be a good thing to add to the `aklabeth` package.

```
#        dh_installdebconf
```

Another one of Debian's cool features is the `debconf` system for putting up a configuration dialog box at install time. `dh_installdebconf` takes care of installing `debconf`'s files into the package. Aklabeth isn't going to use `debconf`, so you can delete this line.

```
#        dh_installlogrotate
```

If your program creates log files, it is a good idea to compress and rotate them on a regular basis to prevent them from growing too big. `logrotate` is a program that does this, and `dh_installlogrotate` can install a `logrotate` config file called `aklabeth.logrotate` and install it into `/etc/logrotate.d/aklabeth`. (This would be useful if Aklabeth used log files, which it doesn't, so just delete this line.)

```
#        dh_installemacsen
```

The `emacs` editor is very powerful, and the secret to that power is the extensive customization that can be done to it using libraries of `lisp` code. If a file containing `emacs lisp` called `aklabeth.emacsen-install` existed, it would be installed as `/usr/lib/emacsen-common/packages/install/aklabeth`. If `aklabeth.emacsen-remove` existed, it would be installed as `/usr/lib/emacsen-common/packages/remove/aklabeth`, and if `aklabeth.emacsen-startup` existed, it would be installed as `/etc/emacs/site-start.d/50aklabeth.el`. Read the `dh_installemacsen(1)` Manpage for more information. Aklabeth doesn't do anything with `emacs`, so you can delete this line.

```
#        dh_installpam
```

PAM (Pluggable Authentication Modules) is the standard method of authenticating and accounting logins on Debian. Given a PAM configuration file called `aklabeth.pam`, `dh_installpam` will install it as `/etc/pam.d/aklabeth`. This is another feature that Aklabeth doesn't use, so this line too can be deleted.

```
#        dh_installmime
```

If a program needs to register additional MIME types with Debian's `mime-support` package, it can do so with `dh_installmime`. It takes a file called `aklabeth.mime` and installs it as `/usr/lib/mime/packages/aklabeth`. This package doesn't do anything with MIME, so the line can be deleted.

```
#       dh_installinit
```

Daemons and other system services should be started by a script in `/etc/init.d`. The script may have one or more configurable options, which should be controlled by a file in `/etc/default`. Additionally, links to this script have to be made in `/etc/rc*.d` for different run levels. `dh_installinit` is a `debhelper` program that takes care of all the necessary steps. If a file called `aklabeth.init` existed, it would be installed as `/etc/init.d/aklabeth`, and if a file called `aklabeth.defaults` existed, it would be installed as `/etc/defaults/aklabeth`. Aklabeth isn't using this either. Delete the line.

```
#       dh_installcron
```

`dh_installcron` installs cron jobs from files called `aklabeth.cron.*` to the relevant directories in `/etc`. For instance, `aklabeth.cron.daily` would be installed as `/etc/cron.daily/aklabeth`. You can also select from `cron.hourly`, `cron.weekly`, `cron.monthly`, and `cron.d`. Delete this line too, as Aklabeth doesn't need cron jobs.

```
#       dh_installinfo
```

The documentation of GNU programs is usually in `info` format. Given a list of `info` pages in a file called `aklabeth.info`, `dh_installinfo` can install them into `/usr/share/info`. Aklabeth has no `info` files, so this line can be deleted.

```
        dh_installman
```

`dh_installman` installs the list of Manpages in `aklabeth.manpages` into the appropriate locations in `/usr/share/man`. Although Aklabeth doesn't currently have a Manpage, one is required by Debian policy, so hold on to this line.

```
        dh_link
```

`dh_link` creates symlinks in packages. It uses a file called `aklabeth.links`, which contains a list of link sources and destinations.

```
        dh_strip
```

`dh_strip` strips debugging information from binaries in the package.

```
        dh_compress
```

`dh_compress` compresses documentation and other files in the package.

```
        dh_fixperms
```

dh_fixperms ensures that the ownership and permissions of files in the package conform to Debian policy.

    #   dh_perl

If your program is using perl, dh_perl will ensure that it has the right dependencies. Aklabeth doesn't, so this line can be removed.

    #   dh_python

If your program uses python, dh_python will add the correct dependencies for you. Aklabeth doesn't use python either, so this line can also be deleted.

    #   dh_makeshlibs

If your package contains libraries, dh_makeshlibs will set up a file that a program like dh_shlibdeps (see following) can use to automatically add dependency information. It will also call ldconfig to include the library in the linkers cache upon installation. Aklabeth doesn't contain libraries, so this line is not needed.

            dh_installdeb

dh_installdeb is responsible for installing package scripts (see following) into the package.

            dh_shlibdeps

dh_shlibdeps scans your package to see which libraries it is using. The packages those libraries belong to are then added to ${shlib:depends} in your package's dependencies.

            dh_gencontrol

dh_gencontrol creates the metadata of the package based on the values in the control file.

            dh_md5sums

This debhelper program adds MD5 sums of all the files to your package. You can check to see whether the package has been tampered with.

            dh_builddeb

And finally, dh_builddeb builds the packages (in the parent directory).

    binary: binary-indep binary-arch

This is the last of the required targets in `rules`. All it does is depend on `binary-indep` and `binary-arch`.

```
.PHONY: build clean binary-indep binary-arch binary install
```

If you are not familiar with GNU `make`, `.PHONY` is a special feature that explicitly says that `build`, `clean`, and so on are target names, not files. This is important because if by some chance (admittedly not very likely) there was a file in the package called, say, `binary-indep`, it would mess up `make`'s dependency checking.

That wraps it up for the `rules` file. There was a lot of information, but this is the most important packaging file. Here is what the edited `rules` file looks like:

```
#!/usr/bin/make -f
# -*- makefile -*-
# Sample debian/rules that uses debhelper.
# GNU copyright 1997 to 1999 by Joey Hess.

# Uncomment this to turn on verbose mode.
#export DH_VERBOSE=1

# These are used for cross-compiling and for saving the configure script
# from having to guess our platform (since we know it already)
DEB_HOST_GNU_TYPE   ?= $(shell dpkg-architecture -qDEB_HOST_GNU_TYPE)
DEB_BUILD_GNU_TYPE  ?= $(shell dpkg-architecture -qDEB_BUILD_GNU_TYPE)

CFLAGS = -Wall -g

ifneq (,$(findstring noopt,$(DEB_BUILD_OPTIONS)))
        CFLAGS += -O0
else
        CFLAGS += -O2
endif

ifeq (,$(findstring nostrip,$(DEB_BUILD_OPTIONS)))
        INSTALL_PROGRAM += -s
endif

config.status: configure
        dh_testdir
        # Add here commands to configure the package.
        CFLAGS="$(CFLAGS)" ./configure --host=$(DEB_HOST_GNU_TYPE) \
        --build=$(DEB_BUILD_GNU_TYPE) --prefix=/usr \
        --mandir=\$${prefix}/share/man --infodir=\$${prefix}/share/info

build: build-stamp

build-stamp:  config.status
        dh_testdir
        # Add here commands to compile the package.
```

```
          $(MAKE)
          touch build-stamp

clean:
          dh_testdir
          dh_testroot
          rm -f build-stamp

          # Add here commands to clean up after the build process.
          -$(MAKE) distclean
ifneq "$(wildcard /usr/share/misc/config.sub)" ""
          cp -f /usr/share/misc/config.sub config.sub
endif
ifneq "$(wildcard /usr/share/misc/config.guess)" ""
          cp -f /usr/share/misc/config.guess config.guess
endif
          dh_clean

install: build
          dh_testdir
          dh_testroot
          dh_clean -k
          dh_installdirs

          # Add here commands to install the package into debian/aklabeth.
          $(MAKE) install DESTDIR=$(CURDIR)/debian/aklabeth

# Build architecture-independent files here.
binary-indep: build install
# We have nothing to do by default.

# Build architecture-dependent files here.
binary-arch: build install
          dh_testdir
          dh_testroot
          dh_installchangelogs ChangeLog
          dh_installdocs
          dh_installmenu
          dh_installman
          dh_strip
          dh_compress
          dh_fixperms
          dh_installdeb
          dh_shlibdeps
          dh_gencontrol
          dh_md5sums
          dh_builddeb

binary: binary-indep binary-arch

.PHONY: build clean binary-indep binary-arch binary install
```

The changelog file

In the "Rebuilding an Existing Package" section of this chapter, you made some changes to the changelog file. In order to build a proper package, you need to learn more about it. Take a look at the template changelog dh_make has made.

```
aklabeth (1.0-1) unstable; urgency=low

  * Initial Release.

 -- Debian Fan <debian@example.com>  Thu, 01 Jan 2004 09:00:00 -0500
```

The first line consists of the name of the source package, followed by the version in parentheses. The version has two parts: the upstream version, then a hyphen, and then the Debian version. Following the version after a space is the distribution. This is meaningful only for official packages. You can leave it as unstable, or you can use testing or stable. Then after a semicolon and a space is an urgency value. This too is meaningful only in the context of official packages. For official packages, the urgency value determines when a package in unstable (assuming it is free of critical bugs) will enter testing. Low-urgency packages take ten days, medium-urgency packages five days, and high-urgency packages two days.

The second line is a bulleted list of notable items about this version of the package. There is only one item right now, which indicates that this is the initial release of the package. As you fix bugs and add features, you can add more items. changelog entries should be in the form of sentences and should be as descriptive as possible.

The third line has the maintainer's name and e-mail address and a date stamp. You may have noticed that the maintainer name is also specified in control. The difference is that the person mentioned in control is the overall "keeper" of the package, the one responsible for it in general. The person mentioned here is the one who actually built this version of the package. Most of the time, the two roles will be occupied by the same person, but that need not be the case.

The changelog file has a very particular layout. Although you could edit it with any ordinary text editor, it would be an error-prone process. Instead, you can use a program from the devscripts package called debchange (it can also be abbreviated to dch). Running dch anywhere in the package directory will start up your favorite text editor with a properly formatted new changelog entry. The entry can also be given on the command line like this:

```
$ dch "My second changelog entry."
```

This makes the changelog look like this:

```
aklabeth (1.0-1) unstable; urgency=low

  * My second changelog entry
  * Initial Release.

 -- Debian Fan <debian@example.com>  Thu, 01 Jan 2004 09:10:00 -0500
```

When you are ready to make a new revision of the package, use the `-i` (increment) option to dch:

```
$ dch -i "Fixed packaging errors."
```

The result is a changelog like this:

```
aklabeth (1.0-2) unstable; urgency=low

  * Fixed packaging errors.

 -- Debian Fan <debian@example.com>  Thu, 01 Jan 2004 09:20:00 -0500

aklabeth (1.0-1) unstable; urgency=low

  * My second changelog entry
  * Initial Release.

 -- Debian Fan <debian@example.com>  Thu, 01 Jan 2004 09:10:00 -0500
```

Perhaps at some point, Aklabeth will come out with a new version, say 2.7. You can change that with the `-v` version of dch:

```
$ dch -v 2.7-1 "New upstream version."
```

The result is a changelog like this:

```
aklabeth (2.7-1) unstable; urgency=low

  * New upstream version.

 -- Debian Fan <debian@example.com>  Thu, 01 Jan 2004 09:30:00 -0500

aklabeth (1.0-2) unstable; urgency=low

  * Fixed packaging errors.

 -- Debian Fan <debian@example.com>  Thu, 01 Jan 2004 09:20:00 -0500

aklabeth (1.0-1) unstable; urgency=low

  * My second changelog entry
  * Initial Release.

 -- Debian Fan <debian@example.com>  Thu, 01 Jan 2004 09:10:00 -0500
```

That's the basics of using dch. You can read the dch(1) Manpage for more information. For now, delete all the modifications you made to the changelog so that it looks like the original version.

The copyright file

The next file to look at is called copyright. It contains information about the copyright and origin of the package. This is the template dh_make creates for this file:

```
This package was debianized by Debian Fan <debian@example.com> on
Thu, 01 Jan 2004 09:00:00 -0500.

It was downloaded from <fill in ftp site>

Upstream Author(s): <put author(s) name and email here>

Copyright:

<Must follow here>
```

For the most part, this is pretty self-explanatory. But I should say something about the copyright part. Here you should put the complete license for the package. (By convention, it can often be found in a file called COPYING or LICENSE.) The only exceptions are for certain commonly used Free Software licenses. The GPL, LGPL, BSD, and Artistic licenses are used by so many packages that it would cause bloat if every copyright file had to include a full version. So instead, copies of these licenses can be found in /usr/share/common-licenses, and it is acceptable to point to those copies instead of including the whole thing. The modified copyright file should look like this:

```
This package was debianized by Debian Fan <debian@example.com> on
Thu, 01 Jan 2004 09:00:00 -0500.

It was downloaded from http://www.autismuk.freeserve.co.uk/

Upstream Author: Paul Robson <autismuk@autismuk.freeserve.co.uk>

Copyright:

Copyright (C) 2004 by Paul Robson

    This program is free software; you can redistribute it and/or modify
    it under the terms of the GNU General Public License as published by
    the Free Software Foundation; either version 2, or (at your option)
    any later version.

    This program is distributed in the hope that it will be useful,
    but WITHOUT ANY WARRANTY; without even the implied warranty of
    MERCHANTABILITY or FITNESS FOR A PARTICULAR PURPOSE.  See the
    GNU General Public License for more details.
```

```
You should have received a copy of the GNU General Public License
along with this program; if not, write to the Free Software Foundation,
Inc., 59 Temple Place - Suite 330, Boston, MA 02111-1307, USA.
```

```
On Debian GNU/Linux systems, the complete text of the GNU General
Public License can be found in '/usr/share/common-licenses/GPL'.
```

The compat file

Debhelper has gone through several changes over the years. The `compat` file has one line, which contains the number 4. This indicates that the package is compatible with the fourth (current) version of the Debhelper API.

Package scripts

A package can contain scripts that are run at one of four points: preinstallation, postinstallation, preremoval, and postremoval. You can include custom code in the scripts to perform any needed tasks. `debhelper` also inserts code into these scripts as needed, which you can choose to keep or to throw away. Even though the names are self-explanatory to some degree, these scripts are described here:

- ✦ The `preinst` script is typically where you would perform any local system-specific configuration the package may need.

- ✦ The `postinst` script is where final package configuration takes place. You can also allow for the installation failing or being aborted here.

- ✦ The `prerm` script is called before the package is removed.

- ✦ The `postrm` script is where final cleanup is done. There is a difference between a package being removed and being purged. When a package is removed, configuration files, log files, and so on are kept behind for the system administrator to dispose of. When a package is purged, all traces of it should be removed. So when you write a `postrm` script, keep this distinction in mind.

Extensive package scripts are not necessary in many cases, but they give your package the opportunity for really deep integration into the system. Bear in mind that `dpkg` runs as root and therefore package scripts will also be run with root privileges, so an error in one of them could be catastrophic. Be extra careful to make sure they work properly and allow for all possible failure modes, no matter how unlikely.

The README.Debian file

The `README.Debian` file is a free-form file in which you can put any piece of information you think the user of this package might want to know. Especially if you have altered the way the package works in such a way that someone familiar with it from outside Debian is likely to be caught by surprise, you should document your changes here. You can also include hints, FAQs, pointers to other resources, anything really. But if you have nothing to say (as in the case of Aklabeth), just delete the file.

The dirs file

`dh_installdirs` looks in the `dirs` file (or `aklabeth.dirs` to use the newer style) to find directories. The name `dirs` is for backward compatibility with older versions of `debhelper` and works only if one `.deb` is being built by the source package. If multiple `.debs` are to be built, you must use the `<packagename>.dirs`-style filenames. The template set up by dh_make looks like this:

```
usr/bin
usr/sbin
```

This means `/usr/bin` and `/usr/sbin` directories will be created. Note that the initial `/` is missing. This is because the directories will be built relative to the package's temporary build directory. Actually, you can get rid of this file, as Aklabeth's makefile will do all the directory installing. But if you need to create additional directories and your package's makefile doesn't handle the task itself, this is the place to do it.

The docs file

`dh_installdocs` looks at the `docs` file (or `aklabeth.docs`) to find documentation to install in the package. As with `dirs`, `docs` is the older, less-preferred name. `aklabeth.docs` should be used, especially for building multiple `.debs`. The template dh_make creates looks like this:

```
NEWS
README
TODO
```

Any other files (or even entire directories) that you may want to install to `/usr/share/doc/aklabeth` can be placed here.

The menu file

dh_make creates a file called `menu.ex`, which is an example of the kind of file `dh_installmenu` can use. It looks like this:

```
?package(aklabeth):needs=X11|text|vc|wm section=Apps/see-menu-manual\
  title="aklabeth" command="/usr/bin/aklabeth"
```

The menu file has several fields. The `package` field is self-explanatory. The `needs` field gives the window manager a hint as to what kind of program this is and what kind of environment it should be run in.

- ✦ `X11` — A graphical program that can just be launched like any other.
- ✦ `text` — A text-based program. The window manager must run it in an xterm or other terminal.
- ✦ `vc` — A program that will work only on the console. These are quite rare.
- ✦ `wm` — Another window manager. The current window manager will have to shut down and then execute this one.

The `section` field is the menu that the application should go in. By perusing the manual for the manual package in `/usr/share/doc/menu/html`, you can see that this needs to be changed to `Games/Adventure`.

The `title` field is the text to be displayed in the menu. The only change needed here is to capitalize `aklabeth`.

The `command` field is the actual command line to be run by the menu entry. It is fine as is. The menu file should be renamed to `aklabeth.menu` and should now look like this:

```
?package(aklabeth):needs=X11 section=Games/Adventure title="Aklabeth"\
 command="/usr/games/aklabeth"
```

The watch file

`dh_make` created a file called `watch.ex`, which looks like this:

```
# Example watch control file for uscan
# Rename this file to "watch" and then you can run the "uscan" command
# to check for upstream updates and more.
# Site          Directory          Pattern          Version Script
version=2
sunsite.unc.edu /pub/Linux/Incoming     aklabeth-(.*)\.tar\.gz   debian
 uupdate
```

This works with a program from the `devscripts` package called `uscan`. The combination of `uscan` and `watch` enables you to automate checking for new upstream versions of your package. Rename `watch.ex` to `watch` and edit it so that it looks like this:

```
version=2
http://autismuk.freeserve.co.uk/aklabeth-(.*)\.tar\.gz  debian  uupdate
```

See the `uscan(1)` Manpage for more information.

The Manpage

dh_make creates not one, but three templates for a manual page. manpage.1.ex is in Troff (see Chapter 10), manpage.sgml.ex is in DocBook SGML, and manpage.xml.ex is in DocBook XML format. You should use one of these to create a Manpage for Aklabeth and delete the other two. If you use either of the DocBook versions, remember to add the code to call docbook-to-man into the rules file and add a build dependency on docbook-to-man. Also bear in mind that as a game, Aklabeth belongs in section 6 of the Manpages, not section 1, which is assumed by the templates. As the last step, create a file called aklabeth.manpages in the debian directory and include the line

```
debian/aklabeth.6
```

This tells dh_installmanpages where to find the Manpage and to install it in the package.

doc-base

Another useful feature of Debian is that documentation can all be centralized through a system called doc-base. As the menu system does for programs, doc-base organizes documentation in a unified topical hierarchy. Front ends to doc-base, such as those found in the dwww, dhelp, or doc-central packages, allow a user to navigate and search the doc-base hierarchy through a Web browser. dh_installdocs can add package documentation to doc-base. dh_make creates an example doc-base control file called aklabeth.doc-base.EX for Aklabeth's documentation. However, Aklabeth doesn't actually have any documentation, so this file can just be removed for this example.

conffiles

dh_make creates a file called conffiles.ex. When filenames are added to it and it is renamed to aklabeth.conffiles, those files are marked in the package as conffiles. That means if a later package upgrade should provide a new version of the file, instead of blindly overwriting it, dpkg will ask whether you want to keep your old version, install the new version, or make a diff between the two.

Since version 3, Debhelper has automatically marked any file installed to /etc as a conffile, so this file isn't really needed anymore. But if you want to declare a conffile outside of /etc for some reason, you can do it through this file.

Other minor files

dh_make also created a number of other files that are used only for very specific circumstances. As far as the Aklabeth package is concerned, all of the files mentioned here can be deleted.

`aklabeth-default.ex` and `init.d.ex` are used by `dh_installinit`. `emacsen-install.ex`, `emacsen-remove.ex`, and `emacsen-startup.ex` are used by `dh_installemacsen`. `cron.d.ex` is used by `dh_installcron`. These Debhelper programs are described briefly in the section on the `rules` file.

Building the Package

When you have all the files tweaked to your liking, you can build the package. Make sure you are in the top-level directory of the source and run this command:

```
$ dpkg-buildpackage -rfakeroot -uc -us
```

After a few screens full of compiler output, `dpkg-buildpackage` should complete. You can use a program from the `devscripts` package called `debc` to examine the contents of the finished `.deb`.

```
$debc
aklabeth_1.0-1_i386.deb
-----------------------

 new debian package, version 2.0.
 size 34182 bytes: control archive= 1931 bytes.
      736 bytes,    16 lines         control
      579 bytes,     9 lines         md5sums
     1072 bytes,    45 lines    *    postinst           #!/bin/sh
     1051 bytes,    41 lines    *    postrm             #!/bin/sh
      917 bytes,    44 lines    *    preinst            #!/bin/sh
      941 bytes,    39 lines    *    prerm              #!/bin/sh
 Package: aklabeth
 Version: 1.0-1
 Section: games
 Priority: optional
 Architecture: i386
 Depends: aalib1 (>= 1.2), libasound2 (>> 1.0.5), libc6 (>= 2.3.2.ds1-4),
libgcc
1 (>= 1:3.3.4-1), libncurses5 (>= 5.4-1), libsdl1.2debian (>> 1.2.7-0),
libstdc+
+5 (>= 1:3.3.4-1), libsvga1, libx11-6 | xlibs (>> 4.1.0), libxext6 | xlibs
(>> 4
.1.0), slang1 (>> 1.4.9dbs-2)
 Installed-Size: 156
 Maintainer: Debian Fan <debian@example.com>
 Description: a role-playing adventure game
  In this game you wander the world, visit dungeons, beat up monsters
  and perform tasks for the legendary Lord British.
  .
  Aklabeth was the first game designed by Richard Garriot, the author
  of the popular Ultima series.
  .
```

```
        Homepage: http://www.autismuk.freeserve.co.uk/
drwxr-xr-x root/root         0 2004-01-01 09:20:00 ./
drwxr-xr-x root/root         0 2004-01-01 09:20:00 ./usr/
drwxr-xr-x root/root         0 2004-01-01 09:20:00 ./usr/games/
-rwxr-xr-x root/root     59976 2004-01-01 09:20:00 ./usr/games/aklabeth
drwxr-xr-x root/root         0 2004-01-01 09:20:00 ./usr/share/
drwxr-xr-x root/root         0 2004-01-01 09:20:00 ./usr/share/doc/
drwxr-xr-x root/root         0 2004-01-01 09:20:00
./usr/share/doc/aklabeth/
-rw-r--r-- root/root        31 2004-01-01 09:20:00
./usr/share/doc/aklabeth/chan
gelog.gz
-rw-r--r-- root/root        89 2004-01-01 09:20:00
./usr/share/doc/aklabeth/NEWS
.gz
-rw-r--r-- root/root       647 2004-01-01 09:20:00
./usr/share/doc/aklabeth/READ
ME
-rw-r--r-- root/root         1 2004-01-01 09:20:00
./usr/share/doc/aklabeth/TODO
-rw-r--r-- root/root      1102 2004-01-01 09:20:00
./usr/share/doc/aklabeth/copy
right
-rw-r--r-- root/root       154 2004-01-01 09:20:00
./usr/share/doc/aklabeth/chan
gelog.Debian.gz
drwxr-xr-x root/root         0 2004-01-01 09:20:00 ./usr/share/man/
drwxr-xr-x root/root         0 2004-01-01 09:20:00 ./usr/share/man/man6/
-rw-r--r-- root/root       974 2004-01-01 09:20:00
./usr/share/man/man6/aklabeth
.6.gz
drwxr-xr-x root/root         0 2004-01-01 09:20:00 ./usr/lib/
drwxr-xr-x root/root         0 2004-01-01 09:20:00 ./usr/lib/menu/
-rw-r--r-- root/root       100 2004-01-01 09:20:00 ./usr/lib/menu/aklabeth
```

Pipe the output of debc through a pager like less if it fills more than one screen. Using debc is a good way of checking to see that everything got installed to the right place with the right permissions and ownership.

If you go up one directory, you see the following files:

✦ aklabeth_1.0-1_i386.deb

✦ aklabeth_1.0.orig.tar.gz

✦ aklabeth_1.0-1.diff.gz

✦ aklabeth_1.0-1.dsc

✦ aklabeth_1.0-1_i386.changes

If the build process didn't work, that is, if you got an error message along the way, you can fix the problem and run dpkg-buildpackage again. Notice that dpkg-buildpackage starts from the very beginning. That's the way it works; first it runs the clean target from `debian/rules` and then the binary target. That's okay for a small package like Aklabeth, which on my Pentium 3–based laptop compiles in about a minute. But imagine compiling some monstrosity like XFree86. If you had spent hours and hours compiling it and just had to fix one packaging error at the end, you would be horrified if `dpkg-buildpackage` cleaned out everything and started you back from the beginning again. Luckily, there is a solution. Recall that `debian/rules` is an executable script and a makefile. You can run it like this:

```
$ fakeroot ./debian/rules binary-arch
```

or with any other target. The building process will pick up from where it left off rather than begin again.

Signing the package

If you have a GNUPG or PGP key, you can cryptographically sign the package as you are building it by using the `-p` option to `dpkg-buildpackage` followed by a signing command with PGP-style command-line arguments, or `-s` followed by a signing command with GNUPG-style command-line arguments. If the key you want to use is not your default key, you can specify a different one by using the `-k` option followed by a key ID. Here are some examples:

```
$ dpkg-buildpackage -rfakeroot -p/usr/local/bin/pgp
$ dpkg-buildpackage -rfakeroot -sgpg -k"debian@example.com"
```

If you want to sign the package after you build it, use the `debsign` program from the `devscripts` package, like so:

```
$ debsign aklabeth_1.0-1_i386.changes
```

A useful capability of `debsign` is to sign files on a remote host. This is useful if you develop on a different computer than the one where your secret key is located. (A PGP or GNUPG key consists of a public and a secret part. You don't want to keep your secret key anywhere not totally under your control.) For instance, if you and your secret key are on your home computer, but you built Aklabeth in a subdirectory of your home directory called `package` on `example.com` where your login name is `debian`, you could sign it like this:

```
$ debsign -rdebian@example.com ~debian/package/aklabeth_1.0-1_i386.changes
```

Quality control

What users appreciate the most about `.debs` in Debian is that they are put together so nicely. This is due to the detailed guidance provided by the Debian Policy Manual. But there's a lot to read there and you might forget a point or two. So to assist you in policy compliance, the `lintian` program has been developed to catch at least the most common packaging mistakes. It is not a panacea. It doesn't cover everything, and like any automated process, it can give some false positives. (You'll know you've become an advanced Debian Developer when you've learned what triggers false positives in `lintian`.) Still, overall, it is a good practice to run your packages through `lintian`. Run it like this:

```
$ lintian aklabeth_1.0-1_i386.changes
```

It gives output like this:

```
W: aklabeth source: out-of-date-standards-version 3.6.0
W: aklabeth: unquoted-string-in-menu-item /usr/lib/menu/aklabeth needs:2
W: aklabeth: unquoted-string-in-menu-item /usr/lib/menu/aklabeth section:2
```

Each line consists of fields separated by colons. The first field is the status of the message. N means the line is a note from `lintian` itself describing a previous line or providing a debugging message. W means it is a warning, something that ought to be fixed but is not urgent. E means it is an error; this type of bug should be fixed straightaway. The second field is the name of the package the message concerns, and the third field is the actual message. The `-i` option to `lintian` goes into more detail about each message:

```
$ lintian -i aklabeth_1.0-1_i386.changes
W: aklabeth source: out-of-date-standards-version 3.6.0
N:
N:   The source package refers to a 'Standards-Version' that is starting to

N:   get out of date, compared to current Policy. You can safely ignore
N:   this warning, but please consider updating the package to current
N:   Policy.
N:
W: aklabeth: unquoted-string-in-menu-item /usr/lib/menu/aklabeth needs:2
N:
N:   The menu item includes a tag with an unquoted string like
N:   section=Games instead of section="Games". This is deprecated. Use a
N:   quoted string instead.
N:
N:    Refer to menu 3.1 for details.
N:
W: aklabeth: unquoted-string-in-menu-item /usr/lib/menu/aklabeth section:2
```

It looks like this package didn't fare too badly. The first warning can be fixed by changing the Standards-version field in the control file from 3.6.0 to 3.6.1. The other two warnings can be fixed by changing the menu file to look like this:

```
?package(aklabeth):needs="X11" section="Games/Adventure" title="Aklabeth"\
command="/usr/games/aklabeth"
```

If you've already made a version of this package public, don't forget to use dch -i to up the revision number of the package. In any case, make proper changelog entries describing the fixes you made to the package before rebuilding it.

Putting it all together

The `devscipts` package has a script called `debuild` that ties the whole package-building process together. It calls `dpkg-buildpackage` using `fakeroot`. It then signs the completed packages with `debsign`, and then it runs `lintian`. You run it from the top-level directory of the source. Its operation can be customized with options that are a mix of those from the programs it runs. You can also specify the name of a rules file target on the command line, and only that target will be run. See the `debuild(1)` Manpage for more information on this program.

Creating Dummy Packages

As mentioned in the section on non-Debian packages, the `equivs` package can be used to create dummy packages to satisfy dependencies for locally installed software. As an example, I show you how to make a dummy package for the VMware Workstation virtual machine software. `/usr/share/doc/equivs/examples` contains samples for a mail transfer agent, a Web server, Star Office 5.0, WordPerfect 8, and Netscape Communicator 4.5 if you want to see some more real-life examples.

Install `equivs` and create an empty directory somewhere. Now change to it and run the following command:

```
$ equivs-control vmware
```

This creates a file called `vmware` that looks like this:

```
Section: misc
Priority: optional
Standards-Version: 3.5.10

Package: <enter package name; defaults to equivs-dummy>
Version: <enter version here; defaults to 1.0>
Maintainer: Your Name <yourname@foo.com>
Pre-Depends: <packages>
Depends: <packages>
Recommends: <packages>
Suggests: <package>
Provides: <(virtual)package>
Architecture: all
Copyright: <copyright file; defaults to GPL2>
Changelog: <changelog file; defaults to a generic changelog>
Readme: <README.Debian file; defaults to a generic one>
Extra-Files: <additional files for the doc directory, comma separated>
Description: <short description; defaults to some wise words>
 long description and info
 .
 second paragraph
```

Looks something like a control file, doesn't it? Most of the fields are exactly the same as you would use in a control file, with just a few exceptions. Extra-Files is where, as the name suggests, you add extra files as a comma-separated list to your "package." Copyright, Changelog, and Readme are given paths to files that fulfill the named functions. But if you don't include them, default files will be generated. Fill in the fields that you need and delete the rest. The result might look like this:

```
Section: misc
Priority: optional
Standards-Version: 3.6.1

Package: vmware-dummy
Version: 1.0
Maintainer: Debian Fan <debian@example.com>
Depends: libc6, libgtk2.0-0
Architecture: all
Description: Dummy package for VMWare workstation
 This is just a quick dummy package I built with equivs to satisfy VMWare
 dependencies.
```

Now run equivs-build like this:

```
$ equivs-build -full vmware
```

This will create the dummy package's packaging scripts and then run debuild on them. When it is finished, you should have a .deb. Install it, and the packaging system will now know about vmware, just as if you had installed a real VMWare .deb. You are better off using a real .deb whenever possible. But for this type of simple usage, equivs is a tool you should consider.

Summary

In this chapter, you learned various ways of building software on your system. You learned how to build non-Debian software in a way that won't cause conflicts with the packages Debian officially provides. You used make-kpkg to build a custom kernel .deb and equivs to build a dummy .deb to trick the packaging system into acknowledging the presence of your locally built software. You learned all the tools and files used to build a full-scale, official-quality Debian package. Armed with this knowledge, you are now free to mold your system the way you want it, not as some vendor wants it to be.

✦   ✦   ✦

Debian Archives

I n Chapter 26 you learned how to create Debian packages. If you just want to use them yourself, there is nothing more to be done. But you may want to distribute your packages to a wider audience. The simplest way to host Debian packages is to just put them on a Web or FTP site somewhere. Users can download them and install them with the command `dpkg -i <packagename.deb>`. But that process deprives users of the power of Debian's `apt` utility. In this chapter, I show you how, with a small amount of effort, you can seamlessly integrate your own `.debs` into the Debian packaging system with all the benefits that entails.

> **Note**
>
> For the rest of this chapter, I refer only to `apt`, but everything that I say here also applies to programs built on top of `apt` such as `aptitude`, `synaptic`, or `wajig`.

`apt` works its magic by operating on special archives. An *archive* is basically an FTP or a Web site with some extra files containing metadata in fixed places where `apt` knows to look. You've used the official Debian archives on a regular basis. They are the ones that the installation process set up for you in `/etc/apt/sources.list`. Creating your own archive is quite simple. For your users, using the archive is even simpler; they just need to add extra lines to `sources.list`.

Hosting an Open Source Project

If you want to contribute your packages to the Debian distribution itself, you can follow the New Maintainer process described in Chapter 25. Or you can try to find an existing maintainer to sponsor uploads for you and then use Debian's own archive. If you would like to maintain your packages independently and they are Open Source, there are a number of sites, detailed in the following sections, that will give you space to host them. Of course, if you already have your own site, you can use that and safely skip the rest of this section, but you still might find it useful, as these sites offer not just space but also an entire project infrastructure including a bug-tracking system, patch manager, version control system, and mailing lists. Remember the discussion of cathedrals and bazaars in Chapter 25? If you want to take full advantage of the Open Source development process, you can't just throw packages out there and consider your task done. You need to provide a mechanism for your users to give feedback and report bugs.

SourceForge

The mother of all Open Source software-hosting sites is SourceForge (`www.sourceforge.net/`), a service provided by a company called VA Software. You can host your project on SourceForge if its license meets the Open Source Definition (`www.opensource.org/`), which is essentially the same as the Debian Free Software Guidelines (see Chapter 25). The GPL, BSD, and Artistic licenses are examples of commonly used licenses. A custom license is also acceptable as long as it can be considered Open Source under the criteria in the Open Source Definition.

If your project is eligible, the first step is to register as a SourceForge user by filling out the form at `http://sourceforge.net/account/register.php` and then logging in as that user. Then visit `https://sourceforge.net/register/` and fill out a form describing your project, what type of software it is, and the license it's under. When you have completed this process, which can take from 15 to 30 minutes, your request will be sent to the SourceForge staff. They will review it (a process that can take a few days, as it is done by hand), and if everything is satisfactory, they will create the infrastructure for your project.

Licenses

Think very carefully about the license you choose and the potential ramifications of releasing software under it. If you want to be absolutely sure that you are picking the correct license to meet your needs, consult a lawyer knowledgeable in the copyright law of your jurisdiction. If you want to avoid legal problems, only such an expert can guide you. I'm sorry, but the courts pay scant attention to the opinions of "this dude who posted on Slashdot."

I hope I'm not sounding too alarmist. In the vast majority of cases, you can release Open Source software using one of the standard licenses without any problems, but it is a sad fact of life that software development can be affected by patents, copyright claims, and lawsuits—more so in an area like Open Source, which is unfamiliar to many people and mostly outside the usual corporate paradigm. The Debian Project has a mailing list at `debian-legal@lists.debian.org` where maintainers can discuss licensing and other legal issues concerning their packages. Debian-legal is also willing to give advice to non–project members on these subjects.

SourceForge provides many services (most of which are available through an easy-to-use Web interface), including the following:

✦ **Domain name:** Your project automatically gets a domain name of `your project.sourceforge.net`. If you already have a domain name, you can delegate it to SourceForge, but note that they do not host DNS or register domains themselves.

✦ **Web space:** This is the most important feature as far as the rest of this chapter is concerned, as this is where you will create your `apt` archive.

✦ **Shell access via** `ssh`**:** This service is mainly for accessing your Web space and other administrative tasks. Only a restricted set of software is installed, and you are supposed to use the server for only project-related purposes. You need shell access to run the programs that will create the metadata for your `apt` archive, as described later in this chapter.

✦ **Download server:** SourceForge runs a distributed network of FTP sites so that if a user wants to access your files, he can visit a local (and presumably higher-bandwidth) mirror. (This isn't especially relevant, as you are going to be serving your packages through a Debian archive.)

✦ **CVS repository:** CVS is the de facto standard version control system in the Open Source world.

✦ **Mailing lists:** You can set up your own e-mail-based discussion groups for your project.

✦ **Project tracker/bug-tracking system:** You can use this to keep track of patches, feature requests, and notes and also as a mechanism for users to report bugs.

✦ **Compile farm:** SourceForge maintains a group of machines running different operating systems on which your project can be automatically compiled. You can use this to check that your source code is portable to different operating systems.

Alioth

Ironically, the software that runs SourceForge isn't Open Source. It was at one point, but VA Software has taken it in proprietary directions. Some developers who didn't like this approach took the last Open Source version and made their own enhancements to it. This forked version is known as Gforge, and there are a number of separate installations of it.

A Gforge installation known as Alioth is run by the Debian Project at `http://alioth.debian.org/`. (Alioth is the name of the capital planet of the Alliance of Independent Systems in the classic Elite video games.) It lacks some services of SourceForge, such as a compile farm, but offers a few additional services, such as support for Subversion, a successor to CVS. Its mission is to support Open Source

projects with some connection to Debian. Just as with SourceForge, you first register as a user at `http://alioth.debian.org/account/register.php` and then
apply to have a project created at `http://alioth.debian.org/register.php`.

Mentors.debian.net

The public repository at `http://mentors.debian.net/` is mainly for people learning Debian packaging and who are in the process of becoming New Maintainers (see
Chapter 25), though other people providing packages are also allowed to use it. It is
not run by the Debian Project. If you would like to host your packages in this repository, go to `http://mentors.debian.net/signup.php` for further information.

Savannah

The Free Software Foundation also has an open variant of the SourceForge code
called Savannah, running at `http://savannah.gnu.org/`. This site is for software
that is officially part of the GNU project. Projects that are Free Software but not
officially under the GNU umbrella can also be hosted on Savannah, but they are
put under the URL `http://savannah.non-gnu.org/`. You can become a user at
`http://savannah.gnu.org/account/register.php`, and after you are logged
in, apply to have a project created at `http://savannah.gnu.org/register.php`.

BerliOs

There is another SourceForge derivative at `http://developer.berlios.de/`.
Hosting your project there requires the familiar drill. Sign up as a user at `http://
developer.berlios.de/account/register.php`. Log in and apply for project
creation at `http://developer.berlios.de/register.php`. BerliOs is based in
Germany, and it offers more support for developers and users who speak languages
other than English than do the other services I've mentioned.

Setting Up a Package Archive

After you have a Web space for your project, you can begin setting up the archive.
This is done via one of two programs: `dpkg-scanpackages`, which is found in the
`dpkg-dev` package, or `apt-ftparchive`, which is in the `apt-utils` package. `dpkg-
scanpackages` can create one type of metadata, the `Packages.gz` file that `apt` looks
for in a binary package archive, but it cannot handle `Sources.gz`, which is used for
source package archives, or release files, which add extra security and give `apt`
additional information on the nature of your archive. As `apt-ftparchive` has all
the features of `dpkg-scanpackages` and more, it is the only one I cover in this
chapter.

If your Web space is on a server running Debian, all is well and good, but if you are using another platform, you will have to port `apt-ftparchive` first. Under Linux it is easy, as you can just grab the source to `apt` from `/pool/main/a/apt/apt_<some version>.tar.gz` on any Debian mirror site and it should compile without problems. A potential hurdle is that sites like SourceForge don't give you access to a C compiler. To get around this hurdle, you can compile it on a comparable system elsewhere (SourceForge runs Red Hat; BerliOs runs SUSE) and copy the files over. If you are using SourceForge, you can download a prebuilt version of `apt-ftparchive` from `http://src.braincells.com/apt4sf.tar.gz`.

To install the prebuilt `apt-ftparchive`, take the following steps:

1. Use the `scp` command to copy the `apt4sf.tar.gz` file to your user account's home directory on SourceForge.

2. Use `ssh` to log in to your account and unpack `apt4sf.tar.gz`.

3. This will create two directories: `bin` and `lib`. Run the following commands (you can add them to your `.bash_profile` file if you want them active every time you log in):

```
$ export PATH=~/bin:$PATH
$ export LD_LIBRARY_PATH=~/lib:$LD_LIBRARY_PATH
```

4. Now you are ready to move on to the next section, which describes how to use `apt-ftparchive`.

If you are using a Web server on another variant of UNIX or, heaven forbid, Windows, things can get a lot trickier. The simplest solution might just be to create the archive, using the procedure described in the next section, on your Debian box and then transfer the whole thing over to the Web server. Make sure you have the same directory structure on both sides or you will have the wrong paths and `apt` won't work.

A simple archive

There are three standard archive layouts supported by `apt-ftparchive`; I refer to these as "simple," "complex," and "Debian style." The differences between them are based on the degree to which packages are sorted and organized. The simple layout looks like this:

```
/debian --+---------packagea/
          |
          +---------packageb/
          |
          +---------packagec/
```

`/debian` in the preceding code is the path as the Web server sees it. The actual path may be `/var/www/debian` or something similar. Each `package dir` directory contains the debianized source of a package plus any `.deb`s that are built from it. No attempt is made to organize the packages in any way.

Build an archive by changing to the directory where you are building the archive and by using the following command:

```
$ apt-ftparchive packages ./ | gzip > Packages.gz
```

The line that users must put into /etc/apt/sources.list to use this archive is

```
deb http://yourserver.com/debian ./
```

You can also create a source line by changing to /debian and issuing the following command:

```
$ apt-ftparchive sources ./ | gzip > Sources.gz
```

The line users must add to /etc/apt/sources.list to use this source archive is

```
deb-src http://yourserver.com/debian ./
```

A complex archive

If you are building multiple sets of packages, for example, for different distributions, and you want to sort them accordingly, you use a layout like the following:

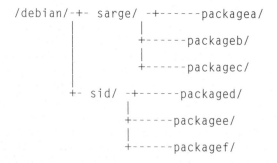

```
/debian/-+- sarge/ -+------packagea/
         |          |
         |          +------packageb/
         |          |
         |          +------packagec/
         |
         +- sid/ -+------packaged/
                  |
                  +------packagee/
                  |
                  +------packagef/
```

Running the following commands will create a package archive using the preceding layout:

```
$ cd debian
$ apt-ftparchive packages sarge/ | gzip > sarge/Packages.gz
$ apt-ftparchive sources sarge/ | gzip > sarge/Sources.gz
$ apt-ftparchive packages sid/ | gzip > sid/Packages.gz
$ apt-ftparchive sources sid/ | gzip > sid/Sources.gz
```

If you want to use the sarge part of the archive with this type of layout, add the following lines to /etc/apt/sources.list:

```
deb http://yourserver.com/debian sarge/
deb-src http://yourserver.com/debian sarge/
```

Or add the following lines if you want to use the `sid` part of the archive:

```
deb http://yourserver.com/debian sid/
deb-src http://yourserver.com/debian sid/
```

You don't have to organize by distribution. You could, for example, have one set of packages for one client and a different set for another.

A Debian-style archive

Now consider the following layout:

```
/debian/dists -- sarge/ -+- main/ -+- binary-i386/ - package/
                 |          |
                 |          +- source/ -+- package/
                 |
                 +- contrib/ -+- binary-i386/ -+- package/
                 |            |
                 |            +- source -+- package/
                 |
                 + - non-free/ -+- binary-i386/ -+- package/
                                |
                                +- source/ -+- package/
```

Whereas the simple archive layout had one level of subdirectories, and the complex layout had two levels, this layout has three levels. Does it look familiar? If you have browsed the directories on, say, `ftp.debian.org`, you will notice this structure. It is the same kind of layout used on official Debian download sites. Debian organizes packages not just by distribution but also by section (main, contrib, or nonfree) within each distribution. Within each section, packages are split up by binary architecture (only i386 is shown in the preceding figure, but the real Debian site would also have alpha, sparc, m68k, and so on), with an additional directory for source packages. Apart from the Debian Project itself, very few people need to build an archive this complex. But if you are one of those people, you can do so by creating the appropriate directories and populating them with packages and then changing to the `sarge` directory and running the following command:

```
$ for i in main contrib non-free; do \
apt-ftparchive packages $i/binary-i386/|gzip > \
$i/binary-i386/Packages.gz; \
apt-ftparchive sources $i/source/|gzip > $i/source/Sources.gz; done
```

You then are able to add lines to `/etc/apt/sources.list` that look like this:

```
deb http://yourserver.com/debian sarge main contrib non-free
deb-src http://yourserver.com/debian sarge main contrib non-free
```

The `dists` and `binary-<architecture>` parts of the layout are not mentioned in the output as they are taken care of by `apt`, which has them hard-coded in.

 Note   Although these examples have assumed that you will be setting up the archive on a Web site, the same principles apply if you want to serve the archive via FTP. From your perspective, it is still just a matter of placing packages and files in a certain directory structure. From the user perspective, the only difference is that the URLs in the lines they have to add to `/etc/apt/sources.list` will begin with `ftp://` instead of `http://`.

The Release file

The last part you need for a complete `apt` archive is a `Release` file. This provides extra metadata about the archive and goes into its top-level directory. So in the simple and complex archive layouts in the preceding sections, the `Release` file would go into `/debian`, whereas in the Debian archive layout, it would go into `/debian/dists/sarge`. In order to create the `Release` file, you first need a configuration file as a source. On a Debian system, you put the configuration file for `apt-ftparchive` into `/etc/apt/`, but it can be anywhere really. You just have to specify the location on the `apt-ftparchive` command line. The configuration file for the Debian archive sample layout in the previous section might look like this:

```
APT
{
  FTPArchive
  {
    Release
    {
      Origin "Wiley";
      Label "Wiley/Sarge";
      Suite "stable";
      Codename "Sarge";
      Architectures "i386";
      Components "main contrib non-free";
      Description "The Debian 3.1 Bible Archive";
    }
  }
}
```

This is what the configuration entries mean:

✦ `Origin`: The organization that is responsible for this archive. This entry is helpful if you have two packages of the same name from different places.

✦ `Label`: A name to describe this archive.

✦ `Suite`: Mostly specific to the Debian Project's way of organization. `Suite` describes which of multiple tiers of distribution this is.

✦ Codename: Can be used as a synonym for Suite.

✦ Architecture: Which architectures are contained in this archive.

✦ Components: For the Debian-style layout mentioned previously, the sections of the archive. Not really relevant for the other layouts.

✦ Description: A brief description of the archive.

Once you have created the configuration file, you can create the Release file by first changing to the directory where the Release file should go — the location of your archive — and then using this command:

```
$ apt-ftparchive -c /location/of/config-file release ./ > Release
```

Apt-ftparchive will copy your configuration, scan the directory you specified and all the ones under it, and write out the MD5 and SHA checksums and size for each Packages.gz, Sources.gz, and Release file it finds. This can be used by security-conscious users who want to be sure the files have not been tampered with. The resulting Release file might look like this:

```
Architectures: i386
Codename: Sarge
Components: main contrib non-free
Date: Thu, 01 Jan 2004 00:00:00 UTC
Description: The Debian 3.1 Bible Archive
Label: Wiley/Sarge
Origin: Wiley
Suite: stable
MD5Sum:
 c1b78ed6d8c2033dd2f6f4db10dd4f72        558 contrib/binary-
i386/Packages.gz
 6d6eb0c4c9e81b4b905af566f4f6fbdb       1023 main/binary-i386/Packages.gz
 f4fc171d170606033ae312ceafa0ba6b       1210 non-free/binary-
i386/Packages.gz
SHA1:
 4261803e98cd58eb213e6ba6497ac61f77fd025f  558 contrib/binary-
i386/Packages.gz
 7486b1a4c55ec8c381f7fec794e50da72824bf09 1023 main/binary-i386/Packages.gz
 33cde973bb7c7923a21b05c463d69f584d6c81ce 1210 non-free/binary-
i386/Packages.gz
```

So that people can trust that the Release file's MD5Sums have not been tampered with, use GnuPG to add a detached signature, as shown in the following line:

```
$ gpg -detach-sign Release > Release.gpg
```

Release.gpg also goes in the archive root alongside the Release file.

Package Signing

One thing people who are familiar with developing RPM packages notice about the `.deb` format is that the packages are not cryptographically signed with GnuPG. Although theoretically such a signature would offer some extra security, Debian's current scheme, in which the `.dsc` and `.changes` files, along with the `Release` file, are signed and contain `MD5Sums`, is good enough for most real-world security scenarios. (`dpkg/apt` will include the GnuPG signature feature and has some experimental support already, but it wasn't production-ready in time for sarge.)

Maintaining the archive on an ongoing basis is quite easy. You just need to remember to regenerate the `Packages`, `Sources`, `Release`, and `Release.gpg` files by following these procedures again, anytime you add or remove a package.

Announcing Your Packages

If you created your packages for public consumption, the public needs to know they exist. You can let people know at `www.apt-get.org/`. This is a third-party site not affiliated with the Debian Project. It allows you to submit your `apt` archive along with a brief description, and it has become quite popular among Debian users looking for `.debs` that are not part of the official distribution. If your archive changes or it is discontinued, be sure to update your entry so that the site remains accurate.

Summary

In this chapter, you learned of some sites that allow you to host an Open Source project for free. You learned how to build and maintain an archive of Debian packages compatible with `apt` and the other package tools built upon it and the different styles of archive layouts. This chapter also covered announcing your archive on `apt-get.org`.

✦   ✦   ✦

What's on the CD-ROMs?

This appendix provides you with information on the contents of the CDs that accompany this book. This book comes with two CDs:

✦ An Installation CD of the first CD of Debian 3.1

✦ A "Live CD" version of the CD based on Debian 3.x

System Requirements

This CD will run on a variety of different systems, and there are no hard limits. Running a graphical desktop environment will require at least a Pentium II or Pentium III system and at least 64 MB of memory. Running the Live CD should be comfortable with a larger amount of memory — often 128 MB. More "bare-bones" systems will run on less powerful computers.

What's on the CDs

The following sections describe the contents of each CD.

Debian Installation CD

The Debian Installation CD is a copy of the official CD-ROM image of the first CD of the Debian distribution. It is the image released and created by the Debian Project. It is *not* a full Debian distribution.

Debian is the largest GNU/Linux distribution in terms of the amount of software included alone. It will release with enough software to fill over a dozen CDs (the exact number hasn't been finalized as of this writing) or a handful of DVDs. Clearly, very few people will want to use the *vast* majority of the software on those CDs. Consequently, the CDs are created by a program that tries to put the most "important" and most popular pieces of software on the first CDs and the less important pieces of software on the later CDs.

The CD that accompanies this book is only the first CD. As a result, it contains the most central pieces of software for someone installing Debian: the Debian installer, important installation-related documentation, the Debian "base" system, essential packages for Debian systems, some installation-related tools, and as many of the most popular pieces of software as would fit on the CD.

The Debian installer shipped is the "next-generation" piece of software for doing installs of Debian systems that has been in development for more than half a decade. This is the first official release of Debian that uses this new installer. Although superficially it may look like the old installer, it is *massively* improved and contains many of the features you'd expect in any mature GNU/Linux distribution, such as automatic hardware detection and automatic and assisted partitioning.

Using only this CD, a user can install a "bare-bones" Debian installation. You can choose to install extra software during the course of the install of the system or after the system is installed by using Debian's advanced package management systems. For many simple workstations and servers, this CD will be everything — or nearly everything — that you need.

If you want a full-fledged graphical environment with a wide assortment of games and applications, this CD will *not* contain everything you need. That said, you can freely get the software you need to do this that is not included on the CD by downloading it over the Internet from within the installer — as much or as little as you need or want. You can also download it from a mirror site near you to maximize download speeds. If, because of bandwidth limitations or other reasons, downloading a large amount of software is simply not an option, you can look online to the list of CD vendors to buy an extra CD or set of CDs. That list is available at `www.debian.org/CD/vendors/`.

Vendors are located in many countries and in many states within the U.S. You should be able to find one near you. Check to make sure that you are buying the latest version of Debian.

To install using the CD, simply put the CD into your drive and reboot your computer. If you do not boot into the Debian installer, check to make sure that your computer is configured to boot from the CD.

The CD also contains a small collection of tools that can be run from Windows. These are in the `tools` directory on the CD. This directory includes software to verify that your CD image was downloaded correctly and that you can use to write floppy disk images directly onto media and to repartition your hard disk—all from within Windows. All of these tools are Free Software/Open Source software.

Finally, the CD contains some amount of documentation. To get the latest version of the install guide, you can go to this Web site:

`www.debian.org/releases/stable/installmanual`

Debian Live CD

This CD also comes with a second "Live" CD, which you can think of as an *installed* Debian distribution on a CD. When a user boots the Live CD, it will bring up a full desktop Linux environment much like one that you will install with the Installation CD. However, this environment will not write anything to hard disk, so no data on the user's computer will be affected. By turning off the computer and popping out the disk, the computer will revert to *exactly* the state it was in before the Live CD was used.

The most famous Live CD is called Knoppix and it was written by Klaus Knopper. Knoppix and its derivatives are all based on Debian systems, and they install and customize Debian packages in the production of their Live CDs. In this way, the CDs provide a snapshot of what a Debian system can be.

I carry a Live CD with me everywhere I go, as it allows me, with a reboot of the machine, to turn *any* system into a Debian system. Combined with a form of removable media—a USB key, for example—it can be a powerful and useful tool for any Debian user on the move.

Live CDs are popular advocacy tools. They are often handed out by GNU/Linux user groups and advocates to those that are interested in exploring a GNU/Linux system but not necessarily ready to make the jump. Using a Live CD can give users a good idea of the type of hardware support that they will be able to expect, as well as provide a good idea of the types of applications and their ability to read or run the documents stored on the Windows system. Many people, once they understand that they can read their e-mail, surf the Web, and edit their Microsoft Word documents, are convinced that GNU/Linux may be for them. The Installation CD and the Live CD complement each other excellently.

Using the Live CD is simple: Place it in the CD drive of the computer and reboot. If the Live CD does not boot, check to make sure that the computer is configured to boot from the CD-ROM drive.

Source Code Coupon

The source code for the Debian install DVD included with this book is available via mail. To order the Debian Linux 3.1 source code, go to `www.wiley.com/go/debinlinuxsource` to download a coupon with further details.

Customer Care

If you have trouble with the CD-ROM, please call the Wiley Product Technical Support phone number at 800-762-2974. Outside the United States, call 1-317-572-3994. You can also contact Wiley Product Technical Support at `http://www.wiley.com/techsupport`. Wiley Publishing will provide technical support only for installation and other general quality-control items. For technical support on the applications themselves, consult the program's vendor or author.

To place additional orders or to request information about other Wiley products, please call 877-762-2974.

✦   ✦   ✦

Debian Constitution

Constitution for the Debian Project (v1.2)

Version 1.2 ratified on October 29th, 2003. Supersedes Version 1.1 ratified on June 21st, 2003, which itself supersedes Version 1.0 ratified on December 2nd, 1998.

1. Introduction

The Debian Project is an association of individuals who have made common cause to create a free operating system.

This document describes the organisational structure for formal decision-making in the Project. It does not describe the goals of the Project or how it achieves them, or contain any policies except those directly related to the decision-making process.

2. Decision-making bodies and individuals

Each decision in the Project is made by one or more of the following:

1. The Developers, by way of General Resolution or an election;

2. The Project Leader;

3. The Technical Committee and/or its Chairman;

4. The individual Developer working on a particular task;

5. Delegates appointed by the Project Leader for specific tasks;

6. The Project Secretary.

Most of the remainder of this document will outline the powers of these bodies, their composition and appointment, and the procedure for their decision-making. The powers of a person or body may be subject to review and/or limitation by others; in this case the reviewing body or person's entry will state this. *In the list above, a person or body is usually listed before any people or bodies whose decisions they can overrule or who they (help) appoint - but not everyone listed earlier can overrule everyone listed later.*

2.1. General rules

1. Nothing in this constitution imposes an obligation on anyone to do work for the Project. A person who does not want to do a task which has been delegated or assigned to them does not need to do it. However, they must not actively work against these rules and decisions properly made under them.

2. A person may hold several posts, except that the Project Leader, Project Secretary and the Chairman of the Technical Committee must be distinct, and that the Leader cannot appoint themselves as their own Delegate.

3. A person may leave the Project or resign from a particular post they hold, at any time, by stating so publicly.

3. Individual Developers

3.1. Powers

An individual Developer may

1. make any technical or nontechnical decision with regard to their own work;

2. propose or sponsor draft General Resolutions;

3. propose themselves as a Project Leader candidate in elections;

4. vote on General Resolutions and in Leadership elections.

3.2. Composition and appointment

1. Developers are volunteers who agree to further the aims of the Project insofar as they participate in it, and who maintain package(s) for the Project or do other work which the Project Leader's Delegate(s) consider worthwhile.

2. The Project Leader's Delegate(s) may choose not to admit new Developers, or expel existing Developers. *If the Developers feel that the Delegates are abusing their authority they can of course override the decision by way of General Resolution - see §4.1(3), §4.2.*

3.3. Procedure
Developers may make these decisions as they see fit.

4. The Developers by way of General Resolution or election

4.1. Powers
Together, the Developers may:

1. Appoint or recall the Project Leader.

2. Amend this constitution, provided they agree with a 3:1 majority.

3. Override any decision by the Project Leader or a Delegate.

4. Override any decision by the Technical Committee, provided they agree with a 2:1 majority.

5. Issue, supersede and withdraw nontechnical policy documents and statements.

   These include documents describing the goals of the project, its relationship with other free software entities, and nontechnical policies such as the free software licence terms that Debian software must meet.

   They may also include position statements about issues of the day.

   1. A Foundation Document is a document or statement regarded as critical to the Project's mission and purposes.

   2. The Foundation Documents are the works entitled Debian Social Contract and Debian Free Software Guidelines.

   3. A Foundation Document requires a 3:1 majority for its supersession. New Foundation Documents are issued and existing ones withdrawn by amending the list of Foundation Documents in this constitution.

6. Together with the Project Leader and SPI, make decisions about property held in trust for purposes related to Debian. (See §9.1.)

4.2. Procedure

1. The Developers follow the Standard Resolution Procedure, below. A resolution or amendment is introduced if proposed by any Developer and sponsored by at least K other Developers, or if proposed by the Project Leader or the Technical Committee.

2. Delaying a decision by the Project Leader or their Delegate:

   1. If the Project Leader or their Delegate, or the Technical Committee, has made a decision, then Developers can override them by passing a resolution to do so; see s4.1(3).

2. If such a resolution is sponsored by at least 2K Developers, or if it is proposed by the Technical Committee, the resolution puts the decision immediately on hold (provided that resolution itself says so).

3. If the original decision was to change a discussion period or a voting period, or the resolution is to override the Technical Committee, then only K Developers need to sponsor the resolution to be able to put the decision immediately on hold.

4. If the decision is put on hold, an immediate vote is held to determine whether the decision will stand until the full vote on the decision is made or whether the implementation of the original decision will be delayed until then. There is no quorum for this immediate procedural vote.

5. If the Project Leader (or the Delegate) withdraws the original decision, the vote becomes moot, and is no longer conducted.

3. Votes are taken by the Project Secretary. Votes, tallies, and results are not revealed during the voting period; after the vote the Project Secretary lists all the votes cast. The voting period is 2 weeks, but may be varied by up to 1 week by the Project Leader.

4. The minimum discussion period is 2 weeks, but may be varied by up to 1 week by the Project Leader. The Project Leader has a casting vote. There is a quorum of 3Q.

5. Proposals, sponsors, amendments, calls for votes and other formal actions are made by announcement on a publicly-readable electronic mailing list designated by the Project Leader's Delegate(s); any Developer may post there.

6. Votes are cast by email in a manner suitable to the Secretary. The Secretary determines for each poll whether voters can change their votes.

7. Q is half of the square root of the number of current Developers. K is Q or 5, whichever is the smaller. Q and K need not be integers and are not rounded.

5. Project Leader

5.1. Powers

The Project Leader may:

1. Appoint Delegates or delegate decisions to the Technical Committee.

    The Leader may define an area of ongoing responsibility or a specific decision and hand it over to another Developer or to the Technical Committee.

    Once a particular decision has been delegated and made the Project Leader may not withdraw that delegation; however, they may withdraw an ongoing delegation of particular area of responsibility.

2. Lend authority to other Developers.

   The Project Leader may make statements of support for points of view or for other members of the project, when asked or otherwise; these statements have force if and only if the Leader would be empowered to make the decision in question.

3. Make any decision which requires urgent action.

   This does not apply to decisions which have only become gradually urgent through lack of relevant action, unless there is a fixed deadline.

4. Make any decision for whom no one else has responsibility.

5. Propose draft General Resolutions and amendments.

6. Together with the Technical Committee, appoint new members to the Committee. (See §6.2.)

7. Use a casting vote when Developers vote.

   The Project Leader also has a normal vote in such ballots.

8. Vary the discussion period for Developers' votes (as above).

9. Lead discussions amongst Developers.

   The Project Leader should attempt to participate in discussions amongst the Developers in a helpful way which seeks to bring the discussion to bear on the key issues at hand. The Project Leader should not use the Leadership position to promote their own personal views.

10. Together with SPI, make decisions affecting property held in trust for purposes related to Debian. (See §9.1.)

5.2. Appointment

1. The Project Leader is elected by the Developers.

2. The election begins nine weeks before the leadership post becomes vacant, or (if it is too late already) immediately.

3. For the following three weeks any Developer may nominate themselves as a candidate Project Leader.

4. For three weeks after that no more candidates may be nominated; candidates should use this time for campaigning (to make their identities and positions known). If there are no candidates at the end of the nomination period then the nomination period is extended for three further weeks, repeatedly if necessary.

5. The next three weeks are the polling period during which Developers may cast their votes. Votes in leadership elections are kept secret, even after the election is finished.

6. The options on the ballot will be those candidates who have nominated themselves and have not yet withdrawn, plus None Of The Above. If None Of The Above wins the election then the election procedure is repeated, many times if necessary.

7. The decision will be made using the method specified in section §A.6 of the Standard Resolution Procedure. The quorum is the same as for a General Resolution (§4.2) and the default option is "None Of The Above".

8. The Project Leader serves for one year from their election.

5.3. Procedure

The Project Leader should attempt to make decisions which are consistent with the consensus of the opinions of the Developers.

Where practical the Project Leader should informally solicit the views of the Developers.

The Project Leader should avoid overemphasizing their own point of view when making decisions in their capacity as Leader.

6. Technical committee

6.1. Powers

The Technical Committee may:

1. Decide on any matter of technical policy.

   This includes the contents of the technical policy manuals, developers' reference materials, example packages and the behaviour of non-experimental package building tools. (In each case the usual maintainer of the relevant software or documentation makes decisions initially, however; see 6.3(5).)

2. Decide any technical matter where Developers' jurisdictions overlap.

   In cases where Developers need to implement compatible technical policies or stances (for example, if they disagree about the priorities of conflicting packages, or about ownership of a command name, or about which package is responsible for a bug that both maintainers agree is a bug, or about who should be the maintainer for a package) the technical committee may decide the matter.

3. Make a decision when asked to do so.

   Any person or body may delegate a decision of their own to the Technical Committee, or seek advice from it.

4. Overrule a Developer (requires a 3:1 majority).

   The Technical Committee may ask a Developer to take a particular technical course of action even if the Developer does not wish to; this requires a 3:1

majority. For example, the Committee may determine that a complaint made by the submitter of a bug is justified and that the submitter's proposed solution should be implemented.

5. Offer advice.

The Technical Committee may make formal announcements about its views on any matter. *Individual members may of course make informal statements about their views and about the likely views of the committee.*

6. Together with the Project Leader, appoint new members to itself or remove existing members. (See §6.2.)

7. Appoint the Chairman of the Technical Committee.

The Chairman is elected by the Committee from its members. All members of the committee are automatically nominated; the committee votes starting one week before the post will become vacant (or immediately, if it is already too late). The members may vote by public acclamation for any fellow committee member, including themselves; there is no default option. The vote finishes when all the members have voted, or when the voting period has ended. The result is determined using the method specified in section A.6 of the Standard Resolution Procedure.

8. The Chairman can stand in for the Leader, together with the Secretary.

As detailed in §7.1(2), the Chairman of the Technical Committee and the Project Secretary may together stand in for the Leader if there is no Leader.

6.2. Composition

1. The Technical Committee consists of up to 8 Developers, and should usually have at least 4 members.

2. When there are fewer than 8 members the Technical Committee may recommend new member(s) to the Project Leader, who may choose (individually) to appoint them or not.

3. When there are 5 members or fewer the Technical Committee may appoint new member(s) until the number of members reaches 6.

4. When there have been 5 members or fewer for at least one week the Project Leader may appoint new member(s) until the number of members reaches 6, at intervals of at least one week per appointment.

5. If the Technical Committee and the Project Leader agree they may remove or replace an existing member of the Technical Committee.

6.3. Procedure

1. The Technical Committee uses the Standard Resolution Procedure.

A draft resolution or amendment may be proposed by any member of the Technical Committee. There is no minimum discussion period; the voting period lasts for up to one week, or until the outcome is no longer in doubt. Members may change their votes. There is a quorum of two.

2. Details regarding voting.

The Chairman has a casting vote. When the Technical Committee votes whether to override a Developer who also happens to be a member of the Committee, that member may not vote (unless they are the Chairman, in which case they may use only their casting vote).

3. Public discussion and decision-making.

Discussion, draft resolutions and amendments, and votes by members of the committee, are made public on the Technical Committee public discussion list. There is no separate secretary for the Committee.

4. Confidentiality of appointments.

The Technical Committee may hold confidential discussions via private email or a private mailing list or other means to discuss appointments to the Committee. However, votes on appointments must be public.

5. No detailed design work.

The Technical Committee does not engage in design of new proposals and policies. Such design work should be carried out by individuals privately or together and discussed in ordinary technical policy and design forums.

The Technical Committee restricts itself to choosing from or adopting compromises between solutions and decisions which have been proposed and reasonably thoroughly discussed elsewhere.

Individual members of the technical committee may of course participate on their own behalf in any aspect of design and policy work.

6. Technical Committee makes decisions only as last resort.

The Technical Committee does not make a technical decision until efforts to resolve it via consensus have been tried and failed, unless it has been asked to make a decision by the person or body who would normally be responsible for it.

7. The Project Secretary

7.1. Powers

The Secretary:

1. Takes votes amongst the Developers, and determines the number and identity of Developers, whenever this is required by the constitution.

2. Can stand in for the Leader, together with the Chairman of the Technical Committee.

If there is no Project Leader then the Chairman of the Technical Committee and the Project Secretary may by joint agreement make decisions if they consider it imperative to do so.

3. Adjudicates any disputes about interpretation of the constitution.

4. May delegate part or all of their authority to someone else, or withdraw such a delegation at any time.

7.2. Appointment

The Project Secretary is appointed by the Project Leader and the current Project Secretary.

If the Project Leader and the current Project Secretary cannot agree on a new appointment they must ask the board of SPI (see §9.1.) to appoint a Secretary.

If there is no Project Secretary or the current Secretary is unavailable and has not delegated authority for a decision then the decision may be made or delegated by the Chairman of the Technical Committee, as Acting Secretary.

The Project Secretary's term of office is 1 year, at which point they or another Secretary must be (re)appointed.

7.3. Procedure

The Project Secretary should make decisions which are fair and reasonable, and preferably consistent with the consensus of the Developers.

When acting together to stand in for an absent Project Leader the Chairman of the Technical Committee and the Project Secretary should make decisions only when absolutely necessary and only when consistent with the consensus of the Developers.

8. The Project Leader's Delegates

8.1. Powers

The Project Leader's Delegates:

1. have powers delegated to them by the Project Leader;

2. may make certain decisions which the Leader may not make directly, including approving or expelling Developers or designating people as Developers who do not maintain packages. *This is to avoid concentration of power, particularly over membership as a Developer, in the hands of the Project Leader.*

8.2. Appointment

The Delegates are appointed by the Project Leader and may be replaced by the Leader at the Leader's discretion. The Project Leader may not make the position as a Delegate conditional on particular decisions by the Delegate, nor may they override a decision made by a Delegate once made.

8.3. Procedure

Delegates may make decisions as they see fit, but should attempt to implement good technical decisions and/or follow consensus opinion.

9. Software in the Public Interest

SPI and Debian are separate organisations who share some goals. Debian is grateful for the legal support framework offered by SPI. *Debian's Developers are currently members of SPI by virtue of their status as Developers.*

9.1. Authority

1. SPI has no authority regarding Debian's technical or nontechnical decisions, except that no decision by Debian with respect to any property held by SPI shall require SPI to act outside its legal authority, and that Debian's constitution may occasionally use SPI as a decision body of last resort.

2. Debian claims no authority over SPI other than that over the use of certain of SPI's property, as described below, though Debian Developers may be granted authority within SPI by SPI's rules.

3. Debian Developers are not agents or employees of SPI, or of each other or of persons in authority in the Debian Project. A person acting as a Developer does so as an individual, on their own behalf.

9.2. Management of property for purposes related to Debian

Since Debian has no authority to hold money or property, any donations for the Debian Project must be made to SPI, which manages such affairs.

SPI have made the following undertakings:

1. SPI will hold money, trademarks and other tangible and intangible property and manage other affairs for purposes related to Debian.

2. Such property will be accounted for separately and held in trust for those purposes, decided on by Debian and SPI according to this section.

3. SPI will not dispose of or use property held in trust for Debian without approval from Debian, which may be granted by the Project Leader or by General Resolution of the Developers.

4. SPI will consider using or disposing of property held in trust for Debian when asked to do so by the Project Leader.

5. SPI will use or dispose of property held in trust for Debian when asked to do so by a General Resolution of the Developers, provided that this is compatible with SPI's legal authority.

6. SPI will notify the Developers by electronic mail to a Debian Project mailing list when it uses or disposes of property held in trust for Debian.

A. Standard Resolution Procedure

These rules apply to communal decision-making by committees and plebiscites, where stated above.

A.1. Proposal

The formal procedure begins when a draft resolution is proposed and sponsored, as required.

A.1. Discussion and Amendment

1. Following the proposal, the resolution may be discussed. Amendments may be made formal by being proposed and sponsored according to the requirements for a new resolution, or directly by the proposer of the original resolution.

2. A formal amendment may be accepted by the resolution's proposer, in which case the formal resolution draft is immediately changed to match.

3. If a formal amendment is not accepted, or one of the sponsors of the resolution does not agree with the acceptance by the proposer of a formal amendment, the amendment remains as an amendment and will be voted on.

4. If an amendment accepted by the original proposer is not to the liking of others, they may propose another amendment to reverse the earlier change (again, they must meet the requirements for proposer and sponsor(s)).

5. The proposer or a resolution may suggest changes to the wordings of amendments; these take effect if the proposer of the amendment agrees and none of the sponsors object. In this case the changed amendments will be voted on instead of the originals.

6. The proposer of a resolution may make changes to correct minor errors (for example, typographical errors or inconsistencies) or changes which do not alter the meaning, providing no one objects within 24 hours. In this case the minimum discussion period is not restarted.

A.2. Calling for a vote

1. The proposer or a sponsor of a motion or an amendment may call for a vote, providing that the minimum discussion period (if any) has elapsed.

2. The proposer or any sponsor of a resolution may call for a vote on that resolution and all related amendments.

3. The person who calls for a vote states what they believe the wordings of the resolution and any relevant amendments are, and consequently what form the ballot should take. However, the final decision on the form of ballot(s) is the Secretary's - see 7.1(1), 7.1(3) and A.3(4).

4. The minimum discussion period is counted from the time the last formal amendment was accepted, or since the whole resolution was proposed if no amendments have been proposed and accepted.

A.3. Voting procedure

1. Each resolution and its related amendments is voted on in a single ballot that includes an option for the original resolution, each amendment, and the default option (where applicable).

2. The default option must not have any supermajority requirements. Options which do not have an explicit supermajority requirement have a 1:1 majority requirement.

3. The votes are counted according to the the rules in A.6. The default option is "Further Discussion", unless specified otherwise.

4. In cases of doubt the Project Secretary shall decide on matters of procedure.

A.4. Withdrawing resolutions or unaccepted amendments

The proposer of a resolution or unaccepted amendment may withdraw it. In this case new proposers may come forward to keep it alive, in which case the first person to do so becomes the new proposer and any others become sponsors if they aren't sponsors already.

A sponsor of a resolution or amendment (unless it has been accepted) may withdraw.

If the withdrawal of the proposer and/or sponsors means that a resolution has no proposer or not enough sponsors it will not be voted on unless this is rectified before the resolution expires.

A.5. Expiry

If a proposed resolution has not been discussed, amended, voted on or otherwise dealt with for 4 weeks the secretary may issue a statement that the issue is being withdrawn. If none of the sponsors of any of the proposals object within a week, the issue is withdrawn.

The secretary may also include suggestions on how to proceed, if appropriate.

A.6. Vote Counting

1. Each voter's ballot ranks the options being voted on. Not all options need be ranked. Ranked options are considered preferred to all unranked options. Voters may rank options equally. Unranked options are considered to be ranked equally with one another. Details of how ballots may be filled out will be included in the Call For Votes.

2. If the ballot has a quorum requirement R any options other than the default option which do not receive at least R votes ranking that option above the default option are dropped from consideration.

3. Any (non-default) option which does not defeat the default option by its required majority ratio is dropped from consideration.

   1. Given two options A and B, V(A,B) is the number of voters who prefer option A over option B.

   2. An option A defeats the default option D by a majority ratio N, if V(A,D) is strictly greater than N * V(D,A).

   3. If a supermajority of S:1 is required for A, its majority ratio is S; otherwise, its majority ratio is 1.

4. From the list of undropped options, we generate a list of pairwise defeats.

   1. An option A defeats an option B, if V(A,B) is strictly greater than V(B,A).

5. From the list of [undropped] pairwise defeats, we generate a set of transitive defeats.

   1. An option A transitively defeats an option C if A defeats C or if there is some other option B where A defeats B and B transitively defeats C.

6. We construct the Schwartz set from the set of transitive defeats.

   1. An option A is in the Schwartz set if for all options B, either A transitively defeats B, or B does not transitively defeat A.

7. If there are defeats between options in the Schwartz set, we drop the weakest such defeats from the list of pairwise defeats, and return to step 5.

   1. A defeat (A,X) is weaker than a defeat (B,Y) if V(A,X) is less than V(B,Y). Also, (A,X) is weaker than (B,Y) if V(A,X) is equal to V(B,Y) and V(X,A) is greater than V(Y,B).

      1. A weakest defeat is a defeat that has no other defeat weaker than it. There may be more than one such defeat.

8. If there are no defeats within the Schwartz set, then the winner is chosen from the options in the Schwartz set. If there is only one such option, it is the winner. If there are multiple options, the elector with the casting vote chooses which of those options wins.

Note: Options which the voters rank above the default option are options they find acceptable. Options ranked below the default options are options they find unacceptable.

When the Standard Resolution Procedure is to be used, the text which refers to it must specify what is sufficient to have a draft resolution proposed and/or sponsored, what the minimum discussion period is, and what the voting period is. It must also specify any supermajority and/or the quorum (and default option) to be used.

B. Use of language and typography

The present indicative ('is', for example) means that the statement is a rule in this constitution. 'May' or 'can' indicates that the person or body has discretion. 'Should' means that it would be considered a good thing if the sentence were obeyed, but it is not binding. *Text marked as a citation, such as this, is rationale and does not form part of the constitution. It may be used only to aid interpretation in cases of doubt.*

✦   ✦   ✦

Index

Continued

Continued

Continued

Continued

Continued

GNU General Public License

Version 2, June 1991

Copyright © 1989, 1991 Free Software Foundation, Inc.

59 Temple Place - Suite 330, Boston, MA 02111-1307, USA

Preamble

The licenses for most software are designed to take away your freedom to share and change it. By contrast, the GNU General Public License is intended to guarantee your freedom to share and change free software—to make sure the software is free for all its users. This General Public License applies to most of the Free Software Foundation's software and to any other program whose authors commit to using it. (Some other Free Software Foundation software is covered by the GNU Library General Public License instead.) You can apply it to your programs, too.

When we speak of free software, we are referring to freedom, not price. Our General Public Licenses are designed to make sure that you have the freedom to distribute copies of free software (and charge for this service if you wish), that you receive source code or can get it if you want it, that you can change the software or use pieces of it in new free programs; and that you know you can do these things.

To protect your rights, we need to make restrictions that forbid anyone to deny you these rights or to ask you to surrender the rights. These restrictions translate to certain responsibilities for you if you distribute copies of the software, or if you modify it.

For example, if you distribute copies of such a program, whether gratis or for a fee, you must give the recipients all the rights that you have. You must make sure that they, too, receive or can get the source code. And you must show them these terms so they know their rights.

We protect your rights with two steps: (1) copyright the software, and (2) offer you this license which gives you legal permission to copy, distribute and/or modify the software.

Also, for each author's protection and ours, we want to make certain that everyone understands that there is no warranty for this free software. If the software is modified by someone else and passed on, we want its recipients to know that what they have is not the original, so that any problems introduced by others will not reflect on the original authors' reputations.

Finally, any free program is threatened constantly by software patents. We wish to avoid the danger that redistributors of a free program will individually obtain patent licenses, in effect making the program proprietary. To prevent this, we have made it clear that any patent must be licensed for everyone's free use or not licensed at all.

The precise terms and conditions for copying, distribution and modification follow.

Terms and Conditions for Copying, Distribution and Modification

0. This License applies to any program or other work which contains a notice placed by the copyright holder saying it may be distributed under the terms of this General Public License. The "Program", below, refers to any such program or work, and a "work based on the Program" means either the Program or any derivative work under copyright law: that is to say, a work containing the Program or a portion of it, either verbatim or with modifications and/or translated into another language. (Hereinafter, translation is included without limitation in the term "modification".) Each licensee is addressed as "you".

Activities other than copying, distribution and modification are not covered by this License; they are outside its scope. The act of running the Program is not restricted, and the output from the Program is covered only if its contents constitute a work based on the Program (independent of having been made by running the Program). Whether that is true depends on what the Program does.

1. You may copy and distribute verbatim copies of the Program's source code as you receive it, in any medium, provided that you conspicuously and appropriately publish on each copy an appropriate copyright notice and disclaimer of warranty; keep intact all the notices that refer to this License and to the absence of any warranty; and give any other recipients of the Program a copy of this License along with the Program.

You may charge a fee for the physical act of transferring a copy, and you may at your option offer warranty protection in exchange for a fee.

2. You may modify your copy or copies of the Program or any portion of it, thus forming a work based on the Program, and copy and distribute such modifications or work under the terms of Section 1 above, provided that you also meet all of these conditions:

    (a) You must cause the modified files to carry prominent notices stating that you changed the files and the date of any change.

    (b) You must cause any work that you distribute or publish, that in whole or in part contains or is derived from the Program or any part thereof, to be licensed as a whole at no charge to all third parties under the terms of this License.

    (c) If the modified program normally reads commands interactively when run, you must cause it, when started running for such interactive use in the most ordinary way, to print or display an announcement including an appropriate copyright notice and a notice that there is no warranty (or else, saying that you provide a warranty) and that users may redistribute the program under these conditions, and telling the user how to view a copy of this License. (Exception: if the Program itself is interactive but does not normally print such an announcement, your work based on the Program is not required to print an announcement.)

These requirements apply to the modified work as a whole. If identifiable sections of that work are not derived from the Program, and can be reasonably considered independent and separate works in themselves, then this License, and its terms, do not apply to those sections when you distribute them as separate works. But when you distribute the same sections as part of a whole which is a work based on the Program, the distribution of the whole must be on the terms of this License, whose permissions for other licensees extend to the entire whole, and thus to each and every part regardless of who wrote it.

Thus, it is not the intent of this section to claim rights or contest your rights to work written entirely by you; rather, the intent is to exercise the right to control the distribution of derivative or collective works based on the Program.

In addition, mere aggregation of another work not based on the Program with the Program (or with a work based on the Program) on a volume of a storage or distribution medium does not bring the other work under the scope of this License.

3. You may copy and distribute the Program (or a work based on it, under Section 2) in object code or executable form under the terms of Sections 1 and 2 above provided that you also do one of the following:

   (a) Accompany it with the complete corresponding machine-readable source code, which must be distributed under the terms of Sections 1 and 2 above on a medium customarily used for software interchange; or,

   (b) Accompany it with a written offer, valid for at least three years, to give any third party, for a charge no more than your cost of physically performing source distribution, a complete machine-readable copy of the corresponding source code, to be distributed under the terms of Sections 1 and 2 above on a medium customarily used for software interchange; or,

   (c) Accompany it with the information you received as to the offer to distribute corresponding source code. (This alternative is allowed only for noncommercial distribution and only if you received the program in object code or executable form with such an offer, in accord with Subsection b above.)

   The source code for a work means the preferred form of the work for making modifications to it. For an executable work, complete source code means all the source code for all modules it contains, plus any associated interface definition files, plus the scripts used to control compilation and installation of the executable. However, as a special exception, the source code distributed need not include anything that is normally distributed (in either source or binary form) with the major components (compiler, kernel, and so on) of the operating system on which the executable runs, unless that component itself accompanies the executable.

   If distribution of executable or object code is made by offering access to copy from a designated place, then offering equivalent access to copy the source code from the same place counts as distribution of the source code, even though third parties are not compelled to copy the source along with the object code.

4. You may not copy, modify, sublicense, or distribute the Program except as expressly provided under this License. Any attempt otherwise to copy, modify, sublicense or distribute the Program is void, and will automatically terminate your rights under this License. However, parties who have received copies, or rights, from you under this License will not have their licenses terminated so long as such parties remain in full compliance.

5. You are not required to accept this License, since you have not signed it. However, nothing else grants you permission to modify or distribute the Program or its derivative works. These actions are prohibited by law if you do not accept this License. Therefore, by modifying or distributing the Program (or any work based on the Program), you indicate your acceptance of this License to do so, and all its terms and conditions for copying, distributing or modifying the Program or works based on it.

6. Each time you redistribute the Program (or any work based on the Program), the recipient automatically receives a license from the original licensor to copy, distribute or modify the Program subject to these terms and conditions. You may not impose any further restrictions on the recipients' exercise of the rights granted herein. You are not responsible for enforcing compliance by third parties to this License.

7. If, as a consequence of a court judgment or allegation of patent infringement or for any other reason (not limited to patent issues), conditions are imposed on you (whether by court order, agreement or otherwise) that contradict the conditions of this License, they do not excuse you from the conditions of this License. If you cannot distribute so as to satisfy simultaneously your obligations under this License and any other pertinent obligations, then as a consequence you may not distribute the Program at all. For example, if a patent license would not permit royalty-free redistribution of the Program by all those who receive copies directly or indirectly through you, then the only way you could satisfy both it and this License would be to refrain entirely from distribution of the Program.

   If any portion of this section is held invalid or unenforceable under any particular circumstance, the balance of the section is intended to apply and the section as a whole is intended to apply in other circumstances.

   It is not the purpose of this section to induce you to infringe any patents or other property right claims or to contest validity of any such claims; this section has the sole purpose of protecting the integrity of the free software distribution system, which is implemented by public license practices. Many people have made generous contributions to the wide range of software distributed through that system in reliance on consistent application of that system; it is up to the author/donor to decide if he or she is willing to distribute software through any other system and a licensee cannot impose that choice.

   This section is intended to make thoroughly clear what is believed to be a consequence of the rest of this License.

8. If the distribution and/or use of the Program is restricted in certain countries either by patents or by copyrighted interfaces, the original copyright holder who places the Program under this License may add an explicit geographical distribution limitation excluding those countries, so that distribution is permitted only in or among countries not thus excluded. In such case, this License incorporates the limitation as if written in the body of this License.

9. The Free Software Foundation may publish revised and/or new versions of the General Public License from time to time. Such new versions will be similar in spirit to the present version, but may differ in detail to address new problems or concerns.

   Each version is given a distinguishing version number. If the Program specifies a version number of this License which applies to it and "any later version", you have the option of following the terms and conditions either of that version or of any later version published by the Free Software Foundation. If the Program does not specify a version number of this License, you may choose any version ever published by the Free Software Foundation.

10. If you wish to incorporate parts of the Program into other free programs whose distribution conditions are different, write to the author to ask for permission. For software which is copyrighted by the Free Software Foundation, write to the Free Software Foundation; we sometimes make exceptions for this. Our decision will be guided by the two goals of preserving the free status of all derivatives of our free software and of promoting the sharing and reuse of software generally.

No Warranty

11. BECAUSE THE PROGRAM IS LICENSED FREE OF CHARGE, THERE IS NO WARRANTY FOR THE PROGRAM, TO THE EXTENT PERMITTED BY APPLICABLE LAW. EXCEPT WHEN OTHERWISE STATED IN WRITING THE COPYRIGHT HOLDERS AND/OR OTHER PARTIES PROVIDE THE PROGRAM "AS IS" WITHOUT WARRANTY OF ANY KIND, EITHER EXPRESSED OR IMPLIED, INCLUDING, BUT NOT LIMITED TO, THE IMPLIED WARRANTIES OF MERCHANTABILITY AND FITNESS FOR A PARTICULAR PURPOSE. THE ENTIRE RISK AS TO THE QUALITY AND PERFORMANCE OF THE PROGRAM IS WITH YOU. SHOULD THE PROGRAM PROVE DEFECTIVE, YOU ASSUME THE COST OF ALL NECESSARY SERVICING, REPAIR OR CORRECTION.

12. IN NO EVENT UNLESS REQUIRED BY APPLICABLE LAW OR AGREED TO IN WRITING WILL ANY COPYRIGHT HOLDER, OR ANY OTHER PARTY WHO MAY MODIFY AND/OR REDISTRIBUTE THE PROGRAM AS PERMITTED ABOVE, BE LIABLE TO YOU FOR DAMAGES, INCLUDING ANY GENERAL, SPECIAL, INCIDENTAL OR CONSEQUENTIAL DAMAGES ARISING OUT OF THE USE OR INABILITY TO USE THE PROGRAM (INCLUDING BUT NOT LIMITED TO LOSS OF DATA OR DATA BEING RENDERED INACCURATE OR LOSSES SUSTAINED BY YOU OR THIRD PARTIES OR A FAILURE OF THE PROGRAM TO OPERATE WITH ANY OTHER PROGRAMS), EVEN IF SUCH HOLDER OR OTHER PARTY HAS BEEN ADVISED OF THE POSSIBILITY OF SUCH DAMAGES.

End of Terms and Conditions